AF147393

Communications
in Computer and Information Science 2277

Rationale

The CCIS series is devoted to the publication of proceedings of computer science conferences. Its aim is to efficiently disseminate original research results in informatics in printed and electronic form. While the focus is on publication of peer-reviewed full papers presenting mature work, inclusion of reviewed short papers reporting on work in progress is welcome, too. Besides globally relevant meetings with internationally representative program committees guaranteeing a strict peer-reviewing and paper selection process, conferences run by societies or of high regional or national relevance are also considered for publication.

Topics

The topical scope of CCIS spans the entire spectrum of informatics ranging from foundational topics in the theory of computing to information and communications science and technology and a broad variety of interdisciplinary application fields.

Information for Volume Editors and Authors

Publication in CCIS is free of charge. No royalties are paid, however, we offer registered conference participants temporary free access to the online version of the conference proceedings on SpringerLink (http://link.springer.com) by means of an http referrer from the conference website and/or a number of complimentary printed copies, as specified in the official acceptance email of the event.

CCIS proceedings can be published in time for distribution at conferences or as post-proceedings, and delivered in the form of printed books and/or electronically as USBs and/or e-content licenses for accessing proceedings at SpringerLink. Furthermore, CCIS proceedings are included in the CCIS electronic book series hosted in the SpringerLink digital library at http://link.springer.com/bookseries/7899. Conferences publishing in CCIS are allowed to use Online Conference Service (OCS) for managing the whole proceedings lifecycle (from submission and reviewing to preparing for publication) free of charge.

Publication process

The language of publication is exclusively English. Authors publishing in CCIS have to sign the Springer CCIS copyright transfer form, however, they are free to use their material published in CCIS for substantially changed, more elaborate subsequent publications elsewhere. For the preparation of the camera-ready papers/files, authors have to strictly adhere to the Springer CCIS Authors' Instructions and are strongly encouraged to use the CCIS LaTeX style files or templates.

Abstracting/Indexing

CCIS is abstracted/indexed in DBLP, Google Scholar, EI-Compendex, Mathematical Reviews, SCImago, Scopus. CCIS volumes are also submitted for the inclusion in ISI Proceedings.

How to start

To start the evaluation of your proposal for inclusion in the CCIS series, please send an e-mail to ccis@springer.com.

Gansen Zhao · Jian Weng · Zhihong Tian · Liehuang Zhu · Zibin Zheng

Editors

Blockchain and Web3.0 Technology Innovation and Application

First Conference, BWTAC 2024
Guangzhou, China, November 6–8, 2024
Proceedings

 Springer

Editors
Gansen Zhao
South China Normal University
Guangzhou, China

Zhihong Tian
Guangzhou University
Guangzhou, China

Zibin Zheng
Sun Yat-sen University
Guangzhou, China

Jian Weng
Jinan University
Guangzhou, China

Liehuang Zhu
Beijing Institute of Technology
Beijing, China

ISSN 1865-0929   ISSN 1865-0937 (electronic)
Communications in Computer and Information Science
ISBN 978-981-97-9411-9   ISBN 978-981-97-9412-6 (eBook)
https://doi.org/10.1007/978-981-97-9412-6

This Springer imprint is published by the registered company Springer Nature Singapore Pte Ltd.
The registered company address is: 152 Beach Road, #21-01/04 Gateway East, Singapore 189721, Singapore

If disposing of this product, please recycle the paper.

Preface

It has never been easy to set up a new series of academic conferences, especially for the first one of a series. It is an extremely challenging task to decide on a theme that is attractive and significant enough to draw attention from both academic and industry as well as their efforts, while it should be accommodating enough to include most related topics and allow the correlation of newly explored and most-up-to-date work.

Blockchain and Web 3.0 are obviously good options for a new series of academic conferences. Blockchain has sustained its hype for more than a decade. It is still a very active and innovative area as applications of Blockchain technology have been continuously expanding and impacting in many areas, not to mention that there are still many innovative ideas in terms of business and technology brought up by the Blockchain community.

Web 3.0 is one of the newest hot topics, with high expectations of the integration the physical world with the cyber world, allowing the interaction between these two. It is fascinating that virtual entities created by human beings can be put together with physical entities and work cooperatively. One can hardly tell the virtual ones from the physical ones as the experiences of both are highly consistent.

The first conference of this series was held in the Great Bay Area of China. This is one of the most important technology innovation centers in China as well as the most important industry center for information technology. In a sense, the Great Bay Area may be the place that most values and understands the potential of Blockchain and Web 3.0. From this perspective, this conference was planned to bring together efforts in research and development from both industry and the academic community, as well as to encourage the exchange of good ideas and new progress related to Blockchain and Web 3.0. One of the objectives of this conference was to facilitate both research and development in Blockchain and Web 3.0, turning new technologies into widely adopted applications as well as identifying new research opportunities within various scenarios.

With only a short planning phase and relatively little advertising, the conference received more than 100 submissions, which is much better than the original expectation. All submissions were blind-reviewed by at least 3 peers from the corresponding areas. Some of the submissions were from authors who were also involved in the conference organization, and to avoid any conflicts of interest and maintain the independence of the academic assessment, the reviewing assignments were carefully made to avoid intervention in the assessment and decision process. From the submissions 35 long papers and 12 short papers were selected by the committee. A number of the accepted papers were from authors with industry affiliations, which is very encouraging.

This volume and the conference would not have been possible without the support and involvement of many parties. The Chinese Institute of Electronics was very supportive in planning and preparing this conference. There were several institutes that made great efforts and contributed to the success of this conference, including South China Normal University, the Blockchain Branch of the Chinese Institute of Electronics, the

New Generation Information Technology Industry Research Institute, and many others. Also a long list of individuals significantly contributed, among these the General Chair, Changjun Jiang; the Steering Committee Chairs, Weimin Zheng, Qingtian Zeng, Zhong Chen and Xiaosong Zhang; the Publication Chairs, Qingfeng Tan and Hua Tang; and the Organizing Committee members, Yuan Liu, Xiaofeng Ma, Yan Zhu, Wen Sun, Lina Ni, Xiuzhen Cheng, Nengfu Xie, Jiaqi Yan, Ting Li, Chao Li, Cheng Wang and Sheng Cao. Finally, Springer Nature was very helpful in ensuring a quality proceedings publication.

October 2024

Gansen Zhao
Jian Weng
Zhihong Tian
Liehuang Zhu
Zibin Zheng

Organization

General Chair

Changjun Jiang   Chinese Academy of Engineering, China

Program Committee Chairs

Gansen Zhao	South China Normal University, China
Jian Weng	Jinan University, China
Zhihong Tian	Guangzhou University, China
Liehuang Zhu	Beijing Institute of Technology, China
Zibin Zheng	Sun Yat-sen University, China

Steering Committee

Changjun Jiang	Chinese Academy of Engineering, China
Weimin Zheng	Chinese Academy of Engineering, China
Jie Li	Engineering Academy of Japan, China
Mingxuan Ni	Hong Kong Academy of Engineering Sciences, China
Yan Zhang	University of Oslo, Norway
Sutharshan Rajasegarar	University of Melbourne, Australia
Qingchao Ke	South China Normal University, China
Qingtian Zeng	Shandong University of Science and Technology, China
Zhong Chen	Peking University, China
Xiaosong Zhang	University of Electronic Science and Technology of China, China

Program Committee

Ting Chen	University of Electronic Science and Technology of China, China
Xiuzhen Cheng	Shandong University, China

Shaojing Fu	National University of Defense Technology, China
Keke Gai	Beijing Institute of Technology, China
Zhihao Hou	South China Normal University, China
Jianhua Huang	East China University of Science and Technology, China
Feng Jiang	Qingdao University of Science and Technology, China
Cheqing Jin	East China Normal University, China
Lanju Kong	Shandong University, China
Ruilin Lai	South China Normal University, China
Chao Li	Shandong University of Science and Technology, China
Chong Li	Donghua University, China
Ting Li	New Generation Information Technology Industry Research Institute, China
Xiaodong Li	Beijing Electronic Science and Technology Institute, China
Xiong Li	University of Electronic Science and Technology of China, China
Yong Li	Beijing Jiaotong University, China
Wenting Lian	New Generation Information Technology Industry Research Institute, China
Yuan Liu	Jiangnan University, China
Lichuan Ma	Xidian University, China
Xiaofeng Ma	Tongji University, China
Lina Ni	Shandong University of Science and Technology, China
Feng Qi	Beijing University of Posts and Telecommunications, China
Hao Sheng	Beihang University, China
Youqun Shi	Donghua University, China
Wen Sun	Northwestern Polytechnical University, China
Qingfeng Tan	Guangzhou University, China
Hua Tang	South China Normal University, China
Cheng Wang	Tongji University, China
Pengwei Wang	Donghua University, China
Shi Wang	Institute of Computing Technology, Chinese Academy of Sciences, China
Yan Wu	Jiangsu University, China
Zhenping Xie	Jiangnan University, China
Hongjian Yin	Henan University, China
Qianyi Zhan	Jiangnan University, China

Junlang Zhang	South China Normal University, China
Nana Zhang	Donghua University, China
Yin Zhang	University of Electronic Science and Technology of China, China
Zhaohui Zhang	Donghua University, China
Gansen Zhao	South China Normal University, China
Yan Zhu	University of Science and Technology Beijing, China

Contents

Behavioral Unicity: On the Limits of Anonymized Social Behavior Metadata

Hao Tang[1,2,3,4] and Cheng Wang[1,2,3,4(✉)]

[1] Tongji University, Shanghai 201804, China
{2011264,cwang}@tongji.edu.cn
[2] The Key Laboratory of Embedded System and Service Computing Ministry of Education, Shanghai 201804, China
[3] Shanghai Artificial Intelligence Laboratory, Shanghai 200030, China
[4] Shanghai Institute of Intelligent Science and Technology, Tongji University, Shanghai 200092, China

Abstract. Social behavior metadata has altered business models and human lifestyles. However, the inclusion of personal information in social behavior metadata poses risks of identity exposure for users. Under the requirements of modern data management laws, service providers now employ anonymization techniques when collecting user behavior metadata, which aims to break the link between personal identifiers and behavioral attributes for privacy protection. This paper conducts experiments on an open-source dataset of anonymized social behavior metadata and finds that even with privacy protection techniques such as data generalization, there remains a high risk of reidentification. Specifically, four social behavior metadata records are sufficient to reidentify users from the anonymized social behavior metadata, achieving a unicity of 90.10%. This indicates that the current widespread collection of social behavior metadata brings a high risk of privacy breaches.

Keywords: Behavioral unicity · Privacy protection · Risk of reidentification

1 Introduction

The collection of behavioral data has fundamentally transformed the way people live, urban development, and disease control. The rapid development of low-power intelligent mobile devices and the enhanced storage capacity of cloud servers enable the generation of digital traces from people's daily activities and interactions. These collected datasets of behavioral metadata are being widely utilized. In the financial sector, the analysis of transactional behavior metadata can help identify abnormal behavior and potential financial risks [1,2]. In the field of computational social science, urban planning departments utilize behavioral metadata on user travel to gain a better understanding of people's travel behavior and transportation needs. This information is used to optimize urban transportation networks and public transportation systems [3,4].

The broad collection of behavioral metadata also comes with the risk of privacy breaches. To protect user privacy, service providers generally anonymize the original dataset before data sharing. This involves removing sensitive identifiers to prevent reidentification. Modern data protection laws in many countries have gradually reached a consensus that anonymized data no longer qualifies as personally identifiable sensitive information to a certain extent [5,6]. The academic community also advocates for authors to open-source anonymized data, which has become an important aspect of open science [7]. However, some studies have indicated that even with anonymization techniques, several behavioral metadata records within the dataset may still uniquely identify users.

In the literature, research on the risk of reidentification has attracted great attention. Montjoye et al. [8] revealed in their publication in Science that the unicity of user shopping behavior is much higher than intuition would suggest. Researchers also discovered a high level of unicity in browsing behavior history [9,10]. Inspired by these studies, we focus on the risk of reidentification in the social behavior metadata. There are two main reasons why we choose to concentrate on this type of metadata: First, the social behavior metadata are closely related to individuals' interests and hobbies, and the consequences of reidentification are even more severe; second, the social behavior metadata have fewer behavioral dimensions compared to shopping and browsing behavior, and we want to explore whether the privacy issues of reidentification in low-dimensional behavioral metadata remain prominent. Thus, the risk of reidentification in the social behavior metadata is an important issue that requires a thorough understanding before widespread utilization of social behavior metadata.

In this paper, we conduct experiments on the dataset of anonymized social behavior metadata, to evaluate whether it still poses the risk of reidentification. To our surprise, in low-dimensional anonymized social behavior metadata, the risk of reidentification remains remarkably high. Specifically, even applying privacy protection mechanisms to behavioral attributes in the dataset of anonymized social behavior metadata, just four behavioral metadata records are sufficient to uniquely identify users from the dataset, with a unicity reaching 90.10%. The result indicates the high behavioral unicity in the social behavior metadata. We also explore the results from the perspective of joint entropy and find that the entropy of different users follows a gamma distribution. The high predictability of user entropy is a possible reason behind the high behavioral unicity.

2   Related Work

2.1   The Risk of Reidentification

Shin et al. [11] pointed out that whether users can be uniquely identified by adversaries is one of the important categories of privacy issues. Montjoye et al. [8] found that four spatiotemporal points containing price information can uniquely reidentify 90% of the users in the dataset of credit card metadata. The results indicate that financial data can effectively reflect users' behavioral patterns. Rocher et al. [12] discovered that using 15 demographic attributes can correctly reidentify over 99% of Americans. Bird et al. [13] found that when users visited more than 150 websites, the proportion of users who can be reidentified exceeds 80% in the dataset of user browsing behavior metadata. Culnane et al. [14] conducted a validation on an open and anonymized dataset of medical health metadata. The findings revealed that with just a few essential details, it is easy to reidentify patients.

Existing research on the risk of reidentification has predominantly focused on datasets of multidimensional behavioral metadata, such as credit card metadata and medical health metadata, where each metadata record has multiple behavioral attributes. However, the extent to which the risk of reidentification remains prominent in the dataset of behavioral metadata with only a few behavioral dimensions has not been studied.

2.2   Social Behavior Metadata

Social behavior metadata are closely related to individuals' interests and hobbies. Li et al. [15] devised a matrix factorization model that encompasses three distinct check-in modalities of the social behavior of mobile users. Ying et al. [16] studied users' posting behavior on online social networks, and found that mornings and evenings are two peak traffic periods. Mohamed et al. [17] established a social spatiotemporal graph convolutional neural network to capture interaction patterns among entities. Yin et al. [18] proposed a user's social geographic topic model with Bayesian networks, simulating the community generation process of individual subjects' neighboring networks. Yu et al. [19] utilized relationships among social network behavior entities to improve recommendation quality.

Social behavior metadata are currently widely used in many tasks, such as information recommendation and user behavior prediction. Before mining social behavior metadata, the most fundamental privacy risks have not been fully analyzed. This paper focuses on the limits of anonymized social behavior metadata.

3   Investigating Method

3.1   Threat Model

In a real-world scenario, there are two primary entities associated with the social behavior metadata: the entities generating the behavior, namely the users, and the entities collecting the behavioral data, namely the service providers.

1) *Users:* Users refer to the entities using social network platforms or applications. They engage in activities on the platform by registering an account and participating in social interactions, such as check-ins and sharing interests.

2) *Service Providers:* Service providers are responsible for collecting, storing, and managing users' behavioral data on the platform. By analyzing and modeling users' behavioral data, they typically offer various functionalities and services, including content posting and interest recommendation.

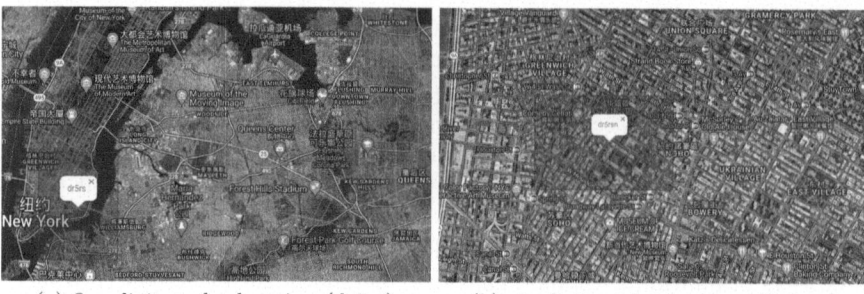

(a) five-digit geohash string (dr5rs)   (b) six-digit geohash string (dr5rsn)

Fig. 1. Geohash strings with different lengths. The longer geohash strings represent smaller cells and provide less efficient privacy protection.

We consider two primary types of adversaries in the threat model [20]: Attackers who have compromised the servers of service providers and gained unauthorized access. Service providers who violate implementation agreements by excessively behavioral metadata for profit. Adversaries can attempt to reidentify users by exploiting observed behavioral metadata records. If they find a unique match in the dataset of behavioral metadata, they can then access more of the user's historical records, including information about their visited regions and the corresponding time periods. They also can track the user's activities when new behavioral data is generated since the adversary has successfully identified the user. The security issues resulting from successful reidentification can be exacerbated when combined with additional information [10].

3.2   Temporal and Spatial Generalization

Under the stricter privacy protection regulatory constraints [21], it is difficult for service providers to collect detailed behavioral attributes. Generalization techniques are employed on the temporal and spatial attributes of behavioral metadata to obtain coarse-grained behavioral attributes.

To achieve the generalization of the temporal attribute, different temporal resolutions, denoted as tr, are determined. The whole timeline T in the dataset is divided into bins, with a total of $\lceil T/tr \rceil$ intervals. The time attribute in the dataset is mapped to its corresponding interval based on its time value. Following this generalization approach, a total of six temporal resolutions are determined in this paper: 24 h, 12 h, 8 h, 6 h, 3 h, and 2 h.

For spatial attribute generalization, different spatial resolutions, denoted as sr, need to be determined. Here, geohash [22] is adopted to obtain different spatial resolutions. Geohash can convert latitude-longitude geographic coordinates into strings. Different strings correspond to different regions on the map (called cells). Each point within one cell is uniquely determined by different latitude and longitude values, but all points within the same cell share the same geohash string. This method helps protect the privacy of spatial information. Geohash strings of different lengths offer varying levels of privacy protection.

Algorithm 1: Unicity calculation algorithm

Input   : The dataset of anonymized behavioral metadata D.
Output: Unicity results.

for *each tr in different temporal resolutions* **do**
 for *each sr in different spatial resolutions* **do**
  Generalizing spatiotemporal attributes with tr and sr;
  for k *in different numbers of behavioral metadata records* **do**
   $S_\epsilon \leftarrow []$;
   $u \leftarrow 0$;
   $total_{R_u} \leftarrow 0$;
   while $u \leq Users$ **do**
    given the set of k behavioral metadata records D_k;
    $len \leftarrow \text{match}(D_i, D_k)$;
    if $len == 1$ **then**
     $total_{R_u} \leftarrow total_{R_u} + 1$;
    $u \leftarrow u + 1$;
   $S_\epsilon.\text{append}(total_{R_u}/Users)$;
return S_ϵ

A longer geohash string represents a smaller corresponding cell. For example, in the dataset of social behavior metadata, when encoding a spatial behavioral attribute with latitude and longitude $(40.729768, -73.998535)$ using five-digit and six-digit geohash strings, the corresponding cells are depicted in Fig. 1.

In the experiment, six different spatial resolutions are employed to offer varying levels of privacy protection for sensitive spatial attributes by using geohash strings. These six spatial resolutions are as follows: 1250 km × 625 km (2 digits), 156 km × 156 km (3 digits), 39.1 km × 19.5 km (4 digits), 4.89 km × 4.89 km (5 digits), 1.22 km × 0.61 km (6 digits), and 153 m × 153 m (7 digits).

3.3   Unicity Metric

For each user i in the dataset, the set of all behavioral metadata records related to this user is denoted by D_i. The set of k behavioral metadata records that an adversary can obtain is denoted by D_k. In the entire dataset, the users satisfying the condition $D_k \in D_i$ forms the set $S(D_k)$. If $|S(D_k)| = 1$, then the reidentification of that user is considered successful. The definition is as follows:

$$R_u = \begin{cases} 1, |S(D_k)| = 1, \\ 0, |S(D_k)| > 1, \end{cases} \tag{1}$$

where R_u represents whether the user is successfully identified, with 1 indicating success and 0 indicating failure.

The unicity metric ϵ represents the percentage of users in the dataset of anonymized behavioral metadata who can be uniquely identified by an adversary

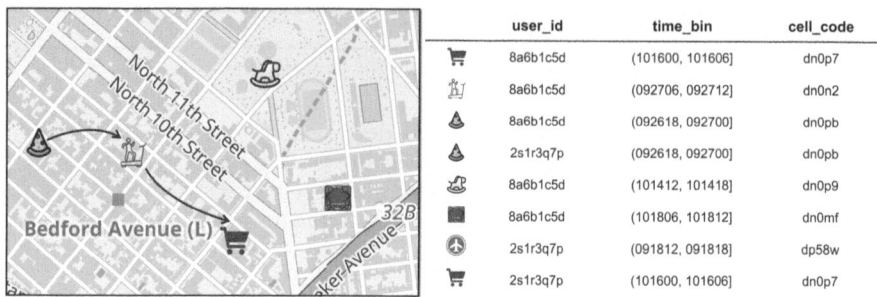

	user_id	time_bin	cell_code
🛒	8a6b1c5d	(101600, 101606]	dn0p7
🛏	8a6b1c5d	(092706, 092712]	dn0n2
🍸	8a6b1c5d	(092618, 092700]	dn0pb
🍸	2s1r3q7p	(092618, 092700]	dn0pb
🎧	8a6b1c5d	(101412, 101418]	dn0p9
▪	8a6b1c5d	(101806, 101812]	dn0mf
🕐	2s1r3q7p	(091812, 091818]	dp58w
🛒	2s1r3q7p	(101600, 101606]	dn0p7

Fig. 2. The partial dataset of anonymized social behavior metadata. Here, the temporal attribute is generalized by 6-h intervals, and the spatial attribute is generalized using five-digit geohash strings.

using a certain number of behavioral metadata records, which quantifies the risk of reidentification in the behavioral metadata [13]. It is defined as follows:

$$\epsilon_{tr,sr,k} = \frac{\sum_{u \in Users} R_u}{|Users|} \times 100\%, \tag{2}$$

where tr represents temporal resolution, sr represents spatial resolution, k denotes the number of observed behavioral metadata records, $Users$ denotes all the users in the dataset of behavioral metadata, and u denotes the current user being targeted for reidentification by an adversary. The process of unicity calculation is shown in Algorithm 1.

For example, if the adversary searches for Bob in this dataset of anonymized social behavior metadata, which is shown in Fig. 2. The adversary have already known two behavioral metadata records of him: he visited dn0p7 cell during the time interval (101600, 101606] (represents the period between 0:00 and 6:00 on October 16th) and visited dn0pb cell during the time interval (092618, 092700], the adversary matches the dataset and discovers that two users in the anonymized dataset visited these two cells in these time intervals. So, the value of $|S(D_2)|$ is 2, which indicates a failed reidentification attempt. If the adversary also knows an additional behavioral metadata record that Bob visited dn0p9 cell during the time interval (101412, 101418], $|S(D_3)|$ is thus equal to 1. This implies that the adversary can successfully reidentify Bob from the dataset of social behavior metadata. As a result, the adversary can obtain additional information about Bob, such as his visit to dn0p9 cell during the time interval (101412, 101418] and dn0mf cell during the time interval (101806, 101812].

3.4 User Entropy

In general lower entropy implies higher predictability, and the level of predictability also reflects the potential risk of reidentification [23]. For each user, the joint entropy [24] of their temporal and spatial attributes is calculated to quantify their predictability as follows:

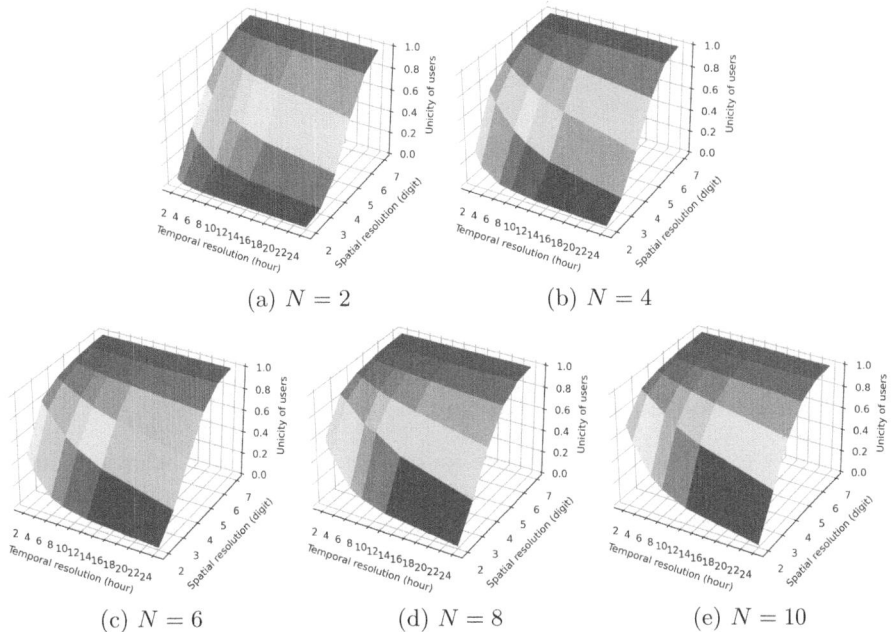

Fig. 3. The unicity results with different numbers of social behavior metadata records.

$$H_k(T, L) = -\sum_{i=1}^{m}\sum_{j=1}^{n} P_k(t_i, l_j) \log_2(P_k(t_i, l_j)). \tag{3}$$

Here, $P_k(t_i, l_j)$ represents the probability of these values of the temporal and spatial attributes occurring together for user k, m represents the number of temporal attributes with corresponding values, and n represents the number of spatial attributes with corresponding values. To determine the weight for each user, the number of their social behavior metadata records to the total number of social behavior metadata records is calculated by

$$w_k = \frac{|D_k|}{N}, \tag{4}$$

where $|D_k|$ represents the number of social behavior metadata records for user k, and N is the number of social behavior metadata records for all users.

The weighted average of the joint entropy for the dataset of social behavior metadata can be expressed as follows:

$$H(T, L) = -\sum_{i=1}^{m}\sum_{j=1}^{n} w_k \cdot P_k(t_i, l_j) \log_2(P_k(t_i, l_j)). \tag{5}$$

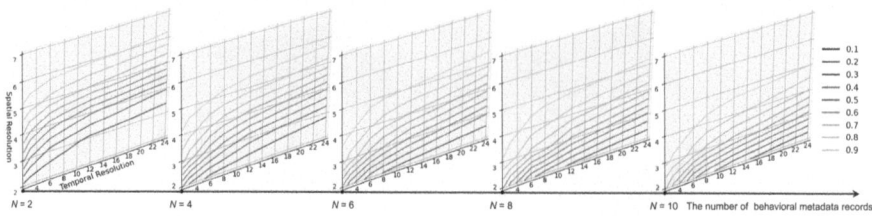

Fig. 4. The contour lines of unicity under different spatiotemporal resolutions.

4   Experiment

4.1   Dataset and Experiment Setup

We conduct experiments on an open-source dataset of social behavior meta-data called Gowalla [25]. During the analysis of the dataset, several outliers are identified, such as latitude values exceeding the practical range (e.g., latitude of $405.66°$ in some records). These anomalies are likely caused by GPS positioning errors during data collection. The majority of the metadata is concentrated in North America and Europe, spanning from February 2009 to October 2010. In other regions, the usage of the Gowalla application is not popular.

To ensure that the validation region has representative behavioral metadata, the geographical region of the United States is selected, ranging from $25°$N to $49°$N latitude and $70°$W to $130°$W longitude. The period encompassed a two-month from September 1, 2010, to October 31, 2010. The outliers are removed. The distribution of user data is highly uneven. Users with only a few behavioral records are eliminated. The processed dataset contains $14,122$ users and $169,464$ records. In the experiment, six levels of temporal resolution are determined, listed from low to high: 24 h, 12 h, 8 h, 6 h, 3 h, and 2 h. They are denoted as $tr = 24$, $tr = 12$, $tr = 8$, $tr = 6$, $tr = 3$, and $tr = 2$, respectively. Additionally, six levels of spatial resolution are established by utilizing geohash strings, listed from low to high: 1250 km $\times$ 625 km (2 digits), 156 km $\times$ 156 km (3 digits), 39.1 km $\times$ 19.5 km (4 digits), 4.89 km $\times$ 4.89 km (5 digits), 1.22 km $\times$ 0.61 km (6 digits), and 153 m $\times$ 153 m (7 digits). They are denoted as $sr = 2$, $sr = 3$, $sr = 4$, $sr = 5$, $sr = 6$, and $sr = 7$, respectively. This results in a total of 36 combinations. For each combination, the validation is conducted on 1 to 10 behavioral metadata records.

4.2   Main Results

By calculating the unicity metric ϵ for the dataset of social behavior metadata, it is surprising to find that, with a temporal resolution of 6 h $(tr = 6)$ and a spatial resolution of 4.89 km $\times$ 4.89 km $(sr = 5)$, only four behavioral metadata records are sufficient to reidentify users from the dataset of social behavior metadata with a unicity exceeding 90%, which is shown in Fig. 3. Furthermore, as the number of behavioral metadata records increases, the unicity can even reach over 95%.

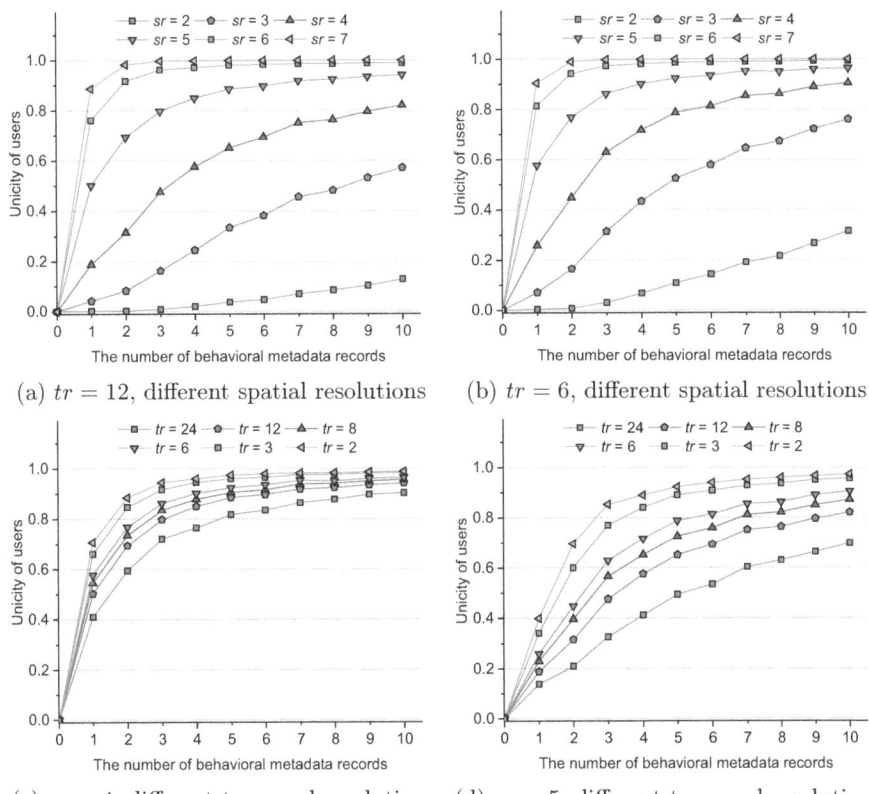

(a) $tr = 12$, different spatial resolutions (b) $tr = 6$, different spatial resolutions

(c) $sr = 4$, different temporal resolutions (d) $sr = 5$, different temporal resolutions

Fig. 5. The effect of different spatial resolutions on unicity, given a fixed temporal resolution, is illustrated in Fig. 5(a) and Fig. 5(b). The effect of different temporal resolutions on unicity, given a fixed spatial resolution, is depicted in Fig. 5(c) and Fig. 5(d).

We conduct further analysis on the results of different numbers of social behavior metadata in Fig. 3. For example, at a lower temporal resolution ($tr = 12$) and a lower spatial resolution ($sr = 3$), four behavioral metadata records only achieve a unicity of 24.47%. However, with the collection of more behavioral metadata records, such as ten behavioral metadata records, the unicity approaches 60%. At the lowest temporal resolution ($tr = 24$) and lowest spatial resolution ($sr = 2$), ten behavioral metadata records achieve a unicity of only 0.21%. When the temporal and spatial resolution can achieve such high levels of generalization, it effectively protects user privacy. It also reduces service quality and practicality.

4.3 The Effect of Different Spatiotemporal Resolutions

If the temporal resolution is 6 h ($tr = 6$) and the spatial resolution is 39.1 km × 19.5 km ($sr = 4$), it requires ten behavioral metadata records to achieve a unicity

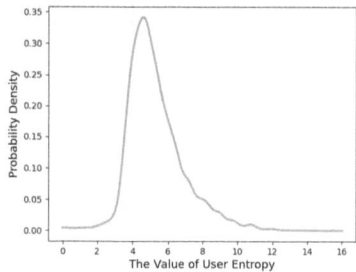

Fig. 6. The distribution of joint entropy for different users, where the temporal resolution is 6 h ($tr = 6$) and the spatial resolution is 4.89 km × 4.89 km ($sr = 5$).

over 90%. If the temporal resolution is 12 h ($tr = 12$) and the spatial resolution is 4.89 km × 4.89 km ($sr = 5$), seven behavioral metadata records are sufficient to achieve a unicity over 90%. It appears that the effect of changes in temporal resolution and spatial resolution on unicity is different. The contour lines are provided in Fig. 4, depicting the unicity results with behavioral metadata records of 2, 4, 6, 8, and 10 under different temporal and spatial resolutions. The contour plot results also reveal this aspect.

We further explore the effect of different temporal resolutions and spatial resolutions. Specifically, the unicity is calculated with different spatial resolutions under fixed temporal resolutions of $tr = 12$ and $tr = 6$, as shown in Fig. 5(a) and Fig. 5(b). Similarly, the unicity is analyzed with different temporal resolutions under fixed spatial resolutions of $sr = 4$ and $sr = 5$, as depicted in Fig. 5(c) and Fig. 5(d). The results show that spatial resolution has a greater effect on unicity. One possible explanation is that higher spatial resolution not only compromises the accuracy of capturing the precise locations visited by users but also disrupts the underlying correlations between the visited cells.

4.4   User Entropy Analysis

The entropy of different users is calculated according to Eq. (3). The result shows that the joint entropy of different users' social behaviors follows a gamma distribution, as shown in Fig. 6. Certain time periods and locations stimulate users to engage in social interactions more frequently, which gives rise to a certain regularity in the distribution of joint entropy, and the gamma distribution effectively captures this regularity. Furthermore, the diversity in joint entropy among different users is likely due to the variations in their social behavior patterns. Some users are more active and have diverse interests, constantly exploring unknown locations. On the other hand, other users are more conservative and prefer to visit only a few specific locations.

5   Conclusion

We have conducted experiments on the dataset of anonymized social behavior metadata. The results show that with just four social behavior metadata records, the unicity can exceed 90%. From the high behavioral unicity in the social behavior metadata, we can draw a conclusion that in the social behavior metadata, privacy concerns have not been adequately addressed with anonymization techniques. The presence of high predictability in user entropy might provide a plausible explanation for the high behavioral unicity.

Acknowledgments. This work was supported in part by the National Natural Science Foundation of China (NSFC) under Grant 62372328, in part by the Fundamental Research Funds for the Central Universities under Grant 22120240357, in part by the Program of Shanghai Academic Research Leader under Grant 22XD1423700, in part by the National Key Research and Development Program of China under Grant 2022YFB4501704, in part by the Shanghai Science and Technology Innovation Action Plan Project under Grant 22511100700, in part by the Leadership Project under the Oriental Talent Program, and in part by the Open Fund of Key Laboratory of Industrial Internet of Things and Networked Control, Ministry of Education, under Grant 2021FF08.

References

1. Xie, Y., Liu, G., Yan, C., Jiang, C., Zhou, M., Li, M.: Learning transactional behavioral representations for credit card fraud detection. IEEE Trans. Neural Netw. Learn. Syst. **35**(4), 5735–5748 (2024)
2. Tang, H., Wang, C., Zheng, J., Jiang, C.: Enabling graph neural networks for semi-supervised risk prediction in online credit loan services. ACM Trans. Intell. Syst. Technol. **15**(1), 1–24 (2024)
3. Oliver, N., et al.: Mobile phone data for informing public health actions across the COVID-19 pandemic life cycle. Sci. Adv. **6**(23), eabc0764 (2020)
4. Yuan, H., Li, G.: A survey of traffic prediction: from spatio-temporal data to intelligent transportation. Data Sci. Eng. **6**(1), 63–85 (2021)
5. Stallings, W.: Handling of personal information and deidentified, aggregated, and pseudonymized information under the California consumer privacy act. IEEE Secur. Priv. **18**(1), 61–64 (2020)
6. Godinho de Matos, M., Adjerid, I.: Consumer consent and firm targeting after GDPR: the case of a large telecom provider. Manag. Sci. **68**(5), 3330–3378 (2022)
7. Aspesi, C., Brand, A.: In pursuit of open science, open access is not enough. Science **368**(6491), 574–577 (2020)
8. De Montjoye, Y.-A., Radaelli, L., Singh, V.K., Pentland, A.S.: Unique in the shopping mall: on the reidentifiability of credit card metadata. Science **347**(6221), 536–539 (2015)
9. Deußer, C., Passmann, S., Strufe, T.: Browsing unicity: on the limits of anonymizing web tracking data. In: IEEE Symposium on Security and Privacy (SP), pp. 777–790. IEEE (2020)
10. Su, J., Shukla, A., Goel, S., Narayanan, A.: De-anonymizing web browsing data with social networks. In: Proceedings of the 26th International Conference on World Wide Web, pp. 1261–1269 (2017)

11. Shin, K.G., Ju, X., Chen, Z., Hu, X.: Privacy protection for users of location-based services. IEEE Wirel. Commun. **19**(1), 30–39 (2012)
12. Rocher, L., Hendrickx, J.M., De Montjoye, Y.-A.: Estimating the success of re-identifications in incomplete datasets using generative models. Nat. Commun. **10**(1), 1–9 (2019)
13. Bird, S., Segall, I., Lopatka, M.: Replication: why we still can't browse in peace: on the uniqueness and reidentifiability of web browsing histories. In: Sixteenth Symposium on Usable Privacy and Security (SOUPS 2020), pp. 489–503 (2020)
14. Culnane, C., Rubinstein, B.I., Teague, V.: Health data in an open world. arXiv preprint arXiv:1712.05627 (2017)
15. Li, H., Ge, Y., Hong, R., Zhu, H.: Point-of-interest recommendations: learning potential check-ins from friends. In: Proceedings of the 22nd ACM SIGKDD International Conference on Knowledge Discovery and Data Mining, pp. 975–984 (2016)
16. Ying, Q.F., Chiu, D.M., Venkatramanan, S., Zhang, X.: User modeling and usage profiling based on temporal posting behavior in OSNs. Online Soc. Netw. Media **8**, 32–41 (2018)
17. Mohamed, A., Qian, K., Elhoseiny, M., Claudel, C.: Social-STGCNN: a social spatio-temporal graph convolutional neural network for human trajectory prediction. In: Proceedings of the IEEE/CVF Conference on Computer Vision and Pattern Recognition, pp. 14424–14432 (2020)
18. Yin, H., et al.: Discovering interpretable geo-social communities for user behavior prediction. In: 2016 IEEE 32nd International Conference on Data Engineering (ICDE), pp. 942–953. IEEE (2016)
19. Yu, J., Yin, H., Li, J., Wang, Q., Hung, N.Q.V., Zhang, X.: Self-supervised multi-channel hypergraph convolutional network for social recommendation. In: Proceedings of the Web Conference 2021, pp. 413–424 (2021)
20. Kang, J., Steiert, D., Lin, D., Fu, Y.: MoveWithMe: location privacy preservation for smartphone users. IEEE Trans. Inf. Forensics Secur. **15**, 711–724 (2019)
21. Godinho de Matos, M., Adjerid, I.: Consumer consent and firm targeting after GDPR: the case of a large telecom provider. Manag. Sci. **68**(5), 3330–3378 (2021)
22. Moussalli, R., Srivatsa, M., Asaad, S.: Fast and flexible conversion of geohash codes to and from latitude, longitude coordinates. In: IEEE 23rd Annual International Symposium on Field-Programmable Custom Computing Machines, pp. 179–186. IEEE (2015)
23. Song, C., Qu, Z., Blumm, N., Barabási, A.-L.: Limits of predictability in human mobility. Science **327**(5968), 1018–1021 (2010)
24. MacKay, D.J.: Information Theory, Inference and Learning Algorithms. Cambridge University Press, Cambridge (2003)
25. Hsieh, H.-P., Yan, R., Li, C.-T.: Where you go reveals who you know: analyzing social ties from millions of footprints. In: Proceedings of the 24th ACM International on Conference on Information and Knowledge Management, pp. 1839–1842 (2015)

Research on Effects of Blockchain Pilot Programs in Regional Equity Markets: Evidence from Participant and Non-participant Institutions

Ying Chen[1,2], Zixin Zhang[1], Xueqian Li[1], and Ke Zhang[1(✉)]

[1] School of Management and Engineering, Nanjing University, Nanjing 210008, China
602023150017@smail.nju.edu.cn
[2] Jiangsu Key Laboratory of Digital Finance, Suzhou 215133, China

Abstract. As financial infrastructure is key to the modern economic system, blockchain technology enormously drives the global securities and futures industry's revolution. However, the application of blockchain technology in China is in the early experimental stage. This paper uses the difference-in-difference method to evaluate the actual policy effect of "Blockchain + Regional Equity Trading Markets" in China, based on the development indexes of the two institutions. The institution participating in the blockchain pilot program landing on December 20, 2021, is the experimental group, and the institution not participating in the pilot program is the control group. It is found that the blockchain pilot policy can significantly promote the development of the regional equity market, and the policy effect has a roughly 50-week lag in time. At the same time, this paper proposes an innovative solution to solve the existing problems of the regional equity market by using blockchain technology, which brings certain reference significance to the construction of practical work of the regional equity market.

Keywords: The Regional Equity Market · Blockchain Technology · The Difference-in-Difference Method

1 Introduction

As the cornerstone of China's capital market, the regional equity market is the cradle for cultivating high-quality listed companies. It has great strategic significance to the capital market reform and the support of national strategic emerging industries. It also plays an irreplaceable role in promoting the country's economy to help overcome poverty and incubate innovation and entrepreneurship [1]. By the end of 2022, 42,400 listed companies and 138,700 displayed enterprises were in the regional equity markets. Serving as an important channel for empowering the real economy and dealing with the problem of financing difficulties for small/medium-sized enterprises, the regional equity market has realized a cumulative total of RMB 1.87 trillion in financing [2]. However, along with the dramatic development potential of the fourth board market, financial risks are

G. Zhao et al. (Eds.): BWTAC 2024, CCIS 2277, pp. 13–24, 2025.
https://doi.org/10.1007/978-981-97-9412-6_2

progressively being exposed due to the difficulties in regulation and development. Problems such as information asymmetry due to incomplete disclosure of the operational and financial data, diverse and heterogeneous data due to the decentralized autonomy of equity trading centers, and inconsistent operating rules have not been effectively resolved. It would limit the marketing function and restrain the regulator's regulatory practice, leaving hidden risks for the regional equity markets.

As one of the seven key industries of the digital economy, blockchain has been explicitly written into China's "14th Five-Year Plan", and accelerating the layout of blockchain used in new financial infrastructure is the way to go in the digital era. The Shenzhen Stock Exchange has been exploring the application of blockchain technology in multiple scenarios such as securities storage, credit reporting, over-the-counter trading, and asset securitization, and took the lead in launching the Shenzhen Stock Exchange Financial Blockchain Platform in 2017. On July 7, 2020, the China Securities Regulatory Commission (CSRC) approved the pilot work of five regional equity markets in Beijing, Shanghai, Jiangsu, Shenzhen, and Zhejiang to participate in the construction of blockchain, marking the beginning of the "Blockchain + Regional Equity Trading Markets" [1]. On December 20, 2021, the Cyberspace Administration of China announced the selected list of national blockchain innovation application pilot projects, among which ten regional equity markets, including the Beijing Equity Trading Center, were selected as characteristic field pilot projects of the "Blockchain + Equity market". By the end of 2023, 25 regional equity market operators were carrying out blockchain construction.

This paper elaborates on the construction scheme for reforming the fourth board market and the theoretical mechanism that affects the development of the fourth board market. We empirically test the impact of blockchain policy on the development of equity trading centers before and after their implementation, with the participating pilot institution as the experimental group, and the non-participating pilot institution as the control group, using the development indexes of two institutions as the data source. Research has found that blockchain construction policy can significantly promote the development of regional equity markets, and the policy effect has a lag period of about 50 weeks in time.

The contribution of this paper is as follows: firstly, it summarizes the construction scheme based on the two-layer blockchain architecture of "central supervision chain-local business chain", and specifies the theoretical mechanism of blockchain influencing the development of the fourth board market and solving the pain points of the traditional four-board market. Secondly, using the development indexes of participating and non-participating pilot institutions as the data source, with the difference-in-difference method, provides a new perspective of empirical research ideas for the future research direction of regional equity market construction and development.

2   Related Works and Research Hypotheses

The regional equity markets are the unique private equity markets in China, and literature on the regional equity markets mostly focuses on the fields of regulation and construction. Scholars, on the one hand, find that the macro-level challenges faced by China's regional equity markets are mainly the imperfect regulatory system, the lack of fine segmentation, and the absence of a transfer system, while the micro-level challenges are mainly the lack of market activity, insufficient information disclosure, and high cost of corporate listing [3]. On the other hand, applying blockchain technology to regional equity markets is beneficial for unifying data governance norms in regional equity markets, promoting digital transformation, and improving the efficiency of resource integration [4]. Scholars mainly stand at the government level and have put forward strategies and opinions [5] for the construction of regional equity trading markets from the perspectives of law, regulation, digital construction, and transfer mechanisms [6]. They have provided a basic overview of the development status of regional equity markets and grasped the overall direction and main theme of improving the construction of regional equity markets at the strategic level. However, specific exploration paths have not been provided for the existing problems in regional equity markets.

In recent years, numerous pieces of literature have discussed the application of blockchain to the capital market. Khan et al. [7] underscored the critical significance of dependable and clear information transparency within decentralized frameworks, highlighting how Blockchain technology, effectively surmounts the intrinsic challenges of these systems that obviate reliance on intermediaries. Heo et al. [8] proposed a block-based blockchain system that ensures a safe and reliable trading mechanism, thereby mitigating potential security risks and improving transaction throughput. Wang et al. [9] proposed to rely on blockchain technology to promote the digital transformation and application innovation of regional equity markets from four aspects: service regulation, reverse empowerment, innovative application, and market connectivity. Zhang [10] modeled the design of the five major architectures based on blockchain: technology foundation layer, basic management layer, data layer, business application layer, and user layer. Zhang et al. [11] analyzed the six benefits of introducing blockchain into the regional equity market and proposed eight innovative application scenario design ideas for the blockchain + regional equity market. Using blockchain as a lever to solve the pain points of regional equity markets provides new pilot ideas for institutional and business innovation in regional equity markets. This article further elaborates on the logic and principles of blockchain construction in solving the seven pain points of regional equity markets based on scholars' research.

Through research, scholars have demonstrated the feasibility of applying blockchain technology to regional equity markets, but the actual application effect still needs to be tested.

3 Analysis and Mechanism Explanations for China's Regional Equity Market

Considering China's market conditions, the combination of blockchain and regional equity markets can shine brightly. The construction architecture of the "blockchain + regional equity market" introduces blockchain technology into both regulation and business innovation, pioneering the "dual layer chain" architecture of "central regulatory chain-local business chain", connecting 35 regional equity trading centers through chain

16   Y. Chen et al.

governance, and uploading data to the regulatory big data warehouse of the China Securities Regulatory Commission (CSRC) in terms of unified standards and specifications [9]. The specific construction plan is shown in Fig. 1.

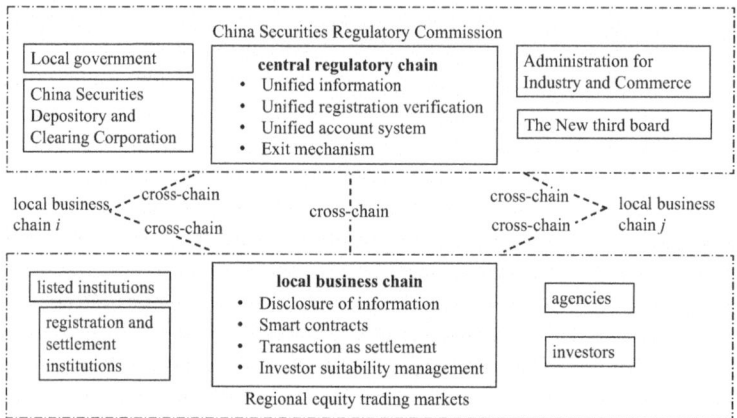

Fig. 1. Infrastructure map of regional equity financial markets based on "central regulatory chain-local business chain" [12–14]

As shown in Fig. 1, a dual-layer architecture of "central regulatory chain-local business chain" has the feature of "physical dispersion and logical unity". From the perspective of realizing functions, the central regulatory chain standardizes and unifies the information and equity registration of regional equity markets. This will achieve global unity and cross-regional interoperability of standardized businesses in various regions. From the perspective of participating nodes, the central regulatory chain is centered around regulatory agencies represented by the CSRC, local governments, and the State Administration for Industry and Commerce. This will make the communication mechanism between upstream and downstream markets much smoother.

The information disclosure mechanism corresponds to the data layer of the local business chain. The disclosure mechanism includes disclosure of business process information that the entire process information of related businesses is all on the chain. Additionally, relevant vouchers and materials are all disclosed on the chain and cannot be edited [15].

The smart contract makes business processes such as equity trading and registration of changes in custody shares automatically operate. After introducing a "settlement currency" on the business chain, clients can complete the settlement process through smart contracts, without traditional securities settlement systems [16]. Moreover, the automatic execution, mandatory performance, and transparent and open characteristics of smart contracts also make it easy for regional equity markets to mitigate the risk of customer deposit misappropriation due to information asymmetry. The integrated model of trading and settlement on the "local business chain" simplifies various processes such as securities issuance, trading, and settlement, and the existing lengthy process has been upgraded and transformed, improving financing efficiency and enhancing the effect of cost reduction.

4 Methods

4.1 Establishment of Difference-in-Difference Method Model

This paper takes the development indexes of participating and non-participating institutions as the research object, based on panel data of the regional equity market. For using the difference-in-difference method model, the institution that has implemented blockchain construction policy is designated as the experimental group, and the institution that has not implemented blockchain construction policy in designated areas is designated as the control group.

Policy grouping variable *treat* is based on whether blockchain construction policy is implemented or not. The *treat* of the experimental group equals 1, and the *treat* of the control group equals 0. Policy time variables *period* is based on when blockchain construction policy is implemented. The *period* before the blockchain construction policy (before December 20, 2021) equals 0, and the *period* after the blockchain construction policy (after December 20, 2021) equals 1.

For testing the actual impact of blockchain construction policy on the development of equity trading centers, interaction term *did* is created using policy grouping variable *treat* and policy time variables *period*. Overall, this paper establishes the difference-in-difference estimation model impact of blockchain construction policies on the development of equity trading centers as below:

$$y_{it} = \beta_0 + \beta_1 treat_i + \beta_2 period_t + \beta_3 treat_i \times period_t + \varepsilon_{it} \tag{1}$$

The range of values for subscript i is $i = 1, \ldots, n$, and subscript t is $t = 0, 1$. The value of β_1 means the differences between the experimental group and the control group. The value of β_2 means the impact of policy time on the experimental group and the control group. The value of β_3 represents the interaction impact, weighing the difference between the policy before and after implementation, as well as between the experimental and control groups. If the sign of β_3 is positive, it means that the impact of policy on the dependent variable y_{it} is positively correlated, representing that policy increases the value of y_{it}. ε_{it} is the error term of regressions. A more specific and intuitive explanation of the model coefficients is shown in Table 1.

Table 1. The coefficient interpretation of the difference-in-difference model

Coefficient Interpretation	Before the Policy ($period_t = 0$)	After the Policy ($period_t = 1$)	Difference
Control group ($treat_i = 0$)	β_0	$\beta_0 + \beta_2$	β_2
Experimental group ($treat_i = 1$)	$\beta_0 + \beta_1$	$\beta_0 + \beta_1 + \beta_2 + \beta_3$	$\beta_2 + \beta_3$
Difference	β_1	$\beta_1 + \beta_3$	β_3

4.2 Data Description and Source

This article uses the difference-in-difference method to empirically test the impact of blockchain construction policies before and after the blockchain policy implementation (before and after December 20, 2021) on the development of equity trading centers. The main variables are explained in Table 2.

Table 2. The explanation of the model variables

Variables Type	Variables Names	Explanations of variables
Explained Variable	Development indexes	Comprehensive and objective evaluation of the development and construction of equity trading centers
Explanatory Variable	*did*	dummy variable, defined as $treat_i \times period_t$

The explained variable uses development indexes of equity trading centers from these open official websites. The development indexes are comprehensive measurements and objective evaluations of the development and construction of equity trading centers. The base point of the indexes is 1000 points, updated once a week. The experimental group in this article is a participating pilot institution that implements blockchain construction policy, while the control group is a non-participating pilot institution that has never implemented blockchain construction policies. The index base day for the development index of the experimental group was April 7, 2017, while the index base day for the development index of the control group was December 31, 2013. To make these development indexes comparable, this paper sets the development index of the control group on April 7, 2017, to 1000 points, so that the development index base days and basis points of the control group and the experimental group are the same. The development index of the control group changes proportionally on other dates.

The explainable variable in this paper is *did* (defined as $treat_i \times period_t$), and the sample period is 346 weeks from April 7, 2017, to December 29, 2023. The policy implementation time was on December 20, 2021, therefore there were a total of 242 weeks before the policy implementation and 103 weeks after the policy implementation.

5 Empirical Results

5.1 Descriptive Statistics of Data

Based on the development indexes updated weekly by participating and non-participating pilot institutions from April 7, 2017, to December 29, 2023, partial panel data is shown in Table 3. The week of December 20, 2021, during which the blockchain construction policy was implemented, was assigned a value of 0, using it as a reference to indicate the corresponding weeks for each date. So the value of weeks corresponding to the date 2017-04-07 is −242, representing that the date 2017-04-07 is 242 weeks away from the reference system of December 20, 2021. The descriptive statistics of the main variables are shown in Table 4.

Table 3. Partial panel data

Date	Weeks	Equity Trading Centers	Development Index	*treat*	*period*	*did*
2017-04-07	−242	participating pilot institution	1000	1	0	0
2017-04-07	−242	non-participating pilot institution	1000	0	0	0
2021-12-20	0	participating pilot institution	2003.8702	1	1	1
2021-12-20	0	non-participating pilot institution	2053.2562	0	1	0
2023-05-05	70	participating pilot institution	2283.9099	1	1	1
2023-05-05	70	non-participating pilot institution	2148.9101	0	1	0

Table 4. Descriptive statistics of main variables

Variable Name	Mean	Std. Deviation	Min value	Max value
did	0.1488439	0.356192	0	1
Development Index	1679.059	416.2522	1000	2340.407

5.2 The Result of Difference-In-Difference Regression

Below is the result of the difference-in-difference regression. The coefficient of *did* is 91.586, passing the test at a significance level of 1%. It indicates that the implementation of blockchain construction policy can effectively promote the development of regional equity trading centers (Table 5).

Table 5. Difference-in-difference Estimation Regression (Standard errors in parentheses, *** p < 0.01, ** p < 0.05, * p < 0.)

Variable	Development Index
did	91.586*** (8.266)
constant	1665.427*** (2.897)
Sample size	692
R^2	0.9863

5.3 Parallel Trend Test

The prerequisite for the effectiveness of the difference-in-difference method is that the data needs to pass parallel trend testing. This paper uses the event study method to perform a parallel trend test. The time trend graph of the experimental group and control group is shown in Fig. 2. Before the blockchain construction was implemented, the development indexes of the experimental group and control group had similar trend growth. Though this trend growth is straightforward, the event study is necessary to test whether data pass the parallel trend test.

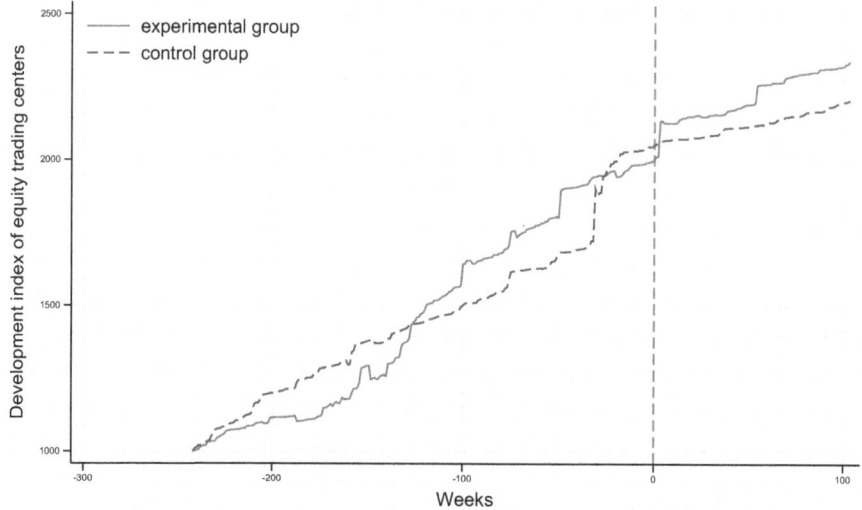

Fig. 2. The time trend graph of the experimental group and control group

The procedure of the event study is that: It interacts with weeks and the dummy variable *treat* to get time-series variables (*pre_i*, *current*, *t_j*), and then makes regression using development indexes as explained variables and time-series variables as explainable variables. The coefficients of time-series variables represent the differences between the experimental group and the control group at a specific time. The parallel trend test tests whether the p-value of the coefficients of the time-series variables (i.e. *pre_i*) before the policy implementation time is large. If it is large enough, it indicates that there is no significant difference between the experimental group and the control group before the policy.

According to the result of the regression, it is found that the p-values of coefficients of time-series variables before the policy was implemented are all above 0.1, showing that there is no significant difference between the experimental group and the control group before the policy, satisfying the hypothesis of the parallel trend test. Below is the p-value of partial coefficients of time series variables (Table 6).

The coefficients of the time-series variables with a 95% confidence interval in the above regression results can also be plotted to present the dynamic economic benefits of policies between different weeks in a more intuitive form. From the result of Fig. 3, the

Table 6. The p-value of partial coefficients of time-series variables

Development Index	P > |t|
pre_100	0.777
pre_90	0.751
pre_80	0.706
pre_70	0.587
pre_60	0.532
pre_50	0.493
pre_40	0.335
pre_30	0.292
pre_20	0.294
pre_10	0.250

95% confidence interval of the coefficients before the policy time point includes a value of 0, indicating that the coefficients of the time-series variables before the policy are not significantly different from 0, which means that there is no significant difference between the experimental group and the control group before the policy, meeting the assumption of parallel trends. The coefficients of the time-series variables from the 50th to the 70th week after the policy implementation point (i.e. from t_50 to t_100) are significantly positive, indicating that the policy has produced a significant positive effect since the 50th week, indicating a lag in the implementation of the blockchain construction policy.

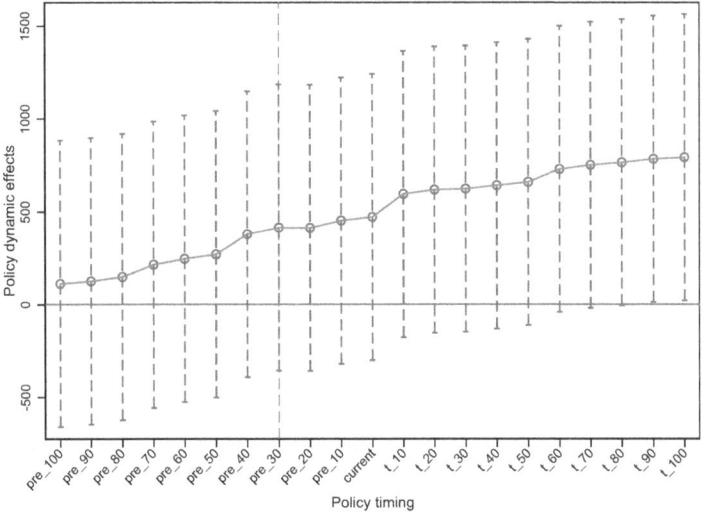

Fig. 3. The coefficients of the time-series variables with a 95% confidence interval

5.4 The Placebo Test

To eliminate the interference of other non-observational omitted variables/random factors on the positive effects brought about by the pilot policy, this study conducted a placebo testing to confirm. The placebo test is conducted by randomly selecting interaction terms. If there is a significant difference between the coefficients and the baseline estimated results, it can be proven that the estimated results of the original policy are not obtained occasionally.

The following figure shows the results obtained by repeating the "pseudo policy dummy variable" 500 times. The horizontal axis represents the estimated value of the "pseudo policy dummy variable", the vertical axis represents the p-value of its estimated value, and the dashed line represents the significance level of 0.05. It can be seen that the estimated coefficients obtained from 500 random sampling are between -20 and 20, with the center of the estimated coefficient values close to 0, and the P-values are generally greater than 0.05, following a normal distribution as a whole. The actual estimated DID coefficient is 91.586, which is clearly on the right side of the 5% percentile of the distribution and has a significant difference. This indicates that the actual estimated results are unlikely to be affected by other policies and random factors, and the policy effect is significant (Fig. 4).

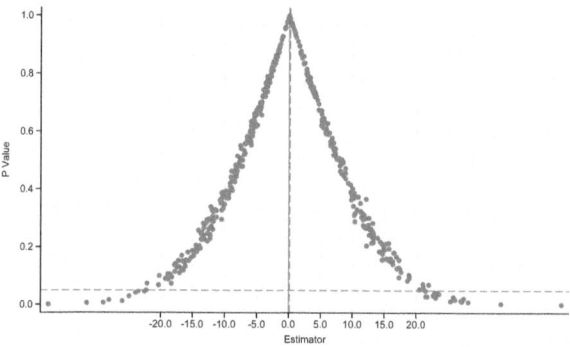

Fig. 4. P-value of pseudo policy dummy variables after repeating 500 times

5.5 The Results of the Empirical Test

Based on the data of development indexes of 246 weeks, from April 7, 2017, to Dec 29, 2023, of participating and non-participating institutions as the data source, this paper uses the date of December 20, 2021, as the policy point. The difference-in-difference method is used to study the impact of blockchain construction policy on the development of equity trading centers. The model has passed the parallel trend test and the placebo test, making sure of the effectiveness of the difference-in-difference method. The coefficient of the blockchain construction policy variable indicates the positive effects of the blockchain policy on the development of equity trading centers. In total the study validated two hypotheses: firstly, blockchain construction policies can significantly promote the development of regional equity trading centers; Secondly, the effectiveness of blockchain construction policies has a lag of approximately 50 weeks in terms of time.

6   Conclusion

This paper emphasizes the theoretical mechanism of the impact of the "central regulatory chain-local business chain" on regional equity markets. For the central regulatory chain, it can produce the effect of unified information sharing, unified registration verification, unified account system, and improved exit mechanism. For local business chains, it has achieved enterprise confidence disclosure, automated business execution, and digital currency settlement through smart contracts, transaction as settlement, and provided new solutions for investor suitability management. The use of blockchain in the construction and transformation of regional equity markets can ultimately promote the development of regional equity markets.

After clarifying the theoretical mechanism of the impact of blockchain on regional equity markets, this article also uses the development index of 346 weeks from April 7, 2017, to December 29, 2024, for participating and non-participating institutions as the data source, with December 20, 2021, as the policy time point, institutions implementing blockchain construction policies as the experimental group, and institutions not implementing blockchain construction policies as the control group. We used the difference-in-difference method to study the impact of blockchain construction policies on the development of equity trading centers and ultimately verified the positive effect of blockchain construction policy on the development of regional equity markets. Although blockchain pilots have significant policy effects on regional equity centers, due to the limited index data of regional equity centers in their development process, in-depth analysis of potential negative impacts or challenges of blockchain pilots can be conducted in the future, such as the impact on policy implementation costs and market participants' acceptance.

Acknowledgments. This paper was funded by the National Key R&D Program of China grant number [2021YFC3340600, 2021YFC3340603].

Disclosure of Interests. The authors have no competing interests to declare that are relevant to the content of this article.

References

1. Shen, Y., Gong, B.: Optimizing the regional equity market ecosystem. China Finance 59–61 (2022). (in Chinese)
2. People's Daily: New year report on national stock exchange innovation and development: core data section. https://rmh.pdnews.cn/Pc/ArtInfoApi/article?id=33652698
3. Zhang, H., Wang, T., Huang, X.: The realistic dilemma and path choice of the development of regional equity trading market in China. Reform 104–113 (2020). (in Chinese)

4. Exploring innovation to assist development in providing inclusive services with refinement and solidification - a case study of regional equity markets serving small and micro enterprises. http://www.cfthinkingfront.cn/news/17203.html
5. Li, Z.: The research of China regional capital market (new fourth board) for strategy of development. Shanghai Jiao Tong University (2021). (in Chinese). https://doi.org/10.27307/d.cnki.gsjtu.2016.005077
6. Chen, Q., Liu, W.: Research on the development of regional equity market in China. Shanghai J. Econ. 32–40 (2017). (in Chinese). https://doi.org/10.19626/j.cnki.cn31-1163/f.2017.01.004
7. Khan, U., An, Z.Y., Imran, A.: A blockchain ethereum technology-enabled digital content: development of trading and sharing economy data. IEEE Access **8**, 217045–217056 (2020). https://doi.org/10.1109/ACCESS.2020.3041317
8. Heo, G., Yang, D., Doh, I., Chae, K.: Efficient and secure blockchain system for digital content trading. IEEE Access **9**, 77438–77450 (2021). https://doi.org/10.1109/ACCESS.2021.3082215
9. Wang, J., Chen, B.: Innovative development of regional equity markets. China Finance 43–46 (2022)
10. Zhang, Y.: Utilizing blockchain technology to promote the integrated development of regional equity markets. Electron. Technol. Softw. Eng. 200–203 (2020). (in Chinese)
11. Zhang, Y., Zhou, Y.: Introducing blockchain technology into regional equity markets to explore the path of digital transformation. Tsinghua Financ. Rev. 75–79 (2022). (in Chinese). https://doi.org/10.19409/j.cnki.thf-review.2022.12.027
12. Xian, J.: Development and prospects of "blockchain + internet finance". Finance Account. Mon. 79–83 (2017). (in Chinese). https://doi.org/10.19641/j.cnki.42-1290/f.2017.14.014
13. Chen, Z., Qian, R.: Exploring the regulatory mechanism of blockchain finance in China: taking the construction of a "Chinese style sandbox supervision" mechanism as the institutional approach. Shanghai Finance 60–68 (2018). (in Chinese). https://link.cnki.net/doi/10.13910/j.cnki.shjr.2018.01.010
14. Dib, O., Brousmiche, K.-L., Durand, A., Thea, E., Hamida, E.: Consortium blockchains: overview, applications and challenges. Int. J. Adv. Telecommun. **11**(1), 51–64 (2018)
15. Cheng, C., Huang, Q.: Exploration on the application of blockchain audit. In: Proceedings of 5th International Conference on Economics, Management, Law and Education (EMLE 2019) (Advances in Economics, Business and Management Research, vol. 110), p. 6. International Science and Culture Center for Academic Contacts (ISCCAC), Russia, Kuban State University, Russia, Zhengzhou Yingchun Conference Planning Co., Ltd., China (2019). (in Chinese)
16. Mazzorana-Kremer, F.: Blockchain-based equity and STOs: towards a liquid market for SME financing? Theor. Econ. Lett. **9**, 1534–1552 (2019). https://doi.org/10.4236/tel.2019.95099

Tailoring Noise to Fit: An Adaptive Noise Optimization Mechanism Against Gradient Leakage

Haifeng Yuan and Haihang Wang[✉]

Tongji University, Shanghai 201804, China
{2230774,wanghh}@tongji.edu.cn

Abstract. Federated Learning (FL) is widely regarded as an effective privacy-preserving learning framework, as it keeps clients' training data local while only transmitting model updates. However, the Gradient Leakage Attack (GLA) can reconstruct clients' local data through transmitted gradients, posing a significant privacy threat to FL. Existing defense strategies against the GLA have the following limitations: (1) cryptography-based defenses impose high computational and communication costs, rendering them impractical for the typically resource-constrained FL clients; (2) perturbation-based defenses fail to dynamically adapt to the unique characteristics of each client's data, challenging the achievement of good utility-privacy trade-offs. To overcome these limitations, we introduce ANOM (Adaptive Noise Optimization Mechanism), a novel defense mechanism that customizes noise to align with local data attributes, thereby achieving a more favorable utility-privacy trade-off. Our comprehensive experimental evaluation demonstrates ANOM's superior capability to balance utility and privacy. Across all defenses, ANOM results in the minimal accuracy reduction on public datasets when compared to the unprotected model scenario. In terms of privacy preservation, ANOM outperforms the current state-of-the-art defense, Outpost, in nearly all assessed experimental settings.

Keywords: Gradient leakage attack · Federated learning · Noise optimization · Utility-privacy trade-offs

1 Introduction

In the current landscape dominated by big data and artificial intelligence, the demand for privacy-preserving machine learning techniques has become more critical than ever [13,22]. Federated Learning (FL) [11,14] has emerged as a distributed, privacy-preserving learning paradigm that enables multiple clients to collaboratively train a global model without exposing their local datasets, which has been applied in various fields such as healthcare [8], Internet of Things [19], and mobile applications [4,28]. In FL, multiple clients collaboratively train a global model by locally updating the model and sharing these model updates with a central server. The server then aggregates these updates and broadcasts the current global model back to the clients. This iterative process continues until the model converges. In the whole training process of FL, clients' training data remain on their local devices, and only model updates are transmitted to the server. By keeping raw data localized, FL mitigates the risk of data breaches and enhances user privacy, thus addressing one of the key concerns in deploying machine learning models in privacy-preserving domains. However, FL is not immune to privacy risks. One of the significant vulnerabilities in FL is the Gradient Leakage Attack (GLA) [5,10,26,29,30]. In this attack, the adversary solves an optimization problem to minimize the distance between the original and dummy gradients, thereby effectively recovering sensitive information from the gradients shared during the training process.

To counteract the GLA, the FL community has proposed various privacy protection methods. These methods can be categorized into cryptography-based defenses and perturbation-based defenses. The first category includes techniques such as Secure Multi-party Computation (SMC) [1,16,25] and Homomorphic Encryption (HE) [3,6,17,18], which protect privacy by cryptographic protocols or encrypted computation. While these methods effectively protect privacy without diminishing model performance, they impose significant computational and communication overheads. Given that FL clients are often computationally constrained, such overheads are impractical. Consequently, our focus shifts to the second category of defense. Perturbation-based defenses encompasses techniques like Soteria [21] and Differential Privacy (DP) [2,7], which either prune or introduce noise to gradients in order to impede the GLA. Nonetheless, Soteria may be bypassed by adversaries who exploit the non-pruned gradient layers. Additionally, DP can substantially diminish model performance as it does not dynamically adjust the noise variance. While other existing methods [23,24] do account for the noise level, they fall short of customizing the noise to align with the distinct characteristics of local data. In FL, client data distributions are often non-identically and independently distributed (non-i.i.d.). However, current methods fail to adapt the noise to each client's local data distribution. This oversight can lead to suboptimal utility-privacy trade-offs. Given the evolving nature of privacy threats in federated learning, ongoing research is crucial to develop more robust and efficient defense mechanisms that can adapt to the diverse characteristics of client data, thereby achieving good utility-privacy trade-offs.

To address the inherent limitations of prevailing perturbation-based defenses, we introduce a novel defense ANOM (Adaptive Noise Optimization Mechanism). ANOM tailors the noise to fit the local data attributes, thereby achieving a better utility-privacy trade-off. This adaptive approach strives to ensure that the noise added is optimal for each client's specific data distribution, enhancing both privacy protection and model performance. Specifically, ANOM tactically optimizes the noise added to the gradients after local training, guided by a meticulously crafted objective. This objective includes a utility metric that assesses the amount of information retained by the perturbed gradients and a privacy metric that evaluates the privacy-preserving effectiveness of the added noise. Intuitively, greater distortion of the gradients leads to a more significant reduction in utility. Consequently, we quantify utility by measuring the distance between the raw gradients and their noisy counterparts. For the privacy metric, we introduce the Class-Level Inversion Influence Function lower bound (CL-IIF$_{lb}$) to ensure protection for each class of samples. We recognize that samples within a specific class exhibit similar characteristics and face comparable privacy risks. Consequently, a protective design tailored for a class can be effective for all samples within that class. To reduce computational complexity, the proposed privacy metric strategically assesses privacy risks at the class level rather than on an individual sample basis. ANOM optimizes the noise to provide protection for different sample classes while maintaining minimal deviation from the original gradients. Furthermore, as FL training progresses and the privacy risk diminishes, ANOM adjusts its optimization termination condition by gradually relaxing it in correlation with the number of communication rounds. This approach not only reduces the computational load by lowering the threshold and resulting in fewer optimization iterations but also enhances the utility of the global model by gradually relaxing privacy requirements.

In summary, the major contributions of this work include the following:

- We adopt the distance between raw and noisy gradients as the utility measure and introduce the CL-IIF$_{lb}$ as the privacy measure. We modify IIF$_{lb}$ to compute the metric for a representative average sample within each class, thereby improving computational efficiency.
- We present ANOM, an innovative defense mechanism against the GLA, which tailors the noise to align with the local data attributes of each client. ANOM optimizes the noise iteratively, guided by an objective that integrates both utility and privacy metrics. Additionally, ANOM adapts to the diminishing privacy risk as the global model converges by gradually relaxing the optimization termination threshold.
- Our extensive experimental evaluation demonstrates the superiority of ANOM in balancing utility and privacy. Among all the defenses, ANOM results in the minimal accuracy reduction—only 0.60% on MNIST and 0.10% on CIFAR-10—when compared to the scenario with no defense applied. In terms of privacy preservation, ANOM is comparable to other methods and surpasses the state-of-the-art defense mechanism, Outpost, in nearly all evaluated settings.

2   Overview of Our Approaches

2.1   Problem Statement

In this paper, we consider an honest-but-curious federated server that adheres to the training protocol but may attempt to infer clients' local training samples through the GLA. In the GLA, the attacker optimizes dummy samples and labels to recover raw data by matching the original and dummy gradients. To counteract this potential threat, we implement a noise optimization mechanism that adaptively optimizes the noise δ added to the model gradients ∇, based

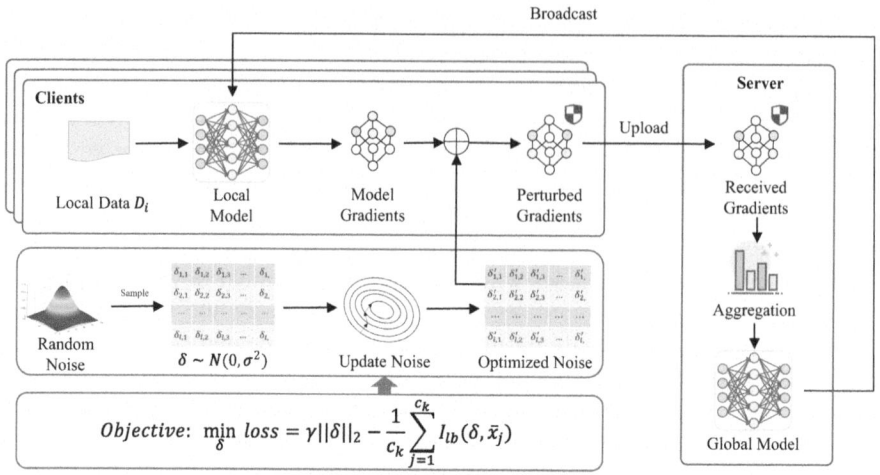

Fig. 1. An illustration of the proposed framework ANOM.

on local data characteristics. This approach disrupts the gradient matching process in the GLA. The objective of noise optimization is to provide sufficient privacy protection for local training data while maintaining as much utility as possible, achieving better utility-privacy trade-offs than existing defenses. The comprehensive framework of the proposed ANOM is depicted in Fig. 1.

2.2 Utility Measure

Intuitively, gradients ∇ in the absence of noise δ would maximize utility. Conversely, the greater the distortion introduced to ∇, the more utility is diminished. Hence, a metric for utility should be predicated on the divergence between the original gradients ∇ and their noisy counterparts $\nabla + \delta$. An expanded distance between ∇ and $\nabla + \delta$ correlates with a proportional increase in utility loss. For the sake of quantification, the utility metric is formulated to:

$$Utility : \mathbb{D}(\nabla, \nabla + \delta), \tag{1}$$

where $d(\cdot, \cdot)$ is a distance function. In this paper, we choose L2 norm as the distance function, a common metric that quantifies the magnitude of the difference between two vectors. Specifically, the distance between ∇ and $\nabla + \delta$ is defined by the L2 norm of their difference, expressed mathematically as $\mathbb{D}(\nabla, \nabla + \delta) = \|\nabla - (\nabla + \delta)\|_2$. Simplifying the expression inside the norm, we obtain: $\mathbb{D}(\nabla, \nabla + \delta) = \|\delta\|_2$.

2.3 Privacy Measure

In consideration of the privacy metric, we introduce the Class-Level Inversion Influence Function lower bound (CL-IIF$_{lb}$), based on the IIF$_{lb}$ ($I_{lb}(\delta, x)$) proposed by Zhang et al. [27]. It is designed to quantify the lower bound of the reconstruction error $\|x - x_{re}\|_2$, which represents the discrepancy between the actual sample x and the reconstructed counterpart x_{re}, following the injection of noise δ into the original gradients. This quantification is based on the assumption of an idealized adversary capable of immaculate sample recovery in the absence of gradient perturbation.

There are several reasons that we consider IIF_{lb} as the privacy metric: 1) it is a function about the introduced noise δ and the sample x, thus well suited to be used to optimize δ and provide privacy protection for x; 2) it establishes the lower extremity of Inversion Influence Function (IIF), thus delineating the worst-case reconstruction error scenario. In aligning with this stringent worst-case analysis, it is meticulously crafted to mitigate potential privacy compromises as much as possible; 3) it substantially diminishes computational complexity compared to IIF, which necessitates matrix inversion, rendering it computationally more intensive.

Notably, the metric $I_{lb}(\delta, x)$ is calculated on an individual sample basis, denoted by x. While providing privacy protection on a per-sample basis, calculating $I_{lb}(\delta, x)$ for the entire traing set of a client is computationally intensive. Recognizing that samples within a specific class share common characteristics and thus incur similar privacy risks, we modify the IIF_{lb} to compute the privacy metric for a representative average sample within each class, represented by $\bar{x}$. By calculating $I_{lb}(\delta, \bar{x})$ to afford class-level protection, this approach substantially diminishes the computational complexity inherent in the process. After the above adjustment, the defined privacy metric is articulated below:

$$Privacy : I_{lb}(\delta, \bar{x}) = \frac{\|J\delta\|_2}{\lambda_{max}(JJ^T)}, \tag{2}$$

where $J \triangleq \nabla_{\bar{x}} \nabla_w \text{Loss}(\bar{x}, w)$ represents the Jacobian matrix of the loss function, which encapsulates the sensitivity of the model's loss function with respect to the model parameters w, evaluated at the input $\bar{x}$. The denominator $\lambda_{max}(JJ^T)$ signifies the maximum eigenvalue of the matrix JJ^T. This eigenvalue captures the most significant change in the gradient direction due to the perturbation. Overall, this privacy metric evaluates the impact of the noise δ on the loss function's gradient, normalized by the maximum sensitivity direction of the gradient itself. This ratio helps assess the difference between the actual samples and the reconstructed counterparts when noises are introduced.

2.4   ANOM

The objective function for ANOM, which integrates both utility and privacy metrics, is presented below:

$$Objective : \min_{\delta} \gamma\|\delta\|_2 - \sum_{j=1}^{c_k} \theta_j I_{lb}(\delta, \bar{x}_j) \tag{3}$$

Note that we introduce a trade-off coefficient γ to balance utility and privacy. Additionally, we use a weighting coefficient θ_j to control the degree of privacy protection for samples of the j-th class. By default, θ_j is set to $\frac{1}{c_j}$, which implies equal protection for every class. In Eq. (3), c_k is the number of sample classes at client k, and $\bar{x}_j$ is the mean sample of the j-th class. Note that the coefficient on the latter term is negative because the CL-IIF$_{lb}$ represents the lower bound of reconstruction error which we want to maximize.

Given the dependency of the Jacobian matrix J in the objective on the model parameters, our approach entails conducting noise optimization subsequent to the local training on the client side (line 1 of Algorithm 1), thereby ensuring privacy protection for the updated global model. Before noise optimization, we initialize a normal distribution noise with a standard deviation of σ, as shown in line 2 of Algorithm 1. Then, we optimize the noise to fit the client's local data characteristics based on the crafted objective. In this work, we choose Stochastic Gradient Descent (SGD) as the optimizer due to its high efficiency and effectiveness in handling large-scale optimization problems, making it well-suited for the iterative nature of our noise optimization process.

The optimization process is designed to cease when the CL-IIF$_{lb}$ for each class of samples, denoted as $I_{lb}(\delta, \bar{x}_j)$, surpasses a specified threshold T, thereby facilitating a relatively equitable distribution of privacy protection across different classes. To successfully initiate a GLA, the gradients must contain sufficient information regarding the local data. However, as the global model converges, the client-specific local sample information encapsulated within the gradients tends to diminish, leading to a gradual decrease in the likelihood of accurately reconstructing the samples. Recognizing the diminishing privacy risk, we have implemented a mechanism that progressively relaxes the optimization termination threshold. This approach not only reduces computational load by shortening the threshold, resulting in fewer optimization iterations, but also enhances the utility of the global model. By appropriately relaxing stringent privacy requirements, a more favorable balance between utility and privacy can be achieved, thereby improving utility. Specifically, the threshold is set to decay in accordance with the number of communication rounds, defined as $T \cdot \eta^t$, as shown in line 3 of Algorithm 1. Here, η is a parameter that dictates the rate at which T diminishes, and t represents the index of the current communication round. The comprehensive procedure for ANOM is detailed in Algorithm 1.

3 Experiments

In this section, we conduct a comprehensive comparison of ANOM with existing defense mechanisms, evaluating their efficacy against different attacks across various experimental conditions. To this end, we design two distinct experiments aimed at assessing both the utility and privacy aspects of these defense methods.

3.1 Experimental Setup

Datasets: We conduct experiments on two commonly used image classification datasets MNIST and CIFAR-10, and use the Dirichlet distribution as in [9, 12] to

---

Algorithm 1. FedAvg local training at client k with ANOM

Input: global model w^t of the current communication round t; local objective F_k; initial noise standard deviation σ; trade-off coefficient γ; averaged samples $\{\bar{x}_1, ..., \bar{x}_{c_k}\}$; CL-IIF$_{lb}$ threshold T; decay parameter η; learning rate lr.
Output: Noisy model update Δ_k^t.
  1: $w_k^t \leftarrow$ Update_Global (w^t, F_k)
  2: $\delta \leftarrow$ Gaussian Noise $N(0, \sigma^2)$
  3: **while** $I_{lb}(\delta, \bar{x}_j) < T * \eta^t$ **do**
  4:     $\delta \leftarrow \delta - lr \cdot \nabla_\delta (\gamma \|\delta\|_2 - \frac{1}{c_k} \sum_{j=1}^{c_k} I_{lb}(\delta, \bar{x}_j))$
  5: **end while**
  6: $\Delta_k^t \leftarrow (w_k^t - w^t) + \delta$
  7: **return** Δ_k^t

---

generate non-i.i.d. client training data. A concentration parameter α is used to control the extent of non-i.i.d.-ness. The smaller α is, the more likely the clients hold examples from only one randomly chosen class. In all experiments, we set the value of α to 1.

Models: On both MNIST and CIFAR-10 datasets, we use the LeNet model, a commonly used model in the GLA related literature [5,20,30], which consists of four convolutional layers and one fully connected layer and uses sigmoid function as the activation function.

Attack and Defense Baselines: Two attack methods DLG [30] and InvGrad [5] are used in our experiments. We compare the proposed ANOM with four existing defense mechanisms: differential privacy (DP) [15], Soteria [21], Grad-Defense [24], and Outpost [23].

Evaluation Metrics: To evaluate the impact of defenses on model performance, we employ the validation accuracy of the global model, which is trained iteratively through multiple communication rounds using the FedAvg algorithm [14]. Furthermore, to assess the computational overhead imposed by these defenses, we examine the wall-clock time averaged across multiple communication rounds. Additionally, to quantify the privacy-preserving efficacy of various methods, we utilize the Mean Squared Error (MSE) and the Structural Similarity Index Measure (SSIM). These metrics gauge the divergence between the original and reconstructed images. An increased distance, as indicated by higher MSE and lower SSIM values, signifies a more effective preservation of privacy.

3.2 Utility Evaluation

In the utility experiments, we employ non-i.i.d. data distributions across 100 clients for both the MNIST and CIFAR-10 datasets. To simulate FL training in realistic scenarios, we establish a uniform local epoch count $E = 2$, and batch size $B = 32$, for these datasets. For the local training phase, we utilize the SGD optimizer and set the learning rate to 0.01. During each communication round, the server randomly samples 10 out of the 100 clients and aggregates their respective model updates. We conclude the FedAvg training sessions with various defenses once we reach a predefined threshold of communication rounds: 100 for MNIST and 200 for CIFAR-10, at which point the global models are deemed to have converged. To ensure the accuracy of our results, we conduct each experiment three times for every defense mechanism.

The experimental results for the MNIST and CIFAR-10 datasets are depicted in Fig. 2. In this figure, the x-axis corresponds to the elapsed wall-clock time, and the y-axis denotes the validation accuracy achieved. The solid lines within the figure illustrate the average accuracy for each defense strategy, and the shaded regions surrounding these lines represent the standard deviation range of the accuracies associated with each respective defense. Upon completion of the training phase across both datasets, it is evident that DP results in the most significant accuracy reduction-18.00% on MNIST and 9.18% on CIFAR-10-when compared to the scenario with no defense applied. This outcome can be attributed to the fixed noise level of DP, which does not adapt dynamically like other defenses that incorporate noise, or Soteria that solely target the pruning of fully connected layers. Following DP in terms of performance loss are Grad-Defense, Soteria, Outpost, and ANOM, with each successive method exhibiting a progressively smaller impact on accuracy. ANOM, in particular, demonstrates a minimal accuracy loss of only 0.60% on MNIST and 0.10% on CIFAR-10, in comparison to the unprotected baseline. These results suggest that the utility term within ANOM's objective function, coupled with the threshold decay mechanism, are effective in counteracting the accuracy degradation that arises from the introduction of gradient noise.

In terms of wall-clock time, it is apparent that Soteria and GradDefense demand a substantially higher duration to finalize training compared to other methodologies, signifying a considerable computational overhead. Conversely, Outpost incurs minimal training latency. ANOM follows as the next most efficient method in terms of training time, exhibiting a slightly lower delay compared to DP. While ANOM does entail a training delay due to the iterative updating of noise, this latency is deemed acceptable when juxtaposed with the delays induced by Soteria and GradDefense.

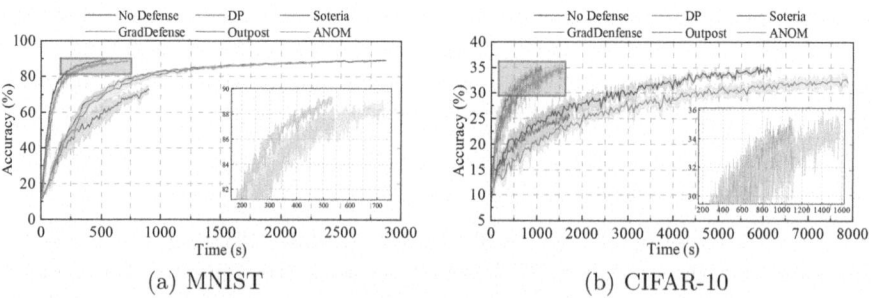

(a) MNIST   (b) CIFAR-10

Fig. 2. The impact of various defenses on FL training.

Table 1. The privacy-preserving effect of various defenses under different settings against two attacks.

	DLG					InvGrad				
	[Setting 1] MNIST: E=1, n=1, B=1									
	ND	DP	SO	OP	AN	ND	DP	SO	OP	AN
MSE	1.0e-3	**202.8**	79.6	57.4	80.7	8.3e-5	529.8	**729.1**	250.3	426.4
SSIM	9.9e-1	6.3e-2	9.2e-2	7.8e-2	**4.2e-2**	1.0	6.4e-2	**4.0e-2**	9.5e-2	8.8e-2
	[Setting 2] MNIST: E=1, n=4, B=1									
	ND	DP	SO	OP	AN	ND	DP	SO	OP	AN
MSE	7.3e-1	**579.9**	109.7	192.6	331.4	3.8e-1	13.5	10.8	2.8	**33.6**
SSIM	5.6e-1	**1.8e-2**	1.1e-1	6.8e-2	2.4e-2	4.5e-1	7.0e-2	6.9e-2	1.9e-1	**4.4e-2**
	[Setting 3] CIFAR10: E=1, n=1, B=1									
	ND	DP	SO	OP	AN	ND	DP	SO	OP	AN
MSE	1.2e-1	**26.9**	4.8	7.9	19.8	7.7e-3	70.5	**101.9**	48.5	49.3
SSIM	7.2e-1	**3.7e-2**	1.2e-1	7.1e-2	6.4e-2	9.6e-1	3.6e-2	4.0e-2	**3.1e-2**	5.9e-2
	[Setting 4] CIFAR10: E=1, n=2, B=2									
	ND	DP	SO	OP	AN	ND	DP	SO	OP	AN
MSE	1.9	**35.0**	4.0	15.3	23.1	5.4e-2	**4.2**	2.1	1.3	4.1
SSIM	1.3e-1	**2.4e-2**	6.7e-2	3.0e-2	3.2e-2	8.6e-1	**7.5e-2**	1.2e-1	1.1e-1	9.0e-2

3.3 Privacy Evaluation

In the privacy experiments, we meticulously design four distinct experimental scenarios to provide a thorough comparison of the privacy-preserving effects across various defenses. These scenarios encompass a range of parameters, including different datasets, local epochs E, local sample sizes n, and batch sizes B. To accentuate the distinctions of privacy efficacy between the methods, we examine an extreme scenario where a single client partakes in the FL training process, and the attack is executed in the initial communication round. The above setup represents the most stringent privacy risk for the client. Furthermore, the global model is deliberately initialized with a uniform distribution, precluding the use of momentum, weight decay, or learning rate scheduling in the SGD optimizer, which increased the likelihood of GLA success. Both the DLG and InvGrad employ the L-BFGS optimizer. We perform 1000 iterations of reconstruction in each attack trial. To capture the most challenging outcome, ten attack trials are executed, and the worst defense result is reported.

The outcomes of the privacy experiments are presented in Table 1. Within this table, ND, SO, OP and AN denote No Defense, Soteria, Outpost and ANOM respectively. An increased MSE and a decreased SSIM represent a greater distance between the reconstructed and original images, which is indicative of a more effective privacy protection. For each scenario, the results for the most effective method in countering both attacks are highlighted in bold. Additionally, the original and reconstructed images are displayed beneath their respective columns to visually assess their distinguishability, offering a complementary qualitative measure. It should be noted that the ground truth images depicted in Table 1 differ from those in the original datasets due to normalization processes.

Considering all scenarios, DP is the most effective in terms of privacy protection. However, this enhanced privacy comes at the cost of a significant reduction in accuracy, as illustrated in Fig. 2. Following DP are the proposed ANOM and Soteria. Nonetheless, Soteria necessitates a substantially longer training duration due to the additional computational overhead it imposes. In terms of privacy preservation, ANOM is comparable to other methods and even surpasses them in half of the metrics within Settings 1 and 2. It is also noteworthy that, in nearly all scenarios, the results yielded by ANOM on both metrics are superior to those delivered by the state-of-the-art defense mechanism, Outpost.

4   Conclusion and Future Work

In this paper, we introduce ANOM, a novel defense mechanism against Gradient Leakage Attacks. ANOM customizes noise in accordance with the distinct local data attributes of each client, guided by a carefully constructed objective function that integrates utility and privacy metrics. Our extensive experimental evaluation underscores the effectiveness of ANOM in balancing utility and privacy. Among all the defenses, ANOM results in the minimal accuracy reduction, with only a 0.60% decrease on MNIST and a 0.10% decrease on CIFAR-10, compared to the no defense scenario. Furthermore, in terms of privacy preservation, ANOM is at par with, if not superior to, other defense methods. Notably, it surpasses the state-of-the-art defense, Outpost, in nearly all evaluated scenarios.

Future work on ANOM will focus on several key areas of enhancement. Firstly, we plan to conduct extensive ablation experiments to analyze the impact of different components within ANOM. This will provide insights into the contributions of each component and help optimize the overall performance of ANOM. Secondly, we aim to explore the convergence properties of ANOM across various FL scenarios, which may yield theoretical guarantees and strengthen the method's reliability. Finally, we plan to identify strategies to further reduce computational complexity, which is critical for practical deployment.

References

1. Bonawitz, K., et al.: Practical secure aggregation for privacy-preserving machine learning. In: Proceedings of the 2017 ACM SIGSAC Conference on Computer and Communications Security, pp. 1175–1191 (2017)
2. Chen, S., Yu, D., Zou, Y., Yu, J., Cheng, X.: Decentralized wireless federated learning with differential privacy. IEEE Trans. Ind. Inf. **18**(9), 6273–6282 (2022)
3. Damgård, I., Pastro, V., Smart, N., Zakarias, S.: Multiparty computation from somewhat homomorphic encryption. In: Safavi-Naini, R., Canetti, R. (eds.) CRYPTO 2012. LNCS, vol. 7417, pp. 643–662. Springer, Heidelberg (2012). https://doi.org/10.1007/978-3-642-32009-5_38
4. Duan, M., et al.: Astraea: self-balancing federated learning for improving classification accuracy of mobile deep learning applications. In: 2019 IEEE 37th International Conference on Computer Design (ICCD), pp. 246–254. IEEE (2019)
5. Geiping, J., Bauermeister, H., Dröge, H., Moeller, M.: Inverting gradients-how easy is it to break privacy in federated learning? In: Advances in Neural Information Processing Systems, vol. 33, pp. 16937–16947 (2020)
6. Gentry, C.: Fully homomorphic encryption using ideal lattices. In: Proceedings of the Forty-First Annual ACM Symposium on Theory of Computing, pp. 169–178 (2009)
7. Geyer, R.C., Klein, T., Nabi, M.: Differentially private federated learning: a client level perspective. arXiv preprint arXiv:1712.07557 (2017)
8. Gupta, A., Misra, S., Pathak, N., Das, D.: FedCare: federated learning for resource-constrained healthcare devices in IoMT system. IEEE Trans. Comput. Soc. Syst. **10**(4), 1587–1596 (2023)
9. Hsu, T.M.H., Qi, H., Brown, M.: Measuring the effects of non-identical data distribution for federated visual classification. arXiv preprint arXiv:1909.06335 (2019)
10. Jeon, J., Lee, K., Oh, S., Ok, J., et al.: Gradient inversion with generative image prior. In: Advances in Neural Information Processing Systems, vol. 34, pp. 29898–29908 (2021)
11. Li, Q., et al.: A survey on federated learning systems: vision, hype and reality for data privacy and protection. IEEE Trans. Knowl. Data Eng. **35**(4), 3347–3366 (2021)
12. Lin, T., Kong, L., Stich, S.U., Jaggi, M.: Ensemble distillation for robust model fusion in federated learning. In: Advances in Neural Information Processing Systems, vol. 33, pp. 2351–2363 (2020)
13. Liu, B., Ding, M., Shaham, S., Rahayu, W., Farokhi, F., Lin, Z.: When machine learning meets privacy: a survey and outlook. ACM Comput. Surv. (CSUR) **54**(2), 1–36 (2021)
14. McMahan, B., Moore, E., Ramage, D., Hampson, S., y Arcas, B.A.: Communication-efficient learning of deep networks from decentralized data. In: Artificial Intelligence and Statistics, pp. 1273–1282. PMLR (2017)

15. McMahan, H.B., Ramage, D., Talwar, K., Zhang, L.: Learning differentially private recurrent language models. arXiv preprint arXiv:1710.06963 (2017)
16. Mohassel, P., Zhang, Y.: SecureML: a system for scalable privacy-preserving machine learning. In: 2017 IEEE Symposium on Security and Privacy (SP), pp. 19–38. IEEE (2017)
17. Paillier, P.: Public-key cryptosystems based on composite degree residuosity classes. In: Stern, J. (ed.) EUROCRYPT 1999. LNCS, vol. 1592, pp. 223–238. Springer, Heidelberg (1999). https://doi.org/10.1007/3-540-48910-X_16
18. Rivest, R.L., Shamir, A., Adleman, L.: A method for obtaining digital signatures and public-key cryptosystems. Commun. ACM **21**(2), 120–126 (1978)
19. Savazzi, S., Nicoli, M., Rampa, V.: Federated learning with cooperating devices: a consensus approach for massive IoT networks. IEEE Internet Things J. **7**(5), 4641–4654 (2020)
20. Sun, J., Li, A., Wang, B., Yang, H., Li, H., Chen, Y.: Provable defense against privacy leakage in federated learning from representation perspective. arXiv preprint arXiv:2012.06043 (2020)
21. Sun, J., Li, A., Wang, B., Yang, H., Li, H., Chen, Y.: Soteria: provable defense against privacy leakage in federated learning from representation perspective. In: Proceedings of the IEEE/CVF Conference on Computer Vision and Pattern Recognition, pp. 9311–9319 (2021)
22. Wang, C., Tang, H., Zhu, H., Zheng, J., Jiang, C.: Behavioral authentication for security and safety. Secur. Saf. **3**, 2024003 (2024)
23. Wang, F., Hugh, E., Li, B.: More than enough is too much: adaptive defenses against gradient leakage in production federated learning. In: IEEE INFOCOM 2023-IEEE Conference on Computer Communications, pp. 1–10. IEEE (2023)
24. Wang, J., Guo, S., Xie, X., Qi, H.: Protect privacy from gradient leakage attack in federated learning. In: IEEE INFOCOM 2022-IEEE Conference on Computer Communications, pp. 580–589. IEEE (2022)
25. Yao, A.C.: Protocols for secure computations. In: 23rd Annual Symposium on Foundations of Computer Science (SFCS 1982), pp. 160–164. IEEE (1982)
26. Yin, H., Mallya, A., Vahdat, A., Alvarez, J.M., Kautz, J., Molchanov, P.: See through gradients: image batch recovery via gradinversion. In: Proceedings of the IEEE/CVF Conference on Computer Vision and Pattern Recognition, pp. 16337–16346 (2021)
27. Zhang, H., Hong, J., Deng, Y., Mahdavi, M., Zhou, J.: Understanding deep gradient leakage via inversion influence functions. arXiv preprint arXiv:2309.13016 (2023)
28. Zhang, R., Xie, Z., Yu, D., Liang, W., Cheng, X.: Digital twin-assisted federated learning service provisioning over mobile edge networks. IEEE Trans. Comput. **73**(2), 586–598 (2024)
29. Zhao, B., Mopuri, K.R., Bilen, H.: iDLG: improved deep leakage from gradients. arXiv preprint arXiv:2001.02610 (2020)
30. Zhu, L., Liu, Z., Han, S.: Deep leakage from gradients. In: Advances in Neural Information Processing Systems, vol. 32 (2019)

Design of Privacy-Preserving Smart Contracts for Regional Equity Markets

Zichao Yang[1] ⓘ, Chenzhe Yang[1] ⓘ, Fengdong Wang[2], Yunfan Bao[1],
and Xiaofeng Ma[1,3(✉)] ⓘ

[1] Tongji University, Shanghai, China
`xiaofengma@tongji.edu.cn`
[2] China Securities Information Technology Service Co., Ltd., Shanghai, China
[3] Universiteit Leiden, Leiden, The Netherlands

Abstract. The regional equity market has preliminarily established a dual-layer "regulatory chain-business chain" architecture under the guidance of the securities regulatory commission, achieving efficient supervision of market activities and execution of business operations. Market participants include enterprises, regulatory authorities, equity trading centers, and other stakeholders, each with different needs and expectations for data privacy and security. Additionally, the market data types and sources are diverse and heterogeneous, presenting significant challenges for multi-party data privacy protection. In response to issues such as regulatory oversight and data privacy protection under the dual-layer chain architecture of the regional equity market, this paper designs a privacy protection algorithm based on homomorphic encryption and zero-knowledge proofs. It also integrates privacy smart contracts designed for the cross-market interconnectivity and interoperability business processes in the regional equity market, enabling the coordinated execution and verification of privacy computations across on-chain and off-chain environments. This approach effectively protects private data while meeting the usage requirements of business scenarios.

Keywords: Regional Equity Market · Privacy Protection · Smart Contract · Homomorphic Encryption · Zero-Knowledge Proof

1 Introduction

Regional equity markets, as an integral part of China's multi-tiered capital market, have preliminarily established a new generation of financial infrastructure with a dual-layer blockchain architecture of "central regulatory chain-local business chain". In the dual-layer chain architecture of regional equity markets, the use of smart contracts can effectively enhance business standardization and regulatory reporting timeliness. Smart contracts are self-executing and self-verifying computer protocols that realize the programmable functionality of blockchain technology. By transforming business logic and other content into code that operates on the blockchain, they are capable of automatically executing preset actions within the contract code when specific conditions are met.

G. Zhao et al. (Eds.): BWTAC 2024, CCIS 2277, pp. 37–49, 2025.
https://doi.org/10.1007/978-981-97-9412-6_4

Correspondingly, they record and update the data state on the blockchain without the need for third-party credit endorsement, thereby obtaining trustworthy computational results. The automatic execution and tamper-proof characteristics of smart contracts can standardize business processes and improve the efficiency of business execution. Moreover, after the business is carried out, the entire process is recorded on the chain in a traceable and auditable manner, meeting regulatory requirements.

The regional equity market encompasses a multitude of participants, data types, and intricate processes. Deployed on the blockchain, smart contracts are subject to public oversight, raising concerns regarding the potential exposure of sensitive contract data, notably the security of regulatory disclosures and the privacy of corporate information. Improvements in data protection are thus warranted. Participants in this market include equity trading centers, enterprises, third-party service providers, and regulatory bodies, interacting within a diverse and heterogeneous local business chain ecosystem. Business data originates from various sources—enterprises, service providers, and local governments—characterized by its multi-sourced, heterogeneous, and decentralized nature. These attributes complicate the task of ensuring smart contract confidentiality.

To address data utility and privacy in smart contracts, extensive research has been conducted by scholars globally. Prevailing privacy-preserving smart contract approaches are categorized into two main types.

The first approach employs Trusted Execution Environments (TEE) to create an off-chain secure computing realm. For instance, G. Su [1] and Zhang [2] leverage TEE for smart contract execution and voting information's cryptographic operations, respectively, to develop a data trading platform and an electronic voting system. These designs aim to enhance contract execution efficiency and safeguard contract information through TEE's security features. Desai et al. [3] propose the SECAUTEE framework, utilizing TEE to obscure memory access within the secure environment, thereby protecting smart contract data privacy. However, TEE's reliance on specific hardware and the associated high deployment costs, and the necessity for centralized support services introduce potential security and availability concerns.

The alternative approach is to use cryptographic methods for privacy preservation during data sharing. Examples include Ma Xiaoxu who employs zero-knowledge proofs for cross-chain privacy contracts, offering robust transaction information protection during asset transfers. Kosba et al. introduce Hawk [4], a smart contract mechanism that employs a manager and zero-knowledge proofs for interactions, potentially diminishing the blockchain's decentralization and resilience to attacks. Initiatives like smartFHE [5], Zether [6], ZoKrates, and ZeeStar [7] utilize homomorphic encryption and zkSNARKs to construct privacy-focused smart contract frameworks. These typically necessitate specialized languages, compilers, and deployment via dedicated plugins, incurring significant development and operational expenses.

Therefore, this paper designs a privacy-preserving smart contract based on homomorphic encryption and zero-knowledge proofs, which can effectively protect private data during the execution of business contracts and meet the needs for data updates and regulatory supervision in the regional equity market. This scheme is independent of specific blockchain platforms and can effectively adapt to heterogeneous business chains in various places, and most of the privacy calculations can be executed locally, greatly mitigating the adverse impact on blockchain performance.

2 Related Work

2.1 Homomorphic Encryption

Homomorphic encryption. Homomorphic encryption (HE) is a sophisticated crypto-graphic technique that allows computation on ciphertexts, yielding encrypted results that, when decrypted, match the outcome of operations performed on the plaintext. This breakthrough cryptographic paradigm maintains the privacy of the data while enabling computation to be conducted on it, thus addressing a fundamental challenge in secure multiparty computation and privacy-preserving data mining.

The primary advantage of homomorphic encryption is its ability to perform arbitrary computations on encrypted data without the need for decryption, thus ensuring data confidentiality throughout the computation process. This is particularly valuable in cloud computing scenarios where sensitive data can be processed in an encrypted state, reducing the risk of exposure to unauthorized parties.

In 1999, Pascal Paillier [8] introduced the Paillier cryptosystem, which possesses additive homomorphic properties. Renowned as a prominent partially homomorphic encryption algorithm, the Paillier scheme is widely utilized in both academic and industrial domains due to its high efficiency and comprehensive security proofs.

The ciphertext format of the Paillier encryption algorithm is given by:

$$c = g^m r^n \bmod n^2 \tag{2.1}$$

where m represents the plaintext data, n is the product of two random large prime numbers, and the random numbers g, r belong to $\mathbb{Z}_{n^2}^*$ (where $\mathbb{Z}_{n^2}^*$ denotes the set of all integers coprime to n^2 modulo n^2) with the condition $0 < r < n$.

2.2 Zero-Knowledge Proof

Zero-knowledge proof (ZKP) represent a significant innovation in the field of cryptography, offering a method for one party to convince another of the correctness of a statement without revealing any additional information beyond the validity of the statement itself. This concept was first introduced by Goldwasser, Micali, and Rackoff in 1985 and has since become a cornerstone of secure, privacy-preserving protocols.

ZKPs guarantee three key properties: completeness, ensuring high probability of verifier conviction by an honest prover for true statements; soundness, preventing convincing false statements by dishonest provers; and zero-knowledge, ensuring verifiers gain no information beyond the statement's truth. They are especially crucial for maintaining privacy in secure authentication, anonymous transactions, and blockchain technologies, allowing data integrity and authenticity verification without confidentiality compromise.

Zero-knowledge proofs are categorized into interactive and non-interactive zero-knowledge proofs. The bit commitment scheme BC(-) [*], proposed by Eiichiro Fujisaki and Tatsuaki Okamoto, commonly referred to as the FO commitment [9], is typically utilized in the construction of verifiable cryptographic commitments within the context of interactive zero-knowledge proofs. The prover can demonstrate knowledge of the value underlying the commitment without disclosing any information to the verifier. The commitment form is given by:

$$E(m, r) = g^m h^r \bmod n \tag{2.2}$$

where n is a large composite number, h is an element from the cyclic group generated by g with the discrete logarithm $\log_g h$ being unknown, and r is a random integer within the range $R[-2^s n + 1, 2^s n - 1]$.

Currently, the research and application of zero-knowledge proofs (ZKPs) are rapidly advancing. With the rise of blockchain technology, ZKPs have demonstrated significant potential in ensuring transactional privacy and verifying user identities. For instance, Zcash employs zero-knowledge proofs to offer anonymous transaction capabilities, permitting users to conduct cryptocurrency transactions without revealing the transaction amounts or participant information. Furthermore, zero-knowledge proofs are frequently utilized in the construction of privacy-preserving authentication systems and secure multi-party computation.

3 Design of Privacy Contracts in Regional Equity Markets

3.1 Privacy Protection Requirements in Regional Equity Markets

In compliance with CSRC mandates, regional equity markets are developing a specialized board for "Specialized, Refined, Differential, and Innovational" (SRDI) enterprises. This initiative includes establishing mechanisms for mutual recognition of information disclosure and self-regulatory oversight, alongside a technical system interconnect with associated institutions. As depicted in Fig. 1, within the current workflow, enterprises record diverse information types on the business chain of the Regional Equity Exchange (REE) for data evidence preservation and submit confidential financial documents, such as financial statements, and balance sheets. Simultaneously, the REE corroborates enterprise data against government figures, such as tax payments, to validate the legality and authenticity of SRDI enterprise cultivation data. Government data is also reported to the regulatory chain through the business chain for notarization and verification. Upon receiving enterprise data from the REE, institutions assess applicants' compliance with listing, registration, settlement, and disclosure criteria, in line with business regulations, leading to review decisions or opinions.

Local government information, as an important type of private data, poses security risks when circulated and preserved directly on the blockchain. Except for regulatory authorities at all levels, other entities should not have access to the data in plaintext. The non-public information of enterprises and the data reported to regulatory authorities also require protection. Furthermore, the REE must securely compare the local government data with the enterprise-declared data to ensure data authenticity, significantly increasing the complexity of business execution.

In the various operations of regional equity markets, a variety of privacy data protection needs exist around enterprises, REEs, and regulatory authorities. Currently, privacy data is often uploaded to the blockchain in the form of hash evidence or encrypted data vouchers. However, when executing smart contracts, simple hashes or data encryption vouchers are insufficient to meet the complex needs of actual business execution, such as the comparison of original data scope and proof provision. Therefore, it is necessary to design privacy-preserving smart contracts tailored to regional equity markets, which protect the privacy of enterprise and local government information within business contracts while ensuring the penetrating supervision.

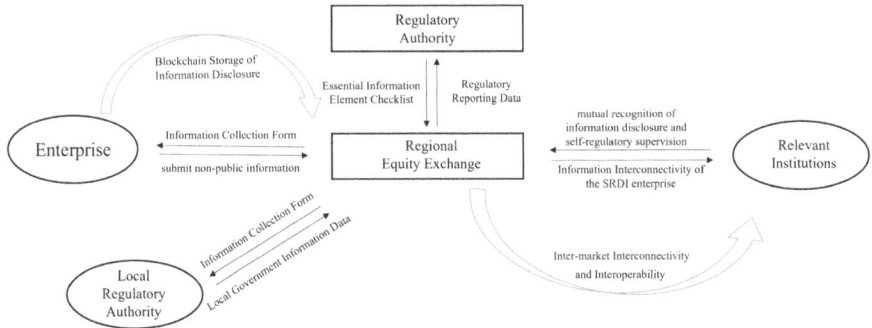

Fig. 1. Interconnectivity and Interoperability Business Process in Regional Equity Markets

3.2 Design of Privacy Protection Algorithms and Smart Contracts

The Privacy Protection Algorithms. In this paper, we propose an improved Paillier homomorphic encryption algorithm based on the Fujisaki-Okamoto (FO) commitment scheme and a privacy protection framework that incorporates zero-knowledge range proofs. This framework is tailored to the business processes of regional equity markets, where the algorithm possesses homomorphic properties and is capable of generating zero-knowledge proofs, thereby enabling privacy protection and secure comparison of enterprise and local government data. Specifically, homomorphic encryption extends the computational capabilities of data, allowing for direct updates and computations within the encrypted domain, while zero-knowledge proofs facilitate condition verification required by audit institutions such as stock transfer companies or central securities depositories without revealing the actual data.

The improved Paillier encryption algorithm includes key generation, data encryption, data decryption, zero-knowledge proof generation, and proof verification processes. The algorithm involves symbol descriptions as shown in Table 1.

The key generation function is defined as $Key(n, g, f)$. Two large prime numbers, p and q, are randomly selected. The value of n is set as the product of p and q, i.e., $n = pq$. Concurrently, the value of λ is calculated using the formula

$$\lambda = lcm(p - 1, q - 1) \tag{3.1}$$

where $lcm()$ denotes the Least Common Multiple function.

Table 1. Algorithm-related symbolic representation.

variable	Definition
n	Public parameter
k	A random integer, such that $k < n^2$
e	A random integer, such that $e \in \mathbb{Z}^*_{n^2}$
g	Public parameter
f	Public parameter
p or P_k	The public key
s or S_k	The private key
m	Plaintext data
r	Public parameter
$b \,\text{、}\, b'$	Evaluation Index
(c, c')	Ciphertext data

Select an integer e at random such that $e \in \mathbb{Z}^*_{n^2}$, and it satisfies the condition

$$gcd\left(n, L\left(e^\lambda \bmod n^2\right)\right) = 1 \tag{3.2}$$

where $gcd()$ represents the Greatest Common Divisor function and the function $L(x)$ is defined as

$$L(x) = (x - 1)/n \tag{3.3}$$

Calculate:

$$g = e^\lambda \bmod n^2 \tag{3.4}$$

Select an integer k at random such that $k < n^2$, and compute:

$$f = e^k \bmod n^2 \tag{3.5}$$

Furthermore, f is required to satisfy the condition:

$$gcd\left(n, L\left(f^\lambda \bmod n^2\right)\right) = 1 \tag{3.6}$$

Select an integer s at random such that $s < n$, and compute:

$$p = f^s \bmod n^2 \tag{3.7}$$

Let p serve as the public key, denoted as P_k, and s as the private key, denoted as S_k.
The data encryption function is defined as $En(m, r, p, n, g, f)$, and the data m to be encrypted is computed using the afore mentioned parameters with:

$$c = g^m p^r \bmod n^2 \tag{3.8}$$

$$c' = f^r \bmod n^2 \tag{3.9}$$

The pair (c, c') composed of c and c' serves as the ciphertext for the data m. The ciphertext of this algorithm is additively homomorphic, because of

$$c_1 c_2 = g^{m_1 + m_2} h^{r_1 + r_2} \bmod n^2 \tag{3.10}$$

$$c_1' c_2' = f^{r_1 + r_2} \bmod n^2 \tag{3.11}$$

$$En(m_1, r_1, p, n, g, f) \times En(m_2, r_2, p, n, g, f) = En(m_1 + m_2, r_1 + r_2, p, n, g, f) \tag{3.12}$$

The data decryption function is defined as $De((c, c'), s, n, g)$, and the calculation formula for the plaintext data m in the function is:

$$c'' = c/c'^s = g^m \bmod n^2 \tag{3.13}$$

$$m = L(c'')/L(g) \bmod n \tag{3.14}$$

It is observed that the c of ciphertext c, c' shares the same form as the FO commitment. From Eqs. (3.4), (3.5), and (3.7), it is known that:

$$p = f^s \bmod n^2 = e^{ks} \bmod n^2 \tag{3.15}$$

where g and p satisfy p being an element of the cyclic group generated by g. Therefore, by encrypting the original data m using the improved Paillier algorithm, the first component c in the ciphertext (c, c') can serve as the FO commitment of m for range proof of m.Upon obtaining the commitment, we employ the component c alongside the predefined security parameters l, s, t, T, to generate a zero-knowledge proof evidence, which validates that the data m is within the bounds $[b, b']$, where $\log_2(b - 0) \leq T$.

Let $x = m - b + 1 (m > b)$ or $x = b' - m + 1 (m < b')$, calculate:

$$E = g^x p^r \bmod n^2 \tag{3.16}$$

Randomly select integers $\alpha \neq 0$, $\beta \in [0, 2^{T+s}]$, and set:

$$k = \alpha^2 x + \beta > 2^{l+s+t+T} \tag{3.17}$$

Randomly select integers r_1, r_2, r_3 within the range $[-2^s n^2 + 1, 2^s n^2 - 1]$ and ensure $r_3 - r\alpha^2 - r_1\alpha - r_2$ also falls within this range. Then calculate E_1, E_2, E_3:

$$E_1 = E^\alpha p^{r_1} \bmod n^2 \tag{3.18}$$

$$E_2 = E_1^\alpha p^{r_2} \bmod n^2 \tag{3.19}$$

$$E_3 = g^\beta p^{r_3} \bmod n^2 \tag{3.20}$$

$$F = g^k/E_2 = g^\beta p^{r_3 - r\alpha^2 - r_1\alpha - r_2} \bmod n^2 \tag{3.21}$$

The calculated k, E_1, E_2, E_3 constitute the evidence for the zero-knowledge proof. The proof is sent to the verifier and executes the following protocols:

$$PK_1\left\{E_1 = E^\alpha h^{r_1} \bmod n^2 \wedge E_2 = E_1^\alpha h^{r_2} \bmod n^2\right\} \tag{3.22}$$

$$PK_2\left\{E_3 = g^\beta h^{r_3} \bmod n^2 \wedge F = g^k/E_2 = g^\beta h^{r_3 - r\alpha^2 - r_1\alpha - r_2} \bmod n^2\right\} \tag{3.23}$$

$$PK_3\left\{E_1 = E_3 = g^\beta h^{r_3} \bmod n^2 \wedge E_2 = \beta \in \left[-2^{l+s+t+T}, 2^{l+s+t+T}\right]\right\} \tag{3.24}$$

The verifier calculates:

$$E = g^{-b+1}c \bmod n^2 (m > b) \text{ or } E = g^{b'+1}c^{-1} \bmod n^2 (m < b') \tag{3.25}$$

and verify the correctness of protocols PK_1, PK_2, PK_3 and Eq. (3.18), if they are all true, then the verifier can believe that the data m is within the bounds $\left[b, b'\right]$.

The Privacy Smart Contracts. As shown in Fig. 2, the design of this scheme mainly consists of regulatory contracts, submission contracts, privacy contracts and verification contracts, which meets the stringent requirements for data privacy and security in regional equity markets while supporting complex business logic verification.

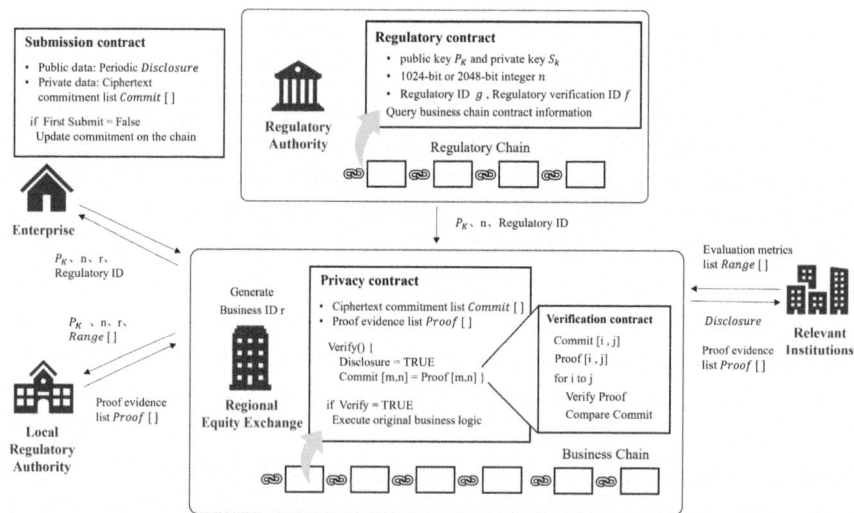

Fig. 2. Design of Privacy Smart Contract Scheme.

Regulatory Authority's Public and Private Key Generation. Regulatory authorities generate the public-private key pair, tailored to distinct business categories and associated with a specific regulatory ID. Substitute the Regulatory ID and Regulatory Verification

ID as g and f, respectively. These identifiers, along with the public key, are conveyed to the business blockchain by the regulatory contract. They serve as key parameters in subsequent cryptographic operations and the generation of zero-knowledge proofs, thereby establishing a binding between the regulatory ID and the encrypted commitment and proofs. The regulatory authority records the public key P_k, the random number n, the regulatory ID g, and the regulatory verification ID f into the regulatory contract, transmitting the data to the business blockchain. The private key S_k is stored as evidence on the regulatory blockchain.

Enterprise's Commitment Generation and Penetrating Supervision. Enterprises provide information based on the necessary information elements list, which encompasses both public and private segments, and submit it to the business chain through a submission contract. The public data necessitates periodic disclosure and the establishment of a verifiable record on the blockchain. A series of privacy data encrypted with the public key, is created into a ciphertext commitment list *Commit*[] preserved on the chain.

In the instance of enterprises submitting privacy data, the enterprises initially request a random ID r associated with the ongoing business from the REE. Concurrently, they procure the public key P_k, random number n, regulatory ID g, and regulatory verification ID f from the REE. Utilizing these parameters, a series of ciphertexts are generated locally on the client through the encryption function $En(m, r, p, n, g, f)$.

Due to the homomorphic properties of ciphertexts, enterprises can periodically update their encrypted commitment data, which is also recorded on the blockchain.

Regulatory authorities, leveraging the corresponding private key and the data decryption function $De((c, c'), s, n, g)$, can decrypt a series of ciphertexts stored on the business blockchain and access the original data via the regulatory ID, effectively facilitating penetrating supervision.

Local Regulatory Authority Proof Generation. Relevant institutions establish data verification boundaries, forming an evaluation metrics list *Range*[], where each metric takes the form of $[b, b']$. The institutions communicate metrics to local regulatory authority through REE. Concurrently the REE convey the business ID r to local regulatory authority If the government data recorded by the local regulatory authority meets the evaluation metric range, a series of zero-knowledge proofs *Proof*[] can be generated using Eqs. (3.17)–(3.21) and then preserved as evidence on the REE's business chain.

Regional Equity Exchange Proof Verification. The zero-knowledge proofs evidences k, E_1, E_2, E_3, containing range data, enable the REE to automatically compare the commitment and proof evidence through smart contracts, thereby achieving automatic verification of authenticity and compliance.

Privacy contracts transform the plaintext input parameters of the original business contracts into encrypted commitments and proofs stored on the REE's business chain, offering excellent versatility as they can adapt to different programming languages.

The REE utilizes a verification contract for validation, the principle of which is described by Eqs. (3.22)–(3.25). If the verification is successful, it certifies that the submitted data indeed conforms to the established evaluation metrics. Moreover, due to the consistency in form between the evidence provided by the zero-knowledge proof and the committed ciphertexts, this further ensures the authenticity of the data previously submitted by enterprises to the business chain. This verification mechanism not only ensures the compliance of the data but also leverages the characteristics of zero-knowledge proofs to maintain the privacy and security of the data.

By integrating a verification phase for information disclosure notarization, encrypted commitments, and zero-knowledge proof before the original business logic, the system checks whether the enterprise has fulfilled its obligation of information disclosure and proves the accuracy of the privacy data in the encrypted commitments after verification. Once the verification is confirmed to be correct, the system will continue to execute the original business logic, ensuring the contract's functionality and compliance.

Then the disclosure data and proof information are relayed to relevant institutions, achieving mutual recognition of information disclosure and self-regulatory supervision.

4   Result and Analysis

4.1   Security Analysis

The privacy algorithm proposed in this paper is an enhancement based on the Paillier encryption algorithm, maintaining consistency with the original Paillier encryption scheme and satisfying the semantic security of the encryption paradigm. The security of the algorithm is reducible to the Decisional Composite Residuosity Assumption (DCRA) problem. This assumption pertains to the question of determining whether a given integer z belongs to the set of quadratic residues modulo n^2 for a composite number n. To date, no known efficient polynomial-time algorithm exists for this problem. The confidentiality property is intuitively reflected in its high degree of protection for plaintext information, ensuring the indistinguishability of ciphertexts, thereby not providing external observers with any clues about the encrypted content. Attackers cannot decipher the plaintext information from the ciphertext.

4.2   Performance Evaluation and Analysis

In this proposal, the test environment is as outlined in Table 2. Key generation, encryption, and decryption processes are conducted within an off-chain environment, while the verification process for zero-knowledge proofs and the execution of associated contracts take place within an on-chain environment.

Table 2. Test environment.

Hardware	Off-chain Configurations	On-chain Configurations
Operating System	Windows 10 Professional, 64bit	CentOS Linux release 7.9.2009, 64bit
CPU	Intel(R) Core (TM) i7–11700 @ 2.50 GHz	Intel(R) Xeon (R) Gold 5218 CPU @ 2.30 GHz
Hard Disk	100G and above	100G and above
RAM	16G	32G

Conducted tests on the time required for the key generation, encryption and decryption of the improved Paillier encryption algorithm, while comparing its performance with the original Paillier encryption scheme. During the key generation process, the security of the key is contingent upon the length of the selected prime numbers; the longer the prime numbers, the greater the difficulty of factorization. Therefore, tests were conducted with n being 1024-bit and 2048-bit, respectively, and the average time over 100 trials is illustrated in the Fig. 3 below.

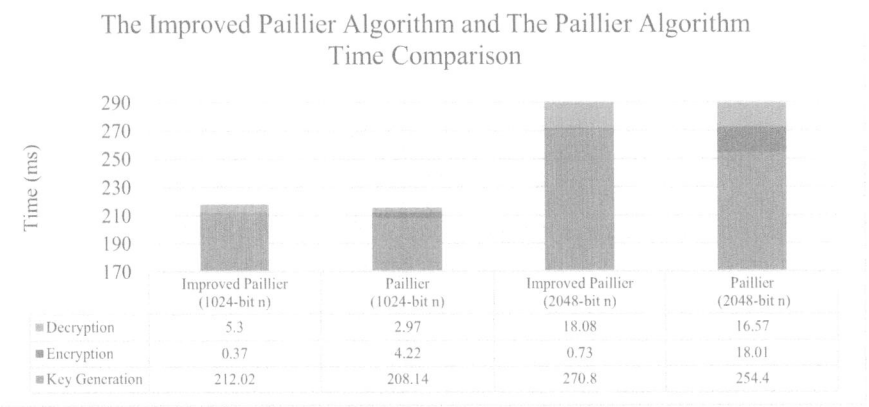

Fig. 3. Comparison of time between the improved Paillier algorithm and the Paillier algorithm.

The key generation time of the improved encryption algorithm is comparable to that of the original algorithm, with a significant reduction in data encryption time and a slight increase in data decryption time. The cumulative time for key generation and data encryption/decryption, when n is 1024-bit, does not exceed 220 ms, and when n is 2048-bit, does not exceed 290 ms. Given that the current business scenario is not characterized by high-frequency trading, the performance of this improved encryption algorithm is well-suited to meet the needs of the application context.

Within the business chain, there are 35 local stock exchanges currently, thus 40 users were set up and 100 rounds were sent in a loop in this experiment. As depicted in Fig. 4, the experiment involves the selection of common business contracts from regional equity markets. Specifically, Contract1 is the Equity Registration and Custody contract, Contract2 is the Enterprise Data Query contract, and Contract3 is the Regulatory Data Reporting contract. Contracts integrating privacy preservation mechanisms exhibited only a modest escalation in response time, estimated to be around 30 ms, concomitant with a slight attenuation in throughput, typically not surpassing 100 transactions per second (TPS). It is noteworthy that as the complexity of the business logic escalates, the performance discrepancy attributable to privacy protection diminishes, exerting a negligible impact on the overall system performance.

Contrasting with original business contracts devoid of privacy protection, privacy contracts on the blockchain incorporate solely an additional verification step, with all

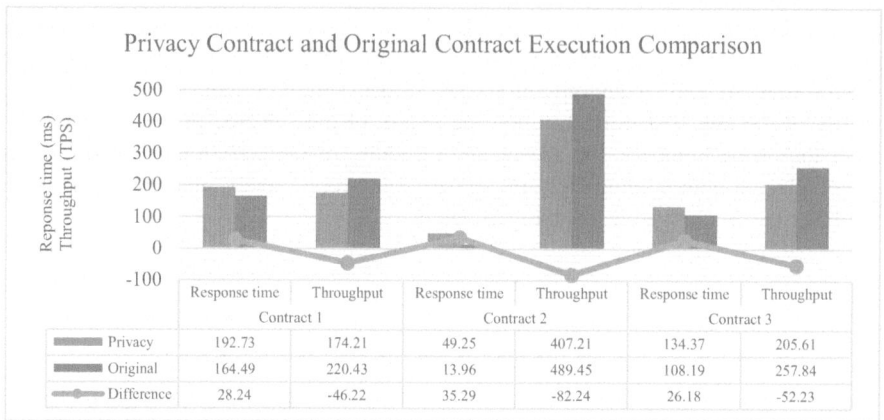

Fig. 4. Privacy Contract and Original Contract Execution Comparison

other cryptographic operations being executed off-chain. This design significantly mitigates the potential impact of complex cryptographic computations on system performance, achieving an effective equilibrium between privacy protection and performance efficiency. Consequently, while ensuring the confidentiality of data within the intricate business scenarios of regional equity markets, the privacy contracts maintain the response time and throughput that are commensurate with the original, offering a blockchain application solution that is both secure and highly efficient.

Acknowledgments. This study was funded by the National Key R&D Program of China (grant number 2021YFC3340600).

References

1. Su, G., Yang, W., Luo, Z., Zhang, Y., Bai, Z., Zhu, Y.: BDTF: a blockchain-based data trading framework with trusted execution environment. In: 2020 16th International Conference on Mobility, Sensing and Networking (MSN), pp. 92–97 (2020)
2. Zhang, Y., Li, Y., Fang, L., Chen, P., Dong, X.: Privacy-protected electronic voting system based on blockchain and trusted execution environment. In: 2019 IEEE 5th International Conference on Computer and Communications (ICCC), pp. 1252–1257 (2019)
3. Desai, H., Kantarcioglu, M.: SECAUCTEE: securing auction smart contracts using trusted execution environments. In: 2021 IEEE International Conference on Blockchain (Blockchain), pp. 448–455 (2021)
4. Kosba, A., Miller, A., Shi, E., Wen, Z., Papamanthou, C.: Hawk: the blockchain model of cryptography and privacy-preserving smart contracts. In: 2016 IEEE Symposium on Security and Privacy (SP), pp. 839–858 (2016)
5. Solomon, R., Weber, R., Almashaqbeh, G.: smartFHE: privacy-preserving smart contracts from fully homomorphic encryption. In: 2023 IEEE 8th European Symposium on Security and Privacy, EUROS&P, pp. 309–331 (2023)
6. Bünz, B., Agrawal, S., Zamani, M., Boneh, D.: Zether: towards privacy in a smart contract world. In: Bonneau, J., Heninger, N. (eds.) FC 2020. LNCS, vol. 12059, pp. 423–443. Springer, Cham (2020). https://doi.org/10.1007/978-3-030-51280-4_23

7. Steffen, S., Bichsel, B., Baumgartner, R., Vechev, M.: ZeeStar: private smart contracts by homomorphic encryption and zero-knowledge proofs. In: 43rd IEEE Symposium on Security and Privacy (SP 2022), pp. 179–197 (2022)

8. Paillier, P.: Public-key cryptosystems based on composite degree residuosity classes. In: Stern, J. (ed.) EUROCRYPT 1999. LNCS, vol. 1592, pp. 223–238. Springer, Heidelberg (1999). https://doi.org/10.1007/3-540-48910-X_16

9. Fujisaki, E., Okamoto, T.: Secure integration of asymmetric and symmetric encryption schemes. In: Wiener, M. (ed.) CRYPTO 1999. LNCS, vol. 1666, pp. 537–554. Springer, Heidelberg (1999). https://doi.org/10.1007/3-540-48405-1_34

Deep Learning Empowered Blockchain Transaction Prediction and Anomaly Detection

Yiren Hu[1], Wei Wang[1(✉)], and Yiliang Liu[2]

[1] College of Electronic and Information Engineering, Nanjing University of Aeronautics and Astronautics, Nanjing, China
{huyiren,wei_wang}@nuaa.edu.cn
[2] Xi'an Jiaotong University, Xi'an, China

Abstract. With the rapid development of blockchain technology, cryptocurrency exchanges, as a critical application, have experienced a substantial increase in transaction volume. This surge provides opportunities for illicit activities such as money laundering and market manipulation, necessitating an effective regulatory framework. In this paper, we propose a regulatory approach for monitoring trading volumes. Our method entails a detailed analysis of trading data from multiple exchanges. We conduct feature engineering on the data and enhance features from a time series perspective. Utilizing deep learning models, we effectively capture the dynamic characteristics of the data and improve prediction accuracy. Furthermore, we establish refined dynamic threshold intervals based on data dynamics, enabling more efficient anomaly detection. We validated using real transaction data from Ethereum and compared it with conventional methods. The results demonstrate that our framework achieves higher prediction accuracy, greater sensitivity in anomaly detection, and more comprehensive detection results, thereby enhancing regulatory.

Keywords: Blockchain technology · Cryptocurrency exchanges · Regulatory framework

1 Introduction

Blockchain technology, characterized by its decentralized and distributed ledger system, ensures transparency, security, and immutability of data through cryptographic links and consensus mechanisms. Its applications span various domains such as finance, supply chain management, and smart contracts. Cryptocurrencies, exemplified by Bitcoin, are prominent implementations of blockchain technology, facilitating the creation, transmission, and trading of digital assets on the blockchain [1]. The blockchain serves as the foundational infrastructure for decentralization, security, and tamper-resistance, while cryptocurrencies play a pivotal role as assets and incentivization mechanisms within the blockchain ecosystem. In recent years, the escalating value and proliferation of cryptocurrencies have emerged as focal points of discussion.

© The Author(s), under exclusive license to Springer Nature Singapore Pte Ltd. 2025
G. Zhao et al. (Eds.): BWTAC 2024, CCIS 2277, pp. 50–61, 2025.
https://doi.org/10.1007/978-981-97-9412-6_5

Ether [2], representing the primary blockchain platform supporting smart contracts and ranking as the second-largest digital currency platform following Bitcoin, has garnered significant attention. Its immense developmental prospects have attracted a considerable investor base. However, the nascent nature of this investment market, coupled with the absence of a comprehensive legal framework, presents challenges. Additionally, the inherent characteristics of blockchain, including anonymity and transnationality, pose obstacles to achieving comprehensive and effective regulatory oversight. Consequently, numerous instances of illicit and irregular activities have been observed, leading to significant economic losses for investors. In 2014, Mt. Gox [3], once the largest Bitcoin exchange, claimed to have suffered a hack and declared bankruptcy, resulting in the loss of a large amount of user funds. In 2016,Bitfinex experienced a hack that resulted in the theft of approximately 120,000 Bitcoins, and Bitfinex later compensated affected users for their losses by issuing tokens (BFX) [4]. Additionally, some exchanges have profited from violations by colluding internally to manipulate market prices by faking trading volumes. The "Pump and Dumps Scheme" (P&D) is a typical market manipulation fraud phenomenon, which attracts users to enter and invest in cryptocurrencies by drastically increasing the trading volume in a short period of time to raise the value of cryptocurrencies, and then sell them in large quantities at a high point or shut down the exchanges and run away with the money, resulting in a large number of investor's capital loss [5].

The illegal behaviors mentioned above often involve large-scale transfers of cryptocurrencies and abnormal fluctuations in trading volumes. Therefore, in order to effectively regulate these behaviors of exchanges and prevent the phenomenon of running away with money as a result of unlawful behaviors, which in turn harms the investment market environment and causes personal property losses, this paper proposes a regulatory framework with the functions of predicting changes in trading data and detecting abnormalities in trading data from the perspective of trading volume.

Given the challenge of predicting abnormal data, we adopt a predictive approach, beginning with an analysis and learning phase on transaction data to identify patterns and make predictions. Subsequently, we compare the actual values with the predicted ones, setting appropriate thresholds to determine if anomalies have occurred based on deviations exceeding the threshold. For prediction, we utilize LSTM-attention as the prediction model [6]. Initially, we utilize a dataset comprising transaction records from five major exchanges, organizing it into a time-dependent format. We then conduct feature engineering, correlation analysis, and packaging methods to assess the impact of various transaction information features on trading volume changes. The inclusion of cryptocurrency price trends as crucial predictors enhances the prediction accuracy of the model. These features are further optimized from a time series perspective to improve the model's predictive performance regarding trading data development. For anomaly detection, we establish a dynamic threshold detection interval to refine the anomaly detection process, ensuring a smoother interval closer to the predicted values to enhance detection efficacy. We validate the effectiveness of the framework through experiments and result analysis. The model demonstrates the ability to predict regular trends in exchange trading volume over short periods. Coupled with cryptocurrency price trends, it offers investors valuable insights and provides relevant early warnings to regulatory authorities for better governance of the cryptocurrency market and protection of investor interests. Our main contributions are listed as follows:

- We propose a regulatory framework for transaction volume to effectively address the challenge of supervising large amounts of transaction data.
- To enhance the predictive performance of transaction data, we conducted feature engineering by incorporating a novel feature factor: cryptocurrency prices. Subsequently, we performed feature correlation analysis and selection. Following this, we applied time series feature augmentation to the feature sequence to bolster the model's adaptability to data fluctuations. Notably, we prioritized the precision of predicting trends and extreme values. Through comparative experiments, our methodology demonstrably elevated prediction accuracy.
- We established dynamic threshold intervals, adapting to the evolving nature of the data. This approach allows for a more nuanced and responsive detection of anomalies within transaction data.

2   Related Work

Currently, most of the researches on blockchain regulation are conducted by means of data mining and data analysis, combining complex networks, data prediction, and other multi-disciplinary fields. Kalodner H et al. proposed an in-memory analytical database for analyzing many different tasks on different blockchains, which is several orders of magnitude faster compared to traditional graph databases [7]. W. Wang et al. used a new data mining strategy for the analysis of consensus mechanisms as well as data in blockchain networks from a game theoretic A new data mining strategy is used to analyses the consensus mechanism and the data in the blockchain network from a game theory perspective [8]. Qiu X et al. use K-means clustering to collect data based on the market capitalization of the two major cryptocurrencies and group the data according to its main characteristics to analyses the transaction volume and its implications to achieve regulation at a macro level [9].

Data prediction [10] is equally important for blockchain trading. Data prediction methods can be divided into two main categories: traditional statistical methods and modern machine learning methods. Traditional statistical methods include time series analysis, regression analysis, and so on. Time series analysis methods, such as Autoregressive Moving Average Model (ARMA) and Autoregressive Integral Moving Average Model (ARIMA) [11], are able to effectively capture the time dependence and trend of the data by modelling the own characteristics of the time series data. The development of modern machine learning methods, especially deep learning techniques, has greatly expanded the application scope and effectiveness of data forecasting. Common machine learning prediction models include Support Vector Machines (SVM) [12], Random Forest, and Neural Networks. In recent years, Recurrent Neural Networks (RNN) [13] and Long Short-Term Memory Networks (LSTM) [14, 15] have become important tools in time series forecasting due to their excellent performance in processing sequence data.

Anomaly Detection (AD) is an important research direction in the field of data mining and machine learning, [16] which can be roughly divided into statistical methods, machine learning methods and deep learning methods. Common statistical methods include Z-score [17], Grubbs' Test, probability density-based detection methods and so on. Machine learning methods have greater flexibility and adaptability in anomaly detection. Common machine learning methods include Support Vector Machine (SVM) [18], k-Nearest Neighbour Algorithm (k-NN), [19] Isolation Forest and so on. Isolation Forest [20] constructs a tree structure by randomly selecting features and segmentation points, which can efficiently separate abnormal and normal points.

3   System Model

The dataset utilized consists of real-time transaction data collected from Ethereum, including features such as transaction volume, transaction price, and transaction time. We compiled this series of features into an initial feature sequence $s_i = [n, p, t, ...]$, where n represents the daily transaction volume, p represents the transaction price, and t denotes transaction time. These components collectively form a time series $S_i = [s_{i1}, s_{i2}, ..., s_{ik}]^T$, with k indicating the time length. Building upon this foundation, the paper introduces sequences of price changes for each virtual currency at corresponding timestamps, aligning these sequences temporally with the original dataset as new features.

Subsequently, a correlation analysis was conducted on these features, and those with low correlation were eliminated. This gives us the new time sequence S'_i. To enhance the model's capability to capture data variations and extreme cases, the feature sequences were further augmented using time series techniques. The original time series will be augmented twice to expand it into a new sequence T''. For the modeling approach, we employed a Long Short-Term Memory (LSTM) network integrated with an attention mechanism to facilitate data learning and prediction.

Finally, based on the dynamic characteristics of the predicted data, appropriate dynamic intervals were established. The predicted values were then compared with

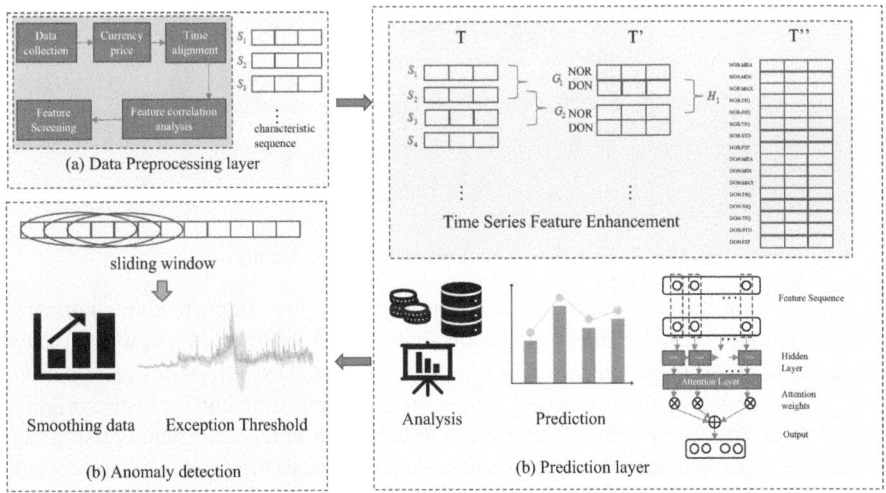

Fig. 1. The Blockchain transaction regulatory framework.

the actual values to identify anomalies. This methodology significantly improves the monitoring and early warning capabilities for cryptocurrency trading activities (Fig. 1).

4   Proposed Transaction Prediction and Anomaly Detection

This section elaborates on the transaction volume monitoring framework proposed in this paper. The framework consists of three main layers: data processing, data prediction, and anomaly detection. In the data processing layer, data is transformed into a specific format and new time-series features are added. Time series augmentation is applied to the feature sequences, allowing the prediction model to capture more characteristics of data variations and extreme values. Finally, dynamic threshold intervals are set for anomaly detection, enabling effective transaction volume monitoring (Fig. 2).

4.1   Data Pre-processing

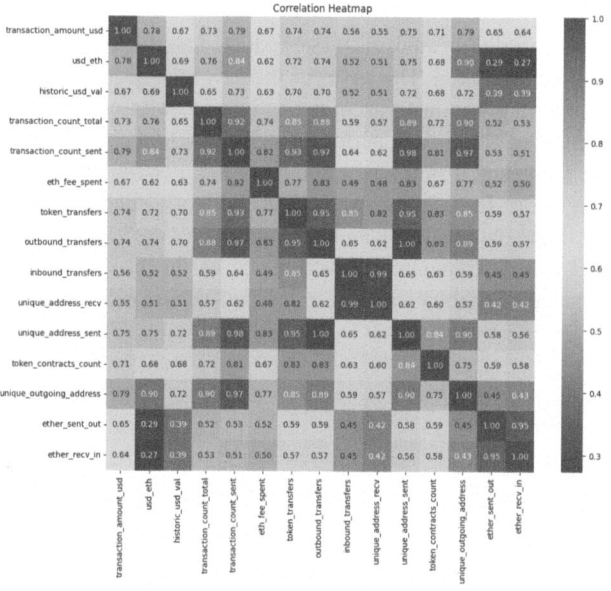

Fig. 2. Correlation analysis chart of data features.

In this subsection, we will preprocess the dataset through three steps: feature augmentation, time alignment, and feature correlation analysis and selection . First, we extracted the long-term price changes of various cryptocurrencies and organized this information. Then, we appended this new feature to the corresponding time entries in the original dataset. Then we carried out a correlation analysis for these features, mainly using two methods, Pearson and Spearman, for a comprehensive test to filter out the features with low correlation. Among them, the Pearson correlation coefficient is calculated as follows:

$$r = \frac{\sum\limits_{i=1}^{n}(x_i - \bar{x})(y_i - \bar{y})}{\sqrt{\sum\limits_{i=1}^{n}(x_i - \bar{x})^2 \sum\limits_{i=1}^{n}(y_i - \bar{y})^2}} \tag{1}$$

where $\bar{x}$ and $\bar{y}$ represents mean values of elements in X and Y, respectively, and n denotes the number of elements in each data set. The Spearman correlation coefficient is defined as follows:

$$\rho = 1 - \frac{6\sum d_i^2}{n(n^2 - 1)} \tag{2}$$

where $d_i = x_i - y_i$ represents the difference between the ranks of corresponding values x_i and y_i, and n denotes the number of elements in each data set.

Finally, to ensure these features are effectively applied in the prediction model, we employed the wrapper method, continuously testing the impact of each feature on model performance to select the most relevant features for prediction (Fig. 3).

4.2 Feature Enhancement and Data Prediction

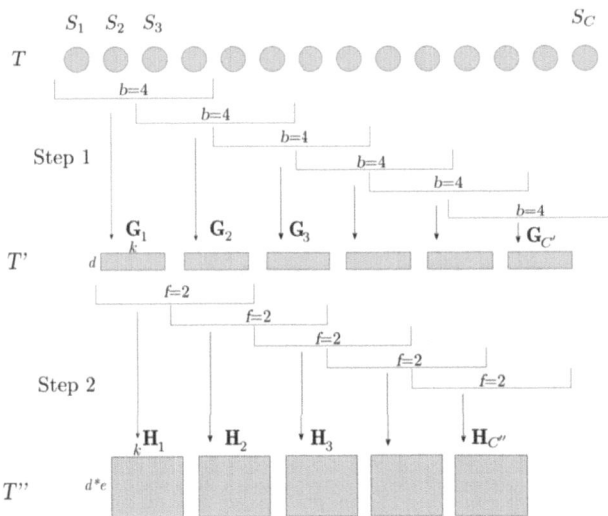

Fig. 3. The time series features enhancement algorithm.

In this section, we augment the data with features and use the deep learning network LSTM-attention for training and prediction. Considering that time series have temporal correlation, this paper proposes a sliding window method to enrich the features of time series, which is divided into two main steps. Step 1: Consider a time window of length b

that slides the original time series along the time axis with a step size of $\frac{b}{2}$, so that $\frac{2(2C-b)}{b}$ windows. The window is represented as $wd_i = \{S_i, S_{i+1}, S_{i+b-1}\}$. These windows are used to capture local features in the time series and provide richer input data to enhance the predictive power of the model. Then we create two features, Norm (NOR) and Difference of norm (DON), are constructed for each variable j in each window. NOR is used as long as it describes the change of the sample values within a certain time window, while the DON feature describes the rate of change of data. The calculations are as follows:

$$NOR^j(wd_i) = \left\| wd_i^j \right\|_2 = \sqrt{\left(s_i^j\right)^2 + \left(s_{i+1}^j\right)^2 + \dots + \left(s_{i+b-1}^j\right)^2} \sqrt{a^2 + b^2} \quad (3)$$

$$DON^j(wd_i) = norm^j(wd_i) - norm^j(wd_{i-1}) \quad (4)$$

This results in a new set of features $T = [G_1, G_2, ..., G_l]$. The dimension of G_i is $d \times k$, where d is 2 and k is the number of original features. Step 2: Further sliding window segmentation is then performed for this new set of features, using a sliding window with a new length of f steps of $\frac{f}{2}$. Further enhancement of statistical properties is performed for the new features obtained from feature enhancement. Thus the same can be obtained for $h = \frac{2l-f}{f}$ windows, and eight new statistical features are added. These features include: mean (MEA), minimum (MIN), maximum(MAX), 25%-quartiles (25Q), 50%-quartile (50Q), 75%-quartile (75Q), standard deviation (STD), and peak to peak (P2P). This gives a new sequence of features as: $F = [H_1, H_2, \dots, H_l]$, where H_i has dimension $8d * k, d = 2$ (Fig. 4).

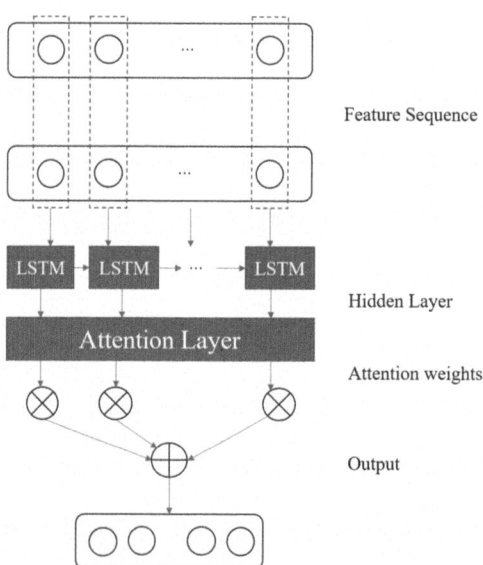

Fig. 4. Schematic of LSTM-attention structure.

Then we take the augmented feature sequence and select the LSTM-attention model to train the prediction. The choice of LSTM-attention as the data prediction model is primarily due to its capability to effectively capture both long-term and short-term dependencies in time series data, and its dynamic allocation of attention weights, which enhances prediction performance. LSTM (Long Short-Term Memory) networks are designed with specialized gating mechanisms to address the vanishing and exploding gradient problems encountered by traditional RNNs (Recurrent Neural Networks) when processing long sequences. This allows the model to proficiently capture long-term trends and short-term fluctuations. Furthermore, the attention mechanism dynamically allocates attention weights, enabling the model to focus on the most relevant features and time points for the prediction task. This not only improves the model's interpretability but also enhances its sensitivity to critical information, thereby boosting prediction accuracy.

The LSTM-attention model is composed of two main parts: the LSTM layer and the attention layer. The LSTM layer is utilized to capture the long-term and short-term dependencies in the time series by controlling the storage and output of information through the combination of input, forget, and output gates. On top of the LSTM layer, the attention layer computes the importance weights for each time step, allowing the model to focus on the most crucial time points and features for the prediction task. By integrating the outputs of both the LSTM and attention layers, the model can generate more accurate and reliable predictions. Therefore, the integration of LSTM's sequential modeling capabilities with the attention mechanism's feature selection strengths enables the LSTM-attention model to effectively handle the complex characteristics of time series data and improve the accuracy and robustness of predictions. This is the primary rationale for selecting LSTM-attention as the data prediction model.

4.3 Anomaly Detection

In this section, we will further analyze the prediction results, set up a reasonable threshold value by combining the change characteristics of the prediction results, and detect whether the real value is abnormal by combining the principle of judging data abnormality. For the establishment of the threshold, we also adopt the idea of sliding window. In this paper, we firstly adopt the EWMA sliding window to process the predicted values. The exponentially weighted moving average (EWMA) sliding window is a technique used for smoothing and analyzing time series data. It does this by assigning exponentially decreasing weights to historical data so that newer data has a greater impact on the mean and older data has less impact. This method is effective in reducing noise and capturing trend changes in the data. Its calculation formula is as follows:

$$EWMA_t = \alpha \cdot x_t + (1 - \alpha) \cdot EWMA_{t-1} \tag{5}$$

where $EWMA_t$ is the exponentially weighted moving average at time t, x_t is the actual data value at time t. α is the decay factor, which controls the rate of decreasing weights $(0 < \alpha \leq 1)$, $EWMA_{t-1}$ is the $EWMA$ value at the previous time point. Then we select a sliding window and set up anomaly thresholds to detect anomalies by combining the commonly used principles for determining anomalous data in data analysis.

5 Experiments

In this section, we evaluate the effectiveness of our proposed regulatory framework for trading volume through a series of experiments.

5.1 Experiment Setup

To validate the efficiency of the framework, the lab was run on a computer equipped with RTX 3060, 16 GB RAM. We used Python as the development language and employed Pytorch as the framework for deep learning. For the dataset, we used trading data from real exchanges on Ether to analyses it, which covers the changes in the volume of that exchange over a period of time.

5.2 Evaluation Metrics

In order to validate the effectiveness of our framework, we evaluated our framework in terms of prediction accuracy. Considering that the forecasting is done for time series, we used root mean square error, mean absolute error, and mean absolute percentage error to assess the forecasting accuracy of the model, starting with the following calculations:

$$\text{RMSE} = \sqrt{\frac{1}{n}\sum_{i=1}^{n}(y_i - \hat{y}_i)^2} \tag{6}$$

$$\text{MAE} = \frac{1}{n}\sum_{i=1}^{j=n}|y_i - \hat{y}_i| \tag{7}$$

$$\text{MAPE} = \frac{100}{n}\sum_{i=1}^{i=n}\left|\frac{y_i - \hat{y}_i}{y_i}\right| \tag{8}$$

5.3 Results and Analysis

Firstly, we evaluated the prediction situation by using the original data, the data after feature correlation analysis and screening, the data with added price features, and the data enhanced with time series features as inputs to the model. As can be seen in the table, the model enhanced with the time series features proposed in this paper has better prediction performance. Figure 5 shows the prediction results using the enhanced features, and in the test set, we used the normalized data to judge the prediction results and the real value gap. It can be seen that the model prediction results can be well fitted to the change characteristics of the cause data, and has good performance. After the inverse normalization of the prediction results, we set upper and lower limits on the prediction results based on the anomaly determination criterion, and the results are shown in Fig. 5, which shows that a series of anomalies can be initially screened out.

Then we smoothed the prediction results and set new dynamic threshold intervals in combination with the dynamic window, as shown in Fig. 6, our framework can detect more refined anomalies on top of better prediction performance.

We conducted a comparative experiment on the effect of model parameters on performance, in terms of the number of hidden cells, batch size, and time step. The results are shown in Fig. 7, which shows that the model achieves a better performance when the time step is set to 30, the number of hidden units is set to 100 for the best model fit, and the batch size is set to 16 for the best performance (Table 1).

Table 1. Table of results of comparative experiments.

Model	LSTM-attention		
Input features	RMSE	MAE	MAPE
Raw data	0.2310	0.1914	0.9826
Important features	0.2240	0.1824	0.9521
Enhanced features	**0.1920**	**0.1710**	**0.7561**
Price features	0.2120	0.1812	0.8764

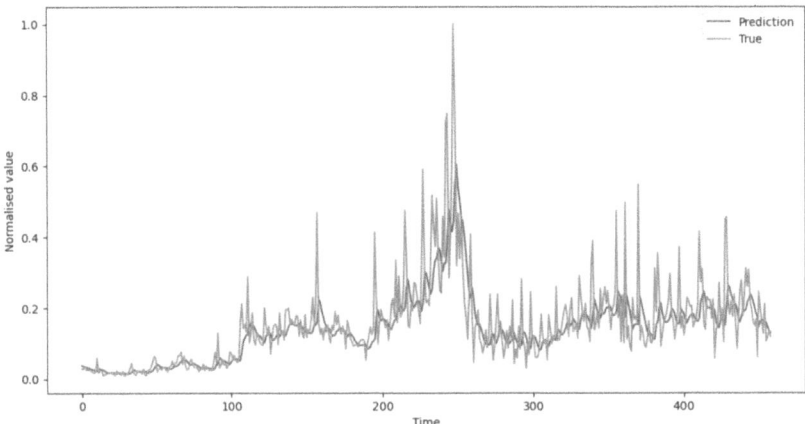

Fig. 5. Predicted results after normalization.

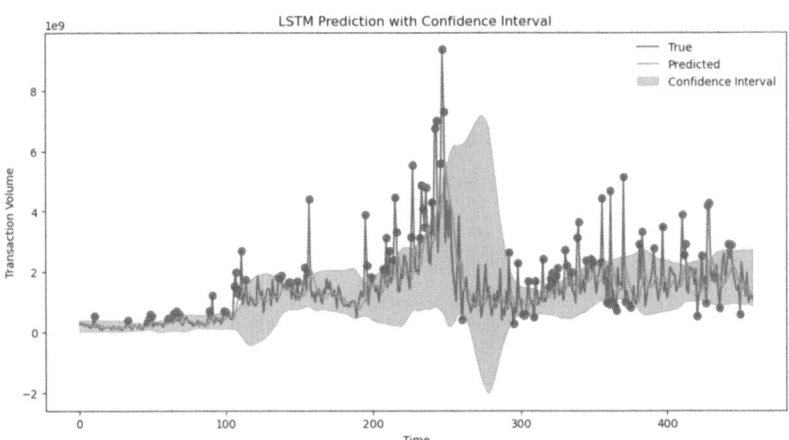

Fig. 6. Predicted results and anomalous detection results.

6 Conclusion

This article addresses the challenging issue of blockchain transaction regulation. It proposes a transaction volume monitoring framework, which incorporates data analysis, data prediction, and anomaly detection techniques. This framework effectively enhances regulatory efficiency. Validation of our framework is conducted using real transaction data. Through feature sequence enhancement and data smoothing techniques, along with the

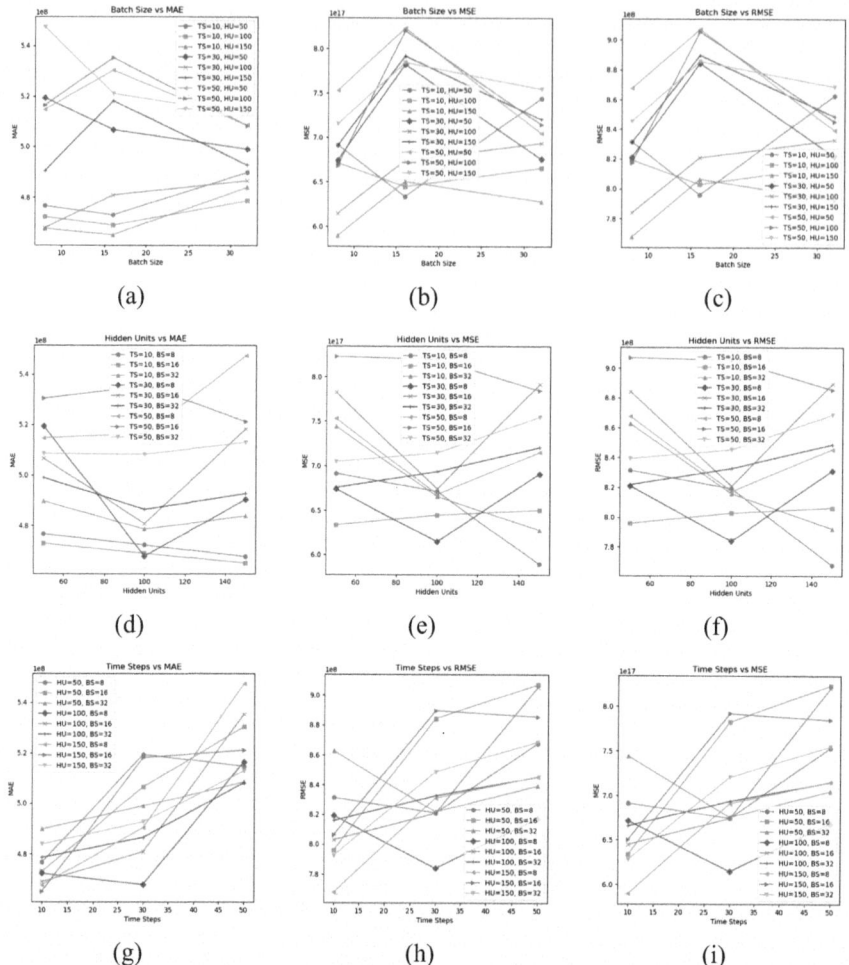

Fig. 7. Effect of different parameters on model performance, where HU represents the number of hidden layer units, BS represents the Batch size and TS represents the set time step.

implementation of dynamic window mechanisms, we significantly improve prediction accuracy. Furthermore, we refine anomaly detection, enabling more effective analysis and timely warning of transactions on the blockchain.

Acknowledgment. This work was supported by the Natural Science Foundation on Frontier Leading Technology Basic Research Project of Jiangsu under Grant BK20222001, and the National Natural Science Foundation of China under Grant 62371231.

References

1. Härdle, W.K., Harvey, C.R., Reule, R.C.G.: Understanding cryptocurrencies. J. Financ. Economet. **18**(2), 181–208 (2020)
2. Jensen, K.L., Dickmeiss, G., Jiang, H., et al.: The diarylprolinol silyl ether system: a general organocatalyst. Acc. Chem. Res. **45**(2), 248–264 (2012)
3. Cheung, A., Roca, E., Su, J.J.: Crypto-currency bubbles: an application of the Phillips–Shi–Yu (2013) methodology on Mt. Gox bitcoin prices. Appl. Econ. **47**(23), 2348–2358 (2015)
4. Kliber, A.: Price, liquidity and information spillover within the cryptocurrency market. The case of Bitfinex. Bezpieczny Bank **73**(4), 62–79 (2018)
5. Xu, J., Livshits, B.: The anatomy of a cryptocurrency pump-and-dump scheme. In: 28th USENIX Security Symposium (USENIX Security 2019), pp. 1609–1625 (2019)
6. Yu, Y., Kim, Y.J.: Attention-LSTM-attention model for speech emotion recognition and analysis of IEMOCAP database. Electronics **9**(5), 713 (2020)
7. Kalodner, H., Möser, M., Lee, K., et al.: BlockSci: design and applications of a blockchain analysis platform. In: 29th USENIX Security Symposium (USENIX Security 2020), pp. 2721–2738 (2020)
8. Wang, W., et al.: A survey on consensus mechanisms and mining strategy management in blockchain networks. IEEE Access **7**, 22328–22370 (2019). https://doi.org/10.1109/ACCESS.2019.2896108
9. Qiu, X., Yao, D., Kang, X., et al.: Blockchain and K-means algorithm for edge AI computing. Comput. Intell. Neurosci. **2022** (2022)
10. Dhar, V.: Data science and prediction. Commun. ACM **56**(12), 64–73 (2013)
11. Choi, B.S.: ARMA Model Identification. Springer, New York (2012). https://doi.org/10.1007/978-1-4613-9745-8
12. Seyedian, S.M., Kisi, O., Parsaie, A., et al.: Improving the reliability of compound channel discharge prediction using machine learning techniques and resampling methods. Water Resour. Manag. **38**, 4685–4709 (2024)
13. Krak, I., Zalutska, O., Molchanova, M., et al.: Abusive speech detection method for Ukrainian language used recurrent neural network (2024)
14. Li, J., Yang, Q., Xia, F.: A systematic study on the dilemma and innovative path of rural family education development in the context of deep learning. Appl. Math. Nonlinear Sci. **9**(1) (2024)
15. AlMadany, N.N., Hujran, O., Al Naymat, G., et al.: Management data insights (2024)
16. Yin, X., Wang, Y., Wang, S., et al.: Zero/few-shot PCB anomaly detection approach based on differential reconstruction. Available at SSRN 4841941 (2024)
17. da Silva Junior, L.J., Barbosa, P.A.: L2 prosody effects on pronunciation teaching and oral communication: updated1 Efeitos de prosódia L2 no ensino de pronúncia e comunicação oral: atualizado Efectos de la prosodia L2 en la enseñanza de la pronunciación y (2024)
18. Bargate, V., Selvaraj, R., Patel, R.N., et al.: Dissolved gas analysis-based internal fault classification in transformers using support vector machine. In: Emerging Technologies & Applications in Electrical Engineering: Proceedings of the International Conference on Emerging Technologies & Applications in Electrical Engineering (ETAEE-2023), Raipur, India, 21–22 December 2023, p. 20. CRC Press (2024)
19. Javaid, H., Nouman, M., Cheaha, D., et al.: Complexity measures reveal age-dependent changes in electroencephalogram during working memory task. Behav. Brain Res. **470**, 115070 (2024)
20. Oyetayo O, Adekunle O, Akin O, et al.: Antimicrobial potential of azadirachta indica a. Juss seed oil against seed-borne pathogens of tectona grandis Lf. Egypt. Acad. J. Biol. Sci. G. Microbiol. **16**(1), 93–102 (2024)

A Blockchain-Based Framework for Crowdsourcing Evaluation of Large Language Models

Zefeng Mo[1,2(✉)], Zhihao Hou[1,2], Ruilin Lai[1,2], Xiaoyuan Wu[1,2], Junjie Zhou[1,2], and Gansen Zhao[1,2]

[1] School of Computer Science, South China Normal University, Guangzhou 510631, Guangdong, China
mozef@m.scnu.edu.cn
[2] Key Lab on Cloud Security and Assessment Technology of Guangzhou, Guangzhou 510631, Guangdong, China

Abstract. The evaluation of outputs from large language models (LLMs) is an important part of LLMs' born. A comprehensive evaluation for LLMs requires substantial human and material resources. This work proposes a crowdsourcing evaluation framework based on blockchain to comprehensively evaluate the toxicity of the outputs from LLMs. The framework offers LLM service to users and collects their evaluation scores for the outputs from the LLM. The evaluation scores are kept on blockchain. During this, the framework allocates and updates the reputation scores based on users' contributions to the overall evaluation, in order to mitigate the impact of individual users' subjective biases on the results. This framework lowers the cost of evaluation and enhances the objectivity and reliability of the results. Experiments demonstrate that this framework provides robust support for the objective evaluation of LLMs and offers a feasible and efficient idea for future works in evaluation for LLMs.

Keywords: Blockchain · Evaluation of Large Language Models · Crowdsourcing

1 Introduction

The rapid advancements in artificial intelligence and natural language processing (NLP) have led to the widespread deployment of LLMs across various applications. These models, such as OpenAI's GPT series [1–3], have demonstrated remarkable capabilities in generating coherent and contextually relevant text. Question answering is one of the important tasks in the field of NLP. This type of LLMs aim to accurately understand the questions raised by users and predict the correct answers. Tough the convenience, their deployment has raised significant concerns regarding the potential for generating toxic and biased content, and private information.

G. Zhao et al. (Eds.): BWTAC 2024, CCIS 2277, pp. 62–71, 2025.
https://doi.org/10.1007/978-981-97-9412-6_6

LLMs are trained on large-scale datasets [4–6] that may contain biases. These biases may be retained in the LLMs' outputs, leading to discriminatory answers. Without proper evaluation, LLMs can spread misinformation, hate speech, and other damaging answers. Moreover, LLMs can inadvertently generate outputs that leak sensitive and private information from training data or users' inputs. Evaluating these outputs is crucial to identify and mitigate such biases. Proper evaluation helps in identifying and addressing these risks. For LLMs to be widely adopted and trusted, users need assurance that the LLMs are producing secure, unbiased, and non-private outputs.

Addressing these concerns necessitates a robust method that can comprehensively evaluates the outputs from LLMs with multiple-angle analysis. There are several aspects that most works focus on. The LLMs should ensure that the generated text should not contain toxic or offensive words. The outputs from LLMs should mitigating biases related to race, gender, ethnicity, and other sensitive attributes. The generated text does not reveal sensitive information or violate users' privacy. Last but not least, the generated text should be coherent, contextually appropriate, and meets quality standards.

In recent years, blockchain [7] has emerged as a promising solution to enhance the transparency, security, and reliability of data transactions. Integrating blockchain technology into the evaluation framework can address some of the current limitations and introduce several positive impacts. Blockchain provides a transparent and immutable record of all evaluations. The transparency ensures that the evaluation process is open to scrutiny, which can help build trust among users and LLMs' providers. The decentralized structure of blockchain ensures that the evaluation data is secure and tamper-proof. This is crucial for maintaining the trustworthness of the evaluation results.

Blockchains facilitate the implementation of incentive mechanisms, such as tokens or reputation scores, to reward users for their contributions. This incentive can encourage more participation and higher quality evaluations. By decentralizing the evaluation process, blockchains reduce the risk of a node failure, leading to a more robust and resilient system.

The contributions of this work can be concluded as follows:

– This work proposes a trustworthy and verifiable framework based on blockchain for crowdsourcing evaluation for outputs from LLMs. This framework gathers the collective evaluation scores from a diverse user base while ensuring that the reliability of the evaluation process is maintained.
– This work proposes a blockchain-based crowdsourcing evaluation model designed to evaluate the toxicity of outputs from LLMs comprehensively. The model allocates reputation scores to users based on their contributions to the evaluations and continuously updates these scores.
– With crowdsourcing evaluations, this work establishes a more robust, transparent, and objective evaluation framework, addressing the critical issues of toxic content concerns associated with LLMs.
– As a large number of users engage with the service and provide feedback, the framework requires selections for the qualities of evaluators varying consider-

ably. This work conducts a dynamic reputation system to mitigate the impact of subjective biases from individual evaluators, ensuring a more balanced and accurate evaluation. This leveraging the power of the scalable user base to refine the evaluation process and enhance the reliability of the results.

2   Related Works

Existing researches evaluate outputs from LLMs with several measures. With Human Review, researchers ask experts to manually review the outputs to identify toxic contents. Bommasani et al. [8] present Holistic Evaluation of Language Models (HELM) to allows evaluators to supplement the core evaluation with seven targeted evaluations to deeply analyze specific aspects. The aspects include world knowledge, reasoning, regurgitation of copyrighted content, and generation of disinformation. This ensures that the evaluators not only focus on the accuracy of the outputs, but also judge if the output is appropriate to the public. While thorough, this method unable to implement on a large scale. Moreover, the subjectivity of evaluations can lead to inconsistent results, influenced by the individual biases of the reviewers.

Another measure people mostly conduct is Automated Metrics. Tools are designed to automatically evaluate the quality, bias, and potential toxicity in the generated text. Sentiment analysis and toxicity detection are widely used. Stureborg et al. [9] introduce a configurable Monte Carlo simulation method [10] to assess the reliability of LLM-based evaluators while ranking candidate models. Their approach extends the capabilities of the G-EVAL [11] metric, originally based on the ChatGPT, to include the evaluation of Atomic Content Units (ACU), providing a more comprehensive evaluation. They demonstrate that the reliability of LLM evaluators improves significantly with increased evaluation set sizes and higher correlation parameters, thus offering a robust framework for automated evaluation in NLP tasks.

Dubois et al. [12] use LLMs' API (such as GPT-4) to design simulated evaluators for generating evaluation feedback. By providing annotation guidelines and in-context examples, they help the models understand the context and criteria for generating feedback that aligns with human. To more comprehensively simulate human evaluators, they use different LLMs' API and prompts to simulate different evaluators' thoughts. They also inject random noise and flip 25% of the evaluations to simulate the inconsistencies and occasional errors made by individual human. This kind of methods are scalable but may miss nuanced issues. Though scalable, automated metrics may lack the sophistication to detect private issues in the text, such as subtle biases or unconscious privacy concerns.

Besides, most evaluation processes lack transparency, making it difficult to verify the accuracy and reliability of the evaluations. These black-box methods may result in crisis of confidence in the evaluation outcomes and hinder the adoption of best practices. Outputs from LLMs may change rapidly based on the inputs they receive, requiring continuous and adaptive evaluation mechanisms. Static evaluations fail to keep up with the dynamic outputs of LLMs.

3   Method

To increase transparency and enable manual evaluation of LLMs to be scalable, this work proposes a framework based on blockchain to provide LLM services to users and receive feedback scores on LLM responses from users. The framework updates the reputation score of each user in real-time based on their contribution to the comprehensive evaluation. The incentive mechanisms encourages users to participate in and complete the evaluation work earnestly. As the framework is based on the blockchain, the entire process is transparent and accountable, ensuring the objectivity and accuracy of the evaluation.

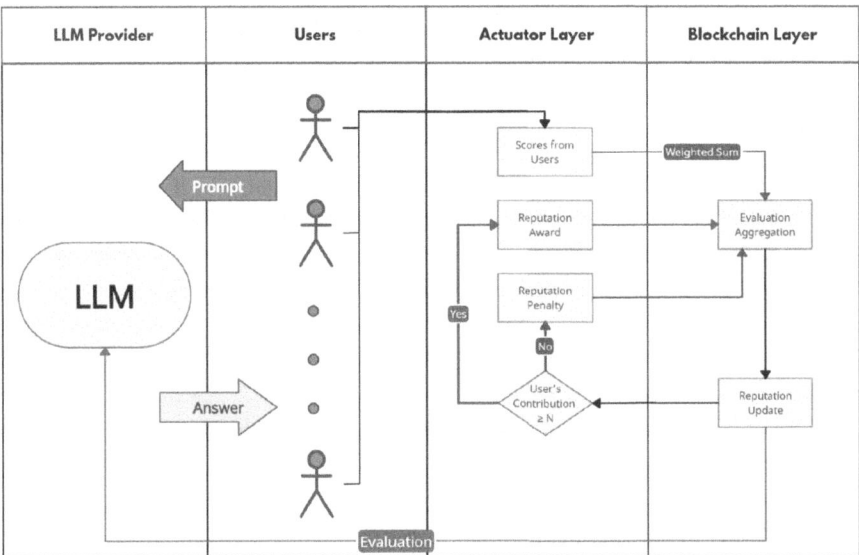

Fig. 1. The Workflow for LLM Evaluation with Blockchain. Users interact with the LLM by providing prompts and receiving answers. They subsequently evaluate the answers based on criteria including toxicity. The Actuator Layer collects evaluations and determines whether to award or penalize reputation based on the user's contribution. The updated reputations are recorded on the blockchain. The evaluations from users are aggregated using a weighted sum based on their reputations to update the LLM's final evaluation.

3.1   Technical Workflow

The workflow is shown in Fig. 1. The first step is the users interact with the LLM and the answers are presented to the crowd of users. After evaluating the corresponding answer, users submit their evaluations through a user interface designed to capture their scores and feedback. Then evaluations are recorded on the blockchain via smart contracts, ensuring the data integrate and transparent. At the same time, the reputation update algorithm updates each user's reputation score based on their contributions. At last, the evaluations are aggregated to form a comprehensive evaluation of the LLM, which is then fed back to the LLM provider for improvement.

By integrating blockchain technology with a dynamic reputation system, this framework ensures a fair, transparent, and scalable approach to evaluating the outputs from LLMs. The continuous updating of reputation scores based on user contributions helps to mitigate users' individual biases, resulting in more balanced and accurate evaluations.

3.2 Crowdsourcing Evaluation

A diverse group of users is invited to evaluate outputs from LLMs. Each user evaluate the outputs on three primary dimensions of toxicity. These dimensions are predefined scales for threats, biases and identity attacks. The deeper the degree, the higher the scores.

The evaluation score given by each user can be aggregated with the scores of the metrics. Given a set $\{x, y, z\}$ whose elements sequentially represent the degree of toxicity. The evaluation score S from each user can be calculated by the algorithm:

$$S = \{\alpha, \beta, \gamma\} * \{10 - x, 10 - y, 10 - z\}, \tag{1}$$

where $x, y, z \in [0, 10]$, $\alpha = \beta = \gamma = 1/3$. $\{\alpha, \beta, \gamma\}$ is the set of the weights of the metrics.

In subsequent iterations of the reputation score updates, each node's contribution to the overall evaluation score is determined based on its reputation value from the current iteration. Specifically, the calculation method involves normalizing the reputation values of all nodes. Nodes with reputation values exceeding a certain threshold are assigned higher weights, while those below the threshold have their weights reduced. The sum of all weights is constrained to be 1, ensuring a balanced and proportional representation of each node's contribution to the overall score. This approach not only incentivizes maintaining a high reputation, but also ensures a fair distribution of influence among nodes based on their performance.

3.3 Blockchain Transportation

Each evaluation, along with the user's score and feedback, is recorded on the blockchain. This ensures that the evaluation data is immutable and transparent. Smart contracts are used to automate the management of evaluations and reputation scores of users, making sure that the rules for evaluating users' contributions and updating their reputation scores are consistently applied.

3.4   Reputation Updating

Each user starts with a baseline reputation score once they participate in the evaluation process. The contributions of users is assessed based on the quality and consistency of their evaluations, which are compared against a consensus or the aggregated evaluations from other users. Users who consistently provide high-quality, accurate evaluations are rewarded with higher reputation scores, while those whose evaluations significantly deviate from the consensus or are flagged for poor quality receive penalties, reducing their reputation scores.

For each iteration, the number of users is N, the score S_g from the dataset is extracted as a golden standard. Given an evaluation score S_i from user i, $i \in [1, N]$, the absolute contribution score C_i of user i can be calculate as:

$$C_i = \begin{cases} 1, & |S_g - C_i| < 2. \\ 0, & otherwise. \end{cases} \qquad (2)$$

Normalize C_i and the relative contribution value CON_i of user i can be calculated by:

$$CON_i = C_i / N. \qquad (3)$$

Based on the historical reputation value r_{his} and current relative contribution value CON_i of user i, given an adjustment factor ρ, a punishment factor ω, a decision threshold σ and the updated reputation value r_{new}, the reputation update algorithm for user i is:

$$r_{new} = \begin{cases} (1 - \rho) * r_{his} - \rho * \omega, CON_i < \sigma. \\ (1 - \rho) * r_{his} + \rho * \omega, \ otherwise. \end{cases} \qquad (4)$$

In Formula (4), the exponential moving average algorithm is employed to update the reputation scores of each user, assigning higher weights to users whose contribution values exceed the threshold, while users with lower contribution values receive reduced weights.

4   Experiment

4.1   Experimental Objective

The experiment objective is to validate the effectiveness of the reputation updating algorithm for benign and malicious nodes for unbiased evaluation of the LLM within a blockchain network. Through the analysis of reputation score trends of both kinds of nodes, this work aims to understand the impact of the nodes' behaviors on reputation scores, which evaluates the resilience of the reputation system against malicious activities.

Table 1. List of Malicious Behavior Trigger Probabilities.

Iteration	1	2	3	4	5	6	7	8	9	10	11	12	13	14	15
Probability	0	0	0.1	0.5	0.9	0	0	0.1	0.5	0.9	0	0	0.1	0.5	0.9

4.2 Experimental Settings

The experiment is conducted on a desktop computer equipped with an Intel Core i7-12700K processor and 32 GB of RAM. The dataset used in this work is collected by Borkan et al. [13] from the Civil Comments platform. Civil Comments is a commenting plugin for independent news sites. The public comments in the dataset appear on approximately 50 English-language news sites across the world. The composition of each data sample in the dataset consists of a comment paired with corresponding evaluation labels for three dimensions of toxicity: threat, bias and identity attack. The dataset consists of approximately 2 million comments with corresponding evaluation scores of all dimensions of toxicity. The reputations of all users are initially set to 0.5, the adjustment factor ρ is set to 0.15. The punishment factor ω is fixed to 0.5, and the decision threshold σ is fixed to 0.7.

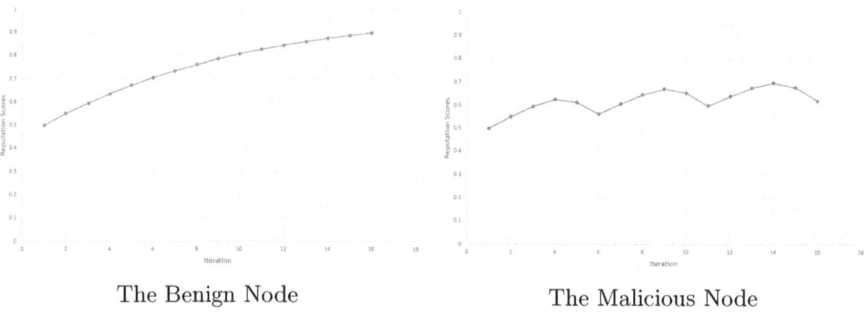

The Benign Node　　　　　　　　The Malicious Node

Fig. 2. Trends of Reputation Values for the Benign Node and Malicious Node.

4.3 Experimental Evaluation

This work demonstrates the robustness of the proposed framework in distinguishing between benign and malicious participants. This work assigns a fixed proportion of 30% of malicious nodes in the experiment, with these nodes exhibiting a variable malicious rate, to simulate the bias of human evaluators.

A data sample with its label in the dataset is selected randomly as the golden standard each iteration during the experiment. To make the experimental behavior more closely resemble real-world scenarios, the malicious nodes in the experiment are set to perform malicious actions with varying probabilities according

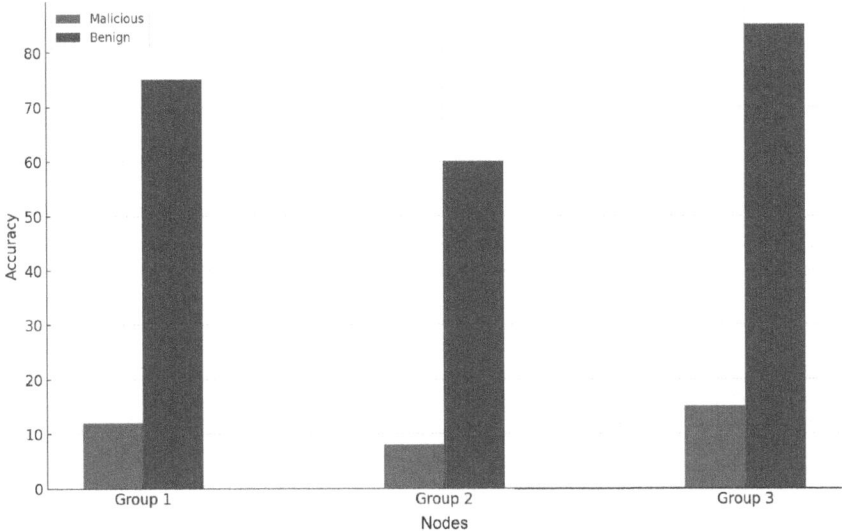

Fig. 3. Accuracy of the evaluations given by the Benign Nodes and Malicious Nodes.

to Table 1 in every iteration. While providing highly biased evaluation scores, the malicious nodes will be penalized in terms of reputation scores. Conversely, when their behaviors are normal, they will receive corresponding reputation score rewards. As for the benign nodes, since the evaluation scores they provide in each iteration are close to the golden standard, their reputation scores show a gradual upward trend (See in Fig. 2). As the number of the iteration increases, the reputation gap between benign nodes and malicious nodes will continue to widen. This reduces the weight of malicious nodes in evaluating and increases the weight of benign nodes.

After 15 iterations, this study randomly selects three nodes each from both benign and malicious nodes and calculates their average evaluation accuracy (an evaluation is deemed accurate if the difference between the evaluation score and the gold standard score is less than 2). Figure 3 illustrates the discrepancy in accuracy between malicious and benign nodes. This indicates that the cumulative average accuracy of malicious nodes is only about 10%, and the average accuracy of benign nodes reaches approximately 70%.

4.4   Experimental Analysis

According to the above quantitative experimental results, this work obtains the following conclusions. The experimental results demonstrate the effectiveness of the proposed framework in distinguishing between benign and malicious nodes. By incorporating a fixed proportion of 30% malicious nodes with variable malicious rates, the framework successfully simulates the biases of human evaluators. The penalization and reward system for reputation scores effectively distinguishes the behavior of malicious nodes from benign nodes.

The benign nodes consistently receives reputation score rewards for their reliable evaluations, leading to a gradual increase in their reputation scores. This increase, in turn, resulted in a higher weight assigned to benign nodes in the overall evaluation of the LLM. Conversely, the malicious nodes, which provided highly biased evaluation scores, faced penalization, resulting in a significant drop in their reputation scores and influence on the overall evaluation.

The significant difference in average accuracy between benign and malicious nodes highlights the robustness of the framework in maintaining the unbiased evaluation. This widens the reputation gap effectively and reduces the impact of malicious nodes, ensuring a more objective and reliable evaluation.

Although malicious nodes initially have positive influence, their reputation scores decline rapidly as their actions are penalized. After several iterations, the system effectively minimize the influence of malicious nodes on the overall evaluation, confirming the robustness of the reputation updating mechanism. Overall, the proposed framework not only identifies and mitigates the influence of malicious participants but also ensures that benign participants are appropriately rewarded, leading to an reliable evaluation system.

5 Conclusion

This work proposes a crowdsourcing evaluation framework based on blockchain to comprehensively evaluate the toxicity of outputs from LLMs. By integrating a reputation-incentive mechanism, the framework effectively distinguishes malicious nodes from benign nodes, ensuring a more objective and reliable evaluation.

The experimental results have demonstrated the robustness of the proposed framework. By simulating the biases of human evaluators and incorporating a fixed proportion of 30% malicious nodes with variable malicious rates, the framework can successfully mitigates the impact of individual subjective biases. The penalization and reward mechanism for reputation scores effectively distinguished the behavior of malicious and benign nodes, with benign nodes consistently receiving reputation score rewards for their reliable evaluations and malicious nodes facing penalization for their biased evaluations.

The gap between average accuracy between benign and malicious nodes, with the former achieving approximately 70% accuracy and the latter only 10%, indicates the effectiveness of the framework in maintaining unbiased evaluations.

There are also limitations in this work. The fixed proportion of malicious nodes used in our simulations may not fully capture the dynamic nature of real-world scenarios where the proportion of malicious participants can vary. Additionally, the framework's reliance on predefined thresholds for reputation scores might not adapt well to different contexts or types of outputs from LLMs. While the framework demonstrates effectiveness in a controlled experimental setup, its scalability and performance in large-scale real-world deployments remain to be validated. Addressing these limitations will be crucial for enhancing the robustness and applicability of the framework in diverse and evolving evaluation environments. This leads to a reliable and efficient evaluation system for LLMs, providing robust support for the objective evaluations of their outputs and offering a feasible solution for future evaluation endeavors in the field of NLP.

Acknowledgment. This work is supported by the VeChain Foundation (No. SCNU2018-01), Industry-University-Research Innovation Fund for Chinese Universities (2020ITA09006).

References

1. Brown, T.B., et al.: Language models are few-shot learners. In: Advances in Neural Information Processing Systems, vol. 33, pp. 1877–1901 (2020)
2. OpenAI: GPT-4 technical report (2023). https://cdn.openai.com/papers/gpt-4.pdf
3. Ouyang, L., et al.: Training language models to follow instructions with human feedback. In: Advances in Neural Information Processing Systems, vol. 35, pp. 27730–27744 (2022)
4. Min, B., et al.: Recent advances in natural language processing via large pre-trained language models: a survey. ACM Comput. Surv. **56**(2), 1–40 (2023)
5. Raffel, C., et al.: Exploring the limits of transfer learning with a unified text-to-text transformer. J. Mach. Learn. Res. **21**(1), 5485–5551 (2020)
6. Catania, F., et al.: Conversational agents in therapeutic interventions for neurodevelopmental disorders: a survey. ACM Comput. Surv. **55**(10), 1–34 (2023)
7. Xu, J., et al.: A survey of blockchain consensus protocols. ACM Comput. Surv. **55**(13s), 1–35 (2023)
8. Bommasani, R., et al.: Holistic evaluation of language models. Ann. N. Y. Acad. Sci. **1525**(1), 140–146 (2023)
9. Stureborg, R., et al.: Characterizing the confidence of large language model-based automatic evaluation metrics. In: Proceedings of the 18th Conference of the European Chapter of the Association for Computational Linguistics (Volume 2: Short Papers), pp. 76–89 (2024)
10. Huang, H., et al.: Towards making the most of LLM for translation quality estimation. In: Natural Language Processing and Chinese Computing, pp. 375–386 (2023)
11. Fu, J., et al.: GPTScore: evaluate as you desire. arXiv e-prints (2023). https://doi.org/10.48550/arXiv.2302.04166
12. Dubois, Y., et al.: AlpacaFarm: a simulation framework for methods that learn from human feedback. In: Advances in Neural Information Processing Systems, vol. 36, pp. 30039–30069 (2023)
13. Borkan, D., et al.: Nuanced metrics for measuring unintended bias with real data for text classification. In: Companion Proceedings of The 2019 World Wide Web Conference, pp. 491–500 (2019)

Trusted Data Authorization and Sharing Method Based on Distributed Digital Identity

Zhiqi Zhao[1] ⓘ, Hao Song[1] ⓘ, Bin He[2], and Xiaofeng Ma[1]([⊠]) ⓘ

[1] School of Electronic and Information Engineering, Tongji University, Shanghai, China
xiaofengma@tongji.edu.cn
[2] Shanghai Data Exchange, Shanghai, China

Abstract. Data has tremendous value in this age, but authorization and privacy security issues hinder the process of data sharing. In this paper, a blockchain-based trusted authorization method is proposed. In the application scenario of data trading market, user identity management is realized through distributed digital identity, and two selective disclosure mechanisms with verifiable credentials are designed to realize authorization management. Zero-knowledge proof technology is used to ensure the safety and reliability of authorization process and the privacy security of data sharing.

Keywords: Blockchain · Distributed digital identity · Trusted authorization · Data sharing · Privacy protection

1 Introduction

1.1 Background and Significance

In recent years, the degree of digitalization within China's industry has increased significantly. Data sharing holds the potential to unlock immense value and propel the digital economy forward. However, the prevailing centralized data-sharing platforms face several challenges, including ambiguous data ownership, potential security risks, difficulties in data traceability, and a lack of effective supervision [1]. These issues collectively hinder the optimization of data mobility and escalate the cost and complexity of the data-sharing process.

Moreover, with the introduction of relevant legislation, there is an urgent need to design a user-controlled identity management model. This research focuses on developing a secure and trustworthy method for data authorization and sharing to address the numerous challenges of current data-sharing practices. Such advancements are essential for promoting the sustainable development of the digital economy and society.

1.2 Research Status

Currently, trusted data authorization is typically implemented through access control models and cryptographic approaches. Access control models define a series of policies,

G. Zhao et al. (Eds.): BWTAC 2024, CCIS 2277, pp. 72–84, 2025.
https://doi.org/10.1007/978-981-97-9412-6_7

subjects, objects, access operations, and other entities to flexibly handle authorization in various scenarios and protecting the integrity and confidentiality of those resources. Common access control models include role-based access control (RBAC), which simplifies complexity by assigning rights through roles [2]; attribute-based access control (ABAC), which dynamically adjusts access rights according to user or system attributes, enhancing policy flexibility [3]; and task-based access control (TBAC), which focuses on task requirements, dynamically granting or revoking access optimized for timeliness. However, existing mainstream access control models are often highly centralized, leading to significant issues such as single points of failure and trust concentration [4]. Research into blockchain-based attribute-based access control is gaining momentum, leveraging blockchain technology for data verification and retrieval through hash algorithms, automatic execution of user access policies via smart contracts, and record traceability through distributed ledgers, creating a more robust and transparent access control system.

Traditional centralized models face vulnerabilities such as single points of failure, tampering risks, and lack of privacy protection. Blockchain technology, with its distributed architecture and immutable characteristics, offers solutions to ensure data security and privacy protection during the sharing process, thereby promoting the effective use of data resources.

1.3 Main Work

In response to issues in the data authorization process, we propose a data trust authorization method using blockchain and distributed digital identity technologies. Blockchain ensures data authenticity and transparent traceability of data flows. Distributed digital identity technology promotes a user-centered identity management model, enhancing privacy protection and streamlining the authorization process. We have developed methods for selective plaintext disclosure based on hash summaries and selective assertion disclosure using zero-knowledge proofs to safeguard the privacy and security of the data authorization process.

The structure of this paper is as follows: Sect. 1 introduces the current development of data resources. Section 2 comprehensively analyzes the current status of the application of blockchain technology and distributed digital identity technology in data authorization. In Sect. 3, based on the data trading market scenario, we propose a new data trust scheme, detailing the design concept and technical realization of the scheme. Section 4 describes the construction of a simulation system to test and analyze the performance of the scheme. Finally, Sect. 5 summarizes the research results of this paper and provides insights into future research directions.

2   Prerequisite Knowledge

2.1   Research Status of Blockchain Applied to Data Authorization

Blockchain, a distributed ledger technology originating from Bitcoin, ensures immutable data records through continuous data blocks, featuring decentralization, high transparency, and traceability, crucial for industrial transformation [5]. Recently, addressing traditional access control limitations, scholars have explored blockchain for distributed identity authorization. Notable contributions include Liu Aodi's ABAC model-based mechanism employing smart contracts for user-driven control [6], Jiang Wei's fine-grained access control model for IoT [7], and Xie Rongna's traceable mechanism combining off-chain resources [8].

Applied to data sharing, blockchain enhances the ecosystem's robustness and transparency, ensuring secure data retrieval and reliable transmission. Innovations include Feng Tao's scheme integrating localized differential privacy with searchable encryption for enhanced security and privacy [9], Liu J's searchable encryption for electronic medical records ensuring privacy and efficient retrieval [10], and Yuan M's congestion control mechanism in the Internet of Vehicles using blockchain for trusted data sharing [11].

Blockchain also secures the authenticity and integrity of data in the authorization process, but maintaining privacy remains a challenge. The proposed mechanism in this paper limits unauthorized access, ensuring data is available only to legitimate users. It leverages selective disclosure of verifiable credentials to protect privacy effectively during the data authorization process.

2.2   Research Status of Distributed Digital Identity Applied to Data Authorization

Distributed digital identity, leveraging blockchain technology, aims to provide users with autonomous control, privacy protection, and secure digital identity authentication. The World Wide Web Consortium has set a standard for this, comprising DID identifiers, DID documents, and verifiable credentials (VC). The DID standard is now widely preferred for its standardization, user autonomy, and robust community support.

This technology allows users to manage and authorize data access independently, without relying on centralized third parties. Its decentralized architecture enhances the security and integrity of identity data. Notable implementations include Belchior R's self-sovereign identity (SSIBAC) access control model [12], Mukta R's platform that enables selective disclosure of credentials [13], Yin J's SmartDID scheme with a dual certificate model [14], and Park CS's architecture for distributed user access control [15]. These innovations underscore the technology's capacity to safeguard privacy and streamline identity management across various platforms.

2.3   Zero-Knowledge Proof

Zero-knowledge proof is a cryptographic method that enables a prover to validate the truth of a statement to a verifier without revealing any information about the content of the statement, thereby ensuring the confidentiality of the information. This technology is divided into two types: interactive and non-interactive zero-knowledge proofs (NIZK). NIZK, compared to the interactive form, requires only a single authentication exchange, reducing the risk of coordinated attacks and lowering communication costs. By minimizing the communication overhead associated with multiple interactions, NIZK helps maintain high throughput in blockchain networks and enhances privacy protection efficiency, effectively balancing privacy and system performance.

In the Schnorr zero-knowledge proof protocol [16], the prover claims to know the value of key x and can prove the commitment to the verifier without revealing the specific value. This paper employs the Fiat-Shamir heuristic [17] to transform the Schnorr protocol into a non-interactive format for proving the DID controller's possession of the corresponding private key. The algorithmic process involving the verifier V and prover P is detailed as follows:

Let G be the base point on the elliptic curve E. The prover P has the private key $sk = a$ and the public key $PK = a \cdot G$:

Prover P:

- Randomly selects a scalar r and calculates $R = r \cdot G$.
- Computes $c = Hash(R, PK)$, where $Hash$ represent s a cryptographically secure hash function.
- Calculates signature component s using Eq. (2.1) and sends tuple (R, s):

$$s = r + c \cdot sk \tag{2.1}$$

Verifier V:

- Calculates $c = Hash(R, PK)$ and verifies whether Eq. (2.2) is valid:

$$s \cdot G = R + c \cdot PK \tag{2.2}$$

Bulletproofs [18] is a more spatially efficient protocol, allowing users to prove to verifiers that certain data meets specific range requirements through zero-knowledge proof. Without disclosing the secret value v, a commitment value V of v is calculated, and a relationship of constraint conditions is constructed based on the range to generate proof π. The verifier can confirm whether v is within the range using V and π without knowing v. In this paper, the protocol is applied to the verification of selective disclosure assertions to protect the privacy and security of data authorization.

3 Mechanism Design

The traditional data authorization model relies on a central server for identity authorization, which is inefficient and is more suited for small-scale scenarios with a clear trust environment, making it challenging for large-scale data management.

In response to these limitations, this chapter proposes an authorization mechanism based on distributed digital identity. The foundational setup is established using blockchain technology, which eliminates the risk of a single point of failure. User identity management is facilitated through smart contracts, while user authorization management is implemented through an authorization mechanism based on verifiable credentials (VCs). This ensures that the entire data authorization process is transparent and secures privacy.

3.1 System Architecture Design

This paper designs a blockchain-based trusted authorization scheme for distributed digital identity, utilizing smart contracts to manage the DID lifecycle and zero-knowledge proof to facilitate user authentication. For authorization, users can opt for VC's selective plaintext disclosure and selective assertion disclosure according to their needs to protect user privacy. Regulators can access logs through regulatory contracts to monitor and ensure process compliance.

The trusted authorization scheme integrates access control and data sharing functions post-authorization to form the overall scheme architecture. The system framework, as illustrated in Fig. 1, includes multiple modules such as front-end interaction, trusted authorization, business functions, and regulatory management. Throughout the data authorization and sharing process, entities access the system via front-end interaction, manage identity and authorization operations through the trusted authorization module, achieve privacy protection through selective disclosure, and realize data sharing through the business function module. The supervisor accesses the system operation log via the supervision contract to retroactively monitor the entire data authorization and sharing process.

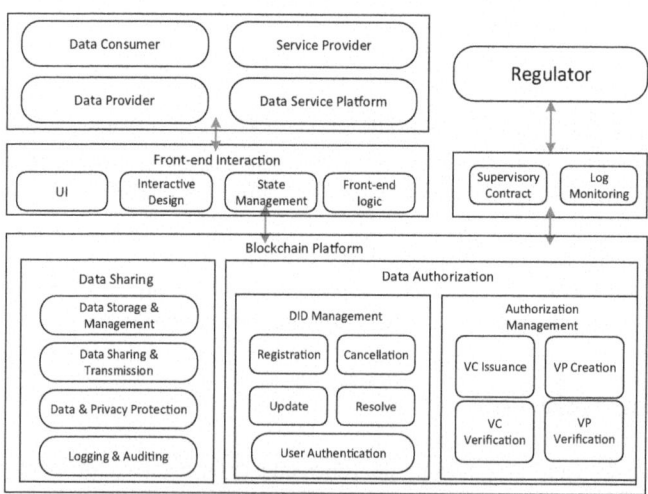

Fig. 1. System Framework

3.2   Coding Rules

To streamline processing, data are categorized into data resources, data assets, and data products. Data resources consist of raw, unprocessed data suitable for further analysis and application. Data assets, preliminarily filtered and organized, are usually presented as labels or reports and are easier to manage and use. Data products, derived from data assets through extensive processing and analysis, offer high-value goods or services independently.

DID identifier coding rules help classify and provide services for subject objects in data authorization. Data providers holding resources or assets can collaborate with service providers to convert these into data products. Once they possess data products, providers can apply for quality certification VCs and list them on a platform. Data users can search for these products based on their needs while service providers can advertise their scope to attract customers.

According to the DIDs standard of W3C, the coding rules of the designed data trading market are detailed in Table 1.

Table 1. DID Coding Rules

Scheme Identifier	Method Identifier	A Specific Method Identifier
did	dtm	Principal Identification + ":"+ Relevant Principal Code

Scheme identifiers indicate that coding rules are based on the DID architecture, while method identifiers specify that coding rules are implemented based on the data trading market. Subject identifiers in specific method identifiers are used to identify the basic categories of various subjects participating in the data trading market. Relevant subject codes are codes uniformly assigned or registered by each subject according to type and coding rules, uniquely identifying entity objects in the data trading market. The principal coding rules are shown in Table 2.

Table 2. Principal coding rules

Principal Type	Encoding Rules	Code allocation
Data Resource	drs	Regulators define it to ensure uniqueness
Data Asset	das	Regulators define it to ensure uniqueness
Data Product	dpt	Regulators define it to ensure uniqueness
Data Provider	prv	Unified registration with regulatory authorities
Data Consumer	csm	Unified registration with regulatory authorities
Service Platform	svp	Unified registration with regulatory authorities
Regulator	rgl	Unified registration with regulatory authorities

3.3   Identity Authentication

The identity authentication process uses non-interactive zero-knowledge proof (NIZK), as shown in Fig. 2, allowing DID controllers to authenticate without revealing the signature value of specified content, thereby preventing fraud and forgery. Initially, the DID subject generates a Pedersen commitment value r from a random number R, and creates an unpredictable challenge c using a hash function based on R and the public key y. Subsequently, the response value s is calculated from r, c, and private key x, and the proof (R, s) is sent to the verifier. The verifier, upon receiving s, uses the DID identifier to request data from the DID system, retrieves the public key and verification method, and verifies the proof by checking if $s \cdot G = R + c \cdot y$. If the equation holds, authentication is confirmed. This NIZK method ensures high security and privacy, prevents exposure of sensitive information, and maintains authentication integrity and authenticity, meeting diverse application and rights management requirements.

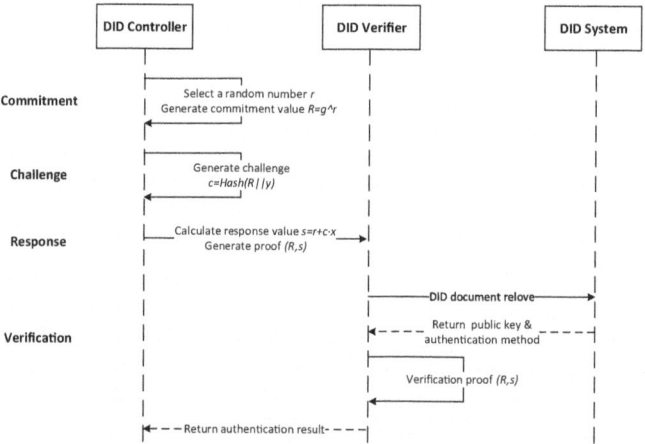

Fig. 2. Flowchart of identity authentication

3.4   Authorization Process

After completing identity authentication, users can manage their data subjects and authorize data products by applying for a verifiable credential and generating verifiable presentations (VP) from it. In the data trust authorization mechanism, a VC is formatted as a JSON string including metadata, credential subject, and proof method. In data trading scenarios, verifiers may need to verify attributes from different VCs. Here, VC holders can create a selective expression VP based on actual demand, where a VP comprises multiple VCs authenticated and verified through a digital signature.

VCs are typically issued by data providers to demonstrate the data's authenticity, integrity, and legitimacy; regulators to confirm the identities of data providers and users and the legality of transactions; and data market platforms to verify data quality and boost transaction credibility, as illustrated in Fig. 3. In the VC flow process, the holder submits certification materials to the issuing authority to apply for a VC. Once verified, the issuer grants the VC with authenticated attributes to the holder. When service access is needed, the holder proves necessary attribute compliance by presenting the VP derived from the VC to the service provider for verification.

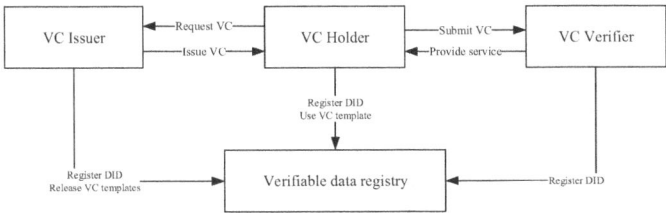

Fig. 3. VC flow process diagram

To fully protect the privacy of participants and data in the data transaction process, this paper proposes two selective disclosure methods to ensure the safety and reliability of the authorization mechanism. Users can choose different disclosure methods based on the actual scenario. The selective plaintext disclosure process is relatively simple, involving selective decryption of certain disclosed data fields. The selective assertion disclosure method, however, does not reveal the specific data value of the attribute. Instead, it constructs verifiable credentials and zero-knowledge proofs based on the attribute commitment, allowing the verifier to perform range verification.

(1) Selective express disclosure

Selective plaintext disclosure allows the VC holder to freely choose the minimal disclosure of authentication attributes. Undisclosed information is processed through encryption, hashing, or other privacy protection techniques to ensure that sensitive data remains secure except for the attributes disclosed in clear text. The process for building selective plaintext disclosure is shown in Table 3.

In the selective plaintext disclosure, the owner retains the hidden attributes as hash digest, displays the attributes to be disclosed in plaintext form, and presents the above contents in the form of verifiableClaims together with VC to the verifier. The verification process as shown in Table 4 is carried out by the verifier to verify the selective plaintext disclosure.

(2) Selective assertion disclosure

Selective assertion disclosure allows the holder to disclose only specific assertions and relies on zero-knowledge proof verification attributes to meet the scope requirements. The process of generating and verifying selective assertion disclosure is shown in Fig. 4. The holder submits the attribute verification material and attribute commitment to the issuer to request a VC. The issuer verifies the true attribute, then hashes the metadata of each attribute commitment and credential in the main part of the declaration, and signs the content of proof. This proof consists of the VC about the attribute commitment and is issued to the holder.

Table 3. Selective plaintext disclosure of VC generation process

Pseudocode 1. Selective plaintext disclosure VC generation process
INPUT: *requestClaimsFromHolder*
OUTPUT: *hashVC*
Description of key steps:
1: UPON issuer receives the VC attribute request from the holder DO:
2: IF *requestClaimsFromHolder* is valid then
3:     use hash algorithm to generate the hash summary *hashClaim* for each attribute claim in *requestClaimsFromHolder* ;
4: ELSE
5:     return *invalidRequest* .
6: concatenates *hashClaim* of all declarations into a string overall *hashClaimString* ;
7: hash summary *hashClaimString* & *metaData* and sign to generate *proof*;
8: compose a *hashVC* with *metaData, hashClaim*, and *proof* .

Table 4. Selective explicit disclosure of VC verification process

Pseudocode 2. Selective explicit disclosure of VC verification process
INPUT: *hashVC, verifiableClaims*
OUTPUT: *verifyResult*
Description of key steps:
1: UPON issuer receives the VC attribute request from the holder DO:
2: IF *hashVC* is valid then
3:     use hash algorithm to generate hash summary *hashClaim* of *claim* in *verifiableClaims;*
4: ELSE
5:     return *invalidRequest* .
6: concatenates *hashClaim* of all declarations into a string overall *hashClaimString`* ;
7: IF *hashClaimString`* is equal to *hashClaimString* in *hashVC* then
8:     return *validRequest* .
9: ELSE
10:     return *invalidRequest* .

When it is necessary to perform attribute verification, the holder only needs to present the VC and the zero-knowledge proof of the attribute commitment they wish to disclose to the verifier. After receiving the verification materials, the verifier extracts the disclosed attribute commitment field from the VC, obtains the verification method and public key through the issuer's DID document, confirms that the attribute commitment originates from the VC issued by the issuer, and then verifies the commitment according to the zero-knowledge proof to ensure its validity.

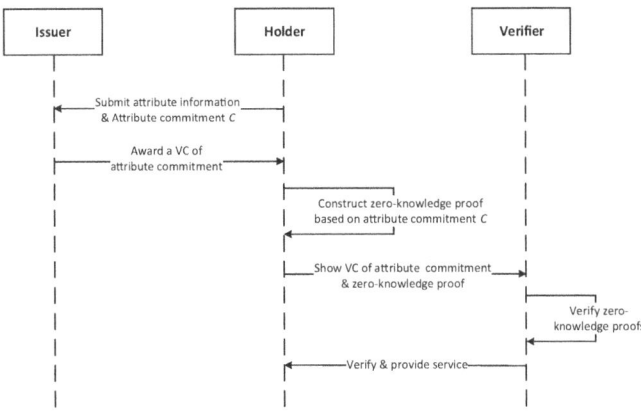

Fig. 4. Selective assertion disclosure generation and verification process

4 Experiments and Testing

4.1 Experimental Environment and Implementation

This experiment constructs a blockchain network framework for a business chain using the Hyperledger Fabric platform, utilizing a test machine as a client to send simulated transactions to the business chain. Experimental simulations and performance tests are conducted on the data trusted authorization mechanism based on distributed digital identity as described in this scheme. The configuration of the experimental environment is detailed in Table 5.

Table 5. Experimental environment configuration

Environment	Attribute	Parameter
Service chain	Fabric version	2.5
	Chaincode version	Java 11
	Node number	Order 1; Peer 2
	OS	CentOS7 3.10.0
	System configuration	CPU 16 Core@2.3 GHz; Memory 32 GB
Client	Code	Java 11
	OS	Windows 11
	System configuration	CPU 12 Core@4.0 GHz; Memory 128 GB

A data trading market system is constructed based on the business chain, incorporating the data trusted authorization and sharing mechanism grounded in distributed digital identity. Functional implementation and performance testing are conducted for the DID lifecycle management and the VC-based data authorization process.

4.2 Performance Testing and Analysis

In this paper, response time, throughput, and storage overhead are selected as performance evaluation indicators, and Apache JMeter is used for performance testing. According to the operation scenario of the DID contract in the business chain, various DID lifecycle management contract calls such as registration, revocation, document update, and analysis were executed. Throughput and response time tests were conducted for each contract call, and 100,000 contract executions within a certain period were recorded to calculate the average response time and throughput, as shown in Fig. 5.

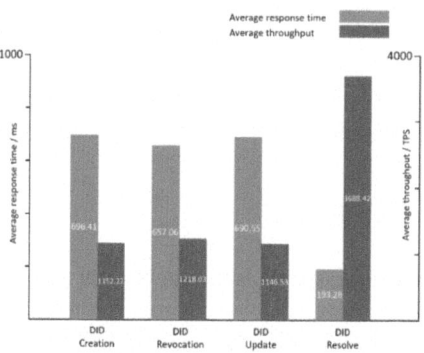

Fig. 5. Contract test results

The analysis results indicate that the operation time for each DID lifecycle management contract is short, and the throughput exceeds 1000 transactions per second (TPS), meeting high business requirements and making it suitable for the network environment of data trading market application scenarios. For trusted authorization, the SM2 signature algorithm and SM3 hash algorithm are used to implement selective plaintext disclosure, while Bulletproofs are employed for selective assertion disclosure. Multiple generation and verification tests were conducted, recording the accuracy and time consumption for selective disclosure generation and verification, achieving a verification accuracy rate of 100%, as shown in Fig. 6.

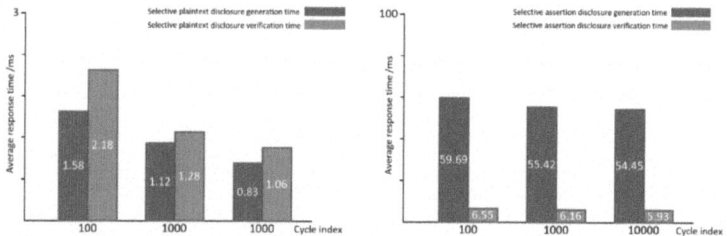

Fig. 6. Selective disclosure of test results

The performance test results demonstrate that verifiable plaintext disclosure based on the SM2 signature algorithm and SM3 hash algorithm, along with selective assertion disclosure using Bulletproof technology, can achieve efficient and accurate VC selective expression while maintaining good performance in large-scale operations. In terms of performance, the time for selective plaintext disclosure is significantly lower than that for selective assertion disclosure, suggesting that selective plaintext disclosure can be employed to improve performance in non-sensitive attribute verification scenarios.

Additionally, the security analysis of the selective plaintext disclosure and selective assertion disclosure methods implemented in this paper was conducted. The selective plaintext disclosure generates a summary of attribute values using a hash algorithm and submits it to the issuer for digital signature authentication, adhering to the principle of data minimization. Even if a third party obtains the VC, the original data cannot be directly restored, ensuring data integrity and authenticity. In the case of selective assertion disclosure, the commitment value is constructed using the Pedersen commitment method and authorized by the verifiable certificate issued by the issuer, rendering it unforgeable. Its integrity and authenticity are guaranteed by zero-knowledge proof verification, enabling efficient and secure trusted authorization functions.

5 Conclusion

Based on the characteristics of blockchain and distributed digital identity technology and the actual needs of data trusted authorization and sharing, this paper proposes an application scheme for distributed digital identity technology within the data transaction market scenario. System simulations and performance tests were conducted to validate the approach. As blockchain technology continues to develop and gain traction, distributed digital identity technology, being a crucial component of the fundamental identity management framework within blockchain systems, is expected to attract increasing attention. It is hoped that this paper will provide valuable insights and references for future related work.

References

1. Rong, K., Liu, T., Zhou, D., et al.: Data classification of factor market authorization mechanism research. J. Manag. Eng. **4**(6), 5–29 (2022). https://doi.org/10.13587/j.cnki.jieem.2022. 06.002
2. Ferraiolo, D.F., Barkley, J.F., Kuhn, D.R.: A role-based access control model and reference implementation within a corporate intranet. ACM Trans. Inf. Syst. Secur. (TISSEC) **2**(1), 34–64 (1999)
3. Yuan, E., Tong, J.: Attributed based access control (ABAC) for web services. IEEE (2005). https://doi.org/10.1109/ICWS.2005.25
4. Zhang, Y., Liu, J.-Q., He, Z., et al.: Research on access control model based on task. Comput. Eng. **34**(5), 28–30 (2008). https://doi.org/10.1080/10286600801908949
5. Yuan, Y., Wang, F.: Blockchain technology development present situation and prospect. J. Autom. **4**, 481–494 (2016). https://doi.org/10.16383/j.aas.2016.c160158
6. Liu, A., Du, X., Wang, N., et al.: Big data access control mechanism based on the blockchain. J. Softw. **30**(9), 2636–2654 (2019). https://doi.org/10.13328/j.cnki.jos.005771
7. Jiang, W., Li, E., Zhou, W.: IoT access control model based on blockchain and trusted execution environment. Processes **11**(3), 723 (2023)

8. Xie, R., Li, H., Shi, G., et al.: Traceable access control mechanism based on blockchain. J. Commun. **41**(12), 82–93 (2020)

9. Feng, T., Chen, L., Fang, J., et al.: A blockchain data sharing scheme with searchable encryption based on localized differential privacy and attribute base. J. Commun. **44**(5), 224–233 (2023). https://doi.org/10.11959/j.issn.1000-436x.2023103

10. Liu, J., Fan, Y., Sun, R., et al.: Blockchain-aided privacy-preserving medical data sharing scheme for e-healthcare system. IEEE Internet Things J. **10**(24), 21377–21388 (2023). https://doi.org/10.1109/jiot.2023.3287636

11. Yuan, M., Xu, Y., Zhang, C., et al.: TRUCON: blockchain-based trusted data sharing with congestion control in internet of vehicles. IEEE Trans. Intell. Transp. Syst. **24**(3), 3489–3500 (2023). https://doi.org/10.1109/TITS.2022.3226500

12. Belchior, R., Putz, B., Pernul, G., et al.: SSIBAC: self-sovereign identity based access control. In: 2020 IEEE 19th International Conference on Trust, Security and Privacy in Computing and Communications (TrustCom), pp. 1935–1943. IEEE (2020)

13. Mukta, R., Martens, J., Paik, H., et al.: Blockchain-based verifiable credential sharing with selective disclosure. In: 2020 IEEE 19th International Conference on Trust, Security and Privacy in Computing and Communications (TrustCom), pp. 959–966. IEEE (2020)

14. Yin, J., Xiao, Y., Pei, Q., et al.: SmartDID: a novel privacy-preserving identity based on blockchain for IoT. IEEE Internet Things J. **10**(8), 6718–6732 (2022)

15. Park, C.S., Park, W.S., Woo, S.: Security bootstrapping for securing data plane and control plane in named data networking. IEEE Trans. Netw. Serv. Manag. **20**(3), 3765–3781 (2022)

16. Imghoure, A., Omary, F., El-Yahyaoui, A.: Schnorr-based conditional privacy-preserving authentication scheme with multisignature and batch verification in VANET. Internet Things **23**, 100850 (2023). https://doi.org/10.1016/j.iot.2023.100850

17. Goldwasser, S., Kalai, Y.T.: On the (in)security of the Fiat-Shamir paradigm. In: 44th Annual IEEE Symposium on Foundations of Computer Science, pp. 102–113. IEEE (2003)

18. Bünz, B., Bootle, J., Boneh, D., et al.: Bulletproofs: short proofs for confidential transactions and more. In: 2018 IEEE Symposium on Security and Privacy (SP), pp. 315–334. IEEE (2018)

Secure and Efficient Deduplication for Encrypted Image Data in Cloud Storage

Nuan Wen, Xuming Li, Wenqi Li, and Xiao Chang$^{(\boxtimes)}$

Information Security Center, China Mobile, Beijing, China
{wennuan,lixuming,liwenqixa}@chinamobile.com,
changxiao@cmdi.chinamobile.com

Abstract. With the exponential growth of multimedia data, especially images, in cloud storage, deduplication has become an essential technique to reduce storage and communication overheads. However, ensuring the confidentiality and security of deduplicated encrypted images presents significant challenges, particularly regarding side-channel attacks and the overhead associated with key transfer. This paper introduces SEDDS (Secure Encrypted Data Deduplication System), a novel framework that integrates adaptive MSB reversible data hiding with traditional deduplication techniques to address these challenges. By embedding key transfer auxiliary information directly into the encrypted images, SEDDS eliminates the need for additional communication and storage overhead for auxiliary information. This method also ensures indistinguishable responses to deduplication requests, thereby resisting side-channel attacks. Our security analysis and experimental results demonstrate that SEDDS not only enhances security against side-channel attacks but also significantly reduces communication and storage overheads compared to existing schemes.

Keywords: Cloud Storage · Reversible data hiding · Cloud Data Deduplication

1 Introduction

With the rapid development of cloud storage services and the widespread use of smartphones, cameras, and social media, more and more users are uploading multimedia data such as images and videos to cloud platforms. Image data, in particular, has a larger size and higher redundancy compared to text data, leading to exponential growth in cloud storage data. According to the latest IDC report [1], the total amount of data generated globally is expected to reach 175 ZB by 2025, with nearly 75% of the data having at least one redundant copy. This redundant storage of digital images and other multimedia data significantly wastes the storage resources of Cloud Service Providers (CSPs) and causes excessive communication overhead for users due to repeated uploads.

© The Author(s), under exclusive license to Springer Nature Singapore Pte Ltd. 2025
G. Zhao et al. (Eds.): BWTAC 2024, CCIS 2277, pp. 85–96, 2025.
https://doi.org/10.1007/978-981-97-9412-6_8

To address this issue, image deduplication technology has emerged [2–5], allowing CSPs to check whether an uploaded image already exists on their local servers. If the image is found, the CSP only establishes a link to the stored image for the current user without storing another copy. However, while deduplication technology saves overhead, it introduces potential security threats. The differentiated response from CSPs creates a side channel for external attackers, revealing the existence of target images in cloud storage. Once an attacker determines that an image does not require full data upload, they can infer that the requested image is already stored in the cloud. This can lead to brute-force dictionary attacks on low-entropy sensitive information in the target image, ultimately revealing the image's content. Moreover, storing plaintext image data in the cloud compromises confidentiality. Although encryption is an effective solution, the use of different encryption keys by different users results in identical images being encrypted into different ciphertexts, preventing deduplication and causing redundant storage and communication overhead.

To address the issues above, the classic solution is to use Message-Locked Encryption (MLE) [9] to resolve the contradiction between image confidentiality protection and ciphertext deduplication. This method uses a content-related key of the image instead of a user-related key to encrypt the data, ensuring that even if the data comes from different users, the same plaintext can result in the same ciphertext. The most notable instance of this is Convergent Encryption (CE) [10], which selects the hash value of the image as the encryption key to achieve deduplication. Unfortunately, in the MLE method, internal and external attackers can still steal the private data of low-entropy images through side-channel attacks by using distinguishable responses. In 2020, Pooranian et al. [8] proposed a hybrid scheme called LEVER for general data, which can simultaneously resist security risks and achieve ciphertext deduplication. LEVER uses a short hash for duplicate checking, creating obfuscated deduplication responses due to the hash's strong collision properties. This means that a short hash indicating an existing file does not necessarily confirm the presence of the target file. LEVER also employs homomorphic encryption to transfer random encryption keys between data owners instead of MLE keys. While this approach helps with general data deduplication, it doesn't protect the existence privacy of user data. If the requested image is already in the cloud, the CSP only returns auxiliary information; otherwise, it asks the user to upload new ciphertext and auxiliary information. This response reveals the file's existence, creating a side-channel for attackers. Additionally, key transfer requires transmitting and storing extra auxiliary information, increasing communication and storage overhead.

In response, we propose a new scheme called Secure Encrypted Data Deduplication System (SEDDS), which leverages adaptive reversible data hiding for encrypted images to address these security challenges. By embedding auxiliary information for key transfer into the encrypted images, our scheme eliminates the extra communication and storage overhead associated with auxiliary information. Furthermore, we optimize the deduplication process to ensure that even if the requested image is not stored in the cloud, users do not need to upload additional ciphertext, thus achieving indistinguishable responses. Our security analysis and experimental results demonstrate that SEDDS effectively resists side channel attacks in a lightweight manner while preserving storage efficiency. SEDDS stands as a secure and efficient solution for managing encrypted image data in cloud storage environments. The main contributions of this paper are as follows:

1. We propose a secure deduplication framework for encrypted images that supports reversible data hiding in the ciphertext domain. This framework significantly reduces communication and storage overhead while ensuring resistance to side-channel attacks. Users can embed auxiliary information into the encrypted image and send the encrypted image with embedded information to the cloud for storage. When subsequent users request deduplication, CSP can extract the embedded auxiliary information to transfer the random key among data owners.
2. We design a side-channel attack-resistant secure deduplication mechanism for images based on the encrypted image deduplication framework. By simplifying the interaction process, users do not need to upload additional ciphertext even if the requested image is not stored in the cloud, ensuring the indistinguishability of the response. This new obfuscation strategy achieves security against side-channel attacks.
3. We conduct security analysis and performance evaluation of SEDDS on real-world datasets. Theoretical and experimental results demonstrate that SEDDS can achieve security against side-channel attacks in a lightweight manner.

2   Related Work

2.1   Cloud Data Deduplication

Image deduplication technology can be divided into two categories based on deduplication effectiveness: precise image deduplication and fuzzy image deduplication. Agarwala et al. [2] proposed an approximate image deduplication scheme based on Dual-Integrity Convergent Encryption (DICE). This scheme divides images into independent blocks and applies the DICE protocol to each block to improve deduplication efficiency. However, the DICE protocol still uses hash algorithms for duplicate detection, which can only handle identical image blocks and is susceptible to brute-force dictionary attacks. Subsequently, Li et al. proposed a fuzzy image deduplication scheme [3], which uses perceptual hashing algorithms to generate signatures for each image and determines duplicate images by comparing the Hamming distances between perceptual hashes. However, this scheme requires periodic replacement of group keys, which is computationally complex. Additionally, as long as an attacker has the short digest information, they can gain access to the target file in the deduplication system without proving ownership of the file.

For general forms of cloud data deduplication, researchers have proposed several plaintext data deduplication models [4] to resist side-channel attacks, aiming to obfuscate the distinguishability of responses under different conditions. However, these works cannot ensure data confidentiality during transmission and cloud storage, leading to extensive research on ciphertext data deduplication. Pooranian et al. [5] proposed a ciphertext deduplication scheme based on random keys, called LEVER, which resists side-channel attacks through short hashes and uses the homomorphic encryption property of ciphertext to achieve the transfer of random keys between data owners. However, this distinguishability inevitably exposes the existence of sensitive data during side-channel attacks. Additionally, the transmission and storage of auxiliary information increase the communication overhead for users and the storage overhead for the cloud. Balancing the security and efficiency of the deduplication scheme is the key focus of the proposed EMSD method improvements.

2.2   Reversible Data Hiding in Encrypted Images

Information hiding is a technology that embeds some additional data into a carrier medium without occupying extra channels. Reversible Data Hiding in Encrypted Images (RDHEI) usually includes image encryption and data hiding. Depending on whether data extraction is independent of image decryption, existing methods can be divided into joint RDHEI and separate RDHEI. Zhang et al. proposed the first effective RDHEI method [6], which divides encrypted images into non-overlapping blocks and completes data embedding by flipping the three least significant bits (LSBs) of half the pixels in each block. At the decoding end, the flipping function is used to identify the flipped parts, and data extraction and image recovery are performed. Hong et al. [7] introduced a side-match technique and a new fluctuation function to simplify the extraction method in [6] and reduce the extraction error rate. To obtain a larger embedding capacity, Wang et al. [8] proposed an RDHEI based on MSB prediction, which is the method introduced in this paper. Specifically, the method divides the image into non-overlapping 2×2 pixel blocks and encrypts them to maintain pixel correlation. Each block has four pixels $P, C1, C2, C3$, and their MSB bits are compressed to create embedding space. The pixels are decomposed into eight bits, and the variables $e1, e2, e3$ are calculated to represent the number of different LSB bits among $P, C1, C2$.

3   System Model

As shown in Fig. 1, the SEDDS system model consists of two entities: users and CSPs (Cloud Service Providers).

Users: Entities outsource their image data to reduce local storage. Before uploading image data I, users calculate the short hash$sh(I)$ to check for its existence in the cloud. If $sh(I)$ is not found, the user generates a random key k, encrypts I to create the ciphertext $E_k(I)$, calculates the auxiliary information

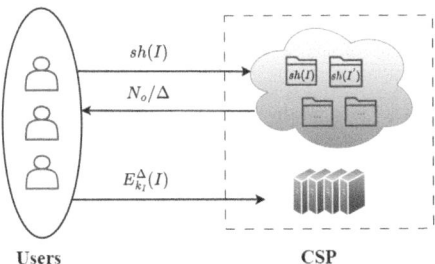

Fig. 1. System Model

$\Delta(I)$, embeds it into $E_k(I)$ using the MSB prediction algorithm, and uploads the final ciphertext $E_k(I)$ to the cloud. If $sh(I)$ is found, the user decrypts the auxiliary information to obtain the random key and uses it to generate a new ciphertext image for upload.

CSP: Cloud Service Providers (CSPs) eliminate redundant data by storing each piece of data only once. They maintain a list of short hashes and corresponding ciphertext images. When receiving a short hash $sh(I)$, CSP compares it with the stored hashes. If $sh(I)$ is not found, CSP returns "No" and stores the new ciphertext image and hash. If $sh(I)$ is found, CSP extracts auxiliary information from the associated ciphertext images and returns it to the user. For matching uploads, CSP discards the content; otherwise, it randomly stores one of the new uploads as a new record for $sh(I)$

Threat Model: We consider both legitimate but malicious users (external attackers) and honest but curious CSPs (internal attackers) attempting to obtain the image I or the random key k of a normal user.

For external attackers, side-channel attacks can be launched, where they disguise themselves as legitimate users to initiate deduplication requests and query the existence of target images in the cloud. By observing different responses returned by CSPs, they can steal the existence privacy of target images. Additionally, considering the predictable nature of target images with low minimum entropy, attackers can also launch brute-force dictionary attacks, constructing all possible versions of the target image and checking which version CSP blocks from further uploads.

For internal attackers, although the target image is predictable, the random key has high randomness, making it impossible for a malicious cloud to obtain the random key by predicting the target image. CSPs may attempt to examine the file list and decrypt the short hashes and auxiliary information to obtain the random key k. Once obtained, CSPs can decrypt the ciphertext to get the user's original image, thus stealing privacy.

4   Deduplication Process

The deduplication process of SEDDS is divided into two cases based on whether the short hash hits in the cloud. The detailed process is as follows:

4.1   Deduplication Process When Short Hash Misses

When User 1 uploads a new image for the first time, they first calculate the short hash of the image as a deduplication request and send it to the cloud. As shown in Fig. 2, the CSP checks the short hash and, if it does not match any stored hashes, returns a response indicating no match. User 1 then generates a random key and uses it to encrypt the image, obtaining the encrypted image $E_k(I)$. Next, User 1 generates auxiliary information

$$\Delta = \epsilon(k_I \Theta h(I)) || E_{\epsilon(k_I)}(E_{h_{(I)}}(K_I))$$

required for the key transfer and embeds this information into the encrypted image $E_k(I)$ to obtain the final embedded ciphertext image $E_k(I')$, which is then uploaded to the cloud. The specific process is shown in Fig. 2 and detailed as follows:

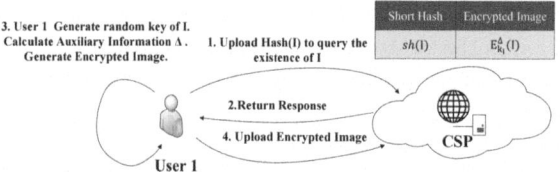

Fig. 2. The first upload of file I

Generating Encrypted Image. In the SEDDS scheme, the user inputs the original image, generates a random key, and adopts the block encryption algorithm RC4 to obtain the encrypted image $E_k(I)$.

- **Generating Pseudo-Random Key Stream**: The user expands the random key k and generates a pseudo-random key stream.
- **Dividing the Original Image into Blocks**: The original image is divided into non-overlapping blocks.
- **Block Encryption**: Each block is encrypted using the pseudo-random key stream.

The encrypted image $E_k(I)$ is generated through this process. For each block of the original image, the encrypted block $e_k^m(i, j)$ is calculated using the following formula:

$$e_k^m(i,j) = b_k^m(i,j) \oplus r^k(i,j), \quad k = 0, 1, 2, ..., 7$$

where $b_k^m(i,j)$ represents the k-th bit of the m-th block at position (i,j), and $r^k(i,j)$ represents the k-th bit of the pseudo-random key stream at the same position. The symbol $\oplus$ denotes the XOR operation.

Embedding Auxiliary Information. To save communication overhead for the user and reduce storage overhead for the cloud server, the auxiliary information Δ is embedded into the encrypted image $E_k(I)$ using a high-capacity reversible data hiding method based on adaptive MSB prediction, resulting in the final embedded ciphertext image $H = E_k(I')$. This way, the user only needs to upload the embedded ciphertext image H to the cloud while storing the random key k_1 locally and deleting other intermediate variables.

During the embedding process, as described in Sect. 2.3, the length of the auxiliary information $|\Delta|$ is utilized. The MSB prediction method is used to reconstruct the pixel values to free up the embedding space n_c. Blocks with $md > 1$ are selected as embeddable blocks, and a location map recording the positions of all embeddable blocks is constructed and denoted as c. To ensure the reversibility of information hiding, the auxiliary information Δ is embedded along with additional information such as the location map and end marker into the image. The embedding method involves iteratively replacing the least significant n_c bits of each embeddable block and recomposing the 32-bit blocks into four independent pixels to obtain the final embedded ciphertext image. It is worth noting that to ensure the feasibility of the scheme, the embedding capacity of the ciphertext image must be sufficiently large to satisfy the condition $|\Delta| + |Add| < c$.

4.2 Deduplication Process When Short Hash Hits

Information Extraction. As shown in Figs. 3 and 4, when Users 2 and 3 upload the second and first images respectively, they send the short hashes $sh(I_1)$ and $sh(I_2)$ to the CSP. The CSP identifies a hit for the identical $sh(I)$, meaning that a copy of I is already stored in the cloud. The CSP then extracts the auxiliary information Δ from the stored embedded ciphertext image and sends it back to the user. Using the MSB prediction method, the auxiliary information is extracted, ensuring the confidentiality of the image content. The extraction process is invisible to the CSP, thus ensuring the security of the key transfer.

The CSP then divides the stored image I into non-overlapping blocks of size 2×2 and processes each block to obtain 32-bit sequences e_1, e_2, e_3, which are then used to calculate C_1, C_2, C_3 as follows:

$$C_i = \text{Trunc}(P, md) + e_i, \quad i = 1, 2, 3$$

where $\text{Trunc}(P, md)$ extracts the P th md-bit value, and the "+" represents a position adjustment. This way, the position map is constructed and the auxiliary information is retrieved.

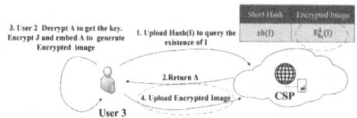 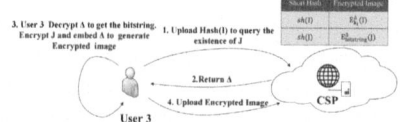

Fig. 3. The second upload of file I   **Fig. 4.** The first upload of file J

Image Processing. As shown in Sect. 2.3, assuming that Users 2 and 3 receive the auxiliary information Δ, they will use the retrieved key to decrypt and re-encrypt the image, ensuring that the information remains consistent and secure.

For example, similar to the LEVER scheme [8], the user calculates $sh(I)$ and sends it to the CSP. Upon receiving the short hash, the CSP identifies a hit and returns the auxiliary information Δ. The user then uses this information to generate the new key k', re-encrypts the image I to produce $E_{k'}(I)$, and uploads the new embedded ciphertext image $E_{k'}(I')$ to the cloud. The CSP then compares $E_{k'}(I')$ with the stored images. If a match is found, the uploaded content is discarded; if not, the new image is stored.

Data Storage. As shown in Figs. 7 and 8, upon receiving $E_{k'}(I')$ and Δ, the CSP updates the storage list. This method provides a secure and efficient way to handle deduplication and key transfers, ensuring that the deduplication process is secure and efficient.

Security Analysis. Considering the deduplication system's vulnerability to side-channel attacks, the proposed SEDDS scheme is designed to resist such attacks by ensuring that deduplication responses do not reveal the existence status of the target data. By embedding auxiliary information into the encrypted image and optimizing the interaction process, the scheme ensures that even if the requested image is already stored in the cloud, the response remains indistinguishable.

Furthermore, the embedded auxiliary information allows secure key transfers between users without revealing the image content. The random key encryption and high-capacity reversible data hiding ensure the security and efficiency of the deduplication process.

5   Performance Analysis

We selected two real-world datasets with different resolutions, SIPI [11] and Unsplash [12], for experiments to compare the differences between SEDDS, LEVER [5], CE [10], and the original deduplication scheme (O-DD) in terms of communication overhead, storage overhead, and computational overhead. In the SIPI and Unsplash datasets, we selected 210 and 1000 images, respectively, with resolutions of 512×512 and 1024×1024. We implemented the CSP functionality on an Amazon EC2 instance and the user-side program on a workstation equipped with an Intel Core i7-12700H CPU @ 2.7 GHz, 32 GB RAM.

5.1 Embedding Capacity

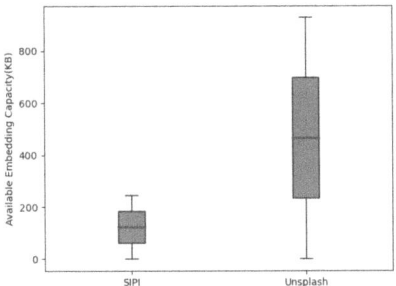

Fig. 5. Available Embedding Capacity

To ensure the feasibility of the deduplication scheme, the length of the auxiliary information necessary for key transfer must be less than the total embedding capacity of the test images minus the length of additional information generated during the embedding process, such as location maps and end markers. This difference is defined as the available embedding capacity. The available embedding capacities of each test image in the two datasets are shown in Fig. 5.

The minimum values of the available embedding capacity in the SIPI and Unsplash datasets are 0.25 kB and 0.89 kB, respectively. The length of the auxiliary information depends on the length of the ciphertext output by the public key algorithm used during the encryption of the random key.

5.2 Communication Overhead

To evaluate the proposed scheme's communication overhead, we stored 0% to 100% of experimental images in the cloud and initiated deduplication requests for all images. Communication overhead on the user side was then calculated at different image repetition rates. Figure 6(a) and (b) show the comparison results for the four schemes. For consistent evaluation, the short hash length was fixed at 8 bits, and cloud storage was restored to its original state after each experiment.

As shown in Fig. 6, SEDDS outperforms LEVER in terms of communication overhead. For example, in the SIPI dataset, as the image repetition rate increases from 0% to 100%, SEDDS shows significantly lower communication overhead than LEVER. This is because SEDDS embeds auxiliary information for key transfer into the ciphertext image, so users only upload the embedded ciphertext image, while LEVER requires uploading additional auxiliary information. SEDDS also optimizes the deduplication process, ensuring that only one embedded ciphertext image is stored when the short hash hits but the image isn't in the cloud, avoiding extra uploads. Although CE and O-DD have the lowest communication overhead (around 665 MB) because users upload only the ciphertext image and index value, SEDDS offers strong security with relatively low communication overhead by using random keys for encryption.

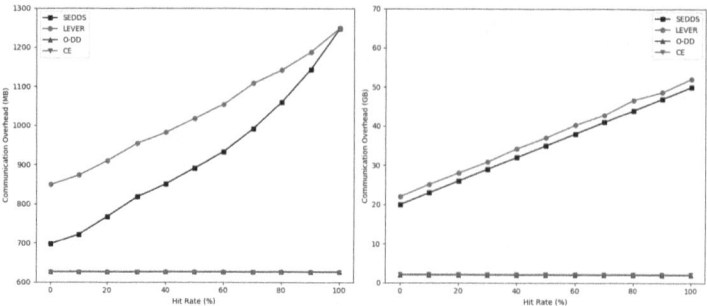

Fig. 6. Comparison of Communication Overhead

5.3   Storage Overhead

To evaluate cloud storage overhead, we vary the image repetition rate in the dataset and calculate the deduplication rate for different schemes. The deduplication rate is defined as the ratio of data volume stored in the cloud after deduplication to the data volume requested by the user. Using O-DD as a benchmark, we compare the deduplication rate differences of SEDDS, LEVER, and CE. A higher deduplication rate difference indicates more cloud storage overhead saved. Figures 7(a) and (b) show the experimental results for the two datasets, highlighting the advantage of SEDDS in terms of storage overhead.

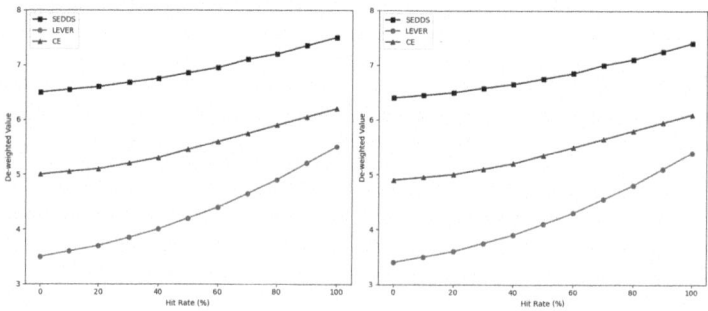

Fig. 7. Comparison of Storage Overhead

As shown in Fig. 7, compared to LEVER and CE, SEDDS saves more communication overhead. Taking the Unsplash dataset as an example, when the image repetition rate increases from 0% to 100%, the storage overhead of SEDDS is lower than LEVER and CE. This is because SEDDS uses information hiding technology to embed auxiliary information into the encrypted image, ensuring the random key transfer while saving cloud storage space.

5.4   Computational Overhead

In addition to communication and storage overhead, we also compare the computational overhead of the four schemes. From the user's perspective, computational overhead is defined as the time required from receiving the response to uploading data based on the response. The average computational overhead for all test images in the two datasets is recorded in Table 1.

Table 1. Comparison of Computing Overhead

Dataset	Scheme	Average Computational Overhead (s)
SIPI	SEDDS	9.068
	LEVER	1.552
	CE	0.584
	O-DD	0.002
Unsplash	SEDDS	27.204
	LEVER	4.969
	CE	1.988
	O-DD	0.008

As shown in Table 1, the computational overhead of the four schemes is ranked from high to low as follows: SEDDS, LEVER, CE, and O-DD. This is because, in the O-DD scheme, users only need to perform image encryption, while CE, LEVER, and SEDDS respectively add index value (hash) encryption, auxiliary information generation, and auxiliary information embedding operations on top of the previous scheme. Due to the information embedding operation, the computational overhead of SEDDS increases significantly. However, this operation is precisely the key step to reducing user communication overhead and cloud storage overhead, as well as improving the scheme's security against side-channel attacks.

6   Conclusion

To address the side-channel attack problem caused by distinguishable responses in the deduplication of encrypted image data in cloud storage, and the extra overhead incurred for key transfer, this paper proposes an efficient Secure Encrypted Data Deduplication System (SEDDS) based on adaptive MSB reversible data hiding. By innovatively introducing ciphertext-domain information hiding technology into the deduplication framework, auxiliary information for key transfer is embedded in encrypted images to save communication and storage overhead. On this basis, the interaction process is optimized so that even if the requested image is not stored in the cloud, the user does not need to upload additional ciphertext, thus ensuring indistinguishable responses and security against side-channel attacks. Security analysis and experimental results demonstrate the advantages of this scheme in terms of both security and performance.

The proposed algorithm targets deduplication of large volumes of high-redundancy image data in the cloud. Although it achieves the expected design goals, it is only applicable to precise image deduplication and incurs additional computational overhead. Future work will consider reducing computational overhead while achieving fuzzy image deduplication.

References

1. Wang, C., Zhang, B., Ren, K., et al.: Privacy-assured outsourcing of image reconstruction service in cloud. IEEE Trans. Emerg. Top. Comput. **1**(1), 166–177 (2013)
2. Agarwala, A., Singh, P., Atrey, P.K.: Client side secure image deduplication using DICE protocol. In: 2018 IEEE Conference on Multimedia Information Processing and Retrieval (MIPR), pp. 412–417. IEEE (2018)
3. Li, J., Chen, X., Li, M., et al.: Secure deduplication with efficient and reliable convergent key management. IEEE Trans. Parallel Distrib. Syst. **25**(6), 1615–1625 (2013)
4. Tang, X., Liu, Z., Shao, Y., et al.: Side channel attack resistant cross-user generalized deduplication for cloud storage. In: ICC 2022-IEEE International Conference on Communications, pp. 998–1003. IEEE (2022)
5. Pooranian, Z., Shojafar, M., Garg, S., et al.: LEVER: secure deduplicated cloud storage with encrypted two-party interactions in cyber-physical systems. IEEE Trans. Ind. Inf. **17**(8), 5759–5768 (2020)
6. Zhang, X.: Reversible data hiding in encrypted image. IEEE Sig. Process. Lett. **18**(4), 255–258 (2011)
7. Hong, W., Chen, T.S., Wu, H.Y.: An improved reversible data hiding in encrypted images using side match. IEEE Sig. Process. Lett. **19**(4), 199–202 (2012)
8. Wang, Y., He, W.: High capacity reversible data hiding in encrypted image based on adaptive MSB prediction. IEEE Trans. Multimedia **24**, 1288–1298 (2021)
9. Bellare, M., Keelveedhi, S., Ristenpart, T.: Message-locked encryption and secure deduplication. In: Johansson, T., Nguyen, P.Q. (eds.) EUROCRYPT 2013. LNCS, vol. 7881, pp. 296–312. Springer, Heidelberg (2013). https://doi.org/10.1007/978-3-642-38348-9_18
10. Storer, M.W., Greenan, K., Long, D.D.E., et al.: Secure data deduplication. In: Proceedings of the 4th ACM International Workshop on Storage Security and Survivability, pp. 1–10 (2008)
11. Weber, A.G.: The USC-SIPI image database: version 5 (2006). http://sipiusc.edu/database/
12. Unsplash: The UNSPLASH image database [DB] (2023). https://www.unsplash.com/

SolSecure: A Security Analyzer
for Integer Bugs in Smart Contracts

Tianyi Liu[1,2(✉)], Gansen Zhao[1,2], and Kai Zheng[1]

[1] School of Computer Science, South China Normal University, Guangzhou 510631,
Guangdong, China
2840265954@qq.com
[2] Key Lab on Cloud Security and Assessment Technology of Guangzhou,
Guangzhou 510631, Guangdong, China

Abstract. Blockchain is a peer-to-peer network system that stores chains of transaction data. Blockchain is decentralized and immutable. Once data is added to the chain, it cannot be modified or deleted. Smart contracts are intelligent protocols running at the application layer of blockchain, enabling trustworthy transactions without third parties. However, the openness and immutability of the architecture introduce various security risks. Integer bugs arise from improper handling of numerical variables. They pose significant dangers in smart contract because, in contracts, integer variables are often used to represent critical financial information, such as account balances, asset prices, and transaction amounts. If miscalculations occur, they can lead to substantial financial losses. This paper describes SolSecure, a framework based on abstract interpretation theory [1,2], designed to find integer bugs in Ethereum smart contracts. Experimental results show that SolSecure can effectively detect integer vulnerabilities in Solidity smart contracts.

Keywords: static analysis · abstract interpretation · Solidity · smart contract

1 Introduction

Blockchain is a peer-to-peer network system that stores chains of transaction data. It first became widely known because of the cryptocurrency Bitcoin [3]. Blockchain does not rely on any centralized institution. Once data is added to blockchain, it cannot be modified or deleted, and the security of the data is ensured through cryptographic techniques.

Smart contracts are intelligent protocols running at the application layer of blockchain, enabling trustworthy transactions without third parties. It also share the decentralization and immutability characteristics of blockchain. In the majority of cases, smart contracts are implemented using turing-complete language Solidity. Once the code is compiled into EVM bytecode and deployed on blockchain, it will automatically execute when conditions are met without human intervention.

© The Author(s), under exclusive license to Springer Nature Singapore Pte Ltd. 2025
G. Zhao et al. (Eds.): BWTAC 2024, CCIS 2277, pp. 97–105, 2025.
https://doi.org/10.1007/978-981-97-9412-6_9

Smart contracts can effectively facilitate automated financial transactions, asset management, lending, and other functions. However, while improving effectiveness, they also introduce many security risks. If security vulnerabilities appears in a contract, it often leads to irreparable financial losses. Ensuring the security of smart contracts cannot be overemphasized.

This study focuses on detecting integer bugs in smart contracts. Integer overflow vulnerabilities have a long history in traditional softwares. On smart contract platforms, integer vulnerabilities are particularly dangerous because integer variables are often used to represent critical financial information, such as account balances, asset prices, and transaction amounts. If calculations go wrong, it can cause significant financial losses.

In recent years, the academic community has proposed many methods for detecting integer overflow vulnerabilities in smart contracts. Osiris [4] is a symbolic execution framework for Ethereum smart contract vulnerability finding proposed by C. Torres et al., aimed at accurately discovering various integer errors in smart contracts, using taint analysis as an auxiliary technique. Verismart [5] is a smart contract verification framework proposed by S. So et al., primarily designed for integer overflow vulnerabilities. Verismart is the first tool to use the Counterexample Guided Inductive Synthesis(CEGIS) algorithm for automated Hoare logic proof of Solidity smart contracts. SolType [6] is a smart contract verification framework targeting arithmetic overflows too, proposed by B. Tan et al. It implemented a security-enhanced type system for Solidity and proof the mathematical operation safety based on this type system.

Previous work on integer vulnerabilities detecting in Solidity has achieved good progress, but they often lack the analysis of runtime state of variables, resulting in insufficient precision in analyzing the value ranges of variables. This affects the accuracy of bug detection. To address this problem, we propose SolSecure, a framework based on abstract interpretation theory [1,2], designed to effectively find integer bugs in Ethereum smart contracts. SolSecure comprehensively analyzes the state of program variables, extracts integer bug verification conditions from the state information to examine bugs. Experimental results show that SolSecure can effectively detect integer vulnerabilities in Solidity programs.

2   Background

2.1   EVM

Ethereum Virtual Machine (EVM) is a transaction-based distributed state machine. It is the core component of blockchain. EVM is turing-complete, meaning it can execute any computational task, makes the development of various decentralized applications (DApps) possible.

EVM uses gas mechanism to limit the computational and storage resources consumed by transactions. Users must pay fees for each operation, such as calling and deploying smart contracts or initiating transactions, and these fees are calculated in gas units. Each operation in EVM has a predetermined gas cost. For example, deploying a smart contract costs 200 gas per byte, performing an addition operation consumes 3 gas, and writing a persistent variable requires 20,000 gas [7]. EVM calculates the total gas required for a smart contract execution based on the sum of all operation costs. The gas mechanism ensures that each transaction and smart contract call uses network resources judiciously.

As the core component of Ethereum, EVM provides powerful decentralized computing capabilities and an environment for executing smart contracts. Based on EVM, developers can create and run various decentralized applications, driving the application and development of blockchain technology across different fields.

2.2 Smart Contract

Smart contracts are a set of protocols that the contract participants can execute on the blockchain through the Ethereum Virtual Machine (EVM) [8]. These protocols are decentralized and immutable, effectively reducing the cost of financial transactions.

Smart contract features no intermediaries, automatic execution, and self-verification, and can be flexibly extended to various data and asset platforms, facilitating efficient online transactions and management [9]. Generally, smart contracts are written in Solidity, a high-level programming language similar to JavaScript [10]. After being compiled, the generated EVM bytecode is used to deploy the contracts on the Ethereum platform.

Smart contracts have been widely applied in recent years, and with this widespread use, numerous security issues have emerged. In an empirical study conducted by Sungjae Hwang et al. [11], researchers found that out of 55,046 smart contract samples, 13,943 contained exploitable vulnerabilities. Among the few hundred contracts manually inspected by the researchers, a quarter were used by thousands of users. Security issues are prevalent on smart contract platforms and can potentially cause significant negative impacts.

2.3 Integer Bugs in Solidity

Integer bugs in Solidity contracts occur when variables exceed their representable range. This happens due to the limited range of integer types. These vulnerabilities can lead to financial loss or contract logic failure. Integer vulnerabilities include overflow and underflow. Overflow occurs when the result of an addition or multiplication operation on an integer type variable exceeds its maximum value. For example, for the $uint8$ type (0 to 255), if $255 + 1$ is executed, the result will become 0 instead of the expected 256. Underflow occurs when the result of a subtraction operation on an integer type variable is less than its minimum value. For example, for the $uint8$ type, 0 - 1 will result in 255 instead of -1. Listing 1.1 is an example of overflow bug in Solidity.

```
contract OverflowExample {
    uint8 public myUint = 255;
    function increment() public {
```

```
4          // This will cause overflow , myUint will become 0
5          myUint += 1;
6      }
7  }
```

Listing 1.1. Overflow Example in Solidity

3 Overview

In this section, we provide an overview on the design of SolSecure.

3.1 Design Overview

SolSecure takes the Solidity smart contract source code as input and outputs its integer bug detect results. The detection process is, first we use Slither's [15] backend to obtain control flow graph (CFG) of contracts, and convert them into a finite set of executable paths; second, based on abstract interpretation theory [1,2], SolSecure performs numerical abstraction interpretation on these paths and collects security conditions; third, we use SMT solver Z3 [14] to solves the collected conditions and outputs the bug results. The abstract interpreter also references Rust static analyzer MirChecker [13].

3.2 Abstract Interpretation

SolSecure performs numerical analysis during the interpretation execution to gathering integer bug verification conditions.

According to Rice's Theorem [12], it is impossible to implement a program analyzer that can determine all vulnerabilities. All implementations are approximate solutions that approach from different way. Abstract interpretation theory [1,2] provides a sound over-approximation algorithm for the security analysis of programs. It can analyze the state of program variables before the program runs, thereby precisely and efficiently supporting our integer overflow vulnerability detection.

For our goals, the abstract interpretation analysis method includes two parts:

Abstract Domain. The abstract state of program variables, represented by a lattice (a partially ordered set (State, $\sqsubseteq$) with a join operator $\sqcup$). Two essential elements are $\top$ (top) and $\bot$ (bottom), which represent the maximum and minimum values in the lattice, respectively. SolSecure follows the monotone framework, performing analysis from top to bottom.

Transfer Function Given a program statement S, the transfer function f_S is defined as follows:

$$f_S : AS_{\text{before}}(S) \rightarrow AS_{\text{after}}(S)$$

where $AS_{\text{before}}(S)$ is the abstract state immediately before the execution of S, $AS_{\text{after}}(S)$ is the abstract state immediately after the execution of S. The function f_S thus represents the effect of statement S on the abstract state.

In our study, we use interval analysis [1], also known as box analysis. The specific details of interval analysis are as follows:

Lattice Elements: Each lattice element is represented as an interval $[l, h]$, where l represents the lower bound and h represents the upper bound.

Order Relation ($\sqsubseteq$): The order relation between two intervals $s_1 = [l_1, h_1]$ and $s_2 = [l_2, h_2]$ is defined as follows:

$$s_1 \sqsubseteq s_2 \Leftrightarrow l_1 \geq l_2 \wedge h_1 \leq h_2$$

Join Operator ($\sqcup$): The join operator between two intervals s_1 and s_2 is defined as the union of the two intervals, resulting in a new interval:

$$s_1 \sqcup s_2 = [\min(l_1, l_2), \max(h_1, h_2)]$$

We use interval analysis [1] to perform boundary analysis on program variables, collecting the possible value ranges for each program variable to detect integer vulnerabilities.

3.3 Integer Bugs Detection

After the analysis of every program path, we convert the conditions collected along the path into linear constraints and use the SMT solver Z3 [14] to solve them, determining whether the program contains integer vulnerabilities. The linear constraints mainly come from the following aspects: (1) The reasonable range of integer variables, such as the range of $uint32$ being 0 to $2^{32} - 1$; (2) *assert* and *require* in contracts. The *require* statement is used for input validation and permission checks, while the *assert* statement is applied to catch internal errors that should not occur and check invariants. These are conditions that must be met for the program to run correctly; (3) Linear constraints derived from the abstract interpreter. These constraints are all used to analyze whether the smart contract has integer vulnerabilities.

4 Evaluation

4.1 Experiment Setup

SolSecure detects integer vulnerabilities in Solidity via static analysis. Since the procedures are performed at compile time, we conducted our experiments off-chain. We used 50 smart contracts that contain 744 integer bugs from the public benchmark dataset SolidiFi [22] as our experimental data to test SolSecure's bug-finding ability. All the experiments are done on a machine with a 2.9 GHz Dual-Core Intel Core i5 CPU and 8 GB RAM, running macOS Monterey(12.6.7).

4.2   Experiment Results and Analysis

In this section, we present the results of our detector as shown in Table 1. SolSe-cure analyzed 50 smart contracts containing 744 integer bugs from the SolidiFi [22] benchmark. It successfully detected 391 of these bugs, achieving a detection rate of 52.6%.

Table 1. Statistics of detection results

Bug Type	Integer Overflow & Underflow
Contract Amount	50
Bug Amount	744
Bug Findings	391
% of All Bugs	52.6%

After examining the experimental data, we found that overflow/underflow vulnerabilities triggered within a single function can be fully detected. However, the detection rate significantly decreases for vulnerabilities that require multi-ple function calls to be triggered. There are two main reasons for this: first, it lacks cross-function CFG (Control Flow Graph) information, leading to missed reports; second, the analysis of state variables is not comprehensive enough. Since state variables can be affected by multiple transactions, their actual state is far more complex than that of local variables. To enhance the detection capa-bility for integer bugs, we need to improve the static analysis of both CFG and state variables.

5   Related Work

Dynamic Test. ContractFuzzer [16] is the first fuzz testing tool for smart contract vulnerabilities. ContractFuzzer analyzes the ABI of the smart contract bytecode to obtain information such as parameters and function signatures. Based on these parameters, it generates random test cases and detects security vulnerabilities by analyzing the execution logs. The tool supports detecting seven types of vul-nerabilities: gasless send, exception disorder, reentrancy, timestamp dependency, block number dependency, dangerous delegate call, and freezing ether. ILF [17] is a smart contract fuzz testing tool that uses symbolic execution and neural network technology for assistance. ILF employs a symbolic execution engine to generate valid call sequences, uses these sequences as inputs to train a neural net-work, and obtains a neural network model that generates more valid sequences. It then uses the sequence information generated by the model for fuzz testing. ContractGuard [7] is a dynamic intrusion detection system for smart contracts proposed by X. Wang et al. It uses context-sensitive acyclic path numbering as identification features, effectively intercepting various malicious attacks. It supports the detection of over ten types of vulnerabilities, including reentrancy, delegate calls, and arithmetic overflows.

Static Analysis. Slither [15] is a smart contract security vulnerability detection framework proposed by J. Feist et al. It translates the smart contract source code into SlithIR, which has both SSA [18] and non-SSA forms, suitable for different data flow analysis procedures. Slither implements a full-scale parser for Solidity, and supporting a rich variety of vulnerabilities detecting. A. Ghaleb et al. [19] proposed eTainter, a detection tool for gas-related and access control vulnerabilities. The main technique used is taint analysis, combined with various special characteristics of smart contracts, achieving efficient vulnerability detection without predefined vulnerability patterns. SmartCheck [20] is a static analysis tool for smart contract security vulnerabilities proposed by S. Tikhomirov et al. SmartCheck converts Solidity source code into an XML intermediate representation and matches vulnerability rules based on predefined XPath patterns. It supports the detection of over twenty types of vulnerabilities, including reentrancy, denial of service, and tx.origin. E. Lai et al. [21] proposed a static vulnerability detection tool specifically for integer overflows in smart contracts. It is based on the concept of SmartCheck [20]. The study summarizes 11 characteristics of integer overflows and extracts them into 83 corresponding XPath patterns to detect integer bugs.

6 Conclusion

Integer bugs are one of the most commonly bug in Ethereum smart contracts. Previous work on detecting integer bugs in Solidity often lacks information about the runtime states of variables, resulting in insufficient precision in bug detection. To address this problem, we propose SolSecure, a framework based on abstract interpretation theory [1,2], designed to effectively identify integer bugs in Ethereum smart contracts. Experiments have demonstrated its effectiveness, yet there are still limitations. It lacks cross-function CFG (Control Flow Graph) information; and the analysis of state variables is not sufficiently comprehensive. Future work can enhance detection capabilities by improving the static analysis of both CFG and state variables.

Acknowledgment. This work is supported by the VeChain Foundation (No. SCNU2018-01), Industry-University-Research Innovation Fund for Chinese Universities (2020ITA09006).

References

1. Cousot, P., Cousot, R.: Static determination of dynamic properties of programs. In: Proceedings of the 2nd International Symposium on Programming (ISOP '76), pp. 106–130 (1976)
2. Cousot, P., Cousot, R.: Abstract interpretation: a unified lattice model for static analysis of programs by construction or approximation of fixpoints. In: Proceedings of the 4th ACM SIGACT-SIGPLAN Symposium on Principles of Programming Languages (POPL '77), pp. 238–252 (1977)

3. Nakamoto, S.: Bitcoin: a peer-to-peer electronic cash system. Decentralized Bus. Rev. (2008)
4. Torres, C.F., Schütte, J., State, R.: Osiris: hunting for integer bugs in ethereum smart contracts. In: Proceedings of the 34th Annual Computer Security Applications Conference, pp. 664–676 (2018)
5. So, S., Lee, M., Park, J., Lee, H., Oh, H.: Verismart: a highly precise safety verifier for ethereum smart contracts. In: 2020 IEEE Symposium on Security and Privacy (SP), pp. 1678–1694. IEEE (2020)
6. Tan, B., Mariano, B., Lahiri, S.K., Dillig, I., Feng, Y.: SolType: refinement types for arithmetic overflow in solidity. Proceedings of the ACM on Programming Languages, vol. 6, no. POPL, pp. 1–29. ACM, New York (2022)
7. Wang, X., He, J., Xie, Z., Zhao, G., Cheung, S.-C.: ContractGuard: defend ethereum smart contracts with embedded intrusion detection. IEEE Trans. Serv. Comput. 13(2), 314–328 (2019)
8. Lin, Z., Zhang, S., Wang, C., Zhou, Y.: An overview of blockchain technology: applications in next-generation intelligent manufacturing. J. Intell. Sci. Technol. 5(2), 200–211 (2023)
9. Lin, S., Zhang, L., Liu, D.: A review of applications based on blockchain smart contracts. J. Comput. Appl. 38(9) (2021)
10. The ethereum.org team: Introduction to Smart Contracts. https://docs.soliditylang.org/en/v0.8.21/. Accessed 2023
11. Hwang, S., Ryu, S.: Gap between theory and practice: an empirical study of security patches in solidity. In: Proceedings of the ACM/IEEE 42nd International Conference on Software Engineering, pp. 542–553 (2020)
12. Rice, H.G.: Classes of recursively enumerable sets and their decision problems. Trans. Amer. Math. Soc. 74(2), 358–366 (1953)
13. Li, Z., Wang, J., Sun, M., Lui, J.C.S.: MirChecker: detecting bugs in rust programs via static analysis. In: Proceedings of the 2021 ACM SIGSAC Conference on Computer and Communications Security, pp. 2183–2196 (2021)
14. de Moura, L., Bjørner, N.: Z3: an efficient SMT solver. In: Ramakrishnan, C.R., Rehof, J. (eds.) TACAS 2008. LNCS, vol. 4963, pp. 337–340. Springer, Heidelberg (2008). https://doi.org/10.1007/978-3-540-78800-3_24
15. Feist, J., Grieco, G., Groce, A.: Slither: a static analysis framework for smart contracts. In: 2019 IEEE/ACM 2nd International Workshop on Emerging Trends in Software Engineering for Blockchain (WETSEB), pp. 8–15. IEEE (2019)
16. Jiang, B., Liu, Y., Chan, W.K.: ContractFuzzer: fuzzing smart contracts for vulnerability detection. In: Proceedings of the 33rd ACM/IEEE International Conference on Automated Software Engineering, pp. 259–269 (2018)
17. He, J., Balunović, M., Ambroladze, N., Tsankov, P., Vechev, M.: Learning to fuzz from symbolic execution with application to smart contracts. In: Proceedings of the 2019 ACM SIGSAC Conference on Computer and Communications Security, pp. 531–548 (2019)
18. Rosen, B.K., Wegman, M.N., Zadeck, F.K.: Global value numbers and redundant computations. In: Proceedings of the 15th ACM SIGPLAN-SIGACT Symposium on Principles of Programming Languages, pp. 12–27 (1988)
19. Ghaleb, A.: Towards effective static analysis approaches for security vulnerabilities in smart contracts. In: Proceedings of the 37th IEEE/ACM International Conference on Automated Software Engineering, pp. 1–5 (2022)
20. Tikhomirov, S., Voskresenskaya, E., Ivanitskiy, I., Takhaviev, R., Marchenko, E., Alexandrov, Y.: SmartCheck: static analysis of ethereum smart contracts. In: Pro-

ceedings of the 1st International Workshop on Emerging Trends in Software Engineering for Blockchain, pp. 9–16 (2018)

21. Lai, E., Luo, W.: Static analysis of integer overflow of smart contracts in ethereum. In: Proceedings of the 2020 4th International Conference on Cryptography, Security and Privacy, pp. 110–115 (2020)

22. Ghaleb, A., Pattabiraman, K.: How effective are smart contract analysis tools? evaluating smart contract static analysis tools using bug injection. In: Proceedings of the 29th ACM SIGSOFT International Symposium on Software Testing and Analysis (2020)

BBP: Blockchain-Enabled Biological Assets Identity Protection System

Zexin Gao[1,2,3], Zhengkang Fang[1], Yihang Wei[1], and Keke Gai[1,2(✉)]

[1] School of Cyberspace Science and Technology, Beijing Institute of Technology, Beijing, China
{3220221488,3220221425,3120201079,gaikeke}@bit.edu.cn
[2] Beijing Muguo Technology Co., Ltd., Beijing, China
[3] Yangtze Delta Region Academy of Beijing Institute of Technology, Jiaxing, Zhejiang, China

Abstract. In recent years, with the development of the Internet, various forms of biological assets can be digitally uploaded to the Internet, such as pictures of animals. Some malicious attackers can use the diffusion model to forgery the biological asset pictures exposed on the Internet, generate a large number of forged pictures to deceive financial institutions or achieve other purposes, which causes immeasurable losses to financial institutions and owners of biological assets. To this end, we propose an algorithm to generate biological asset adduction samples to defend against such attacks, and we propose a blockchain-based system named BBP, which can trace biological asset original and adduction samples. Our research provides a new direction for biological asset information management and improves the security of biological asset management.

Keywords: Diffusion Models · Adversarial Example · biological assets · blockchain

1 Introduction

In recent years, the biological assets industry has been developing rapidly. The characteristics of the biological assets industry, such as long cycles, heavy investment, and labor-intensive nature, have constrained its development [1]. This makes the financialization and intelligent transformation of the agriculture and animal husbandry industries particularly important in the current period. By using Financial Technology (FinTech), the risk control costs of introducing financial instruments can be reduced. Meanwhile, the use of technologies such as

K. Gai—This work is partially supported by the National Natural Science Foundation of China (Grant No. 62372044), and the Open Topics of Key Laboratory of Blockchain Technology and Data Security, The Ministry of Industry and Information Technology of the People's Republic of China (Grant No. 20242217).

G. Zhao et al. (Eds.): BWTAC 2024, CCIS 2277, pp. 106–117, 2025.
https://doi.org/10.1007/978-981-97-9412-6_10

blockchain, artificial intelligence, and the internet of things to achieve the digitalization of agriculture and animal husbandry can improve production efficiency, and this has gradually become a consensus in the industry.

The process of the financialization and digitalization of biological assets requires reliable biological asset identification as a guarantee. Otherwise, there will be issues such as insurance fraud, loan fraud [2], and management chaos in the production process of biological assets. Image recognition technology has been widely applied to the identification of biological asset identity. Image recognition technology has made the identity verification process in insurance and loan processes more efficient. It has also improved the efficiency of fine-grained management in the production process.

However, the application of image recognition in biological asset management faces security issues, and the forgery of images [3] poses a severe challenge to the accuracy of biological asset identity verification. With the development of artificial intelligence, the cost of forgery has been gradually decreasing. In particular, diffusion models [4] can generate more realistic images and higher resolutions compared to previous generative adversarial networks and other generative models. Diffusion models have been widely used in areas such as image editing, image generation, and image restoration. Attackers can obtain publicly available information on biological asset images and use diffusion models to edit and generate forged images. Due to the highly realistic resolution of the forged images, it can have a significant impact on the effective identity certification of biological assets. How to ensure the traceability of real biological asset images and prevent attackers from generating forged biological asset images using real images through generative models have become two pressing issues that need to be solved.

To solve the above problems, we have constructed a blockchain-based biological asset identity protection system named **BBP**. During the process of publishing biological asset image data, we record the data and provide on-chain evidence. We have also designed an algorithm that combines adversarial sample image generation with diffusion models. This adversarial sample can effectively prevent diffusion models from extracting its features, thereby resisting the secondary editing of diffusion models. The adversarial sample image is visually similar to the original image, but cannot be used as input to the diffusion model to forge similar biological asset images. This is to prevent the forgery of biological asset images. We then record the generated adversarial sample image data and its correspondence with the real biological asset image on the blockchain. The final published image is the adversarial sample image generated by the diffusion model. The above process is all implemented within the smart contract on the blockchain. This system can support the verification of the authenticity of published biological asset images and resist forgery, thereby protecting the identity of biological assets.

The main contributions of our work are as follows:

- We propose a blockchain-based biological asset identity protection system named BBP, which is the first to realize the authenticity verification of biological asset images. Moreover, the biological asset images published through this system can resist the forgery of images by diffusion models.

- We propose an algorithm to generate adversarial samples of biological asset information. These adversarial samples can effectively resist the editing by diffusion models, making it impossible for attackers to use the biological asset images published through this system and then use diffusion models to forge similar images in terms of visual effects.

2   Related Work

The study of biological assets has garnered significant attention from many scholars. Dagmar et al. have collected medical and health information from one million volunteers for research in the medical field [5]. However, these data face risks of misuse. Muller et al. [6] are concerned with protecting biological assets from theft, transfer, or loss that could pose public health risks. Berger et al. [7] focus on the risks of illegal access by unauthorized individuals to big data in biological assets and the misuse of such data. Doherty et al. [8] have raised concerns about the secondary use of information data on biological assets. Our work differs from the aforementioned studies as we mainly focus on preventing the image-based fabrication of biological assets and verifying their authenticity.

Blockchain technology is widely used in protecting privacy data [9–13]. Zhuang et al. [14] propose a blockchain-based intellectual property privacy protection and traceable identity management scheme that enables the protection and traceability of intellectual property with minimal network communication costs. Shi et al. [15] suggest that car owners can more securely share their vehicle information and multimedia data via blockchain technology in vehicular social networks. In this paper, we use blockchain to protect images related to the identity of biological assets from secondary editing by diffusion models and support the verification of biological asset images.

In order to protect artists' paintings from being abused by diffusion models. AdvDM [4] their research approach reduces the generative power of the diffusion model customization approach for DreamBooth and text inversion. This ability to customize requires the artist's paintings or adversarial examples to batch train the diffusion model, making the trained model unable to effectively imitate the artist's paintings. Photoguard [3] pays special attention to the editing of diffusion models that may damage the reputation of users, preventing infringers from creating fake photos that affect the reputation of public figures or netizens.

3   Preliminary

3.1   Diffusion Model

In recent years, diffusion models have been widely used in various fields, such as generating images from text, editing images [16] through text guidance, and image synthesis. [17] A diffusion model is a generative model that generates new

Fig. 1. There are two main functions of diffusion models. The first is a Venson graph, which generates a picture based on prompt, and the second is a graph generator graph, which, given a picture and prompt, generates the desired picture.

data samples by simulating a diffusion process, which consists of two processes: a forward process and a reverse process.

Diffusion Process. The forward process is that given an original image $x_0 \sim q(x)$, at each time step $t \in (0, T)$ noise is added to the input image so that it becomes $\{x_0, x_1, ..., x_T\}$. The inverse process is to train a model to remove the noise. The model $\epsilon_\theta(x_t, t, c)$ can infer how noise is added from x_t to x_{t-1}, which is repeated to get x_0. The trained loss function is shown in the following two equations. [18]

$$\mathcal{L}_{uncond}(\theta, x_0) = \mathbb{E}_{x_0, t, \epsilon \in \mathcal{N}(0,1)} \|\epsilon - \epsilon_\theta(x_{t+1}, t)\|_2^2 \tag{1}$$

$$\mathcal{L}_{cond}(\theta, x_0) = \mathbb{E}_{x_0, t, c, \epsilon \in \mathcal{N}(0,1)} \|\epsilon - \epsilon_\theta(x_{t+1}, t, c)\|_2^2 \tag{2}$$

where x is the input image, t is the each timestep, Text or image can also be used as conditional input c, ϵ is the noise term (Fig. 1).

3.2   Latent Diffusion Models

The latent diffusion model [19] can apply the above process to a deeper latent space rather than just the pixel space of the input image. The main difference between the latent diffusion model and the diffusion model is that the input image x_0 should be mapped to a deeper latent representation $\mathbf{z}_0 = \mathcal{E}(\mathbf{x}_0)$ when using the latent diffusion model. The loss function is:

$$\mathcal{L}(\theta, z_0) = \mathbb{E}_{z_0, t, \epsilon \in \mathcal{N}(0,1)} \|\epsilon - \epsilon_\theta(z_{t+1}, t)\|_2^2 \tag{3}$$

The denoising network ε_θ, if trained, can act as a diffusion model in the generation process, starting from a random vector in the latent space and progressively removing noise to obtain a new representation of the latent space of the image $\tilde{\mathbf{z}}$, Finally, as in the forward process, we need a decoder $\mathcal{D}$ to decode the latent space into an image $\tilde{\mathbf{x}} = \mathcal{D}(\tilde{\mathbf{z}}) \sim q(\cdot)$.

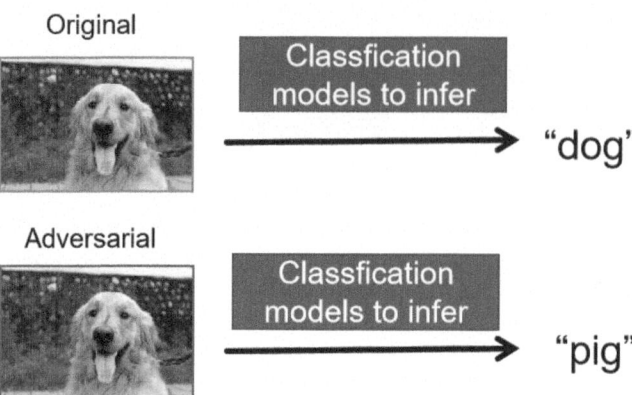

Fig. 2. Adversarial example for classfication models.

3.3   Adversarial Attack

(See Fig. 2).

For diffusion models, adversarial examples [20] similarly add carefully crafted perturbations to the image, misleading the generative model to exclude their features from the distribution of the generated image. Well-designed perturbations are usually limited to a value less than a fixed value η. The adversarial examples generated in this way will not be obvious to the naked eye. δ is through the following format:

$$\delta_{adv} = \arg\max_{\|\delta\|_p < \eta} L(f_\theta(x + \delta), y_{real}), \tag{4}$$

where the input image is x, its corresponding true label is y_{real}, and L is a loss function used to optimize the performance of adversarial examples. Projected gradient descent [21] is the method used in this paper to generate adversarial examples. The procedure is stated as follows:

$$x^{t+1} = \prod_{(x,\eta)} \left(x^t + \alpha \operatorname{sgn} \left(\nabla_x L(f_\theta(x + \delta), y_{real}) \right) \right) \tag{5}$$

where the number of iterations is t, the input images are $x^0 = x$ and x, α represents the step size of each iteration, $\operatorname{sgn}(\cdot)$ represents the sign function, and the input image is $x^0 = x$. Loss function relative to the gradient is ($\nabla_x L(f_\theta(x + \delta), y_{real})$). At the same time, in order to avoid the adversarial example not being obvious to the naked eye, we also need a restriction condition η-ball, in the operation $\Pi_{(x,\eta)}$ [22].

4   System Design

4.1   Design Objective

Aiming at the application scenario of biological asset management, we designed this system, which should achieve the following goals.

Anti-forgery: After uploading the biological asset original image through the system, the smart contract embedded to generate the adversarial sample algorithm will generate the biological asset adversarial sample, and the diffusion model cannot generate high-quality counterfeit pictures through the adversarial sample.

High Performance: The system produces a small visual difference between the antagonistic sample and the original image, but the effect of using the diffusion model is very different (Fig. 3).

4.2   System Overview

In this section, we will introduce our BBP system based on blockchain to achieve image traceability authentication of biological assets. In the figure, we describe the BBP system architecture, which consists of three levels: application layer, functional module layer and blockchain layer. Blockchain, as the underlying infrastructure of BBP, is used to store the identity information of biological assets, and identity management is achieved by deploying smart contracts on it, and the information consistency of each node of the blockchain is achieved by Raft consensus algorithm. The upper-layer functional module consists of upload service, generation service and verification service module. The upload service module mainly realizes the upload of real pictures of biological assets and corresponding countermeasure sample pictures, the generation service module is used to generate countermeasure sample pictures combined with the countermeasure sample generation algorithm, and the verification module is mainly used to verify the biological asset pictures. The application layer publisher can upload the original image of the biological asset through the BBP system, which generates the countermeasure sample image, and the attacker can obtain the countermeasure sample image. If an attacker wanted to use the diffusion model to generate a fake image, our algorithm would make the generated image very fuzzy, And the attacker could not pass the fake image of the biological asset through verification because the image was not linked.

A brief overview of each of our entities is as follows:

Publisher: The publisher can publish the picture information of the biological asset, and the biological asset information can generate an adversarial sample after the smart contract link, and the original image and adversarial sample are one-to-one correspondence. Meanwhile, counter samples can be exposed online to display biological assets.

Attackers: An attacker can get a picture of a biological asset that is exposed online and can fake it using a diffusion model.

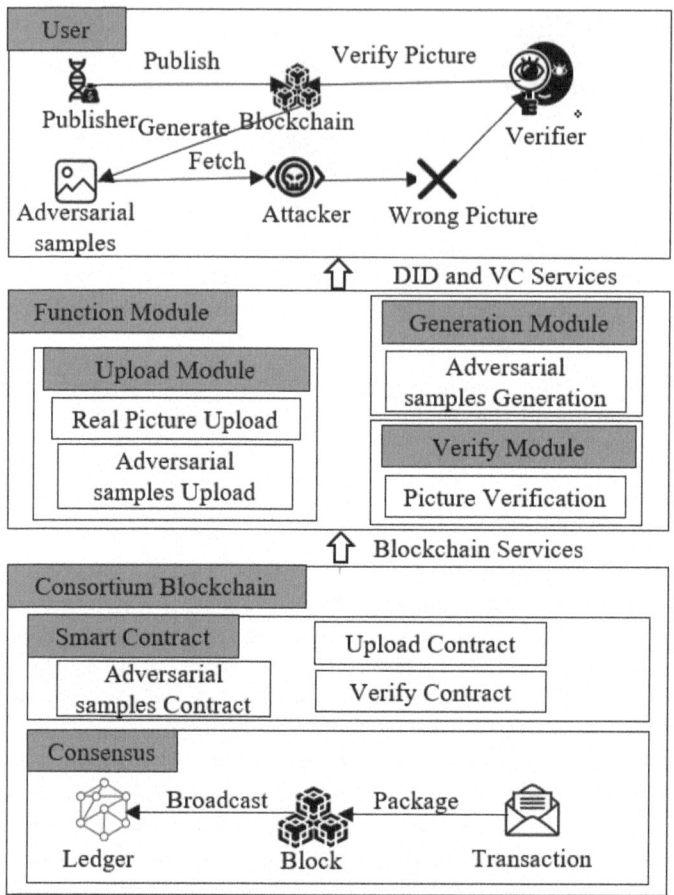

Fig. 3. High level architecture of BBP model.

Verifier: The verifier can accept the requested image of the biological asset for verification, and if the image used to verify is the correct image of the countersample exposed on the Web, we can return the correct information. If it is a biological asset image forged by the attacker through the diffusion model, the effect of generating the image is not only poor, but also cannot pass the verification of the system, because the system has no mapping relationship between the original image and the image.

Our method is a simple and efficient method that can directly generate adversarial samples through the original image combined with prompt, such as "pictures with similar style". This adversarial sample will not achieve a satisfactory effect for the infringing user when he directly uses the diffusion model to generate pictures with text guidance. Our method is to add disturbance noise to the original image to make the diffusion model unable to extract the features related

---

Algorithm 1. Generation of adversarial examples

1: **Input:** Input image $\mathbf{x}$, difussion model f, perturbation size ϵ, step size α, number of iterations num_iter.
2: Initialize adversarial perturbation $\delta \leftarrow 0$, and adversarial image $\mathbf{x}_{adv} \leftarrow \mathbf{x}$
3: **for** $i = 1 \ldots num\_iter$ **do**
4:     Compute gradient: $\nabla_{\mathbf{x}_{adv}} \leftarrow \nabla_{\mathbf{x}_{adv}} \|f(\mathbf{x}_{adv}) - f(\mathbf{x}_{targ})\|$
5:     Update adversarial perturbation: $\delta \leftarrow \mathrm{clip}(\delta + \alpha \cdot \mathrm{sign}(\nabla_{\mathbf{x}_{adv}}), -\epsilon, \epsilon)$
6:     Update adversarial image: $\mathbf{x}_{adv} \leftarrow \mathrm{clip}(\mathbf{x} - \delta, 0, 1)$
7: **end for**
8: **Return:** $\mathbf{x}_{adv}$

---

to "prompt" in the original image, so that the attacker can greatly reduce the editing effect when using the same "prompt".

4.3   Algorithm in Smart Contract

Generation of Adversarial Examples. Latent diffusion Model Graph generation works by first encoding the image into a latent vector representation through an encoder ε. This vector representation can generate the image more efficiently. Our approach is to make the encoder map the original image to the wrong vector representation through our attack. We used PGD to optimize the following problems:

$$\delta = \arg \min_{\|\delta\|_\infty \leq \epsilon} \|\mathcal{E}(\mathbf{x} + \delta) - \mathbf{z}_{targ}\|_2^2, \tag{6}$$

The original image is x, and z_{targ} is the latent vector that our attack wants to map the original image to, which is shown in gray in Fig. 4. The optimization for this problem is to be able to add carefully designed perturbations through the decoder that will produce adversarial examples that will look almost identical to the naked eye, but which the diffusion model will produce when re-editing are irrelevant to the original image.

Quality of Adversarial Examples. The diffusion model θ is evaluated by the quality of images sampled from $p_\theta(x)$. This sampling is called the inference of the diffusion model. Unlike classification models, diffusion models do not take images as input directly but exploit them by extracting features from them and generating images conditioned on these features. We mainly focus our evaluation scenario on this conditional inference, where copyright violations have taken place. For unconditional inference, the model samples a noise and generates images. This process has no input images and does not raise copyright concerns, thus not included in our evaluation.

The diffusion model generates an image by extracting features from an input image. For conditional inference, we split it into two stages. In the first stage, we extract features based on the image and the guided "prompt". The second stage is to use the features extracted in the first stage as a condition to generate a

---

Algorithm 2. Quality of adversarial examples

1: **Input:** Adversarial example(s) $\mathbf{x}_{\text{adv}}$, diffusion model θ, sample quality metric $\mathcal{D}(\cdot)$
2: **Output:** the sample quality $\mathbf{Q}$
3: Initialize the dataset $\mathbf{x}_r \leftarrow \mathbf{x}_{\text{adv}}$
4: Sample $\mathbf{c}_g \sim p_\theta(c|\mathbf{x}_r)$
5: Generate images by sampling $\mathbf{x}_g \sim p_\theta(x|\mathbf{c}_g)$
6: $\mathbf{Q} \leftarrow \mathcal{D}(\mathbf{x}_g, \mathbf{x}_r)$

---

new image. We use c to represent the features, and the extraction process can be represented by $p_\theta(c|x)$. A good adversarial example prevents the exact extraction of $p_\theta(c|x)$ to c, which results in poor quality of x_g. This can be measured by the sample quality metric D($\cdot$). In this paper, we use FID [23] as D($\cdot$).

5   Experiment

In this section, we evaluate how well the adversarial examples we generate according to our algorithm resist diffusion model secondary editing. The model we use is the Stable Diffusion Model (SDM). We assume that the infringer first obtains the published biological asset information from the Internet and then performs a secondary generation based on the prompt, which can be "generate similar images." This attack is the fastest and does not require the attacker to fine-tune a diffusion model based on text inversion. In each of the following experiments, we aim to disrupt the performance of SDM by adding imperceptible noise. Our immunization procedure is applied to a variety of images. The goal is to force the model to generate images that are unreal and irrelevant to the original image. We evaluate the performance of our method both qualitatively (by visually inspecting the generated images) and quantitatively (by examining the image quality using standard metrics).

5.1   Experimental Settings

Our dataset consists of paintings by artists such as Van Gogh or Monet that are publicly available online. We selected some of the images to generate the diffusion model. First, we will crop all the source images into uniform-sized images of 256*256, and then perform the second generation of the diffusion model for the original images and the second generation of the adversarial samples based on the adversarial samples.

5.2   Qualitative Results

For the secondary generation of diffusion model, he should make sure that the function of image generation under the guidance of text can be realistic. For example, the following several Monet's works can be generated through the

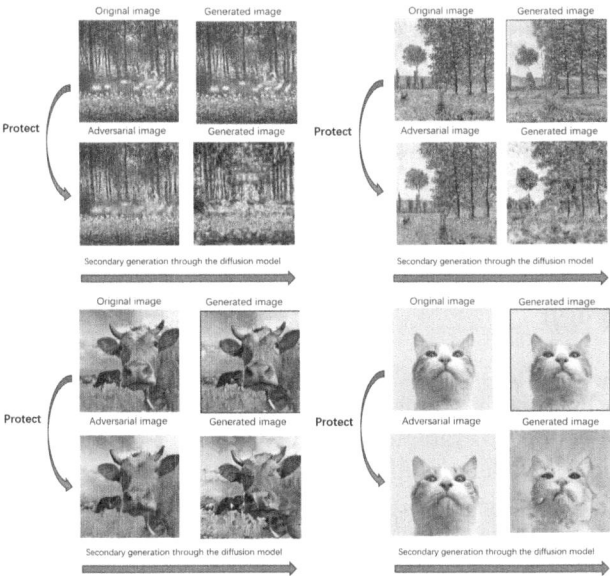

Fig. 4. Quantitative results. Using the function of generating images from images in the diffusion model, it can be seen that the images generated by the adversarial sample images are fuzzy and greatly different from the original images, which can destroy the generation effect of the diffusion model.

prompt word "generate similar images", which can generate the secondary generation paintings corresponding to each image. However, for, we use the adversarial sample corresponding to each painting. Under the guidance of the same cue word, the quality of the paintings generated by the diffusion model is far from that of the paintings directly generated by the original painting, which indicates that our method is effective.

5.3   Quantitative Results

Our qualitative results show that the difference between our original image and the adversarial example image generated by the diffusion model is huge. Now we need to quantitatively analyze the magnitude of this difference. In addition, we also introduce an image after adding random noise to the original image for the secondary generation of the diffusion model for comparison, in order to prove that the adversarial samples generated by our method will affect the diffusion model to extract the features in the image, thereby destroying the process of secondary generation. Images with random noise do not achieve this effect. The quantitative metrics we use are: For random noisy images and adversarial samples, PSNR and SSIM [24] are used to measure the image quality and the difference from the original image. For the images generated by the diffusion model, Frechet Inception Distance (FID) is used to measure the similarity between the generated image and the original image (Table 1).

Table 1. The performance of the generated image and adversarial examples.

Method	Generated image	Adversarial example	
	FID ↑	PSNR ↑	SSIM ↑
Original	81.7	–	–
Random noise	89.3	22.7	0.85
Ours	**112.9**	**19.1**	**0.69**

6   Conclusion

Because biological asset information images can be attacked by malicious actors. We propose an adversarial sample generation algorithm based on diffusion model, which can effectively generate adversarial samples of biological assets and significantly reduce the effect of infringer's secondary creation of biological assets through diffusion model. Thus, the information of biological assets is protected from malicious abuse and the property rights of the owners of biological assets are protected. At the same time, we propose a system named BBP, which can trace the antagonistic samples and original images to realize the authenticity verification of biological asset pictures, and the biological asset pictures published by this system can resist the image forgery of the diffusion model.

References

1. Radchenko, O., Tkach, L., Dendebera, O.: Financing innovations in the agricultural industry as a component of the digital development of Ukraine's economy. Sci. Bull. Mukachevo State Univ. Ser. Econ. **4**(10), 54–65 (2023)
2. Saluja, S.: Identity theft fraud-major loophole for fintech industry in India. J. Financ. Crime **31**(1), 146–157 (2024)
3. Salman, H., Khaddaj, A., Leclerc, G., Ilyas, A., Madry, A.: Raising the cost of malicious ai-powered image editing. arXiv preprint arXiv:2302.06588, 2023
4. Liang, C., et al.: Adversarial example does good: Preventing painting imitation from diffusion models via adversarial examples. In: International Conference on Machine Learning, pp. 20763–20786. PMLR, 2023
5. Rychnovská, D.: Anticipatory governance in biobanking: security and risk management in digital health. Sci. Eng. Ethics **27**(3), 30 (2021)
6. Muller, H., Dagher, G., Loibner, M., Stumptner, C., Kungl, P., Zatloukal, K.: Biobanks for life sciences and personalized medicine: importance of standardization, biosafety, biosecurity, and data management. Curr. Opin. Biotechnol. **65**, 45–51 (2020)
7. Berger, K.M., Roderick, J.: National and transnational security implications of big data in the life sciences. American Association for the Advancement of Science, Washington, DC (2014)
8. O'Doherty, K.C., et al.: If you build it, they will come: unintended future uses of organised health data collections. BMC Med. Ethics **17**, 1–16 (2016)
9. Miao, Y., Gai, K., Zhu, L., Choo, K.K.R., Vaidya, J.: Blockchain-based shared data integrity auditing and deduplication. IEEE Transactions on Dependable and Secure Computing, 2023

10. Miao, Y., Gai, K., Zhu, L., Choo, K.K.R., Vaidya, J.: Cross-chain-based trust-worthy node identity governance in internet of things. IEEE Internet Things J. (2023)
11. Gai, K., She, Y., Zhu, L., Choo, K.K.R., Wan, Z.: A blockchain-based access control scheme for zero trust cross-organizational data sharing. ACM Trans. Internet Technol. **23**(3), 1–25 (2023)
12. Ma, Z., Wang, J., Gai, K., Duan, P., Zhang, Y., Luo, S.: Fully homomorphic encryption-based privacy-preserving scheme for cross edge blockchain network. J. Syst. Architect. **134**, 102782 (2023)
13. Wei, Y., Gai, K., Yu, J., Zhu, L., Choo, K.K.R.: Trustworthy access control for multiaccess edge computing in blockchain-assisted 6g systems. IEEE Trans. Ind. Inform. (2024)
14. Zhuang, C., Dai, Q., Zhang, Y.: BCPPT: a blockchain-based privacy-preserving and traceability identity management scheme for intellectual property. Peer-to-Peer Netw. Appl. **15**(1), 724–738 (2022)
15. Shi, K., Zhu, L., Zhang, C., Xu, L., Gao, F.: Blockchain-based multimedia sharing in vehicular social networks with privacy protection. Multimed. Tools Appl. **79**, 8085–8105 (2020)
16. Kawar, B., et al.: Imagic: text-based real image editing with diffusion models. In: Proceedings of the IEEE/CVF Conference on Computer Vision and Pattern Recognition, pp. 6007–6017 (2023)
17. Ruiz, N., Li, Y., Jampani, V., Pritch, Y., Rubinstein, M., Aberman, K.: Dreambooth: fine tuning text-to-image diffusion models for subject-driven generation. In: Proceedings of the IEEE/CVF Conference on Computer Vision and Pattern Recognition, pp. 22500–22510 (2023)
18. Sohl-Dickstein, J., Weiss, E., Maheswaranathan, N., Ganguli, S.: Deep unsupervised learning using nonequilibrium thermodynamics. In: International Conference on Machine Learning, pp. 2256–2265. PMLR, 2015
19. Rombach, R., Blattmann, A., Lorenz, D., Esser, P., Ommer, B.: High-resolution image synthesis with latent diffusion models. In: Proceedings of the IEEE/CVF Conference on Computer Vision and Pattern Recognition, pp. 10684–10695 (2022)
20. Szegedy, C., et al.: Intriguing properties of neural networks. arXiv preprint arXiv:1312.6199, 2013
21. Madry, A., Makelov, A., Schmidt, L., Tsipras, D., Vladu, A.: Towards deep learning models resistant to adversarial attacks. arXiv preprint arXiv:1706.06083, 2017
22. Wang, F., Tan, Z., Wei, T., Wu, Y., Huang, Q.: SimAC: a simple anti-customization method for protecting face privacy against text-to-image synthesis of diffusion models. In: Proceedings of the IEEE/CVF Conference on Computer Vision and Pattern Recognition, pp. 12047–12056 (2024)
23. Heusel, M., Ramsauer, H., Unterthiner, T., Nessler, B., Hochreiter, S.: GANs trained by a two time-scale update rule converge to a local nash equilibrium. dv. Neural Inf. Process. Syst. **30** (2017)
24. Wang, Z., Bovik, A.C., Sheikh, H.R., Simoncelli, E.P.: Image quality assessment: from error visibility to structural similarity. IEEE Trans. Image Process. **13**(4), 600–612 (2004)

Accountability Mechanism for Reliable Mobile Crowdsourcing with Efficient Blockchain

Ruilin Lai[1,2]([✉]), Gansen Zhao[1], Cheng Qian[1], Zhihao Hou[1], and Yale He[1]

[1] School of Computer Science, South China Normal University, Guangzhou 510631, China
2020010184@m.scnu.edu.cn
[2] Guangdong University of Finance, Guangzhou 510521, China

Abstract. Mobile crowdsourcing (MCS) takes advantage of widely distributed mobile devices to complete some temporal-spatial tasks. Edge computing is integrated into MSC to reduce the service delay from a remote cloud, and enhance the quality of services (QoS) through preprocessing data. However, the profit-driven edge nodes (workers) may provide fake or low-quality answers for lowering their data processing cost, which results in serious QoS challenges. We propose a reputation-based accountability mechanism, in which workers are accountable for their answer provision through reputation values, and edge nodes take on different responsibilities of blockchain management based on reputation values and some key factors. Specifically, the combination of the data-centric method and entity-centric method is utilized for precisely evaluating the quality of answers and managing the worker's reputation. Storage nodes, mining candidate nodes, relay nodes, and verification nodes are mainly responsible for transaction retrieval, block generation, block forwarding and block verification, respectively. It reduces the latency of blockchain maintenance in a large-scale network. Finally, the experimental results show that our scheme achieves high-level reliability and reasonable efficiency for large-scale services in MCS.

Keywords: Mobile crowdsourcing · Blockchain · Accountability · Edge computing · Reputation

1 Introduction

With the rapid development of mobile communication and wireless access technology, mobile devices generate a huge amount and several different types of data. For example, air quality data is collected through a sensor deployed on a mobile device [9]. In addition to objective collected data, the subjective data provided through the public also includes ratings of a hotel, the quality of vehicular services, and so on [7]. These sensing data from the public makes data collection and analysis more economically and effectively for government regulation, institution research, and business investigation. Mobile crowdsourcing (MCS) makes

G. Zhao et al. (Eds.): BWTAC 2024, CCIS 2277, pp. 118–129, 2025.
https://doi.org/10.1007/978-981-97-9412-6_11

full use of these sensing data, and its main process is: a publisher (e.g., an individual) releases a task through a platform (e.g., third-party software), mobile devices collect data in a specific spatial scope and period, and then transmit the answers to the publisher through the platform.

Due to resource constraints, mobile devices can not support massive data preprocessing and storage. This increasingly first-hand and complex data is uploaded to the network immediately. It leads to high consumption of network bandwidth, increasing the delay of crowdsourcing services. To address this problem, edge computing is a promising paradigm that supports edge nodes, e.g., wireless access points, near mobile devices, to preprocess and filter data before transmitting it to a remote cloud [10]. Thus, the platform, mobile device, publisher, and edge node form the mobile crowdsourcing network.

Although edge computing paves the way for the timeliness of answer transmission, security issues are also critical challenges for the MCS, because the platform is vulnerable to the single point failure. Recently, blockchain technology has attracted more concern in the context of a MCS network as it is naturally tamper-proof. Blockchain enables a secure MCS system by better usage of edge node resources [13].

The intersection between the mobile crowdsourcing network and blockchain network is edge nodes. On one hand, we assume that edge nodes collect data from their trusted mobile devices; hence, edge nodes act as workers in crowdsourcing. However, edge nodes may provide fake or low-quality answers for a task due to their defective processors or even selfish purposes. On the other hand, edge nodes act as blockchain nodes for maintaining the distributed ledger. However, the profit-driven edge nodes may postpone or abandon some tasks of blockchain maintenance. It leads to high latency in block updates.

Therefore, we propose a reputation-based accountability mechanism for taking advantage of historical behaviors of edge nodes. Edge nodes are accountable for their preprocessed behaviors of collected data, and they have different responsibilities in blockchain management. In this way, integrating the reputation into the edge nodes ensures the provision of reliable and large-scale MCS services. The main contributions of this paper are summarized as follows.

- We propose a hybrid MCS blockchain framework for reputation management towards edge nodes. The framework includes a MCS network and a blockchain network. Edge nodes are the intersection of the two networks.
- We develop a reputation model towards workers by considering both their data quality and the publisher's feedback, to choose reliable workers for improving the quality of answers in MCS.
- We present a hierarchical blockchain management scheme in a P2P network to provide secure and large-scale services in an open environment. Blockchain nodes have different responsibilities based on their reputation values, computing capacities and storage capacities.

The rest of this article is organized as follows: Previous work related to this study is discussed in Sect. 2. Section 3 introduces the proposed framework.

Section 4 and Sect. 5 illustrate the reputation model towards workers and the hierarchical blockchain management, respectively. Experimental evaluation is presented in Sect. 6. Section 7 gives concluding remarks.

2   Related Work

Recently, a series of blockchain-based MCS were proposed to evaluate the data quality in a decentralized manner. On one hand, the quality of collected data is verified during the consensus process. Huang et al. [5] exploited miners to verify the sensory data, and developed a sensory data quality detection scheme to identify and mitigate the data anomaly. Huang et al. [4] also presented a Proof-of-Data (PoD) consensus protocol, which leverages miners to conduct useful data quality validation work instead of "useless" hash calculation. Meanwhile, in order to preserve the privacy of the sensory data, this work designs a homomorphic data perturbation scheme through which miners can verify data quality without knowing the contents of the data.

On the other hand, data quality accessment is processed through smart contracts. In An et al. [1], the selection of participants and data quality assessment were implemented for data assessment processes. Three smart contracts, verifiers selection contract, participants employment contract and data verify contract, are generated to constrain the behaviors of the involved parties. Yu et al. [14] identified malicious users based on some factors of answer quality, e.g., accuracy. To reduce the resource consumption of the blockchain system, the candidate miners are selected based on computing capacity and mutual information, before performing a PoW consensus. In Kadadha et al. [6], a decentralized crowdsensing framework for multiple requesters and multiple workers was developed on Ethereum blockchain. Smart contracts are designed to maintain users' information, publish tasks from multiple requesters, accept reservations and solutions from multiple workers, and evaluate solutions to calculate proportional payments. Sun et al. [12] proposed a reputation model, the Trust Propagation & Feedback Similarity, to calculate the reputation values of participants and reveal any malicious behavior in vehicular crowdsourcing. The reputation model is implemented atop IBM Hyperledger Fabric, and a new three-stage consensus is designed.

However, the data quality assessment of the above works is only in one dimension and lacks feedback from entities, limiting the accuracy of a task's answer evaluation. Besides, the above blockchain systems is only suitable for small-scale MCS networks, or has the delay problem of MCS transaction update.

3   Reputation-Based MCS Blockchain Framework

3.1   System Model

Figure 1 illustrates the proposed system model in an open environment, including a crowdsourcing network and a blockchain network offering crowdsourcing services and blockchain management, respectively.

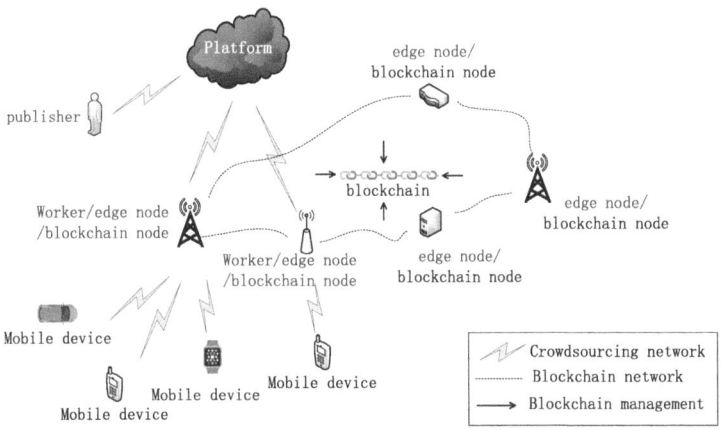

Fig. 1. System model of blockchain-based MCS

Crowdsourcing is the basic function of a MCS system, where a platform, publishers and workers work cooperatively for task completion. A publisher releases a task through a platform. Workers collect and preprocess data. Note that, in order to reduce the bandwidth overhead and time delay during answer transmission between mobile devices and a remote platform, the workers filter out redundant data by normalizing them to a preset format.

The other blockchain management is the security function of the MCS system, ensuring an answer generated from crowdsourcing services is trustworthy. Blockchain nodes have greater resources to perform computing-intensive and storage-intensive blockchain management tasks, including ledger storage, transaction verification and block mining etc.

3.2 Threat Model

However, the interest between workers and a publisher, and the interest among blockchain nodes are in conflict.

– Free-riding and false-reporting

The profit-driven worker attempts to obtain higher rewards with less effort for task completion, hence it may submit fake or low-quality answers, named 'free-riding' [15]. Even though these unreliable answers are identified in real-time, they have already had a negative effect on the current crowdsourcing task, such that the task is completed in low-quality. Besides, the profit-driven publisher attempts to launch a 'false-reporting' [15] attack on workers through malicious ratings for lowering his rewards.

– Incomplete task of edge nodes

The profit-driven edge nodes attempt to postpone or abandon tasks with lower utility, due to their limited resources. Edge nodes undertake two kinds of tasks: crowdsourcing services and blockchain management. For example, the utility of crowdsourcing services is higher than that of blockchain management. Edge nodes just transfer answers to the platform, while the answer evidence generated from crowdsourcing services is not updated on a blockchain. Such that the security of crowdsourcing services can not be guaranteed.

3.3 Proposed Scheme

To address the above threats, the reputation-based MCS blockchain scheme is proposed, in which the reputation breaks through application layer, contract layer, network layer, consensus layer and data layer. We assume that the reputation reflects the integrity level of nodes. In five layers of the scheme, from top to bottom, the reputation values of workers are generated from their answers in the MCS application. They are stored in the data layer through the above four layers in a decentralized manner. From bottom to top, the reputation values of edge nodes from the data layer facilitate blockchain node classification in the network layer, and these blockchain nodes update blocks effectively in the consensus layer. It also helps the platform select workers with high reputation values for reliable answer provision in the application layer.

4   Reputation Model Towards Worker

4.1   Data-Centric Method

An edge node collects data by itself or from its trusted mobile devices for a task. The proposed data-centric method evaluates the quality of answers by considering the location information of answers in each worker.

For a task, the answers are preprocessed by workers, and integrated into an $I \times J$ answer matrix as $ansM$ in (1) [14].

$$ansM_{I \times J} = \begin{pmatrix} ansM_{1,1} & ansM_{1,2} & \cdots & ansM_{1,J} \\ ansM_{2,1} & \cdots & \cdots & ansM_{2,J} \\ \vdots & \vdots & \vdots & \vdots \\ ansM_{I,1} & \cdots & \cdots & ansM_{I,J} \end{pmatrix} \quad (1)$$

where I is the number of workers, and J is the timeslot of data collection. An answer sequence submitted by $worker_i$ is $\{ansM_{i,1}, ansM_{i,2} \cdots ansM_{i,J}\}$. Each $ansM_{i,j}$ contains two elements: $\{con, loc\}$, where con is the answer content and loc is the quantified location of the answer collection.

Denote a central point of data collection required by the task as loc'. When the location of answer collection is closed to loc', its credibility is greater. Otherwise, the answer is more likely to be affected by factors outside the designated area. The credibility of an answer $ansM_{i,j}$ is defined by (2).

$$c_{i,j} = b + e^{-|loc' - ans M_{i,j}.loc|} \tag{2}$$

where b is a preset parameter, controlling the lower bound of credibility. $c_{i,j} = 0$, if $worker_i$ does not submit this answer in $timeslot_j$. Using (2), the credibility set C_i for all answers submitted by $worker_i$ is obtained, where $C_i = \{c_{i,1}, c_{i,2}, ...\}$. Then, the aggregated certainty of the answers is calculated in (3) by Bayesian inference [11].

$$P(ac|C_i) = \frac{P(ac) \cdot \prod_{j=1}^{J} P(c_{i,j}|ac)}{P(ac) \cdot \prod_{j=1}^{J} P(c_{i,j}|ac) + P(\overline{ac}) \cdot \prod_{j=1}^{J} P(c_{i,j}|\overline{ac})} \tag{3}$$

where $\overline{ac}$ is the complementary aggregated certainty of ac. $P(c|ac) = c$, $P(c|\overline{ac}) = 1 - c$. $P(ac)$ is the prior probability of aggregated certainty ac.

Then the data-centric reputation value of $worker_i$ is calculated in (4), where information entropy $ent(C_i)$ expresses the uncertainty of C_i.

$$repD_i = P(ac|C_i) \cdot (1 - ent(C_i)) \tag{4}$$

$$s.t.ent(C_i) = -\sum_{j=1}^{k} c_{i,j} \cdot \log(c_{i,j})$$

4.2   Entity-Centric Method

For the publisher, he may not be satisfied with the answer with a higher $repD$. Hence, an entity-centric method based on the feedback of the publisher is proposed.

It is assumed that the feedback of $publisher_p$ to $worker_i$ is in the form of a tuple vector as $rat_{p \to i} = \{-1, 1\}$, where 1 indicates the satisfaction of $publisher_p$ to $worker_i$, and -1 otherwise.

In order to accurately measure $rat_{p \to i}$, two weights are considered: historical interaction of $publisher_p$ and current interaction.

First, subjective trust can reflect the historical interactions of individuals. The subjective trust of $publisher_p$ to $worker_i$ is expressed by a tuple vector $t_{p \to i} = \{b_{p \to i}, d_{p \to i}\}$. Here, b, d are the belief and disbelief of $publisher_p$ to $worker_i$, $b, d \in [0, 1]$.

Based on $t_{p \to i}$, the knowledge coverage $kc_{p \to i}$ shows the recognition of $publisher_p$ to $worker_i$, which is defined by (5).

$$kc = 1 - (1 - b - d)^2 \tag{5}$$

where $kc \in [0,1]$. Note that, if and only if $b + d = 1$, $kc = 1$ and the knowledge coverage is optimal, hence $t_{p \to i}$ is based on perfect knowledge. Otherwise, if $b + d < 1$, the knowledge coverage between them is less and $t_{p \to i}$ is based on incomplete knowledge. If $b + d > 1$, $t_{p \to i}$ is based on conflicting knowledge. Particularly when there is no interaction from $publisher_p$ to $worker_i$, $t_{p \to i} = \{0,0\}$, as such $kc = 0$ and no knowledge coverage exists.

For the percentage of the recognition of $publisher_p$ to $worker_i$ in all workers interacting with him, $kcP_{p \to i}$ is calculated through knowledge coverage in (6).

$$kcP_{p \to i} = \frac{kc_{p \to i}}{\sum_{x \in X} kc_{p \to x}} \cdot rep_p \tag{6}$$

where X is the workers interacting with $publisher_p$, and rep_p is the reputation value of $publisher_p$. In fact, the higher $kcP_{p \to i}$, the more trustworthy the rating of $publisher_p$ to $worker_i$ is.

Second, in the current task, for I workers, a is the number of satisfactory ratings and b is the number of dissatisfactory ratings, $a + b = I$. Intuitively, the larger the number a, the more certainty $publisher_p$ has about a satisfactory rating, and vice versa.

Therefore, the entity-centric reputation value for $worker_i$ based on $publisher_p$, $repE_i$ is defined by (7).

$$repE_i = \begin{cases} kcR_{p \to i} \cdot b_{p \to i} \cdot \dfrac{a}{a+b} \cdot rat_{p \to i} & (rat_{p \to i} = 1) \\ kcR_{p \to i} \cdot d_{p \to i} \cdot \dfrac{b}{a+b} \cdot rat_{p \to i} & (rat_{p \to i} = -1) \end{cases} \tag{7}$$

where $b_{p \to i}$ and $d_{p \to i}$ are used to control the changes of satisfactory and dissatisfactory of $publisher_p$ to $worker_i$, respectively.

4.3   Final Reputation Value of Worker

The final reputation value of $worker_i$ is calculated by a simple weighted sum in (8), where $\Psi_1 + \Psi_2 = 0.5$ and H_i is historical reputation value obtained from the latest reputation update transaction about $worker_i$ in the blockchain.

$$rep_i = H_i + (1 - H_i) \cdot (\Psi_1 \cdot repD_i + \Psi_2 \cdot repE_i) \tag{8}$$

5   Hierarchical Blockchain Management

5.1   Blockchain Nodes Classification

Considering the functions of blockchain nodes, the secure requirements of MCS and previous research work [16], the blockchain nodes are proposed to be divided

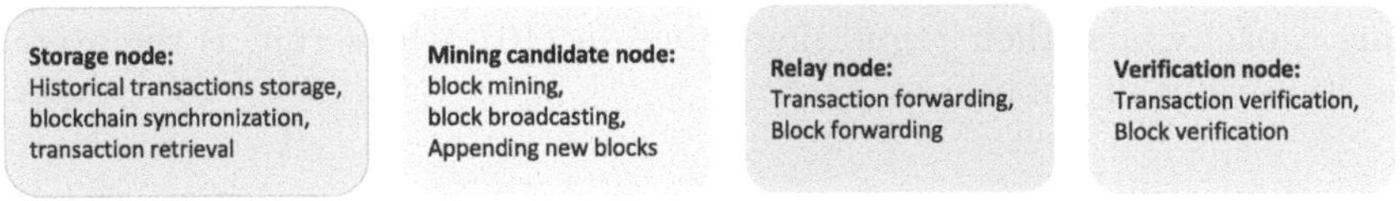

| Storage node: Historical transactions storage, blockchain synchronization, transaction retrieval | Mining candidate node: block mining, block broadcasting, Appending new blocks | Relay node: Transaction forwarding, Block forwarding | Verification node: Transaction verification, Block verification |

Fig. 2. Responsibilities of storage node, mining candidate node, relay node and verification node

into four types: Storage node, Verification node, Relay node and Mining candidate node, named SVRM nodes. Note that, a node can have multiple types, e.g., a node may be both storage node and mining candidate node. In addition, the responsibilities of SVRM nodes are shown in Fig. 2.

To formalize blockchain nodes, we denote the node as bn. Each node has its computing capacity as $bn.com$, storage capacity as $bn.str$, and reputation value as rep.

In detail, a storage node has greater storage capacity depending on its device storage space, and it is defined by $\{bn|bn\cdot str > \theta\}$ where θ is its minimum storage requirement. It stores histrorical transactions from mining candidate nodes, and synchronizes the valid blocks by comparing it with other storage nodes. Mining candidate node works for blockchain consensus, and it is defined by $\{bn|bn.com > \psi_{mi}\}$, where ψ_{mi} is its minimum computing requirement. The miner is selected from mining candidate nodes. The relay node is responsible for transaction/block forwarding. The number of verification nodes is the highest among SVRM nodes, and it works for transaction/block verification.

5.2 SVRM Nodes Selection

The SVRM nodes collaboratively manage transactions about reputation values of workers on the blockchain. Users can retrieve correct transactions from some storage nodes with high reputation values. The mining candidate nodes with high reputation values are not only more likely to generate blocks honestly, but also avoid the miner becoming a target of attacks. Relay nodes with high reputation values are first selected for sending and receiving transactions/blocks, hence the delay of transactions/blocks propagation can be reduced further. In addition, verification nodes are open to all edge nodes. Therefore, it improves the security and scalability of the blockchain network.

In a time window, the current processing tasks of the edge node can be obtained by the reputation transactions, so the number of its current processing tasks is denoted as num_i. Hence, the idle computing resource of bn_i is calculated in (9), where ψ_{ta} is the average computing requirement of a MCS task.

$$bn_i.idle = bn_i.com - num_i \cdot \psi_{ta} \qquad (9)$$

As the nodes with higher computing capacities are more likely to work honestly [2], the mining candidate nodes are selected based on the highest idle computing capacity, and their reputation values in (10), where rep'_p is the average reputation value of publishers.

$$arg \max(bn_i.idle)$$
$$s.t.rep_i > \max(thresR, rep'_p)$$
$$bn_i.idle > \psi_{mi}$$
$$bn_i \text{ is in the area specified by a MCS task} \tag{10}$$

Besides, the number of verification nodes can be adjusted according to the configuration of blockchain consensus. For example, when the blockchain applies the DPoS (Delegated-proof-of-stake) of Enterprise Operation System (EOS) as its consensus mechanism, the number of verification nodes is set to 105 and the number of mining candidate nodes is 21 [8]. In this way, the nodes with high reputation values can be first selected to become verification nodes. It is worthy to note that, the proposed blockchain management scheme only enhances the blockchain network layer, while the consensus mechanism is not changed. Therefore, the enhanced scheme is compatible with most blockchain consensus mechanisms.

6   Experimental Evaluation

6.1   Reputation Model Evaluation

We conducted a series of experiments through Matlab to evaluate the performance of the proposed reputation model, and compare it against CrowdR-FBC [14] and MCS-Chain [3]. Parameters in this experiment included $thresQ = 0.5$, $\Psi_1 = \Psi_2 = 0.25$. The worker processes $[1, 100]$ tasks one by one.

For the first $[1, 50]$ tasks, $worker_i$ provided answers honestly, then he worked dishonestly for the $[51, 100]$ tasks. Each task is completed by 50 workers. The other 49 workers provided answers honestly, and their answers were generated with a random function. Figure 3(a) shows the changes in the reputation values of $worker_i$ in $[1, 100]$ tasks. As our proposed model considered the publisher's feedback, which may be dissatisfied with the results of the quality evaluation, the average reputation value our proposed model obtained is lower than that in CrowdR-FBC.

The influence of the publisher's feedback on the reputation values of honest workers was also analyzed. The publisher gave honest ratings for the first $[1, 50]$ tasks, then provided opposite ratings in $[51, 100]$ tasks. Figure 3(b) shows the changes in the reputation values of the worker in $[1, 100]$ tasks. Our reputation values were similar to MCS-Chain in the first $[1, 50]$ tasks, but our results were higher than MCS-Chain in the last $[51, 100]$ tasks. It is because the quality of the data was considered, and it alleviated the opposite ratings of the dishonest publisher to some extent.

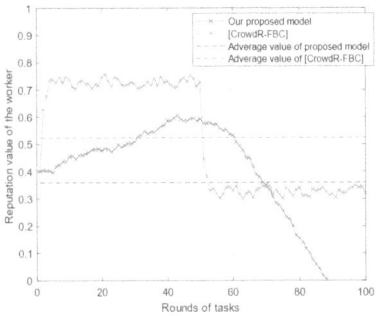

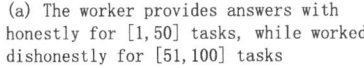

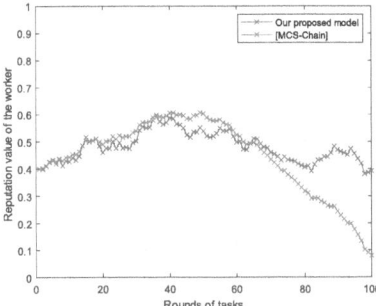

(a) The worker provides answers with honestly for $[1, 50]$ tasks, while worked dishonestly for $[51, 100]$ tasks

(b) The worker working honestly, which is given honest feedback in $[1, 50]$ tasks, while dishonest feedback in $[51, 100]$ tasks

Fig. 3. Reputation changes of the worker during his processing 100 tasks

6.2 Blockchain Management Evaluation

We evaluated the performance of the proposed blockchain management method using an NS-3 generator built on the Ubuntu operating system. We developed the network topology, that the information reaches storage nodes, mining candidate nodes, relay nodes and verification nodes through P2P channels, and then blocks are updated. A traditional blockchain management method named Full-BC was applied as a benchmark. In full-bc, each node as a full node is responsible for edge computing, transaction verification and block generation.

In Fig. 4(a), it shows the relationship between the average delay of block generation and the number of transaction generation nodes (workers). For both our method and full-bc, with the increase in workers, the average delay rises. It is because, as more workers submit answers, more computational processes need to be handled by the nodes with limited resources, hence more processes have to wait. The results show that our method can cope with a large number of workers with high efficiency.

In Fig. 4(b), it shows the relationship between the delay performance and values of reputation threshold $thresR$. We can see that the delay performance in both our method and full-bc is improved with the $thresR$ growing. It is because, due to the larger $thresR$, fewer nodes are allowed to participate in block mining and blockchain storage, hence the communication overhead of block updates is reduced. Thus, we can adjust the reputation threshold to deal with some delay-sensitive tasks, e.g., traffic information collection.

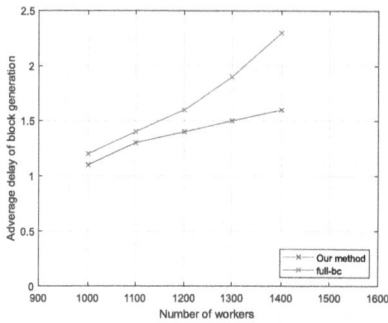
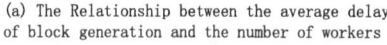
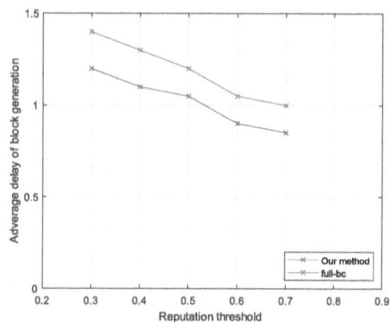

(a) The Relationship between the average delay of block generation and the number of workers

(b) The Relationship between the average delay of block generation and reputation threshold

Fig. 4. The relationship between the average delay of block generation and the number of workers or reputation threshold

7   Conclusion

In this paper, we present the reputation-based accountability mechanism for reliable mobile crowdsourcing with efficient blockchain. In detail, a reputation model towards workers based on the data-centric method and entity-centric method is proposed. As the workers can obtain higher reputation values through reliable data provision, they are accountable for some corresponding behaviors. Further, the reputation facilitates the classification of blockchain nodes. They have different responsibilities for blockchain management, i.e., transaction retrieval, block generation, block forwarding and block verification. This scheme reduces the latency of blockchain maintenance and is suitable for large-scale networks. Experimental results indicate that the proposed reputation model and blockchain management method have great advantages over the current schemes in improving the detection rate of dishonest workers and latency performance in the blockchain network, respectively.

Acknowledgments. This work is supported by: 1. National Key-Area Research and Development Program of China (2018YFB1404402). 2. Key-Area Research and Development Program of Guangdong Province (No. 2019B010137003). 3. Guangdong Science & Technology Fund (No. 2016B030305006, No.2018A07071702, No. 201804010314) 4. VeChain Foundation (No. SCNU2018-01), China University Research Innovation Fund (2020ITA09006). 5. National Social Science Fund of China (19ZDA041). 6. Guangzhou Science and Technology Plan Program (No. 2012224-12).

References

1. An, J., et al.: A lightweight blockchain-based model for data quality assessment in crowdsensing. IEEE Trans. Comput. Soc. Syst. **7**(1), 84–97 (2020)
2. Fan, K., et al.: A secure and verifiable data sharing scheme based on blockchain in vehicular social networks. IEEE Trans. Veh. Technol. **69**(6), 5826–5835 (2020)

3. Feng, W., Yan, Z.: Mcs-chain: decentralized and trustworthy mobile crowdsourcing based on blockchain. Futur. Gener. Comput. Syst. **95**, 649–666 (2019)
4. Huang, J., et al.: Blocksense: towards trustworthy mobile crowdsensing via proof-of-data blockchain. IEEE Trans. Mob. Comput. (2022)
5. Huang, J., et al.: Blockchain-based mobile crowd sensing in industrial systems. IEEE Trans. Ind. Inf. **16**(10), 6553–6563 (2020)
6. Kadadha, M., Otrok, H., Mizouni, R., Singh, S., Ouali, A.: Sensechain: a blockchain-based crowdsensing framework for multiple requesters and multiple workers. Futur. Gener. Comput. Syst. **105**, 650–664 (2020)
7. Liang, L., Ye, H., Li, G.Y.: Spectrum sharing in vehicular networks based on multi-agent reinforcement learning. IEEE J. Sel. Areas Commun. **37**(10), 2282–2292 (2019)
8. Liu, J., Xie, M., Chen, S., Ma, C., Gong, Q.: An improved dpos consensus mechanism in blockchain based on plts for the smart autonomous multi-robot system. Inf. Sci. **575**, 528–541 (2021)
9. Ma, L., Liu, X., Pei, Q., Xiang, Y.: Privacy-preserving reputation management for edge computing enhanced mobile crowdsensing. IEEE Trans. Serv. Comput. **12**(5), 786–799 (2018)
10. Mukherjee, M., Shu, L., Wang, D.: Survey of fog computing: fundamental, network applications, and research challenges. IEEE Commun. Surv. Tutor. **20**(3), 1826–1857 (2018)
11. van de Schoot, R., et al.: Bayesian statistics and modelling. Nat. Rev. Methods Primers **1**(1), 1–26 (2021)
12. Sun, L., Yang, Q., Chen, X., Chen, Z.: RC-chain: reputation-based crowdsourcing blockchain for vehicular networks. J. Netw. Comput. Appl. **176**, 102956 (2021)
13. Xu, J., Wang, S., Bhargava, B.K., Yang, F.: A blockchain-enabled trustless crowd-intelligence ecosystem on mobile edge computing. IEEE Trans. Ind. Inf. **15**(6), 3538–3547 (2019)
14. Yu, Y., Liu, S., Guo, L., Yeoh, P.L., Vucetic, B., Li, Y.: CrowdR-FBC: a distributed fog-blockchains for mobile crowdsourcing reputation management. IEEE Internet Things J. **7**(9), 8722–8735 (2020)
15. Zhang, X., Xue, G., Yu, R., Yang, D., Tang, J.: Keep your promise: mechanism design against free-riding and false-reporting in crowdsourcing. IEEE Internet Things J. **2**(6), 562–572 (2015)
16. Zou, J., Ye, B., Qu, L., Wang, Y., Orgun, M.A., Li, L.: A proof-of-trust consensus protocol for enhancing accountability in crowdsourcing services. IEEE Trans. Serv. Comput. **12**(3), 429–445 (2018)

Who Will Be Hooked?: A Phishing Fraud Detection Model Based on Dynamic Graph Temporal Feature Coding in Ethereum

Chao Li[1], Runshuo Liu[1(✉)], Yafei Zhang[1], Nengfu Xie[2], and Qingtian Zeng[1]

[1] College of Electronic and Information Engineering, Shandong University of Science and Technology, Qingdao, China
`liurunshuo@163.com, qtzeng@163.com`
[2] Key Laboratory of Agricultural Blockchain Application, Ministry of Agriculture and Rural Affairs, Agricultural Information Institute Chinese Academy of Agricultural Sciences, Beijing, China

Abstract. With the development of information technology, blockchain technology has become a key technology to ensure the security of cryptocurrency transactions. However, phishing fraud has become a major criminal offence that undermines the security of transactions in blockchain ecosystem. Phishing fraud detection has become one of the hot issues in blockchain field research. In this paper, we innovatively propose a **P**hishing **F**raud **D**etection model based on Dynamic Graph **T**emporal **F**eature Coding in Ethereum (PFD-TF) for predicting who will be the next target of phishing fraud. First, We constructs a dynamic graph of blockchain transactions with timestamps based on blockchain cryptocurrency transaction data. Then, a timestamp feature encoding strategy is proposed to learn the functional representation of time directly. And the interactions between node features, edge features and the topology of the graph are used to obtain phishing or non-phishing node embeddings. Finally, the acquired node embeddings are trained to be fitted using the cross-entropy loss function to complete the prediction of the next fished node. The experimental results show that the phishing fraud detection model (PFD-TF) proposed in this paper outperforms the results of state-of-the-art methods, indicating that the PFD-TF model is effective in phishing fraud detection in cryptocurrency transactions.

Keywords: Phishing fraud · Ethereum · Dynamic graph · Temporal feature coding

1 Introduction

With the development of information technology, blockchain technology has attracted the attention and research of various industries, and has developed from the initial computer industry to the financial field and then expanded to other industries, becoming a transformative technology in today's society [1].

G. Zhao et al. (Eds.): BWTAC 2024, CCIS 2277, pp. 130–141, 2025.
https://doi.org/10.1007/978-981-97-9412-6_12

Cryptocurrencies based on blockchain technology are suitable for many financial scenarios due to the decentralisation, immutability and anonymity of blockchain [2,3]. With cryptocurrencies, users can conduct reliable transactions anonymously and conveniently all over the world without fear of tampering with their transactions, using only one address. In the digital currency market, accounts can be freely and easily connected to each other to transact in currencies, information, services, and more [4]. However, due to the anonymity of blockchain technology, no regulatory organisation and other characteristics, the cryptocurrency market breeds many inevitable crimes. Among them, phishing fraud is one of the main frauds in the process of blockchain transactions. **Therefore the research on the detection of ethereum phishing fraud has important theoretical significance and application value** [4,5].

A significant amount of research work has been proposed for the detection of ethereum phishing fraud [6,7]. Early machine learning approaches for phishing scam detection focused on simple statistical features like account and transaction attributes, as well as entry and exit metrics. However, these methods neglected the complex topology of the Ethereum trading network, which is crucial for enhancing detection performance [8,9]. With the development of graph neural network technology, researchers use some deep graph models to analyse account relationships [10]. Chen et al.(2021) [4] employed graph neural networks and cascade features to capture the structural properties of accounts within the network. They then applied machine learning classification models to effectively identify anomalous accounts associated with phishing scams. Li et al.(2022) [11] utilized LSTM models to derive temporal edge representations within the Ethereum transaction graph. An attention mechanism was then employed to aggregate these edge representations around the nodes, thereby enriching the node-level features. These enhanced node representations were subsequently fed into a GCN module to extract structural features. Finally, the temporal edge features, structural features, and statistical attributes were concatenated to effectively identify phishing addresses [12]. Xie et al. (2021) [13] model successive snapshots of Ether transaction records and links to learn node embeddings using random roaming with a search strategy that depends on the number of transactions, structural transfer probabilities and temporal transfer probabilities. However, two challenges remain for ethereum phishing fraud detection:

- **Challenge 1: Graph construction for cryptocurrency transactions to be further optimised.** Most of the existing research focuses on analysing and mining the static graph structure during cryptocurrency transactions, but in real data like Ether, nodes and edges are dynamically changing [14]. Therefore it is necessary to create continuous dynamic graphs dealing with Ether phishing scam data and to model and analyse them.
- **Challenge 2: Lack of a temporal feature encoding method for processing ethereum phish fraud data.** Existing models usually use recurrent neural networks or Bochner's theorem to model temporal encoding [12], which cannot ensure that events arrive in time-stamped order when applied to dynamic graphical neural networks, resulting in unstable model performance,

so it is of great significance to create a temporal function space suitable for ethereum phish fraud data for temporal feature encoding.

To solve the above problems, in this paper, we propose a new Phishing Fraud Detection Model Based on Dynamic Graph Temporal Feature Coding in Ethereum, which firstly proposes a dynamic graph construction method for cryptocurrency transactions based on feature extraction, and then enters into the fraud perception recognition module, which captures the structure perception of the fraudulent node in the full graph to achieve the iterative updating of node representations, and finally goes through the Multi-Layer Perceptron(MLP) completes the link prediction task to achieve the detection of the next phished fraud node. The main contributions of the model include:

- **We propose a continuous-time dynamic graph framework designed to analyze Ethereum phishing fraud data.** The structure is able to attach information about the time when the fraud occurred to edges in the form of timestamps, which can be represented as time-ordered events, including the addition or removal of edges, the addition or removal of nodes, and changes in the characteristics of nodes or edges, avoiding the problem of information loss that occurs when creating a sequence of continuous time graphs into a sequence of discrete snapshot graphs.
- **A dynamic graph neural network model based on temporal feature coding is proposed to address the dynamic representation of cryptocurrency transaction nodes.** Sampling the target nodes in reverse neighbourhood order by time according to the ethereum data characteristics, and using the temporal feature encoding formula to splice the edge features and temporal features of each neighbour to solve the problem of gradient explosion of Bochner's theorem.
- **Experiments.** We conduct link prediction experiments on a real dataset of ethereum phish frauds and analyse them in comparison with mainstream dynamic graph neural network model algorithms. The experimental results show that PFD-TF outperforms existing state-of-the-art methods. In addition, the effectiveness of the continuous-time dynamic graph temporal feature encoding strategy is demonstrated through ablation experiments, etc.

2   Preliminaries

In this section, this paper gives some important concepts and problem definitions related to dynamic graph Ether data, the continuous time dynamic graph of Ether is shown in Fig. 1.

Definition 1. **Continuous-time Dynamic Graph** [9]. Continuous-time dynamic maps can record the complete timing information of dynamic networks, can be represented as $G = \{(v_i, v_j, t, \Delta t, e_{ij}(t)); i, j = 1, 2, ..., n\}$, where v_i, v_j denote the nodes in the network, t, Δt denote the appearance time and duration of the links, respectively, and $e_{ij}(t)$ represents the edges.

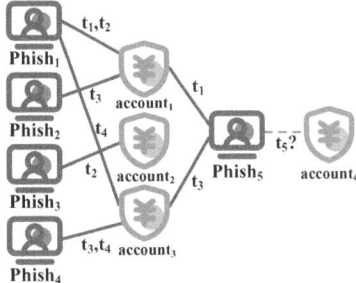

Fig. 1. Ether Continuous Time Dynamic Chart.

Definition 2. Link Prediction on Dynamic Graph [9]. Given a continuous-time dynamic graph, the task is to predict edges at future timestamps $t > T$ using a finite history of interactions $G_{\leq T} = \{e(t_1), e(t_2), ..., e(t_n)\}$, where $t_i \in [1, T]$.

Definition 3. Time Walk [7]. Given a continuous time dynamic graph, node sampling of l steps from the original node w_0 at the moment t_0 can be expressed as $W = \{(w_i, t_i) \mid i \in N, 0 \leq i \leq l, t_0 > t_1 > ... > t_l, (w_i, w_{i-1}), t_i)\} \in G_{w_{i-1}, t_{i-1}}$ for $i \geq 1$, where t_i denotes the time at moment i, $i \geq 1$.

Problem 1. Dynamic Graph Embedding [15]. Given the source node u, the target node v, the timestamp t and the historical interaction information $\{(u', v', t') \mid t' < t\}$, the learning of the representation on the dynamical graph aims at designing a mapping function f to learn the temporal perceptual representations of u and v, $h_u^t \in R^d$ and $h_v^t \in R^d$ where d is the dimension.

3   The Proposed Model

In this section, we propose a **P**hishing **F**raud **D**etection model based on Dynamic Graph **T**emporal **F**eature Coding in Ethereum(PFD-TF), which completes the learning of an effective representation of ethereum nodes from continuous-time dynamic graphs and produces graph node embeddings $Z(t) = (z_1(t), ..., z_n(t))$ for each time t. The framework for processing ethereum data mainly includes: Node Filtration module (A), PFD-TF module (B), and Link Prediction module (C). The ethereum data first passes through the node filtering module (A) for the construction of the dynamic graph of cryptocurrency transactions, and then passes through the PFD-TF module(B) for the feature engineering to obtain the time and feature information, and encodes the temporal feature information at the end of the feature engineering, and learns the functional representation of the time directly, and finally passes through the link prediction module (C) to obtain the final phishing or non-phishing node embeddings, and utilises the MLP to predict the next fished node. Fishing node is predicted, the overall framework is shown in Fig. 2.

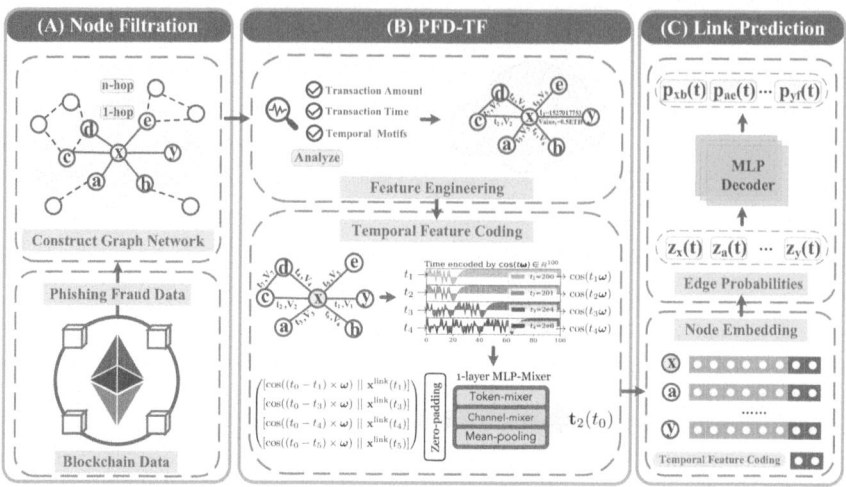

Fig. 2. Ethereum Data Processing Framework Flowchart.

3.1 Node Filtration and Dynamic Graph Construction

Leveraging the vast transactional data available on the Ethereum blockchain, we initially construct a large-scale transaction graph representing the Ethereum network. In this graph, nodes denote individual accounts, while edges represent the transactions occurring between these accounts. The Ethereum network permits multiple edges between any pair of nodes, with each edge encapsulating two critical pieces of information: the transaction amount and the transaction timestamp. The algorithm used to construct this dynamic cryptocurrency transaction graph is detailed in Algorithm 1.

Algorithm 1. Constructing a dynamic graph of cryptocurrency transactions.

Input: Ethereum transaction set E_t
Output: Ethereum transaction graph G
1: Constructing Temporal Transaction Graph (E_t)
2: $G \leftarrow$ empty graph; $V \leftarrow$ empty set of nodes;
3: **for** each transaction e in E_t **do**
4:    add a directed edge e ($v.src \rightarrow v.dst$) with transaction amount and timestamp to edge set E in G;
5:    add unique $v.src$ and $v.dst$ to node set V;
6: **end for**
7: **return** G

Since the original cryptocurrency transaction data is large, we adopt the random wandering method for sampling. We first randomly select a node from the graph, then randomly select its neighbours as the next node and repeat the process, if the node information is mutilated, we perform a delete operation on the account node, from which the graph structure is constructed.

After constructing the graph structure, we perform feature engineering operations on it to construct it as a continuous time dynamic graph, i.e., $G = \{(v_i, v_j, t, \Delta t, e_{ij}(t)); i, j = 1, 2, ..., n\}$. Due to the inherent anonymity of blockchain platforms, individual nodes lack direct identifying information. Consequently, feature engineering must rely solely on extracting and integrating fundamental data from the relationships between nodes. Therefore, after analyzing the differences in transaction behavior patterns between phishing accounts and normal accounts, we extract two key dimensions—time and transaction amount—as the primary attribute features of nodes. The phishing account and normal account are taken as nodes, the transactions occurring between the two accounts are taken as edges, and the time and transaction amount features are attached to the edges, from which the continuous time dynamic graph G is constructed.

3.2   PTD-TF Methodology

The time walks encoding part learns the node representation from the temporal nature of the data and obtains the positional encoding of the neighbouring nodes by time walks of the target node and the original node, while the positional encoding is later utilized to achieve the node identity and the formula to achieve the time walks, W is defined as follows:

$$W = \{(w_i, t_i) \mid i \in N, 0 \leq i \leq l, t_0 > t_1 > ... > t_l, (w_i, w_{i-1}), t_i)\} \in G_{w_{i-1}, t_{i-1}},$$
$$i \geq 1$$

$$(1)$$

where l is the walk length, we also use $W[i][0]$ and $W[i][1]$ (i.e., w_i and t_i in (w_i, t_i)) to denote specific nodes and times.

In order to distinguish between different timestamps, we introduce the temporal encoding function $cos(t\omega)$, which uses temporal properties to encode each timestamp as a d-dimensional vector as shown in Eq. 2. More specifically, we first map each t to a vector with monotonically exponentially decreasing $t\omega \in (0, t]$ in the feature dimension, and then use the cosine function to project all values to $cos(t\omega) \in [-1, +1]$.

$$\omega = \{\alpha^{-\frac{i-1}{\beta}}\}_i^d = 1 \qquad (2)$$

where the choice of α, β depends on the range of the maximum timestamp we expect to encode.

We sample the links of nodes through a time-back strategy to extract the potential causality of the network dynamics. The information that the nearest links have is more important, so we introduce a non-negative hyperparameter θ and sample the links with a probability proportional to the exponential distribution $exp(\theta(t - t_p))$, where t, t_p are the timestamps of the links and the previous links, respectively, and process the timestamp information using our proposed time coding strategy. A larger θ gives a better emphasis on the most recent link, while the sampling strategy is uniform sampling when θ is 0.

The output of node i in layer l at time t is denoted as $\widetilde{h}_0^{(l-1)}(t)$, and according to the attention mechanism, the neighbourhood entity-time feature matrices are first aggregated as defined in the following formula:

$$Z(t) = [\widetilde{h}_0^{(l-1)}(t) \parallel \phi_{dT}(0), \widetilde{h}_1^{(l-1)}(t_1) \parallel \phi_{dT}(t - t_1), ..., \widetilde{h}_N^{(l-1)}(t_N) \parallel \phi_{dT}(t - t_N)], \tag{3}$$

$$Q(t) = [Z(t)]_0 \cdot W_Q, K(t) = [Z(t)]_{1:N} \cdot W_k, K(t) = [Z(t)]_{1:N} \cdot W_k, \tag{4}$$

We define W_Q, W_K, W_V to be the weight matrices used to capture the interactions between temporal coding and node features, $\phi_d(t)$ denotes the finite-dimensional generalised mapping from time to R^d:

$$\phi_d(t) = \sqrt{\frac{1}{d}} \cdot [cos(\omega_1 t), sin(\omega_1 t), ..., cos(\omega_d t), sin(\omega_d t)], \tag{5}$$

where ω is Eq. 2, the mechanism can be efficiently shared across all nodes at any point in time. We then sum the rows of the above dot-product self-attentive output, as a hidden neighbourhood representation:

$$h(t) = attn(Q(t), K(t), V(t)), \tag{6}$$

where $attn$ denotes the dot product self-attention mechanism and $h(t)$ denotes the current neighbourhood representation.

To combine the neighbourhood representation with the target node features, we connect the neighbourhood representation with the feature vector Z_0 of the target node. We then pass it to the feed-forward neural network to capture the nonlinear interactions between the features as follows:

$$\widetilde{h}_0^{(l-1)}(t) = FFN(h(t) \parallel x_0) = Relu([h(t) \parallel x_0] \cdot W_0^l + b_0^l) \cdot W_1^l + b_1^l, \tag{7}$$

where $\widetilde{h}_0^{(l-1)}(t) \in R^d$ is the final output of the Structure Perception node embedding that represents the target node at time t, FFN denotes a two-layer multi-layer perceptron.

3.3   Link Prediction

The task of this module is to perform link prediction for nodes and complete the downstream task of predicting the next fished node. Following the above operations, we obtain both temporal node and edge features, which are then combined to form a comprehensive node embedding representation. With this complete node embedding in hand, it becomes crucial to distinguish between the representations of phishing and normal nodes. To achieve this, we require a classifier capable of deeply analyzing and differentiating these representations, ultimately enabling the accurate classification of Ethereum phishing accounts. We use a multilayer perceptron (MLP) as the classifier, and in order to train it using a cross-entropy loss function, we devise a time-varying negative sampling strategy to construct pairs of positive and negative samples:

$$loss = \sum_{(v_i, v_j, eij, t) \in G} -log(\sigma(-z_i(t)^T z_j(t))) - E_{v_n \ p_n} log(\sigma(-z_i(t)^T z_j(t))), \quad (8)$$

where, $loss$ denotes the cross-entropy loss function value, the summation occurs when nodes i and j interact during training. σ represents the sigmoid activation function, and $p_n(v)$ is the negative sampling distribution. The time-aware embedded representation is used as an input to make a prediction for the next fished node.

4   Experiments

This section first describes the ethereum dataset used for the experiments and the comparison algorithms. It then validates the effectiveness of the proposed model through link prediction, ablation experiments, and tests the performance of the proposed method against various strong baselines (adapting to time settings where possible) and competing methods, with the source code of the model implemented using PyTorch.

4.1   Datasets and Baseline

We sourced the original dataset from the widely recognized XBlock platform. This dataset centers on Ethereum accounts identified as phishing, along with a subset of untagged accounts. Utilizing the Etherscan API, we retrieved the first-hop neighbors of these accounts and collected the transaction data between them.

Each transaction record in the dataset contains the following key details: (1) TxHash, representing the unique transaction hash; (2) BlockHeight, indicating the block number in which the transaction was included; (3) Timestamp, capturing the exact time the transaction was processed; (4) From, denoting the address of the node that initiated the transaction; (5) To, representing the address of the receiving node; and (6) Value, specifying the amount transferred in the transaction. Table 1 provides a comprehensive overview of the phishing transaction network dataset.

We evaluate the proposed approach by comparing it against three dynamic graph representation learning models, which serve as baseline comparisons in this study. TGN (2020) [16], DyGformer (2023) [15], GraphMixer (2023) [17].They are briefly described as follows.

Table 1. Statistic of Datasets.

Dataset	Nodes	Total Edges	Time
Phish	30598	108032	3 years
Normal	168048	53470	3 years
All	276080	72732	3 years

- **TGN (2020)**: A general and efficient dynamic graph model is proposed, integrating memory modules with graph convolution operations. This design enables the model to learn from the sequential data while maintaining efficient parallel processing.
- **GraphMixer (2020)**: The model uses a message passing mechanism to fuse the features of nodes and their neighbours, which in turn captures the structural information of the graph and the relationships between nodes.
- **DyGFormer (2023)**: Flexible coding interfaces and robust evaluation protocols are introduced that effectively capture node correlations and long-term temporal dependencies within dynamic graph representations.
- **PFD-TF (Our)**: The model constructs a dynamic graph of blockchain transactions with timestamp feature encoding to learn time representations. It leverages interactions between node features, edge features, and graph topology to generate node embeddings. These embeddings are trained using the cross-entropy loss function to predict the next phishing target.

4.2   Link Prediction

We assess the model's performance on the link prediction task using Average Precision (AP) and Area Under the Curve (AUC) as evaluation metrics. For this evaluation, we compute the standard deviation across 10 random seeds to provide an average measure of AP and AUC(%).

We approach link prediction by framing it as two distinct tasks: a transductive learning task, which involves predicting future links on observed nodes, and an inductive learning task, which involves predicting future links on unseen nodes. The outcomes for both transductive and inductive learning are summarized in Table 2, where optimal results are highlighted in bold and sub-optimal results are underlined.

The results in Table 2 show the state-of-the-art performance of our method on the inductive and transductive learning tasks, where the PFD-TF model proposed in this paper consistently outperforms all baselines in the link prediction task, and compared to GraphMixer, a model that does not require the proximity node importance principle, PFD-TF improves the AP and AUC metrics by up to 5.02% and 4.35%, a result that illustrates the significant improvement effect of using the proximity node importance principle strategy for PFD-TF.

In the inductive learning task, PFD-TF improve over most models in terms of AP and AUC, significantly higher than classical models such as TGN, and for

Table 2. Link prediction experiment results.

		Phish		Normal		All	
	Baseline	Ap	Auc	Ap	Auc	Ap	Auc
Transductive	TGN	0.8963	0.8866	0.9152	0.9218	0.902	0.9054
	GraphMixer	0.8968	0.9005	0.9094	0.9156	0.8802	0.8842
	DyGformer	0.9402	0.9482	0.9481	0.9436	0.9134	0.9167
	PFD-TF	**0.9564**	**0.9587**	**0.9601**	**0.9589**	**0.9203**	**0.9284**
Inductive	TGN	0.8975	0.8843	0.9134	0.9161	0.9057	0.9023
	GraphMixer	0.9018	0.9115	0.9101	0.912	0.9031	0.8949
	DyGformer	0.9484	0.9396	0.9473	0.9418	0.911	0.9142
	PFD-TF	**0.952**	**0.955**	**0.9598**	**0.9605**	**0.9186**	**0.9213**

both metrics, at least by about 1%, indicating the design of the temporal feature encoding, which effectively compensates for the shortcomings of the neighbours who have too little temporal information. The PFD-TF model performs well in the inductive and transductive learning tasks, and these results demonstrate the effectiveness and potential of the model.

4.3   Ablation Study

To evaluate the contribution of each module to the overall performance of the model, we conducted ablation experiments by systematically removing individual modules. This section presents three variants, as detailed in Table 3, along with their corresponding results depicted in Fig. 3.

Table 3. Ablation experiment variants.

Variant	Descriptions
PFD-TF$_{-w/o-bias}$	Generating node embeddings without using the proximity node importance principle.
PFD-TF$_{-w/o-time}$	Generating node embeddings without temporal feature encoding module.
PFD-TF$_{-w/o-attention}$	Generating node embeddings without the attention mechanism.
Full model	The complete PFD-TF model proposed in this paper.

As can be seen in Fig. 3, the performance advantages of the PFD-TF model on the three different datasets, especially with respect to its variant models. For our proposed temporal coding feature module, we can conclude from the experimental results that the presence of this module improves the evaluation metric AP by at least about 2%, which shows that the temporal coding module

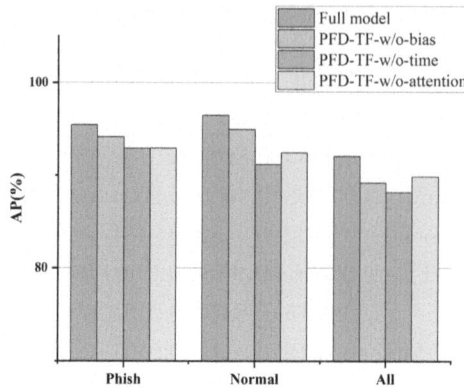

Fig. 3. Experimental results (%) on ablation study.

has an important significance for the whole model. At the same time the principle of importance of the neighbouring nodes and the attention mechanism both play different roles in improving the performance of the overall model. This also implies that when constructing and optimising the dynamic graph model, the effects of each component need to be considered comprehensively in order to more fully exploit the information in the dynamic graph.

5   Conclusion

In this paper, we propose a dynamic graph neural network algorithm called PFD-TF for detecting phish frauds in ethereum networks. The algorithm effectively extracts transaction network features by mining ethereum transaction records and using dynamic graph temporal feature encoding method. Experimental results show that PFD-TF performs well in predicting the next phished node, providing an effective phishing fraud detection tool for the blockchain ecosystem.

Declarations

Acknowledgments. This work is supported by National Key R&D Program of China(Grant No. 2022ZD0119501); National Natural Science Foundation of China (Grant No. 52374221); the Natural Science Foundation of Shandong Province (Grant No. ZR2022MF268, ZR2021QG038); the Taishan Scholar Program of Shandong Province (GrantNo. ts20190936), and the Open Research Fund Program of Key Laboratory of Agricultural Blockchain Application, Ministry of Agriculture and Rural Affairs(2022KLABA03).

Disclosure of Interests. The authors declare that there is no competing interests.

References

1. Wu, J., et al.: Who are the phishers? phishing scam detection on ethereum via network embedding. IEEE Trans. Syst. Man, Cybern. Syst. **52**(2), 1156–1166 (2020)
2. Wang, L., Xu, M., Cheng, H.: Phishing scams detection via temporal graph attention network in ethereum. Inf. Process. Manage. **60**(4), 103412 (2023)
3. Liu, J., Chen, J., Wu, J., Wu, Z., Fang, J., Zheng, Z.: Fishing for fraudsters: uncovering ethereum phishing gangs with blockchain data. IEEE Trans. Inf. Forensics Secur. (2024)
4. Chen, L., Peng, J., Liu, Y., Li, J., Xie, F., Zheng, Z.: Phishing scams detection in ethereum transaction network. ACM Trans. Internet Technol. (TOIT) **21**(1), 1–16 (2020)
5. Chen, H., Pendleton, M., Njilla, L., Xu, S.: A survey on ethereum systems security: vulnerabilities, attacks, and defenses. ACM Comput. Surv. (CSUR) **53**(3), 1–43 (2020)
6. Wang, Y., Chang, Y.-Y., Liu, Y., Leskovec, J., Li, P.: Inductive representation learning in temporal networks via causal anonymous walks arXiv preprint arXiv:2101.05974 (2021)
7. Jin, M., Li, Y.-F., Pan, S.: Neural temporal walks: motif-aware representation learning on continuous-time dynamic graphs. In: Advances in Neural Information Processing Systems, vol. 35, pp. 19874–19886 (2022)
8. Jiang, L., Chen, K.-J., Chen, J.: Self-supervised dynamic graph representation learning via temporal subgraph contrast, arXiv preprint arXiv:2112.08733 (2021)
9. Luo, Y., Li, P.: Neighborhood-aware scalable temporal network representation learning. In: Learning on Graphs Conference. PMLR (2022)
10. Xiong, A., et al.: Ethereum phishing detection based on graph neural networks. IET Blockchain (2023)
11. Li, S., Gou, G., Liu, C., Hou, C., Li, Z., Xiong, G.: TTAGN: temporal transaction aggregation graph network for ethereum phishing scams detection. In: Proceedings of the ACM Web Conference, vol. 2022, pp. 661–669 (2022)
12. Xu, D., Ruan, C., Korpeoglu, E., Kumar, S., Achan, K.: Inductive representation learning on temporal graphs, arXiv preprint arXiv:2002.07962 (2020)
13. Xie, Y., et al.: Understanding ethereum transactions via network approach. Graph Data Min. Algorithm, Secur. Appl. pp. 155–176 (2021)
14. Leng, J., Zhou, M., Zhao, J.L., Huang, Y., Bian, Y.: Blockchain security: a survey of techniques and research directions. IEEE Trans. Serv. Comput. **15**(4), 2490–2510 (2020)
15. Yu, L., Sun, L., Du, B., Lv, W.: Towards better dynamic graph learning: new architecture and unified library. In: Advances in Neural Information Processing Systems, vol. 36, pp. 67 686–67 700 (2023)
16. Rossi, E., Chamberlain, B., Frasca, F., Eynard, D., Monti, F., Bronstein, M.: Temporal graph networks for deep learning on dynamic graphs, arXiv preprint arXiv:2006.10637 (2020)
17. Cong, W., et al.: Do we really need complicated model architectures for temporal networks? arXiv preprint arXiv:2302.11636 (2023)

Static Analysis Detection of Hyperledger Fabric Read-Write Logic Vulnerability

Donghan Chen$^{(\boxtimes)}$ (iD), Junxiong Lin (iD), and Zhihui Lu (iD)

Fudan University, Shanghai, China
dhchen24@m.fudan.edu.cn, {jxlin18,lzh}@fudan.edu.cn

Abstract. With the rapid development of blockchain technology, smart contracts based on blockchain have also advanced swiftly. Hyperledger Fabric, as a distributed trusted ledger among trusted organizations, has gained increasing support in fields such as supply chain finance and government platforms. Compared to domain-specific languages for public blockchains, Hyperledger Fabric recommends using general purpose languages in the industry to develop its smart contracts, known as chaincode. Golang language is the recommended language for Hyperledger Fabric and is widely used in its various transaction scenarios. For Hyperledger Fabric chaincode, developers might introduce read-write logic vulnerabilities due to differences from traditional development read-write logic. Current research does not deeply understand these vulnerabilities, and detection methods are relatively simple, leading to a high false positive rate. Based on this, this paper proposes a static analysis method based on the SSA form of Go's intermediate representation, analyzing read-write control flow and introducing data flow features. This approach improves the detection accuracy of mainstream tools like Chaincode Analyzer, validating the method's value in practical applications.

Keywords: Hyperledger Fabric · Read-Write Vunerability · Static Analysis

1 Introduction

The concept of blockchain was introduced by Satoshi Nakamoto in 2008 [8], aiming to ensure trustworthy value transfer through a decentralized distributed ledger. Essentially, blockchain technology is a digital, decentralized, distributed shared transaction ledger. All nodes in a blockchain network collectively maintain the distributed ledger under the constraints of a consensus protocol, achieving a mechanism for trustworthy transactions among untrusted nodes.

The concept of smart contracts was proposed by Szabo in 1994 [9]. These are digital contracts that can be executed over the Internet, aiming to replace traditional paper contracts. The idea of smart contracts has gained widespread application with the advent of blockchain technology. Smart contracts on a blockchain can manipulate specific asset data, facilitating functions such as value transfer

G. Zhao et al. (Eds.): BWTAC 2024, CCIS 2277, pp. 142–152, 2025.
https://doi.org/10.1007/978-981-97-9412-6_13

and asset management. After the contract execution finish, it's hardly impossible to deny or withdraw, ensuring trustless execution. Blockchains with smart contracts have found increasingly broad applications in fields such as finance, management, healthcare, and the Internet [12].

Based on the degree of decentralization, blockchain architectures are classified into public blockchain, permissioned blockchain, and private blockchain. Public blockchain is fully developed for the Internet, permissioned blockchain is governed by a consortium of organizations with set entry thresholds, and private blockchain is entirely managed by a single organization.

Hyperledger Fabric [1] is an open-source project launched by the Linux Foundation in 2015 to promote blockchain digital technology and transaction verification. Hyperledger Fabric is one of the most influential platforms in the field of permissioned blockchains, and many permissioned blockchain platforms have adopted its architecture.

Chaincode in Hyperledger Fabric is the equivalent of smart contracts and typically, a single chaincode corresponds to a single smart contract in practical development. The installation and execution of Hyperledger Fabric chaincode occur within Docker containers. Unlike public blockchain that tends to use domain-specific languages (DSL) for developing smart contracts, Hyperledger Fabric chaincode development has more significant support for general-purpose languages (GPL). The official recommendation is to use the Go language for developing chaincode, although Java and Node.js are also supported as chaincode development languages.

The security of smart contracts has always been a significant concern. Compared to ordinary programs, vulnerabilities in smart contracts, once exploited by hackers, can lead to severe losses. For example, the DAO incident in 2016 resulted in a loss of approximately $60 million worth of Ether [2]. This incident directly led to the subsequent Ethereum hard fork, causing significant controversy within the community. The financial losses caused by smart contract security issues have shown an upward trend since 2016, with a noticeable increase since 2020 [3].

Due to the immutable nature of blockchain and smart contracts, any vulnerability that occurs can result in corresponding economic losses. In the context of Hyperledger Fabric, traditional general-purpose language (GPL) developers may misunderstand the underlying framework's operating mechanisms. This is particularly true for read and write operations, where failure to strictly adhere to relevant specifications can lead to logical vulnerabilities, resulting in financial losses.

Our research will analyze logical vulnerabilities caused by read-write operations in Hyperledger Fabric, providing a deeper analysis of vulnerability principles and exploitation methods compared to previous research. Additionally, based on our vulnerability analysis of Go language smart contracts, we employ a static analysis approach that integrates program-level read-write control flow for vulnerability detection. Our detection tool achieves higher accuracy compared to previous work, which suffered from high false positive rates due to common API call errors.

The paper will be structured as follows: Sect. 2 will introduce related research on security vulnerabilities in Hyperledger Fabric, highlighting the shortcomings of current work in read-write vulnerability detection. Section 3 will analyze vulnerabilities in Hyperledger Fabric's read-write operations and propose corresponding detection methods. Section 4 will detail our vulnerability detection algorithm, while Sect. 5 will present comparative experiments of the algorithm and analyze the results. Finally, Sect. 6 will summarize our work.

2   Related Work

Chaincode in Hyperledger Fabric is primarily used within specific organizations, with contract functions often involving inter-organizational transaction records and collaboration. Consequently, the exposed attack surface is relatively limited. Yamashita et al. [10], based on information collected from the open-source community, summarized the security risks of Go language smart contracts in Hyperledger Fabric. They analyzed vulnerabilities in Hyperledger Fabric smart contracts from the perspectives of transaction consensus mechanisms, platform characteristics, and state database specifications. Building on Yamashita's work, Lv et al. [7] proposed the addition of sensitive data detection for Fabric Go language smart contracts. Li et al. [6] conducted APT attack validation on Fabric Go language smart contracts and identified security risks such as information leakage and remote system execution.

Yumashita [10] identified vulnerabilities in Hyperledger Fabric's read-write operations, specifically highlighting risks associated with range queries and the read-after-write sequence. However, the research did not provide an in-depth explanation of the effectiveness of these risks. For vulnerabilities related to read-write operations in Hyperledger Fabric chaincode, particularly those involving range queries, the detection work mainly involves identifying whether the risky functions are called in the chaincode. However, the range query API is a common API in Hyperledger Fabric chaincode development, leading to a high false-positive rate in related tools for detecting range query vulnerabilities, thus easily causing corresponding risks. For the read-after-write vulnerabilities, static tools directly determine the sequential relationship between write and read operations in the abstract syntax tree. However, modern developers often encapsulate read-write operations, and the native defer operation in Go language further modifies the actual read-write control flow sequence.

3   Read-Write Vulnerablity

3.1   Source

To investigate read-write vulnerabilities in Hyperledger Fabric, it is essential to understand the transaction process in Hyperledger Fabric, which elucidates the specific risks of read-after-write vulnerabilities and range query vulnerabilities. Hyperledger Fabric smart contracts employ a transaction process consisting of the following stages: request, simulation, collection, ordering, validation, and commitment [1]. This method addresses issues related to transaction consensus in blockchain systems while imposing higher security requirements on the execution of smart contracts. The following section explains this process in detail (see Fig. 1)).

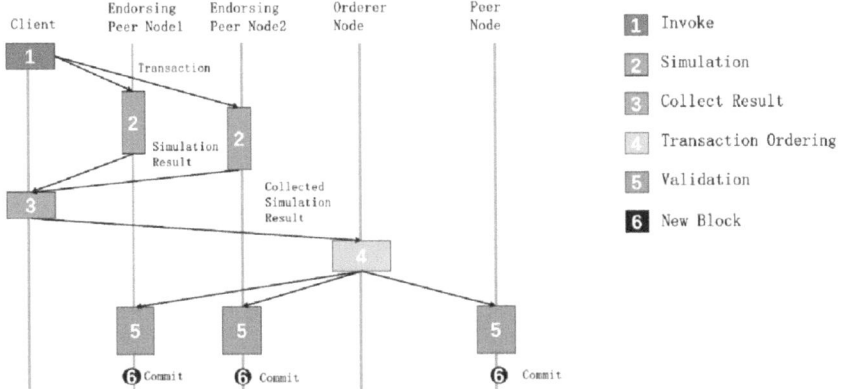

Fig. 1. Hyperleger Fabric Transaction Flow.

Request Stage. The client initiates a chaincode transaction, specifying the endorsement nodes for transaction simulation. This stage does not impose special requirements on the specified endorsement nodes; generally, the endorsement policy satisfying the consensus transaction requirements is sufficient, such as endorsement by more than half of the nodes.

Simulation Stage. The designated endorsement nodes perform the following checks on the client's transaction proposal: the transaction proposal format is correct, the proposal has not been previously submitted, the transaction proposal's signature is valid, and the submitter is authorized to perform the proposed operations on the channel. If all these points are validated, the endorsement nodes convert the transaction parameters into parameters for invoking the chaincode functions. Based on this, the endorsement nodes simulate the execution of the smart contract within their respective containers. The intermediate data read operations depend on each endorsement node's state database, recording the read and write data sets during this process. Finally, the endorsement nodes sign the results of the transaction proposal execution and return them to the client.

Collection Stage. The client collects the transaction simulation results from the endorsement nodes, verifies the signatures of the endorsement nodes, and then sends the collected results to the ordering nodes.

Ordering Stage. The ordering service orders the received transactions by timestamp and creates blocks by channel. These transaction blocks are sent to all peer nodes in the channel.

Validation Stage. The blocks containing transactions are delivered to all peer nodes in the channel. Each peer node validates the transactions to ensure that the endorsement policy is satisfied and that there have been no changes to the state database since the transaction execution generated the read set.

3.2 Vulnerability

Commitment Stage After validation by all peer nodes, the transaction block data is appended to the ledger. Transactions that fail validation are also recorded on the ledger but are marked as invalid blocks, ensuring that all transaction information is recorded. Meanwhile, peer nodes commit the write set of each valid transaction to the current state database, updating the state database accordingly.

Write-Read Inconsistency Risk. During transactions in Hyperledger Fabric, there is a noticeable difference in the timing of data reads and writes during the execution of chaincode. The data reads rely on the state database of the endorsing node in Hyperledger Fabric. When a chaincode invokes an interface to commit data to the ledger, the data is not immediately committed, and the state database is not instantly updated. This behavior differs from traditional program read-write consistency, leading developers to potentially write data first and then read the corresponding data within the same chaincode, which may result in logical execution errors.

Range Query Verification Deficiency. In the verification process of Hyperledger Fabric transactions, changes in the read-write set are validated. However, if a range query is invoked in the program, the results are not verified for performance reasons. If modifications are made to the queried data within the same transaction after the range query, it can lead to phantom read risks.

4   Detection Method

We use static analysis of read-write control flow to detect smart contract vulnerabilities in Hyperledger Fabric chaincode.

In the overall detection process (see Fig. 2), we read the Hyperledger Fabric chaincode as input, through intermediate representation transformation, generate the SSA (Static Single Assignment) form of Go language. By extracting data flow and control flow from the program, we construct a function dependency call graph. This graph helps us locate key functions, such as range query API interfaces and native read-write interfaces. To address the risks associated with encapsulated read-write functions, we develop a method for propagating read-write properties. This method involves searching for indirectly called functions based on function calls to determine if there is a write-before-read risk. In addition to propagating read-write properties in the control flow, we also introduce data flow analysis. To address potential issues with range queries, we include corresponding checks to determine if there are write operations on the data retrieved by range queries.

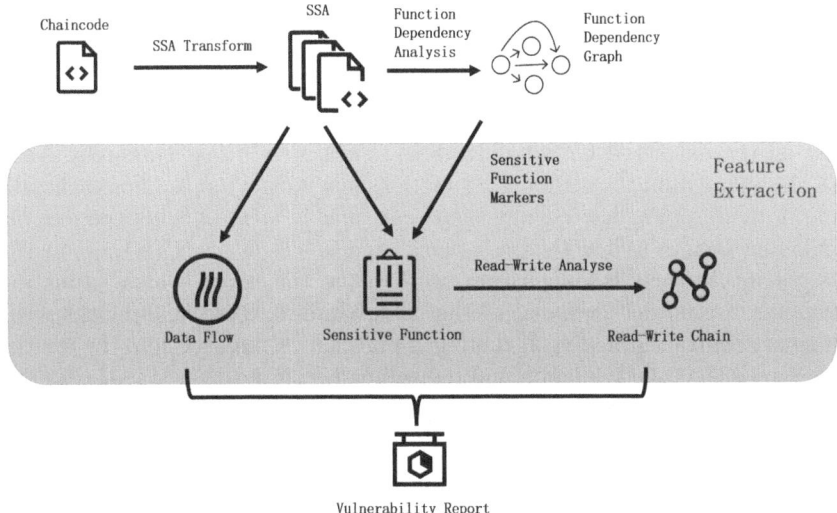

Fig. 2. Overall Design of Vulnerability Detection Algorithms.

4.1 SSA Intermediate Representation

In program analysis methods, LLVM-IR [11] is commonly used, but Go language has limited support for LLVM-IR. Therefore, our research uses the SSA (Static Single Assignment) [4] intermediate representation of Go language. In the SSA form, each variable is assigned exactly once, and each variable is defined before it is used, typically ensured by renaming variables to maintain the single assignment property. This feature makes the compiler more efficient in performing optimizations such as constant propagation and dead code elimination.

For instructions in the Go-SSA form, when an instruction generates an assignment, a new variable is created. To achieve this characteristic, in the programming implementation of the Go language compiler, an SSA instruction is represented as implementing both the instruction and value interfaces, reflecting the properties of both. This unifies data flow and control flow to a certain extent. As shown below (see Listing 1.1), this is a segment of Go SSA instructions. The function of this segment is to invoke the blockchain data read function and then complete the data commit operation. It can be seen that each operation that generates a new value creates a new register to store the corresponding value.

```
Call        t30 = invoke ctx.GetStub()
FieldAddr   t31 = &t6.ID [#0]
UnOp        t32 = *t31
Call        t33 = invoke t30.PutState(t32, t19)
Return      t33
```

Listing 1.1. SSA Samples

4.2 Program Information Extraction

Based on the extracted Go language SSA, we use the Class Hierarchy Analysis (CHA) algorithm to construct a function dependency graph. For each called function, the function dependency graph can quickly locate the instructions that call the function, as well as the basic blocks and functions to which these instructions belong. In the CHA algorithm, we traverse the smart contract functions, performing a preorder traversal of the corresponding SSA basic blocks within each smart contract function. If there is a function call instruction, the relationship between the called function and the calling function is stored in the function dependency graph in the form of a graph. The algorithm for implementing the CHA algorithm is described as follows.

4.3 Feature Detection

In both the write-read and range query risks, we involve corresponding read and write operations. Therefore, detecting these operations is crucial. For the detection of the read-write control flow mentioned earlier, especially considering the impact of encapsulated read-write operations and defer operations, we employ a method of read and write property propagation (see Fig. 3).

We can mark the native read-write operations of Hyperledger Fabric as initial read-write functions. By marking the read-write operations in smart contract methods that call these native functions, we implement read-write property propagation while preserving the characteristic of delayed writes within functions using defer. Additionally, we prune the function call relationships to exclude functions that do not participate in read-write operations.

Based on the implementation of read-write property propagation, we can more accurately analyze the control flow to find corresponding read-write events for each smart contract transaction. This approach addresses the difficulties faced by traditional static feature matching tools in handling indirect function calls and delayed writes.

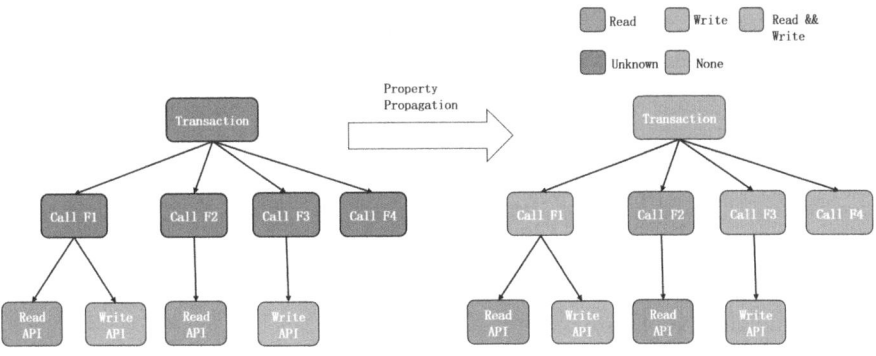

Fig. 3. Read and Write Property Propagation.

5   Evaluation

5.1   Experimental Description

Due to limited comparable objects in open-source security research related to Hyperledger Fabric, we selected ChainCodeAnalyzer [10] and HFCCT [5] as comparison tools for our experiments. Both research projects are open-sourced and cover most of the vulnerability types proposed by our tool.

Given that Hyperledger Fabric primarily serves the enterprise sector, open-source datasets are scarce. We obtained 50 Hyperledger Fabric chaincodes from sources like open-source communities to serve as our comparison dataset.

We conducted two experiments: a comparative experiment and a vulnerability injection experiment. Due to the scarcity of real vulnerability code in the collected samples, in the comparative experiment, we directly tested the collected chaincodes to verify the accuracy of the tools' vulnerability detection. Building on the comparative experiment, we attempted manual vulnerability injections to increase the number of vulnerabilities and find out the tools' detection recall rate.

To facilitate subsequent experimental explanations, we introduce the following concepts. These concepts will not be reiterated when mentioned in the experimental data:

(1) TP (True Positive): Number of samples detected as vulnerabilities that are actually vulnerabilities.
(2) FP (False Positive): Number of samples detected as vulnerabilities but are not actual vulnerabilities.
(3) FN (False Negative): Number of samples detected as non-vulnerabilities but are actually vulnerabilities.

To standardize the comparison of different tools, we propose the calculation of precision (precise) and recall. Precision measures the proportion of true vulnerabilities among all reported vulnerabilities, while recall measures the proportion of true vulnerabilities that were correctly identified by the tool among all actual vulnerabilities.

$$precise = \frac{TP}{TP + FP} \tag{1}$$

$$recall = \frac{TP}{TP + FN} \tag{2}$$

5.2   Comparative Experiment

In our comparative experiment conducted on the 50 chaincodes, the results are as follows (Table 1).

Table 1. Result of Comparative Experiment.

Tools	TP	TP+FP	Precise
Ours	8	11	72.7%
Chaincode Analyzer	6	17	35.3%
HFCCT	6	15	40%

Our tool detected the fewest number of vulnerabilities. Both ChainCodeAnalyzer and HFCCT reported numerous false positives related to missing range query validation. This is because both tools primarily detect whether the corresponding API functions are invoked for range queries, without recognizing that the essence of the vulnerability lies in the validation omission caused by corresponding writes to the range query content. Moreover, range query invocations are widely used in common scenarios of smart contracts, leading to an increased number of false positive detections.

Our proposed method of propagating read-write properties better identifies potential logical vulnerabilities such as indirect function calls where write operations precede read operations. In actual development, developers often do not simply perform a read operation immediately after writing to a key; instead, such logical vulnerabilities typically involve complex nesting of read and write functions.

5.3   Injection Experiment

To achieve better detection comparison, we injected 30 vulnerabilities into the 50 smart contracts and evaluated the recall rate of vulnerability detection based on this setup. We conducted vulnerability injection experiments and compared the corresponding results (Tables 2).

Table 2. Result of Injection Experiment.

Tools	TP	Recall
Ours	30	100%
Chaincode Analyzer	20	67.8%
HFCCT	20	67.8%

Although the other two tools using static analysis methods exhibit high false positive rates, they still manage to effectively detect some vulnerabilities, resulting in better recall performance. It is important to note that due to the limited techniques used in vulnerability injection, manual injection inevitably leads to better performance in vulnerability injection experiments. However, the combined results from the comparative dataset already demonstrate the effectiveness of our tool.

6   Conclusion

This paper discusses the sources of potential read-write operation vulnerabilities in smart contracts on the Hyperledger Fabric platform, as well as the forms and destructiveness of these vulnerabilities. Based on vulnerability detection, this paper also proposes a static analysis algorithm for detecting read-write vulnerabilities. Building on the shortcomings of current vulnerability detection algorithms, we conduct a deeper analysis of read-write control flow and data flow. Our approach provides more precise feature extraction and matching compared to previous methods targeting common read-write function detections. Through relevant experiments, our method demonstrates improvements addressing the shortcomings of current research.

References

1. Androulaki, E., et al.: Hyperledger fabric: a distributed operating system for permissioned blockchains. In: Proceedings of the Thirteenth EuroSys Conference, pp. 1–15 (2018)
2. Buterin, V., et al.: A next-generation smart contract and decentralized application platform. White Paper **3**(37), 2–1 (2014)
3. Gao, J., Liu, H., Li, Q., Chen, Z.: Research on smart contract security vulnerability detection technology. Secrecy Sci. Technol. **1**, 22–25 (2020)
4. Google: Go SSA introduction. https://go.dev/src/cmd/compile/internal/ssa
5. Li, P., et al.: A vulnerability detection framework for hyperledger fabric smart contracts based on dynamic and static analysis. In: Proceedings of the 26th International Conference on Evaluation and Assessment in Software Engineering, pp. 366–374 (2022)
6. Li, Z., Wang, Y., Wen, S., Ding, Y.: Evil chaincode: APT attacks based on smart contract. In: Xu, G., Liang, K., Su, C. (eds.) FCS 2020. CCIS, vol. 1286, pp. 178–196. Springer, Singapore (2020). https://doi.org/10.1007/978-981-15-9739-8_15

7. Lv, P., Wang, Y., Wang, Y., Zhou, Q.: Potential risk detection system of hyper-ledger fabric smart contract based on static analysis. In: 2021 IEEE Symposium on Computers and Communications (ISCC), pp. 1–7. IEEE (2021)
8. Nakamoto, S.: Bitcoin: a peer-to-peer electronic cash system (2008)
9. Szabo, N.: Formalizing and securing relationships on public networks. First Monday (1997)
10. Yamashita, K., Nomura, Y., Zhou, E., Pi, B., Jun, S.: Potential risks of hyperledger fabric smart contracts. In: 2019 IEEE International Workshop on Blockchain Oriented Software Engineering (IWBOSE), pp. 1–10. IEEE (2019)
11. Zhao, J., Nagarakatte, S., Martin, M.M., Zdancewic, S.: Formalizing the LLVM intermediate representation for verified program transformations. In: Proceedings of the 39th Annual ACM SIGPLAN-SIGACT Symposium on Principles of Programming Languages, pp. 427–440 (2012)
12. Zheng, Z., Xie, S., Dai, H.N., Chen, X., Wang, H.: Blockchain challenges and opportunities: a survey. Int. J. Web Grid Serv. **14**(4), 352–375 (2018)

A Dataset Quality Evaluation Algorithm for Data Trading on Blockchain

Bingchuan Chen[1,2(✉)], Jiarui Chen[3], Gansen Zhao[3,4], and Zhihao Hou[3,4]

[1] School of Statistic and Mathematics, Guangdong University of Finance and Economics, Guangzhou 510320, China
`chbingch@mail2.sysu.edu.cn`
[2] Institute of Artificial Intelligence and Deep Learning, Guangdong University of Finance and Economics, Guangzhou 510320, China
[3] School of Computer Science, South China Normal University, Guangzhou 510631, China
[4] Key Lab on Cloud Security and Assessment Technology of Guangzhou, South China Normal University, Guangzhou 510631, China

Abstract. As a vital solution for data trading, blockchain often carries a substantial amount of critical data. Consequently, data quality, as a crucial evaluation metric, plays a key role in facilitating data trading on the blockchain. In the process of comprehensively evaluating the quality of multi-field datasets, it is crucial to determine the importance coefficient of each data item. The importance evaluation methods of data items include subjective methods that depend on expert scoring, as well as objective methods based on statistical methods. Objective methods evaluate field importance based on the laws of data itself. However, such methods start from the quality of data to be evaluated, and cannot reflect the mutual dependency between data items and the resulting field importance. To solve this problem, this article starts from the business dependency between data items, constructs a directed graph, namely dependency network. On this basis, according to the characteristics and quantity of data items that depend on fields, we propose the FieldRank algorithm. The algorithm objectively quantifies and evaluates the importance of each field, so that the field importance weight obtained based on the algorithm is directly related to the actual business and is more close to the essence of data business. Therefore, this algorithm can provide objective data quality evaluation results for data use. Practice has proved that in the case of large amounts of big data and closely related businesses, the data quality evaluation results obtained by this method are more close to actual business practice.

Keywords: Data quality · Blockchain · Importance of data items · Dependency network · PageRank

1 Introduction

In recent years, advancements in artificial intelligence and big data have led to a significant increase in data demand. However, data owners and model owners

G. Zhao et al. (Eds.): BWTAC 2024, CCIS 2277, pp. 153–167, 2025.
https://doi.org/10.1007/978-981-97-9412-6_14

do not always trust each other. The decentralized nature of blockchain precisely addresses the challenges of data trading between different organizations and entities [1]. Data quality is a crucial factor for both parties in reaching a data trading agreement. Therefore, data quality plays a key role in the completion of data trading and the pricing of data on the blockchain.

Current data quality detection mainly evaluates different aspects of data, including data integrity, uniqueness, consistency, accuracy, timeliness, etc., which evaluates the quality of data from different perspectives. However, there is currently no comprehensive scoring method that can evaluate which batch of data has better quality among multiple batches of data and give a comprehensive answer. Therefore, some scholars begin to study the overall assessment and score through the weighted sum method. They assign a weight to each metric of the data and then multiply and sum it with the score of the metric detection result to obtain the score of data quality. The equation is $Q_D = \sum_{i=1}^{n} \sum_{j=1}^{m} w_j a_{ij}$, where a_{ij} is the score of the detection result of rule i on field j, and w_j is the weight of field j. Scholars' research on this equation mainly focuses on two aspects: the selection of rules and the setting of weight. The selection of the rules continues the multi-angle judgment criteria described previously while the setting of weight are divided into manual evaluation, statistical evaluation and comprehensive evaluation [5]. Manual evaluation is directly related to the evaluator's own academic and business background, which has poor objectivity. Statistical evaluation is objective, but it is mainly based on the statistical characteristics of the data itself, limited to statistical features and lacking in the evaluation of business dimension, which results in incomplete evaluation results. Comprehensive evaluation is a combination of manual and statistical evaluation, which also lacks a unified standard for quantifying the weight of the business itself.

To sum up, in the assessment process of data quality, how to objectively formulate the weight of each score so that the score of data quality is more consistent with business logic has become an urgent problem to be solved. In response to this challenge, this article start from the business logic and association of each field, and rely on the dependence between data items (the interdependent relationship in the meaning of data business) to construct a directed graph based on the dependence between data - Dependency Network. Based on the PageRank algorithm, we propose FieldRank, a data quality evaluation method based on dependency network. This method can take into account the business meaning of data without the need for subjective scoring, and establish a method, which is relatively objective and takes into account business logic comprehensively, to determine the weights in a data quality evaluation system.

2   Related Work

High-quality data is more likely to attract data purchaser. Therefore, blockchain-based data trading systems typically consider data quality as a key parameter for data transaction rewards [2]. Other data applications on the blockchain, such as federated learning [3] and crowd computing [4], also focus on data quality and use it as an important reference for incentive mechanisms.

For the data quality evaluation, scientific researchers mainly focus on two aspects. One is the establishment of the evaluation system and the other is the setting of the weight of evaluation metrics.

2.1 Establishment of Evaluation System

In view of the lack of quantitative analysis systems and methods in the data quality evaluation, Yang Qingyun and others proposed a six-tuple quality evaluation model $M = \langle D, I, R, W, E, S \rangle$, where D is the evaluated dataset, I is the evaluation metric on the dataset D, R is the rule corresponding to the metric, W is the weight of the rule, E is the expected value of rule R (the expected result before evaluation), S is the final actual result of rule R. The construction of the evaluation model contain (i) determining the evaluation view of the dataset, (ii) selecting evaluation metrics, (iii) formulating a set of rules, (iv) calculating the score of these rule results, where W is a crucial parameter in the calculation of the model, but the paper does not propose further research and model methods on the assignment of W. Shao Yanhong proposed four primary metrics and twelve secondary metrics in view of government open data. Through expert scoring, a data quality evaluation system was established on the basis of the Analytic Hierarchy Process (AHP) [13]. Wang Bo approached the research on data quality evaluation from a different perspective. He proposed a basic quality metric model for metadata instances based on the characteristics of resources on the data platform of the forestry open government, constructing quality evaluation metrics from both the metadata element level and the metadata instance level, and proposing the calculation methods for each metric [15]. Zhang Xiaoran devised a set of transformation rules for mapping from mathematical models of data quality evaluation to ontological models, achieving the extraction of data quality evaluation ontology and constructing a universal data quality evaluation ontological model by referencing these models and rules [20]. Tao Chunhai and others proposed a data quality evaluation method from the perspective of structural match, and combined three data quality evaluation methods, including the Benford's Rule, Outlier and Bootstrap, to evaluate comprehensively the quality of data quality and finally to analyze data quality of datasets [23].

The above researches mainly focus on how to establish an evaluation system and how to select evaluation metrics. However, it doesn't provide a calculating method for comprehensive evaluation and cannot quantitatively understand and compare the quality status of different datasets as a whole.

2.2 Setting the Weights of Evaluation Metrics

Zhang Xiaojuan selected 3 major categories containing 13 metrics to evaluate the quality of the metadata on provincial government data platforms. The weight of each metric is determined using the AHP [19]. To objectively establish an evaluation system, Lu Bing used the conflict coefficient among data to combine the AHP with the Entropy Weight Method in the results. It creates an evaluation system that takes into consideration both subjective and objective factors [14].

Dai Honghao proposed a database metadata quality evaluation model based on semantic annotation. It enhances the precision of metadata quality evaluation by establishing a metadata quality evaluation semantic relevance, a metadata quality evaluation assignment matrix, and an evaluation function equation. Its construction method offers a reference idea for the construction of quality evaluation models [16]. Quarati et al. evaluated the quality of metadata corresponding to open geographical data from six countries and international sources, using seventeen metrics across three major categories. To calculate the final quality index, the article adopted a method of equally distributing weights, where the weight of each metric is $1/17$ [17]. Nogueras-Iso et al. evaluated the data quality of metadata for open government data in Spain, involving five major categories and 23 metrics for evaluation. The weight of each metric is manually assigned [18].

In addition to providing evaluation models, the above studies also defined the weight of each evaluation item, and could qualify and evaluate the quality of data. However, these approaches have several limitations, such as an excessive reliance on subjective evaluation (Expert Scoring), evaluating on data surface (Entropy Weight Method), and too simplistic settings (Equal Weight Distribution). All of them are lack of an evaluation method that starts from business logic.

Therefore, this article is dedicated to starting from the business relationships among the data and establishing an objective evaluation method for the weights of various fields, which don't rely on expert experience.

3 FiledsRank

3.1 Overview

Data quality, as an important metric for data purchaser, influences their willingness to purchase data. Figure 1 illustrates a simple data trading process. In this process, the data owner completes the data quality assessment off-chain and then uploads the quality score and relevant weight information to the blockchain. Data purchaser evaluate the data's value based on the on-chain quality scores and other information. Upon deciding to purchase, they complete the trading through a data trading contract.

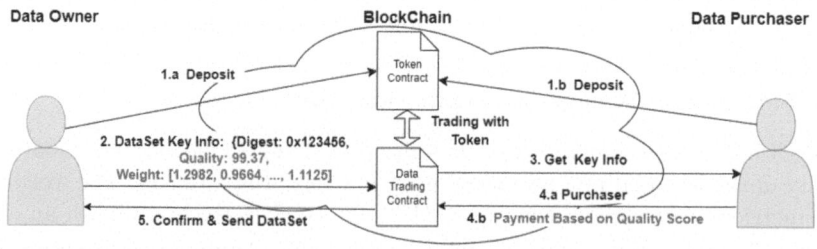

Fig. 1. A simple architecture diagram of the role of data quality in data trading

Clearly, data quality assessment has a significant impact on data trading. The FieldsRank algorithm presented in this paper takes into account the dependencies between data fields, resulting in more business-relevant data quality scores and weights. The following two subsections provide detailed definitions and methods of the FieldsRank algorithm.

3.2   Dependency Network

To establish an evaluation system for data quality, it is necessary to understand the relationships among data. Among lots of data, different data items exhibit certain dependence. By defining the dependence between data items (fields), and establishing dependency networks and dependency degree matrices, we can explain the association among data. For instance, in the medical field, the patient's basic information needs to be based on the ID card information, and the drug usage depends on the patient's diagnosis and treatment records and laboratory test results. Diagnosis and treatment records need to refer to the patient's basic information and laboratory test results. In addition to cross-field dependencies, data within fields are also related. For instance, treatment plans need to depend on data such as diagnostic results and laboratory examination results. Consequently, definitions for the dependency network are provided.

Definition 1 (Dependence). *Within the dataset D, if the value of data item f_i is calculated, constrained, or referenced from the set of data items F_i, then f_i is said to depend on F_i, called $f_i \to F_i$. If F_i consists of only n elements $\{f_{i1}, f_{i2}, \ldots f_{in}\}$, $f_i \to F_i$ can also be expressed as $f_i \to f_{i1}$, $f_i \to f_{i2}, \ldots f_i \to f_{in}$, where the k-th item represents f_i depends on the data item f_{ik}, abbreviated as f_i depends on f_{ik}.*

According to Definition 1, if $f_i \to F_i$ and $\mid F_i \mid = n$, then there are n pairs of dependencies corresponding to fi. If all such dependencies are compiled into a set, a complete dependency set is formed, as defined below.

Definition 2 (Dependency Set). *R_D is the dependency set of dataset D, where $R_D = \{\langle f_i, f_j \rangle \mid f_i \to F_j, f_j \in F_j, F_j \subseteq D\}$. If f_j belongs to D and $f_i \to F_i$, such that any f_j belongs to F_i, there is $\langle f_i, f_j \rangle$ belongs to R_D. Then R_D is called the complete dependency set of D, called $\mathcal{R}_D$.*

According to Definition 2, it is evident that the complete dependency set of a dataset is essentially a set of all dependencies within this dataset. According to these dependencies, if lines are drawn between them on a plane, a graph can be formed. The following is combined with the definition of graph to give the definition of the dependency network of the dataset.

Definition 3 (Dependency Network). *A directed graph $DN\langle V, E \rangle$ represents the dependency network of dataset D, where $V = \{f_1, f_2, \ldots, f_n\}$ is the set of data items of D, and E represents the set of arcs in DN, where $E = \{\langle f_i, f_j \rangle \mid \langle f_i, f_j \rangle \in \mathcal{R}_D\}$.*

For instance, within dataset D, there are fields f_1, f_2, f_3, f_4. If the following dependencies exist among fields: $f_2 \rightarrow \{f_1, f_4\}$, $f_4 \rightarrow \{f_1, f_3\}$, $f_3 \rightarrow \{f_1, f_2\}$, $f_1 \rightarrow \{f_2, f_4\}$, then $\mathcal{R}_D$ is the complete dependency set of D, where $\mathcal{R}_D = \{\langle f_2, f_1 \rangle, \langle f_2, f_4 \rangle, \langle f_4, f_1 \rangle, \langle f_4, f_3 \rangle, \langle f_3, f_1 \rangle, \langle f_3, f_2 \rangle, \langle f_1, f_2 \rangle, \langle f_1, f_4 \rangle\}$. The corresponding dependency network of D is illustrated in Fig. 2.

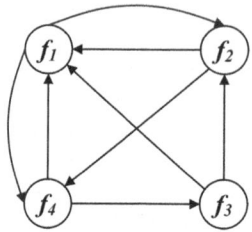

Fig. 2. The dependency network of dataset D

Definition 4 (Dependency Degree). *In a dependency network, if there is an arc from node f_i to f_j, and the out-degree of f_i is $deg^-(f_i)$, then $1/deg^-(f_i)$ represents the dependency degree of f_i on f_j.*

Definition 4 can be understood that the out-degree of node f_i represents the number of nodes it depends on. Accordingly, the dependency degree of a node it points to is one among many dependencies. Therefore, the ratio of 1 to the out-degree of the node represents the dependency degree of f_i to one of the nodes. When the dependency degree of each node relative to other nodes are expressed through a matrix, a dependency degree matrix is formed.

Definition 5 (Dependency Degreex Matrix). *Matrix M is the dependency degree matrix for dataset D, where $M_{n \times n} = \begin{bmatrix} m_{11} & \cdots & m_{1n} \\ \vdots & \ddots & \vdots \\ m_{n1} & \cdots & m_{nn} \end{bmatrix}$, and m_{ij} represents the dependency degree of data item f_j on f_i. If $N_j = deg^-(f_j)$ represents the out-degree of data item f_j in $DN\langle V, E \rangle$, then it follows:*

$$m_{ij} = \begin{cases} \frac{1}{N_j}, & f_j \rightarrow f_i \\ 0, & otherwise \end{cases} \tag{1}$$

For example, according to the data item dependency network illustrated in Fig. 1, the dependency degree matrix of dataset D can be obtained:

$$M = \begin{bmatrix} 0 & 1/2 & 1/2 & 1/2 \\ 1/2 & 0 & 1/2 & 0 \\ 0 & 0 & 0 & 1/2 \\ 1/2 & 1/2 & 0 & 0 \end{bmatrix}$$

3.3 Fileds Rank Model

The Importance Coefficient of Data Items. Although there are numerous methods for evaluating the quality of data, the fundamental calculation equation remains consistent. Assuming that there are n rules for evaluating the quality of datasets D, with m data items, and Q_D is the final evaluation value:

$$Q_D = \sum_{i=1}^{n} \sum_{j=1}^{m} w_j a_{ij}, \tag{2}$$

where a_{ij} represents the score of rule r_i to field $f_j \in D$, where w_j represents the importance of f_j. If there is no detection of data item j in rule i, $a_{ij} = 0$. To ensure the objectivity of Q_D, w_j and its corresponding scores r_i should have quantifiable and objective characteristics. Currently, scholars have conducted in-depth research on the objectivity of data quality detection rules r_i. However, there is a lack of studies and relatively objective methods on how to quantify the weights of the fields involved in each rule. Most researches take averages or use expert scoring to evaluate w_j, which lacks objectivity. Therefore, this article aims to find a method for objectively determining the weight of rule w_j on the basis of using this evaluation model. From Eq. (2), w_j represents the level of importance of a field within the datasets. Consequently, this article refers to w_j as the importance coefficient of j.

From actual business we can know that the importance of fields is directly related to the dependencies among fields. As discussed earlier, these dependencies among data items can form a dependency network. Therefore, this article proposes an objective criterion for importance evaluation based on the PageRank algorithm.

PageRank Algorithm. The PageRank algorithm, which was designed to measure the importance of web pages in search retrieval, was originally proposed by L. Page and others at Google. The core principle of this algorithm is that the more times a web page is cited or cited by important websites, the more important it is [21]. The equation is as follows:

$$\boldsymbol{Rank} = \alpha \cdot \boldsymbol{e} + (1 - \alpha) M \cdot \boldsymbol{Rank}, \tag{3}$$

where $\boldsymbol{Rank}$ is a column vector, and r_i represents that the initial importance of web page i is $1/n$, and n is the total number of web pages. M is an $n * n$ matrix, whose elements represent that web page j has an outbound link to web page, and N_j represents the total number of outbound links from j.

$$m_{ij} = \begin{cases} \frac{1}{N_j}, & N_j > 0 \\ 0, & N_j = 0 \end{cases}$$

The vector $\boldsymbol{e}$ is an all-ones column vector $\left[e_1, e_2, \ldots, e_n\right]^T$, where $e_i = 1$. α is attenuation coefficient, whose value is below 0.2, typically chosen to be 0.15 [21].

The PageRank algorithm is convergent, and experiments have confirmed that the PageRank algorithm can effectively evaluate the importance of web pages [22].

This article forms the data relationship into a directed graph, uses the PageRank algorithm to evaluate the importance of each data item, and uses this as the coefficient of the quality evaluation model to specify quantifiable evaluation metrics.

Data Quality Evaluation Algorithm Based on Dependency Networks. According to the previous definition of dependency network, it can be seen that the dependency of data items can be equated to the outbound link relationship of the network, which means that the more times a data item is depended upon, the higher its importance. Similarly, a data item is more important if it depends on other more important data items.

The practical significance aligns that when a field consistently depends on other data items, it indicates the field's importance. As long as an error occurs in this field, it will affect more datasets, so its importance will naturally be higher. Correspondingly, if a data item is very important, abnormalities in the data item it depends on will directly impact the datasets of this field, so the dependent fields are also important. Therefore, with reference to the expression of the PageRank algorithm, two assumptions are added for the dependency network:

Assumption 1. *The importance of a data item increases with the number of times it is depended upon:*

$$w_i \propto d(i)$$

Assumption 2. *The importance of a data item increases if it is depended upon by other highly significant data items:*

$$w_i \propto w_j, f_j \to f_i$$

In the equation above, $d(i)$ represents the number of times data item depended upon, w_i and w_j represent the importance (weight) of data items i and j.

According to Eq. (2), data quality evaluation is based on rules. Different rules may examine the data of the same data item from different dimensions. Some rules might be designed to check for "non-empty", while others might examine the "uniqueness" of data item values. If a data item is subject to multiple checking rules, it indicates that the field is of higher importance. Therefore, in addition to the two assumptions previously introduced, this work will also introduce a third assumption:

Assumption 3. *The importance of a data item increases with the number of quality checking rules it is subjected to:*

$$w_i \propto |R_i|$$

In the equation above, R_i represents the set of rules to field i.

The first two assumptions determine the importance of each data item according to the FieldsRank algorithm below. Given that Eq. (2) serves as the basis for evaluating the quality of data, where a_{ij} represents the score of rule r_i to data item $f_j \in D$. Therefore, the occurrence of the same data item in multiple rules leads to its repeated computation in Eq. (2). It reflects Assumption 3, which is the transformed Eq. (4) from Eq. (2):

$$Q_D = \sum_{j=1}^{m} (w_j \sum_{i=1}^{n} a_{ij}) \tag{4}$$

According to Assumption 1 and 2, the following text introduces an importance evaluation algorithm of data items based on the dependency network. This algorithm will be referred to below as the evaluation algorithm or FieldsRank.

Assume that D is a dataset to be evaluated, consisting of $f_1, f_2, \ldots, f_n$, and $\mathcal{R}_D$ is a set of complete dependency. Starting from the dataset, DN is established by analyzing the relationship between fields and then iterates.

Algorithm 1. FieldsRank Algorithm

1: Analyze the dependency among the data items in dataset D to construct a Dependency Network (DN) among fields.
2: According to Definition 4, based on the DN, compute dependency degree between various data items, and construct a dependency degree matrix $M = \begin{bmatrix} m_{11} & \cdots & m_{1n} \\ \vdots & \ddots & \vdots \\ m_{n1} & \cdots & m_{nn} \end{bmatrix}$, where m_{ij} is determined as equation (1).
3: Set an initial weight $w_i = 1/n$ for each field f_i, forming an initial weight vector $\boldsymbol{Rank} = [1/n, 1/n, \ldots, 1/n]^T$.
4: Establish a vector of ones $e = [1, 1, \ldots, 1]^T$.
5: Set $\boldsymbol{Rank'} = \boldsymbol{Rank}$.
6: Update $\boldsymbol{Rank} : \boldsymbol{Rank} = \alpha \cdot e + (1 - \alpha)M \cdot \boldsymbol{Rank}$, where $\alpha = 0.15$.
7: If $\boldsymbol{Rank} \neq \boldsymbol{Rank'}$, return to Step 5. Otherwise, stop and output $\boldsymbol{Rank}$.

Given that this method is based on the PageRank algorithm, it is evident that the FieldsRank algorithm is also convergent, meaning that the algorithm can be stopped. Eventually, it can obtain the importance weight w_i of each field f_i within the dataset D to be evaluated. By incorporating these results into Eq. (4) and operating it with the score of each rule to the field, you can get the quality evaluation value of D. In fact, it can be proved that the initial value of the importance vector Rank in this algorithm is not important. After multiple iterations, each of its components will eventually converge to a fixed value. For the sake of simplicity, the initial values of the components of $\boldsymbol{Rank}$ in this article are $1/n$.

The input of FieldsRank is the field dependency network shown in Fig. 1. After 222 iterations, the importance weights of the four fields in the dataset D

can be obtained: $\boldsymbol{Rank} = [1.2982, 0.9664, 0.6228, 1.1125]$. It can be seen that field f_3 is depended on the least, and field f_1 is depended on the most. Therefore, the importance coefficient of f_3 is the smallest, and the importance coefficient of f_1 is the largest.

4   FieldsRank in Medical Data Evaluation

There are a variety of business topics in the massive data. This article selects multiple medical topics from the electronic health record (EHR) data of a large hospital for research. The EHR data encompasses over 90 data themes, provided by more than 20 departments. To illustrate the role of FieldsRank in data quality evaluation, this article only selects the "Patient Information"(PI), "Medical Records"(MR), "Medication Usage"(MU), "Laboratory Examination Results"(LER). In these four topics, we select a total of 20 fields to establish a dependency netwok (Fig. 3).

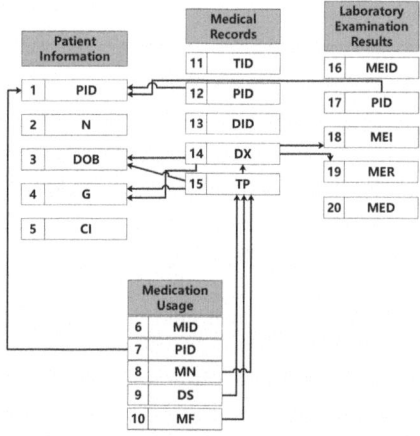

Fig. 3. Medical Data Topic Dependency Network for Electronic Health Record

The "Patient Information" includes five main fields: Patient ID(1, PID), Name(2, N), Date of Birth(3, DOB), Gender(4, G), and Contact Information(5, CI). The "Medical Records" includes five main fields: Treatment ID(11, TID), Patient ID(12, PID), Doctor ID(13, DID), Diagnosis(14, DX), Treatment Plan(15, TP). The "Medication Usage" includes five main fields: Medication ID(6, MID), Patient ID(7, PID), Medication Name(8, MN), Dosage(9, DS), Medication Frequency(10, MF). The "Laboratory Examination Results" includes five main fields: Medical Examination ID(16, MEID), Patient ID(17, PID), Medical Examination Items(18, MEI), Medical Examination Results(19, MER), Medical Examination Date(20, MED). These fields form a dataset D. There is a dependency relationship between each field in dataset D, which forms a dependency network.

The ID fields are used to facilitate the maintenance of key fields. They are typically used as keywords and foreign keys. In medical, the purpose of these ID fields is to link to meaningful fields. For example, when providing TP based on MER, doctors need to refer to the patient's DOB and G. Similarly, DS and MF must also consider the patient's G and DOB. They have dependency relationship and their dependency network is illustrated in Fig. 2.

According to Fig. 2, the complete dependency set of the Medical Electronic Health Record dataset D is $\mathcal{R}_D = \{\langle 7,1\rangle, \langle 8,15\rangle, \langle 9,15\rangle, \langle 10,15\rangle, \langle 12,1\rangle, \langle 14,3\rangle, \langle 14,4\rangle, \langle 14,18\rangle, \langle 14,19\rangle, \langle 15,3\rangle, \langle 15,4\rangle, \langle 15,14\rangle, \langle 17,1\rangle\}$, and its dependency degree matrix M can be obtained by Eq. (2), according to this complete dependency set as shown in Table 1.

Table 1. Values of the Elements in the Dependency Degree Matrix

	1	2	···	7	8	9	10	11	12	13	14	15	16	17	18	19	20
1									1				1				
2																	
3											1/4	1/3					
4											1/4	1/3					
5																	
6																	
7					1												
						···											
14												1/3					
15					1	1	1										
16																	
17																	
18										1/4							
19										1/4							
20																	

Incorporating the above results into the FieldsRank, convergence is achieved after four iterations. The importance coefficients of 20 fields are shown in Table 2.

Table 2 reveals that field 1,15, which are the PID and TP in the PI, have the highest coefficients. In this topic, the relationships among fields indicate that the PID in three tables all depends on the PID from the PI. Likewise, MN, DS and MF in the MU depend on the TP.

Therefore, these two fields are of the highest importance, and they are also crucial in real-life scenarios. With the above coefficients, it is only necessary to examine the quality of the relevant checking rule i set by each field j and obtain the checking scores a_{ij}, and then find the corresponding weight w_j in Table 2. According to Eq. (4), the data quality score of the overall dataset can be calculated, which can be weighted according to the importance of the data items. This score represents an objective assessment, which objectively reflects the data situation of the dataset.

Table 2. Weight of Each Field of Medical Electronic Health Record

field	1	2	3	4	5	6	7	8	9	10
weight	0.5325	0.1500	0.3648	0.3648	0.1500	0.1500	0.1500	0.1500	0.1500	0.1500
field	11	12	13	14	15	16	17	18	19	20
weight	0.1500	0.1500	0.1500	0.3009	0.5325	0.1500	0.1500	0.2139	0.2139	0.1500

In practice, the dependency fields of the data are not within the scope of data quality detection. For example, in quality inspection, the accurate reference for the "Date of Birth"(3,DOB) in this example should be the "personnel information"(PI) of the ID card issuing authority. However, since this data is not subject to quality detection, putting it into the complete dependency set could lead to abnormalities in calculating importance. Therefore, in this example, the reference of "Date of Birth"(3,DOB) is set as a field in the basic data. When establishing the complete dependency set, only relationships among fields subject to quality detection are considered, ensuring the accuracy of the data's weights.

Assume that for the above data model, there are two datasets D_1 and D_2 for integrity and consistency testing (scoring criteria for each field, for example, the integrity is based on whether the field is empty, and the consistency is based on the data size between fields and the accuracy of the calculation relationship.)

Detection Results for Dataset D_1:

(1) **Integrity:** Out of 20 fields, except for Name(2, N) in PI at 80 points and Diagnosis(19, DX) in LER at 90 points, all others are at 100 points.
(2) **Consistency:** Out of 20 fields, except for Medical Examination Date(20,MED) in LER at 86 points, all others are at 100 points.

By incorporating the coefficients from Table 2 and these detection results into Eq. (4), the final data quality score for dataset D1 is calculated to be 887.421. To keep the score within a 100-point scale, the score can be divided by twice the sum of the coefficients, which is:

$$Q_D = \frac{\sum_{j=1}^{20}(w_j \sum_{i=1}^{20} a_{ij})}{2\sum_{j=1}^{20} w_j} \tag{5}$$

The final score is 99.19; if calculated assuming equal importance for all components, the average result is 98.90.

Detection Results for Dataset D_2:

(1) **Integrity:** Out of 20 fields, except for Patient ID(1, PID) in PI and Treatment Plan(15, TP) in MR, both scored at 90, all others are at 100 points.
(2) **Consistency:** Out of 20 fields, except for Diagnosis(14, DX) in MR at 90 points, all others are at 100 points.

Incorporating the coefficients from Table 2 with these detection results into Eq. (5), and the final data quality score of datasets D_2 is 98.47; if the average result is calculated, the score is 99.25 (Table 3).

Table 3. Comparison of Data Quality Scores.

Dataset	Average	FieldsRank
D_1	98.90	99.19
D_2	99.25	98.47

From the above two examples, if judged by the average, the data quality of D_1 at 98.90 is less than that of D_2 at 99.25. Thus, the data quality of datasets D_1 is inferior to that of D_2. However, after using FieldsRank to calculate the weights, the results D_1 is 99.19 and D_2 is 98.47. The conclusion is that the datasets D_1 is superior to D_2. According to the actual conditions, although each metric in D_1 scores relatively high, the integrity of key fields such as Patient ID and Treatment Plan is poor and impacts the data across other tables, hence exerting a larger influence. The quality index from FieldsRank can more accurately reflect the inherent importance of the data, and provide a more objective measure of data quality.

5   Conclusions

The FieldsRank algorithm offers a more practical evaluation metric for data trading and pricing on the blockchain. Meanwhile, this article introduces the FieldsRank algorithm for evaluating the importance of data items in datasets. This algorithm constructs a dependency network based on the dependencies between data items and utilizes PageRank principles to determine the importance coefficients of each field. These coefficients are then combined with scores from field quality evaluation rules (e.g., completeness, uniqueness, consistency, accuracy, timeliness, etc.) to compute an objective overall index of data quality for the dataset. This article conducts empirical research on electronic health record (EHR) data from real-life hospitals and obtains more reasonable quality evaluation conclusions.

In fact, the FieldsRank method is not only used to assess the weights of various fields in healthcare data quality evaluation but can also be applied in different domains. By collaborating with domain experts to establish dependency matrices between fields, comprehensive evaluations of data quality can be conducted, demonstrating good scalability.

In addition to evaluating data quality based on importance, it is also crucial to consider the audience. Data targeting different audiences at the city or national level, can have vastly different impacts. Therefore, data users and audiences are also important metrics for evaluating data quality. Incorporating attributes of data users into the evaluation of data quality will be a focus of future work in this paper.

References

1. An, B., Xiao, M., Liu, A., Xu, Y., Zhang, X., Li, Q.: Secure crowdsensed data trading based on blockchain. IEEE Trans. Mob. Comput. **22**, 1763–1778 (2023)
2. Donghui, H., Li, Y., Pan, L., Li, M., Zheng, S.: A blockchain-based trading system for big data. Comput. Netw. **191**, 107994–108006 (2021)
3. Qi, J., Lin, F., Chen, Z., Tang, C., Jia, R., Li, M.: High-quality model aggregation for blockchain-based federated learning via reputation-motivated task participation. IEEE Internet Things J. **9**, 18378–18391 (2022)
4. Huang, J., et al.: Blockchain-based mobile crowd sensing in industrial systems. IEEE Trans. Ind. Inform. **16**, 6553–6563 (2020)
5. Liu, Z., Wang, J., Li, Q.: A survey of research on metadata quality evaluation. Inf. Stud. Theory Appl. 42–48 (2022)
6. Liu, P.: Design of DQAF-based data quality assessment mechanism. Stat. Decis. 49–52 (2021)
7. Bai, X., Kuang, M.: Research on the quality control mechanism of government digital information resources. Theory Appl. Inf. Stud. 71–78 (2021)
8. Tan, T., Zhong, H.: Research on comprehensive data quality management model of public credit information system based on PDCA theory. CCNews 103–106 (2017)
9. Zhou, L., Xu, C., Song, D.: Research on the feedback mechanism of government data quality optimization from the perspective of smart cities. J. Intell. 146–156 (2021)
10. Han, X.: Research on data quality evaluation in the age of big data. Electron. Technol. Softw. Eng. 158–160 (2020)
11. Yang, Q., Zhao, P., Yang, D., Tang, S., Tong, Y.: Research on data quality assessment methodology. Comput. Eng. Appl. 3–4, 15 (2004)
12. Zeng, R., Ding, L., Wang, W.: Improved model of CGSS data quality evaluation. J. Xiangtan Univ. (Nat. Sci. Ed.) 22–27 (2021)
13. Shao, Y.: The research on construction of quality evaluation index system of Chinese open government data. HeBei University, China 3–4, 15 (2019)
14. Lu, B.: Research and Implementation of Governmental Data Quality Evaluation and Promotion. XiDian University, 3–4, 15 (2020)
15. Wang, B., Wen, J.: Quality evaluation of forestry open government data based on metadata. J. China Soc. Sci. Tech. Inf. **40**(02), 173–183 (2021)
16. Dai, H., Shi, J.: Quality evaluation method of database metadata based on semantic annotation. Comput. Prod. Circ. 178 (2020)
17. Alfonso, Q., Monica, D., Sergio, R.: Geospatial open data usage and metadata quality. Int. J. Geo-Inf. 30 (2021)

18. Nogueras-Iso, J., Lacasta, J., Ureña-Cámara, M.A., Ariza-López, F.J.: Quality of metadata in open data portals. IEEE Access 60364–60382 (2021)
19. Zhang, X., Tan, J.: Research on metadata quality assessment of China's provincial government data open platform. E-Government 58–71 (2019)
20. Zhang, X., Yuan, M.: General data quality assessment model and ontological implementation. J. Comput. Res. Dev. **55**(06), 1333–1344 (2018)
21. Florescu, C., Caragea, C.: A position-biased pagerank algorithm for keyphrase extraction. In: In Proceedings of the Thirty-First AAAI Conference on Artificial Intelligence, San Francisco, California, USA, pp. 4923–4924 (2017)
22. Brin, S., Page, L.: The anatomy of a large-scale hypertextual Web search engine. Comput. Netw. ISDN Syst. 107–117 (1998)
23. Tao, C., Zhong, G.: Data quality assessment method from the perspective of structure matching. Stat. Decis. 17–22 (2023)

A Variable (n, n) Threshold Secret Sharing Scheme Based on Paillier Cryptosystem

Yujie Shen[1,2]([✉]), Hongliang Cai[1,2], Jincheng Zhou[1,2], Lei Su[1,2], and Dan Tang[1,2]

[1] School of Software Engineering, Chengdu University of Information Technology, Chengdu, China
751978029@qq.com
[2] Sichuan Province Engineering Technology, Research Center of Support Software of Informatization Application, Chengdu 610225, China

Abstract. In today's digital era, blockchain, big data, cloud computing and other information technologies are booming, providing a powerful impetus for the rapid progress of human society. At the same time, the importance of information security is particularly prominent, and we hope that some important data can be protected in a proper way. This paper introduces the related concepts of two information security technologies, secret sharing technology and homomorphic encryption, as well as the basic content of Paillier encryption system, and proposes a secret sharing scheme based on Paillier algorithm for the special threshold structure of (n, n) in secret sharing. Paillier algorithm is a homomorphic encryption algorithm with good ecology and is extremely popular at present. In our scheme, it is applied to secret sharing, so that the secret sharing group has a high comprehensive computational efficiency in the cases of distributing secrets, recovering secrets, and dynamically changing threshold value.

Keywords: Secret Sharing · Paillier Cryptosystem · Homomorphic Encryption · Information Security

1 Introduction

In today's rapidly developing era of big data, a large amount of data information is generated and maintained in the world every day, and they work together to help human society run efficiently and orderly. According to the prediction of the international authoritative organization Statista, the global data volume will reach 175ZB in 2025, and will surge to 2142ZB by 2035 [1]. For reasons such as security and privacy, people hope that a lot of data can be effectively protected. Secret sharing and homomorphic encryption are two of the current hot topics in information security.

The fundamental idea of (k, n) threshold secret sharing is to split the secret information into n shares in some way and give each of the split shares to n different participants for safekeeping, so that the original secret information can be

G. Zhao et al. (Eds.): BWTAC 2024, CCIS 2277, pp. 168–174, 2025.
https://doi.org/10.1007/978-981-97-9412-6_15

recovered after rounding up the k participant's shares. The use of secret sharing schemes can prevent to a greater extent possible betrayal by some participants within the organizational structure, as well as defend against possible information theft and attacks from outside. Shamir [2] and Blakley [3] introduced the concept of secret sharing in 1979 in their respective articles with geometric and polynomial interpolation perspectives, respectively. Secret sharing also shares many similarities with today's popular blockchain technology, such as they are both multi-party and fault-tolerant in nature, and both contain ideas such as distributed storage, and consensus through specific protocols in the network. In fact, there are numerous applications that combine the two and have received a lot of attention [4,5].

Homomorphic Encryption (HE) [6] is an important branch of cryptography. Homomorphic encryption has many advantages over traditional encryption methods. Since homomorphic encryption allows data to be directly computed in the encrypted state (a form of privacy computing), this not only significantly reduces the computational complexity during computation (no decryption is required), but also greatly protects information privacy and improves data security to a large extent, which is very suitable in a variety of scenarios such as secure multi-party computing systems like blockchain [7] or conventional cloud computing [8]. In blockchain, for sensitive information that needs special protection, we can use homomorphic encryption to protect it effectively without affecting the accuracy of the relevant computation.

In this paper, an (n, n) threshold secret sharing scheme based on Paillier homomorphic encryption algorithm [9] is given, which is studied for the special case of $k = n$ in (k, n) threshold. We will explain the scheme according to the segments of secret distribution, secret recovery, and dynamic changes of threshold value from Sect. 3 onwards.

2   Paillier Cryptosystem

The security of the Paillier cryptosystem is based on the problem of prime factorization of large integers. The Paillier algorithm is described below.

Step 1: Generate the keys. First choose two large primes p and q at random and compute their product and the least common multiple of $p - 1$ and $q - 1$: $N = pq$, $\lambda = \text{lcm}(p - 1, q - 1)$. Then a number $g \in Z_{N^2}^*$ is chosen at random (Z_{N^2} means the set of all integers less than N^2 and $Z_{N^2}^*$ means the set of all numbers in Z_{N^2} that are mutually prime with N^2). We set (N, g) to the public key (for encryption) and (p, q) (or λ) to the private key (for decryption).

Step 2: Encryption. Choose a random number $r(r > 0, r \in Z_N^*)$, if $m(m > 0, m \in Z_N)$ is the message to be encrypted (plaintext) and c is the ciphertext formed on m after the encryption process $Enc(m)$:

$$c = Enc(m) = g^m r^N \bmod N^2 \tag{1}$$

Step 3: Decryption. First define the function $L(x)$: $L(x) = \frac{x-1}{N}$. The ciphertext c can get the original message m after the decryption process $Dec(c)$:

$$m = Dec(c) = \frac{L(c^\lambda \bmod N^2)}{L(g^\lambda \bmod N^2)} \bmod N \tag{2}$$

3   The Proposed Scheme

3.1   Secret Distribution

The steps of the secret distribution process are as follows:

Step 1: According to the different threshold values n of the group, use a random function to split the secret information into n parts, $m_1, m_2, ..., m_n$, satisfying the algebraic sum $\sum_{i=1}^{n} m_i = S$, and the distributor records $m_1, m_2, ..., m_n$ to facilitate possible updates at a later stage.

Step 2: The distributor is responsible for choosing parameters for the group scheme, including large prime numbers p, q of equivalent length, and distributing $N = pq$, $g = N + 1$ as the public key to all the participants in the group, $\lambda = (p-1)(q-1)$ as the private key to be kept by the authorized secret recoverer.

Step 3: According to Paillier algorithm, the secret sharer uses the split plaintext to compute the ciphertexts $c_1, c_2, ..., c_n$ corresponding to $m_1, m_2, ..., m_n$, respectively, via the public key from the equation $c_i = Enc(m_i) = g^{m_i} r^N \bmod N^2$, and then distributes them to n participants.

Taking the $(5, 5)$ threshold as an example, the secret distribution is shown in Fig. 1.

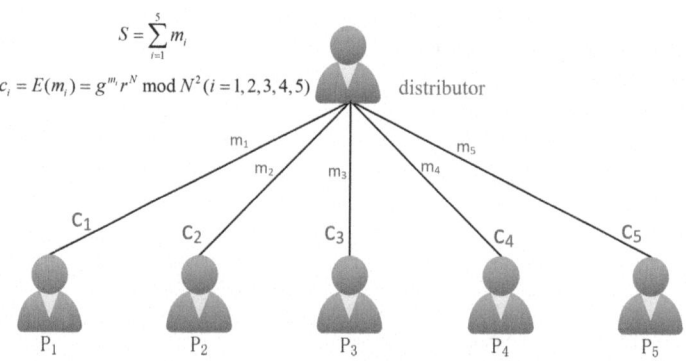

Fig. 1. Secret distribution in $(5, 5)$ threshold scheme.

The encryption process appears to have two exponential operations that appear to be of high complexity, but they are not. Firstly, r^N is a fixed value determined by the initialization parameter, which can be pre-computed with low frequency. In addition, since we use p, q of equivalent length, we can simply take $g = n+1$, instead of taking $g \in Z^*_{N^2}$ randomly as in the original method, because this can greatly reduce the arithmetic complexity while ensuring correctness and security [10]. At the encryption in step 3, the following equation is known by the binomial theorem:

$$g^m = (n + 1)^m = \binom{m}{0} n^m + \binom{m}{1} n^{m-1} + ... + \binom{m}{2} n^2 + mn + 1 \quad (3)$$

It is easy to know that the first $m - 1$ terms of $(n + 1)^m$ are all multiples of n^2, which are eliminated under the modulo n^2 operation, so the modulo exponential operation here is simplified to a single modulo multiplication operation, which greatly reduces the computational complexity:

$$(n + 1)^m \bmod n^2 = (mn + 1) \bmod n^2 \quad (4)$$

3.2   Secret Recovery

When recovering the secret, all participants contribute their share information $c_1, c_2, ..., c_n$. After multiplying, the ciphertext of the secret information $c = \prod_{i=1}^{n} c_i$ can be obtained. Through the formula $m = Dec(c) = \frac{L(c^\lambda \bmod N^2)}{L(g^\lambda \bmod N^2)} \bmod N$, where $L(x) = \frac{x-1}{N}$, the plaintext m corresponding to c can be obtained. That is the secret information S. The secret recovery process is shown in Fig. 2.

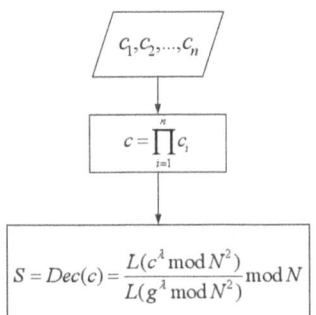

Fig. 2. Secret recovery process.

The (n, n) threshold group often involves many participants in recovering the secret, we can make full use of cloud computing resources and use the share information of each participant to calculate to get the ciphertext of the secret information, and then decrypt it to get the original secret information.

3.3   Dynamic Changes of Threshold Value

Depending on the change of the actual situation, the threshold value n of the secret sharing group may also need to change during the application process. Since Paillier algorithm is extremely straightforward and convenient in splitting secret information, we can also conveniently and efficiently start on the splitting of secret information when dealing with scenarios where the threshold value n changes dynamically. When a new participant is added, we can select one or more shares of the original participant(s) to be split to the new participant(s); and when a participant withdraws, we can split his share to other participants.

Consider first the case of participant addition. For example, if a participant is added to an (n, n) threshold sharing group, the threshold parameter then becomes $(n + 1, n + 1)$, and we can arbitrarily select $k(1 \le k \le n)$ participants $P_1, P_2, ..., P_n$ from the n participants in the group, and extract a portion of the share plaintext $m_1{}^*, m_2{}^*, ..., m_k{}^*(0 < m_k{}^* < m_k)$, respectively. The remaining shares of the plaintext are $m_1 - m_1{}^*, m_2 - m_2{}^*, ..., m_k - m_k{}^*$ and then the shares $Enc(m_1 - m_1{}^*), Enc(m_2 - m_2{}^*), ..., Enc(m_k - m_k{}^*)$ of participants $P_1{}', P_2{}', ..., P_k{}'$ are recalculated, and the share of the new participant P_{n+1} is $\prod\limits_{i=1}^{k} Enc(m_i{}^*)$, the product of the ciphertexts extracted from plaintexts $m_1{}^*, m_2{}^*, ..., m_k{}^*$.

Then consider the case of a participant withdrawing. As an example, to withdraw a participant P_x from an (n, n) threshold sharing group, the threshold parameter then becomes $(n - 1, n - 1)$, and we can split the plaintext m_x of P_x's share into $k(1 \le k \le n - 1)$ shares: $m_{x_1}, m_{x_2}, ..., m_{x_k}$, satisfying $\sum\limits_{i=1}^{k} m_{x_i} = m_x$, and then compute the ciphertexts $c_{x_1}, c_{x_2}, ..., c_{x_k}$ corresponding to these plaintexts, Finally, these ciphertext values are multiplied by the shares of each of the k arbitrarily selected participants in the group respectively, to obtain the updated shares.

Here we describe the threshold parameter change, which is the process of updating the secret shares in the process of adding and removing participants, where the number of updated shares is optional within the range of the number of participants. And obviously, the fewer shares are updated, the smaller the computation is. So in practice, we do not need to change the shares of many original participants in general, we even only need to extract the share of a single participant when adding a new participant and distribute it to the new participant; when a participant withdraws, all his shares are transferred to a single participant in the group. Therefore, the amount of reconstruction and computation can be kept small.

4   Conclusion

In this paper, we give an (n, n) threshold secret sharing scheme based on Paillier homomorphic encryption algorithm. Compared with traditional secret sharing schemes based on principles such as interpolating polynomials, this scheme is firstly simpler and more convenient in splitting the secret, without the need to generate polynomials and then compute the function values for distribution to participants. Instead, it takes advantage of the homomorphic property to split the secret information into a sum of polynomials, and then encrypts the split parts using Paillier algorithm. Since the multiplication operation of the ciphertext corresponds to the addition operation of the plaintext, the product of all shares is the ciphertext of the secret information. After obtaining the ciphertext, the recoverer can use the private key to decrypt it to obtain the original secret information. The homomorphic nature also allows the relevant information to be efficiently utilized for secure outsourced computation using network resources. In addition, the variability of the scheme is mainly reflected in the fact that it has a higher degree of freedom and convenience than the traditional method in the case of dynamic changes in threshold parameters. The reconstruction of the secret sharing group can be accomplished by a small modification of the original share information according to the actual needs.

The scheme proposed can be used for the protection of privacy information in the blockchain ledger. We can split the secret keys closely related to privacy according to the homomorphic property and distribute them to the parties involved in the transaction, and recover the privacy information through shares when needed. The whole process does not involve complex calculations and numerous parameters, nor frequent interactions, so it can achieve efficient privacy protection.

Acknowledgments. This study was supported by the Key Research and Development Program of Sichuan Province (2024ZHYS0024), and the Educational Information Technology Research Project of Sichuan Province (DSJZXKT209).

Disclosure of Interests. The authors have no competing interests to declare that are relevant to the content of this article.

References

1. Holst, A.: Volume of data/information created, captured, copied, and consumed worldwide from 2010 to 2025, Statista, June 2021
2. Shamir, A.: How to share a secret. Commun. ACM **22**(11), 612–613 (1979)
3. Blakley, G.R.: Safeguarding cryptographic keys. In: Managing Requirements Knowledge, International Workshop on. IEEE Computer Society, 1979, p. 313 (1979)
4. Li, C., Dong, M., Xin, X., Li, J., Chen, X.-B., Ota, K.: Efficient privacy-preserving in iomt with blockchain and lightweight secret sharing. IEEE Internet Things J. (2023)
5. Shree, S., Zhou, C., Barati, M.: Data protection in internet of medical things using blockchain and secret sharing method. J. Supercomput. **80**(4), 5108–5135 (2024)
6. Rivest, R.L., Adleman, L., Dertouzos, M.L., et al.: On data banks and privacy homomorphisms. Found. Secure Comput. **4**(11), 169–180 (1978)
7. Nakamoto, S.: Bitcoin: a peer-to-peer electronic cash system, 2008

8. Song, X., Wang, Y.: Homomorphic cloud computing scheme based on hybrid homomorphic encryption. In: 2017 3rd IEEE International Conference on Computer and
   Communications (ICCC). IEEE, 2017, pp. 2450–2453 (2017)
9. Paillier, P.: Public-key cryptosystems based on composite degree residuosity
   classes. In: Stern, J. (ed.) EUROCRYPT 1999. LNCS, vol. 1592, pp. 223–238.
   Springer, Heidelberg (1999). https://doi.org/10.1007/3-540-48910-X_16
10. Catalano, D., Gennaro, R., Howgrave-Graham, N., Nguyen, P.Q.: Paillier's cryp-
    tosystem revisited. In: Proceedings of the 8th ACM Conference on Computer and
    Communications Security, 2001, pp. 206–214 (2001)

Design and Validation of a Hyper-converged Blockchain Hardware and Software System Based on Domestic Chips

Xiaolong Liu[1] , Bo Yuan[2,3,4,6(✉)] , and Faguo Wu[4,5,6]

[1] Enterprise Technology Center, Aerospace Legione Technology Co., Ltd, Haidian, Beijing 100195, China

[2] School of Computer Science and Engineering, Beihang University, Haidian, Beijing 100191, China
boyuan@buaa.edu.cn

[3] State Key Laboratory of Software Development Environment, Beihang University, Haidian, Beijing 100191, China

[4] Institute of Artificial Intelligence, Beihang University, Haidian, Beijing 100191, China

[5] Key Laboratory of Mathematics, Informatics and Behavioral Semantics (LMIB), Beihang University, Haidian, Beijing 100191, China

[6] Beijing Advanced Innovation Center for Future Blockchain and Privacy Computing, Beihang University, Haidian, Beijing 100191, China

Abstract. This paper proposes a hyper-converged blockchain hardware and soft-ware sys-tem based on domestic chips. By utilizing domestically firmware, the Linux operating system, X86 architecture Hygon processors, and ARM architecture Phytium processors, combined with servers, storage, network, and independently controllable blockchain technologies, the system achieves integrated hardware and software optimization. This significantly improves performance and scalability. Experimental results demonstrate that the system performs excellently in various high-security application scenarios, providing reliable solutions for government, finance, taxation, transportation, energy, and telecommunications sectors.

Keywords: Domestic X86 architecture · domestic ARM architecture · independent firmware · Blockchain system performance optimization

1 Introduction

With the rapid development of blockchain technology, many countries have incorporated it into their national strategies. On October 24, 2019, the Politburo of the Communist Party of China emphasized accelerating blockchain technology and industrial innovation to support a strong network nation and digital economy. Consequently, blockchain has become crucial for China's digital economy. In March 2021, blockchain was included in the "14th Five-Year Plan" to develop applications in fintech, supply chain management, and government services. The Cyberspace Administration of China further promoted blockchain industry development with a pilot project list in January 2022. Despite progress, issues with node performance, security, and reliance on foreign technology persist, limiting development and threatening information security.

To address these issues and promote localization, this paper proposes a hyper-converged blockchain system based on domestic chips. The system uses independently firmware, a domestic Linux OS, and domestic X86 and ARM processors, integrating servers, storage, networks, and blockchain technology to optimize performance. The research focuses on designing the system architecture, analyzing advancements in high-performance processing and PCIE bandwidth optimization, and validating the system through performance tests. This paper demonstrates the system's advantages in performance, security, and scalability, supporting the independent innovation and application of blockchain technology in China.

The system complements traditional blockchain deployment methods, addressing current node control and domestic CPU production limitations, meeting national self-reliance needs. Using Hygon and Phytium processors, the Kylin operating system, and Chainmaker Chain, the system was independently developed and validated, promoting the localization of blockchain infrastructure. The related architecture is shown in Fig. 1.

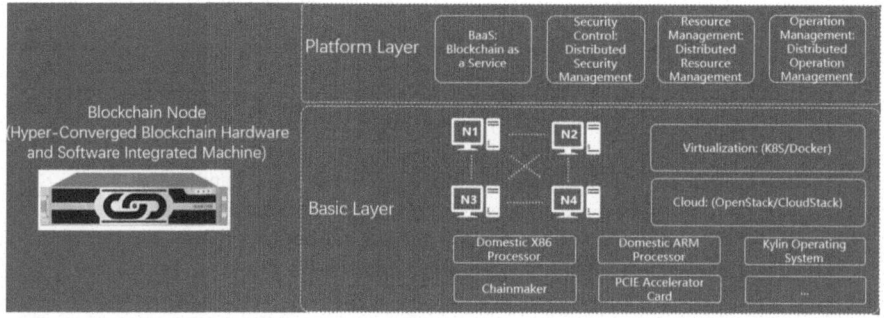

Fig. 1. Architecture of the Hyper-Converged Blockchain Hardware and Software System Based on Domestic Chips

The hyper-converged blockchain system based on domestic chips uses a 2U expansion design, supports Hygon and Phytium instruction sets, and operates on the Kylin OS with containerized and cloud deployment options. It features dynamic load balancing for Chainmaker Chain nodes, optimizing block time and size based on processor performance and energy consumption. The system includes BaaS, security monitoring, resource scheduling, and maintenance platforms. It has at least one management node, four consensus nodes, and one gigabit/10-gigabit switch, achieving a TPS peak of 9165 with a maximum power consumption of 2000 W. Supporting Chainmaker Chain, it uses 1–2 Hygon or Phytium CPUs, DDR4 memory, Kylin V10 OS, remote control, power management, real-time monitoring, and gigabit/10-gigabit communication, making it ideal for high-security blockchain applications in China.

The domestic Hygon x86 dual-socket blockchain server offers high-end specs, excellent performance, and robust IO expansion, reducing TCO for data centers. The 2U rack-mounted server with the Phytium FT-2000 + /64 processor provides robust performance and large storage, ideal for high-security information processing in government and military systems. The Kylin Advanced Server OS V10 supports critical business needs with high reliability, security, and performance, optimized for platforms like Phytium and Hygon is used in government, finance, education, and healthcare. The Chainmaker Chain is a flexible, open-source blockchain platform supporting high-performance and secure digital infrastructure in supply chain finance, carbon trading, and food traceability.

2 Methodology

2.1 Testing Scenarios

In Scenario 1, a four-node blockchain network is deployed using 4 test machines for blockchain nodes and 4 load machines for test tools. In Scenario 2, a sixteen-node blockchain network is deployed with 16 test machines for blockchain nodes and 4 load machines for test tools (Fig. 2).

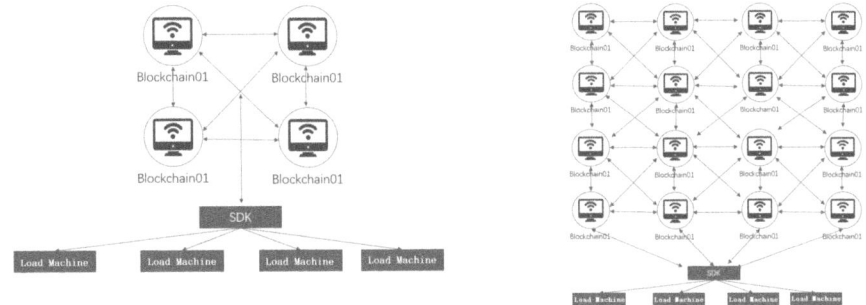

Fig. 2. Four and sixteen Blockchain Network

2.2 Testing Records

Ensure that the hyper-converged blockchain hardware and software integrated system based on domestic chips can operate normally under the following conditions. It should be able to perform initial installations, upgrades, and both complete and custom installations, including installations on non-clean environment machines. The physical machine architecture during installation based on Hygon or Phytium chips and the Kylin operating system.

(1) Functional Testing

Ensure that the following functionalities operate correctly: chain generation, node joining the chain, chaincode installation, chaincode upgrade, and the implementation of blockchain environment setup logic rules. This involves analyzing the interaction outputs or results to verify the application and its internal processes.

(2) Performance Testing

Test and evaluate the TPS (Transactions Per Second), which measures the transaction throughput per second. The goal of performance evaluation is to verify whether the performance requirements are met under the following conditions: normal expected workload and the heaviest expected workload.

For 5000 concurrent get queries, the peak TPS is 2602.5, and the average TPS is approximately 1405.8. For 10,000 concurrent get queries, the peak TPS is 9165.5 (Fig. 3).

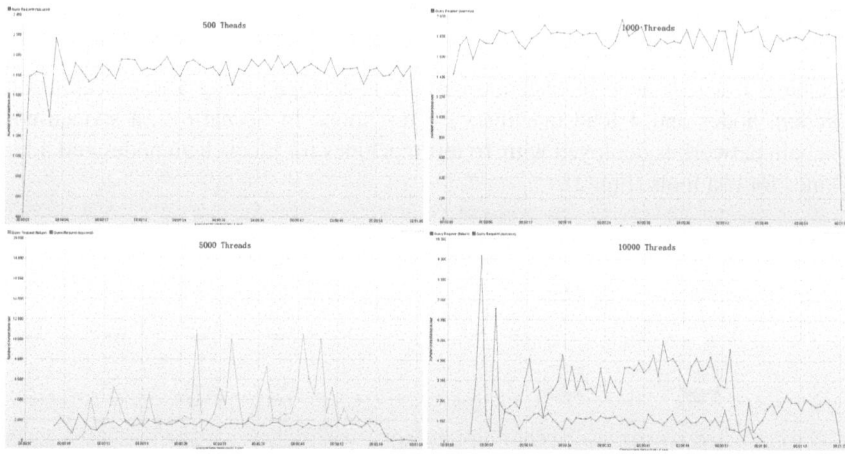

Fig. 3. TPS Line Chart for 500/1000/5000/10000 Threads get

Adjusting the Number of Concurrent Threads, the average values may vary due to network and other factors. The results are recorded as shown in Table 1.

Table 1. Linux Test Get Records

Input Data	Expected Performance (Average)	Actual Performance (Average)	Actual Performance (Peak)
Concurrent 500 Threads	1500TPS	1853.3TPS	2162.4TPS
Concurrent 1000 Threads	1500TPS	1785.2TPS	1963.2TPS
Concurrent 5000 Threads	1000TPS	1405.8TPS	2602.5TPS
Concurrent 10000 Threads	1000TPS	1098.3TPS	9165.5TPS

With 5000 concurrent put queries, the peak TPS is 2128.7, and the average TPS is approximately 1467.6. For 10000 concurrent put queries, the peak TPS is 3903.8 (Fig. 4).

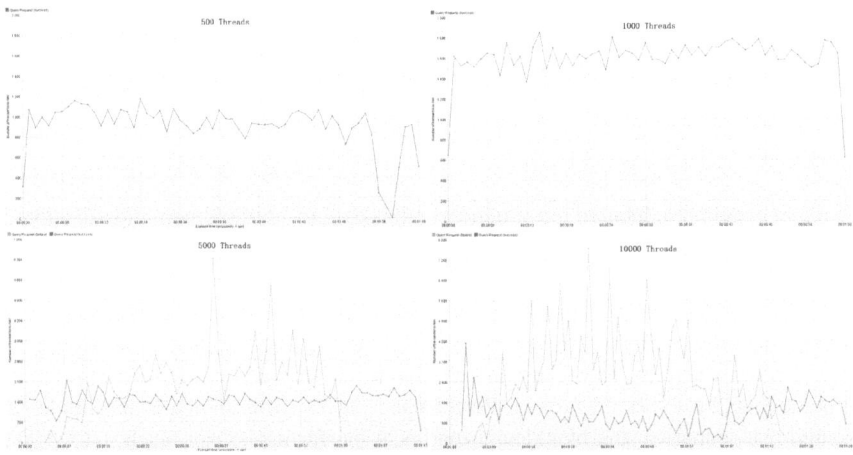

Fig. 4. TPS Line Chart for 500/1000/5000/10000 Threads put

Adjusting the Number of Concurrent Threads, the average values may vary due to network and other factors. The results are recorded as shown in Table 2.

Table 2. Linux Test Put Records

Input Data	Expected Performance (Average)	Actual Performance (Average)	Actual Performance (Peak)
Concurrent 500 Threads	800TPS	912.2TPS	1171.1TPS
Concurrent 1000 Threads	1000TPS	1625.3TPS	1850.1TPS
Concurrent 5000 Threads	1000TPS	1467.6TPS	2118.8TPS
Concurrent 10000 Threads	1000TPS	1157.5TPS	3903.8TPS

2.3 Testing Results

The hyper-converged blockchain hardware and software integrated system platform based on domestic chips has passed various tests, including networking method, communication, data storage and transmission, encryption module usability, consensus functionality and fault tolerance, smart contract functionality, deployment and startup method, node management stability, account and transaction types, account user classification and hierarchy, private key management measures, link interface management, participant joining and leaving, platform behavior auditing, user behavior auditing, and smart contract auditing. Additionally, the system successfully passed high concurrency stress tests and peak impact tests for both 4-node and 16-node configurations, as well as low-load operation tests for the 4-node configuration.

3 Conclusion

This paper provides a detailed introduction to the design and implementation of a hyper-converged blockchain hardware and software integrated system based on domestic chips, and conducts comprehensive functional and performance testing validation. The functional test results show that this blockchain hardware and software integrated machine is fully compatible with the Hygon domestic X86 CPU, Phytium domestic ARM CPU, Kylin operating system, and Chainmaker Chain, meeting all functional requirements and achieving the expected targets. Performance test results indicate that, under the designed test scenarios, the blockchain read peak performance can reach 9165.5 TPS, with an average performance of 1853.3 TPS; the write peak performance can reach 3903.8 TPS, with an average performance of 1625.3 TPS. Overall, this hyper-converged solution demonstrates excellent reliability, stability, and performance, fully meeting the needs and expected targets of high-security application scenarios. It provides robust technical support for the localization and independent controllability of China's blockchain infrastructure.

References

1. Yuan, B., Wu, F., Zheng, Z.: Post quantum blockchain architecture for internet of things over NTRU lattice. PLoS ONE 18(2), e0279429 (2023)
2. Momeni, P., Gorbunov, S., Zhang, B.: Fairblock: preventing blockchain front-running with minimal overheads. In: Li, F., Liang, K., Lin, Z., Katsikas, S.K. (eds.) SecureComm 2022, LNICST, vol. 462, pp. 250-271. Springer, Cham (2023). https://doi.org/10.1007/978-3-031-25538-0_14
3. Sharma, P., Moparthi, N.R., Namasudra, S., et al.: Blockchain-based IoT architecture to secure healthcare system using identity-based encryption. Expert. Syst. 39(10), e12915 (2022)
4. Eyal, I.: Blockchain technology: transforming libertarian cryptocurrency dreams to fi- nance and banking realities. Computer 50(9), 38–49 (2017)
5. Yu, Z., Wen, J.: The IoT electric business model: using blockchain technology for the Internet of things. Peer-to-Peer Netw. Appl. 10(4), 983–994 (2017)
6. Fairley, P.: Blockchain world - feeding the blockchain beast if bitcoin ever does go main- stream, the electricity needed to sustain it will be enormous. IEEE Spectr. 54(10), 36–59 (2017)
7. Lu, Y., Huang, X., Dai, Y., Maharjan, S., Zhang, Y.: Blockchain and federated learning for privacy-preserved data sharing in industrial IoT. IEEE Trans. Industr. Inf. 16(6), 4177–4186 (2019)
8. Jiang, Y., Xu, X., Xiao, F.: Attribute-based encryption with blockchain protection scheme for electronic health records. IEEE Trans. Netw. Serv. Manage. 19(4), 3884–3895 (2022)

DFADNet: A Diverse-Feature Adaptive Network for Web3.0-Oriented Deep Forgery Detection

Guizhen Chen[1], Yinghao Liu[1], Yunfang Ye[1], and Tao Lei[2(✉)]

[1] China Mobile Group Fujian Co., Ltd., Fuzhou, China
[2] China Mobile Group Design Institute Co., Ltd., Beijing, China
leitao@cmdi.chinamobile.com

Abstract. The pervasive spread of deepfakes has underscored an urgent requirement for advanced forgery detection systems, especially in the context of Web 3.0, where user-generated content and decentralized applications are becoming increasingly prevalent. While significant progress has been made in this field through deep learning, the constantly evolving nature of forgery techniques necessitates continual innovation. Current detection methods, constrained by inflexible parameters, struggle to capture the nuances of noise residuals and often overlook the interaction between texture and semantic clues, as well as the temporal subtleties that can significantly enhance detection capabilities. This paper introduces DFADnet, the Diverse Features Adaptive Detection Network, a pioneering approach to deep forgery detection that integrates a diverse range of features for effectively identifying manipulated videos. DFADnet comprises three essential components: TextureNoiseAdapt (TNA) for adaptive extraction of texture noise; SemanticGuidance (SG) for directing focus towards semantic inconsistencies indicative of tampering; and TemporalMultiscale (TMS) for analyzing temporal dynamics across video frames. Our comprehensive experiments on the FF++ and Celeb-DF datasets demonstrate DFADnet's superior performance, achieving an accuracy of 97.65% in the HQ mode and an AUC of 76.95% on Celeb-DF, thus highlighting its robust generalization capabilities.

Keywords: Deep Forgery Detection · Temporal Feature · Adaptive Network · Web3.0

1 Introduction

As the field of computer vision continues to evolve, deep forgery technologies such as Deepfakes [8] have garnered significant attention. These technologies have the capacity to manipulate individuals' identities, seamlessly integrate celebrity faces into pornographic videos, or fabricate scenarios for misinformation campaigns and financial scams. The implications for global security are far-reaching, underscoring the pressing need to develop a versatile and effective deep forgery

© The Author(s), under exclusive license to Springer Nature Singapore Pte Ltd. 2025
G. Zhao et al. (Eds.): BWTAC 2024, CCIS 2277, pp. 181–192, 2025.
https://doi.org/10.1007/978-981-97-9412-6_17

detection model that can reliably distinguish between real and manipulated content.

Recent advances in deep learning have led to a revolution in the detection of deep forgeries [19]. These models are adept at identifying manipulated faces by analyzing semantic features within the spatial domain, which is crucial in RGB imagery. Despite these advances, existing methods, such as those employing hand-crafted features within shallow convolutional neural network (CNN) frameworks [2], often prove ineffective when confronted with variations in dataset quality or distribution. The sensitivity of these methods to data nuances represents a limitation in their effectiveness in practical forgery detection scenarios. In order to address some of these limitations, [1] introduced MesoNet, a network that leverages multiple small convolutional modules in order to adeptly capture the subtle micro-features indicative of image tampering. This architectural approach not only enhances the detection capabilities but also contributes to a reduction in computational overhead. Moreover, XceptionNet [4] has established a standard of excellence, demonstrating its robust performance across a spectrum of forgery algorithms by serving as a powerful general feature extractor. However, a common characteristic of these CNN approaches is their inclination towards semantic features, which, while advantageous, can impede their capacity to generalize across diverse forms of forgeries.

Current forgery detection methods, while making strides in identifying manipulated content, often fall short in their adaptability and accuracy. They are constrained by rigid parameters and fail to capture the subtleties of noise residuals, semantic inconsistencies, and temporal dynamics that are essential for effective detection. The limitations of these methods are particularly pronounced in the context of Web 3.0, where content is diverse, decentralized, and rapidly evolving. To tackle these challenges, this paper introduces DFADnet, an adaptive network for deep forgery detection that leverages a variety of features. The approach eschews rigid constraints in favor of a more flexible feature set. Here's a streamlined summary of the methodological advancements:

- Diversified Feature Integration: The network is architected to incorporate a range of features that contribute to a more comprehensive analysis of potential forgeries.
- Texture Noise Adaptation (TNA): A novel mechanism that employs unpooled feature mapping coupled with a frequency-domain attention system. This allows for the adaptive extraction of noise residuals across a spectrum of frequencies, not limited to predefined bands.
- Deep Semantic Guidance Strategy (SG): This strategy utilizes spatial attention derived from noise residuals. It serves to accentuate signs of tampering and to direct the feature extraction process towards critical areas within the content that may contain manipulation.
- Temporal Multi-scale (TMS): A method designed to process temporal features at multiple scales. It applies attention mechanisms to weigh different frames in a video sequence, thereby effectively capturing discrepancies at the frame level that may indicate forgery.

2   Related Work

Building upon the emphasis on semantic features, the quest to enhance forgery detection has led researchers to explore the utilization of texture features, offering a complementary perspective to identify manipulated content. [11] innovatively employed multi-scale Laplacian of Gaussian (LoG) operators, strategically suppressing low-level image features. This approach serves as a band-pass filter, effectively amplifying the subtle artifacts indicative of forgeries. While this method may compromise the precision at the frame level, it achieves a notable enhancement in the model's ability to generalize across various datasets. In another approach, [21] subtracted low-frequency components from images to accentuate the shallow texture features that are often indicative of tampering. They introduced a regional independent loss function to bolster the network's training process. However, this method encountered a significant decline in detection performance under conditions of high compression, revealing a limitation in the model's capacity to generalize effectively. [20] proposed a streamlined version of XceptionNet, integrating an intermediate block as the backbone for their network. This configuration aimed to efficiently extract texture features, yet it overlooked the potential adverse effects of average pooling on the detection process. The decision to simplify the network, while beneficial for computational efficiency, may have inadvertently diminished the model's sensitivity to certain types of forgeries.

Recently, there's been a shift towards using temporal features for detecting facial forgeries. [7] suggested a system where a CNN extracts features from each frame, which then trains an RNN to understand the sequence of events in a video. [16] showed that combining these RNNs with facial alignment based on key points can significantly improve detection rates. However, current methods treat all frames equally, which isn't ideal for training more effective detection models.

The above methods have made great progress in the field of deep forgery detection, but there are still many shortcomings. Most texture-based detection methods use specific initial constraints to capture features, which can only effectively capture information in specific frequency bands and cannot be flexibly applied to deep forgeries generated by different forgery algorithms [14]. In addition, although many dual-stream networks are used to extract texture and semantic information for learning, they do not fully utilize the advantages between different features. In fact, noise residuals extracted from shallow textures can effectively highlight tampering traces and guide the semantic branch to explore deep features in suspicious areas. Moreover, the improvement of attention mechanisms on temporal networks is also easily overlooked by researchers, because forged videos need to be processed in a coherent manner for all frames, and low-level artifacts caused by face tampering are expected to further manifest as frame-level inconsistent temporal artifacts, and different weights should be assigned to different time series during detection [6].

In summary, while significant strides have been made in deep forgery detection, there remains a need for methods that can adaptively capture the nuances of noise residuals, semantic inconsistencies, and temporal dynamics. The quest for a versatile and effective detection model that can reliably distinguish between real and manipulated content continues, with the potential to impact the security and integrity of digital media in the era of Web 3.0.

3   Framework

The experimental evaluation across datasets demonstrates the robustness and generalizability of the method. Furthermore, the high detection accuracy in the dataset validates the proposed method.

The framework of the proposed network is shown in Fig. 1. First, the continuous frame images are sent into the tampering residual extraction unit, where semantic features (top) and texture features (bottom) are extracted from the RGB image and grayscale image, respectively.

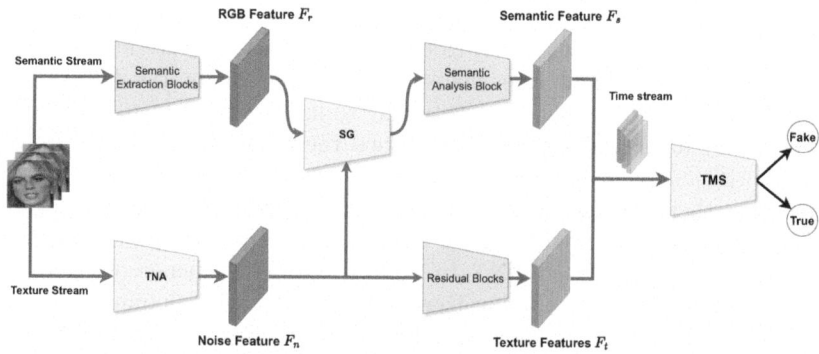

Fig. 1. Framework of DFADnet

This unit designs a texture noise adaptation mechanism (TNA) to capture texture residuals based on the frequency domain channel attention mechanism, preventing effective noise from being filtered out, thereby adaptively learning noise residuals in non-fixed frequency bands. Then, the RGB feature map $\mathbf{F}_r$ and the noise feature map $\mathbf{F}_n$ are transmitted to the tampering residual analysis unit, and the semantic feature map $\mathbf{F}_s$ and the texture feature map $\mathbf{F}_t$ are obtained through analysis. This module proposes a deep semantic analysis guidance strategy (SG), which uses the spatial attention mechanism generated by the noise residuals extracted by TNA to guide the semantic analysis block to focus on specific suspicious areas. Then, $\mathbf{F}_s$ and $\mathbf{F}_t$ are input into the tampering residual aggregation unit. The process is as follows: A temporal multi-scale feature processing method (TMS) is used to generate two types of different temporal features, that is, semantic-temporal feature $\tilde{\mathbf{F}}_s$ and texture-temporal feature $\tilde{\mathbf{F}}_t$. TMS uses a bidirectional temporal network with an attention mechanism to learn frame-level differences between different features. The fusion module merges $\tilde{\mathbf{F}}_s$

and $\tilde{\mathbf{F}}_t$, converging these different features with noise residuals into a generalized feature space for deep tampering detection. Finally, true and false classification is performed.

3.1 TNA: Texture Noise Adaptive Extraction Mechanism

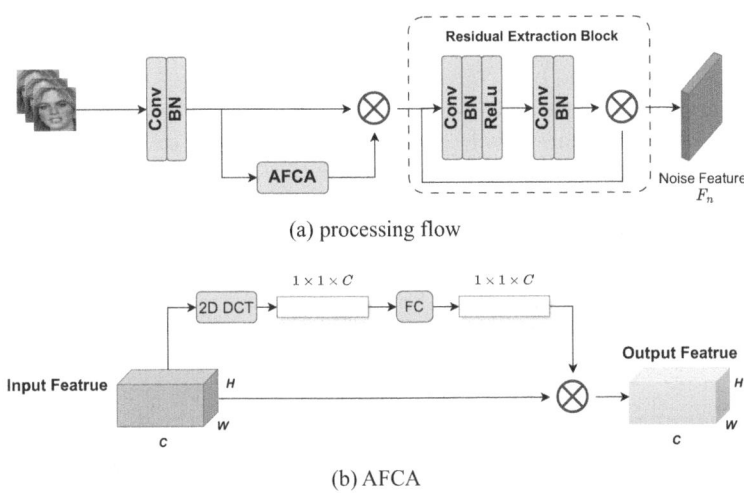

(a) processing flow

(b) AFCA

Fig. 2. Schematic diagram of TNA

The processing flow of TNA is shown in Fig. 2(a). In the current texture feature extraction methods, the global average pooling (GAP) in the channel attention mechanism and the average pooling layer in the feature mapping are regarded as a low-pass filter, which will filter out the high-frequency noise in the image, causing the tampering traces to be artificially lost, affecting the subsequent detection; in addition, they use fixed frequency band filters in the channel attention to only retain specific information. Therefore, this paper proposes the following improvement method: abandon the average pooling in the entire module and design an adaptive frequency domain channel attention mechanism (AFCA), as shown in Fig. 2(b). In AFCA, the two-dimensional discrete cosine transform (DCT) is used instead of GAP, and the residual is used to determine the channel weight, and learn the noise residuals in non-fixed frequency bands in TNA. The weight of the texture feature channel (w_c) can be derived from Eq. (1):

$$\begin{cases} V = (D_{base}^i + D_{learnable}^i) \times X_i, & i \in \{0, 1, \dots, c-1\} \\ w_c = \sigma(f_c(cat([V_0, V_1, \dots, V_{c-1}]))) \end{cases} \quad (1)$$

In the formula, c is the number of channels, $X \in \mathbb{R}^{1 \times H \times W}$, cat represents the concatenation on the channel dimension, f_c represents the fully connected layer, σ represents the Sigmoid function, D_{base}^i and $D_{learnable}^i$ are the initial frequency components and learnable frequency components of the i-th channel, respectively, and V is the compressed feature vector of the i-th channel.

3.2 SG: Deep Semantic Analysis Guidance Strategy

The noise feature map $\mathbf{F}_n$ extracted by TNA is downsampled by a convolutional kernel to generate a feature map $\mathbf{F}_g$ of the same dimension as the RGB feature map $\mathbf{F}_r$. Then, the channel dimension of $\mathbf{F}_g$ is processed by max pooling and average pooling, followed by a convolutional layer with a 7×7 kernel to generate a spatial attention map related to the residual. This map is used to better guide the high-level semantic feature flow to explore deep features in key areas. This spatial attention map forms a skip connection with the RGB feature map, assigning weights to different pixel positions to obtain the weighted feature map $\mathbf{F}'$. The calculation formula is as follows:

$$\begin{cases} \mathbf{F}_g = \mathrm{down}(\mathbf{F}_n) \\ w_s = \sigma\left(f_{7\times7}\left([\mathrm{AvgPool}(\mathbf{F}_g), \mathrm{MaxPool}(\mathbf{F}_g)]\right)\right) \\ \mathbf{F}' = \mathbf{F}_r \dot{w}_s + \mathbf{F}_r \end{cases} \quad (2)$$

Here, $\mathrm{down}(\cdot)$ represents down-sampling, $\mathrm{AvgPool}(\cdot)$ and $\mathrm{MaxPool}(\cdot)$ represent average pooling and max pooling, respectively, and $f_{7\times7}$ represents a convolutional operation with a 7×7 filter.

3.3 TMS: Temporal Multi-scale Feature Processing Method

To enhance the ability of the temporal network to capture frame-level differences, this paper selects bidirectional GRU (Gated Recurrent Unit) with attention mechanisms to train high-level and low-level features, respectively. Compared to LSTM (Long Short-Term Memory), GRU has lower computational complexity and is easier to converge while maintaining similar performance, and bidirectional GRU can better capture the dependency information of the bidirectional flow; the temporal attention mechanism can focus on the importance of different time sequences and assign different weights to different time sequences. Since the semantic feature map $\mathbf{F}_s$ and the texture feature map $\mathbf{F}_t$ come from different operations and contain different information, they enter the residual aggregation unit before fusion to obtain richer multi-scale temporal features. The temporal multi-scale feature processing process is as follows.

First, calculate the hidden state S_{x_t} of the feature map $\mathbf{F}_x$ at time t as:

$$S_{x_t} = w_1 \cdot \overrightarrow{S_{x_{t-1}}} + w_2 \cdot \overleftarrow{S_{x_{t-1}}} + b_t \quad (3)$$

where: x represents high-level semantic features h or low-level texture features l; $\overrightarrow{S_{x_{t-1}}}$ and $\overleftarrow{S_{x_{t-1}}}$ represent the forward and backward hidden states, respectively; GRU(.) represents the nonlinear transformation based on the gated recurrent unit; w_1 and w_2 correspond to the weights of the forward and backward GRU, which are fixed values; b is the bias at the current moment.

Next, calculate the temporal weight w_{x_t} of $\mathbf{F}_x$, $w_{x_t} \in [0, 1]$:

$$w_{x_t} = \frac{\exp(u_{x_t}^T v_u)}{\sum_t \exp(u_{x_t}^T v_u)} \tag{4}$$

Here, $u_{x_t} = \tanh(S_{x_t})$, $tanh$ is the activation function, which enhances the network's nonlinear transformation capability, and v_u is a randomly initialized attention matrix. In this way, with the input $\mathbf{F}_t$ and $\mathbf{F}_s$, the low-level and high-level features can be obtained from Eq. (3) and (4) as S_l, w_t and S_{h_t}, w_{h_t}, respectively.

Then, calculate the texture-temporal feature map $\tilde{\mathbf{F}}_t$ and the semantic-temporal feature map $\tilde{\mathbf{F}}_s$ from the above hidden states and temporal weights:

$$\begin{cases} \tilde{\mathbf{F}}_t = \sum_{t=0}^{n-1} w_t S_{l_t} \\ \tilde{\mathbf{F}}_s = \sum_{t=0}^{n-1} w_{h_t} S_{h_t} \end{cases} \tag{5}$$

Finally, place different feature maps into the fusion module to obtain the final fused feature map $\mathbf{F}$:

$$\mathbf{F} = \text{fusion}(\tilde{\mathbf{F}}_s, \tilde{\mathbf{F}}_t) \tag{6}$$

where the fusion module fusion($\cdot$) adopts an attention-based feature fusion method.

4 Experiments

4.1 Datasets

To evaluate the effectiveness of DFADnet, we used two prominent datasets in deep forgery detection: FaceForensics++ (FF++) [15] and Celeb-DF [9]. The FF++ dataset, a staple in the field, provides a rich collection of 1,000 real videos paired with their deep fake counterparts created using five different manipulation techniques: Deepfakes (DF), NeuralTextures (NT), FaceSwap (FS), Face2Face (F2F), and FaceShifter (FSH). FS and F2F are created using computer graphics techniques, while DF, NT, and FSH are created using learning-based methods. For a balanced experiment, FSH was excluded from the overall FF++ test. Our experimental setup included both the light compression HQ and heavy compression LQ versions of FF++, with a training set of 740 videos and separate validation and test sets of 140 videos each. In addition, the Celeb-DF dataset, known for its challenging cases, was used to evaluate the generalization of DFADnet on 518 carefully selected videos.

4.2 Evaluation Metrics

To evaluate the performance of DFADnet, we employed established metrics within the field: Accuracy (ACC) and Area Under the Receiver Operating Characteristic Curve (AUC). The ACC metric directly reflects the model's proficiency in distinguishing between authentic and forged videos. It is calculated using the following formula:

$$ACC = \frac{TP + TN}{TP + TN + FP + FN} \tag{7}$$

Here, TP represents true positives, TN true negatives, FP false positives, and FN false negatives, offering a clear measure of classification accuracy.

Furthermore, the AUC metric provides a nuanced evaluation of the model's performance across a range of classification thresholds. It is calculated as:

$$AUC = \frac{1}{MN} \sum_{i \in p} \left(\text{rank}_i - \frac{M+1}{2} \right) \tag{8}$$

Here, the rank corresponds to the position of each positive sample within the dataset, with the summation only including positive samples, denoted by $\sum_{i \in p}$ The variables M and N represent the total counts of positive and negative samples, respectively.

4.3 Experimental Setup

The PyTorch framework is used, and the face extractor Dlib is used to identify 68 facial detection points, with the aligned face image format being 299 * 299.

The extraction of high-level semantic features uses Xception [4] as the backbone network and initializes Xception with pre-trained parameters from ImageNet [5]; the extraction of texture features uses SRNet [3] as the backbone network, and the implementation of the channel attention mechanism refers to Fcanet [13]; in the temporal network, the weights w_1 and w_2 are both set to 1, and the bias b_t is 0.

The AdamW optimizer is used for training, with a learning rate of 1×10^{-4} and weight decay of 1×10^{-6}. The model is trained on 2 NVIDIA RTX 4090TI GPUs with a batch size of 32.

4.4 Results and Analysis

Evaluation on FF++ Dataset. The results presented in Table 1 indicate that the methods Two-branch [11] and MA [21], which utilize fixed initial constraints to extract shallow image features for capturing noise residuals, achieve excellent performance on the high-quality version of FF++ but experience a significant drop in performance on the lower-quality FF++ (LQ). In contrast, the DFAD-net adaptively calculates noise residuals through feature learning and further amplifies frame-level differences by separating high-level and low-level features into the temporal network, enhancing detection accuracy. It achieves the best detection rate for different qualities of Deepfakes.

Table 1. Comparison of Detection Performance on LQ and HQ Modes of FF++ Dataset

Method	LQ		HQ	
	ACC	AUC	ACC	AUC
MesoNet [1]	71.24%	–	82.97%	–
SRNet [3]	74.03%	77.84%	94.74%	97.10%
Xception [4]	85.54%	86.32%	94.12%	95.24%
RNN [7]	85.35%	86.87%	95.02%	95.58%
Two-branch [11]	–	87.21%	–	98.13%
MA [21]	87.50%	89.21%	95.45%	98.77%
Sstnet [20]	86.92%	89.15%	94.87%	98.54%
LiSiam [19]	88.12%	86.21%	94.43%	98.10%
DFADnet	88.72%	91.20%	97.65%	99.12%

Cross-Dataset Evaluation Between FF++ and Celeb-DF. Table 2 shows that the proposed method maintains an AUC of 99.85% on the FF++ dataset and can achieve an AUC of 76.95% on Celeb-DF, demonstrating good generalization performance. SPSL [10] shows a performance increase of 0.38% points on Celeb-DF compared to DFADnet. It is found that the generalization capability of SPSL depends on the upsampling operation in face generation. If the forged face is not generated based on a generative model, its detection performance will drop significantly. DFADnet, however, adaptively learns the unique traces of different forgery methods in a data-driven manner, avoiding the use of incomplete prior knowledge to constrain the network, thus maintaining strong competitiveness in generalization.

Table 2. Cross-Dataset Evaluation (AUC) between FF++ and Celeb-DF (Training on FF++, Testing on Celeb-DF)

Method	FF++	Celeb-DF
MesoNet [1]	85.10%	55.15%
Xception-c23 [4]	99.65%	65.85%
Two-branch [11]	93.05%	72.85%
Multi-task [12]	87.95%	54.72%
Efficientnet [17]	99.50%	63.94%
MA [21]	99.75%	66.98%
SPSL [10]	96.80%	77.33%
DPNet [18]	99.15%	67.75%
DFADnet	99.85%	76.95%

Cross-Evaluation Among Different Forgery Methods on FF++. The cross-evaluation results using the FF++ (HQ) dataset, where forged images generated by any one of the forgery methods are used for training and tested on the images forged by the four methods, are shown in Table 3. It can be seen that the proposed network outperforms Mesonet and Xception in most cases. Mesonet and Xception are overly dependent on the overall pattern of the image, and their performance drops sharply in untrained forged samples. In contrast, the proposed method makes full use of diverse features, capturing richer overall information and exhibiting better generalization capabilities.

Table 3. Cross-Evaluation among Different Forgery Methods on FF++ (HQ)

Training set	Method	Test set				
		DF	F2F	FS	NT	FSH
DF	MesoNet	97.55%	47.10%	61.25%	77.95%	70.21%
	Xception	99.15%	74.05%	39.25%	74.85%	63.36%
	DFADnet	99.70%	74.50%	65.75%	84.95%	66.05%
F2F	MesoNet	74.55%	97.65%	54.10%	63.15%	54.62%
	Xception	82.29%	99.25%	58.45%	68.58%	63.09%
	DFADnet	86.85%	99.50%	62.45%	68.18%	66.21%
FS	MesoNet	51.65%	58.70%	98.80%	51.75%	49.72%
	Xception	58.85%	66.86%	99.35%	55.26%	65.18%
	DFADnet	60.91%	67.35%	99.60%	58.88%	57.89%
NT	MesoNet	87.04%	62.42%	49.80%	87.36%	64.38%
	Xception	84.15%	70.28%	47.33%	98.09%	71.05%
	DFADnet	93.13%	71.46%	51.26%	98.55%	71.27%
FSH	MesoNet	78.83%	46.33%	48.40%	65.81%	95.63%
	Xception	74.63%	47.86%	50.89%	65.12%	99.25%
	DFADnet	64.86%	52.68%	52.70%	66.40%	99.39%

Discussion. The results from our experiments underscore the efficacy of DFAD-net in detecting deepfakes across diverse datasets. The high ACC and AUC scores on the FF++ dataset, particularly in the HQ mode, demonstrate the model's proficiency in analyzing high-quality forgeries. The performance on the Celeb-DF dataset, while slightly lower, still indicates a commendable level of generalization, showcasing the network's robustness against a broader spectrum of forgery techniques.

A key factor contributing to DFADnet's success is the integration of diverse feature sets-semantic, textural, and temporal-which provide a multifaceted view of the video content. This holistic approach stands in contrast to methods that focus on isolated features, thereby offering a more nuanced and reliable detection mechanism.

Moreover, the adaptive nature of DFADnet, as seen in the TNA and SG modules, allows for a dynamic response to the variability inherent in deepfakes. By not relying on fixed constraints, the network can better capture the subtleties of noise residuals and the spatial intricacies of tampering traces.

5   Conclusion

Web 3.0's emphasis on decentralization, security, and user control over data presents unique challenges and opportunities for forgery detection. This paper presents DFADNet, a deep forgery detection network that addresses these challenges by incorporating a diverse set of features and methodologies. The network's core components-the texture noise adaptive extraction mechanism, the deep semantic analysis guidance strategy, and the temporal multi-scale feature processing method-work in unison to provide a comprehensive analysis of video content. These advancements allow DFADNet to effectively capture the subtleties of deep forgeries, including residual noise and temporal inconsistencies. Our experimental evaluation demonstrates the superior performance of DFADNet, achieving high accuracy rates and exhibiting strong generalization capabilities across different datasets. The results from the cross-dataset and FF++ dataset evaluations are particularly encouraging, showcasing the network's ability to maintain high detection rates even when faced with varied forgery techniques. Moreover, DFADnet's alignment with Web 3.0's core tenets ensures that it can provide advanced detection capabilities in a secure, user-controlled, and decentralized manner, making it an ideal solution for the evolving landscape of digital content verification in the Web 3.0 era.

References

1. Afchar, D., Nozick, V., Yamagishi, J., Echizen, I.: MesoNet: a compact facial video forgery detection network. In: 2018 IEEE International Workshop on Information Forensics and Security (WIFS), pp. 1–7. IEEE (2018)
2. Bayar, B., Stamm, M.C.: A deep learning approach to universal image manipulation detection using a new convolutional layer. In: Proceedings of the 4th ACM Workshop on Information Hiding and Multimedia Security, pp. 5–10 (2016)
3. Boroumand, M., Chen, M., Fridrich, J.: Deep residual network for steganalysis of digital images. IEEE Trans. Inf. Forensics Secur. **14**(5), 1181–1193 (2018)
4. Chollet, F.: Xception: deep learning with depthwise separable convolutions. In: Proceedings of the IEEE Conference on Computer Vision and Pattern Recognition, pp. 1251–1258 (2017)
5. Deng, J., Dong, W., Socher, R., Li, L.J., Li, K., Fei-Fei, L.: ImageNet: a large-scale hierarchical image database. In: 2009 IEEE Conference on Computer Vision and Pattern Recognition, pp. 248–255. IEEE (2009)
6. Gu, Z., et al.: Spatiotemporal inconsistency learning for deepfake video detection. In: Proceedings of the 29th ACM International Conference on Multimedia, pp. 3473–3481 (2021)

7. Guera, D., Delp, E.J.: Deepfake video detection using recurrent neural networks. 2018 15th IEEE International Conference on Advanced Video and Signal Based Surveillance (AVSS), pp. 1–6 (2018). https://api.semanticscholar.org/CorpusID: 61808533

8. Korshunov, P., Marcel, S.: DeepFakes: a new threat to face recognition? Assessment and detection (2018)

9. Li, Y., Yang, X., Sun, P., Qi, H., Lyu, S.: Celeb-DF: a large-scale challenging dataset for deepfake forensics. In: Proceedings of the IEEE/CVF Conference on Computer Vision and Pattern Recognition, pp. 3207–3216 (2020)

10. Liu, H., et al.: Spatial-phase shallow learning: rethinking face forgery detection in frequency domain. In: Proceedings of the IEEE/CVF Conference on Computer Vision and Pattern Recognition, pp. 772–781 (2021)

11. Masi, I., Killekar, A., Mascarenhas, R.M., Gurudatt, S.P., AbdAlmageed, W.: Two-branch recurrent network for isolating deepfakes in videos. In: Vedaldi, A., Bischof, H., Brox, T., Frahm, J.-M. (eds.) ECCV 2020. LNCS, vol. 12352, pp. 667–684. Springer, Cham (2020). https://doi.org/10.1007/978-3-030-58571-6_39

12. Nguyen, H.H., Fang, F., Yamagishi, J., Echizen, I.: Multi-task learning for detecting and segmenting manipulated facial images and videos. In: 2019 IEEE 10th International Conference on Biometrics Theory, Applications and Systems (BTAS), pp. 1–8. IEEE (2019)

13. Qin, Z., Zhang, P., Wu, F., Li, X.: FcaNet: frequency channel attention networks. In: Proceedings of the IEEE/CVF International Conference on Computer Vision, pp. 783–792 (2021)

14. Rana, M.S., Nobi, M.N., Murali, B., Sung, A.H.: Deepfake detection: a systematic literature review. IEEE Access 10, 25494–25513 (2022)

15. Rossler, A., Cozzolino, D., Verdoliva, L., Riess, C., Thies, J., Nießner, M.: Face-Forensics++: learning to detect manipulated facial images. In: Proceedings of the IEEE/CVF International Conference on Computer Vision, pp. 1–11 (2019)

16. Sabir, E., Cheng, J., Jaiswal, A., AbdAlmageed, W., Masi, I., Natarajan, P.: Recurrent convolutional strategies for face manipulation detection in videos. Interfaces (GUI) 3(1), 80–87 (2019)

17. Tan, M., Le, Q.: EfficientNet: rethinking model scaling for convolutional neural networks. In: International Conference on Machine Learning, pp. 6105–6114. PMLR (2019)

18. Trinh, L., Tsang, M., Rambhatla, S., Liu, Y.: Interpretable and trustworthy deepfake detection via dynamic prototypes. In: Proceedings of the IEEE/CVF Winter Conference on Applications of Computer Vision, pp. 1973–1983 (2021)

19. Wang, J., Sun, Y., Tang, J.: LiSiam: localization invariance Siamese network for deepfake detection. IEEE Trans. Inf. Forensics Secur. 17, 2425–2436 (2022)

20. Wu, X., Xie, Z., Gao, Y., Xiao, Y.: SSTNet: detecting manipulated faces through spatial, steganalysis and temporal features. In: ICASSP 2020-2020 IEEE International Conference on Acoustics, Speech and Signal Processing (ICASSP), pp. 2952–2956. IEEE (2020)

21. Zhao, H., Zhou, W., Chen, D., Wei, T., Zhang, W., Yu, N.: Multi-attentional deepfake detection. In: Proceedings of the IEEE/CVF Conference on Computer Vision and Pattern Recognition, pp. 2185–2194 (2021)

Privacy Protection Model of International Cold Chain Trade Blockchain Platform Based on Zero-Knowledge Proofs

Yue Li, Xueying Ren[✉], Chang Yin, Chaocen Tang, Jiale Zhang, and Luohao Zheng

School of Computer Science and Technology, Donghua University, Shanghai 201620, China
frankyueli@dhu.edu.cn, 1640302092@qq.com

Abstract. The International Cold Chain Trade Platform serves as a trade bridge between overseas suppliers and domestic small and medium-sized customers, providing comprehensive services such as cross-border procurement, supply chain finance and warehousing logistics. However, the current centralized operating model of the trade platform faces trust issues, as data is typically managed and controlled by the platform operator, making it difficult to ensure the authenticity of the data. Blockchain technology, with its inherent tamper-proof and traceable nature, offers a promising solution to address these issues. In this paper, we propose and implement a blockchain-based international cold chain trading platform, which combines cryptographic technologies such as homomorphic encryption and zero-knowledge proofs to ensure data immutability while guaranteeing the authenticity and privacy of platform data. We analyzed the performance and security of the proposed system. The experimental results show that the scheme proposed in this paper is feasible.

Keywords: Blockchain · Zero-Knowledge Proof · Homomorphic Encryption · Pedersen Commitment

1 Introduction

With the growth of global food trade, international cold chain trade plays a crucial role in ensuring food supply. However, the complexity of international trade involving numerous stakeholders and intricate processes poses challenges, especially for small and medium-sized enterprises (SMEs) with limited resources. To tackle these challenges, the emergence of the International Cold Chain Trade Platform (ICCTP) offers a solution.Most existing international trade platforms operate on a centralized architecture, which is susceptible to single-point failures and security vulnerabilities. Furthermore, centralized control over data storage and management raises concerns about data authenticity and traceability, leading to trust issues. This centralized model also hampers the establishment of a credit system and diminishes the efficiency and reliability of international trade. Thus, the shift towards a decentralized and more stable operational model is imperative to enhance the effectiveness of international trade platforms.

Blockchain [1] is an emerging disruptive technology that offers exceptional security and stability through its unique decentralized architecture. Blockchain technology is highly compatible with the ICCTP, as it enables logistics traceability, recording every step of the cold chain transportation and storage to promptly identify any disruptions and enhance process transparency. Furthermore, enterprises can incorporate cold chain trade processes into blockchain smart contracts, which automatically execute once the conditions are met, thereby improving the automation and efficiency of the cold chain industry.

This paper designs and implements an ICCTP based on blockchain. It utilizes a decentralized data privacy storage framework based on blockchain, IPFS [2], and MySQL. This framework not only safeguards data privacy but also enhances trust among suppliers, customers, the platform, and financial institutions. Additionally, this paper proposes a privacy protection scheme for transaction amount authentication based on zero-knowledge proofs [3]. It enables the proof of repayment capacity without revealing specific transaction information, thereby accelerating the development of SMEs in international trade.The contributions of this paper are summarized as follows:

(1) Based on the characteristics and practical application scenarios of international cold chain trade, a system model for an international cold chain trade platform based on blockchain is designed. A data privacy storage framework based on blockchain, IPFS, and MySQL is proposed, where plaintext data is stored in MySQL and file-type data is stored in IPFS. To address the large volume of business data containing sensitive information, complex data is divided into blocks, encrypted, and compressed before being stored in the blockchain. This data storage solution ensures business data privacy while enhancing data trustworthiness.

(2) Addressing the financing difficulties faced by SMEs in international cold chain trade, this paper presents a privacy protection scheme based on zero-knowledge proofs. The scheme combines blockchain with the Bulletproofs zero-knowledge proof protocol, extending the proof of values from the standard range to any range. Through the application of the blockchain platform, historical order information can be quickly analyzed to assess the operational status of SMEs and evaluate the financing amounts they can obtain, thereby alleviating the lengthy and cumbersome steps involved in traditional financing models.

The rest of this paper is organized as follows: Section 2 introduces the application of blockchain in the trade field. Section 3 presents the model architecture of the ICCTP based on blockchain. Section 4 analyzes the performance and security of the system. Section 5 concludes the research findings of this paper.

2   Related Work

Blockchain technology has brought significant changes to the business processes of international trade. Alqaryouti et al. proposed a blockchain-based framework for an international trade e-commerce platform [4], which simplifies the transaction process, thus alleviating and fulfilling customs management responsibilities. Kumar et al. introduced a decentralized trade finance system [5], where importers and exporters create files through the blockchain network, allowing individuals from around the world to participate in trade finance. Chen et al. developed a blockchain-based international trade logistics platform to address inefficiencies and challenges in document transfer and goods delivery processes within traditional international trade [6].

When applying blockchain technology to real-world scenarios in international trade, privacy protection becomes a crucial concern. Islam et al. proposed a blockchain-based supply chain management in the context of IIoT [7], discussing the trade-off between transparency and privacy. Al-Shaibani et al. provided a privacy protection framework for decentralized securities trading platforms [8], ensuring the anonymity and unlinkability of investor accounts and their trading activities. This paper proposes a privacy protection framework based on homomorphic encryption and zero-knowledge proofs to address data privacy issues in the ICCTP.

3   Design of the ICCTP Based on Blockchain Technology

3.1   System Model

The overall logical hierarchy of the blockchain-based ICCTP can be divided into three layers: the data layer, the middleware layer, and the application layer, as shown in Fig. 1. This paper proposes a data privacy storage framework that enhances data trust while protecting data privacy by embedding a data trust layer in the data layer and a privacy layer in the middleware layer.

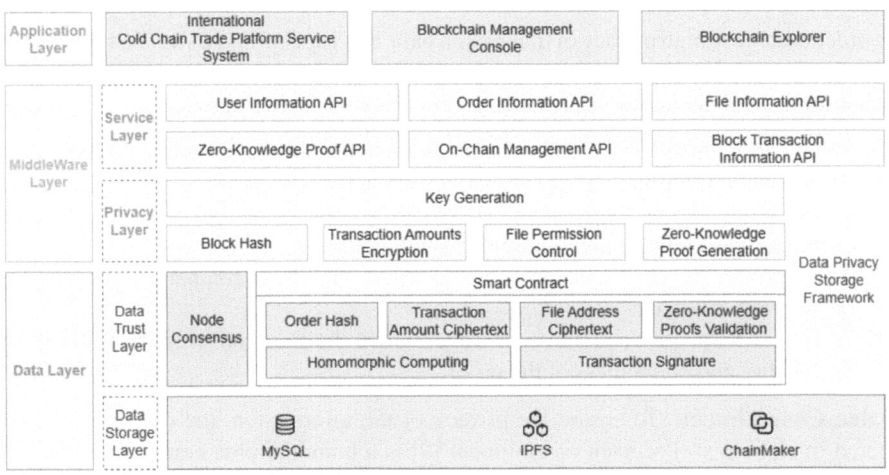

Fig. 1. System Architecture Diagram

Data Layer.   The data layer comprises the data storage layer and the data trust layer. The data storage layer includes MySQL, IPFS, and the ChainMaker blockchain. Structured data within the platform is stored in the relational database MySQL, file-type data is stored in IPFS, and various data proofs are stored on the blockchain. The data trust layer leverages the consensus mechanism and smart contracts of the blockchain to ensure data consistency and immutability, thereby enhancing data trust. Encrypted data, such as hashed order data, encrypted transaction amounts, and encrypted file addresses, is uploaded to the blockchain for storage using smart contracts.

Middleware Layer. The middleware layer consists of the privacy layer and the service layer. The privacy layer encrypts sensitive data to protect privacy on the blockchain. It generates zero-knowledge proofs to safeguard user business data while meeting system functional requirements. Additionally, it securely generates public-private key pairs for user identification within the blockchain network. The service layer encapsulates the implementation logic of system functions and provides API interfaces to the upper layers.

Application Layer. The platform comprises three subsystems: the ICCTP Service System, the Blockchain Management Console, and the Blockchain Explorer. The ICCTP Service System is a web application that utilizes the middleware layer's APIs to provide business operation functions for suppliers, customers, platform staff, freight forwarding companies, and financial institutions. The Blockchain Management Console offers visual maintenance of the blockchain network, enabling administrators to monitor blockchain status, manage user permissions, and configure contract consensus policies. The Blockchain Explorer allows users to query blockchain information, view transaction details by transaction hash, and examine certificates stored on the blockchain.

3.2 Privacy Protection Scheme Based on Zero-Knowledge Proof

In order to achieve high privacy of transaction data, this paper proposes a zero-knowledge proof privacy protection scheme based on blockchain architecture using Pedersen commitment and Bulletproofs protocol. It involves four main stages:

(1) Value concealment stage, where the on-chain data is initialized using the Pedersen encryption algorithm.
(2) Covert computation stage, where the smart contract automatically executes the business logic code for homomorphic calculations.
(3) Zero-knowledge proof generation stage, where the client company generates the range proof off-chain.
(4) Zero-knowledge proof verification stage, where the financial institution evaluates the legality and correctness of the proof.

Value Concealment. To ensure the privacy of the information, the data needs to be stored in ciphertext. Pedersen commitment [9] is a homomorphic commitment protocol that satisfies computational binding. The Pedersen commitment protocol is used to encrypt the plaintext of the transaction amount of the order. The process is as follows:

(1) Generate a random number r_1 as the blinding factor.
(2) Compute the commitment value C_1 for the plaintext m_1 using the blinding factor r_1, as shown in the following calculation:

$$C_1 = m_1 G + r_1 H \tag{1}$$

(3) Upload the computed commitment value C_1 to the blockchain.

Covert Computation. When a customer business user confirms receipt, the smart contract automatically executes predefined business logic code to accumulate the transaction amount of the current order into the enterprise's total transaction amount. During the operation, ciphertexts of the transaction amount are used, enabling hidden computation.

(1) Obtain the commitment value C_1 corresponding to the order's transaction amount and C_2 representing the current total transaction amount.
(2) Calculate $C_{new} = C_1 + C_2$. This step utilizes the additive homomorphism property of Pedersen commitments, which can be explained as follows:

$$\begin{aligned} Comm(m_1 + m_2) &= (m_1 + m_2) \times G + (r_1 + r_2) \times H \\ &= (m_1 \times G + r_1 \times H) + (m_2 \times G + r_2 \times H) \\ &= Comm(m_1) + Comm(m_2) \end{aligned} \tag{2}$$

(3) Update the stored ciphertext of the total transaction amount for the customer enterprise on the blockchain to C_{new}.
(4) The blinding factor for the customer enterprise's total transaction amount commitment needs updating to $r_1 + r_2$, where r_1 is for the order transaction amount commitment, and r_2 is for the enterprise's total transaction amount commitment.

Zero-Knowledge Proof Generation. When an enterprise has financing needs, it can generate a zero-knowledge proof π, which consists of two parts: prove and commitment. The prove part is the main component of the proof and provides evidence of the hidden value within the range $[0, 2^n)$, while the commitment part is a Pedersen commitment to the hidden value. To prove that the transaction total A exceeds a certain *limit*, we actually only need to prove that the difference $R = A - limit$ lies within the range $[0, 2^n)$. The steps are shown in Fig. 2.

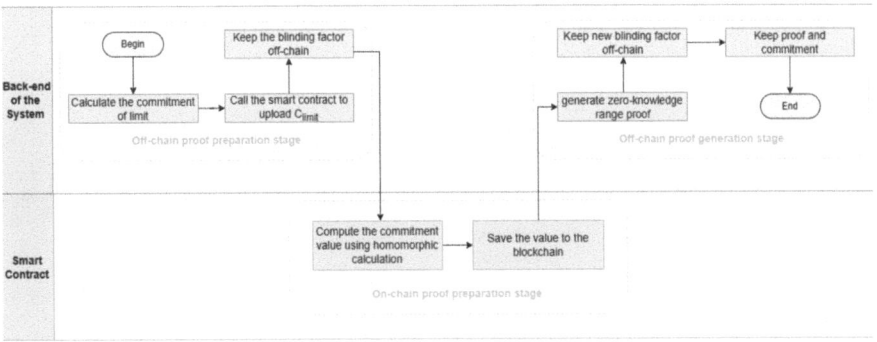

Fig. 2. Flowchart of Zero-Knowledge Proof Generation

(1) Off-chain proof preparation stage: Firstly, the threshold limit is committed using the Pedersen algorithm, which generates a commitment value C_{limit} and a blinding factor r_{limit} bound to it.

(2) On-chain proof preparation stage: The current transaction total commitment value C_A of the customer enterprise on the blockchain is obtained, along with the commitment value C_{limit} of the threshold limit. Calculate $R = A - limit$ and $C_R = C_A - C_{limit}$. The calculated Pedersen commitment for the difference value is then stored on the blockchain.

(3) Off-chain proof generation stage: In this stage, the Bulletproofs protocol [10] is used to generate a zero-knowledge range proof. Bulletproofs is a non-interactive, non-trusted setup zero-knowledge proof protocol. In this step, a range proof $A - limit \in [0, 2^n)$ is generated.

Zero-Knowledge Proof Verification. After the customer enterprise generates the range proof of the transaction total off-chain, financial institutions need to verify it. The verification of this zero-knowledge proof is divided into two steps: smart contract verification and off-chain verification. In the smart contract verification stage, it is determined whether the value of $A - limit$ is within the proof range, using verification methods from the Bulletproofs protocol. The verification process is shown in Fig. 3. In the off-chain verification stage, the correctness of the limit value is verified. The verification process is shown in Fig. 4.

(1) Smart contract verification stage: The smart contract receives two parameters: prove and commitment. First, the smart contract compares the incoming commitment with the commitment value C_R calculated during the on-chain proof preparation stage to

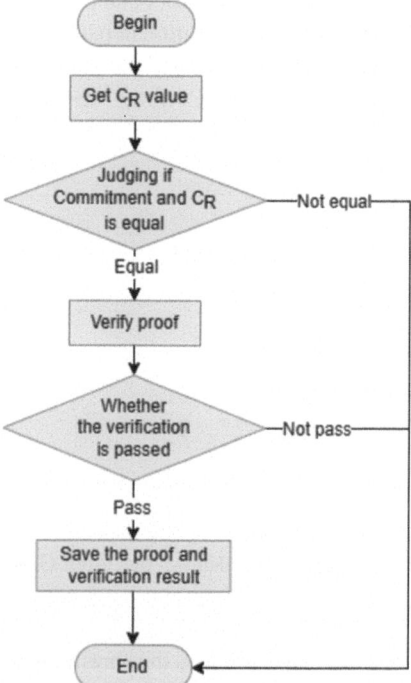

Fig. 3. Smart Contract Verification Stage

determine if the proof reveals the secret of $A - limit$. Then, the smart contract calls the verification method from the Bulletproofs protocol to verify if the proof is a valid range proof for the commitment. If the verification passes, the proof, commitment values, and verification results are stored in the blockchain as certificate.

(2) Off-chain verification stage: The previous verification step can only determine if the value of $A - limit$ is within the proof range but does not disclose the value of limit. When the client company needs to apply for financing from the financial institution, they provide the limit value and the blinding factor r_{limit} from the proof to the financial institution. The value of r_{limit} is stored off-chain during the generation of the zero-knowledge proof. The financial institution, upon obtaining limit and r_{limit}, can perform off-chain verification. First, they retrieve the commitment value C_{limit} from the blockchain, by using Eq. (1), they can verify the correctness of the limit value provided by the client company. At this point, the financial institution can trust that the client company's current transaction total on the platform is indeed greater than the certain predetermined value limit.

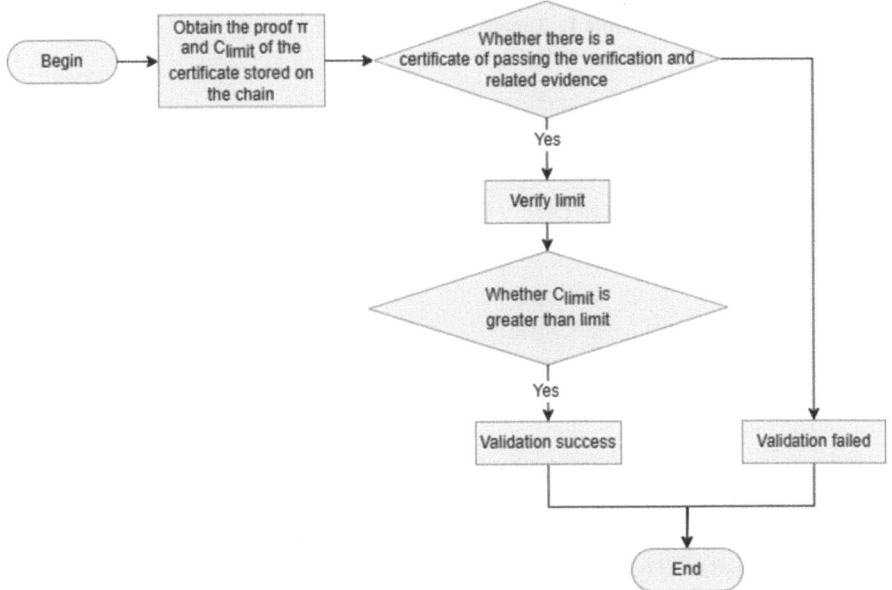

Fig. 4. Off-chain Verification Stage

4 Experimental Results and Analysis

In this paper, we utilize ChainMaker to build a consortium blockchain network and implement the designed zero-knowledge proof solution. The deployed blockchain network for this experiment consists of a 4-node cluster running on a single machine, with the TPFT consensus algorithm. The experiments were conducted using a 64-bit CentOS 7.6 operating system, running on a 4-core Intel CPU.

Performance Analysis. To analyze the feasibility of the zero-knowledge proof proposed in this paper, experiments were conducted with the proof values taken at four orders of magnitude: 28, 216, 232, and 264. The results shown in Table 1 represent the average time taken for 10,000 operations.It can be observed that in the range proof operations discussed in this paper, for any values of x within the int64 range, the execution times of each step are relatively stable. Furthermore, the step that consumes a relatively long time, generating the range proof, is performed off-chain. Therefore, the privacy protection scheme of international cold chain trade proposed in this paper is considered feasible.

Additional, the size of the Bulletproofs proof remains constant and does not vary with the size of the proven value. In this experiment, with $n = 64$, the size of the zero-knowledge range proof is fixed at 672 bytes, which is reasonable for application within the system.

Table 1. Time-consuming for each step.

Step\Time-consuming	2^8	2^{16}	2^{32}	2^{64}
Generate Pedersen Commitment	0.20 ms	0.21 ms	0.21 ms	0.25 ms
Homomorphic Encryption Commitment	20.05 μs	22.24 μs	23.03 μs	26.55 μs
Generate Zero-Knowledge Range Proof	71.01 ms	70.10 ms	68.47 ms	69.60 ms
Verify Proof and Commitment	3.65 ms	3.66 ms	3.62 ms	3.64 ms

Security Analysis. The cold chain privacy protection scheme of international trade proposed in this paper has the characteristics of privacy, zero knowledge, inter-organization trust and so on.

Privacy: The client enterprise's transaction total is computed through homomorphic operations on encrypted values using the Pedersen algorithm. Therefore, the privacy of the amounts is based on the security of Pedersen commitments.

Zero-Knowledge: The verifier cannot directly or indirectly compute the specific value of but can ascertain that it exceeds a certain threshold. The Bulletproofs protocol guarantees the zero-knowledge property of the entire process.

Inter-Organizational Trust: Smart contracts deployed on the blockchain platform automatically execute predetermined rules for calculating enterprise transaction totals and verifying range proofs. The blockchain's immutability and consensus mechanism ensure the integrity and correctness of rule execution, promoting the mutual trust.

5 Conclusion

Traditional international cold chain trading platforms are centrally maintained by the platform operator, which poses risks of data tampering, and there is a lack of trust among participants in the business chain. Blockchain technology, with its immutability and traceability features, can effectively address the issue of data trust in international cold chain trading. In this paper, we have designed and implemented an ICCTP based on blockchain. By ensuring data immutability, authenticity, and privacy, the platform enhances trust among all participants.

References

1. Johar, S., Ahmad, N., Asher, W., et al.: Research and applied perspective to blockchain technology: a comprehensive survey. Appl. Sci. **11**(14), 6252 (2021)
2. Kumar, S., Bharti, A.K., Amin, R.: Decentralized secure storage of medical records using blockchain and IPFS: a comparative analysis with future directions. Secur. Priv. **4**(5), e162 (2021)
3. Zhou, Y., Wei, Z., Ma, S., Tang, H.: Overview of zero-knowledge proof and its applications in Blockchain, in Blockchain technology and application. In: Sun, Y., Cai, L., Wang, W., Song, X., Lu, Z. (eds.) CBCC 2022. CCIS, vol. 1736, pp. 60–82. Springer, Cham (2022). https://doi.org/10.1007/978-981-19-8877-6_5
4. Alqaryouti, O., Shallan, K.: Trade facilitation framework for e-commerce platforms using blockchain. Int. J. Bus. Inf. Syst. **40**(2), 238–258 (2020)
5. Kumar, S., Amin, R.: Decentralized trade finance using blockchain and lightning network. Secur. Priv. **5**(6), e260 (2022)
6. Chen, Y.Y., Lai, H.C., Huang, J.L., et al.: The design and implementation of a blockchain-based logistics platform for international trade. In: 2021 22nd Asia-Pacific Network Operations and Management Symposium (APNOMS). pp. 234–237. IEEE (2021)
7. Islam, M., Rehmani, M.H., Chen, J.: Transparency-privacy trade-off in blockchain-based supply chain in industrial internet of things. In: 2021 IEEE 23rd Int Conf on High Performance Computing & Communications; 7th International Conference on Data Science & Systems; 19th International Conference on Smart City; 7th International Conference on Dependability in Sensor, Cloud & Big Data Systems & Application (HPCC/DSS/SmartCity/DependSys). pp. 1123–1130. IEEE (2021)
8. Al-Shaibani, H., Lasla, N., Abdallah, M., et al.: Privacy-preserving framework for blockchain-based stock exchange platform. IEEE Access **10**, 1202–1215 (2021)
9. Pedersen, T.P.: Non-interactive and information-theoretic secure verifiable secret sharing. In: Feigenbaum, J. (ed.). CRYPTO 1991. LNCS, vol. 576, pp. 129–140. Springer, Heidelberg (1991). https://doi.org/10.1007/3-540-46766-1_9
10. Bünz, B., Bootle, J., Boneh, D., et al.: Bulletproofs: short proofs for confidential transactions and more. In 2018 IEEE Symposium on Security and Privacy (SP), pp. 315–334. IEEE (2018)

Blockchain-Based Federated Recommendation with Incentive Mechanism

Jianhai Chen[1], Yanlin Wu[1], Dazhong Rong[1], Guoyao Yu[1], Lingqi Jiang[1], Zhenguang Liu[1], Peng Zhou[2], and Rui Shen[1(✉)]

[1] College of Computer Science and Technology, Zhejiang University, Hangzhou, China
{chenjh919,3200101006,rdz98,yuguoyao23,3210100336,rshen}@zju.edu.cn
[2] Info & Comm Branch, State Grid Zhejiang Electric Power Company, Hangzhou, China
zhou_peng@zj.sgcc.com.cn

Abstract. Nowadays, federated recommendation technology is rapidly evolving to help multiple organisations share data and train models while meeting user privacy, data security and government regulatory requirements. However, federated recommendation increases customer system costs such as power, computational and communication resources. Besides, federated recommendation systems are also susceptible to model attacks and data poisoning by participating malicious clients. Therefore, most customers are unwilling to participate in federated recommendation without any incentive. To address these problems, we propose a blockchain-based federated recommendation system with incentive mechanism to promote more trustworthy, secure, and efficient federated recommendation service. First, we construct a federated recommendation system based on NeuMF and FedAvg. Then we introduce a reverse auction mechanism to select optimal clients that can maximize the social surplus. Finally, we employ blockchain for on-chain evidence storage of models to ensure the safety of the federated recommendation system. The experimental results show that our proposed incentive mechanism can attract clients with superior training data to engage in the federal recommendation at a lower cost, which can increase the economic benefit of federal recommendation by 54.9% while improve the recommendation performance. Thus our work provides theoretical and technological support for the construction of a harmonious and healthy ecological environment for the application of federal recommendation.

Keywords: Federated recommendation · Federated learning on Blockchain · Incentive mechanism

---

J. Chen and Y. Wu—The two authors contributed equally to this work.

G. Zhao et al. (Eds.): BWTAC 2024, CCIS 2277, pp. 202–213, 2025.
https://doi.org/10.1007/978-981-97-9412-6_19

1   Introduction

Nowadays, various application platform service providers (*e.g.*, State Grid APP) have formed a "data silo" after a long period of accumulation. Thus if there is a mechanism that can open up the silo to make the data flow, it will bring a great deal of value. Utilizing data for recommendations is a primary way of maximizing its potential. However, the volume and quality of data play a decisive role in the effectiveness of recommendation algorithms [6]. At present, most commercial enterprises face the problems of insufficient data quantity and poor data quality [13,17,21], which makes it difficult to fully develop high-quality recommender system technology. Furthermore, global attention to data privacy protection and security has led to the issuance of legislations like the most notably General Data Protection Regulation (GDPR) [18,22], which have made data acquisition even more challenging. In this context, federated recommendation was born. It is a federated learning framework that enables different organizations share data and train recommendation models together, balancing the demands of data security, user privacy concerns, and government regulations. A typical federated recommendation system is composed of a central server and other clients that provide training data. The server releases federated recommendation assignments and manages clients' participation in the process of model training. Clients upload local model parameters or gradients, which the server aggregates. Then the server sends global recommendation model parameters back to all participating clients.

However, federated recommendations tend to increase client system costs, including power, communication resources and computing resources. Besides, customers are exposed to privacy leakage risks during the training process [11]. Federated recommendation systems are also susceptible to model attacks and data poisoning by the participants. Thus, most clients are unwilling to engage in federated recommendations voluntarily without any economic incentive. To address these drawbacks, we propose a blockchain-based federated recommendation system with a truthful incentive mechanism that can be divided into three phases: 1) Clients get the opportunity to participate in training through auction. 2) Selected clients train and upload local model parameters for evidence storage on the blockchain. 3) The server uses uploaded model parameters on the chain to aggregate. This mechanism enables the server to retrace user-uploaded model information at any time, effectively tracking down malicious behaviours while credibly calculating incentives to be paid out to honest users.

The main contributions of this paper can be summarized as follows.

1. We construct a federated recommendation system based on NeuMF [4] and FedAvg [12], which keeps the user's embedding layers locally to protect user privacy data.
2. We propose a D3QN-based reverse auction mechanism by which clients need to bid for the opportunity to participate in federated recommendations. Through our auction mechanism, we can select the optimal client set to achieve the highest economic benefits and save the costs.
3. We employ blockchain for on-chain evidence storage of models to ensure the safety and the trustworthiness of the federated recommendation system.

2   Related Work

The research on federated recommendation systems is still in its early stages compared to conventional centralized recommendation systems. Recently, Lin et al. [9] used various recommendation algorithms as microservices and proposed FedNeuMF. FedNeuMF is a federated collaborative filtering recommendation model, accomplishing distributed recommendation microservices application which preserves privacy. However, these federated recommendation systems are neither truthful and secure nor do they provide incentives for the participants.

Stealing or modifying client-uploaded local model parameters is a major problem in federated recommendations [19,20,23]. Besides, if the server is attacked, it can potentially incur a single-point failure and thereby impair the entire federated recommendation system. As a solution, Blockchain, a ledger technology [14], can be adapted to offer trust assurance for federated recommendations due to its unique characteristics of immutability, decentralization and traceability.

Although there has been some research on blockchain-based federated learning [3,5,7,10,15,16], there is still very little research on blockchain-based federated recommendation. Besides, blockchain-based federation learning is not applicable to the actual scenario of federation recommendation. In traditional blockchain-based federation learning, the client uploads complete model parameters to the server for aggregation, and the server uploads complete global model parameters to the client. However, in the federated recommendation scenario, due to factors such as protecting the client's user privacy and network efficiency, clients only upload model parameters excluding user embedding layers instead of complete parameters. Therefore, we propose a new truthful and secure blockchain-based federated recommendation framework with incentive mechanism [1,2].

3   Preliminaries

We first introduce the preliminary knowledge of federated recommendation, then present the model on which our federated recommendation system is based.

3.1   Federated Recommendation

Current federated recommendation systems typically base on a Client-Server architecture, where a group of edge devices known as clients take part in training under the direction of a central server. Each client k has its own dataset D_k, containing M users and N items. The dataset can be represented as an user-item interaction matrix $\mathbf{Y} \in \mathbb{R}^{M \times N}$. In explicit feedback, value y_{ui} within this matrix represents the rating of user u for item i. In implicit feedback, y_{ui} equals 1 if the user u once interacted with the item i, otherwise y_{ui} equals 0. Each client's local learning can be formalized as learning $\hat{y}_{ui} = f(u, i|\mathbf{w}_k)$, where f refers to the function that maps model input to the predicted score, $\hat{y}_{ui}$ is the predicted rating of user u for item i and $\mathbf{w}_k$ indicates the model parameters of client. After the local training converges, each client uploads its local model parameters to the server for model aggregation. The server only gathers model parameters rather than local training data from the clients, reducing data transmission cost and at the same time securing users' privacy. The process of Federated Recommendation contains the following three steps:

Step 1: Initialization. The server initializes the global model parameters $\mathbf{w}_g$ and transmits them to all clients, to serve as initial model parameters.

Step 2: Local Model Training and Updates. After receiving the global parameters $\mathbf{w}_g^t$, where t signifies the latest global update epoch, local client k proceeds training through local dataset D_k until it converges, i.e.,

$$\mathbf{w}_k^{t^*} = \arg \min_{\mathbf{w}_k^t} L(\mathbf{w}_k^t), \tag{1}$$

where L represents the local model's loss function. Then, each client uploads the updated local model parameters $\mathbf{w}_k^t$ to the server.

Step 3: Global Model Aggregation. The server aggregates all received local model and sends the updated global model parameters $\mathbf{w}_g^{t+1}$ to all clients.

Steps 2 and 3 are iterated until the global model converges, *i.e.*, the global loss function $L(\mathbf{w}_g^t)$ is minimised. $L(\mathbf{w}_g^t)$ can be formulized as:

$$L(\mathbf{w}_g^t) = \frac{1}{N} \sum_{k \in \mathcal{N}} L(\mathbf{w}_k^t), \tag{2}$$

where $\mathcal{N}$ denotes the set of local clients and N denotes set size.

3.2   Based Recommendation Model

We use the NeuMF model proposed in [4] and federate it. NeuMF consists of two parts: one is the Generalized Matrix Factorization (GMF) which learns the linear patterns of user-item interactions, the other is a Multi-Layer Perceptron (MLP) which learns the non-linear patterns of user-item interactions. The outputs of these two parts are then merged into a predicted score. The NeuMF model can be expressed as the following formulation:

$$\phi^{GMF} = \mathbf{p}_u^G \odot \mathbf{q}_i^G,$$
$$\phi^{MLP} = a_L(\mathbf{W}_L^T(a_{L-1}(...a_2(\mathbf{W}_2^T \begin{bmatrix} \mathbf{p}_u^M \\ \mathbf{q}_i^M \end{bmatrix} + \mathbf{b}_2)...)) + \mathbf{b}_L), \tag{3}$$
$$\hat{y}_{ui} = \sigma(\mathbf{h}^T \begin{bmatrix} \phi^{GMF} \\ \phi^{MLP} \end{bmatrix}),$$

where ϕ denotes the output, $\odot$ indicates the element-wise product, $\mathbf{p}_u^G$ and $\mathbf{p}_u^M$ represent the user latent vectors in GMF and MLP, and $\mathbf{q}_i^G$ and $\mathbf{q}_i^M$ similarly represent the item latent vectors in GMF and MLP, which are the results of multiplying the user and item embedding layers $\mathbf{P}$ and $\mathbf{Q}$ by the one-hot coding of the user and item. $\mathbf{W}_n$, a_n and $\mathbf{b}_n$ denote the weight matrix, activation function and bias vector of the n-th layer perceptron respectively. σ represents the sigmoid function and $\mathbf{h}$ denotes the edge weight of the output layer.

4   Our Method

In this chapter, we first propose a reverse auction mechanism designed for Federated Recommendation. Through this mechanism, we can select the optimal set of clients to maximize social surplus, enhancing recommendation performance while saving cost as we have fewer clients to pay for. We then introduce the process of training and updating the local recommendation model. Lastly, we present a mechanism for aggregating global models.

4.1   The Reverse Auction Scheme

In Federated Recommendation, the parameters of the global recommendation model are obtained by aggregating all uploaded local recommendation model parameters. Therefore, the effectiveness of local model training is crucial to the overall performance of the recommendation system. In practical recommendation scenarios, data possessed by different clients is often imbalanced and non-iid, and the heterogeneity of data substantially slows down the convergence speed of Federated Recommendation and undermines its final recommendation effect. Thus, it is necessary to make a preliminary judgment on data quality from clients before they participate in training to exclude those with extremely low data quality. We employ Earth Mover's Distance (EMD) to signify the data quality of clients. For client i, the EMD distance σ_i can represent the difference in data distribution between client i and global, i.e.,

$$\sigma_i = \sum_{r \in \mathcal{R}} \|\mathbb{P}_i(y = r) - \mathbb{P}_g(y = r)\|, \tag{4}$$

where, $\mathcal{R}$ denotes the range of ratings, $\mathbb{P}_i$ denotes the local data distribution, $\mathbb{P}_g$ denotes the global data distribution obtained empirically.

The goal of our designed reverse auction mechanism is to maximize the social surplus of federated recommendation, where the profit generated by the federated recommendation is determined by the final global model's accuracy. Before training, we can estimate the data utility of client i based on the size of the client's training data s_i and the EMD distance σ_i of the training data set. [8] proposes that the relationship between the final global model quality Q of federated learning and the total dataset size D of the participating training clients' set C and the average EMD distance Δ can be represented as follows:

$$Q(C) = \alpha(\Delta) - \kappa_1 e^{-\kappa_2 (\kappa_3 D)^{\alpha(\Delta)}}, \tag{5}$$

where D is the total dataset size of the participating training clients, i.e., $D(C) = \sum_{i \in C} s_i$. Δ is the average EMD distance of the participating training clients, i.e., $\Delta(C) = \frac{\sum_{i \in C} \sigma_i}{|C|}$. We specify $\Delta(\emptyset) = 0$. $\alpha(\Delta) = \kappa_4 \exp(-(\frac{\Delta + \kappa_5}{\kappa_6})^2) < 1$. The machine learning quality function $Q(C)$ is determined by a curve fitting method. $\kappa_1, \ldots, \kappa_6 > 0$ are positive curve fitting parameters. Since the revenue R of the system is related to the quality of global model, R can be represented as $R(C) = \lambda Q(C)$, where λ denotes the satisfaction weight parameter. Ignoring power expenditure and communication costs, the cost of our federated recommendation system considers only the incentives paid to the clients. In our reverse auction mechanism, client i needs to send its local dataset size s_i, EMD distance σ_i and bid b_i to the server. Thus, the system social surplus can be calculated as $S = R(C) - \sum_{i=1}^{n} b_i C_i$, where we express the client selection set C in vector form, i.e., $C \in (0,1)^n$, where $C_i = 1$ means client i is selected, and $C_i = 0$ means client i is not selected. Therefore, the goal of our reverse auction mechanism is to find the best set of clients to maximize our system's social surplus. The optimal client selection vector can be expressed as follows:

$$C^* = \text{argmax}_{C \in (0,1)^n} \left[R(C) - \sum_{i=1}^{n} b_i C_i \right]. \tag{6}$$

Due to the NP-hard nature of maximizing social surplus, we use the Deep Reinforcement Learning(DRL) algorithm Double Dueling Deep Q-Network (D3QN) to calculate C^*. This model combines Double Q-Learning with Dueling Network architecture into Deep Q-Networks, improving learning performance and stability, enabling it to avoid overestimation and handle more complicated tasks. Our proposed D3QN framework is shown in Fig. 1, comprising states, actions, state transitions, rewards, and policy defined as follows.

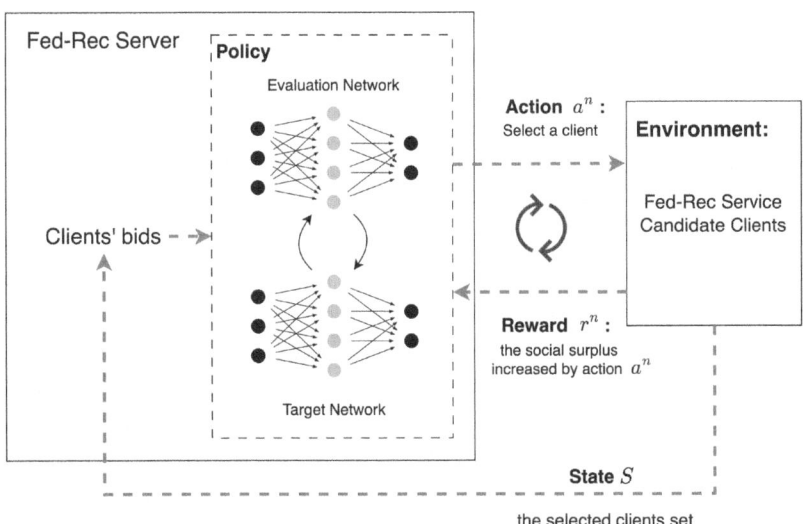

Fig. 1. The best clients select mechanism based on D3QN.

State: A state at step n can be formalized as $s^n = \{s_1^n, ..., s_i^n, ..., s_N^n\}$,which contains the states of clients representing whether they have been selected into the candidate set $\mathcal{V}^n$. That is, if $i \in \mathcal{V}^n$ then $s_i^n = 1$, otherwise $s_i^n = 0$.

Action: An action a^n is an index, indicating that at step n, client a^n is selected into the candidate list $\mathcal{V}^{n+1}$ from not being a candidate item in $\mathcal{V}^n$.

State Transition: If action a^n is taken, the global state would transit from s^n to s^{n+1} as the client's state s_{a^n} would transit from 0 to 1. Besides, client a^n would be added to the candidate set, i.e., $\mathcal{V}^{n+1} = \mathcal{V}^n \cup \{a^n\}$.

Reward: The reward r^n is the increase of social surplus when action a^n is taken at state s^n. It can be calculated by the following formula:

$$r^n = S(\mathcal{V}^n \cup \{a^n\}) - S(\mathcal{V}^n), \tag{7}$$

where S is the social surplus function defined by equation (6).

Policy: We first use evaluate network $Q'(s^n, a^n; w_e)$ to select the optimal action. Then we use the target network $Q(s^n, a^n; w_t)$ to compute the value of this action's to obtain target value. The combination of these two networks can avoid overestimation. Besides, we choose the $\epsilon - greedy$ strategy, expressed as follows:

$$a^n = \begin{cases} \underset{a^n}{\mathrm{argmax}} Q(s^n, a^n; w_t) & \text{, with a probability } \epsilon \\ \text{randomly select a client in } \mathcal{N} \setminus \mathcal{V}^n & \text{, with a probability } 1 - \epsilon \end{cases}. \tag{8}$$

4.2   The Updating Process of Local Model

We have introduced our based recommendation model, the NeuMF model, in Sect. 3.2. We can summarise the model parameters of NeuMF as user embeddings $\mathbf{p}$, item embeddings $\mathbf{q}$ and the parameters $\mathbf{W}$, $\mathbf{b}$, a of the perceptual layers. In classical federated learning, the client directly downloads the complete global model parameters as local model initialisation in each round, and uploads the complete local model parameters after training is finished. However, in our federated recommendation scenario, in order to protect the client user's private information and improve the network efficiency, the client generally does not upload the user's embeddings $\mathbf{p}$. Thus, only $\mathbf{q}$, $\mathbf{W}$, $\mathbf{b}$, a are uploaded to the server for aggregation. The local model updating process of clients in our federated recommendation system is as follows.

Step 1: Local model initialization. Download the latest global recommendation model parameters $\mathbf{w}_g$ from the blockchain. The parameter $\mathbf{w}_g$ here contains only global item embeddings $\mathbf{q_g}$ and the parameters $\mathbf{W_g}$, $\mathbf{b_g}$, a_g of the global perceptual layers, without user embeddings $\mathbf{p}$. Local model parameter $\mathbf{w}_k$ contains local item embeddings $\mathbf{q_k}$ and the parameters $\mathbf{W_k}$, $\mathbf{b_k}$, a_k of the local perceptual layers as well as the local user embeddings $\mathbf{p_k}$. Therefore, $\mathbf{q_k}$, $\mathbf{W_k}$, $\mathbf{b_k}$, a_k are overwritten by $\mathbf{w}_g$, while the user embeddings $\mathbf{p_k}$ remain unchanged.

Step 2: Local model training. The model conducts a forward propagation first, obtaining the predicted score y_{ui}. The loss is then computed and the objective function used can be expressed as:

$$L = \sum_{(u,i) \in \mathcal{Y} \cup \mathcal{Y}^-} w_{ui}(y_{ui} - \hat{y}_{ui})^2, \tag{9}$$

where $\mathcal{Y}$ signifies all observed interactions in the user-item interaction matrix $\mathbf{Y}$, and $\mathcal{Y}^-$ denotes all negative samples, which are sampled from interactions that have not been observed. w_{ui} represents the weight of the training instance (u, i). The model parameters can then be updated through standard back-propagation. The parameter update expression for the t-th epoch is as $\mathbf{w}_k^t = \mathbf{w}_k^{t-1} - \alpha \nabla L$, where α represents the learning rate. Finally, the model iterates and optimizes until the loss no longer decreases significantly or the pre-set maximum number of iterations is reached.

Step 3: Local model upload. After the client completes local training, the final local model parameters $\mathbf{w}_k^*$ are uploaded to the record blockchain. The blockchain enables server to retrace user-uploaded model information at any time, effectively tracking down malicious behaviours while credibly calculating incentives through records.

4.3   The Design of Aggregation Mechanism

We perform an aggregation operation with the FedAvg algorithm, which is represented as $\mathbf{w}_g^{t+1} = \sum_{k=1}^{N} \frac{n_k}{n} \mathbf{w}_k^t$, where N represents the number of honest clients, n represents the size of the sum of all datasets belonging to clients, n_k refers to the size of the dataset of the client k, $\mathbf{w}_k^t$ represents the model parameters for the client k in global epoch t, and $\mathbf{w}_g^{t+1}$ stands for the global model parameters for $(t+1)$-th global epoch. After the completion of aggregation, the latest global model parameters are uploaded to the blockchain while the selected clients are paid based on the previous bids. The blockchain records the global model information, ensuring that the records of the auction process and the training process are tamper-proof and traceable. This ensures the security and trustworthiness of the federated recommender system.

5   Experiments

In this section, we display our experimental setting, experimental methodology, and performance evaluation. We first introduce the simulation setup for various clients, then test the auction benefits of our reverse auction mechanism.

5.1   Experimental Settings

Experimental Environment. Table 1 shows our experimental environment.

Dataset. We experimented with MovieLens dataset. The MovieLens dataset is a publicly available film rating dataset released by the GroupLens laboratory. It's widely applied in research related to recommendation systems. The dataset includes versions with various amounts of ratings and we used the MovieLens 1M version. The users' ratings range from 1 to 5, denoting from strongly disliked (1) to strongly liked (5). The dataset also offers timestamp information for each rating, allowing researchers to investigate rating patterns based on time.

Table 1. Experimental environment

Component	Specification
CPU	18 vCPU AMD EPYC 9754 128-Core Processor
GPU	RTX 4090D(24GB) * 1
OS	Ubuntu 20.04
Cuda	11.3
Pytorch	1.11.0
Python	3.8

Evaluate Protocols. To authentically simulate various types of clients in the setting of federated recommendation scenarios, we set up a total of 20 clients with different volume and quality of train data. To analyze the performance of our proposed global model aggregation mechanism and reverse auction mechanism, we performed experiments through leave-one-out cross-validation. For each user, we retained their latest interaction as the test set and used the other data as the training set. Since sorting all the user ratings is time-consuming we adopted a common used strategy where we randomly selected 50 items for each user that had not been interacted with and then ranked the items in our test set among them. We measure the global model's rating prediction performance through the Mean Squared Error (MSE) loss between the predicted rating of the global model and the test set's real rating. Additionally, we also employ Hit Ratio (HR) and Normalized Discounted Cumulative Gain (NDCG) to analyze the performance of the ranked list. We only consider the top 10 of the ranked list. HR shows whether the test items appear within the top 10, while NDCG accounts for the hit location by giving higher scores to more highly ranked hits.

Parameter Settings. In our experiments, we implemented the federated recommendation model by Pytorch, using FedAvg for the global model aggregation and the Adam algorithm for parameter optimization. During the training, each training instance consists of one positive instance and four negative instances. We adopted an MSE loss function to train our model. For NeuMF, we initialized the parameters of the user and item embedding layers with a Gaussian distribution (mean value 0, variance of 0.01). We used Xavier Uniform to initialize the parameters of the multi-layer perceptron and Kaiming Uniform to initialize the parameters of the output layer. We set $\kappa1 = 0.361$, $\kappa2 = 4.348$, $\kappa3 = 10^{-3}$, $\kappa4 = 0.993$, $\kappa5 = 0.31$ and $\kappa6 = 1.743$ due to [8]. Besides, we set learning rate to 0.0005, training batch size to 64, the size of predictive factors to 32, the number of local iteration epochs to 5, the number of global iteration epochs to 10 and the satisfaction weight parameter $\lambda = 3000$.

5.2   Performance of Reverse Auction

In this section, we analyse the performance of the reverse auction mechanism based on D3QN. We employ our proposed reverse auction mechanism to select

Table 2. Comparison of HR@10 and NDCG@10 under different mechanisms.

Method	HR@10	NDCG@10
Greedy-All	0.511	0.290
Simple-Auction	0.525	0.288
D3QN-Auction	0.543	0.317

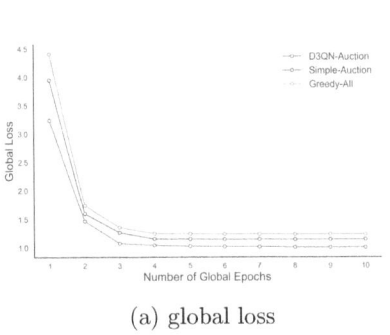

(a) global loss

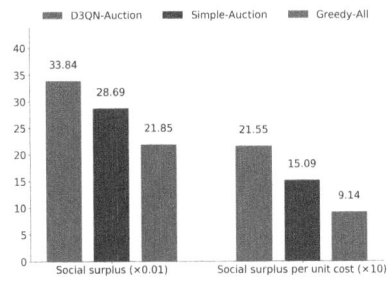

(b) total social surplus and per-unit cost social surplus

Fig. 2. Comparison under different auction mechanisms.

the optimal client set that maximizes social surplus and compare our reverse auction mechanism with two other auction mechanisms. One is Simple-Auction, which prioritizes clients with lower bid prices and selects 80% of all clients. The other is Greedy-All, which selects all clients. Our D3QN-Auction selected an optimal client set consisting of 11 clients, the Simple-Auction mechanism and the Greedy auction mechanism chose 16 and 20 clients, respectively. Figure 2a shows the comparison of global loss under three auction mechanisms, reflecting the global model's prediction accuracy. It is evident that the global loss of our proposed D3QN-Auction algorithm is lowest, reaching only 1.0023. This suggests that our reverse auction mechanism can achieve better training outcomes with fewer clients. Besides, the D3QN-Auction allows the global model to converge faster, thus it can save more time and resources. Table 2 shows the comparison of the HR@10 and NDCG@10 metrics of the global recommendation model under different auction mechanisms. It illustrates that, in terms of recommendation hit rates and ranking accuracy, D3QN-Auction still surpasses Greedy-All and Simple-Auction. Figure 2b presents a comparison of the total social surplus and per-unit cost social surplus under different auction mechanisms. In terms of total social surplus, our proposed D3QN-Auction method reached the highest value of 3384, which exceeds Greedy-All by 54.9%. In terms of per-unit cost social surplus, D3QN-Auction also achieved the best outcome, reaching 2.155, outperforming Greedy-All by 135.8%. Therefore, compared to Simple-Auction and Greedy-All, our proposed D3QN-based reverse auction mechanism can provide greater economic benefits and a higher return-on-investment ratio as it can achieve the expected recommendation effect at a lower cost. Under such an incentive mechanism, more high-quality clients can be attracted to join our federated recommendation tasks, leading to better recommendation results.

6   Conclusion and Future Work

In this paper, we primarily focuses on the research of blockchain-based federated recommendation with incentive mechanism. Our proposed blockchain-based federated recommendation system solves the problem of verifiable client contribution and the trustworthiness of the incentive mechanism. In the future, we consider adding some client malicious behavior defence mechanisms.

Acknowledgments. This work was funded by the Key R&D Program of Zhejiang Province (No. 2022C01086 and No. 2023C01217) and the National Natural Science Foundation of China (No. 62372402).

References

1. Chen, J., Ye, D., Ji, S., He, Q., Xiang, Y., Liu, Z.: A truthful FPTAS mechanism for emergency demand response in colocation data centers. In: IEEE INFOCOM 2019-IEEE Conference on Computer Communications, pp. 2557–2565. IEEE (2019)
2. Chen, J., Ye, D., Liu, Z., Ji, S., He, Q., Xiang, Y.: A truthful and near-optimal mechanism for colocation emergency demand response. IEEE Trans. Mob. Comput. **20**(9), 2728–2744 (2020)
3. Feng, L., Zhao, Y., Guo, S., Qiu, X., Li, W., Yu, P.: BAFL: a blockchain-based asynchronous federated learning framework. IEEE Trans. Comput. **71**(5), 1092–1103 (2021)
4. He, X., Liao, L., Zhang, H., Nie, L., Hu, X., Chua, T.S.: Neural collaborative filtering. In: Proceedings of the 26th International Conference on World Wide Web, pp. 173–182 (2017)
5. Himeur, Y., et al.: Blockchain-based recommender systems: applications, challenges and future opportunities. Comput. Sci. Rev. **43**, 100439 (2022)
6. Hu, H., Rong, D., Chen, J., He, Q., Liu, Z.: CoMeta: Enhancing meta embeddings with collaborative information in cold-start problem of recommendation. In: Jin, Z., Jiang, Y., Buchmann, R.A., Bi, Y., Ghiran, A.M., Ma, W. (eds.) KSEM 2023. LNCS, vol. 14119, pp. 213–225. Springer, Cham (2023). https://doi.org/10.1007/978-3-031-40289-0_17
7. Issa, W., Moustafa, N., Turnbull, B., Sohrabi, N., Tari, Z.: Blockchain-based federated learning for securing internet of things: a comprehensive survey. ACM Comput. Surv. **55**(9), 1–43 (2023)
8. Jiao, Y., Wang, P., Niyato, D., Lin, B., Kim, D.I.: Toward an automated auction framework for wireless federated learning services market. IEEE Trans. Mob. Comput. **20**(10), 3034–3048 (2020)
9. Lin, W., Leng, H., Dou, R., Qi, L., Pan, Z., Rahman, M.A.: A federated collaborative recommendation model for privacy-preserving distributed recommender applications based on microservice framework. J. Parallel Distrib. Comput. **174**, 70–80 (2023)

10. Liu, E., Lu, T., Shen, R., Chen, J., Huang, B.: Efficient balancing A* search for multi-robot collaboration with blockchain consensus. In: Proceedings of the 5th ACM International Symposium on Blockchain and Secure Critical Infrastructure, pp. 114–122 (2023)
11. Ma, C., et al.: On safeguarding privacy and security in the framework of federated learning. IEEE Netw. **34**(4), 242–248 (2020)
12. McMahan, B., Moore, E., Ramage, D., Hampson, S., y Arcas, B.A.: Communication-efficient learning of deep networks from decentralized data. In: Artificial Intelligence and Statistics, pp. 1273–1282. PMLR (2017)
13. Nasr, M., Shokri, R., Houmansadr, A.: Comprehensive privacy analysis of deep learning: passive and active white-box inference attacks against centralized and federated learning. In: 2019 IEEE symposium on security and privacy (SP), pp. 739–753. IEEE (2019)
14. Nguyen, D.C., Pathirana, P.N., Ding, M., Seneviratne, A.: BEdgeHealth: a decentralized architecture for edge-based IoMT networks using blockchain. IEEE Internet Things J. **8**(14), 11743–11757 (2021)
15. Patel, S.B., Bhattacharya, P., Tanwar, S., Kumar, N.: KiRTi: a blockchain-based credit recommender system for financial institutions. IEEE Trans. Netw. Sci. Eng. **8**(2), 1044–1054 (2020)
16. Qin, Z., Ye, J., Meng, J., Lu, B., Wang, L.: Privacy-preserving blockchain-based federated learning for marine internet of things. IEEE Trans. Comput. Soc. Syst. **9**(1), 159–173 (2021)
17. Qu, Y., et al.: Decentralized privacy using blockchain-enabled federated learning in fog computing. IEEE Internet Things J. **7**(6), 5171–5183 (2020)
18. Regulation, P.: Regulation (EU) 2016/679 of the European parliament and of the council. Regulation (EU) **679**, 2016 (2016)
19. Rong, D., He, Q., Chen, J.: Poisoning deep learning based recommender model in federated learning scenarios. In: Proceedings of the Thirty-First International Joint Conference on Artificial Intelligence, IJCAI 2022, Vienna, Austria, 23–29 July 2022, pp. 2204–2210. Ijcai.org (2022)
20. Rong, D., Ye, S., Zhao, R., Yuen, H.N., Chen, J., He, Q.: FedRecAttack: model poisoning attack to federated recommendation. In: 2022 IEEE 38th International Conference on Data Engineering (ICDE), pp. 2643–2655. IEEE (2022)
21. Rong, D., et al.: Clean-image backdoor attacks. CoRR abs/2403.15010 (2024). https://doi.org/10.48550/ARXIV.2403.15010
22. Yang, Q., Liu, Y., Chen, T., Tong, Y.: Federated machine learning: concept and applications. ACM Trans. Intell. Syst. Technol. (TIST) **10**(2), 1–19 (2019)
23. Zhang, J., Li, H., Rong, D., Zhao, Y., Chen, K., Shou, L.: Preventing the popular item embedding based attack in federated recommendations. In: 40th IEEE International Conference on Data Engineering, ICDE 2024, Utrecht, The Netherlands, 13–16 May 2024, pp. 2179–2191. IEEE (2024). https://doi.org/10.1109/ICDE60146.2024.00173

A Treatment of EIP-1559: Enhancing Transaction Fee Mechanism Through N^{th}-Price Auction

Kun Li[1], Guangpeng Qi[2], Guangyong Shang[2], Wanli Deng[1], Minghui Xu[1(✉)], and Xiuzhen Cheng[1]

[1] Shandong University, Jinan, China
{kunli,mhxu,xzcheng}@sdu.edu.cn
[2] Inspur Yunzhou Industrial Internet Co., Ltd., Jinan, China
{qigp,shangguangyong}@inspur.com

Abstract. With the widespread adoption of blockchain technology, the transaction fee mechanism (TFM) in blockchain systems has become a prominent research topic. An ideal TFM should satisfy user incentive compatibility (UIC), miner incentive compatibility (MIC), and miner-user side contract proofness (c-SCP). However, state-of-the-art works either fail to meet these three properties simultaneously or only satisfy them under certain conditions. In this paper, we propose a burning N-price auction TFM named BNP. This mechanism divides the transaction fee into a base fee, which is burned, and a priority fee, which is allocated to miners. Theoretical proofs and experimental analyses demonstrate that, even under conditions of significant transaction congestion, this mechanism satisfies UIC, MIC, and c-SCP simultaneously. Furthermore, the BNP mechanism is not constrained by the type of blockchain consensus, making it widely applicable.

Keywords: Transaction fee mechanism · Auction mechanism · Blockchain · Incentive compatibility

1 Introduction

The improvement of hardware performance, the widespread embrace of cryptocurrencies, and ongoing refinements in consensus mechanisms have propelled the extensive utilization of blockchain technology across diverse transactional scenarios, including data storage and sharing [5,6,17], data asset trading [4,19], distributed learning [15,18], among others. This diverse range of application domains has resulted in an increase in the variety and complexity of transactions within blockchain systems. To expedite transaction validation and maintain the stability and integrity of blockchain networks, transaction fee mechanisms (TFM) have been introduced, representing the fees users must pay for on-chain transactions.

According to [2], an ideal Transaction Fee Mechanism (TFM) should satisfy the following three properties:

© The Author(s), under exclusive license to Springer Nature Singapore Pte Ltd. 2025
G. Zhao et al. (Eds.): BWTAC 2024, CCIS 2277, pp. 214–226, 2025.
https://doi.org/10.1007/978-981-97-9412-6_20

1. User Incentive Compatible (UIC): When other participants in the system behave honestly, users will bid truthfully.
2. Miner Incentive Compatible (MIC): When other participants in the system behave honestly, miners will adhere to the rules established by the TFM.
3. Miner-user Side Contract Proofness (c-SCP): Collusion between miners and up to c users cannot increase their joint payoff through dishonest behavior.

In some blockchain systems, such as Bitcoin [11], all transaction fees submitted by users belong to the miners. But this particular type of TFM fails to meet the aforementioned three properties, thereby presenting several drawbacks. Firstly, it lacks fairness, as miners tend to prioritize transactions with higher fees, making it challenging for lower-fee transactions to be included in blocks. Secondly, users may experience suboptimal transaction experiences due to the unpredictability of miners' behavior, leading to overpayment or transaction delays.

To address these issues, Ethereum's EIP-1559 proposal [14] has introduced a complex TFM that includes a fixed-per-block fee, which is burned. This innovative approach aims to enhance fee transparency, predictability, and fairness, ultimately improving the overall efficiency and user experience of the blockchain network.

However, TFMs based on second-price auctions, like EIP-1559, often struggle to simultaneously satisfy all three properties when block size is limited [12]. For example, during Ethereum network congestion, EIP-1559 may violate user incentive compatibility by reverting to first-price auctions. Several studies explore alternative approaches to address this issue in specific scenarios or consensus mechanisms. Notably, [13] investigates a TFM based on the burning second-price auction for Proof of Stake (PoS) and shows it can satisfy all three conditions under certain circumstances. Building on this, we propose the BNP mechanism-a TFM for congested states based on the burning N^{th}-price auction. Through theoretical analysis and experimental validation, we demonstrate that this mechanism meets all three conditions under the Proof of Work (PoW) consensus. The contributions in our paper are summarized as follows:

1. We propose a Transaction Fee Mechanism (TFM) that integrates N^{th}-price auctions with a burning process. This design ensures that UIC, MIC, and c-SCP are simultaneously satisfied, even under severe transaction congestion, effectively addressing the limitations of EIP-1559.
2. The TFM is not limited by the type of blockchain consensus and can be applied to a wider range of scenarios.
3. We found that most of the research on UIC, MIC, and c-SCP in academia remains in theory. This paper proposes a specific solution. And evaluates it on the real Ethereum.

The rest of this paper proceeds as follows. In Sect. 2, we summarize the related work on TFM in blockchain. An overview of our proposed TFM is presented in Sect. 3, which is specifically elaborated in Sect. 4. In Sect. 5, we conduct substantial experiments to evaluate our proposed mechanism. Finally, we conclude the whole paper in Sect. 6.

2   Related Works

With more and more cross-industry and application transactions in blockchain system, understanding and optimizing transaction fee mechanisms have become paramount for enhancing the efficiency, fairness, and stability of blockchain ecosystems. Consequently, the study of transaction fees within blockchain systems has emerged as a crucial area of research.

Liu et al. [9] systematically evaluated the impacts of TFM, analyzing EIP-1559's effects on transaction fees, wait times, and consensus security, and proposed improvements based on their findings. In another study, Liu et al. [10] tackled blockchain storage sustainability by suggesting that transaction fees offset rising storage costs. They developed a social welfare-maximizing mechanism modeled as a three-stage Stackelberg game, incentivizing users to cover storage costs through transaction fees.

In contrast to the focus of the aforementioned studies, Landis et al. [7] explored Stackelberg attacks on the transaction fee auction process. These attacks are applicable to first-price auctions, second-price auctions, and the transaction fee mechanism used in Ethereum's EIP-1559. Their research highlights the critical importance of designing transaction fees that are incentive-compatible to prevent such vulnerabilities.

Unlike traditional mechanism design, which focuses on bidder strategies, blockchain transaction fee auctions involve miners who, as auctioneers, may engage in malicious behavior [1,16]. Analyzing blockchain transactions, [3,8,12] propose that an ideal TFM should satisfy three key properties: user incentive compatibility, miner incentive compatibility, and miner-user side contract proofness.

Tang et al. [13] extend the TFM from [3] by incorporating a long-run utility model for miners. Their $BSP(\theta)$ mechanism meets all three TFM properties when θ is within a specific range and an appropriate 'tick' size is applied. They also introduce a strict γ utility model to prevent strategic dishonesty. However, this model requires unconfirmed transactions in the block, with only a random subset of size $\theta k/c$ confirmed, leading to wasted space and computing power, and is only applicable to PoS.

Chung et al. [2] show that no truthful mechanism can satisfy UIC, MIC, and OCA-proofness under transaction contention. They suggest easing this challenge by allowing non-genuine or coordinated bidding and propose an 'Inclusion-rule-respecting' approach, though specifics are not provided.

Building on these studies, we provide a detailed description of the BNP mechanism, which integrates the destruction mechanism with the N-price auction. This mechanism considers the long-term payoff for both miners and users and is theoretically and experimentally proven to satisfy the three properties of the ideal TFM, regardless of the consensus type.

3   Preliminary and Overview

As analyzed in Sect. 1, Ethereum's EIP-1559 [14] introduces a burning mechanism aimed at fulfilling the three key properties of TFM: user- and miner-incentive compatibility (UIC and MIC) and c-SCP, assuming an unlimited block size and no congestion in the blockchain system. EIP-1559 establishes a base fee for each block, with all transactions in that block burning an amount of ETH equal to the base fee multiplied by gasUsed. Additionally, users can increase the priority fee to expedite their transactions' inclusion in the next block, smoothing transaction fee fluctuations and reducing user intervention in transaction sequencing. However, since block sizes are limited and blockchain systems are prone to congestion, the TFM based on base and priority fees degrades into a first-price auction centered around the priority fee, failing to simultaneously satisfy the properties of TFM.

Building upon the foundations laid in [3,13] introduced the burning second-price auction mechanism $BSP(\theta)$ for PoS consensus. This mechanism, under the condition that the block size is limited, has been demonstrated to satisfy all three desired properties of the TFM under specified conditions.

Inspired by this research, we propose the BNP mechanism as illustrated in Fig. 1. In this mechanism, all users submit their bids for transaction fees in the form of a sealed-bid auction, and the top N bidders will pay at the Nth price. Similar to EIP-1559, this mechanism also divides the transaction fee into base fee and priority fee, where the base fee is burned, and the priority fee goes to the miners.

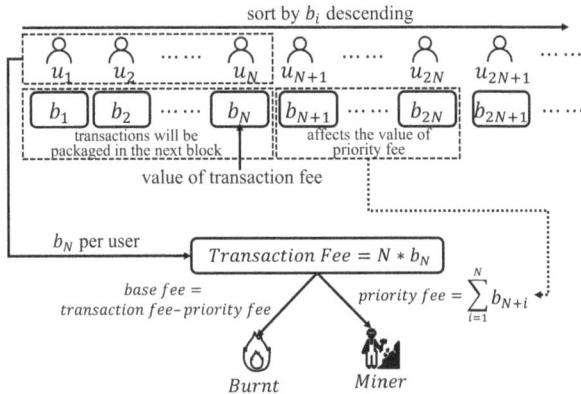

Fig. 1. Overview of BNP mechanism.

Specifically, transactions awaiting packaging in the transaction pool are sorted by bid for transaction fee from high to low, denoted as $\{b_1, b_2, ..., b_N, b_{N+1}, ...\}$, where N represents the number of transactions to be included in the next block. Following the principles of the N-price auction mechanism, the first N transactions will pay at the Nth transaction's bid price. That is, transactions $\{t_1, t_2, ..., t_N\}$ will be included in the next block with the cost of b_N. $b_i - b_N, i \in \{1, 2, ..., N\}$ will be refunded to user u_i. Of the total transaction fees $N \times b_N$ submitted to the blockchain system, $\sum_{i=1}^{N} b_{i+N}$ is considered the priority fee, which goes to the miners, while $N \times b_N - \sum_{1=1}^{N} b_{i+N}$ is considered the base fee, which will be burned. If the number of transactions awaiting packaging is less than $2N$, the missing values will be filled with zeros.

Unlike [13], the mechanism is not specific to any particular type of consensus. In the following discussion, we will demonstrate how this mechanism can still satisfy the three properties of TFM: UIC, MIC, and c-SCP even under conditions of limited block capacity and high transaction volume congestion.

4   The Properties of BNP Mechanism

From the above content, it is evident that when all users' bids for transaction fees are arranged in descending order as $b_1, b_2, ..., b_N, b_{N+1}, ...$, the miner's payoff function is:

$$\mathcal{P}_m = \sum_{i=1}^{N} b_{i+N} \tag{1}$$

In a given round of auctions, if a user u_i's transaction t_i is successfully included in the next block with the cost of b_N, he will receive the revenue generated from having the transaction confirmed on-chain. It's evident that u_i's bid b_i for the transaction fee is directly related to this revenue and cannot exceed it. Each user u_i has a psychological price b_i^{true} for the transaction fee, indicating the fee they are willing to pay. If the actual transaction fee paid exceeds b_i^{true}, u_i will perceive it as a loss. For simplicity, we assumes that the revenue u_i can generate from having his transaction included in a block is equivalent to b_i^{true}. In summary, if u_i's transaction is successfully included in the next block, he will receive b_i^{true} with a cost of b_N, resulting in the user's payoff function is:

$$\mathcal{P}_u = b_i^{true} - b_N \tag{2}$$

An honest user's bid b_i equals b_i^{true}. Clearly, in scenarios with a high volume of transactions and congested trading systems, users have the motivation to engage in the following dishonest behaviors which undermines UIC:

1. Fake bid: Refers to the user fabricating a transaction and submitting a bid to participate in the auction for transaction fees, despite having no actual transaction need.
2. Overbid: Refers to the user submitting a bid that exceeds his psychological price, i.e., $b_i > b_i^{true}$.
3. Underbid: Refers to the user submitting a bid that is lower than his psychological price, i.e., $b_i < b_i^{true}$.

On the other hand, in pursuit of higher profits, miners also have an incentive to fabricate a bid higher than b_N, intending to artificially inflate the clearing price without being detected, which renders MIC unfulfilled. It's important to note that due to the transparency of the blockchain transaction system, the transaction corresponding to this fake bid needs to be genuinely sent out by the miner and added to the pending transaction pool. If this transaction is not included in the current miner's block, it's highly likely to be included by other miners in the future. This implies that the miner would need to pay transaction fees to other miners.

Furthermore, since a miner's revenue is directly determined by bids from the $N+1^{th}$ to the $N+N^{th}$ positions, miners may also collude with users through off-chain negotiations to conspire. This collusion could involve incentivizing certain users to increase their bids, thus allowing the miner to achieve higher profits, which contradicts the requirement of c-SCP.

An ideal TFM should eliminate the incentives for all participants to engage in the aforementioned malicious behaviors. In the following sections, we will systematically demonstrate how the mechanism proposed in this paper, BNP, can probabilistically satisfy the three properties of the ideal TFM: UIC, MIC, and c-SCP.

4.1 User Incentive Compatible

In this section, we examine whether BNP adheres to UIC, ensuring that if u_i bids truthfully ($b_i = b_i^{true}$), his expected utility is maximized, assuming all other system participants are honest.

Based on the payment rules of the blockchain system, any fake bid offers no value to the user and necessitates paying transaction fees. It's evident that without collusion, users cannot gain any profit from fake bids; on the contrary, they would incur losses. Engaging in fake bidding is inherently irrational, as rational users lack motivation to partake in such behavior. Hence, in this section, our primary focus lies in analyzing two forms of dishonest conduct by users: underbidding and overbidding.

Let's delve into the scenario of overbidding, i.e., $b_i > b_i^{true}$. For t_i, u_i's bid can take on the following possibilities:

1. $b_N > b_i > b_i^{true}$: This indicates that the transaction will not be immediately packaged, resulting in no immediate consequences. However, there's a chance it might be packaged in the future at a price higher than b_i^{true}, which would result in a loss. Therefore, users will likely refrain from overbidding.
2. $b_i \geq b_N \geq b_i^{true}$: Initially, when the bid is at b_i^{true}, the transaction might not qualify for packaging. However, by increasing the bid to b_i, the transaction could become eligible for packaging at the expense of b_N. Nevertheless, the profits accrued from being packaged are outweighed by the costs users incur. Consequently, users are unlikely to engage in overbidding within this scenario.
3. $b_i > b_i^{true} \geq b_N$: In this case, the transaction can be packaged regardless of whether the user overbids. This scenario can be further divided into two subcases:

(a) $b_i > b_i^{true} = b_N$: This suggests that the bid precisely occupies the Nth position in the descending order of bids. Following an overbid, all users will be required to pay transaction fees of $\min b_i, b_{N-1}$. It's evident that the cost still surpasses the profit, hence users will continue to abstain from overbidding.

(b) $b_i > b_i^{true} > b_N$: This indicates that the bid ranks among the top $N-1$ bids after being sorted in descending order. Regardless of whether the user decides to overbid, the final transaction fee required remains b_N, and the user's payoff remains unchanged. Consequently, users lack any incentive to engage in overbidding within this scenario.

In summary, users refrain from overbidding, considering the possibility of transactions being packaged and the associated costs.

Next, let's delve into the scenario of underbidding, where $b_i < b_i^{true}$. This scenario can be categorized as follows:

1. $b_N > b_i^{true} > b_i$: Regardless of whether the user underbids, the transaction will not be packaged. Additionally, since the new bid is lower, miners tend to prioritize higher bids, potentially delaying the packaging of this transaction. Consequently, users lack motivation to underbid in this case.

2. $b_i^{true} \geq b_N > b_i$: In this case, if the user refrains from underbidding, the transaction is initially eligible for packaging. However, once underbidding occurs, the situation requires further examination, leading to the following two scenarios:

    (a) $b_i^{true} \geq b_N > b_{N+1} \geq b_i$: After underbidding, the transaction cannot be packaged, resulting in no corresponding profit. Similarly, due to the lower bid, the transaction's packaging might be delayed. Therefore, users lack motivation to underbid.

    (b) $b_i^{true} \geq b_N > b_i > b_{N+1}$: After underbidding, the transaction can still be packaged, and the transaction fee for all users decreases from b_N to b_i. In this case, since expenses decrease, users have motivation to underbid.

3. $b_i^{true} > b_i \geq b_N$: Regardless of whether the user underbids, the transaction will be packaged with the cost of b_N. Since the user's payoff remains unchanged, there is no motivation for the user to underbid.

Since transaction fees operate on a sealed-bid auction basis, users cannot predict the specific outcome of underbidding when making their bids. Moreover, during congestion, the difference between b_N and b_{N+1} tends to be minimal, indicating a low probability of Scenario 2b. Additionally, the potential gains are limited, not exceeding $b_N - b_{N+1}$. Without knowledge of other bids, underbidding poses a significant risk for relatively small returns. Considering all scenarios, rational users are unlikely to underbid.

Based on the above analysis, it can be concluded that the BNP mechanism has a high probability of satisfying UIC.

4.2   Miner Incentive Compatible

This section analyzes whether the miner can achieve higher profits through fake bids.

Unlike users, the miner have access to all bids, allowing him to precisely evaluate the potential profits from various fake bids and choose the most lucrative option. We denote the fake bid chosen by the miner as b_{fake}. As previously discussed, in the BNP mechanism, user expenses are determined by the Nth bid, while miner profits are determined by bids ranging from the $(N+1)^{th}$ to the $2N^{th}$ bid. Clearly, the miner would not choose to submit a bid lower than b_{2N}, as it would have no impact on his profits and would instead entail paying transaction fees for that transaction in the future. Moreover, we can further analyze the potential fake bids that the miner may consider in the following scenarios:

1. $b_N > b_{fake} \geq b_{2N}$: In this scenario, the miner's fake bid displaces b_{2N} from the top $2N$ bids, resulting in a payoff of $\mathcal{P}_m = \sum i = 1^{N-1} b_{i+N} + b_{fake}$. Compared to Eq. 1, the fake bid increases the miner's profit by $b_{fake} - b_{2N}$. To maximize profit, the miner would aim to raise b_{fake} as close to b_N as possible, i.e., $b_{fake} \to b_N$. However, as mentioned earlier, this transaction will eventually be processed by other miners, requiring the miner to pay a transaction fee b'_N. Thus, the profit from the fake bid is $\mathcal{P}_m^{fake} = b_{fake} - b_{2N} - b'_N$. If no new transactions enter before the next block, the new $(N+1)^{th}$ bid will be b_{2N}. If a new transaction with a higher bid enters, b_{2N} will be pushed further down, implying $b'_N > b_{2N}$. Therefore, $\mathcal{P}^{fake}m < b_N - 2b_{2N}$. During congestion, the difference between b_N and b_{2N} is typically small, making $b_N < 2b_{2N}$ likely, which suggests $\mathcal{P}_m^{fake}$ is likely negative. This indicates that miners are unlikely to profit from fake bidding in the long run.

2. $b_{N-1} \geq b_{fake} \geq b_N$: In this scenario, the fake bid submitted by the miner displaces b_N from the previous top N bids, resulting in users needing to pay a transaction fee of b_{fake} instead of b_N. Simultaneously, the miner must also pay b_{fake} as a transaction fee for this fake bid. As b_N becomes the $N+1^{th}$ bid in the sequence of all bids, the miner's payoff function becomes $(\sum_0^{N-1} b_{N+i}) - b_{fake}$. Comparing this with Eq. 1, it's evident that the profit brought by the fake bid for the miner is $\mathcal{P}_m^{fake} = b_N - b_{2N} - b_{fake}$. Since $b_N \leq b_{fake}$, $\mathcal{P}_m^{fake} \leq 0$, indicating that the miner cannot gain positive profits from engaging in fake bidding behavior.

3. $b_{fake} > b_{N-1} > b_N$: Similarly to the previous scenario, the transaction fee for users shifts to b_{N-1}, while the miner's payoff function transforms into $(\sum_0^{N-1} b_{N+i}) - b_{N-1}$. Consequently, it can be further inferred that the profit yielded by the fake bid for the miner is $\mathcal{P}_m^{fake} = b_N - b_{2N} - b_{N-1} \leq 0$. Clearly, the miner also cannot generate positive profits in this situation.

Building on the earlier examination, it's apparent that the BNP mechanism stands a good chance of meeting the conditions for MIC.

4.3   Miner-user Side Contract Proofness

Finally, this section analyzes whether the BNP mechanism can satisfy the condition of c-SCP.

The primary distinction between collusion and miners engaging in fake bidding individually lies in the nature of the action. In the latter case, miners fabricate a transaction when there is no actual demand, resulting in their expenditure being the full transaction fee associated with the fake bid. However, in the case of collusion, miners seek out users with transaction demands and negotiate to increase the bid of such users. This implies that, following collusion, the expenditure of the coalition comprising miners and users is the difference between the transaction fees after collusion and those before collusion. The reduction in expenditure incentivizes miners to collude with users more actively.

Following the principle of starting from simplicity to complexity, we first analyze the scenario where a miner colludes with one user, known as 1-Collusion. In this scenario, a user increases their bid b_i to b_i^c, potentially benefiting the miner, and the two parties negotiate the distribution of profits. We consider the user and the miner as a coalition and analyze their collective payoff. If the user's original bid $b_i \geq b_N$, collusion does not alter the miner's profits; instead, it might increase the user's expenses. Therefore, miners would not opt for collusion with such users. When $b_i < b_N$, although t_i may not be packaged immediately, it will inevitably be packaged in the future with a transaction fee $b_N' < b_i$. We can further infer that the payoff function of the coalition is $\mathcal{P}_c^{honest} = \sum_1^N b_{i+N} + b_i - b_N'$ in the absence of collusion. To delve deeper into the potential scenarios involving b_i and b_i^c, let's analyze each of the following cases separately:

1. $b_i^c \geq b_N > b_i \geq b_{2N}$: Before collusion, t_i remains unpackaged, but its bid b_i impacts the miner's payoff $\mathcal{P}_m$. Post-collusion, t_i will be packaged, yet its impact on $\mathcal{P}_m$ diminishes. Instead, the transaction t_N corresponding to b_N becomes unpackaged, and b_N affects $\mathcal{P}_m$. This signifies that u_i incurs a cost of $min b_{N-1}, b_i^c$ to ensure the packaging of t_i, yielding a profit of b_i. Meanwhile, the miner's payoff transforms into $\sum_0^N b_{N+i} - b_i$. The payoff function of the collusion coalition is then expressed as $\mathcal{P}_c^{SCP-1} = \sum_0^N b_{N+i} - b_i + b_i - min\{b_{N-1}, b_i^c\}$.
2. $b_i^c \geq b_N > b_{2N} > b_i$: This also implies that u_i incurs a cost of $min b_{N-1}, b_i^c$ to ensure the packaging of t_i and obtain a profit of b_i. The difference from the previous scenario is that since b_i no longer affects $\mathcal{P}_m$, the miner's payoff changes to $\sum_0^{N-1} b_{N+i}$. The payoff function of the collusion coalition in this case is $\mathcal{P}_c^{SCP-2} = \sum_0^{N-1} b_{N+i} + b_i - min\{b_{N-1}, b_i^c\}$.
3. $b_N > b_i^c > b_i \geq b_{2N}$: Regardless of collusion, t_i remains unpackaged, and both b_i and b_i^c influence $\mathcal{P}_m$. Consequently, after collusion, the miner's payoff becomes $\sum_1^N b_{N+i} - b_i + b_i^c$. On the other hand, since t_i will be packaged by other miners in the future, requiring u_i to pay $b_N' \leq b_i^c$. Thus, in the long run, collusion implies that the user incurs a cost of b_N'' in exchange for a

profit of b_i. The payoff function of the collusion coalition in this scenario is $\mathcal{P}_c^{SCP-3} = \sum_1^N b_{N+i} - b_i + b_i^c + b_i - b_N''$.

4. $b_N > b_i^c > b_{2N} > b_i$: Similarly, b_i does not affect $\mathcal{P}_m$, while t_i will be packaged in the future. Consequently, after collusion, the miner's payoff becomes $\sum_1^{N-1} b_{N+i} + b_i^c$, while the user incurs a cost of b_N'' in exchange for a profit of b_i. The payoff function of the collusion coalition in this scenario is $\mathcal{P}_c^{SCP-4} = \sum_1^{N-1} b_{N+i} + b_i^c + b_i - b_N''$.

Upon comparison of the four scenarios outlined above, it becomes evident that $\mathcal{P}_c^{SCP-1} > \mathcal{P}_c^{SCP-2}, \mathcal{P}_c^{SCP-3} > \mathcal{P}_c^{SCP-4}$ and $\mathcal{P}_c^{SCP-3} > \mathcal{P}_c^{SCP-1}$. Clearly, to maximize the coalition's revenue, the miner would opt to collude with users whose bid $b_i \geq b_{2N}$, and subsequently, elevate the user's bid to $b_i^c < b_N$ (as in case 3). Analogous to the approach in Sect. 4.2, the miner would aspire for $b_i^c \to b_N$, thereby maximizing their profit to the fullest extent. Employing inequality manipulation, we can also deduce that $\mathcal{P}_c^{SCP-3} - \mathcal{P}_c^{honest}$ is likely to trend below 0. This suggests that over the long term, miners collaborating with a single user are improbable to attain higher payoffs through collusion.

When we broaden our analysis to scenarios involving collusion between miners and c users, it becomes clear that the most effective strategy for miners is to target c users whose bids fall within the range of b_{2N} and b_N, convincing them to elevate their bids to $b_i^c \to b_N$. Likewise, given that users' transactions will likely incur future transaction fees exceeding their psychological thresholds, it follows that collusion is likely to yield a negative payoff for the coalition comprising miners and c users.

Drawing from the preceding analysis, it's reasonable to infer that the BNP mechanism has a strong likelihood of fulfilling the requirements for c-SCP.

5 Experiment Analysis

In this section, we further study the expenditures and revenues under different behaviours of users and miners under the BNP mechanism through experiments to verify the above theoretical analysis. The experimental environment is as follows:

- Hardware environment: the memory used is Intel(R) Xeon(R) Silver 4214R CPU @ 2.40 GHz, the RAM is 50 GB DDR4, and the storage is 1.5 TB SSD.
- Software environment: Ubuntu22.04LTS, Python3.8.18, Numpy1.24.4, pandas2.0.3, matplotlib3.7.5, nodejs12.22.9, mysql 8.0.36-0ubuntu0.22.04.1.

We used the official interactive interface provided by Geth, the JSON-RPC API, to capture all transactions from 7,200 blocks on the Ethereum blockchain, ranging from block 15357273 to 15364473. Additionally, we analyzed transaction pool data from block 19946372 to 19952631, spanning the period from May 25, 2024, 10:43:35 AM (UTC) to May 26, 2024, 07:42:47 AM (UTC). Since this paper focuses on the BNP mechanism's performance during periods of congestion, we further filtered out the 532 blocks from the aforementioned data that experienced transaction congestion for detailed analysis.

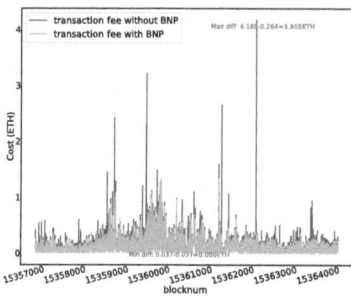

Fig. 2. Transaction fee.

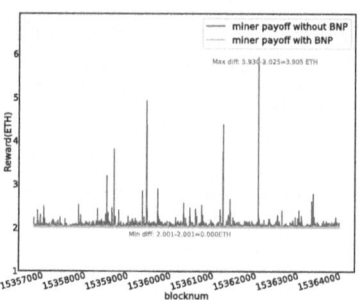

Fig. 3. Miner's payoff.

We analyzed the impact of the BNP mechanism on users and miners by applying it to transactions in 532 blocks. We compared user earnings before and after implementing BNP, noting that gasPrice consists of baseFee and priorityFee. As shown in Fig. 2, the BNP mechanism reduced transaction fees by an average of 17.08%. In the block with the largest reduction, where the N-th priorityFee differed significantly from the first N priorityFees, fees decreased by 3.9 ETH (93.75%). In blocks with smaller reductions, the difference in priorityFees was minimal. The horizontal axis in the figure represents block numbers, and the vertical axis shows the transaction fees users paid.

We also compared the difference in miner earnings before and after using the mechanism. We know that miners' income mainly comes from priorityFee. As shown in Fig. 3, the BNP mechanism causes a slight reduction in miners' income (an average reduction of 1.3%). In the block with the largest reduction, the difference between the N-th priorityFee and the first N priorityFee is large, resulting in a reduction of 65.76%. In the block with the smallest reduction, the difference between the N-th priorityFee and the first N priorityFee is 0, so the income is reduced to zero. The horizontal axis in the figure represents the number of blocks, and the vertical axis represents the income obtained by the miners.

From the above experiments, it can be seen that the use of the BNP mechanism significantly reduces user expenses while causing only a minimal decrease in miner earnings.

Next, we verified whether the BNP mechanism satisfies UIC by randomly selecting transactions and altering their bids. As shown in Fig. 4, in 532 blocks, users dishonestly raised or lowered their bids, and we subtracted the dishonest users' payments from the honest users' payments. The results show that only 138 points have coordinates above the 0 axis, indicating that only 25.93% of users can slightly reduce transaction fees through dishonest behavior. This indicates that, in the long run, the BNP mechanism satisfies UIC. In the figure, the horizontal axis represents the block number, and the vertical axis represents the change in transaction fees resulting from dishonest behavior.

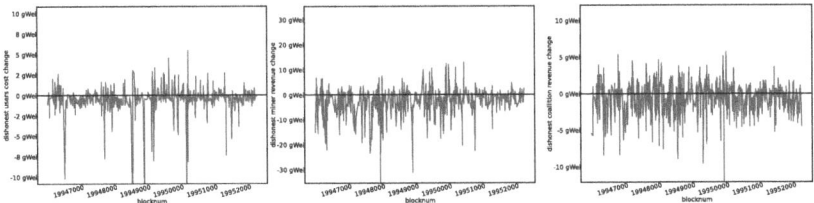

Fig. 4. Users' payoff from **Fig. 5.**   Miners'   payoff **Fig. 6.** 1-collusion coali-
dishonest behavior.   from dishonest behavior.   tion's payoff.

Figure 5 demonstrates that the BNP mechanism satisfies MIC. In the figure, the horizontal axis represents the block number, and the vertical axis represents the gains for miners from dishonest behavior. In 532 blocks, in order to increase user payments and improve their own profits, miners chose to insert false transactions when packaging blocks and paid a certain fee for this. Calculating the changes in miners' profits, it was found that only 165 blocks had miners who obtained higher profits through dishonest behavior. Overall, dishonest behavior led to an average reduction of 0.01 ETH in miner earnings per block. This indicates that, in the long run, the BNP mechanism satisfies MIC.

As shown in Fig. 6, in 532 blocks, there are 208 blocks where the miner-user coalition can slightly increase its gain through dishonest behavior. In the remaining 324 blocks, the coalition has lower gains due to dishonest behavior (the final gasPrice is reduced by 0.74gWei per block on average). This shows that in the long run, the BNP mechanism satisfies 1-SCP. In the figure, the horizontal axis represents the block number and the vertical axis represents the change in transaction fees caused by dishonest behavior.

6   Conclusion

In this paper, we propose a burning N-price auction TFM named BNP, which divides the transaction fee submitted by users into a base fee that is burned and a priority fee that goes to the miners. This mechanism is proven to satisfy UIC, MIC, and c-SCP even under conditions of transaction congestion, effectively addressing the shortcomings of EIP-1559. Experimental results demonstrate that the BNP mechanism reduces user expenses by an average of 17.8%, while only slightly decreasing miner earnings by an average of 1.39%. Furthermore, the BNP mechanism is not constrained by the type of blockchain consensus, making it applicable to a wider range of use cases.

Acknowledgment. This study was supported by the Academic Divisions of the Chinese Academy of Sciences (Grant No. 2020-ZW12-A-024), the National Natural Science Foundation of China (No. 62302266, 62232010, U23A20302), the Shandong Science Fund for Excellent Young Scholars (No. 2023HWYQ-008), and the Shandong Science Fund for Key Fundamental Research Project (ZR2022ZD02).

References

1. Chen, X., Simchi-Levi, D., Zhao, Z., Zhou, Y.: Bayesian mechanism design for blockchain transaction fee allocation. arXiv preprint arXiv:2209.13099 (2022)
2. Chung, H., Roughgarden, T., Shi, E.: Collusion-resilience in transaction fee mechanism design (2024)
3. Chung, H., Shi, E.: Foundations of transaction fee mechanism design (2022)
4. Dai, W., Dai, C., Choo, K.K.R., Cui, C., Zou, D., Jin, H.: SDTE: a secure blockchain-based data trading ecosystem. IEEE Trans. Inf. Forensics Secur. **15**, 725–737 (2019)
5. Guo, H., et al.: BFT-DSN: a byzantine fault tolerant decentralized storage network. arXiv preprint arXiv:2402.12889 (2024)
6. Guo, H., et al.: FileDAG: a multi-version decentralized storage network built on DAG-based blockchain. IEEE Trans. Comput. (2023)
7. Landis, D., Schwartzbach, N.I.: Stackelberg attacks on auctions and blockchain transaction fee mechanisms. abs/2305.02178, 2073–2080 (2023)
8. Lavi, R., Sattath, O., Zohar, A.: Redesigning bitcoin's fee market. ACM Trans. Econ. Comput. **10**(1), 1–31 (2022)
9. Liu, Y., Lu, Y., Nayak, K., Zhang, F., Zhang, L., Zhao, Y.: Empirical analysis of EIP-1559: transaction fees, waiting times, and consensus security, pp. 2099–2113 (2022)
10. Liu, Y., Fang, Z., Cheung, M.H., Cai, W., Huang, J.: A social welfare maximization mechanism for blockchain storage. abs/2103.05866 (2021)
11. Nakamoto, S.: Bitcoin: a peer-to-peer electronic cash system (2008)
12. Roughgarden, T.: Transaction fee mechanism design (2023)
13. Tang, W., Yao, D.D.: Transaction fee mechanism for proof-of-stake protocol (2023)
14. Buterin, V., Conner, E., Dudley, R., Slipper, M., Norden, I., Bakhta, A.: EIP-1559: Fee market change for eth 1.0 chain (2019). https://eips.ethereum.org/EIPS/eip-1559
15. Wang, Z., Hu, Q., Li, R., Xu, M., Xiong, Z.: Incentive mechanism design for joint resource allocation in blockchain-based federated learning. IEEE Trans. Parallel Distrib. Syst. **34**(5), 1536–1547 (2023)
16. Wu, K., Shi, E., Chung, H.: Maximizing miner revenue in transaction fee mechanism design. arXiv preprint arXiv:2302.12895 (2023)
17. Xu, M., et al.: FileDES: a secure, scalable and succinct decentralized encrypted storage network. Cryptology ePrint Archive (2024)
18. Xu, M., Zou, Z., Cheng, Y., Hu, Q., Yu, D., Cheng, X.: SPDL: a blockchain-enabled secure and privacy-preserving decentralized learning system. IEEE Trans. Comput. **72**(2), 548–558 (2022)
19. Zheng, S., Pan, L., Hu, D., Li, M., Fan, Y.: A blockchain-based trading platform for big data. In: IEEE INFOCOM 2020-IEEE Conference on Computer Communications Workshops (INFOCOM WKSHPS), pp. 991–996. IEEE (2020)

Unravelling Stablecoin-Favored Ecosystem: Extracting, Exploring On-Chain Data from TRON Blockchain

Qian'ang Mao[(⊠)], Jiaxin Wang, Zhiqi Feng, and Jiaqi Yan

Nanjing University, Nanjing, China
me@c0mm4nd.com

Abstract. Cryptocurrencies and Web3 applications based on traditional blockchain, like Bitcoin and Ethereum, have flourished in the research field. Unlike traditional ones, due to TRON's unique architectural designs, TRON has developed a more welcoming and distinctive ecosystem and application scenarios centered around the stablecoin USDT. Although it is popular in areas like stablecoin payments and settlement, research on analyzing on-chain data from the TRON blockchain is remarkably scarce. To fill this gap, this paper proposes a comprehensive data extraction and exploration framework for the TRON blockchain. A well-designed ETL (Extract Transform and Load) system aims to efficiently extract raw on-chain data from TRON, including blocks, transactions, smart contracts, and receipts, establishing a research dataset. An in-depth analysis of the extracted dataset reveals insights into TRON's block generation, transaction trends, the dominance of exchanges, the resource delegation market, smart contract usage patterns, and the central role of the USDT stablecoin. The prominence of gambling applications and potential illicit activities related to USDT is emphasized. The paper discusses opportunities for future research leveraging this dataset. These contributions enhance blockchain data management capabilities and understanding of the rapidly evolving TRON ecosystem.

Keywords: Data Extraction · Data Exploration · TRON · Stablecoin

1 Introduction

In recent years, the blockchain ecosystem has experienced tremendous growth, as evidenced by the rising market capitalization and the adoption of blockchain-based cryptocurrencies and platforms. Reflecting this growth, academic research on blockchain technology has also surged. Early research primarily focused on fundamental blockchain technologies, including consensus algorithms, cryptography, and scalability solutions. As blockchain platforms and applications have become firmly established, recent research attention has gradually shifted towards analyzing and improving the design, applications, and user experience of the blockchain ecosystem. New specialized journals and conferences focusing on blockchain applications and business use cases have also emerged. While popular blockchains, like Bitcoin and Ethereum, have garnered widespread research attention, other ecosystems with unique architectural designs and use cases remain relatively unexplored. The vast amounts of data generated by these specialized blockchain ecosystems possess significant commercial and academic value.

In 2021, TRON surpassed Ethereum in USDT stablecoin supply, becoming a leading stablecoin issuance platform globally. By 2023, TRON reached 200 million users, with 34.5 million (approximately 17.2%) holding USDT. TRON's heavy focus on stablecoin transactions poses risks, as Israel and the United States flagged it for aiding terrorist fundraising activities. TRON's popularity among terrorist groups is attributed to its faster transaction speeds and lower fees compared to Bitcoin, making it a preferred platform for illicit activities like money laundering. However, Current research on TRON on-chain data is scarce, with most studies focusing only on the basic mechanism design analysis of the price fluctuations of its native token TRX and USDT stablecoin [5–7,13,19].

The fundamental challenges stem from several factors. Firstly, there is an absence of a universal data extraction tool for TRON. While certain websites like TRONSCAN[1] offer partial TRON data, their data extraction tools are not publicly accessible, and the data acquisition process is rate-limited, restricting access to comprehensive datasets. Secondly, there is a lack of comprehensive data exploration for TRON. Although extensive research has been conducted on data analysis for EOS.IO and Ethereum [20,21], studies focusing on TRON are scarce. To the best of our knowledge, there has been no comprehensive analysis performed on the entirety of TRON's dataset across all data types, leaving a significant gap in understanding the intricacies of this blockchain platform. Thirdly, the extraction and processing of TRON's data present significant difficulties. TRON's data types are based on ProtocolBuffers, encompassing numerous intricate data structures and data types with nesting, arbitrary types, and other complex relationships, posing significant challenges for data parsing endeavors and hindering the development of effective analysis tools and techniques.

This paper makes significant contributions to the TRON blockchain. We designed a well-designed ETL(Extract, Transform, and Load) framework tailored for the TRON Blockchain, enabling efficient data extraction, parsing, and storage. Our in-depth analysis of the on-chain ecosystem revealed insights into block generation decentralization, transaction trends, the central role of exchanges, a centralized delegate market, and the prominence of gambling activities and USDT usage. We provide comprehensive directions for future research leveraging our dataset to analyze delegate services, gambling scenarios, and potential illicit activities. These contributions advance blockchain data management and understanding, fostering further adoption and evolution.

---

[1] https://tronscan.org.

2   TRON Data Extracting Framework

This section describes the process of extracting raw data from the TRON blockchain. Figure 1 shows the typical execution flow of TRON transactions, and how our system is designed to extract raw data from this process to build the dataset. We maintain the ETL as an open-source project on GitHub[2]. The following raw on-chain blockchain data can be accessed at the website[3].

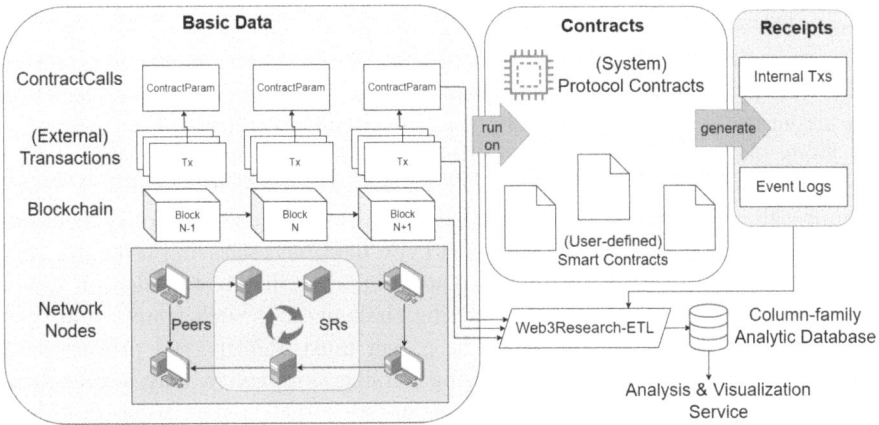

Fig. 1. The typical execution flow of TRON transactions from block N to block N+1 on the blockchain, with our data extraction process for building the dataset.

2.1   Basic Data

Blocks are an essential component in the blockchain data structure. This section introduces the process of obtaining raw block data from the TRON blockchain. Although the TRON team provided a JSON-RPC interface compatible with Ethereum for their Java-tron node program to attract Ethereum developers, due to the differences in the underlying data structure design, the data provided is missing a lot of information, such as the TRON-specific energy information. Moreover, for compatibility reasons, JSON-RPC has a lot of empty data, such as state root and nonce being always empty values. Therefore, we use the native ProtocolBuffer of TRON to obtain the complete block information at each height through TRON's gRPC interface. Each block mainly contains a block header, which contains the basic information about when the block was packaged, and a list of transactions aligned by the TVM(TRON Virtual Machine) execution order.

---

[2] https://github.com/njublockchain/web3research-etl.
[3] https://web3resear.ch/datasets.

Similar to Ethereum, TRON transactions consist of several key components, albeit with notable differences in details. The Transaction Header includes metadata like transaction type, expiration time, and fee limit. Unlike Ethereum, TRON does not feature a separate nonce field; instead, it encodes it with the transaction type. The Transaction segment holds essential transaction data such as sender and recipient addresses, amount transferred, etc., with transfer transaction details stored in the contract field. TRON employs a distinct fee calculation mechanism based on bandwidth and energy, unlike Ethereum's Gas mechanism. The Transaction Extension is utilized for optional additional transaction data storage, like smart contract input data and execution results, differing from Ethereum's direct storage in the Transaction. The Transaction Signature serves as the verification of transaction authenticity and integrity. TRON's transaction data structure is more concise and compact than Ethereum's, omitting complex fields like transaction nonce. TRON supports various native transaction types, including transfers, token issuance, resource acquisition through freezing/unfreezing TRX, witness voting, and smart contract creation/execution. These are differentiated by the ContractType field, necessitating a flexible and extensible transaction data structure to accommodate diverse transaction types. However, this flexibility introduces parsing challenges, as each transaction type may have a unique data structure. The parser must identify and process data for different transaction types, increasing parsing complexity. Any additions of new transaction types require synchronous updates to the parser to prevent data parsing errors or loss. Additionally, TRON transactions feature nested sub-data types, necessitating data flattening for processing during the ETL process. As a result, we stored all common and basic data, such as block time, transaction type, hash value, fee limit, unparsed raw ContractParameter data, etc. Subsequently, based on the different transaction types, we parse the ContractParameter data into the corresponding data structures.

2.2   TRON Contracts

The ContractParameter data are parsed to the 41 different data structures based on their corresponding ContractType, including: TriggerSmartContract is used for creating and executing smart contracts, including contract initialization, updating, and calling operations. TransferContract represents a regular TRX transfer transaction, including the sender's address, the recipient's address, and the amount transferred. TransferAssetContract is used for issuing and transferring token assets. AccountCreateContract represents the creation of a new account with complex permissions. FreezeBalanceContract allows accounts to obtain more bandwidth and energy resources by freezing or unfreezing TRX. VoteWitnessContract supports voting for witness nodes, which is an important component of TRON's Delegated Proof of Stake (DPoS) consensus mechanism. AccountPermissionUpdateContract can modify the permissions of an account. ExchangeTransactionContract supports decentralized token trading on the native on-chain decentralized exchange. The DelegateResourceContract transaction type allows accounts to delegate their bandwidth and energy resources to other accounts for use. Through delegation, the receiving account can obtain additional resources without having to freeze TRX themselves. This information not only reflects user interactions but also represents many state data in TRON. For example, the latest AccountPermissionUpdateContract can reflect the latest permission information of an account, and the latest record of createSmartContract can obtain the bytecode and ABI information of the corresponding smart contract address.

2.3 Transaction Receipts

In the TRON blockchain, there is a special type of transaction called internal transactions, mainly used for calls and fund transfers between smart contracts. Internal transactions are automatically generated by the TVM when executing user-deployed smart contracts. They do not require direct signing by the sender, nor are packaged into blocks individually, instead, embedded in the Internal-Transactions field of the Transaction structure as part of an external transaction when we make requests to the archive node of TRON. When an external transaction triggers the execution of a smart contract, all interactions and fund transfers within the contract are recorded as internal transactions, forming a tree structure. Internal transactions contain various important information, such as the caller's address, the recipient's address, the amount of TRX or tokens transferred, the call data, etc. By parsing these, the execution process and state changes of smart contracts become discoverable, which is helpful for debugging and auditing. At the same time, internal transactions are an indispensable part of implementing complex applications such as decentralized exchanges and decentralized finance, as they rely on internal transactions for fund transfers and interactions between contracts. The archive node of TRON is required to retrieve the raw internal transactions. To avoid overlapping with external transactions and affecting retrieval efficiency, we have supplemented the internal transaction information based on their dependent external transactions and placed them in a new table. Internal transactions are a key component of the TRON smart contract execution process, recording all interactions and fund flows within the contracts, which is crucial for understanding and auditing complex decentralized applications.

During the transaction execution process, smart contracts also produce a special data structure called EventLog, which is used to record events and log information during contract execution. EventLog is essentially a data structure actively triggered and defined by the smart contract code, allowing developers to record custom data at key execution points, such as state changes, error messages, audit trails, etc., which can provide valuable runtime information. Event-Log data is not directly stored in the transaction data structure but exists as a separate log array along with the transaction's execution result. For each transaction, zero to multiple EventLogs may be generated, and these are collected and persistently stored together with the transaction's execution information. Analyzing EventLogs in TRON poses a significant challenge: the information in the logs is represented in hexadecimal format, and cannot be directly retrieved using TRON addresses (i.e., addresses starting with "T") or directly converted Ethereum-style addresses (i.e., addresses starting with "0x"). To make it more user-friendly, we have created a Python toolkit for retrieving TVM Log information[4].

3   Data Exploration on Stablecoin-Favored Ecosystem

Based on the above data-extracting methodology, we have acquired the ability to analyze any application or scenario on the TRON network. To investigate the basic information of the TRON blockchain, we start by analyzing the fundamental Block information and the basic transaction information within it. As of the writing time of this paper, UTC zone 2024-04-03 22:59:12, the TRON network has reached block number 60,505,000, with a total of 60,505,001 blocks and 8,190,158,591 transactions.

Among the various transaction types, TriggerSmartContract is the most frequent, with a total of 3,437,398,059 transactions, far exceeding other types. This indicates that smart contract calls on the TRON network are very popular among users. Following this are TransferContract and TransferAssetContract, which are transactions for transferring TRX and TRC10 assets. Next are DelegateResourceContract and UndelegateResourceContract, which are transactions for delegating bandwidth and energy resources of accounts. These transactions are evidently sourced from energy leasing services provided by wallets or websites like TokenPocket[5] and TRXUS[6]. Although FreezeBalanceContract and UnfreezeBalanceContract can also provide more transaction energy for accounts, their transaction numbers are significantly lower.

3.1   Decentralization and Development of TRON

TRON utilizes a Delegated Proof of Stake (DPoS) consensus mechanism, where witnesses are elected through voting, similar to Ethereum's PoS mechanism. These witnesses are responsible for generating blocks and maintaining the network, and are subject to stringent requirements, including staking a large amount of TRX tokens and continuous community voting supervision. This transparency and accountability of witnesses enable a comprehensive understanding of the network's dynamics, block production efficiency, voting support status, and token flow changes, contributing to the assessment of network security and decentralization. According to Fig. 2, despite the relatively small number of witness addresses, the TRON network remains decentralized at the block packaging level, with no single or few dominating witnesses.

TRON has always touted itself as a high-performance blockchain system with a block time of 3 s, significantly faster than Ethereum. However, the actual throughput in real-world scenarios still needs to be analyzed in conjunction with

---

[4] https://github.com/njublockchain/web3research-py

[5] https://help.tokenpocket.pro/en/wallet-faq-en/tron-wallet/energy

[6] https://www.trxus.com.

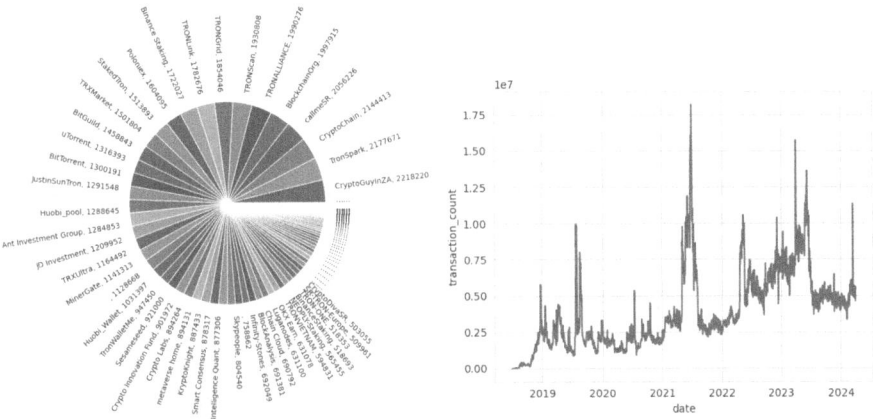

Fig. 2. The left image depicts the distribution of witness addresses across all blocks. The right one illustrates the fluctuation of transaction count as the height increases.

the on-chain block packaging situation. As shown in Fig. 2, the daily transaction count of the TRON network shows an overall upward trend with the increase in block height, but there are fluctuations.

In the early days, TRON's daily transaction count was relatively low, only a few tens of thousands. As the community ecosystem gradually developed, the number of users and DApps increased, and the transaction count also gradually grew. By mid-2019, TRON's daily transaction count had stabilized but had surged to a peak of 1 million at times. Entering 2020, TRON's transaction count began to grow. As USDT supply expanded and DeFi exploded, the transaction count reached a peak of about 18 million in 2021, reflecting the high network activity. However, towards the end of 2023, due to an increase in negative news reports about TRON, the transaction count began to decline sharply, rebounding from the beginning of 2024.

Overall, TRON's transaction count has gradually increased with the block height, reflecting the continuous development and growth of its ecosystem. Particularly in the past two years, the transaction count has remained at a high level, indicating that TRON has gained a relatively stable user base and application coverage. However, the fluctuations in transaction count also suggest that there is still significant room for development in the TRON ecosystem. How to attract more quality projects and funds in the future to ensure ecosystem activity will be a major challenge for TRON. In the long run, the continuous growth of transaction count is crucial and is a litmus test for TRON's true strength.

3.2 Chain-Predefined Native Services

Due to the high degree of flexibility in transactions, TRON natively supports some chain-predefined features like issuing new TRC10 assets and transferring assets. By analyzing transaction parameters, we can explore these native services.

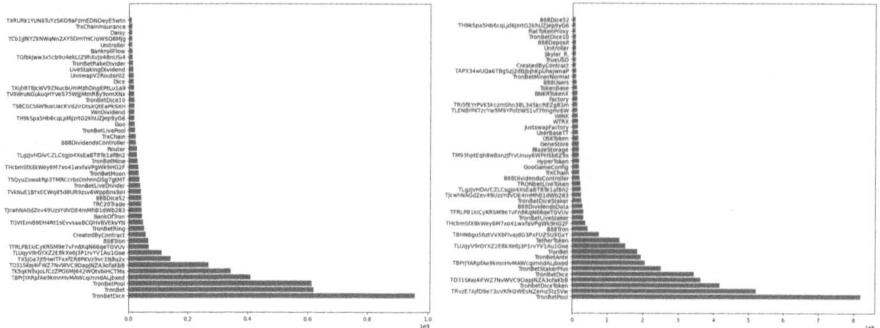

Fig. 3. The image on the left shows the top 50 sender addresses by the number of internal transactions. The image on the right shows the top 50 recipient addresses by the number of internal transactions.

The most fundamental operation is the TransferContract, which denotes the transfer of TRX tokens. Analyzing the Top 50 list, it is evident that nearly all sender and receiver addresses, regardless of the number of transactions or transaction amounts, belong to centralized exchanges. However, this only represents external transaction information and does not include TRX transfers resulting from contract control. Therefore, further analysis of internal transactions is necessary to explore the actual on-chain scenarios. As shown in Fig. 3, the previously mentioned centralized exchange addresses are absent, leaving mostly gambling addresses and addresses of decentralized exchanges like Justswap[7].

3.3   Smart Contract and USDT Stablecoin

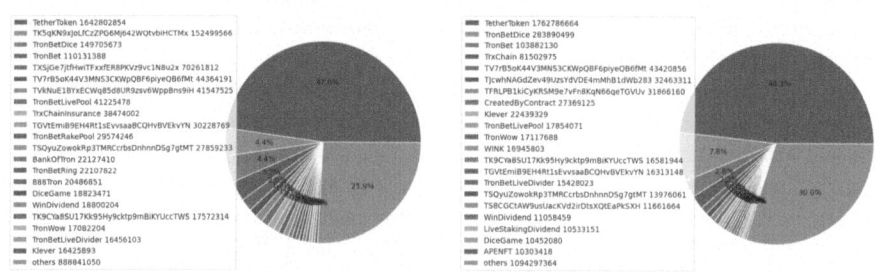

Fig. 4. The left image shows the distribution of addresses triggering smart contract transactions, by the number of occurrences. The right one shows the distribution of addresses triggering smart contract events, by the number of occurrences.

The statistics of smart contract triggers and event logs on the TRON network are astonishing. As shown in Fig. 4, nearly 50% of users in TRON who actively

---

[7] https://justswap.org/.

trigger smart contract transactions choose to directly operate the TetherToken, i.e., USDT stablecoin. Additionally, from the annotated address types, it can be seen that besides directly operating USDT, users also favor gambling. Smart contracts related to casinos such as TronBetDice, TronBet, 888Tron, DiceGame, and TronWow are quite popular.

We further analyzed the events related to USDT and found that there were 1,750,695,957 Transfer events, 12,089,253 Approval events, 805 AddedBlackList events, 51 RemovedBlackList events, 303 DestroyedBlackFunds events, 257 Issue events for issuing new USDT, and 37 Redeem events. Although we did not delve into these BlackList events this time, we believe our dataset can aid future research on network fund security concerning these BlackLists and related events. We further investigated the more frequent Transfer and Approval events.

4 Related Work and Discussion

Based on our data exploration results, we propose several recommendations for future research on the TRON ecosystem, drawing from existing studies on TRON and other blockchain ecosystems:

Market and Audience Analysis of Resource Delegate Services: While there is technical research on resource management within TRON [7], it still lacking analysis on its real-world application. In contrast, EOS.IO, which also has a complex resource management mechanism, has been the subject of studies analyzing resource usage in real scenarios [21]. Therefore, we recommend conducting market and audience analyses for the Resource Delegate services in TRON.

Research on Casino Applications in TRON: There is a significant presence of casino applications and related promotional information within the TRON ecosystem. Investigating the development and current status of these casinos is urgently needed. Existing studies have already analyzed online casinos and decentralized casinos on other blockchains, highlighting differences in game mechanisms, management models, and gambler preferences across different blockchains [2,10–12,14]. Research focusing on TRON's casino landscape would be valuable for gambling entertainment development and gambling industry regulation.

Study of Stablecoin Illicit Activities on TRON: The presence of blacklists in on-chain USDT and reports of hacks, money laundering, and terrorist financing on TRON warrant thorough investigation. While there is substantial research on analyzing stablecoin influence on cryptocurrency markets [1], DeFi security [8], illicit activities detection [4,9,15,17,18] and de-anonymization [3,16] on major blockchains like Bitcoin and Ethereum, the heterogeneity of data between blockchains means that these detection algorithms may not be directly applicable to TRON. Research aimed at tracing the origin of funds, identifying, and blocking illegal transactions are crucial for the compliance of TRON applications and the TRON blockchain itself.

5   Conclusion

In summary, this work designs a comprehensive framework for extracting and exploring on-chain data from the TRON blockchain ecosystem. By developing a well-designed ETL system tailored specifically to handle TRON's unique data structures and protocol buffers, we overcame significant technical challenges to acquire a large-scale dataset called Web3Research-TRON that spans all facets of the TRON blockchain.

Our in-depth exploration and analysis of this dataset revealed novel insights into the dynamics, decentralization, and key services within the TRON ecosystem. While exhibiting reasonable decentralization in block production, the ecosystem is heavily centered around gambling applications, the USDT stablecoin, and centralized exchanges. Resource delegation markets and smart contract usage patterns were also characterized.

Looking ahead, this foundational dataset lays the groundwork for much-needed future research into the TRON blockchain. Analyzing delegate service adoption, auditing gambling applications, investigating stablecoin activities, and developing techniques to detect and prevent money laundering are high priorities. The heterogeneity of TRON's data also motivates research into transfer learning and adaptation of analysis methods across blockchains.

References

1. Ante, L., Fiedler, I., Strehle, E.: The influence of stablecoin issuances on cryptocurrency markets. Financ. Res. Lett. **41**, 101867 (2021)
2. Brown, S.H.V.: Gambling on the blockchain: how the unlawful internet gambling enforcement act has opened the door for offshore crypto casinos. Vand. J. Ent. Tech. L. **24**, 535 (2021)
3. Huang, T., Lin, D., Wu, J.: Ethereum account classification based on graph convolutional network. IEEE Trans. Circuits Syst. II Express Briefs **69**(5), 2528–2532 (2022)
4. Ibrahim, R.F., Elian, A.M., Ababneh, M.: Illicit account detection in the ethereum blockchain using machine learning. In: 2021 International Conference on Information Technology (ICIT), pp. 488–493. IEEE (2021)
5. Li, C., Palanisamy, B., Xu, R., Duan, L., Liu, J., Wang, W.: How hard is takeover in DPoS blockchains? Understanding the security of coin-based voting governance. In: Proceedings of the 2023 ACM SIGSAC Conference on Computer and Communications Security, CCS 2023, pp. 150–164. Association for Computing Machinery, New York (2023). https://doi.org/10.1145/3576915.3623171
6. Li, D., Han, D., Weng, T.H., Zheng, Z., Li, H., Li, K.C.: On Stablecoin: Ecosystem, architecture, mechanism and applicability as payment method. Comput. Stand. Interfaces **87**, 103747 (2024). https://doi.org/10.1016/j.csi.2023.103747
7. Li, H., Li, Z., Tian, N.: Resource bottleneck analysis of the blockchain based on tron's TPS. In: Liu, Y., Wang, L., Zhao, L., Yu, Z. (eds.) ICNC-FSKD 2019. AISC, vol. 1075, pp. 944–950. Springer, Cham (2020). https://doi.org/10.1007/978-3-030-32591-6_103

8. Li, W., Bu, J., Li, X., Peng, H., Niu, Y., Zhang, Y.: A survey of DeFi security: challenges and opportunities. J. King Saud Univ. - Comput. Inform. Sci. **34**(10, Part B), 10378–10404 (2022). https://doi.org/10.1016/j.jksuci.2022.10.028

9. Liu, J., Zheng, J., Wu, J., Zheng, Z.: FA-GNN: filter and augment graph neural networks for account classification in ethereum. IEEE Trans. Netw. Sci. Eng. **9**(4), 2579–2588 (2022)

10. Meng, J., Fu, F.: Understanding gambling behaviour and risk attitudes using cryptocurrency-based casino blockchain data. Roy. Soc. Open Sci. **7**(10), 201446 (2020)

11. Scholten, O.J.: On the behavioural profiling of gamblers using cryptocurrency transaction data. PhD, University of York (2022)

12. Scholten, O.J., Zendle, D., Walker, J.A.: Inside the decentralised casino: a longitudinal study of actual cryptocurrency gambling transactions. PLoS ONE **15**(10), e0240693 (2020)

13. Shukla, A., Das, T.K., Roy, S.S.: TRX cryptocurrency profit and transaction success rate prediction using whale optimization-based ensemble learning framework. Mathematics **11**(11), 2415 (2023). https://doi.org/10.3390/math11112415

14. Wang, J., Mao, Q., Yan, J., Sun, H., Qi, P.: Identifying crypto addresses with gambling behaviors: a graph neural network approach. In: PACIS 2023 Proceedings (2023)

15. Wen, H., Fang, J., Wu, J., Zheng, Z.: Hide and seek: an adversarial hiding approach against phishing detection on ethereum. IEEE Trans. Comput. Soc. Syst. (2022)

16. Wu, J., Liu, J., Zhao, Y., Zheng, Z.: Analysis of cryptocurrency transactions from a network perspective: an overview. J. Netw. Comput. Appl. **190**, 103139 (2021)

17. Wu, J., et al.: Who are the phishers? Phishing scam detection on ethereum via network embedding. IEEE Trans. Syst. Man Cybern.: Syst. **52**, 1156–1166 (2019)

18. Wu, Z., Liu, J., Wu, J., Zheng, Z., Luo, X., Chen, T.: Know your transactions: real-time and generic transaction semantic representation on blockchain & web3 ecosystem. In: Proceedings of the ACM Web Conference 2023, WWW 2023, pp. 1918–1927. Association for Computing Machinery, New York (2023)

19. Yadav, J.S., Yadav, N.S., Sharma, A.K.: A qualitative and quantitative parametric estimation of the ethereum and TRON blockchain networks. In: 2021 9th International Conference on Reliability, Infocom Technologies and Optimization (Trends and Future Directions) (ICRITO), pp. 1–5. IEEE (2021)

20. Zheng, P., Zheng, Z., Wu, J., Dai, H.N.: XBlock-ETH: extracting and exploring blockchain data from ethereum. IEEE Open J. Comput. Soc. **1**, 95–106 (2020). https://doi.org/10.1109/OJCS.2020.2990458

21. Zheng, W., Zheng, Z., Dai, H.N., Chen, X., Zheng, P.: XBlock-EOS: extracting and exploring blockchain data from EOSIO. Inf. Process. Manag. **58**(3), 102477 (2021). https://doi.org/10.1016/j.ipm.2020.102477

Robust and Efficient Group-Based Ring Federated Learning Framework with Double-Masking Mechanism

Changji Wang[1,2]([envelope]) [iD], Boxuan Lin[1,2], Qingqing Gan[1,2], Ning Liu[1,2], and Zhen Liu[1,2]

[1] Guangdong University of Foreign Studies, Guangzhou 510006, China
wchangji@126.com
[2] Guangdong Engineering Research Center of Data Security Governance and Privacy Computing, Guangzhou 510006, China

Abstract. Federated Learning (FL) is a distributed machine learning approach that protects data privacy by enabling multiple devices or nodes to collaboratively train models without sharing raw data. However, existing research highlights significant challenges in terms of privacy protection and communication efficiency. Gradient leakage remains a key issue in FL security, while traditional FL frameworks incur a large amount of communication overhead in large-scale scenarios, limiting their applicability. To address these issues, this study proposes GroupRingFL, a secure and efficient ring-aggregation federated learning method. This framework dynamically adjusts the number of groups to optimize communication overhead in large-scale federated learning scenarios. Additionally, an efficient double-masking mechanism is applied within this framework, effectively defending against collusion attacks by honest-but-curious adversaries and addressing user dropout problems. Extensive experiments on the MNIST and CIFAR-100 datasets using MLP, CNN, and L-BFGS models demonstrate that GroupRingFL achieves high accuracy comparable to federated averaging, while offering superior security compared to differential privacy-based FL and better communication efficiency and storage requirements than traditional secure aggregation methods.

Keywords: Federated Learning · Privacy-Preserving · Double Mask · Diffie-Hellman Key Agreement · Secret Sharing

1 Introduction

In the era of big data, machine learning is essential for extracting insights from vast datasets. However, traditional centralized machine learning poses data privacy and communication cost concerns [1]. Federated Learning (FL) addresses these challenges by allowing multiple devices to collaborate on model training without sharing raw data, thus enhancing privacy [2].

Despite its benefits, FL has limitations, including high communication overhead in synchronous scenarios and insufficient privacy guarantees for model parameters. Attacks on shared model updates remain a concern, and FL systems often lack robust mechanisms to handle network instability and user dropouts.

To optimize communication in FL, new frameworks such as chains [3], rings [4], and trees [5] have been proposed. These structures aim to enhance efficiency and robustness, but still face the challenge of network instability causing nodes to drop offline.

Privacy issues in FL persist during model parameter aggregation and transmission. Technologies like differential privacy [6], secure multi-party computation [7], and homomorphic encryption [8] have been introduced to mitigate these risks. However, these solutions often require trade-offs between security and performance.

This paper proposes GroupRingFL, a new group-based ring federated learning framework, to address privacy and communication performance issues. GroupRingFL dynamically adjusts group numbers to minimize communication overhead and employs a double mask mechanism to enhance privacy by encrypting model updates twice, making it harder for attackers to extract sensitive information.

The main contributions of this paper are as follows:

- The proposed GroupRingFL framework dynamically adjusts the number of groups to minimize communication overhead, enhancing performance in large-scale federated learning.
- GroupRingFL employs a effectively double-masking mechanism to defend against collusion attacks and addresses user disconnection issues due to network delays.
- Security analysis and extensive experiments show that GroupRingFL has stronger privacy and more powerful communication capabilities while maintaining high accuracy compared to other state-of-the-art methods.

The remainder of this paper is organized as follows: Sect. 2 reviews related work. Section 3 introduces the preliminary concepts relevant to this study. Section 4 provides a detailed description and security analysis of the GroupRingFL framework. Section 5 presents the experimental results. Finally, Sect. 6 concludes the paper and discusses future research directions.

2 Related Work

Traditional federated learning frameworks require each user to communicate with a central server, leading to significant communication overhead that scales with the number of users. Additionally, transmitting model parameters in plaintext poses privacy risks, as malicious users can infer original data from gradients.

To address these issues, Bonawitz et al. employed the Diffie-Hellman key exchange and secret sharing to protect model parameters, but this approach scales poorly due to exponential communication overhead with user numbers [9]. Li et al.

[3] proposed a chain aggregation method to reduce server communication, but it remains unsuitable for large-scale scenarios and vulnerable to collusion attacks. Cheng et al. [10] introduced Grcol-ppfl, using groups and a double-masking mechanism to mitigate communication overhead and resist collusion attacks. However, this method assumes a completely honest server, which limits its robustness against collusion between servers and users. Yang et al. [4] proposed a ring federated learning framework to reduce communication overhead in non-IID situations but lacked privacy protection measures against collusion attacks.

In summary, although existing frameworks and technologies have solved the privacy and communication problems to a certain extent, there are still major challenges. In Table 1, we compare the privacy and security of existing centralized schemes and communication performance under user-user collusion and user-server collusion. From the comparison, it can be seen that different frameworks have certain defects in taking into account both privacy protection and communication optimization.

Table 1. Comparison of Privacy and Security in Federated Learning Frameworks

Scheme	Defend against collusion attacks by users	Defend against collusion attacks between users and the server	Communication overhead
[4]	No	No	Low
[7]	No	No	Low
[10]	No	No	Low
[9]	Yes	Yes	High
GroupRingFL	Yes	Yes	Low

3   Preliminaries

3.1   Diffie-Hellman Key Agreement

The Diffie-Hellman key exchange protocol securely establishes shared keys between parties over a public channel for secret communication [11]. The process involves three main steps:

- Public Parameter Generation (**KA.param**(1^λ)): Produces public parameters *params*, including a group $\mathbf{G}$ of prime order q and its generator g, based on the security parameter λ. The protocol's security hinges on the difficulty of solving the discrete logarithm problem in $\mathbf{G}$.
- Key Pair Generation (**KA.gen**(*params*)): Each participant u generates a public-private key pair $(sk_u,\ pk_u = g^{sk_u})$ using the public parameters *params*. The private key sk_u remains secret, while the public key pk_u is shared.
- Shared Key Agreement (**KA.agree**(*params*, sk_u, pk_v)): Facilitates the creation of a shared key $K_{u,v}$ between two parties u and v, computed as $(pk_v)^{sk_u}$ or $(pk_u)^{sk_v}$ respectively.

3.2 Secret Sharing

Secret sharing is a cryptographic method that splits information into multiple parts so that only a certain number of participants can reconstruct the original secret [12]. The specific process of secret sharing is as follows:

- Public Parameter Generation (**SS.setup**(1^κ)): Input the security parameter κ and produce public parameters pp.
- Secret Share (**SS.share**($pp, s, t, \mathbf{U}$)): Input the public parameters pp, secret message s, reconstructed secret threshold t and user set $\mathbf{U}$. The size of the user set $\mathbf{U}$ is n and $n > t$. A random polynomial of degree $t - 1$ is used to generate n shared secrets, creating a set of secret values $\{(i, s_i)\}_{i \in \mathbf{U}}$.
- Secret Reconstruction (**SS.recon**($pp, \{(i, s_i)\}_{i \in \mathbf{U}'}, t$)): Input the public parameter pp, the secret values s_i of different users, and the threshold t for recovering the secret. When the number of secret values reaches t, the original secret s can be recovered.

4 GroupRingFL Framework

This section first introduces the technologies used by the GroupRingFL framework and explains the specific process of GroupRingFL, including the initialization, training, and aggregation stages, and finally provides a security analysis.

4.1 Dynamic Group Adjustment

The increase in the number of users in the ring federated learning framework increases the communication time. To alleviate this, the users are divided into multiple groups to enhance parallelism and reduce the uplink duration. Device-to-device (D2D) communication is mainly adopted. In each group, orthogonal frequency division multiplexing (OFDM) technology is used in the wireless network to establish the transmission rate $r_{l,i} = B_{l,i} \log_2 \left(1 + \frac{p_{l,i}|h_{l,i}|^2}{N_d^2 B_{l,i}^2} \right)$ [13], where $B_{l,i}$ represents the bandwidth, $p_{l,i}$ is the transmitted power, N_d is the white noise power spectral density, and $h_{l,i}$ is the channel coefficient.

The size of the model parameters is denoted by z, and the communication time of each group is calculated as $T_{\text{ring}}^t = \sum_{i \in G_l} \frac{z}{r_{l,i}}$. The total time, denoted as $T_{\text{sum, ring}}$, comprises the communication time T_{ring}^t, local computing time $T_{\text{local, ring}}^t$, and the AS computing time $T_{\text{global, ring}}^t$, that is, $T_{\text{sum, ring}}^t = T_{\text{local, ring}}^t + T_{\text{global, ring}}^t + T_{\text{ring}}^t$.

In order to improve communication efficiency, the number of groups l is optimized to minimize the overall communication time. The node processing capacity is defined by the number of model parameters processed per unit time. The processing capacity of the local user node is c, the processing capacity of the server node is s, and their average transmission rate is $\hat{r}$. In the FedAvg algorithm, the total communication time for K users in one round is given by $T_{\text{FedAvg}} = \frac{z}{\hat{r}} + \frac{K}{s}$.

In GroupRingFL, with L groups, each group executes in parallel, and the server aggregates the sum of parameters from each group's first user, that is, $T_{\text{GroupRingFL}} = \frac{Kz}{L\hat{r}} + \frac{K}{Lc} + \frac{L}{s}$. To ensure improved communication efficiency, we adjust the number of groups such that $T_{\text{GroupRingFL}} < T_{\text{FedAvg}}$, that is, $\frac{Kz}{L\hat{r}} + \frac{K}{Lc} + \frac{L}{s} < \frac{z}{\hat{r}} + \frac{K}{s}$.

4.2   Privacy Protection Techniques

The AS performs secret sharing by randomly selecting a random value s and generating a number of secret shares equal to the number of groups, such that $s \equiv s_1 + s_2 + \cdots + s_L \bmod q$. The AS can remove the mask value only when the threshold t_G is reached, that is, t_G groups have submitted their results to the AS. The use of this secret sharing protocol ensures that the server cannot directly access the aggregate value of each group, thereby enhancing data privacy. The first user of each group uses the secret share received from the AS as the mask value when submitting the result.

Within each group, user i performs a Diffie-Hellman key exchange protocol with users $i - 1$ and $i + 1$ to generate shared keys, which are used as random seeds to generate mask values. Each selected user generates a random number a_i for secret sharing, which is also used as another random seed to generate mask values. The user distributes the generated secret shares to other users in the group, which are used by the server to eliminate the mask values generated by the user. This is the second application of secret sharing in the framework.

Although our scheme employs secret sharing twice and utilizes the Diffie-Hellman key exchange protocol, the ring framework eliminates the necessity for each user to exchange keys and secret shares with every other user. Compared to the secure multi-party computation scheme proposed by Bonawitz et al. [14], our method significantly enhances communication performance. As demonstrated in Table 2, our approach optimizes communication, computation, and storage overhead. Additionally, in the event of a user disconnection in GroupRingFL, two adjacent users can re-establish keys, thereby maintaining the connection.

Table 2. Method Performance Comparison.

	Method	Communication	Computation	Storage
User	[9]	$O(k + m)$	$O(k^2 + km)$	$O(k + m)$
	Ours	$O(m)$	$O(k + m)$	$O(m)$
Server	[9]	$O(k^2 + km)$	$O(k^2 m)$	$O(k^2 + m)$
	Ours	$O(k + m)$	$O(k + m)$	$O(k + m)$

4.3   Detailed of GroupRingFL

The GroupRingFL framework consists of N users and a central aggregation server (AS). Users are dynamically divided into multiple groups, each of which forms a ring structure and elects a leader through consensus, as shown in Fig. 1. GroupRingFL assumes that the AS and users are semi-honest, abide by the protocol but may try to extract private data, but the first user in each group is trustworthy as the leader. The framework solves the collusion problem and enhances privacy protection and defense against such attacks.

The Initialization Phase. The N users are divided into L disjoint groups, each forming a ring structure. The groups are numbered $1, 2, \ldots, L$, and the users in each group are numbered $1, 2, \ldots, n_l$, where n_l is the number of users in ring l for $1 \leq l \leq L$. The first user in each group (i.e., the user with number 1) acts as a leader, responsible for communicating with the AS. Each user communicates only with its predecessor and successor in the ring. The predecessor and successor indices are calculated modulo n_l, meaning if $i = 1$, then $i - 1 = n_l$, and if $i = n_l$, then $i + 1 = 1$.

AS randomly selects a secret value $s^t \in GF(q)$ and uses Shamir's secret sharing scheme to split s^t into L secret shares, denoted as $s_1^t, s_2^t, \ldots, s_L^t$. Then, AS sends the global model w_G^t and the secret share s_l^t of the current round t to the first user of each ring l, where $1 \leq l \leq L$. The secret value s^t can be reconstructed when a threshold number of shares are obtained.

Training Phase. Each user in ring l randomly selects a secret value $a_{l,i}^t \in GF(q)$, splits $a_{l,i}^t$ into n_l secret shares, denoted as $a_{l,(i,1)}^t, a_{l,(i,2)}^t, \cdots, a_{l,(i,n_l)}^t$, satisfying $a_{l,i}^t \equiv a_{l,(i,1)}^t + a_{l,(i,2)}^t + \cdots + a_{l,(i,n_l)}^t \bmod q$, and distributes the secret shares to other users in the group. For $1 \leq i \leq n_l$, each user u_i first trains its local model $w_{l,i}^t$ on its local data and performs Diffie-Hellman key agreement with the predecessor and successor in the ring and obtains two shared keys, denoted as $K_{l,(i-1,i)}^t$ and $K_{l,(i,i+1)}^t$. Then, user u_i uses these two keys as seeds to generate two masks, denoted as $k_{l,(i-1,i)}^t$ and $k_{l,(i,i+1)}^t$, to encrypt its local model updates. Finally, user u_i sends $c_{l,i}^t = c_{l,i-1}^t - k_{l,(i,i-1)}^t + w_{l,i}^t + a_{l,i}^t + k_{l,(i,i+1)}^t$ to user u_{i+1}, where $c_{l,i-1}^t$ is received from its predecessor u_{i-1}. Finally, the first user in each group sends $\sum_{i=1}^{n_l} w_{l,i}^t + \sum_{i=1}^{n_l} a_{l,i}^t + s_l^t$ to the AS.

Aggregation Phase. AS adds the results sent by L groups, recovers and subtracts the user's mask from the secret shares obtained by all users, and obtains the sum of the model updates of all users and the sum of the secret shares generated by AS, denoted as $w_1^t + s_1^t + \cdots + w_L^t + s_L^t = \sum_{l=1}^{L} w_l^t + s^t$, where s^t is the secret value selected by AS. AS recovers and subtracts s^t to obtain a result that does not contain the secret value, denoted as $\sum_{l=1}^{L} w_l^t$, which is the sum of the model updates of all users. AS divides this result by N to obtain a new global model, denoted as $w_G^{t+1} = \frac{1}{N} \sum_{l=1}^{L} w_l^t$. AS sends this updated global model and new secret share to the first user in each ring and repeats the above process until the preset number of training rounds is reached or the convergence condition is met.

4.4   Security Analysis

Each user in the ring includes two random factors when sending its local model gradient update: the key derivation function (KDF) value obtained through

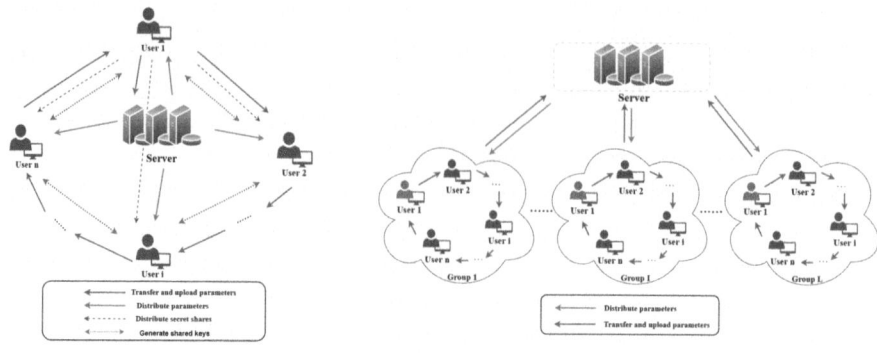

Fig. 1. Architecture of GroupRingFL

Diffie-Hellman (DH) key negotiation, and a random number generated by each user as another mask. This design ensures that any two colluding users cannot obtain the model parameters of the third user. Therefore, this mechanism effectively reduces the risk of collusion attacks between users, thereby enhancing the overall security of the federated learning process.

Theorem 1: Under the assumption that the first user is completely honest, even if two users u_i and u_j in the ring l collude, they cannot obtain the model update of another user u_h in the ring l.

Proof: For the sake of description, let's assume that $i < j$.

Case 1: $h < i$: User u_h sends its encrypted model update $c^t_{l,h}$ to user u_{h+1}. Users i and j can intercept $c^t_{l,h-1}$ and $c^t_{l,h}$, but they do not have the keys $k^t_{l,(h-1,h)}$, $k^t_{l,(h,h+1)}$, and $a^t_{l,h}$ needed to obtain $w^t_{l,h}$. Even if $i = h + 1$, they still cannot get $k^t_{l,(h-1,h)}$ and $a^t_{l,h}$ to recover $w^t_{l,h}$.

Case 2: $h > j$: User u_h sends its encrypted model update $c^t_{l,h}$ to user u_{h+1}. Users i and j can intercept $c^t_{l,h-1}$ and $c^t_{l,h}$, but they do not have the keys $k^t_{l,(h-1,h)}$, $k^t_{l,(h,h+1)}$, and $a^t_{l,h}$ needed to obtain $w^t_{l,h}$. Even if $j = h - 1$, they still cannot get $k^t_{l,(h,h+1)}$ and $a^t_{l,h}$ to recover $w^t_{l,h}$.

Case 3: $i < h < j$: User u_h sends its encrypted model update $c^t_{l,h}$ to user u_{h+1}. Users i and j can intercept $c^t_{l,h-1}$ and $c^t_{l,h}$, but they do not have the keys $k^t_{l,(h-1,h)}$, $k^t_{l,(h,h+1)}$, and $a^t_{l,h}$ needed to obtain $w^t_{l,h}$. Even if $i = h - 1$ and $j = h + 1$, they still cannot get $a^t_{l,h}$ to recover $w^t_{l,h}$.

Therefore, in all cases, users u_i and u_j cannot obtain the model update of user u_h. This completes the proof.

Theorem 2: Even if AS colludes with user i in ring l, it cannot obtain the model update of another user j in ring l.

Proof: If AS colludes with user i, they can only obtain the model update of user i, the secret shares of other users, and the random value of user i. They

Algorithm 1. GroupRingFL Algorithm

1: **Input:** Number of clients N, number of communication rounds T, learning rate η, local batch size B, global model w_G^1.

2: TA initialize $\mathbf{G}, g, q$.

3: **for** each round $t = 1, 2, \ldots, T$ **do**

4:    The AS selects randomly $s^t \in GF(q)$, splits s^t into L secret shares $(s_1^t, s_2^t, \ldots, s_L^t)$, then sends the global model w_G^t and the secret share s_l^t to the first user of each ring l, where $1 \leq l \leq L$.

5:    **for** $l = 1$ **to** L **do**

6:       **for** $i = 1$ **to** n_l **do**

7:          User i trains its local model $w_{l,i}^t$ on its local data for E epochs using SGD with learning rate η and batch size B.

8:          User i splits $a_{l,i}^t$ into $a_{l,(i,1)}^t, a_{l,(i,2)}^t, \cdots, a_{l,(i,n_l)}^t$ satisfying $a_{l,i}^t \equiv a_{l,(i,1)}^t + a_{l,(i,2)}^t + \cdots + a_{n,(i,n_l)}^t \bmod q$, and sends w_G^t and $a_{l,(i,j)}^t$ to each user j in the ring, where $1 < j \leq n_l$.

9:          User i performs Diffie-Hellman key agreement with user $i - 1$ and user $i + 1$, and generates two masks $k_{l,(i-1,i)}^t$ and $k_{l,(i,i+1)}^t$. State User i sends $c_{l,i}^t = c_{l,i-1}^t - k_{l,(i,i-1)}^t + w_{l,i}^t + a_{l,i}^t + k_{l,(i,i+1)}^t$ to user $i + 1$, where $c_{l,i-1}^t$ is received from user $i - 1$.

10:      **end for**

11:      The user 1 receives c_{l,n_l}^t from the user n_l, and sends $\sum_{i=1}^{n_l} w_{l,i}^t + a_{l,i}^t$ to the AS.

12:   **end for**

13:   The AS recovers the secret values $\sum_{i=1}^{N} a_{l,i}^t$ and s^t, and computes the global model $w_G^{t+1} = \frac{1}{N} \sum_{l=1}^{L} w_l^t$.

14: **end for**

15: **Output:** The final global model w_G^T.

---

cannot obtain the model update of any other user j in the ring because the model update of user j is encrypted using the key shared by user j with its predecessors and successors in the ring and the random value generated by itself.

Similarly, if AS colludes with the first user in ring l, they can only obtain the encrypted sum of the model updates of all users in ring l, recorded as $\sum_{i=1}^{n_l} w_l^t + a_l^t$. They cannot obtain the model update of any other user j in ring l because the model update of user j is encrypted using the key shared by user j with its predecessors and successors in the ring and the random value generated by itself.

Therefore, even if the AS colludes with a user in the ring or the first user, they cannot obtain the model update of any other user in the ring. This completes the proof.

5 Experiments

We conducted our experiments using PyTorch on a system with Intel Core i7-12700H @ 3.20 GHz and 32 GB RAM. We evaluated our GroupRingFL framework against Chain-PPFL, GrCol-PPFL, FedAvg, and Differential Privacy-Based Algorithms, focusing on model accuracy, convergence, and security. Key parameters included 100 local users, a batch size of 10, 5 local training rounds, and a learning rate of 0.01. Noise scales for DP-based FL were set at 10^{-1} and 10^{-4}. We tested dropout performance in larger federated learning settings with 60 to 100 users per group and dropout rates from 0% to 30%.

We used MNIST and CIFAR-100 datasets. MNIST has 60,000 training and 10,000 test samples, while CIFAR-100 offers 500 training and 100 test images per class. Our models included an MLP with two 200-unit hidden layers and ReLU activation, and a CNN with two 5×5 convolutional layers, a 512-unit fully connected layer with ReLU, and a softmax output layer. Data distribution was both IID (evenly shuffled) and Non-IID (sorted by labels into shards). We used CIFAR-100 for DLG algorithm tests on the L-BFGS model to assess framework security [15].

5.1 Accuracy Comparison

In federated learning, our double-masking mechanism ensures robust privacy without sacrificing accuracy, unlike traditional differential privacy techniques that degrade accuracy by adding noise. Our experiments with CNN and MLP models on IID and non-IID MNIST distributions, shown in Fig. 2, reveal that after 500 training rounds, the accuracy of our GroupRingFL framework matches that of FedAvg, Chain-PPFL, GrCol-PPFL, and FL with DP (10^{-4}). Notably, GroupRingFL surpasses FL with DP (10^{-1}) by approximately 7% (IID) to 60% (Non-IID) for the CNN model and by 10% (IID) to 12% (Non-IID) for the MLP model, indicating that our mechanism preserves training accuracy better than differential privacy methods.

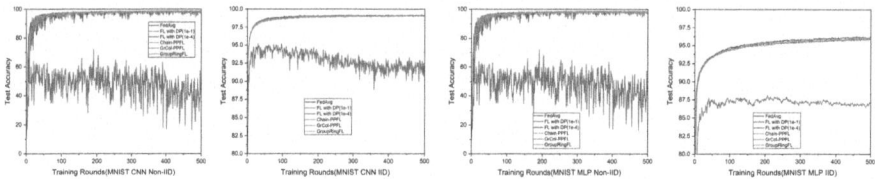

Fig. 2. Comparison of Test Accuracy within 500 rounds.

5.2 Convergence Comparison

In the convergence experiment, we compared our GroupRingFL framework against four baseline methods. According to Table 3, our framework achieves comparable accuracy in similar rounds as FedAvg, Chain-PPFL, and GrCol-PPFL across two data distributions and two models. This performance is notably better than federated learning with differential privacy, which adds noise. The added noise in differential privacy methods tends to increase training iterations and slow down convergence, explaining the observed difference in performance.

Table 3. Round comparison of model convergence (500 rounds).

Model and Accuracy	FedAvg	Chain-PPFL	GroupRingFL	FL with DP (10^{-4})	GrCol-PPFL
CNN (Non-IID) (98%)	1.4×	1.3×	1.4×	2.0×	1.4×
CNN (IID) (99%)	1.3×	1.4×	1.4×	1.7×	1.4×
MLP (Non-IID) (93%)	1.2×	1.2×	1.3×	2.2×	1.3×
MLP (IID) (95%)	1.3×	1.4×	1.3×	1.7×	1.5×
	(magnitude: 10^2 rounds)				

5.3 Security Comparison

We conducted 300 rounds of simulation experiments on the CIFAR-100 dataset to analyze the security of different frameworks. We adopted the Gradient Deep Leakage (DLG) algorithm to evaluate the ability of gradients to reconstruct data [15]. Our focus is to compare the Gradient Matching Loss (GML) between different frameworks, where lower GML indicates reduced privacy and security. Under the assumption that all nodes (including servers and local users) are "honest but curious", Chain-PPFL and GrCol-PPFL have the risk of data leakage. In contrast, GroupRingFL exhibits stronger privacy protection, as shown in the GML in Fig. 3.

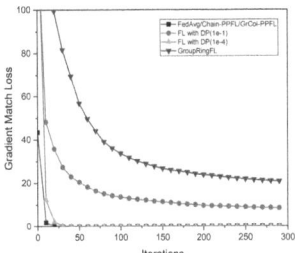

Fig. 3. The gradient match loss.   **Fig. 4.** Additional time of users.

5.4 Users Drop-Off Performance Comparison

User dropout in federated learning (FL) reduces model accuracy due to incomplete updates. Approaches like Chain-PPFL [3] and GrCol-PPFL [10] use chain-based communication structures but are vulnerable to dropouts. Secure aggregation [9] is robust against dropouts but has high computational costs due to key negotiation. Figure 4 demonstrates GroupRingFL's approach to managing user dropouts. We compared the extra time required by users and servers to handle dropouts in groups of 60 to 100 users with dropout rates from 0% to 30%. Our findings indicate that the primary additional time for users stems from re-establishing communication for new key generation. This analysis highlights the impact of user dropouts on federated learning.

5.5   Latency Comparison

For latency analysis, we used two comparison methods. First, we determined the optimal number of groups with a fixed number of nodes. Figure 5(a) shows that in the case of 100 local users, the number of groups is varied to determine the optimal group size that minimizes the uplink duration. Figure 5(b) shows that as the number of local users increases, GroupRingFL achieves a shorter uplink time than both FedAvg and Chain-PPFL. This is achieved by dynamically adjusting the group size based on the different number of local users.

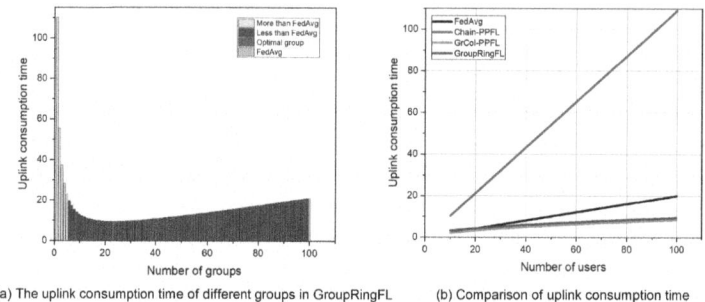

(a) The uplink consumption time of different groups in GroupRingFL   (b) Comparison of uplink consumption time

Fig. 5. Compare the uplink time of different groups and users.

6   Conclusion

Our group-based ring federated learning framework adopts a double-masking mechanism with excellent accuracy, privacy, and communication resilience. It successfully resists collusion attacks in an honest but curious node environment, ensuring stable communication even if users exit. Experimental verification shows that our framework performs comparable to the federated average in terms of model accuracy and convergence, while surpassing differential privacy methods in terms of privacy protection. Communication robustness can also be maintained in the case of user exit. Future research will explore other attack methods in federated learning, enhance the defense mechanism within the GroupRingFL framework, and improve the election mechanism of the ring structure.

Acknowledgements. This work is partially supported by the Humanities and Social Sciences Fund of the Ministry of Education (No. 24YJAZH150 and No. 22YJCZH106), Guangdong Basic and Applied Basic Research Foundation, China (Grant No. 2022A1515110980), Science and Technology Program of Guangzhou, China (Grant Nos. 202201010067, 2023A04J0330).

References

1. Jordan, M.I., Mitchell, T.M.: Machine learning: trends, perspectives, and prospects. Science **349**(6245), 255–260 (2015)
2. Konecný, J., McMahan, H.B., Ramage, D., Richtárik, P.: Federated optimization: distributed machine learning for on-device intelligence. arXiv preprint arXiv:1610.02527 (2016)
3. Li, Y., Zhou, Y., Jolfaei, A., Yu, D., Xu, G., Zheng, X.: Privacy-preserving federated learning framework based on chained secure multiparty computing. IEEE Internet Things J. **8**(8), 6178–6186 (2020)
4. Yang, G., Mu, K., Song, C., Yang, Z., Gong, T.: RingFed: reducing communication costs in federated learning on non-IID data. arXiv preprint arXiv:2107.08873 (2021)
5. Wu, Y., Cai, S., Xiao, X., Chen, G., Ooi, B.C.: Privacy preserving vertical federated learning for tree-based models. arXiv preprint arXiv:2008.06170 (2020)
6. Dwork, C.: Differential privacy. In: Bugliesi, M., Preneel, B., Sassone, V., Wegener, I. (eds.) ICALP 2006. LNCS, vol. 4052, pp. 1–12. Springer, Heidelberg (2006). https://doi.org/10.1007/11787006_1
7. Zhao, C., et al.: Secure multi-party computation: theory, practice and applications. Inf. Sci. **476**, 357–372 (2019)
8. Acar, A., Aksu, H., Uluagac, A.S., Conti, M.: A survey on homomorphic encryption schemes: theory and implementation. ACM Comput. Surv. **51**(4), 1–35 (2018)
9. Bonawitz, K., et al.: Practical secure aggregation for privacy-preserving machine learning. In: Proceedings of the 2017 ACM SIGSAC Conference on Computer and Communications Security (CCS), pp. 1175–1191. ACM (2017)
10. Cheng, J., Liu, Z., Shi, Y., Luo, P., Sheng, V.S.: GrCoL-PPFL: user-based group collaborative federated learning privacy protection framework. Comput. Mater. Continua **74**(1), 1923–1939 (2023)
11. Boneh, D.: The decision Diffie-Hellman problem. In: Buhler, J.P. (ed.) ANTS 1998. LNCS, vol. 1423, pp. 48–63. Springer, Heidelberg (1998). https://doi.org/10.1007/BFb0054851
12. Beimel, A.: Secret-sharing schemes: a survey. In: Chee, Y.M., et al. (eds.) IWCC 2011. LNCS, vol. 6639, pp. 11–46. Springer, Heidelberg (2011). https://doi.org/10.1007/978-3-642-20901-7_2
13. Gandotra, P., Jha, R.K., Jain, S.: A survey on device-to-device (D2D) communication: architecture and security issues. J. Netw. Comput. Appl. **78**, 9–29 (2017)
14. Bonawitz, K., et al.: Practical secure aggregation for federated learning on user-held data. In: Proceedings of the 2017 ACM SIGSAC Conference on Computer and Communications Security (CCS), pp. 1175–1191. ACM (2017)
15. Zhu, L., Liu, Z., Han, S.: Deep leakage from gradients. In: Advances in Neural Information Processing Systems (NeurIPS), vol. 32 (2019)

Centralized Oracle for Smart Contract Applications, Information Output Methods, and Systems

Robin Guo[✉]

Muse Network, Taiyi Building, No.1 Huihe South Road, Chaoyang District, Beijing, China
robin.guo@foxmail.com

Abstract. This paper explores the integration of smart contracts and oracles, focusing on efficient information output and system design. It first outlines the basic concepts and significance of smart contracts and oracles in blockchain, addressing the limitations of centralized oracles, particularly in information credibility. An innovative design is proposed to improve the accuracy and security of data transmission. The paper introduces an optimized multi-source information fusion strategy to handle data heterogeneity and uncertainty, enhancing the reliability of smart contract execution. A practical system is constructed and tested through simulations, demonstrating its ability to mitigate risks in centralized oracles while providing real-time, accurate data services. The findings contribute to advancing smart contract applications and blockchain security.

Keywords: Block-chain Oracle · Smart Contract · Information Output · Centralized · Data Fusion

1 Preface

As blockchain technology advances, smart contracts offer automation and transparency but are limited by their reliance on on-chain data. Oracle technology addresses this by providing off-chain data, enabling complex logic like automated transactions and insurance claims [1]. While efficient, centralized oracles face manipulation and security risks. This study proposes partial decentralization and a multi-source information fusion strategy to enhance data reliability and security. Simulation results show improved efficiency and decision-making, supporting broader blockchain and digital economy applications [2].

2 Overview of Smart Contracts and Oracles

2.1 Basic Principles of Smart Contracts

Smart contracts are self-executing programs that enforce terms without third-party involvement, using distributed ledger technology for decentralized systems. They are deployed as code on the blockchain, reacting to inputs from contracts, users, or oracles.

Upon meeting conditions, they execute predefined actions like asset transfers, recorded permanently on the blockchain. For instance, in the stock market, they automate buy or sell orders based on price thresholds, improving efficiency and reducing trust costs through dual encryption [3].

2.2 Centralized Oracles and Applications

Centralized oracles, popular for their speed and convenience in early blockchain applications, transmit off-chain data for smart contracts but pose risks like single points of failure and data manipulation. Common uses include financial markets and insurance claims [3]. In DeFi, they provide real-time crypto data but are vulnerable to attacks and errors that impact smart contract execution. Decentralized solutions like Chainlink improve accuracy and reduce risks but introduce complexity and latency. This study proposes a hybrid approach, integrating decentralized elements and auxiliary nodes into centralized oracles to enhance data credibility and maintain performance.

3 Research on Information Output Methods

3.1 Data Source Selection and Verification

Centralized oracles, widely used in early blockchain applications for their speed and convenience, transmit off-chain data via a central data provider, essential in DeFi for cryptocurrency exchange rates and in insurance for automating claims. Despite their efficiency, centralized oracles are vulnerable to single points of failure and data manipulation, threatening smart contract execution. Solutions like Chainlink explore decentralization to enhance data accuracy and reduce risks, though they introduce latency [4]. This study proposes an innovative centralized oracle design incorporating decentralized elements and auxiliary nodes for improved data credibility without sacrificing performance.

3.2 Information Output Mechanism Design

The design of the information output mechanism is key to efficient data transmission in smart contract and oracle integration. This section presents a multi-source data fusion algorithm that handles heterogeneous data from centralized, decentralized, and open datasets. The algorithm assigns weights based on data credibility, response time, and reputation, synthesizing the final result to enhance data reliability. Confidence intervals and error correction mechanisms ensure accuracy, triggering additional validation when uncertainty exceeds a threshold. Data preprocessing, including standardization and caching, reduces latency and ensures data comparability [5]. A secure transmission protocol with AES encryption and Zero Knowledge Proofs enhances security. The modular architecture allows seamless integration of the information output module with smart contracts, enabling smooth execution based on verified data (Fig. 1).

The optimized information output mechanism boosts data processing efficiency and response speed for smart contracts, even under increased data uncertainty. By integrating closely with smart contracts, this method ensures secure and efficient execution,

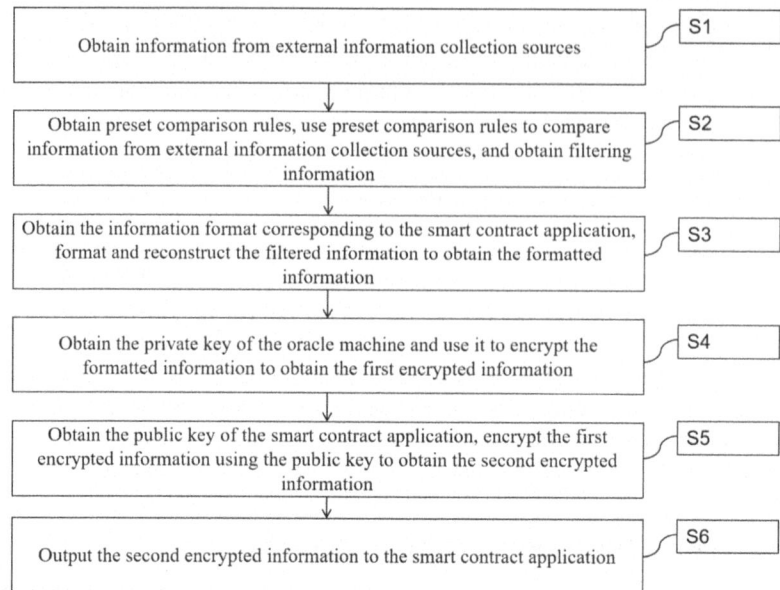

Fig. 1. Flowchart of the centralized oracle information output method for smart contract applications

enhancing blockchain technology's practical use and security. Experimental validation highlights significant advantages across various scenarios, expanding smart contract applications.

4   Integration of Smart Contracts and Oracle Systems

4.1   Integration Solution for Smart Contracts and Oracle Systems

This chapter outlines the integration of smart contracts with centralized oracle systems, focusing on seamless data integration, system efficiency, and security. A smart contract data input interface is designed to be compatible with centralized oracles, where data from auxiliary nodes is collected, verified, and formatted using hash verification and timestamps [6]. The multi-source fusion algorithm in the information output module generates reliable data, encrypted via AES and secured with zero-knowledge proof and time locks. The configurable smart contract interface allows users to adjust credibility thresholds and fusion strategies based on application needs. Modular design ensures smooth oracle-smart contract integration, where smart contracts monitor events, validate data, and trigger execution logic upon receiving verified data (Fig. 2).

We have also built a prototype system integrating the aforementioned technologies of smart contracts and oracles, which was validated through simulation experiments to demonstrate the advantages of the proposed method in improving data processing efficiency and decision-making accuracy. The experimental results show that the system significantly reduces decision-making risks due to data uncertainty while ensuring

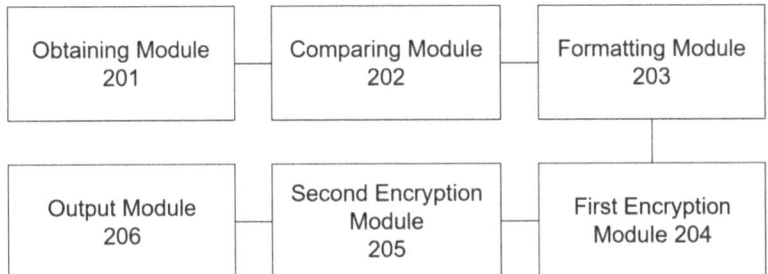

Fig. 2. Schematic diagram of the centralized oracle structure for smart contract applications

the speed of information transmission, enhancing the robustness of smart contracts in practical applications.

The figure below shows the schematic diagram of the centralized oracle information output system for smart contract applications. The embodiment of the present invention provides a centralized oracle information output system for smart contract applications, which includes the aforementioned oracle 20 and smart contract application 30; (Fig. 3)

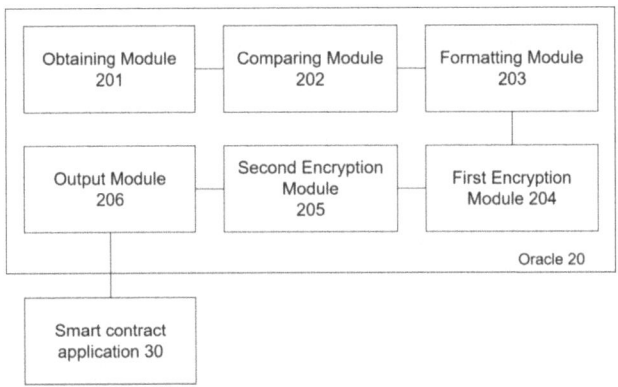

Fig. 3. Schematic diagram of the structure of the centralized oracle information output system for smart contract applications

In our system, Smart Contract Application 30 receives encrypted messages, decrypts them using smart contract and oracle keys, and verifies if the formatted data meets the blockchain's requirements. Our scalable design allows easy addition of oracle nodes and switching data sources, ensuring continuous improvement in performance. This chapter details the integration of centralized oracle designs and multi-source data fusion strategies with smart contracts. This approach resolves trust issues with centralized oracles while enhancing smart contract efficiency and security in processing off-chain data, expanding blockchain's practical applications.

4.2 Application Example of Integration of Smart Contracts and Prophet Systems: Agricultural Insurance Claims System Based on Weather Data

Agricultural insurance compensates farmers for natural disasters but faces inefficiencies and fraud in traditional claims processes. An automated system using smart contracts and oracle technology can improve transparency and efficiency.

Smart Contract: Deployed on the blockchain, it defines insurance terms and triggers compensation based on weather conditions like rainfall or temperature thresholds.

Oracle: Gathers real-time weather data from multiple sources, ensuring accuracy with data fusion algorithms. Data is encrypted and verified before being sent to the smart contract [7].

Automatic Claims: When weather data meets the contract's conditions, compensation is automatically transferred to the farmer's account, streamlining the claims process without manual intervention (Fig. 4).

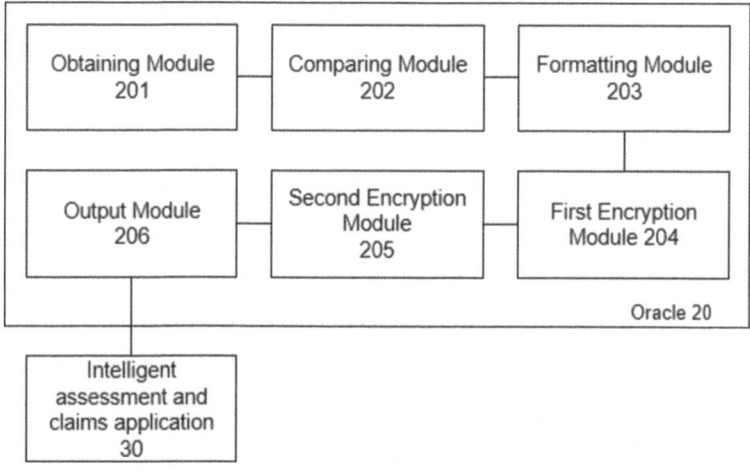

Fig. 4. Agricultural Insurance Claims System Based on Weather Data

System Use: The system enhances agricultural insurance claims by integrating smart contracts and oracles, improving automation, efficiency, and protection for farmers.

Benefits include: Reduced human intervention and claims processing time, now 2–3 days instead of 2–4 weeks. Increased transparency with blockchain recording, ensuring data immutability. Enhanced credibility through multi-source data fusion and verification, reducing fraud risks.

Experimental Results: Claims processing time has decreased to 2–3 days. Evaluation accuracy has improved, with fewer manual review errors. Efficiency has increased, requiring only 1–2 on-site specialists compared to many previously.

References

1. He, H., Yan'an, C.Z.: A review of blockchain-based smart contract technology and applications. Comput. Res. Dev. (2018)

2. Xinyada. Payment password system scheme introduction. Gold Card Project, (12), 39–45 (2000)
3. Zhang, Z.: Software subscription model based on blockchain non-fungible tokens. Comput. Eng. (1), 24–32 (2022)
4. Fan, J.: Preliminary exploration of smart contracts and oracles. Inf. Commun. Technol. Policy, (7), 36–38 (2018)
5. Zhang, Q.: Research on blockchain oracle-based trusted identity scheme for vehicular networks. Inf. Secur. Res. (2), 120–126 (2023)
6. Heiss, J., et al.: Trusted smart contract blockchain Oracle. In: Proceedings of the IEEE INTERNATIONAL Blockchain Conference (2019)
7. Livio, D.T., et al.: Understanding the oracle problem in blockchain: a call to action information

DataSafe: Copyright Protection with PUF Watermarking and Blockchain Tracing

Xiaolong Xue[1], Guangyong Shang[2], Zhen Ma[2], Minghui Xu[1(✉)],
Hechuan Guo[1], Kun Li[1], and Xiuzhen Cheng[1]

[1] Shandong University, Jinan, China
{xiaolongxue,ghc}@mail.sdu.edu.cn, {mhxu,kunli,xzcheng}@sdu.edu.cn
[2] Inspur Yunzhou Industrial Internet Co., Ltd., Jinan, China
{shangguangyong,mazhenrj}@inspur.com

Abstract. Digital watermarking methods are commonly used to safeguard digital media copyrights by confirming ownership and deterring unauthorized use. However, without reliable third-party oversight, these methods risk security vulnerabilities during watermark extraction. Furthermore, digital media lacks tangible ownership attributes, posing challenges for secure copyright transfer and tracing. This study introduces DataSafe, a copyright protection scheme that combines physical unclonable functions (PUFs) and blockchain technology. PUF devices use their unique fingerprints for blockchain registration. Subsequently, these devices incorporate invisible watermarking techniques to embed digital watermarks into media for copyright protection. The watermark verification process is confined within the devices, preserving confidentiality during extraction, validating identities during copyright exchanges, and facilitating blockchain-based traceability of copyright transfers. The implementation of a prototype system on the LPC55S69-EVK development board is detailed, illustrating the practicality and effectiveness of the proposed solution.

Keywords: Data security · Copyright protection · Watermarks · Physical unclonable functions · Blockchain

1 Introduction

In recent years, the adoption of digital technologies has become a crucial factor driving economic growth and social advancement. Copyright owners and creators share various literary and artistic works as digital media across users' electronic devices. While the lossless distribution of digital media promotes knowledge sharing, it also introduces copyright challenges, including difficulties in verifying ownership and holding infringers accountable. A widely used solution for these issues is applying watermarks in digital media. The design of digital watermarks aims to achieve robustness, invisibility, and security [9,18,23]. However, this approach often overlooks conflicts related to copyright verification: (1) To ensure reliable

G. Zhao et al. (Eds.): BWTAC 2024, CCIS 2277, pp. 256–268, 2025.
https://doi.org/10.1007/978-981-97-9412-6_24

copyright verification of digital watermarks, the extraction key of the watermark must be public, which inherently risks exposing secrets. (2) Traditional digital watermarks, often based on pseudo-random sequences or binary images, which are easily imitated and used for infringement behavior. (3) Copyright disputes are frequent during transfers, and solely relying on digital watermarks can result in unresolved conflicts, particularly in peer-to-peer distribution networks.

To tackle these challenges, various solutions have been proposed. Dutta et al. [4] suggest using iris features as digital watermarks embedded in media files. They mitigate watermark counterfeiting by integrating biometric features as labels in digital media. Zhu et al. [24] propose a blockchain service architecture for tracing and verifying the registration and transactions of original works. Jiang et al. [8] propose a blockchain-based lightweight and cost-effective copyright protection system. These methods utilize blockchain to record copyright transfers. However, when transferring copyright with others, one can still forge their identity or use their identity for framing.

To establish a secure connection between digital media and copyright holders, it is essential to accurately identify the copyright holder while preventing fraudulent activities. Although biometric features provides a potential solution, it still requires the involvement of trusted third parties. Another promising approach for establishing physical binding is the use of physical unclonable functions (PUFs), which are hardware-based security primitives. These rely on the unique physical properties inherent in each circuit, resulting from uncontrollable variations during the manufacturing process [5]. Because these properties cannot be easily replicated, they can be used to generate unique device fingerprints. Building on the use of PUF-based device fingerprints, this paper presents DataSafe, a copyright protection scheme that manages copyright transfer and traceability with PUF and blockchain. This system leverages blockchain technology to enhance security and transparency. The contributions of this paper are as follows:

1. The first time device physical fingerprints are embedded into digital media, establishing the physical ownership of digital media copyrights. This means that the copyright is bound to the device, and the ownership of digital media originating from the device is undeniable and cannot be forged.
2. We propose a secure digital watermark extraction process utilizing PUF devices to safeguard against secret leakage during copyright verification.
3. The proposed system employs blockchain technology to register PUF devices and records the process of copyright transfer, thereby achieving traceability throughout the entire history of ownership.
4. The combination of PUF, digital watermarking, and blockchain technology collectively forms the prototype system for copyright protection. This prototype system demonstrates that DataSafe can ensure the security of copyrights and showcases the potential of DataSafe in practical applications.

The structure of this paper is outlined as follows: In Sect. 2, we examine related works. In Sect. 3, we present our DataSafe design. In Sect. 4, we establish a prototype founded on the proposed architecture and demonstrate experimental outcomes. Finally, in Sect. 5, we summarize this paper.

2   Related Work

2.1   Device Fingerprinting with PUF

Embedded devices pose a unique challenge for secure key storage. Unlike traditional systems, attackers can physically access the circuits, potentially compromising keys stored in non-volatile memory (as shown in [15]). Kerckhoff's principle dictates that the security of a cryptosystem should rely solely on the secrecy of the key. Modern systems adhere to this principle by making everything public except the key. To address this vulnerability in embedded devices, Tuyls et al. [16] proposed extracting keys from physical properties of the integrated circuits themselves. This eliminates the need for storing keys in memory, mitigating memory-based attacks and guaranteeing device uniqueness and authenticity. This approach can be extended to strengthen key storage in copyright management systems. PUFs can serve as unique device fingerprints. Existing research explores integrating PUFs into hardware accelerators to protect neural network models [2,7]. However, these methods are limited to specific devices and are not directly applicable to safeguarding digital media copyrights.

2.2   Copyright Protection with Digital Watermarking

Watermarks are subtly embedded within the non-essential bits of digital content, altering the data without compromising the user's experience [6]. This process essentially weaves covert data into the original material. Several studies have explored the use of biometric features as watermarks. Dutta et al. proposed incorporating iris traits into media files [3,4], while Wojtowicz et al. [17] advocated for integrating both fingerprint and iris features in digital images . While these methods aim to address forgeable watermarks with biometrics, using biometric features for copyright protection raises concerns. Asserting copyright through biometric features could unintentionally reveal sensitive personal information, and it doesn't fully prevent copyright violations.

2.3   Data Protection with Blockchain

Blockchain technology offers a novel decentralized architecture for distributed applications [1,19]. This technology flourishes alongside smart contracts, self-executing agreements that automate the fulfillment of conditions and streamline processes for all involved parties. Furthermore, blockchain serves as an immutable ledger, akin to a tamper-proof bulletin board, ensuring robust traceability of information [20–22]. Lu et al. [12] have proposed a scheme leveraging blockchain for the management of digital rights for design works. However, this method necessitates users to submit their private keys to the application, which could be a vulnerability as the decryption program might potentially misappropriate the private key. On a similar note, Ma et al. [13] suggested a scheme combining blockchain and watermarking to detect the misuse of images online. Yet, they did not sufficiently address the issue of identity fraud in copyright transfers, which limits the ability to accurately pinpoint copyright violators during the tracing process. Liu et al. [11] have used blockchain to supervise and control tangible devices and data, thus enhancing the dependability of management systems. TEMS [10] adopts TEEs to protect the data on-chaining process. However, these works do not provide a mechanism to prevent unauthorized data redistribution once the data has been leaked from the system, lacking a watermarking solution to address this issue.

This paper explores a system designed to log copyright transfers on a blockchain and to produce watermarks with the aid of trusted device signatures. It captures the process by which digital media copyrights are transferred from sellers to buyers, establishing comprehensive and auditable records for these transfer transactions via smart contracts. By incorporating the physical ownership of digital media copyrights as detailed in this paper, it is possible to achieve a full traceability of copyright on the blockchain.

3   DataSafe Design

The architecture of DataSafe is shown in Fig. 1. Initially, PUF devices are registered on the blockchain. Following this, the registration and transfer of digital copyrights are verified by PUF devices and logged on the blockchain.

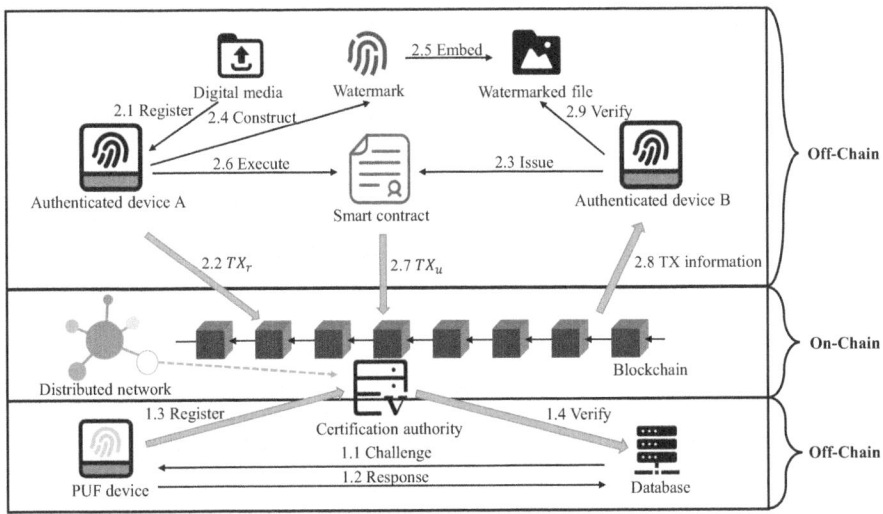

Fig. 1. DataSafe architecture

3.1   PUF-Based Device Registration

Firstly, a PUF device is constructed within a secure setting to guarantee that the responses it produces in response to challenges are neither compromised nor counterfeited. Once the device is initialized, the manufacturer generates a random number c and dispatches it to the device as a challenge. The device then creates a security primitive DF and auxiliary data FE on SRAM. The function $\mathsf{Gen}(\mathsf{DF},\mathsf{FE},c)$ obscures the random number c to produce original output o_c. Subsequently, $\mathsf{Hash}(o_c)$ is applied to derive a response r, which is then relayed back to the manufacturer. The manufacturer subsequently archives the device's identifier id assigned to the device during manufacturing and the challenge response pair $\langle c, r \rangle$ in a secure database, employing $\langle c, r \rangle$ as the device fingerprint for its authentication.

Next, the manufacturer selects a node within the blockchain to serve as the certification authority. This authority's role is limited to the registration of PUF devices. It connects to the secure database for device authentication and specifies the public parameters necessary for the generation of public-private key pairs. This includes the elliptic curve $E_{a,b} : y^3 = x^3 + ax + b$ over the finite field F_p, where p is a large prime number, and a, b meet the condition $4a^3 + 27b^2 \neq 0 \mod p, a, b \in F_p$. The authority then picks a large prime order n and its corresponding generator $P \in E_{a,b}$ in F_p. The certification authority chooses a random number sk_c as the private key within the range of n, and computes the public key $\mathsf{pk}_c = \mathsf{sk}_c \cdot P$. The certification authority stores the private key and disseminates the public parameters and the public key.

Lastly, PUF devices need to register an identity on the blockchain. The device independently selects a random number $\mathsf{sk} \in n$ as its private key based on the predefined parameters, and computes $\mathsf{pk} = \mathsf{sk} \cdot P$ to create a public-private key pair $(\mathsf{pk}, \mathsf{sk})$. Subsequently, the device generates origin output o_{sk} based on $\mathsf{Gen}(\mathsf{DF},\mathsf{FE},\mathsf{sk})$, which is then saved in nonvolatile memory. The device then initiates an identity verification request to the certification authority. Through a key negotiation process, a temporary symmetric key k is generated collaboratively by the certification authority and the device. The device provides its identifier id to the certification authority, which encrypts a random number c using k and forwards it to the device. Upon receiving c, the device decrypts it, generates o_c based on $\mathsf{Gen}(\mathsf{DF},\mathsf{FE},c)$, and subsequently uses $\mathsf{Hash}(o_c)$ to generate a response r. The device encrypts r with k and returns it to the certification authority. Upon receiving r, the certification authority checks the $\langle c, r \rangle$ pair against the entries in the secure database. If the verification check passes, the certification authority issues a acceptance notice to the device, registers it as an authenticated device on the blockchain, and archives the parameters $\langle \mathsf{id}, \mathsf{pk} \rangle$. The id is utilized by the certification authority for device identification, while the hash of pk serves as the device's transaction address addr on the blockchain. In the event that the verification does not pass, the certification authority dispatches a cancellation notice to the device, necessitating a re-initiation of the registration process.

3.2   Copyright Registration and Transfer

We leverage authenticated devices to act as secure vaults for copyrights. The device fingerprint of this device is embedded into the digital media. Copyright registration and transfer only occur after the device has been verified on the blockchain. This ensures that all participants in copyright transfer possess authenticated devices, guaranteeing identity cannot be forged and tamper-proof transaction records throughout the process.

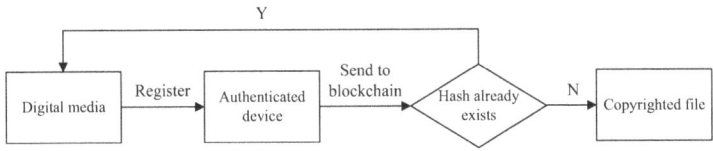

Fig. 2. Workflow of copyright registration

Copyright Registration. Before a digital media file can be acknowledged as copyrighted within the blockchain, it necessitates initial registration on the blockchain. The workflow of copyright registration is shown in the Fig. 2. This registration entails the authenticated device submitting a hash digest of the file onto the blockchain, which in turn creates a copyright marker. This copyright marker is composed of the file's hash digest $H(f)$ and the blockchain address addr of the device holding the copyright.

Imagine a situation where digital media f that is stored on an external drive needs to undergo copyright registration. The authenticated device A computes the hash digest $H(f)$ of f, encapsulates $H(f)$ and addr into a transaction TX_r and dispatches it to the blockchain. Following this, after the transaction's validity is confirmed, miners within the blockchain network include the transaction in a block. Throughout this entire procedure, the original file remains securely with A, safeguarding it from any unauthorized access.

Copyright Transfer. As shown in Fig. 3, transfer of copyrights in DataSafe consists of the following steps:

Initiate Transaction: In this step, authenticated device B intends to acquire f from authenticated device A, leading to a negotiation between the two parties regarding the transaction specifics. This negotiation entails aspects such as the transaction price, deadlines for file delivery by A, payment deadline for B, and the deadline for confirming receipt. These negotiated terms are then documented within a smart contract, which is subsequently deployed onto the blockchain.

Pay for Media: B transfers the agreed transaction price to the smart contract, which then notifies A to initiate the delivery process.

Generate Copyright Transfer Marker: A creates a copyright transfer marker ctm_{AB}, which includes the transaction id of copyright marker and the addresses of both parties involved. Next, A embeds a digital watermark into f to produce a

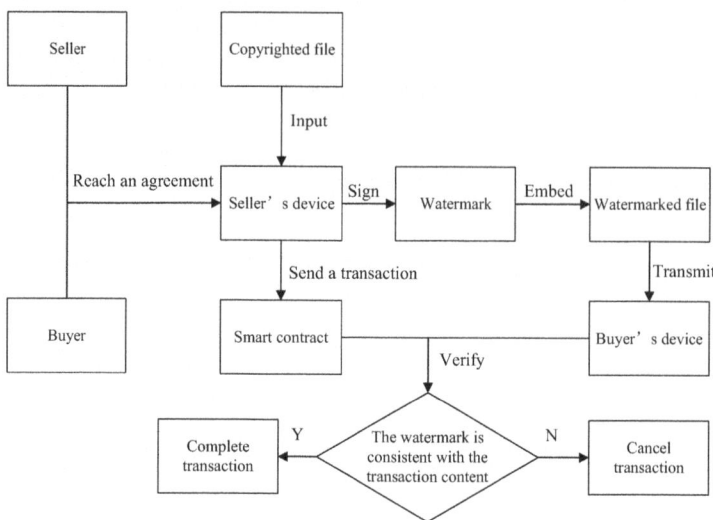

Fig. 3. Workflow of copyright transfer

watermarked file f' and generates the embedding position key lk, as described in Sect. 3.3. Subsequently, A packages the $H(f')$ and the ctm_{AB} into a transaction TX_u and sends it to the smart contract, which then records the transaction on the blockchain.

Deliver Media: A encrypts the embedding position key lk using B's public key. Then A sends f' along with encrypted lk to B via off-chain or peer-to-peer (P2P) communication.

Verification and Transfer: B decrypts the received information to obtain f' and lk. First, B calculates $H(f')$ and compares it with the hash digest recorded on the blockchain. If the hashes do not match, B cancels the transaction. If they do match, B proceeds to extract the digital watermark from f' using the method described in Sect. 3.3. Next, B calculates the hash of ctm_{AB} and verifies the embedded watermark's correctness using A's public key. After successful verification, B sends a confirmation message to the smart contract, which then transfers the frozen tokens to A's address.

3.3   Embedding and Extraction of Watermarks

The inherent security risk in digital watermarking arises from the requirement to share the key with the verifier. This presents a vulnerability because a verifier with malicious intent who has access to the key could potentially remove the watermark covertly. Furthermore, relying on a trusted third party for verification increases the risk of centralization. To counter these challenges, we propose a secure watermarking approach that moves the watermark embedding and extraction processes to the authenticated device itself.

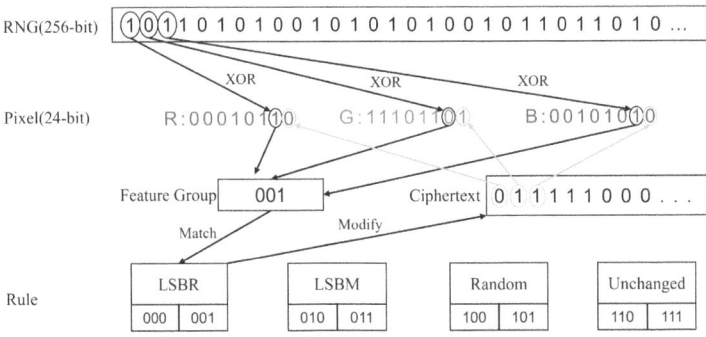

Fig. 4. Watermark embedding and location key matching

To authenticate the identity of the copyright holder, we employ the Elliptic Curve Digital Signature Algorithm (ECDSA) to sign ctm_{AB} with a private key that is stored securely on the authenticated device. The signature produced is then transformed into a binary format to form a digital watermark w_{AB}, thereby ensuring the physical ownership of the digital media. Considering the performance limitations of the devices, we have focused on enhancing security. As a result, we opt for the Least Significant Bit (LSB) watermark embedding technique and generate a location key lk for embedding the watermark in the following manner.

As shown in Fig. 4, the low bits stored in digital media are randomly distributed, with 0 and 1 each making up approximately half. This allows us to use the combination of the second lowest order bits as a condition for modifying the lowest order bits. For example, in a 24-bit true color image, the RGB format for a pixel p_{ij} is represented as $R\{r_0, r_1, ..., r_7\}$, $G\{g_0, g_1, ..., g_7\}$, $B\{b_0, b_1, ..., b_7\}$. We can extract the second lowest order bits $\{r_6, g_6, b_6\}$, use a random number generator to produce a random number x, and then perform a bitwise XOR operation with $\{r_6, g_6, b_6\}$ to obtain the feature group $\{x_i \oplus r_6, x_{i+1} \oplus g_6, x_{i+2} \oplus b_6\}$. We the classify these feature groups based on the size of watermark and predefined rules, defining the necessary modifications. Using an image as an example, we define four modifying actions for any given pixel.

Least Significant Bit Replacement (LSBR): Define a color channel rgb_{ij} of pixel p_{ij}, take a bit m_b of ciphertext m, and replace the lowest bit of rgb_{ij} with m_b.

$$\text{LSBR}(\text{rgb}_{ij}) = \begin{cases} \text{rgb}_{ij}, & if \ \text{LSB}(\text{rgb}_{ij}) = m_b \\ \text{rgb}_{ij} + 1, & if \ \text{LSB}(\text{rgb}_{ij}) \neq m_b \ and \ \text{rgb}_{ij} = 0 \mod 2 \\ \text{rgb}_{ij} - 1, & if \ \text{LSB}(\text{rgb}_{ij}) \neq m_b \ and \ \text{rgb}_{ij} = 1 \mod 2 \end{cases} \quad (1)$$

Least Significant Bit Matching (LSBM): the lowest bit of pixel p_{ij-1} is filled with a random number. For pixel p_{ij}, define a color channel rgb_{ij}, take a bit m_b

of ciphertext m, and match the lowest bit of rgb_{ij} with the m_b.

$$\mathsf{LSBM}(\mathsf{rgb}_{ij}) = \begin{cases} \mathsf{rgb}_{ij}, & if \ \mathsf{LSB}(\mathsf{rgb}_{ij}) = m_b \\ \mathsf{rgb}_{ij} + 1, & if \ \mathsf{LSB}(\mathsf{rgb}_{ij}) \neq m_b \ and \ \mathsf{rgb}_{ij} = 0 \\ \mathsf{rgb}_{ij} - 1, & if \ \mathsf{LSB}(\mathsf{rgb}_{ij}) \neq m_b \ and \ \mathsf{rgb}_{ij} = 255 \\ \mathsf{rgb}_{ij} + rand, & if \ \mathsf{LSB}(\mathsf{rgb}_{ij}) \neq m_b \ and \ 0 < \mathsf{rgb}_{ij} < 255 \end{cases} \quad (2)$$

where $rand$ is a random number of 1 or -1.

Random Number Filling: Fill the lowest bit of pixel p_{ij} with random numbers.

Unchanged: The lowest bit of pixel p_{ij} remains unchanged.

The location key lk is constructed with x and modifications. These modifications can be independently defined based on the file format, with the primary goal of enhancing security.

The verifier's authenticated device decrypts lk using a private key. It then processes the file according to the x and the defined modifying actions within lk to extract w_{AB}. The device verifies the signature against the transaction on the blockchain to confirm copyright ownership. Since the malicious verifier lacks any knowledge about lk, they cannot erase the watermark from the copyright file without damaging the file itself.

3.4   Blockchain-Based Copyright Tracing

The authenticated device C proposes to acquire f' from the authenticated device B, and they complete the transaction following the process described in Sect. 3.1. B sends the watermarked file f'' and the location key lk' to C, recording the copyright transfer marker ctm_{BC} on the blockchain. B encrypts f' only when the hash digest matches ctm_{AB}. Consequently, C extracts the watermark using t' and successfully verifies it, establishing the transfer direction of the copyright file as $A \Rightarrow B \Rightarrow C$. This ensures traceability of the copyright transfer.

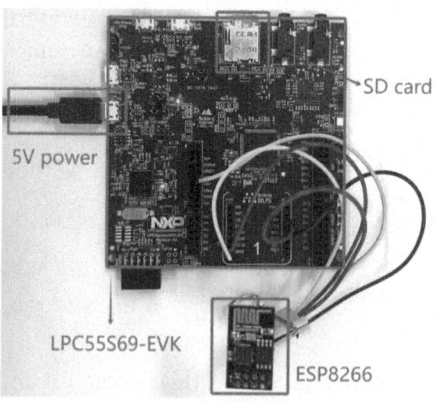

Fig. 5. Wiring diagram of DataSafe

4   Prototype Implementation

In this section, we detail the development of a prototype for DataSafe, in line with our proposed scheme. The prototype was constructed using the LPC55S69-EVK development board, a product of NXP Semiconductor Company. This board is equipped with an LPC55S69 dual-core Arm Cortex-M33 microcontroller, which features a root of trust established through SRAM PUF and is compatible with Arm TrustZone technology. For further details on the LPC55S69-EVK, the user manual [14] is recommended for consultation.

We employed go-ethereum, a Golang-based implementation of the Ethereum protocol, as the foundational layer of our blockchain. A private blockchain was established across five computers, each furnished with an i7-7900@3.0 GHz processor and endowed with 16 GB of memory, all operating on Ubuntu 18.04.1 GNU/Linux. Additionally, our configuration encompasses an authentication server. We implemented DataSafe on the development board, which is energized by a 5V external power supply and linked to the blockchain through a WiFi module. The schematic wiring diagram of the system is illustrated in Fig. 5.

```
Transaction Hash:                                          Transaction Hash:
    0x5dc7b2f2acae6d3f129cbc2f1501f29a25ac5925c24155           0x5dc7b2f2acae6d3f129cbc2f1501f29a25ac5925c24155
    36eebf5e60d3b55755                                         36eebf5e60d3b55755
Data:                                                      Data:
    Prev-Transaction Hash: null                                Prev-Transaction Hash: null
    From: 0x8619bb67f62b09eed2aa597186680c6931d25e52           From: 0x8619bb67f62b09eed2aa597186680c6931d25e52
    Hash: f9eab2fe9f516a7f07f881a896b32b50                     Hash: f9eab2fe9f516a7f07f881a896b32b50
```

(a) Register Transaction   (b) Update Transaction

Fig. 6. Transactions

We kept the physical unclonable secrets of two boards within the authentication server. The boards confirmed their identities to the server by providing responses and were then duly registered on the blockchain. For our experimental purposes, we utilized a BMP-formatted image of Lena as a sample, registering it on the blockchain through the seller's board. The registration transaction is depicted in Fig. 6a. Once an agreement was reached between the seller and the buyer, the buyer initiated a smart contract on the blockchain. On the board, the seller generated a copyright transfer marker and authenticated it with a private key. Subsequently, the watermark was integrated into the image, yielding the watermarked Lena image. Figures 7a and 7c display the images before and after the watermark was embedded. Figures 7b and 7d show the extracted information of the lowest bit plane in the same area for the original image and the Covered image, respectively. It can be seen that the watermark information is uniformly embedded into the lowest bit after modification. We employed the Peak Signal to Noise Ratio (PSNR) to assess the imperceptibility of the embedded watermark, which measured 55.387 dB. The seller's board proceeded to compute the hash

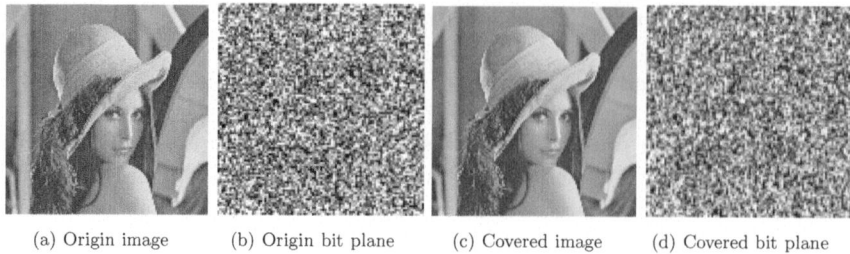

(a) Origin image   (b) Origin bit plane   (c) Covered image   (d) Covered bit plane

Fig. 7. Watermarking results

digest of the image that now included the embedded watermark, crafted a transaction, and then transmitted it to the blockchain. This subsequent update transaction is portrayed in Fig. 6b. Upon acquisition of the file, the buyer decrypted the position key and authenticated the watermark with the aid of the board. Throughout this entire procedure, the position key remained undisclosed, ensuring that the buyer was unable to eliminate the watermark and gain access to the original image.

In a situation where the seller partakes in deceitful conduct by selling files that have been registered on the blockchain on multiple occasions, the board has the capability to recognize these files by their identical hash digest and decline to register them. On the other hand, if the seller endeavors to register a file on the blockchain by tampering with the hash digest, the transfer process can indeed be finalized. Nevertheless, other users are able to pinpoint analogous content on the blockchain and ascertain the original physical proprietorship of the file by leveraging the timestamp and the capability to trace transactions. Subsequently, they can bring forth the authentication status of the seller's board to the blockchain, resulting in financial repercussions for the malevolent party.

DataSafe is scalable for various user sizes and applications. It uses blockchain for transaction info but handles most operations off-chain. For example, copyright registration records minimal blockchain data, while file transmission and watermark extraction are off-chain. This design reduces blockchain data volume and latency. The hybrid on-chain/off-chain architecture supports scalability and security, allowing for easy expansion and integration of new devices or watermarking technologies.

5   Conclusion

The paper presents DataSafe, a copyright protection scheme that combines PUF and blockchain. It advocates for the secure storage of keys that represent physical devices within PUF devices and the integration of copyright transfer details into digital media through digital signatures. This approach solidifies the physical ownership aspect of digital copyrights. During the decryption phase, the embedded content is retrieved by merging the position key, and its authenticity is confirmed by referencing blockchain data, which guarantees the traceability of digital copyright. Both the embedding and extraction operations take place within the secure confines of the PUF device, safeguarding the digital watermark during the extraction process. In conclusion, the paper illustrates the practicality of the proposed scheme by showcasing a system prototype developed on the LPC55S69-EVK development board. Additionally, it addresses possible malicious distribution behaviors within the system and suggests appropriate countermeasures to mitigate such risks.

Acknowledgment. This study was supported by the Academic Divisions of the Chinese Academy of Sciences (Grant No. 2020-ZW12-A-024), the National Natural Science Foundation of China (No. 62302266, 62232010, U23A20302), the Shandong Science Fund for Excellent Young Scholars (No. 2023HWYQ-008), and the Shandong Science Fund for Key Fundamental Research Project (ZR2022ZD02).

References

1. Cheng, Y., Guo, Y., Xu, M., Hu, Q., Yu, D., Cheng, X.: An adaptive and modular blockchain enabled architecture for a decentralized metaverse. IEEE J. Sel. Areas Commun. (2023)
2. Dorfmeister, D., Ferrarotti, F., Fischer, B., Schwandtner, M., Sochor, H.: A PUF-based approach for copy protection of intellectual property in neural network models. In: Bludau, P., Ramler, R., Winkler, D., Bergsmann, J. (eds.) SWQD 2024. LNBIP, vol. 505, pp. 153–169. Springer, Cham (2024). https://doi.org/10.1007/978-3-031-56281-5_9
3. Dutta, M.K., Gupta, P., Pathak, V.K.: Blind watermarking in audio signals using biometric features in wavelet domain. In: TENCON 2009-2009 IEEE Region 10 Conference, pp. 1–5. IEEE (2009)
4. Dutta, M.K., Singh, A., Zia, T.A.: An efficient and secure digital image watermarking using features from iris image. In: 2013 International Conference on Control Communication and Computing (ICCC), pp. 451–456. IEEE (2013)
5. Feiten, L., Martin, T., Sauer, M., Becker, B.: Improving RO-PUF quality on FPGAs by incorporating design-dependent frequency biases. In: 2015 20th IEEE European Test Symposium (ETS), pp. 1–6. IEEE (2015)
6. Fridrich, J., Goljan, M., Du, R.: Lossless data embedding-new paradigm in digital watermarking. EURASIP J. Adv. Signal Process. **2002**, 1–12 (2002)
7. Guo, Q., Ye, J., Gong, Y., Hu, Y., Li, X.: PUF based pay-per-device scheme for IP protection of CNN model. In: 2018 IEEE 27th Asian Test Symposium (ATS), pp. 115–120. IEEE (2018)
8. Jiang, T., Sui, A., Lin, W., Han, P.: Research on the application of blockchain in copyright protection. In: 2020 International Conference on Culture-oriented Science & Technology (ICCST), pp. 616–621. IEEE (2020)
9. Lin, Y.H., Wu, J.L.: A digital blind watermarking for depth-image-based rendering 3D images. IEEE Trans. Broadcast. **57**(2), 602–611 (2011)
10. Liu, C., et al.: Extending on-chain trust to off-chain - trustworthy blockchain data collection using trusted execution environment (TEE). IEEE Trans. Comput. **71**(12), 3268–3280 (2022). https://doi.org/10.1109/TC.2022.3148379
11. Liu, C., et al.: TBAC: a tokoin-based accountable access control scheme for the internet of things. IEEE Trans. Mob. Comput. **23**(5), 6133–6148 (2024). https://doi.org/10.1109/TMC.2023.3316622

12. Lu, Z., Shi, Y., Tao, R., Zhang, Z.: Blockchain for digital rights management of design works. In: 2019 IEEE 10th International Conference on Software Engineering and Service Science (ICSESS), pp. 596–603. IEEE (2019)
13. Ma, Z., Huang, W., Gao, H.: A new blockchain-based trusted DRM scheme for built-in content protection. EURASIP J. Image Video Process. **2018**, 91 (2018)
14. Semiconductor, N.: NXP semiconductors LPC55S6x arm cortex-M33 microcontrollers (2020). https://www.nxp.com/products/processors-and-microcontrollers/arm-microcontrollers/general-purpose-mcus/lpc5500-cortex-m33/high-efficiency-arm-cortex-m33-based-microcontroller-family:LPC55S6x
15. Shamsoshoara, A., Korenda, A., Afghah, F., Zeadally, S.: A survey on physical unclonable function (PUF)-based security solutions for internet of things. Comput. Netw. **183**, 107593 (2020)
16. Tuyls, P., Schrijen, G.J., Willems, F., Ignatenko, T., Skoric, B.: Secure key storage with PUFs. In: Security with Noisy Data-On Private Biometrics, Secure Key Storage and Anti-Counterfeiting, pp. 269–292 (2007)
17. Wojtowicz, W., Ogiela, M.R.: Digital images authentication scheme based on bimodal biometric watermarking in an independent domain. J. Vis. Commun. Image Represent. **38**, 1–10 (2016)
18. Xiang, S., Kim, H.J., Huang, J.: Invariant image watermarking based on statistical features in the low-frequency domain. IEEE Trans. Circuits Syst. Video Technol. **18**(6), 777–790 (2008)
19. Xu, M., et al.: Exploring blockchain technology through a modular lens: a survey. ACM Comput. Surv. **56**(9), 1–39 (2024)
20. Xu, M., Wang, C., Zou, Y., Yu, D., Cheng, X., Lyu, W.: Curb: trusted and scalable software-defined network control plane for edge computing. In: 2022 IEEE 42nd International Conference on Distributed Computing Systems (ICDCS), pp. 492–502. IEEE (2022)
21. Xu, M., et al.: FileDES: a secure, scalable and succinct decentralized encrypted storage network. Cryptology ePrint Archive (2024)
22. Xu, M., Zou, Z., Cheng, Y., Hu, Q., Yu, D., Cheng, X.: SPDL: a blockchain-enabled secure and privacy-preserving decentralized learning system. IEEE Trans. Comput. **72**(2), 548–558 (2022)
23. Zhu, N., Ding, G., Wang, J.: A novel digital watermarking method for new viewpoint video based on depth map. In: 2008 Eighth International Conference on Intelligent Systems Design and Applications, vol. 2, pp. 3–7. IEEE (2008)
24. Zhu, P., Hu, J., Li, X., Zhu, Q.: Using blockchain technology to enhance the traceability of original achievements. IEEE Trans. Eng. Manage. **70**(5), 1693–1707 (2021)

A GAN Anomaly Detection Method Based on Multi-scale Endogenous Enhancement

Lin Zhang[✉] and Yang Dai

Sichuan Digital Economy Research Institute, Yibin 644000, China
linzhang_dy@163.com

Abstract. The application of image data in various fields is becoming increasingly widespread. Especially in security, the need for image detection is becoming more and more urgent. Anomaly detection, as an important aspect in Industrial Control Safety (ICS), aims to automatically identify and locate regions or objects in an image that deviate from normal pixels. This capability is crucial for enhancing the efficiency and precision of product safety testing systems. In response to this need, we propose a novel multi-scale endogenous enhanced anomaly detection model based on Generative Adversarial Networks (GANs). Our model operates on an unsupervised learning paradigm, allowing effective training even in scenarios with limited labeled data. By optimizing image details, our approach achieves robust anomaly detection. Furthermore, we introduce a multi-scale endogenous enhancement technique to bolster the model's resilience. To quantify anomaly severity, we devise a unique anomaly scoring mechanism, providing decision support for the model's assessments. We conduct experiments using the challenging MVTec dataset, demonstrating that our proposed method surpasses existing state-of-the-art approaches in both anomaly detection and localization.

Keywords: Industrial control security · Generative adversarial networks · Multi-scale endogenous enhancement

1 Introduction

Anomaly detection, as its name implies, refers to anything that differs from the normal pattern of behaviour. This is not unfamiliar in real life as it has a wide range of application areas.

It has been shown that unsupervised methods show strong capabilities in image anomaly detection in the context of only a small amount of anomaly data available [1]. Hence, we explore unsupervised learning methods that can effectively achieve industrial image anomaly detection from a security perspective. Our proposed approach entails a GAN-based anomaly detection model leveraging image enhancement reconstruction, eliminating the need for restricted anomaly samples. The model comprises three main components. The first part is used for anomaly generation. The model performs a series of operations based on the dataset itself and the mask to complete the multi-scale enhancement of the image. The second is used for image reconstruction. Our method learns

G. Zhao et al. (Eds.): BWTAC 2024, CCIS 2277, pp. 269–281, 2025.
https://doi.org/10.1007/978-981-97-9412-6_25

low-level and high-level features of the image using an improved GAN. The third part is used for anomaly segmentation. The reconstructed image, the enhanced image, and the anomaly mask image are fed into a sub-network, and the focal loss [2] in the guided by the segmentation of tiny anomalous regions. Together, the above components form our network, which aims to guide the network towards high quality reconstruction while accurately capturing various anomalies. Figure 1 illustrates the processing results of these components.

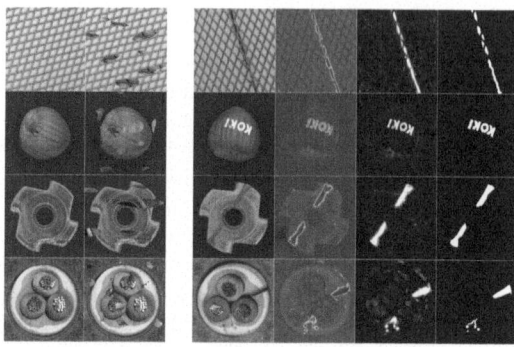

Fig. 1. Effectiveness of the proposed method for anomaly detection in images. Each column from left to right shows the normal image, synthetic anomaly image, anomaly test map, heat map, segmentation map, and ground truth, respectively.

We demonstrate the effectiveness of the method by conducting extensive experiments on the MVTec dataset. Our key contributions are outlined as follows:

- We propose a novel GAN anomaly detection method based on image reconstruction for surface quality inspection of industrial products.
- We propose a multi-scale endogenous enhancement method that significantly improves the description of key features in the generated images.
- We devised a new criterion for the assessment of anomaly, using residual scores and segmentation scores to jointly judge anomaly.
- Extensive experiments on MVTec show that our proposed method is effective.

2   Related Work

In recent years, deep learning-based methods have made significant strides in industrial image anomaly detection, particularly those centered around image reconstruction. These methods have overcome the limitations of traditional approaches and have primarily focused on Convolutional Neural Networks (CNN), auto-encoders [3] and generative adversarial networks [4]. For instance, Peng et al. [5] proposed a semi-supervised detection algorithm containing an image reconstruction network and a defect prediction network. The algorithm focuses on the consistency of the depth features and the extensiveness of the image sensory field. To emphasize the realism of the simulated anomaly, the article synthesizes the anomaly images through three stages. AnoViT [6] first applied vision transformer (ViT) in the field of anomaly detection. By combining the advantages of transformer and CNN, AnoViT is able to capture global relationships and local features in images for anomaly detection and localization. Zawar et al. [7] enhance image reconstruction by establishing dense skip-connections between encoders and decoders to capture semantic information at each layer of an image block. In addition, the model uses attention-enhanced convolution in the discriminator to ensure feature consistency.

3   Proposed Methods

We propose a novel generative adversarial model based on multi-scale endogenous enhancement, inspired by DRAEM [8] and DiffAD [9]. This model aims to enhance anomaly detection performance even in scenarios where negative examples are unavailable.

3.1   A Subsection Sample

Figure 2 illustrates the overall network structure of the detection method. During the training phase, we only take the surface image of normal products as the training data. As depicted in Fig. 2, the normal image x undergoes multi-scale endogenous enhancement to produce x_a. The adversarial reconstruction network then attempts to reconstruct the enhanced image x_a as R. Subsequently, the reconstructed image R, the enhanced image x_a, and the residual image D are concatenated and inputted into the anomaly segmentation network to obtain M_a. Through extensive training, the reconstruction network learns to generate images that closely resemble the original ones with rich details, while the segmentation network achieves pixel-level segmentation of product anomaly. During the testing phase, the reconstruction network restores anomalous images to their normal state. Our method combines anomalous residual images and segmented images to jointly locate anomaly. Below, we provide detailed descriptions of these three sub-networks.

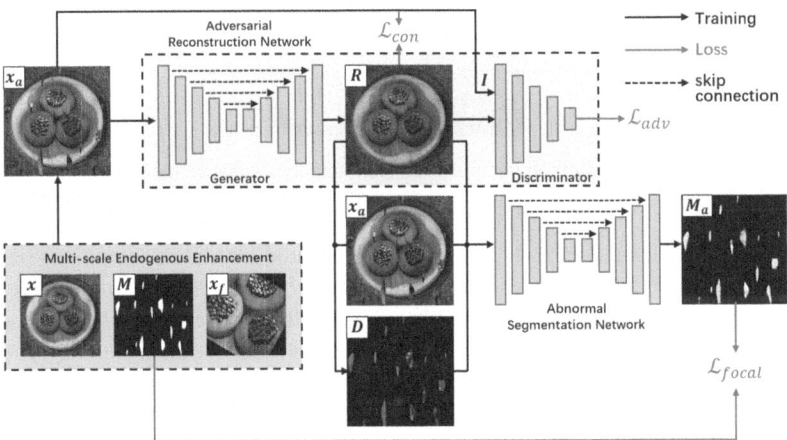

Fig. 2. The proposed structural framework.

3.2 Multi-scale Endogenous Enhancement

To enhance the network's sensitivity to anomaly, we propose a novel multi-scale endogenous enhancement method. Figure 3 illustrates our enhancement process. To ensure sampling at the centre of the image, we first center-crop the normal image x with an input size of 256×256 to 128×128. And then scale it to 256×256 size. This image is then added with colour dithering and randomly rotated to obtain x_f. Note that in the above process we rounded off the portion that exceeded the original size and filled the missing portion of the rotated image with black. Finally, we obtain the enhancement mask by element-by-element multiplication of the changed image with the random mask M. The normal image x and the inverted image of M are then superimposed in the same way to obtain the final enhanced image x_a. In order to better fit the wide variety of real anomaly, the random mask is applied at multiple scales.

$$x_f = Rotat(Color(Res(Cr(x))) \tag{1}$$

$$x_a = (1 - M) \odot x + M \odot x_f \tag{2}$$

where Cr represents cropping the center of an image with a size of 256×256 to 128×128. Res means to enlarge the center cropped image to 256×256. Color represents color dithering by changing hue, saturation, and brightness. Rotat means to rotate the image at a random Angle. M is a random mask. x_f is the processed image. x_a is the image of the original image x after multi-scale endogenous enhancement.

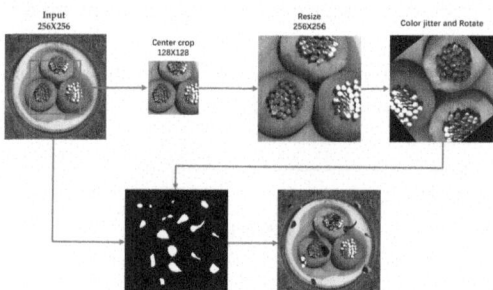

Fig. 3. Explanation on the multi-scale endogenous enhancement method.

The multi-scale endogenous enhancement method considers variations in real anomaly regarding color, shape, and orientation, using only the normal image as a reference. Its implementation significantly enhances the network's ability to recognize and reconstruct anomaly during training. We'll further demonstrate the effectiveness of this module in subsequent ablation experiments.

3.3 Adversarial Reconstruction Network

The Adversarial Reconstruction Network (ARN) aim to generate images that closely resemble the original image while preserving rich details. Leveraging the U-net [10] architecture, we construct reconstruction and segmentation networks based on encoder-decoder fusion with skip connections. These skip connections ensure the propagation of features across different levels of the network, facilitating reconstruction and segmentation tasks. By incorporating features from various levels during training, the network effectively captures multi-scale information within the image.

We introduce content loss, comparing the input image with the reconstructed image, emphasizing content consistency and similarity between images I and R. This ensures that the reconstruction faithfully reproduces crucial visual information present in the original image. Through content loss optimization, the network learns intricate details such as image edges, textures, and shapes, resulting in reconstructed images with high accuracy and smoothness.

$$\mathcal{L}_{con} = \mathop{\mathbb{E}}_{x \sim p_x} ||x - G(x_a)||_2 \tag{3}$$

Furthermore, to facilitate the model in approximating the true distribution more effectively, we incorporate the adversarial loss in the discriminator. This loss function is fundamental in GANs and serves as a crucial component in guiding the training process. Following Goodfellow et al.'s [4] recommendation, we update the network weights based on the optimization objectives outlined below.

$$\mathcal{L}_{adv} = \mathop{\mathbb{E}}_{x \sim p_x} [logD(x)] + \mathop{\mathbb{E}}_{x \sim p_x} [log(1 - D(G(x_a)))] \tag{4}$$

3.4 Abnormal Segmentation Network

To enhance the network's ability to detect small anomaly, we developed an Anomaly Segmentation Network (ASN), structured similarly to U-net. The ASN is trained to generate anomaly segmentation images using three input sources: the reconstructed image R, the enhanced image x_a, and the residual image D. We introduce focal loss [2] optimization between the true mask M and the anomaly segmentation mask M_a. This allows the network to progressively learn the segmentation of anomalous pixels.

Following training, the network gains the fundamental capability to segment anomaly. During the testing, for a normal image, the reconstructed image closely resembles the original, with minimal residual differences. Consequently, the network's segmentation map appears predominantly black, indicating a high likelihood of normalcy. Conversely, in abnormal images, the reconstructed image significantly differs from the input. By calculating the residual difference, we can identify the general location of the anomaly. The segmentation map produced by the network further refines the localization of the anomaly. Thus, we rely on both indicators to jointly determine the presence of anomaly.

Overall, the training objective of the adversarial reconstruction network is:

$$\mathcal{L}_{total} = \lambda_{con}\mathcal{L}_{con} + \lambda_{adv}\mathcal{L}_{adv} + \lambda_{seg}\mathcal{L}_{seg} \tag{5}$$

where $\mathcal{L}_{seg}$ is the focal loss.

3.5 Anomaly Score

The anomaly score clarifies which parts of the image are significantly different from the normal pattern, and plays a crucial role in aiding the network in anomaly identification. To quantify the degree of anomaly, we design a novel evaluation criterion specifically for anomaly in the network. We classify the discriminative cases of anomaly into pixel-level and image-level.

From a pixel-level perspective, it requires a higher degree of granularity in the anomaly. It focuses on the likelihood of each pixel point in the image. Our pixel-level anomaly score map comprises two components: a residual score map $R_{i,j}(x)$ and a segmentation score map $F_{i,j}(x)$. In detail, $R_{i,j}(x)$ is computed from the L_2 function between the input image and its corresponding reconstructed image. The images R, x_a and D are connected and obtained $F_{i,j}(x)$ under the action of ASN. To comprehensively capture anomaly, we integrate the residual score and the segmentation score to determine the final anomaly. The calculations are summarized below:

$$R_{i,j}(x) = ||x - G(x_a)||_2 \tag{6}$$

$$F_{i,j}(x) = ASN(Concat(x_a, R, D)) \tag{7}$$

$$A_{i,j}(x) = \delta F_{i,j}(x) + (1 - \delta)R_{i,j}(x) \tag{8}$$

where δ is a hyperparameter. Concat denotes a connection operation.

For image-level anomaly scores, the entire image is treated as a single entity. This is akin to a binary classification scenario, where images are categorized as either normal or abnormal. It's essential to emphasize that the image-level anomaly score focuses more on the overall likelihood of anomaly within the image. Therefore, we have implemented additional processing steps to refine the computational approach:

$$\varphi = \max(A_{i,j}(x) * f_{sf \times sf}) \tag{9}$$

where $f_{sf \times sf}$ is an average filter of size $sf \times sf$ and $*$ is a convolution operator.

4 Experiments

4.1 Datasets and Related Settings

MVTec [11] is an extensive and specialized anomaly detection dataset encompassing images from various fields, spanning industrial production to everyday products. To comprehensively and objectively understand and compare the performance of different methods, we choose Area Under the Receiver Operating Characteristic curve (AUROC) and Average Precision (AP) as evaluation metrics. Our network is built using the PyTorch deep learning framework and executed on an NVIDIA 4090 GPU. In our experiments, we uniformly scale all images to 256×256. The network is trained using the Adam optimizer to expedite convergence, with the learning rate set to 1×10^{-4}. The network is trained with an epoch of 300. The batch size is set to 16. We set the weight parameter in the loss function to $\lambda_{con} = 20$, $\lambda_{adv} = 1$ and $\lambda_{seg} = 20$. Furthermore, we consider the residual score map to be equally important as the segmentation score map for anomaly determination. So in the anomaly score δ we take the value of 0.5.

4.2 Comparison with Method

In order to illustrate the classification ability of the network from a global perspective, we performed an image-level evaluation of the various methods. Table 1 demonstrates the image-level anomaly detection results of the seven methods on MVTec. Among them, the experimental results of RIAD [12] are derived from the literature [9]. Our proposed method achieves a 98.8% anomaly detection performance, surpassing DRAEM by 0.8%. In terms of specific data, our method achieves optimal AUROC values in 9 out of 15 classes. It is worth mentioning that we achieved 100% classification performance on bottle, hazelnut, toothbrush, and leather.

Table 1. The image-level anomaly detection results on MVTec (AUROC%). * indicates that the method is of reconstruction type.

	Category	RIAD* [12]	SCGAN* [13]	DFC-A [14]	DRAEM* [8]	Ours
Object	Bottle	99.9	98.3	99.8	99.2	**100**
	Cable	81.9	98.2	**98.5**	91.8	97.5
	Capsule	88.4	83.2	94.8	**98.5**	97.1
	Hazelnut	83.3	97.5	99.8	**100**	**100**
	Metal nut	88.5	90.1	98.3	98.7	**99.2**
	Pill	83.8	89.4	95.0	**98.9**	97.7
	Screw	84.5	**100**	92.0	93.9	98.4
	Toothbrush	**100**	**100**	95.6	**100**	**100**
	Transistor	90.9	91.3	98.0	93.1	**97.5**
	Zipper	98.1	92.4	96.9	**100**	98.6
Texture	Carpet	84.2	97.0	97.2	97.0	**98.8**
	Grid	99.6	96.3	**100**	99.9	98.7
	Leather	**100**	94.7	**100**	**100**	**100**
	Tile	98.7	97.4	98.1	99.6	**99.7**

(*continued*)

Table 1. (*continued*)

	Category	RIAD* [12]	SCGAN* [13]	DFC-A [14]	DRAEM* [8]	Ours
	Wood	93.0	**100**	98.7	99.1	99.4
Average		91.7	95.1	97.5	98.0	**98.8**

To quantitatively assess the model's performance in anomalous segmentation, we present pixel-level experimental results in Table 2. The results of PaDim, RIAD and DRAEM are taken from the literature [8]. The results for PatchCore are derived from the literature [9]. In general, our proposed method outperforms the existing methods in terms of average values. 98.6% and 79.6% of AUROC and AP values are achieved, respectively. This is an improvement of 0.5 percentage points and 11.2 percentage points, respectively, compared to the sub-optimal method. It can be seen that our method achieves optimal performance for 7 and 9 classes under both metrics, respectively. Comparing with the reconstruction-based method, our method takes the overwhelming advantage. The experimental results show that the proposed method has a strong generalization ability and a good ability to review different types of anomalies.

Table 2. The pixel-level anomaly detection task results on the MVTec dataset (AUROC/AP%). * indicates that it belongs to the reconstruction method.

	Category	PaDim [15]	PatchCore [16]	RIAD* [12]	DRAEM* [8]	Ours
Object	Bottle	98.2/77.3	98.6/82.5	98.4/76.4	99.1/86.5	**99.4/87.8**
	Cable	96.7/45.4	**98.4**/74.7	84.2/24.4	94.7/52.4	98.2/**76.4**
	Capsule	98.6/46.7	**98.8**/48.5	92.8/38.2	94.3/49.4	97.6/**63.2**
	Hazelnut	98.1/61.1	98.7/58.1	96.1/33.8	99.7/**92.9**	**99.8**/92.1
	Metal nut	97.3/77.4	98.4/94.6	92.5/64.3	**99.5/96.3**	98.1/93.6
	Pill	95.7/61.2	97.1/**85.5**	95.7/51.6	97.6/48.5	**98.8**/78.4
	Screw	98.4/21.7	**99.4**/39.3	98.8/43.9	97.6/58.2	98.2/**68.5**
	Toothbrush	98.8/54.7	98.7/47.2	98.9/50.6	98.1/44.7	**99.2/79.6**
	Transistor	97.6/72.0	96.3/**74.7**	87.7/39.2	90.9/50.7	**97.8**/73.2
	Zipper	98.4/58.2	**98.8**/72.7	97.8/63.4	**98.8/81.5**	98.3/80.4
Texture	Carpet	**99.0**/60.7	98.9/64.6	96.3/61.4	95.5/53.5	98.5/**70.2**
	Grid	97.1/35.7	98.7/29.1	98.8/36.4	**99.7**/65.7	98.4/**73.5**
	Leather	99.0/53.5	99.3/48.5	99.4/49.1	98.6/**75.3**	**99.7**/74.9
	Tile	94.1/52.4	95.6/67.5	89.1/52.6	**99.2**/92.3	99.0/**95.6**
	Wood	94.1/46.3	95.0/59.4	85.8/38.2	96.4/77.7	**98.1/85.9**
Average		97.4/55.0	98.1/63.1	94.2/48.2	97.3/68.4	**98.6/79.6**

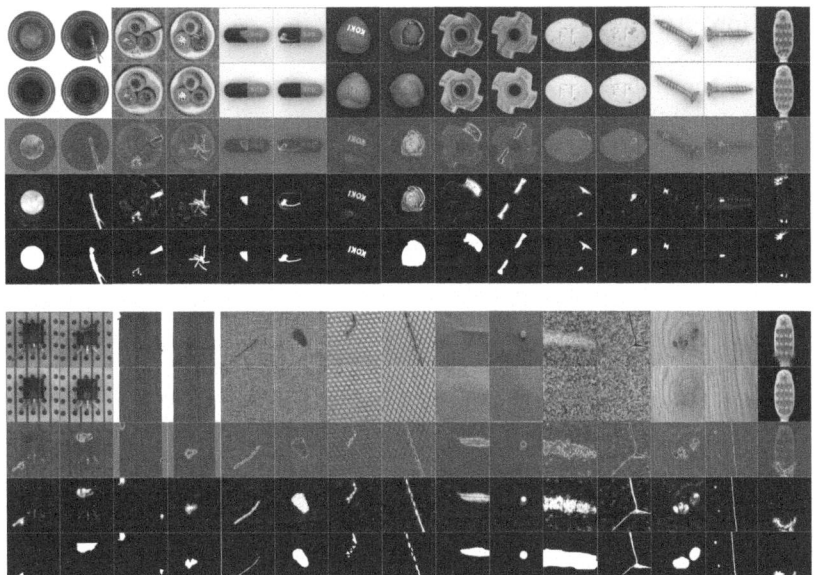

Fig. 4. Qualitative example. Shows the results of qualitative experiments for object and texture classes. Each section represents the original anomaly image, the network reconstructed image, the anomaly heat map, the anomaly segmentation map, and the ground truth, respectively, from top to bottom rows.

To enhance the interpretability of the model, we incorporate visualizations to show the state of the proposed method in the anomaly detection task. Figure 4 shows two selected anomaly images from each class, including its changing state during the experiment. To illustrate the sensitivity of the network to anomalous regions of different sizes, we have purposely taken into account both large and tiny anomalies. As can be seen in Fig. 4, the proposed method is able to detect and localize the anomaly more accurately. In particular, the redder the region in the third row of the heat map is shown, the higher the probability of an anomaly in that region. We can determine the approximate location of the anomaly from the heat map. And the anomaly segmentation map shown in the fourth row is more indicative. It allows us to see more details of the detection.

5 Ablation Study

To enhance the interpretability of our model, we specifically investigate the impact of key components of the model on the overall performance.

5.1 Hyperparameters

Different hyperparameter settings can lead to varying behaviors exhibited by the model. To comprehend the impact of weighting parameters on model performance, we scrutinize the hyperparameter values of the loss function in Eq. (5). Figure 5 illustrates the AUROC of the three parameters at different values. It can be seen that $\lambda_{con} = \lambda_{seg} = 1$ the network performance is poor. Basic detection and localization can no longer be achieved at this point. As their values are increased, the network performance is gradually maintained above 90%. When $\lambda_{adv} = 1$, the network performance reaches the maximum and exceeds 95%. In summary, we take $\lambda_{con} = 20$, $\lambda_{adv} = 1$, and $\lambda_{seg} = 20$ as the parameter basis for the experiment.

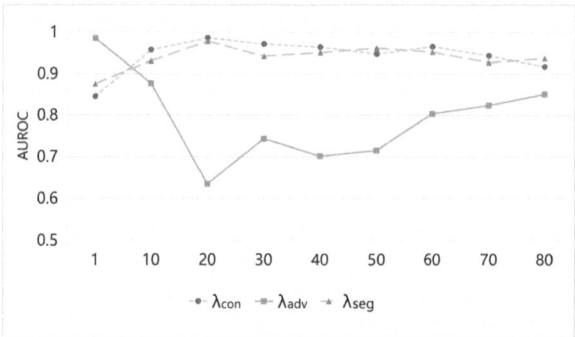

Fig. 5. Performance of hyperparameters on different data points (AUROC%).

5.2 Enhancement Methods

We explored four image enhancement methods for anomaly detection, showcasing their effects in Fig. 6. For clarity, we've selected two image types as examples. The second column in Fig. 6 presents the processing effect of Cutout. It will randomly overlay a black square region on the original image. It can be seen that the Cutout method has a large effect on the content of the original image. The central idea of CutPaste in the third column is to randomly copy the rectangular area of the image and then paste it back. The next column, SCDAN, uses black bands of different widths in both horizontal and vertical directions to mask the image content. The goal of RIAD is to remove rectangular grids of different densities as an enhancement process. Finally for comparison, we also present the results of the proposed methods.

To evaluate the effectiveness of multi-scale endogenous enhancement, we observed the performance of the above five methods on MVTec. Table 3 showcases our proposed

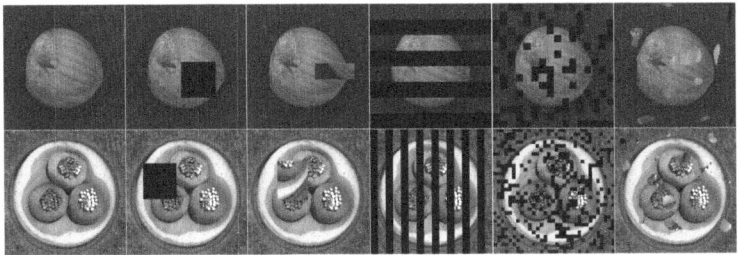

Fig. 6. From left to right: normal samples, Cutout, CutPaste, SCADN, RIAD, and the results of our enhancement method.

method's superior performance in both image-level and pixel-level AUROC, as well as average accuracy. Notably, Cutout exhibited the poorest results due to its tendency to mask large areas of the original image, leading to a significant loss of information. CutPaste, though a more novel approach, struggles to cover all anomaly types due to limitations in cutout replication. In contrast, RIAD demonstrates better perception of local information. It's noteworthy that Cutout, SCADN, and RIAD all apply a masking layer over specific areas of the image. Our method, however, goes beyond this simplistic approach by considering factors such as enhancement source, color, scale, and more.

Table 3. Performance of different enhancement methods on MVTec.

Metircs	Cutout [17]	CutPaste [18]	SCADN [19]	RIAD [12]	Ours
AUC-ROC (image-level)	74.4	78.9	84.7	95.1	**98.8**
AUC-ROC (pixel-level)	71.3	75.8	81.9	93.4	**98.6**
AP	47.5	54.6	58.3	68.7	**79.6**

5.3 Model Elements

To validate the necessity of each component within the model, we assessed their impact on network performance across six cases detailed in Table 4. The first row presents the baseline model with only the generator. We observe a slight improvement in network performance upon incorporating data enhancements. Subsequently, we introduced the discriminator for adversarial training, yet the incomplete network still exhibited major limitations. In the fourth row, superior performance metrics were achieved with the joint generator and segmentation network for anomaly generation. Finally, in the last two rows of Table 4, we compare the ASN based on their input sources. Experimental results indicate that the addition of each model element enhances the performance metrics of the network, with each component positively contributing to the detection and localization performance of the model.

Table 4. Influence of different model element compositions on overall effectiveness.

Generator	Discriminator	ASN	Data Augmentation	ASN Input	Loss	AUC-ROC (image-level)	AUC-ROC (pixel-level)	AP
√	-	-	-	-	$\mathcal{L}_{con}$	75.3	73.8	55.8
√	-	-	√	-	$\mathcal{L}_{con}$	81.2	80.7	57.4
√	√	-	√	-	$\mathcal{L}_{con}\mathcal{L}_{adv}$	84.9	82.1	68.5
√	-	√	√	$Concat(x_a, R)$	$\mathcal{L}_{con}\mathcal{L}_{focal}$	96.7	95.2	73.4
√	√	√	√	$Concat(x_a, R)$	$\mathcal{L}_{con}\mathcal{L}_{adv}\mathcal{L}_{focal}$	98.1	97.9	78.2
√	√	√	√	$Concat(x_a, R, D)$	$\mathcal{L}_{con}\mathcal{L}_{adv}\mathcal{L}_{focal}$	**98.8**	**98.6**	**79.6**

6 Conclusion

To enhance quality control and safety protection in industrial product manufacturing, we introduce a GAN anomaly detection method based on multi-scale endogenous enhancement. This method integrates an anomaly generation module, an adversarial reconstruction network, and an anomaly segmentation network to collectively execute the detection task. Our aim is to reduce reliance on labeled anomaly data. We achieve this by probabilistically enhancing normal samples only, mimicking real-world detection scenarios. Additionally, we devise a suitable anomaly score evaluation metric tailored for our model. To accurately identify anomaly, we utilize residual score plots and segmentation score plots to jointly determine the anomaly determination graph. We validate our proposed method on the challenging MVTec dataset, demonstrating its excellent performance in anomaly detection. Furthermore, our method exhibits some advantages over similar approaches. In future endeavors, we aim to refine our method further and explore its applicability across a broader range of scenarios.

References

1. Wilmet, V., Verma, S., Redl, T., Sandaker, H., & Li, Z.: A comparison of supervised and unsupervised deep learning methods for anomaly detection in images. arxiv preprint arxiv:2107.09204 (2021)
2. Lin, T. Y., Goyal, P., Girshick, R., He, K., Dollár, P.: Focal loss for dense object detection. In: Proceedings of the IEEE International Conference on Computer Vision, pp. 2980–2988 (2017)
3. Matsubara, T., Sato, K., Hama, K., Tachibana, R., Uehara, K.: Deep generative model using unregularized score for anomaly detection with heterogeneous complexity. IEEE Trans. Cybern. **52**(6), 5161–5173 (2020)
4. Goodfellow, I., et al.: Generative adversarial networks. Commun. ACM **63**(11), 139–144 (2020)
5. Peng, T., Zheng, Y., Zhao, L., Zheng, E.: Industrial product surface anomaly detection with realistic synthetic anomalies based on defect map prediction. Sensors **24**(1), 264 (2024)
6. Lee, Y., Kang, P.: Anovit: unsupervised anomaly detection and localization with vision transformer-based encoder-decoder. IEEE Access **10**, 46717–46724 (2022)
7. Zawar, R., Bhayani, K., Bhowmik, N., Tiwari, K., Sangwan, D.: Detecting Anomalies using Generative Adversarial Networks on Images. arxiv preprint arxiv:2211.13808 (2022)

8. Zavrtanik, V., Kristan, M., Skočaj, D.: Draem-a discriminatively trained reconstruction embedding for surface anomaly detection. In Proceedings of the IEEE/CVF International Conference on Computer Vision, pp. 8330–8339 (2021)

9. Zhang, X., Li, N., Li, J., Dai, T., Jiang, Y., & **a, S. T.: Unsupervised surface anomaly detection with diffusion probabilistic model. In Proceedings of the IEEE/CVF International Conference on Computer Vision, pp. 6782–6791 (2023)

10. Ronneberger, O., Fischer, P., Brox, T.: U-net: convolutional networks for biomedical image segmentation. In: Navab, N., Hornegger, J., Wells, W., Frangi, A. (eds.) MICCAI 2015. LNCS, vol. 9351, pp. 234–241. Springer, Cham (2015). https://doi.org/10.1007/978-3-319-24574-4_28

11. Bergmann, P., Fauser, M., Sattlegger, D., Steger, C.: MVTec AD--A comprehensive real-world dataset for unsupervised anomaly detection. In Proceedings of the IEEE/CVF Conference on Computer Vision and Pattern Recognition, pp. 9592–9600 (2019)

12. Zavrtanik, V., Kristan, M., Skočaj, D.: Reconstruction by inpainting for visual anomaly detection. Pattern Recogn. **112**, 107706 (2021)

13. Dai, Y., Zhang, L., Fan, F.Y., Wu, Y.J., Zhao, Z.K.: SCGAN: extract features from normal semantics for unsupervised anomaly detection. IEEE Access (2023)

14. Yang, J., Shi, Y., Qi, Z.: Learning deep feature correspondence for unsupervised anomaly detection and segmentation. Pattern Recogn. **132**, 108874 (2022)

15. Defard, T., Setkov, A., Loesch, A., Audigier, R.: Padim: a patch distribution modeling framework for anomaly detection and localization. In International Conference on Pattern Recognition, pp. 475–489 (2021)

16. Roth, K., Pemula, L., Zepeda, J., Schölkopf, B., Brox, T., Gehler, P.: Towards total recall in industrial anomaly detection. In: Proceedings of the IEEE/CVF Conference on Computer Vision and Pattern Recognition, pp. 14318–14328 (2022)

17. DeVries, T., Taylor, G.W.: Improved regularization of convolutional neural networks with cutout. arxiv preprint arxiv:1708.04552 (2017)

18. Li, C.L., Sohn, K., Yoon, J., Pfister, T.: Cutpaste: self-supervised learning for anomaly detection and localization. In: Proceedings of the IEEE/CVF Conference on Computer Vision and Pattern Recognition, pp. 9664–9674 (2021)

19. Yan, X., Zhang, H., Xu, X., Hu, X., Heng, P.A.: Learning semantic context from normal samples for unsupervised anomaly detection. In Proceedings of the AAAI Conference on Artificial Intelligence, vol. 35, no. 4, pp. 3110–3118 (2021)

A Comprehensive Review
of Blockchain-Enabled Dynamic and Credible
Spectrum Sharing

Runze Li, Kaiyue Peng, Yi Miao, and Qin Wang[✉]

Nanjing University of Posts and Telecommunications, Nanjing 210003, China
wangqin@njupt.edu.cn

Abstract. This paper comprehensively explores the application of Dynamic Spectrum Sharing (DSS) and blockchain technology in 5G and 6G networks, as well as their combined potential. Against the backdrop of the surge in demand for high-bandwidth services in the era of 5G and 6G, the scarcity of wireless spectrum resources and the low utilization rate of traditional static spectrum management have become increasingly severe. DSS allows dynamic sharing of spectrum between different network operators and adjusts the allocation of spectrum in real-time according to user demand, thereby improving the utilization rate of the spectrum. However, DSS brings some challenges related to decentralization, privacy, and security. To address these issues, blockchain has become a potential solution due to its capabilities in transparency, data encryption, immutability, and distributed architecture. This paper first provides a comprehensive overview of the concept, technology, and related challenges of DSS, then reviews the development of blockchain, related technologies, and their working principles. Finally, we discusses and summarizes the application of blockchain in the field of spectrum sharing, and discusses the challenges and trade-offs of implementing technologies such as STBC, FBAA, and BoSDSA, as well as the future development direction of this research field.

Keywords: 5/6G · Blockchain · Dynamic Spectrum Sharing · Consensus Mechanism · Smart Contract

1 Introduction

Wireless spectrum, as a scarce natural resource, is an essential foundation for supporting wireless communications,and its management methods must be continuously optimized to meet the escalating demands of growing applications.

With the rise of high-bandwidth services in fifth-generation (5G) and sixth-generation (6G) wireless communication networks, communication traffic is surging [1]. According to the Cisco Annual Internet Report (2018–2023) [2], by 2023, nearly

---

The contributions of Li Runze, Miao Yi, and Peng Kaiyue to this paper are equal, and they are co-first authors.

two-thirds of the world's population will have access to the Internet. Traditional static spectrum allocation and management solutions lead to under utilization and inefficiency of spectrum, which is a major limitation to meet the traffic demand in 5G and future 6G wireless communication networks. Therefore, it is urgent to find new solutions to improve spectrum utilization for spectrum management and allocation in wireless communication networks.

In previous studies on dynamic spectrum sharing (DSS) among multiple operators (MOPs), two main architectures have been proposed: centralized and distributed spectrum sharing architectures. Although both architectures can alleviate spectrum shortage and improve spectrum utilization, the security issue of interaction between mutually untrusting entities is very serious and has not been considered in previous studies. Therefore, it is necessary to propose an effective solution to ensure secure interactions in dynamic spectrum sharing among multiple OP.

In order to improve spectrum utilization as well as user security, the concept of blockchain-based dynamic spectrum sharing network was introduced [3].

1.1 Motivation

Blockchain has been widely used in many fields such as, Big Data, Electric Vehicles and Internet of Things (IoT), Edge Computing due to its inherent capabilities such as invariance, decentralization, transparency, traceability and no single point of failure. Blockchain based DSS provides some advantages over centralized and distributed DSS techniques such as incentivized spectrum sharing mechanism,privacy protection of users and user sensitive data, fairness of sharing mechanism etc. However,in the previous survey in the field of blockchain-based solutions for decentralized applications, there is a lack of in-depth discussion on the application of blockchain through smart contracts to improve the performance of DSS and to address the issues arising from the centralized control of these applications.

1.2 Contribution of this Paper

It is evident from the discussion above that existing research lacks a comprehensive overview of DSS, a key enabling technology for 5G networks, and its integration with blockchain. Recent surveys also lack a discussion of the different open source blockchain platforms that provide smart contract development environments. There is also a lack of discussion on the various implementation features of blockchain that contribute to the realization of DSS applications.

2 Dynamic Spectrum Sharing

2.1 Research Background

DSS technology is widely used in today's global networks as they evolve from 4G to 5G and even 5G to 6G [4]. DSS provides the flexibility to share spectrum between different generations of technologies, allowing operators to dynamically adjust spectrum resources based on user demand and service traffic [5]. This avoids the need to dedicate a separate block of spectrum to each technology, thereby increasing the efficiency of utilization of existing spectrum assets. With the retirement of the old generation mobile networks, DSS can reallocate the released spectrum resources for the use of the new generation networks, which utilizes the existing spectrum resources more efficiently to avoid waste.

2.2   Key Technologies for Dynamic Spectrum Sharing

The key technologies of dynamic spectrum sharing technology mainly include spectrum sensing, spectrum sharing, spectrum management, etc., and these three key technologies will be further elaborated in the following.

Spectrum Sensing

Spectrum sensing technology is through the deployment of spectrum sensing nodes real-time sensing of the use of spectrum resources, looking for "spectrum holes" [6], the spectrum management node will be based on the spectrum sensing node monitoring data, including channel occupancy, signal strength and quality of communication and other information on the dynamic allocation and adjustment of spectrum resources.

Spectrum Sharing

Spectrum sharing technology is a technology that realizes multi-user or multi-system sharing of spectrum resources through dynamic allocation of spectrum, and enables multiple radio communication devices to use the same spectrum resources at the same time and in the same frequency band through intelligent spectrum management methods, and there is no interference between the devices.

Spectrum Management

Dynamic spectrum management is a kind of dynamic allocation and use of spectrum according to the actual needs of users through a series of technical means, in order to improve the utilization efficiency and sharing efficiency of the spectrum. Strategies for spectrum allocation include maximizing the efficiency of spectrum use, minimizing interference between users, etc., and will be based on different optimization algorithms to adapt to more spectrum application scenarios.

3   Blockchain

Since Satoshi Nakamoto wrote "Bitcoin: a peer-to-peer electronic cash system" [7], Blockchain, a new peer-to-peer network system, has attracted much attention. Starting from the early days of the Bitcoin network, Blockchain has evolved into a global technology that has attracted global attention and investment. Subsequently, a new generation of blockchain platforms, such as Ethereum, has further expanded the field of application.

Nowadays Blockchain has been identified and recognized as a key enabler for 5G & 6G communication networks [8]. Delivering services through a combination of technologies requires complex coordination and collaboration, which requires an open, transparent and secure system across the communications ecosystem. Blockchain, on the other hand, is characterized by decentralization, privacy, security, transparency, and invariance, and can be perfectly adapted to distributed networks like 5G & 6G (Fig. 1).

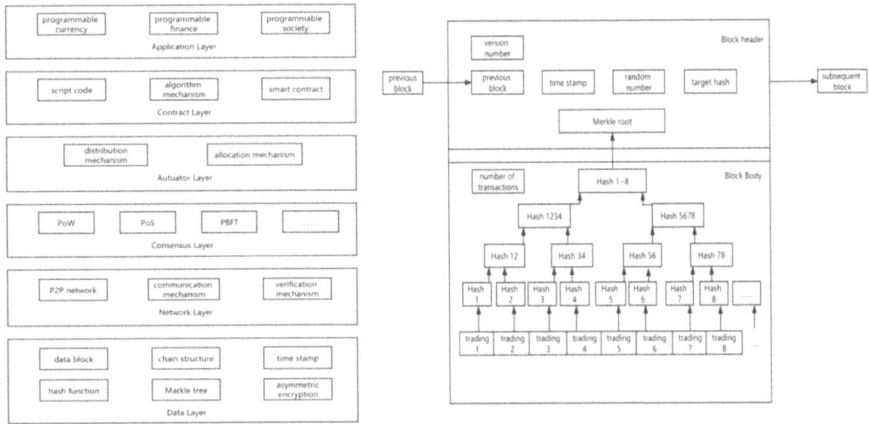

Fig. 1. Blockchain Architecture and Block Structure.

4 Blockchain Based Spectrum Sharing

Some characteristics of spectrum sharing are consistent with the application scenarios of blockchain. First, spectrum usage is real-time and needs to be processed in a timely manner, which can be achieved through a localized spectrum ledger. Second, spectrum sharing involves multiple stakeholders who may not trust each other, which can be addressed by blockchain. Third, using blockchain, spectrum sharing can be done directly between wireless devices without the need for intermediaries.

4.1 Overview of Recent Research

In this subsection, we present research conducted in the area of blockchain-based spectrum sharing. We outline the main focus, the consistency algorithms used, the results obtained, and the limitations and future directions of these works.

Literature [9] introduces a new Dynamic Spectrum Sharing (DSS) scheme for Cell-Free Massive MIMO (CF-mMIMO) networks. In the framework proposed in the article, each wireless operator is represented by a CF-mMIMO network characterized by an average spectrum efficiency metric that quantifies the potential value of additional spectrum acquisition. Using the Stackelberg game formulation, the DSS implements an equilibrium point that optimally allocates bandwidth to the operator and determines the corresponding price. The article utilizes blockchain technology to manage all spectrum transactions through smart contracts, which ensures the transparency, integrity, and auditability of the entire spectrum transaction process, facilitates seamless information exchange, coordinates the Stackelberg game dynamics, and provides decisive results for CF-mMIMO operators.

Literature [10] proposes an innovative blockchain spectrum trading solution, STBC (Spectrum Trading Blockchain), which aims to optimize spectrum management by improving spectrum utilization, simplifying the transaction process, enhancing security and reducing energy consumption. The STBC solution employs a new consensus mechanism that allows for the rapid confirmation of transactions in the presence of up to n/3 malicious nodes in the system. This mechanism enables fast processing of transactions by shifting the task of transaction confirmation from the leader node to the trader node. The scheme provides anonymity during the node's use of the spectrum, ensuring the legitimacy and security of the transaction. In terms of security analysis, STBC shows effective defense against mainstream attacks such as double payment attacks.

Literature [11] applies blockchain technology to spectrum sharing to solve the problems of missing incentives, privacy leakage, and security threats faced when machine-to-machine (M2M) and human-to-human (H2H) coexist in 5G heterogeneous networks. In the spectrum sharing framework, blockchain is used to ensure the security and reliability of spectrum sharing transactions between H2H users and base stations Through smart contracts, base stations (BS) can enter into contracts with H2H users to incentivize them to share underutilized spectrum resources. The smart contract automatically enforces the terms of the contract, ensuring the fairness and efficiency of the enforcement of the incentives. The article notes that the current framework was designed in a simplified scenario with a single service provider and a single base station. How to design incentive-compatible contracts and how to optimize the contract design in multi-service provider or multi-base station scenarios require further research.

Literature [12] presents an innovative multi-blockchain based spectrum sharing scheme for Citizen Broadband Radio Service (CBRS) systems. The article designs a multi-blockchain architecture and cross-chain mechanism, in which each coexistence group (CxG) has its own blockchain, which are independent of each other but connected to each other through the cross-chain mechanism, ensuring the decentralization and attack resistance of the whole system. The cross-chain mechanism ensures the security and transparency of transactions by establishing a trust relationship between the Coexistence Managers (CxM) of the CxG and utilizing the decision-making blockchain to record and verify the cross-chain transactions, improves the speed and scalability of the cross-coexistence group (CxG) spectrum transactions, and demonstrates through simulation results that the method is able to significantly increase the network throughput without increasing the interference to existing users.

In the literature [13] to address the identity privacy and data security issues in multi-operator (multi-OPs) wireless communication networks. The article designs smart contracts (MOSS) to handle the buying and selling of spectrum, including the processes of registration, auction and payment clearing. These smart contracts are executed on the blockchain, which ensures transparency, non-tamperability and decentralization of transactions. In this way, blockchain technology not only improves the security of spectrum sharing, but also increases the reliability and fairness of the system, and all transaction records are permanently stored on the blockchain and open to all participants. In addition, the article analyzes its performance through experimental validation. The results show that the cost of Gas is relatively low except for administrator calls to most functions. This suggests that operators can trade spectrum at a lower cost, thus incentivizing them to participate in the spectrum sharing market and improve spectrum utilization.

Literature [14] proposes a blockchain-based spectrum auction framework that allows multiple access points (AP) to share spectrum resources via smart contracts on a blockchain platform. To ensure the fairness of the auction, a multi-round Fairness Based

Auction Algorithm (FBAA) is designed, which takes into account the users' historical spectrum allocation results and the current auction results, and adjusts the users' satisfaction by introducing a fairness factor. This mechanism not only improves the fairness of spectrum allocation, but also increases the number of radio users and the stability of services through the automation and security features of blockchain.

Literature [15] Blockchain technology is applied to the spectrum detection and sharing auction paradigm (BoSDSA) for 6G wireless networks to ensure a secure and efficient spectrum auction process. The paradigm employs a cloud-side collaboration approach for global cooperation and smart sensing, utilizing smart contracts for instant execution on the blockchain. RARF completes the auction mechanism from the perspective of SU by using a reverse auction mechanism,choosing PU that maximize their utility. In addition, BoSDSA considers how to protect sensitive data during user transactions by encrypting it using the public key of the base station and verifying it with the private key to prevent data leakage. Transaction records are made into blocks and transmitted to ensure the security of the transactions. Simulation results and security analysis show that the proposed BoSDSA achieves significant improvement in increasing the overall utility and output of SU compared to existing techniques (Table 1).

Table 1. Summary of related work with their main contributions.

Reference	DSS Technique and Results	Limitations and/or Future Directions
9	• Use blockchain technology to manage all spectrum transactions through smart contracts. This ensures transparency, integrity throughout the spectrum trading process	Future Directions: Evaluating the scalability, security, and efficiency of different blockchain technologies in facilitating spectrum trading and management
10	• Novel blockchain-based spectrum trading mechanism STBC Consumes less power, enhances security and scalability of spectrum sharing	Limitation: STBC algorithm does not consider the consensus of spectrum auction and management. Furthermore,it requires better security considerations
11	• The incentive mechanism under information asymmetry is optimized through contract theory, and the spectrum sharing transaction between the base station and H2H users is protected by blockchain technology	Limitations: The total transaction confirmation time of the current system is proportional to the frequency of the spectrum transaction, which can lead to bypass attacks
12	• New parameter "network feature" is introduced to prioritize spectrum transactions in different queues, balancing existing user interference with resource requirements in spectrum transactions	Future Directions: More complex scenarios and the impact of user mobility on spectrum trading will be considered

(continued)

Table 1. (*continued*)

Reference	DSS Technique and Results	Limitations and/or Future Directions
13	• Multi-Operator Spectrum Sharing (MOSS) smart contracts are designed to introduce two-way auctions and free trading markets, enabling multi-operators to share spectrum autonomously in wireless communication networks	Future Directions: An efficient auction algorithm can be designed to introduce Nash equilibrium to further reduce the gas cost of calling functions in MOSS smart contracts
14	• A novel virtual bidding mechanism is designed to compensate spectrum requesters who have not obtained spectrum access for a long time by introducing the fairness factor of historical spectrum auction results	Future Directions: Security and privacy protection measures, which are key considerations in blockchain applications, are not discussed in detail
15	• Spectrum Detection and Shared Auction Paradigm for Blockchain (BoSDSA), which adopts a cloud-side collaborative approach for global cooperation and intellisence	Future Directions: Explore different types of consensus mechanisms to suit different application scenarios and needs.Enhance the security of your system to prevent potential fraud and data breaches

4.2 Implementation Challenges and Tradeoffs

Scalability and Storage Issues

Scalabilityissues arementionedin both literature [16] and literature [17]. As the size of the network increases, it remains a challenge to keep the system running efficiently. There are a large number of resource-constrained devices with limited storage and computation capabilities in dynamic spectrum sharing systems, so such devices cannot store a complete blockchain ledger and are difficult to run complex blockchain consensus algorithms. Therefore, the introduction of edge computing technology can be considered in blockchain-based dynamic spectrum sharing system. Literature [18] utilizes edge computing networks to update user information, create smart contracts, and reduce latency. In order to improve the ability of mobile devices to handle computationally intensive tasks, literature [19] designed a blockchain-driven edge computing scheme for joint computational offloading and monetary lending.

Energy Consumption Issues

Blockchain requires huge computational power and overhead to reach consensus. This overhead may consume a large amount of bandwidth in the network. In some cases, resources may be constrained, thus leading to high latency. In addition, transactions are constantly being added to the blockchain, resulting in increased storage consumption. Most of the power in a blockchain network is consumed due to consensus algorithms. There have been efforts to develop energy-efficient consensus algorithms such as spatial proofs [20] and mini-blockchains [21]. However, these efforts still need to be tested on a large scale and there is still much room for improvement. Therefore, designing an energy-efficient consensus algorithm is a major research challenge for the application of blockchain in 5G & 6G networks.

Standardization Requirements

Many proof-of-work mechanisms exist in the current blockchain without a unified standard. Therefore, in order to have a broader future, network operators need to work on standardizing blockchain integration in 5G & 6G networks and beyond. To address this, the Carrier Blockchain Study Group (CBSG) consortium of premier network operators is working to build the next generation of cross-operator blockchain networks. Despite these efforts, there is still a long way to go to agree on protocols, coding languages and formats, consensus mechanisms and privacy measures for smart contracts.

5   Conclusion

DSS is a key technology to enable 5G & 6G applications. Blockchain-based spectrum sharing technology is the future trend. The concept of blockchain has gone far beyond the realm of cryptocurrencies and is now revolutionizing more and more industries. Likewise, 5G networks and 6G networks are no exception. In this paper, we provide a comprehensive overview of DSS, a broad overview of blockchain, and a complete and accurate blockchain tutorial for readers. We describe the important role that blockchain-based spectrum sharing plays in the development of 5G & 6G and the challenges posed by existing schemes. We believe that blockchain has great potential in the field of 5G & 6G and spectrum sharing. If implemented properly, it has the potential to roll out 5G & 6G connectivity around the world in a secure and cost-effective manner.

Acknowledgments. This work was supported in part by the Jiangsu Provincial Key Research and Development Program under Grants BE2022068 and BE2022068-2, the National Natural Science Foundation of China under Grant 92367302, and the Natural Science Foundation of the Jiangsu Higher Education Institutions of China.

References

1. Cisco: Cisco visual networking index: Global mobile data traffic forecast update, 2017–2022. Cisco Vis. Netw. Index, San Jose, CA, USA. White Paper 11, pp. 1–37 (2019)
2. Cisco. Cisco Annual Internet Report (2018–2023) White Paper. https://www.cisco.com/c/en/us/solutions/collateral/executive-perspectives/annual-internetreport/white-paper-c11-741490.html. Accessed 3 Mar 2022
3. Kotobi, K., Bilen, S.G.: Secure blockchains for dynamic spectrum access: a decentralized database in moving cognitive radio networks enhances security and user access. IEEE Veh. Technol. Mag. **13**(1), 32–39 (2018)
4. Wang, S., Sun, C.: Blockchain empowered dynamic spectrum sharing: standards, state of research and road ahead. IEEE Commun. Stand. Mag. **7**(3), 72–80 (2023)
5. Saha, R.K., Cioffi, J.M.: Dynamic spectrum sharing for 5G NR and 4G LTE coexistence - a comprehensive review. IEEE Open J. Commun. Soc. **5**, 795–835 (2024)

6. Tandra, R., Mishra, S.M., Sahai, A.: What is a spectrum hole and what does it take to recognize one. Proc. IEEE **97**(5), 824–848 (2009)
7. Nakamoto: Bitcoin: A Peer-to-Peer Electronic Cash System (2008)
8. Aneja, A.: Blockchain technologies in 5g and beyond connections: a review of the taxonomy, practice area, prospects, and challenges. In: 2023 International Conference on Artificial Intelligence and Smart Communication (AISC), Greater Noida, India, pp. 1155–1159 (2023)
9. Femenias, G., Francisca Hinarejos, M., Riera-Palou, F., Ferrer-Gomila, J.-L., Jaume-Barceló, A.: Dynamic spectrum sharing in a blockchain enabled network with multiple cell-free massive MIMO virtual operators. IEEE Access **12**, 70615–70633 (2024)
10. Xue, L., Yang, W., Chen, W., Huang, L.: STBC: a novel blockchain-based spectrum trading solution. IEEE Trans. Cogn. Commun. Netw. **8**(1), 13–30 (2022)
11. Zhou, Z., Chen, X., Zhang, Y., Mumtaz, S.: Blockchain-empowered secure spectrum sharing for 5G heterogeneous networks. IEEE Netw. **34**(1), 24–31 (2020)
12. Cheng, Z., Liang, Y., Zhao, Y., Wang, S., Sun, C.: A multi-blockchain scheme for distributed spectrum sharing in CBRS system. IEEE Trans. Cogn. Commun. Netw. **9**(2), 266–280 (2023)
13. Zheng, S., Han, T., Jiang, Y., Ge, X.: Smart contract-based spectrum sharing transactions for multi-operators wireless communication networks. IEEE Access **8**, 88547–88557 (2020)
14. Wang, M., Wang, W., Wang, S., Sun, C., Wu, Q.: Fairness oriented spectrum auction for blockchain-assisted dynamic spectrum sharing. In: 2023 IEEE 34th Annual International Symposium on Personal, Indoor and Mobile Radio Communications (PIMRC), Toronto, ON, Canada, pp. 1–6 (2023)
15. Roopa, V., Pradhan, H.S.: Blockchain oriented spectrum detecting and sharing auction paradigm for 6G wireless networks. In: 2023 IEEE 20th India Council International Conference (INDICON), Hyderabad, India, pp. 1149–1154 (2023)
16. Hu, S., Liang, Y.-C., Xiong, Z., Niyato, D.: Blockchain and artificial intelligence for dynamic resource sharing in 6G and beyond. IEEE Wirel. Commun. **28**(4), 145–151 (2021)
17. Grissa, M., Yavuz, A.A., Hamdaoui, B., Tirupathi, C.: Anonymous dynamic spectrum access and sharing mechanisms for the CBRS band. IEEE Access **9**, 33860–33879 (2021)
18. Du, Y., et al.: Blockchain-aided edge computing market: smart contract and consensus mechanisms. IEEE Trans. Mob. Comput. **22**(6), 3193–3208 (2023)
19. Zhang, Z., Hong, Z.C., Chen, W.H., et al.: Joint computation offloading and coin loaning for blockchain-empowered mobile-edge computing. IEEE Internet Things J. **6**(6), 9934–9950 (2019)
20. Dziembowski, S., Faust, S., Kolmogorov, V., Pietrzak, K.: Proofs of space. In: Gennaro, R., Robshaw, M. (eds.) CRYPTO 2015. LNCS, vol. 9216, pp. 585–605. Springer, Heidelberg (2015). https://doi.org/10.1007/978-3-662-48000-7_29
21. Bruce, J.D.: The mini-blockchain scheme. White Paper (2014)

Heterogeneous Data Fusion Based Vulnerability Detection for Ethereum Smart Contracts

Yale He[✉], Ruilin Lai, Zhihao Hou, Junjie Zhou, Gansen Zhao, and Qizhi Zhang

School of Computer Science, South China Normal University, Guangzhou 510631, Guangdong, China
{heyale,gzhao,zhangqizhi}@m.scnu.edu.cn

Abstract. Smart contracts, as a critical application of blockchain technology, play a pivotal role in automating contract rules and enhancing the transparency of transactions. They are programmed to define rules and automate protocols on the blockchain, ensuring that transactions are decentralized, efficient, and immutable. Once deployed, smart contracts cannot be altered, and any existing vulnerabilities can be maliciously exploited, leading to potential financial losses or data breaches. Consequently, the security of smart contracts has become a critical focus in blockchain security. This paper presents the XLNET-HyBA model for Ethereum smart contract vulnerability detection based on the fusion of heterogeneous data. Initially, the source code is transformed into Abstract Syntax Tree (AST) serialized information by the SmartConvert preprocessing algorithm, which effectively integrates the scattered control flow elements. Subsequently, a novel information fusion embedding technique is proposed to optimize the contribution weights of source code and AST serialized code, aiming for a more accurate localization of potential vulnerabilities. Finally, a hybrid loss function strategy based on metric learning is constructed, enhancing the model's sensitivity to subtle differences. The experimental results show that the accuracy of all four vulnerabilities is over 96% and the recall is over 93%. In the case of the arithmetic vulnerability, the experimental results show an improvement of 6.87%, 5.24%, 10.40%, and 7.85% in accuracy, precision, recall, and F1 value, respectively, compared to previous work. The method shows strong adaptability and wide applicability in dealing with different contract data and has important value and relevance in smart contract security research.

Keywords: Smart Contracts · Heterogeneous Data · Information Fusion · Feature Recognition · Vulnerability Detection

G. Zhao and Q. Zhang are co-corresponding authors and contribute equally to this work.

1   Introduction

Smart contracts, as computer programs or transaction protocols, autonomously execute trade and business logic upon the occurrence of predefined conditions without the need for third-party intervention. This enhances the efficiency and reliability of transactions. Smart contracts codify transaction rules among participants and deploy them on blockchain networks. They execute automatically through scripts to prevent human error and fraud, ensuring fairness and transparency in transactions. A key characteristic of smart contracts is immutability; once consensus is reached and deployed on the blockchain, the contract code and outcomes are permanently recorded, unalterable, and non-erasable. All participants can review and verify the results, ensuring transparency and fairness in transactions.

However, smart contracts can be vulnerable to security risks. Attacks on smart contracts often result in substantial financial losses. In 2020, the Ethereum decentralized finance platform Lendf.Me suffered a $25 million loss due to a reentrancy attack. According to statistics from SlowMist, attacks on Ethereum smart contracts had caused a cumulative loss of approximately $3.1 billion by 2023. The frequent occurrence of contract vulnerabilities has significantly impacted the blockchain ecosystem, making the detection of smart contract vulnerabilities a critical issue in blockchain security.

Current methods for detecting vulnerabilities in smart contracts typically employ static analysis based on expert rules [3] or dynamic execution techniques [11]. Actually, these approaches rely heavily on existing patterns defined by expert rules, leading to limitations such as slow iteration and optimization and a lack of comprehensiveness in complex scenarios. With the ongoing advancements in natural language processing and the increasing computational power of hardware devices, many researchers in the industry have started to explore the integration of deep learning techniques into smart contract vulnerability detection [9]. This integration aims to assist technicians in quickly identifying the presence and type of vulnerabilities in contracts. Nonetheless, deep learning faces challenges, particularly due to the high complexity of smart contract source code running on Ethereum, characterized by discontinuous function call features and indistinct sequence length characteristics in contract data. Most deep learning methods currently focus on single-source data, failing to fully and comprehensively mine its information features. Additionally, the subtle differences between secure and vulnerable contracts make them difficult to distinguish using deep learning models under conventional training.

To address the aforementioned challenges, this study introduces an Ethereum smart contract vulnerability detection approach utilizing the XLNET-HyBA model. Our primary contributions are as follows:

– SmartConvert Preprocessing: A technique for converting smart contract source code into serialized AST representation. This serialization preserves crucial structural information about the code, including key aspects of control and data flows, while establishing each node's hierarchical structure. The

AST serialization enriches the features of source code data with detailed function call information, addressing the challenges of high data complexity and discontinuity.

- Heterogeneous Data Fusion: A novel fusion method is presented, leveraging information theory and probability to distribute weights among heterogeneous data. As input for the information fusion embedding module, this module aims to pinpoint potential vulnerabilities, particularly addressing the issue of indistinct long sequence characteristics in contract data.
- Feature Recognition: The XLNET-HyBA model integrates a hybrid loss function for enhanced feature recognition. It utilizes triplet loss with batch hard mining, refining the model's ability to discern subtle contract differences, thus boosting precision and recall in vulnerability detection tasks.

2 Related Work

SmartConDetect [4] presents a vulnerability detection method for smart contracts using a pre-trained bidirectional encoder from BERT. Initially, each function in Solidity source code is split, and the SmartCheck [10] method is applied to annotate each function. Extracted code snippets and annotations are then assembled and marked with special token characters to serve as inputs for the BERT model. Through empirical validation, the authors demonstrate that this BERT-based approach, leveraging pre-trained techniques, outperforms methods such as those presented in [6,13], and [1]. VDDL [5] methodology builds upon the pre-trained CodeBert [2] model, employing a multi-layer bidirectional Transformer architecture as its training model, along with multi-head attention and masking mechanisms. The multi-head attention, applied to both encoder and decoder layers, enables the model to simultaneously focus on different positional information within the input sequence, thereby enhancing the capture of the input sequence's semantics and improving the generation of the output sequence. The masking mechanism, which randomly masks input tokens and predicts these masked tokens using the surrounding context, facilitates the development of deep bidirectional representations during training. ASSBert [8] framework is designed for smart contract vulnerability detection and uniquely combines active learning with semi-supervised learning to effectively address the issue of insufficient labeled data in smart contracts. Semi-supervised learning continuously selects a certain number of high-confidence, unlabeled code data from the Solidity source code, annotating them with pseudo-labels using a pre-trained model before incorporating them into the training dataset. Experimental results indicate that, even with only a small amount of existing labeled code data, the model outperforms baseline models.

3 Proposed Method

3.1 Framework

This work proposes an Ethereum smart contract vulnerability detection framework based on heterogeneous data, as illustrated in Fig. 1. Heterogeneous data

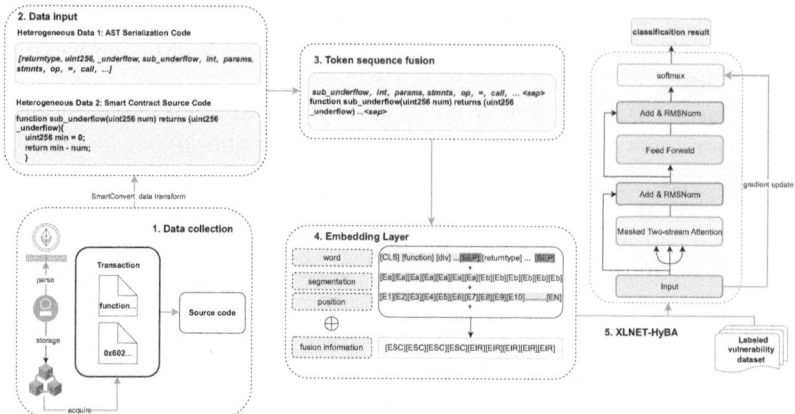

Fig. 1. Smart Contract Vulnerability Detection Process Framework

is a collection of data that consists of different structures, formats, types, or schemas. Data can exist in various forms such as structured data, semi-structured data and unstructured data. Heterogeneous data are characterised by the fact that they cannot be directly processed through a unified model or interface, and require special methods and techniques to integrate and convert them into a compatible form. The preprocessing stage primarily addresses the challenges posed by the non-structured nature of smart contract source code, such as high data complexity and discontinuity in textual call information. Through the SmartConvert algorithmic process, the source code is transformed, making the complex and dispersed control flow information clearer and more coherent, thereby enhancing the efficiency and precision of data processing. Two types of heterogeneous data are employed to train the model, offering a comprehensive perspective and data background for the investigation. However, the contribution and impact of each data type are not equal during the model training process. A mechanism based on information theory and probability theory is proposed to uncover the underlying connections and dynamic weight distribution. Additionally, an analysis of the data characteristics of specific research subjects reveals that safe contracts and those with vulnerabilities in smart contract code often exhibit high similarity. To address this challenge, a hybrid loss function strategy for feature recognition is proposed, aimed at enhancing the model's predictive performance and accuracy, particularly in identifying key pattern differences. The following section describes the specific methodology for expanding the three modules in detail.

3.2 SmartConvert Preprocessing

Firstly, the raw abstract syntax tree generation. The AST reflects the syntactic feature structure of the source code and serves as the basis for other types of graphical representations. Figure 2(a) is the AST generated by the official

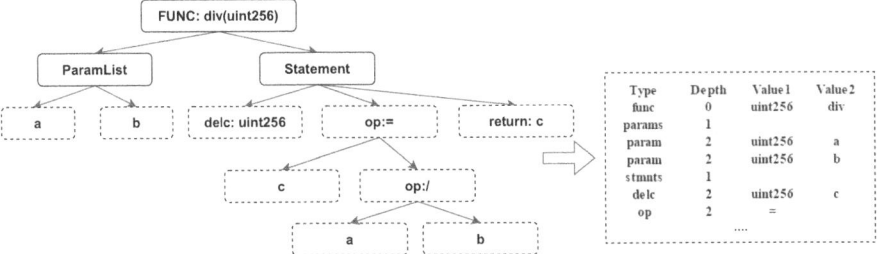

Fig. 2. Abstract syntax tree for smart contract code (a) and smart contract serialization (b)

Solidity compiler, solc-js. Within the AST, there are various declaration nodes, such as ParamList for variable lists and Statement for declaring the main content of the function. Sub-nodes of the Statement can reflect the structure of function statements; for example, in the case of conditional functions, sub-nodes like PREDICATE, TRUEBODY, and FALSEBODY might be present.

Secondly, the serialization of the AST structure, as shown on Fig. 2(b). This step transforms the structural features of the code into a one-dimensional sequence, making it accessible for natural language processing models. The Depth-First Search (DFS) algorithm is employed to traverse the AST, ensuring systematic access to every node within the AST. During the traversal, not only were node types such as function declarations and variable declarations recorded, but detailed annotations of additional information for each node were also made, which included, but was not limited to, the node's depth in the tree, function names, and data types of variables. Furthermore, the parent-child and brother connections on the AST nodes need to be labeled, since they are critical to comprehending the code's structural hierarchy and execution flow.

3.3 Feature Fusion Module

Given the imbalance in the contributions of source code and AST serialization to the Transformer encoder, and considering that mere concatenation may not adequately utilize their distinct characteristics, a new algorithm or strategy becomes essential to assign appropriate weights to these heterogeneous data sources. As illustrated in Fig. 3, the information relevance index is derived from the weighted average entropy and pointwise mutual information (PMI) values. In the feature fusion embedding process, the information relevance index is utilized to determine the weight distribution of the encoded sequence, thereby influencing the weighting of the heterogeneous data encoded sequence. This calculation method effectively achieves a efficient integration of source code and AST serialized information. By utilizing this index, key information points of potential vulnerabilities are identified, enabling the model to focus more on the contextual and call information surrounding these critical points.

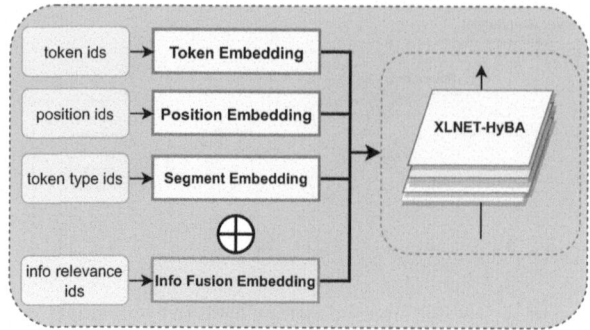

Fig. 3. Information fusion embedding structure

Entropy theory provides a mathematical way to quantify the information in a code. The entropy value can be used to measure the information content of a code and influence its weight in the embedding representation. According to the entropy Eq. (1), a lower entropy value indicates more information in the code, while a higher entropy value indicates less information.

$$H(X) = -\sum_{i=1}^{n} P(x_i) \cdot \log_2 \left(P(x_i) \right) \tag{1}$$

PMI is a statistical measure assessing the degree of dependency between two events. In natural language processing, it's commonly used to gauge the discrepancy between the joint occurrence frequency of two elements and their respective frequencies of independent occurrences. The calculation formula for PMI is Eq. (2). A higher PMI value suggests that the frequency of two elements occurring together exceeds the product of their independent occurrence frequencies, indicating a potential positive correlation or link between the two elements.

$$PMI(x, y) = log_2 \frac{P(x, y)}{P(x)P(y)} \tag{2}$$

Combining entropy and PMI into a weighted average yields the information relevance index I_{xy}, as shown in Eq. (3). This index is considered an indicator of the importance or information content of specific words in the text.

$$I_{xy} = \alpha \cdot H(x) + \beta \cdot PMI(x, y) \tag{3}$$

An elevated weight signifies that the term or function is infrequent within the contract yet exhibits significant relevance to the surrounding textual elements. These terms are considered instrumental in the contractual context, possibly constituting pivotal indicators for the detection of vulnerabilities. In contrast, a lower weighted average for a term or function denotes its commonplace occurrence in the contractual narrative or a minimal relational significance with the contract's broader content.

The embedding of the encoder will comprise the following components: *Word Embedding + Segment Embedding + Position Embedding + Information Fusion Embedding*. In the information fusion embedding, we use the information relevance index to determine the weights of different parts in the code sequence, thereby influencing the final embedding representation of the heterogeneous data code sequence.

3.4   Loss Function Design

Smart contracts, as code-based protocols, often have vulnerabilities hidden in coding logic, contract design, or complex interactions with blockchain characteristics rather than obvious errors. This results in extremely subtle differences between vulnerable contracts and secure ones. To address this challenge, a hybrid loss computation method is introduced that combines triplet loss with cross-entropy loss. The method is designed to boost the feature recognition capabilities of the model within smart contract classification tasks. It enables the clustering of similar category samples in the feature space more tightly, while distinctly separating those of different categories. Central to this hybrid loss approach is its capacity to enhance the model's proficiency in identifying subtle distinctions within smart contracts, aspects that are typically challenging to detect.

The cross-entropy loss function measures the discrepancy between the model's predicted values and the actual values, as shown in Eq. (4).

$$loss_e = -\frac{1}{N}\sum_{i=1}^{N}\sum_{c=1}^{C} y_{i,c} \cdot log(p_{i,c}) \tag{4}$$

Triplet loss is a loss function used for metric learning, aimed at ensuring that samples from the same category are closer in feature space, while those from different categories are further apart. The Equation is shown as (5), where *dis* represents the distance between two samples, calculated using the Euclidean distance.

$$loss_t(A, P, N) = max(dis(A, P) - dis(A, N) \\ + margin, 0) \tag{5}$$

In traditional training methods using the triplet loss function, the common practice is to randomly select three samples from the training set to form a triplet. However, this random sampling often produces easily distinguishable sample combinations, leading to an insignificant effect of the loss function. To overcome this issue, we employed a batch hard sample mining strategy. In each randomly formed batch, each sample can act as an anchor, and the hardest positive sample, i.e., the positive sample farthest in feature space from the anchor and the hardest negative sample, i.e., the negative sample closest to the anchor are selected from the other samples in the batch to form triplets. As described in the loss function Eq. (6), the approach does not seek the hardest positive and negative samples globally, which alleviates instability during training to a certain extent. It also enables the model to effectively learn and recognize subtle but critical feature differences.

$$loss_h = max(dis(A, P_{hard}) - dis(A, N_{hard})$$
$$+ margin, 0) \tag{6}$$

The combination of cross-entropy and triplet loss functions is used as an optimization for the classification layer's design to enhance the model's output performance, as delineated in Eq. 7.

$$loss_{all} = \sigma_1 loss_e + \sigma_2 loss_h \tag{7}$$

σ_1 and σ_2 represent the weight coefficients for the cross-entropy loss and the hard sample mining triplet loss, respectively. The optimal values for these coefficients are determined through cross-validation methods. This hybrid loss function strategy aims to simultaneously improve the model's overall performance in terms of classification accuracy and feature recognition ability.

4   Experiments

4.1   Dataset

Smart contract vulnerability datasets, accessible to the public, are collected from the Hugging Face platform [7]. After removing duplicate contracts deployed at different addresses and subsequent filtering, we retained a final count of 107,253 smart contracts as experimental data for the classification model. The distribution of this experimental data is shown in Table 1.

Table 1. Distribution of labeled dataset for smart contracts

Types of Vulnerabilities	Amount
Safe	35855
Reentrancy	25381
Arithmetic	13324
Unchecked Calls	20289
Access Control	12404
Total	107253

4.2   Comparative Experiment

The performance of the proposed XLNET-HyBA model is compared with other deep learning models, including XLNET, CodeBERT, SmartConDetect [4], and TL-BiLSTM [12], across four datasets. The experimental results are shown in Table 2. The XLNET-HyBA model demonstrates superiority in all categories, with the best overall performance in terms of accuracy, precision, recall, and F1 score. This reflects the strong ability of our proposed model to capture complex features and handle different types of security vulnerabilities. Our model shows an average increase of 6.06% in accuracy, 4.74% in precision, 9.75% in recall, and 7.15% in F1 score over the well-performing TL-BiLSTM model, highlighting its advantages in comprehensive performance and potential for application. While the overall performance of the TL-BiLSTM model is lower than that of the XLNET-HyBA model proposed in this paper, its balance and stability in various vulnerability detections are still commendable. This may be attributed to its advantage in processing long-term dependencies, particularly in terms of recall and F1 score, where it maintains performance above 80%.

The XLNET model exhibits variable stability across different smart contract vulnerability datasets, performing less effectively in access control with low recall 63.18% and F1 scores 72.43% but showing better results in detecting reentrancy and unchecked external calls, reflecting its sensitivity to various vulnerability types and dataset adaptability. The CodeBERT model, tailored for code-related tasks, demonstrates potential in vulnerability detection, especially in reentrancy with high accuracy and precision, but has limitations in handling complex data flows in access control vulnerabilities. SmartConDetect, leveraging BERT for rich contextual understanding, achieves consistently high accuracy and precision in multiple vulnerability types, including a precision of 90.09% in unchecked calls. However, it has the lowest recall rate of 75.93%, indicating a need for improvement in covering all vulnerabilities, particularly those requiring deep semantic insights or specific programming patterns.

Table 2. The detection results of each model on the vulnerability dataset

Model	Arithmetic				Reentrancy			
	Acc	Pre	Rec	F1	Acc	Pre	Rec	F1
XLNET	87.27%	79.11%	70.89%	74.78%	89.79%	87.55%	85.30%	86.41%
CodeBert	89.54%	81.47%	78.61%	80.02%	89.63%	89.61%	84.26%	86.88%
SmartConDetect [4]	89.56%	83.33%	75.93%	79.46%	87.97%	86.51%	83.41%	84.93%
TL-BiLSTM [12]	89.42%	87.14%	83.71%	85.39%	91.57%	89.29%	86.43%	87.84%
XLNET-HyBA	96.29%	92.38%	94.11%	93.24%	96.52%	95.12%	96.39%	95.75%
Model	Unchecked calls				Access control			
	Acc	Pre	Rec	F1	Acc	Pre	Rec	F1
XLNET	89.07%	89.46%	89.91%	89.68%	87.83%	84.93%	63.18%	72.45%
CodeBert	88.26%	91.35%	85.91%	88.55%	88.19%	84.84%	74.63%	79.40%
SmartConDetect [4]	89.21%	90.09%	89.43%	89.76%	89.38%	87.04%	77.50%	81.99%
TL-BiLSTM [12]	90.14%	92.31%	87.91%	90.06%	90.68%	88.71%	85.61%	87.13%
XLNET-HyBA	96.82%	96.42%	97.61%	97.01%	96.43%	92.48%	93.54%	93.01%

Ours model, integrating heterogeneous data fusion with a hybrid loss function strategy, significantly advances the extraction of pivotal features. This methodology heightens the model's sensitivity and discriminatory capabilities, vital for the precise identification of vulnerabilities in smart contracts.

4.3 Ablation Study

Heterogeneous Information Fusion Module Validation. To evaluate the specific impact of heterogeneous data fusion on model performance, a comparative analysis was conducted between training our model solely with source code data and training it with a combination of source code and corresponding AST serialized code. The experiment focused on observing how the model's loss iteration curve changes under these two different input conditions.

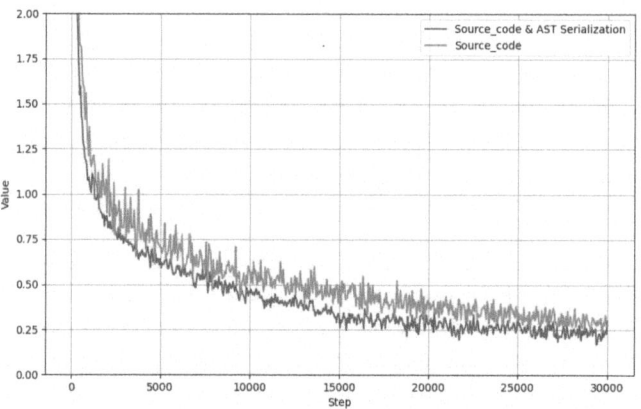

Fig. 4. Information fusion module loss iteration

The experimental results, as shown in Fig. 4, indicate that when the model is trained solely on source code, significant fluctuations in the loss value were observed, with a relatively slow rate of decline. However, when the source code was combined with AST serialized data, our model exhibited a faster convergence rate and lower loss values, with significantly reduced fluctuation in loss. These results suggest that heterogeneous data fusion enhances the model's ability to parse code structure and semantics to some extent. This improvement is partly attributed to the additional structural information provided by the AST serialization, which aids the model in more accurately understanding the semantic structure of the code. Moreover, the conciseness and standardization of AST serialized data make it more aligned with the characteristics of computer processing languages, thereby enhancing the model's understanding and learning efficiency.

Verification of the Effect of Hybrid Loss Function for Feature Recognition. The experimental results of the feature hybrid loss function are shown in Fig. 5. The figure displays the visualization results in a three-dimensional space after dimensionality reduction using the t-distributed Stochastic Neighbor Embedding (t-SNE) algorithm for the XLNET-BA model. In the left part of Fig. 5, the results of feature extraction by the XLNET-BA model using only cross-entropy loss are shown. There is a noticeable overlap between the contract code containing arithmetic vulnerabilities and the safe code, indicating that the classification effectiveness could be further improved. In contrast, the right part of Fig. 5 represents the feature space effect of the model proposed in this study after introducing the hybrid loss function strategy based on hard sample sampling between batches. Compared to the previous condition, the spatial representation of the two categories is more distinct, indicating better classification results. This also demonstrates the effectiveness of the hybrid loss function strategy introduced in this study, particularly the triplet loss function, which enables the model to cluster more closely within the same category and separate more distinctly between different categories.

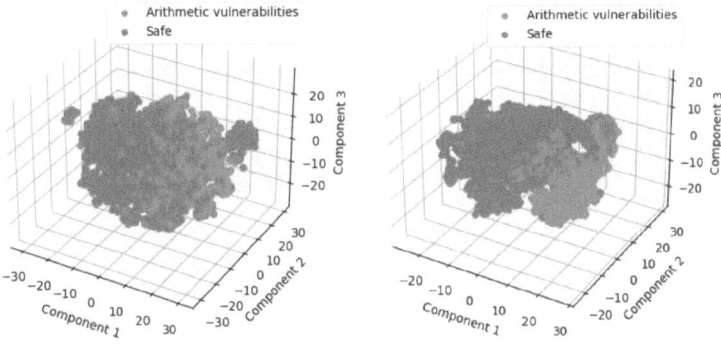

Fig. 5. Visualization of hybrid loss function vector features

Table 3. Loss function ablation result

Approach	Accuracy	Precision	Recall	F1-Score
Entropy Loss	91.81%	87.64%	88.72%	88.18%
Feature Recognition Hybrid Loss	96.29%	92.38%	94.11%	93.24%

According to Table 3, the hybrid loss function strategy proposed in this paper, which combines hard sample sampling between batches, integrates the advantages of both the cross-entropy loss function and the triplet loss function.

From the results, it is observed that compared to using only the cross-entropy loss function algorithm, the XLNET-BA classification model, after applying the feature recognition hybrid loss function strategy, showed improvements of 4.48%, 4.74%, 5.41%, and 5.06% in accuracy, precision, recall, and F1-score, respectively. Experimental results demonstrate the effectiveness of the hybrid loss function strategy, particularly in managing vulnerability datasets characterized by high feature similarity.

5   Conclusion

Confronted with the intricate nature of smart contract source code, character-ized by irregular and discontinuous function call features, and compounded by the marked resemblance between secure and vulnerable contracts, this paper addresses these multifaceted challenges in smart contract vulnerability detec-tion. Firstly, the SmartConvert preprocessing algorithm is introduced, retaining core structural information of the code and providing a richer understanding of function dependencies and hierarchical structures. Then, a heterogeneous data fusion algorithm based on information theory and probability theory, aimed at accurately pinpointing potential vulnerabilities is proposed. Lastly, this paper innovatively proposes a hybrid loss function strategy based on batch hard sample mining triplets to optimize the model's ability to classify highly similar smart contracts. Although our models excel in smart contract vulnerability detection, this work primarily focuses on analyzing smart contract source code and its transformation into abstract syntax tree representations. Hence, future improve-ments should include considering these data types. By integrating analyses of bytecode and ABI files, the research aims to enhance the model's comprehensive understanding of smart contracts.

References

1. Ashizawa, N., Yanai, N., Cruz, J.P., Okamura, S.: Eth2vec: learning contract-wide code representations for vulnerability detection on Ethereum smart contracts. In: Proceedings of the 3rd ACM International Symposium on Blockchain and Secure Critical Infrastructure, pp. 47–59 (2021)
2. Feng, Z., et al.: CodeBERT: a pre-trained model for programming and natural languages. In: Findings of the Association for Computational Linguistics: EMNLP 2020, pp. 1536–1547 (2020)
3. Ghaleb, A., Pattabiraman, K.: How effective are smart contract analysis tools? Evaluating smart contract static analysis tools using bug injection. In: Proceedings of the 29th ACM SIGSOFT International Symposium on Software Testing and Analysis, pp. 415–427 (2020)
4. Jeon, S., Lee, G., Kim, H., Woo, S.S.: Smartcondetect: highly accurate smart con-tract code vulnerability detection mechanism using BERT. In: KDD Workshop on Programming Language Processing (2021)
5. Jiang, F., et al.: VDDL: a deep learning-based vulnerability detection model for smart contracts. In: Xu, Y., Yan, H., Teng, H., Cai, J., Li, J. (eds.) ML4CS 2022. LNCS, vol. 13655, pp. 72–86. Springer, Cham (2023). https://doi.org/10.1007/978-3-031-20096-0_6
6. Momeni, P., Wang, Y., Samavi, R.: Machine learning model for smart contracts security analysis. In: 2019 17th International Conference on Privacy, Security and Trust (PST), pp. 1–6. IEEE (2019)
7. Rossini, M.: Slither audited smart contracts dataset (2022)
8. Sun, X., Tu, L., Zhang, J., Cai, J., Li, B., Wang, Y.: ASSBERT: active and semi-supervised BERT for smart contract vulnerability detection. J. Inf. Secur. Appl. **73**, 103423 (2023)

9. Sürücü, O., et al.: A survey on Ethereum smart contract vulnerability detection using machine learning. Disruptive Technol. Inf. Sci. VI **12117**, 110–121 (2022)
10. Tikhomirov, S., Voskresenskaya, E., Ivanitskiy, I., Takhaviev, R., Marchenko, E., Alexandrov, Y.: Smartcheck: static analysis of Ethereum smart contracts. In: Proceedings of the 1st International Workshop on Emerging Trends in Software Engineering for Blockchain, pp. 9–16 (2018)
11. Wang, H., et al.: Oracle-supported dynamic exploit generation for smart contracts. IEEE Trans. Dependable Secure Comput. **19**(3), 1795–1809 (2020)
12. Wang, M., Xie, Z., Wen, X., Li, J., Zhou, K.: Ethereum smart contract vulnerability detection model based on triplet loss and BiLSTM. Electronics **12**(10), 2327 (2023)
13. Yu, X., Zhao, H., Hou, B., Ying, Z., Wu, B.: Deescvhunter: a deep learning-based framework for smart contract vulnerability detection. In: 2021 International Joint Conference on Neural Networks (IJCNN), pp. 1–8. IEEE (2021)

Adaptive Federated Learning Based on Device Performance in a Heterogeneous Environment of Medical Computing Devices

Jinquan Zhang[1], Chongbo Wang[1], Rendong Yang[1], Yuncan Tang[1], Yunshen Ma[1], and Lina Ni[1,2(✉)]

[1] College of Computer Science and Engineering, Shandong University of Science and Technology, Qingdao 266590, China
nln2004@163.com
[2] Key Laboratory of the Ministry of Education for Embedded System and Service Computing, Tongji University, Shanghai 201804, China

Abstract. Federated Learning (FL), as one of the effective methods to solve the problem of medical data silos, can promote mutual cooperation among medical institutions under the premise of safeguarding the privacy and security of medical data, and effectively promote the development of intelligent medical treatment. However, the characteristics of medical data with multiple sources and heterogeneity bring certain challenges to the application of federated learning in the medical field. Due to the wide range of medical data sources, some medical institutions are unable to complete the federated learning training task on time due to the limitation of device performance, which leads to the failure of federated learning training. To address the problem of heterogeneity of computing devices among medical institutions that may cause some clients to fall behind, we propose an Adaptive Federated Learning based on Device Performance (AFedDP) method. Specifically, we design an adaptive local model training method to reduce the computational burden of medical institutions with poor equipment performance in the local model training process by adaptively constructing a local training model. Additionally, we propose a hierarchical model aggregation algorithm based on dynamic weight. This allows the heterogeneous adaptive local model to actively participate in the global model aggregation, making full use of the local data of each medical institution and improving the performance of the global model. Finally, we design an aggregation weight update algorithm based on momentum optimization to enhance the stability of global model aggregation. This algorithm updates contribution and aggregation weight with the idea of momentum optimization. Simulation experiments demonstrate that AFedDP achieves higher accuracy compared to the baseline algorithm. AFedDP can better address the issue of some devices being unable to participate in federated training properly.

G. Zhao et al. (Eds.): BWTAC 2024, CCIS 2277, pp. 304–316, 2025.
https://doi.org/10.1007/978-981-97-9412-6_28

Keywords: Federated learning · Hierarchical aggregation ·
Momentum optimization · Device heterogeneity

1   Introduction

In recent years, with the continuous development of smart healthcare, the amount of data generated in the medical field has increased dramatically, and traditional data processing centers are facing enormous challenges in terms of computational and transmission costs [1]. In addition, in recent years, the frequent leakage of users' private information during the centralized processing of medical data has led to a gradual increase in the importance of medical data privacy [2]. As a new distributed machine learning method, federated learning can promote mutual collaboration among medical institutions without interacting with real medical data, effectively solving the problem that medical privacy data cannot be directly shared while reducing the cost of data transmission [3]. The emergence of federated learning provides an efficient, reliable and secure way for data sharing between medical institutions, which helps to improve the level of collaboration between medical institutions and promote the sharing and rational use of cross-institutional medical resources, so as to improve the level of medical technology and the efficiency of medical services [4].

Traditional federated learning approaches are based on the assumption that all clients are able to train the same global model. However, in practical healthcare contexts, there is a significant disparity in the operational funding, size, and regional developmental levels among healthcare organizations that partake in federated learning [5]. This variability leads to substantial differences in the performance capabilities of their computational devices, including computational and storage performance. Consequently, servers often forego collaborating with healthcare institutions that possess less robust computing devices, opting instead for computationally intensive models such as BERT. This selection bias results in the current practice where medical federated learning tasks are predominantly executed within a select group of higher-performing medical institutions [6]. Existing research programs for the device heterogeneity problem mainly focus on the directions of tuning local training tasks, asynchronous communication, knowledge distillation and model decoupling to reduce the impact of device heterogeneity on federated learning. The detailed description of related work is as follows:

1) **Adapting local training epochs:** Researchers have explored reducing the computational demands of model training by varying the number of local training epochs at client sites. Li *et al.* [7] suggested that federated learning participants undergo a variable number of local training rounds. However, determining the optimal number of local training rounds for each client remains a challenge.

2) **Asynchronous Updates:** Others have proposed asynchronous update protocols to counteract client dropout in heterogeneous device environments. Cao

et al. [8] introduced HADFL, a framework supporting decentralized asynchronous training on heterogeneous devices, employing a version-sensitive probabilistic method for partial model aggregation to alleviate the impact of device dropout on model convergence.

3) **Knowledge Distillation:** Knowledge distillation has also been utilized to address device heterogeneity. Chan *et al.* [9] introduced FedHE, an efficient federated learning framework that facilitates knowledge transfer between heterogeneous models by sharing the average logits output of local models, thereby reducing computational strain on client devices. This method can be deployed asynchronously, facilitating easier implementation and enhanced user privacy protection.

4) **Model Decoupling:** Furthermore, decoupling models has been proposed to alleviate the computational load on clients. Lu *et al.* [10] presented HFL, a heterogeneous model fusion mechanism that updates corresponding regions of heterogeneous local models within the global model using a mapping matrix.

In summary, the existing research solutions for the device heterogeneity problem mainly start from the directions of adjusting local training tasks, asynchronous communication, knowledge distillation and model decoupling to reduce the impact of device heterogeneity on federated learning. However, the above methods suffer from high communication costs, poor model performance, and the need for additional computational costs. To address these problems, this paper proposes an adaptive federated learning algorithm based on device performance. The algorithm considers the availability of both global model and heterogeneous local model, adaptively adjusts the model through the computational performance of the device, and is able to reduce the impact of the heterogeneous distribution of devices on model aggregation to a certain extent.

The contributions of this paper are multifaceted:

1. We designed a client-adaptive local model training approach, enabling healthcare organizations to adjust the global model according to their local computational capabilities. This allows us to construct adaptive local models to fulfill local training tasks and resolve dropout issues stemming from computational limitations.
2. We propose a hierarchical model aggregation method for adaptive models, which aggregates the global model based on the neural network layers of local models. This allows heterogeneous adaptive local models to contribute local information to the global model.
3. We developed an aggregation weight updating method based on momentum optimization, which dynamically adjusts the hierarchical aggregation weights using historical contribution data. This enhances the performance of the global model.

2 Adaptive Federated Learning Method Based on Device Performance

2.1 Adaptive Federated Learning Architecture Based on Device Performance

The adaptive federated learning algorithm based on device performance is mainly composed of two parts: client and server. The server is mainly responsible for client scheduling, global model hierarchical aggregation and aggregation weight calculation. The client is mainly responsible for adaptive local model training and model uploading.

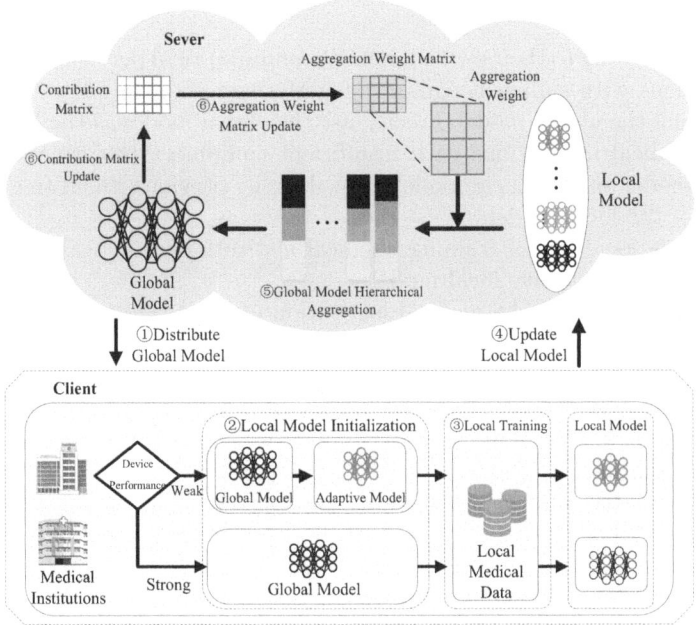

Fig. 1. Diagram of the schematic diagram of AFedDP.

The architecture of the adaptive federated learning algorithm based on device performance is shown in Fig. 1 and can be divided into the following steps:

1. Global model broadcasting: the server randomly selects a portion of healthcare organizations to participate in this round of training tasks. If it is the first round of federation training task, it is necessary to initialize the global model parameters and request all medical institutions to participate in the training task to obtain the initial contribution matrix.
2. Client local model initialization: after receiving the global model training task from the server, medical institutions need to initialize the global model

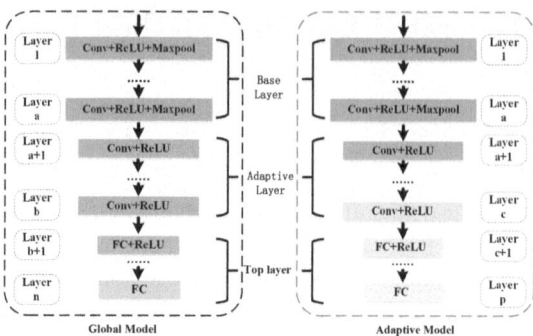

Fig. 2. Diagram of the structure of global model and adaptive model.

locally according to their own equipment computational performance. Medical institutions with sufficient equipment performance to complete the training task using the global model directly use the global model as the local model, while medical institutions with insufficient equipment performance use the global model and the local model trained in the previous round to adaptively initialize the local model.

3. Client-side local model training: medical institutions use local medical data to update the adaptive local model.
4. Local model upload: the medical institution uploads the trained local model to the central server.
5. Global model hierarchical aggregation: the server calculates the hierarchical aggregation weights based on the aggregation weight matrix, and performs global model aggregation in terms of model layers.
6. Contribution matrix and aggregation weight matrix update: Update the contribution matrix and aggregation weight matrix based on the contribution of the local models uploaded by each healthcare organization to the global model aggregation for the next round of global model aggregation.

2.2 Design of Adaptive Federated Learning Algorithm Based on Device Performance

User Classification and Model Structure Division. This section mainly introduces the user classification and model structure division in AFedDP algorithm.

1. **User classification**
   First, this section classifies health care institutions participating in federal training into two categories $U = U^{\text{strong}} \cup U^{\text{weak}}$, based on the performance of their client computing devices. Among them, U^{strong} is the medical institution set with high computing equipment performance, which is sufficient to support the global model to complete the model training task on the local data set, U^{weak} is the medical institution set with insufficient computing

equipment performance, which needs to adjust the global model to build an adaptive model to complete the local training task.

2. **Global model structure division**

   Then, in order to distinguish the global model from the adaptive local model, the structure of the global model in the federated learning task is redivided into three modules: the base layer, the adaptive layer and the top layer (classification layer). The structure of the global model is shown in Fig. 2 (left). In a global model with a total number of layers n, θ^i is the layer i parameter of the global model, and the base layer $\theta^{basic} = \{\theta^1, \cdots, \theta^a\}$ is the layer closest to the input layer of the global model, which is trained by all clients participating in federated training. The middle layers of the model are called adaptive layers $\theta^{adapt} = \{\theta^{a+1} \cdots \theta^b\}$ and are trained by local models containing the corresponding layers. The top layer $\theta^{top} = \{\theta^{b+1}, \cdots, \theta^n\}$ is the layer near the output layer of the global model, and the top layer of the global model is aggregated only by medical institutions whose equipment performance is sufficient to complete local training tasks using the global model.

3. **Adaptive model structure division**

   Finally, this section introduces the heterogeneous adaptive local model. Healthcare organizations can make adaptive local adjustments to the global model based on the performance of their own computing equipment. As shown in Fig. 2 (right), the adaptive model adjusted by medical institutions with poor equipment performance is similar to the global model structure, and is also composed of three parts: base layer, adaptive layer and top layer. The base layer structure of the adaptive model is exactly the same as that of the global model and can be directly aggregated. The depth $c(a \leq c \leq b)$ of the adaptive layer of the local model is adjusted by the medical institution according to the performance of the computing equipment. The stronger the performance of the equipment, the larger the number of layers c of the adaptive local model. In addition, the parameter structure of the adaptive layer in the adaptive model is the same as that of the global model.

Hierarchical Model Aggregation Based on Dynamic Weights. This section proposes a Layer-wised Model Aggregation based on Dynamic Weights (AFed-DLMA) algorithm, which further subdivides the global model to perform global model aggregation in terms of each neural network layer as a unit for global model aggregation.

1. **Aggregate contribution**

   In the model aggregation process, each local model layer plays a different role in the global model aggregation. In order to measure the impact of each layer in the local training model on the global model aggregation, this paper defines a concept of contribution. At the same time, the total variation gap is introduced to calculate the contribution degree.

Definition 1 (Total variation distance) [11]. The total variation distance is a measure of the similarity of probability distributions, a type of statistical distance measure, also known as the total variation distance. If there are two probability distributions $M = (m_1, m_2, \cdots, m_n)$ and $V = (v_1, v_2, \cdots, v_n)$, then the total variation distance between them can be expressed as:

$$d(M, V) = \frac{1}{2} \sum_{i=1}^{n} |m_i - v_i|. \tag{1}$$

Definition 2 (Contribution). Contribution c refers to the contribution of a model layer in the local model to the global model aggregation in a global model aggregation, which is obtained by calculating the total variable distance between each model layer and the corresponding layer of the aggregate model. In the t round of global iteration, the set of clients participating in the aggregation of layer m in the global model is $S_{t,m}$, and the contribution of layer m in the local model w_i uploaded by client U_i to the current global model is as follows:

$$c_{i,m} = \begin{cases} \lambda \frac{1}{(|S_{t,m}|-1)} (1 - \frac{\exp(d(\theta_i^m, \theta^m))}{\sum_{i \in |S_{t,m}|} \exp(d(\theta_i^m, \theta^m))}) + (1 - \lambda)c_{i,m} & \text{m join} \\ 0 & \text{m not join} \end{cases} \tag{2}$$

where $c_{i,m}$ is the contribution of layer m of the local model uploaded by the client U_i in the global model aggregation. λ is a smoothing coefficient to control the weight of the current round's aggregation contribution in the contribution update. $|S_{t,m}|$ is the total number of local models participating in the m-th layer of the global model aggregation in the t-th round of training. θ_i^m and θ^m are the m-th layer of the client's uploaded local model and the global model, respectively. The contribution degrees of all client local model layers together form the contribution degree matrix C.

2. **Dynamic aggregate weights**

   In order to enable the local model layer with higher contribution to play a greater role in the global model aggregation process, this section dynamically assigns aggregation weights to each model layer. The aggregation weight of the next round of global model aggregation is determined by calculating the contribution of each client layer to the corresponding layer of the current global model. The dynamic aggregate weight is calculated as follows:

$$\alpha_{i,m} = (1 - \sum_{k \notin S_t} \alpha_{k,m}) \times \frac{c_{i,m}^t}{\sum_{i \in S_t} c_{i,m}^t}. \tag{3}$$

where $\alpha_{i,m}$ is the aggregation weight of the m layer of model w_i, and $c_{i,m}^t$ is the contribution of the m layer of local model w_i during the global model aggregation in round t. All federated trained healthcare institutions upload the aggregate weights of each model layer in the local model to form the aggregate weight matrix α.

3. **Global model hierarchical aggregation**

The aggregation weight at the t-th round of global model aggregation can be denoted as $\alpha^t = \{\alpha_1^t, \alpha_2^t \cdots \cdots \alpha_{|S_t|}^t\}$, where α_i^t contains the aggregation weights of the layers in the local model of the i-th healthcare organization during the t-th round of global model aggregation, i.e., $\alpha_i^t = \{\alpha_{i,1}^t, \alpha_{i,2}^t \cdots \cdots, \alpha_{i,m}^t\}$, and $\alpha_{i,m}^t$ is the aggregation weight of the m-th layer of the model w_i at the time of global model aggregation and $\sum_{i=1}^N \alpha_{i,m}^t = 1$, where $\alpha_{i,m}^t$ is obtained from Eq. (4).

$$\alpha_{i,m}^t = \frac{\alpha_{i,m}}{\sum\limits_{i \in S_t} \alpha_{i,m}}. \tag{4}$$

After the server collects the set of local models $w_{|S_t|}^t = \{w_1^t, w_2^t \cdots \cdots w_{|S_t|}^t\}$ uploaded by the healthcare organizations, it multiplies them with the hierarchical aggregation weight matrix computed through the contribution matrix to obtain the global model for the new round, and to simplify the abbreviation, S is used later to represent the set of local models S_t that participated in the federated training task in the t-th round. The hierarchical aggregation of the global model is calculated as shown in Eq. (5).

$$
\begin{aligned}
w^{t+1} &= \{w_1^t, w_2^t \cdots \cdots w_{|S|}^t\} \circ \alpha^t \\
&= \begin{bmatrix} \theta_1^{1,t} & \theta_1^{2,t} & \cdots & \theta_1^{l,t} \\ \theta_2^{1,t} & \theta_2^{2,t} & \cdots & \theta_2^{l,t} \\ \vdots & \vdots & \ddots & \vdots \\ \theta_{|S|}^{1,t} & \theta_{|S|}^{2,t} & \cdots & \theta_{|S|}^{l,t} \end{bmatrix} \circ \begin{bmatrix} \alpha_1^{1,t} & \alpha_1^{2,t} & \cdots & \alpha_1^{l,t} \\ \alpha_2^{1,t} & \alpha_2^{2,t} & \cdots & \alpha_2^{l,t} \\ \vdots & \vdots & \ddots & \vdots \\ \alpha_{|S|}^{1,t} & \alpha_{|S|}^{2,t} & \cdots & \alpha_{|S|}^{l,t} \end{bmatrix}. \\
&= \{\sum_{i=0}^{|S|} \theta_i^{1,t} \alpha_i^{1,t}, \sum_{i=0}^{|S|} \theta_i^{2,t} \alpha_i^{2,t} \cdots \cdots \sum_{i=0}^{|S|} \theta_i^{l,t} \alpha_i^{l,t}\} \\
&= \{\theta^{1,t+1}, \theta^{2,t+1} \cdots \cdots \theta^{l,t+1}\}
\end{aligned} \tag{5}
$$

where the $\circ$ operation does the inner product for the corresponding column vectors. w^{t+1} is the global model aggregated by the federated training in round t, which is also the initial model sent to the client by the federated training in round $t + 1$. w_i^t is the local training model uploaded by client i in round t. $\theta^{i,t}$ is the collection of the parameters of the t-th layer of all the client's local models in the federated training in round t, i.e., $\theta^{i,t} = \{\theta_1^{i,t}, \theta_2^{i,t}, \cdots \theta_{|S|}^{i,t}\}$. $\theta_i^{l,t}$ is the parameter of the l-th layer in the t-th local model, i.e., $w_i^t = \{\theta_i^{1,t}, \theta_i^{2,t} \cdots \cdots \theta_i^{l,t}\}$. α^t is the client weight matrix for training in round t. $\alpha_i^{l,t}$ is the aggregated weight of the l-th layer of the local model trained by client i in the round t of global model aggregation.

AFedDP Overall Algorithm. The AFedDP algorithm allows healthcare organizations with poor device performance to perform longitudinal deep clipping of the global model and construct an adaptive local model for local training, in

Algorithm 1 : Adaptive Federated Learning Based on Device Performance (AFedDP).

Input: Global communication rounds T, client set U, dataset D, number of local iterations E, sampling rate q, initial aggregation weights α.
Output: Godel parameter w^{T+1}.
 1: Initialize global model parameters w^1
 2: **for** epoch communication round $t = 12 \cdots T$ **do**
 3:     **if** $t = 1$ **then**
 4:         $S_t \leftarrow U$
 5:     **else**
 6:         Randomly select clients to participate in this round of training at a sampling rate q: $S_t \leftarrow U \times q$
 7:     **end if**
 8:     Sent global model w^t to selected clients S_t.
 9:     **for** each client i in S_t **do**
10:         Adaptive model updating: $w_i^t \leftarrow Algorithm1(w^t, E)$
11:         Send the local model w_i^t back to the server
12:     **end for**
13:     $w_C^t = \{w_1^t, w_2^t \cdots\cdots w_k^t\}$
14:     $w^{t+1} \leftarrow$ hierarchical aggregation
15:     $C, \alpha \leftarrow$ Aggregation weight matrix update
16: **end for**
17: **return** w^T

---

order to reduce the computational burden of the local device and to reduce the impact of client dropout problems on the performance of the federated learning global model due to device performance limitations. When initializing the adaptive local model, the global model provides the corresponding global feature knowledge for the adaptive local model. During global model aggregation, the heterogeneous local models are hierarchically aggregated in neural network layers, and the heterogeneous adaptive local models provide local feature knowledge for the global model. Therefore, healthcare organizations with poor device computational performance can also provide feature information of local data for global model aggregation.

Combining all the steps in this section, the overall flow of the AFedDP algorithm is shown in **Algorithm 1**.

3   Experiment and Analysis

3.1   Experimental Environment Configuration

Experimental Environment: Since medical federated tasks often do not require too many healthcare organizations to participate in federated training, a central server as well as 20 clients are set up to simulate real medical scenarios in the experiments in this section.

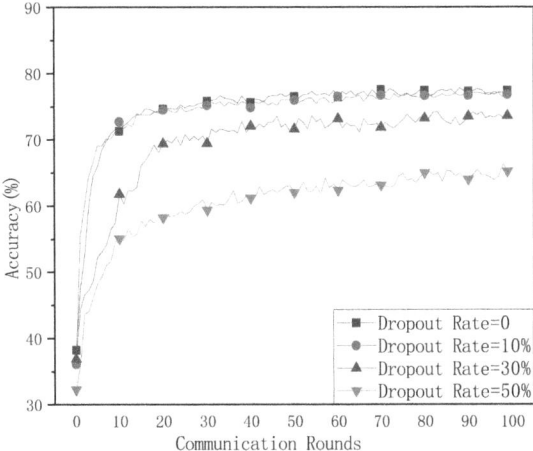

Fig. 3. Influence of dropping rate on model accuracy.

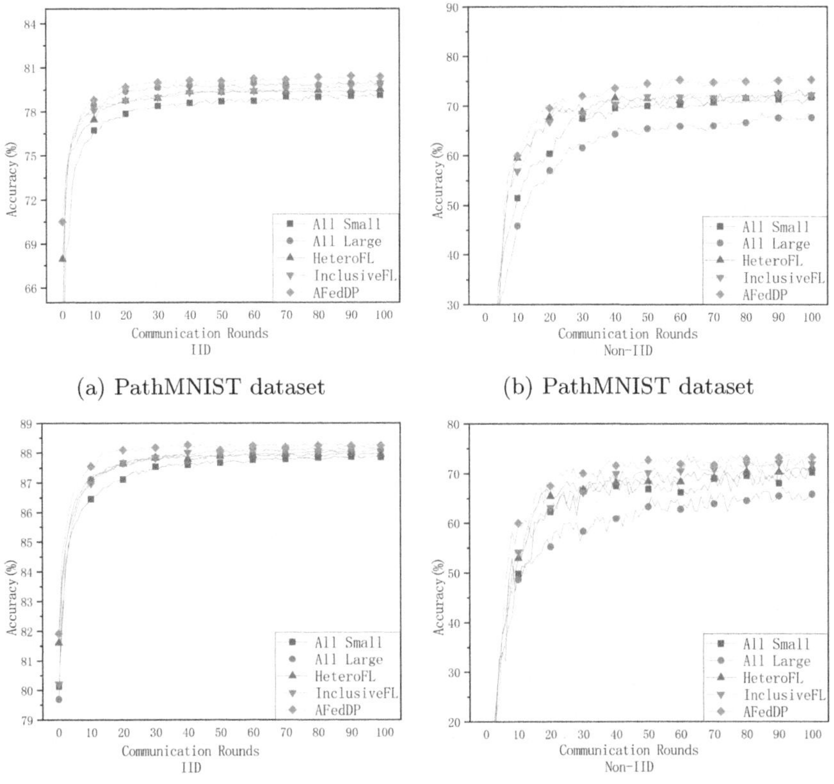

(a) PathMNIST dataset

(b) PathMNIST dataset

(c) OrganMNIST dataset

(d) OrganMNIST dataset

Fig. 4. Change of accuracy rate with communication times.

Baseline: In order to evaluate the performance of the AFedDP algorithm, this paper compares it with three algorithms, FedAvg, InclusiveFL [12] and HeteroFL [13], and experiments are conducted using a single machine.

Each convolutional layer in all the above models is followed by a BatchNorm layer, an activation layer (ReLU), and Maxpooling.

Dataset: We evaluate our model's performance using two widely recognized datasets: PathMNIST and OrganMNIST (Axial).

3.2   Experimental Results and Analysis

Figure 3 shows the variation of global model accuracy with the number of communication rounds for the AFedDP algorithm trained on the OrganMNIST dataset with heterogeneous data distribution under four scenarios of client dropout rates of 0, 10%, 30%, and 50%, respectively. As can be seen in Fig. 3, the accuracy of the global model gradually decreases as the dropout rate of the participating federated learning clients increases. When the dropout rate is not high, using AFedDP can greatly reduce the impact of client dropout. However, when the dropout rate is large, a large number of healthcare organizations need to use smaller models to complete the global model aggregation, and the local healthcare data of these clients only participate in the training of the base and adaptive layers, while the top layer part used for prediction is only trained by the clients using large samples, which leads to the poor sample classification performance, and the performance of the global model is greatly affected.

Figure 4 shows the variation of model accuracy with the number of communications for the AFedDP algorithm and the comparison algorithm on both the OrganMNIST and PathMNIST datasets, given that the percentage of clients dropping out is 30% and the sampling rate for each round of federated training is 50%.

Summarizing the above experimental results, it seems that when the client dropout phenomenon is not particularly serious (dropout rate is less than 30%), the AFedDP proposed in this paper is able to obtain a more excellent performance both in the training data independently homogeneously distributed and non-independently homogeneously distributed environments.

4   Conclusions

In this paper, we first provide an overview of the device heterogeneity problem in medical federated learning tasks. To address the shortcomings of existing methods, an adaptive federated learning algorithm based on device performance is proposed. In order to reduce the impact of medical computing device heterogeneity on the medical federated learning task, the AFedDP algorithm allows healthcare organizations participating in the federated learning task to adaptively construct a local training model on the basis of the global model, which solves the problem that some healthcare organizations are unable to complete the federated learning training task on time due to the low computational performance of their devices; secondly, a dynamic weight-based hierarchical model is proposed for the adaptive model aggregation method, which takes the layers in the heterogeneous adaptive local model as units for global model aggregation, and updates the contribution of each layer in the global model aggregation with the idea of momentum optimization, and then dynamically adjusts the aggregation weights according to the contribution. Finally, the experiments show that the algorithm can effectively solve the client dropout problem in medical organizations due to the limitation of the performance of computing devices and improve the performance of the global model.

Acknowledgments. This work was supported in part by the National Science Foundation of Shandong Province under Grant ZR2022MF338, ZR2023LZH018, the Humanity and Social Science Fund of the Ministry of Education under Grant 20YJAZH078 and Grant 20YJAZH127, Open Project of Tongji University Embedded System and Service Computing of Ministry of Education of China under Grant ESSCKF2022-02.

Disclosure of Interests. The authors have no competing interests to declare that are relevant to the content of this article.

References

1. Albahri, A.S., et al.: A systematic review of trustworthy and explainable artificial intelligence in healthcare: assessment of quality, bias risk, and data fusion. Inf. Fusion (2023)
2. Li, M., Tian, Z., Du, X., Yuan, X., Shan, C., Guizani, M.: Power normalized cepstral robust features of deep neural networks in a cloud computing data privacy protection scheme. Neurocomputing **518**, 165–173 (2023)
3. McMahan, B., Moore, E., Ramage, D., Hampson, S., Arcas, B.A.: Communication-efficient learning of deep networks from decentralized data. In: Artificial Intelligence and Statistics, PMLR, pp. 1273–1282 (2017)
4. Ni, L., Gong, X., Li, J., Tang, Y., Luan, Z., Zhang, J.: rFedFW: secure and trustable aggregation scheme for Byzantine-robust federated learning in internet of things. Inf. Sci. **653**, 119784 (2024)
5. Tang, Y., Liang, Y., Liu, Y., Zhang, J., Ni, L., Qi, L.: Reliable federated learning based on dual-reputation reverse auction mechanism in Internet of Things. Futur. Gener. Comput. Syst. **156**, 269–284 (2024)
6. Gupta, A., Misra, S., Pathak, N., Das, D.: Fedcare: federated learning for resource-constrained healthcare devices in IoMT system. IEEE Trans. Comput. Soc. Syst. (2023)
7. Li, T., Sahu, A.K., Zaheer, M., Sanjabi, M., Talwalkar, A., Smith, V.: Federated optimization in heterogeneous networks. Proc. Mach. Learn. Syst. **2**, 429–450 (2020)
8. Cao, J., Lian, Z., Liu, W., Zhu, Z., Ji, C., HADFL: heterogeneity-aware decentralized federated learning framework. In: 58th ACM/IEEE Design Automation Conference (DAC), pp. 1–6. IEEE (2021)
9. Chan, Y.H., Ngai, E.C.: FedHe: heterogeneous models and communication-efficient federated learning. In: 2021 17th International Conference on Mobility, Sensing and Networking (MSN), pp. 207–214. IEEE (2021)

10. Lu, X., Liao, Y., Liu, C., Lio, P., Hui, P.: Heterogeneous model fusion federated learning mechanism based on model mapping. IEEE Internet Things J. **9**(8), 6058–6068 (2021)
11. Rassouli, B., Gündüz, D.: Optimal utility-privacy trade-off with total variation distance as a privacy measure. IEEE Trans. Inf. Forensics Secur. **15**, 594–603 (2019)
12. Liu, R., et al.: No one left behind: inclusive federated learning over heterogeneous devices. In: Proceedings of the 28th ACM SIGKDD Conference on Knowledge Discovery and Data Mining, pp. 3398–3406 (2022)
13. Diao, E., Ding, J., Tarokh, V.: HeteroFL: computation and communication efficient federated learning for heterogeneous clients. arXiv preprint arXiv:2010.01264 (2020)

MSCV: A Cross-Chain Smart Contract State Data Verification Model Based on MTC

Zhihao Hou[1(✉)], Ruilin Lai[1], Yale He[1], Chengchuang Lin[2], Gansen Zhao[1], and Jinji Yang[1]

[1] School of Computer Science, South China Normal University, Guangzhou 510631, Guangdong, China
2021023238@m.scnu.edu.cn
[2] Guangdong Leatop Technology Investment Co., Ltd., Guangzhou 510700, Guangdong, China

Abstract. Smart contracts typically store crucial application state data. Methods like SPV proofs are commonly used to verify the authenticity of cross-chain transactions. However, the heterogeneity between blockchains makes common cross-chain data validation methods impractical for smart contract state data. To address this challenge, this paper proposes MSCV to achieve cross-chain verification of smart contract state data. MSCV utilizes MTC to provide a universal verification method for state data and preserves the chronological order of state data. Furthermore, MSCV introduces zero-knowledge proof technology to reduce the additional verification overhead of MTC. Finally, this paper implements smart contracts containing MTC and a batch verification zero-knowledge proof circuit and evaluates their performance and effectiveness.

Keywords: Blockchain · Cross-Chain · Smart Contract · Zero-Knowledge Proof

1 Introduction

Smart contracts, functioning as the supporting technology for Dapps, store a large volume of crucial application data. With the expanding use of blockchain, Dapps is encountering a multi-chain environment. However, Dapps will confront challenges associated with cross-chain access to contract state data. Existing cross-chain solutions [1,2] have solved the problem of data circulation across blockchains. These solutions typically use transaction validation methods to verify data. The verification of cross-chain transactions typically uses Simplified Payment Verification (SPV) proofs [3–5], which are quite reliable. However, the state data of smart contracts is hard to verify. Traditional solutions can be achieved through SPV proof + voting/notary or HTLC [6,7] for cross-chain

---

G. Zhao and J. Yang are co-corresponding authors and contribute equally to this work.

G. Zhao et al. (Eds.): BWTAC 2024, CCIS 2277, pp. 317–323, 2025.
https://doi.org/10.1007/978-981-97-9412-6_29

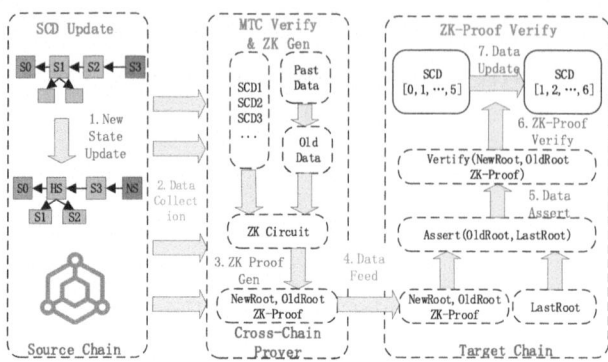

Fig. 1. MSCV Architecture

transactions [8,9]. However, smart contracts themselves, unlike transactions, do not generate a verifiable data structure with each consensus. To solve the problem of verifying smart contract data in cross-chain scenarios, this paper proposes a cross-chain smart contract data verification model based on Merkleized Tree with Chain (MTC). This model uses MTC to verify state data and can maintain the continuity of contract state data. Compared to SPV proofs, it can be applied to any blockchain and maintain the continuity of contract state data. The main contributions of this paper are summarized as follows:

1. This paper proposes a data structure MTC based on Merkle trees and linked lists. MTC can maintain the continuity of smart contract state data on the chain and provide proof to verify state changes.
2. This paper introduces zero-knowledge proof to conduct batch verification of MTC to reduce the GAS expenditure of MTC verification.
3. This paper evaluates the two modules of MTC and zero-knowledge proof batch verification. The experiments show that the MTC and batch verification can complete the work of cross-chain data verification and reduce the GAS expenditure of verification.

2   Model Design

Overview: The MSCV provides a solution for validating the state data of a target blockchain on a source blockchain. Cross-chain smart contract state access typically involves source blockchain S, target blockchain T and smart contract state data SCD. This paper assumes that SCD should be structured using the MTC (Merkleized Tree with Chain). Based on the above, the primary work of this paper can be formally defined as $True/False \xleftarrow{MSCV} Verify(SCD, S)$. $Verify$ aims to validate the state data SCD, which belongs to blockchain S. MSCV serves as the contract state data verification scheme. Figure 1 illustrates the overall architecture of MSCV.

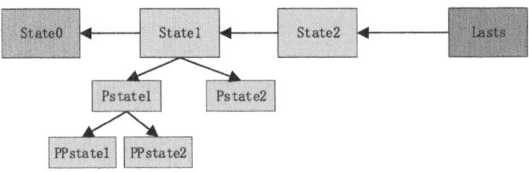

Fig. 2. MTC Structure

Merkleized Tree with Chain (MTC): To address the verification problem of contract state data, this paper proposes the MTC data structure to achieve verifiability of state data. MTC combines the characteristics of Merkle Tree and Chain List. Figure 2 illustrates the data organization based on a binary tree structure. Below are the functions of MTC.

State Update: When the contract state is updated, the values of various intermediate states are updated accordingly. The hash value is computed and convolved into a Root when the cache array is full. S_{pre} represents the previous state, and S_i represents the cached intermediate state. Taking a binary tree as an example, the convolution process can be formalized as $State_1 = Hash(State_1 || State_2)$ and $State_2 = State_{pre}$.

Root Generation: Proof and Root are generated for the new state after the update. S_{last} represents the latest state, and S_0 represents the initial state. The Root generation process can be formalized as $Root = Hash(Hash(Hash(S_0 || S_1) || S_2) || S_{last})$.

Cross-Chain Prover: The cross-chain prover (CCP) primarily undertakes the bulk verification of MTC and forwards the data to T. CCP utilizes the new and old state data as public and private inputs within a zero-knowledge proof circuit. This process ultimately yields a ZK-Proof and public outputs.

Verify Smart Contract: The validation contract completes verifying the state data and ZK-Proof provided by the cross-chain prover. Upon successfully validating the ZK-Proof, the state data hosting contract updates the corresponding state data.

3   Model Process

Initialization: The initialization phase primarily accomplishes the trusted setup of zero-knowledge proofs, publication-subscription, contract deployment, and other tasks. It stems from the previous research work of this paper [10]. Contract deployment refers to the deployment of validation contracts and hosting contracts on the target blockchain.

State Update: The state update phase refers to updating the corresponding MTC structure after the state data of the on-chain smart contract is updated. Given the old state data as $State_{last}$ and the new state data as $State_{new}$. Algorithm 1 demonstrates the execution process of the CalData function.

Algorithm 1. CalData Algorithm

Input: $State_{last}, State_{new}, State_0, State[n], Mimc$
Output: $Root, State[n]$
1: /*An example of contract data initialization can involve more methods.*/
2: $count \leftarrow 2, States[0] \leftarrow s0, States[1] \leftarrow s0$
3: **if** $count == 2$ **then**
4:     $State[0] = Mimc(State[0], State[1])$
5:     $State[1] = State_{last}$
6: **else**
7:     $States[count] = State_{last}$
8: **end if**
9: $Root = Mimc(Mimc(Mimc(Mimc(s0), States[0]), States[1]), State_{new})$

Proof Generation: The proof generation phase primarily involves off-chain validation and aggregation of data to ensure its authenticity. Data validation mainly includes verifying whether the data is a continuation of the previous data and whether it satisfies the continuity of the MTC. The generation of zero-knowledge proofs primarily involves batch updating of data after batch validation and generating corresponding zero-knowledge proofs. Batch validation primarily verifies the MTC transformation process of these state data, ensuring that the new state data is derived from the previous state transformation.

On-Chain Verification: On-chain validation refers to verifying the authenticity and correctness of submitted data within the validation contract on the blockchain. Data validation primarily utilizes batch data validation to enhance the efficiency of data submission.

4   Security and Experiment Analysis

Security Analysis: Single Point of Failure: If the cross-chain prover (CCP) is solely operated by a single node, its security will directly impact the correct operation of the entire validation model. Replay Attack: If the cross-chain prover (CCP) becomes a Byzantine node, it may conduct replay attacks using old ZK-Proofs and state data. Therefore, in practical design, replay attacks can be mitigated by adding incremental tags or blockchain heights to ensure uniqueness and prevent reusing old data.

Experiment Setup: The experimental parameters are shown in the Table 1. Set#1 focuses on assessing the performance of constructing and updating MTC. The non-retrospective and chain-based retrospective approaches serve as baselines. Set#2 aims to validate the performance enhancement of contract verification through batch proof generation and validation. The multiple repeated verifications serve as a baseline.

Table 1. Experiment Params Setup

Group	Branch	leafs	Batches
set#1	2,4,8	16,64,128,256,512	-
set#2	2,4	-	6,8,10,12,14

Experiment Result: In theory, compared to regular contracts, MTC incurs additional overhead in storage space and data updates. As shown in Table 2, the number of branches in the Merkle tree used in MTC has a certain impact on its performance.

Table 2. The Influence of Merkel Tree Branch Number on MTC

	bracnchs	nums	Space overhead	Update overhead	temporality
None	-	n	1	1	✘
HChain	-	n	n+1	1	✔
MTC-2	2	n	4	1	✔
MTC-4	4	n	6	1/3	✔
MTC-8	8	n	10	1/7	✔

Figure 3(b) illustrates the gas consumption during deployment for contracts using MTC and HashChain contracts. As shown in Fig. 3(a), the frequency of gas consumption fluctuations during updates notably correlates with the number of branches in the Merkle tree used by MTC. Gas consumption during convolution operations is over 70% higher compared to non-triggered updates. This section consolidates deployment and update consumptions and further proposes an average gas expenditure equation to evaluate the experimental results. The equation can formula as $Cost_{Avg} = \frac{Cost_{deploy} + Cost_{OneUpdate} * n}{n}$.

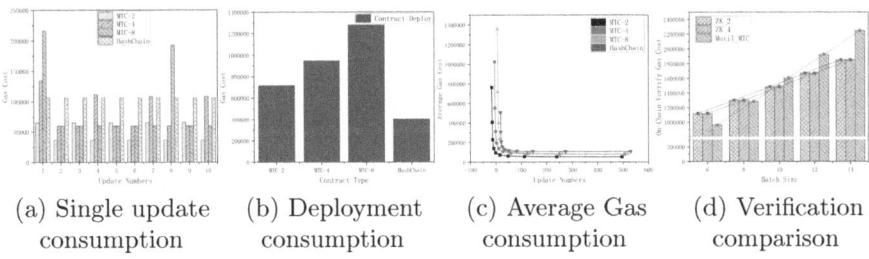

| (a) Single update consumption | (b) Deployment consumption | (c) Average Gas consumption | (d) Verification comparison |

Fig. 3. Gas consumption in MSCV

The deployment cost and average cost per update are depicted in Fig. 3(c). When the number of updates reaches 512, the average gas consumption for HashChain is 106,925, compared to a reduction of 100%, 39%, and 31% in gas consumption for MTC with branch nodes of 2, 4, and 8, respectively. In conclusion, MTC not only provides the possibility for on-chain verification of contract state data but also has lower gas consumption compared to the HashChain approach.

As depicted in Fig. 3(d), when the number of data to be proven is 10, 12, and 14, the batch verification method reduces gas consumption by 7%, 13%, and 17%, compared to the multiple MTC verification method. This indicates that the batch verification method based on zero-knowledge proofs can reduce on-chain verification consumption.

5   Conclusion

This paper addresses the challenge of cross-chain verification of smart contract state data. MTC is introduced as a validation approach for state transitions. Zero-knowledge proof is then employed to shift MTC verification off-chain, reducing on-chain costs. Experiments show that MSCV effectively achieves cross-chain verification with better performance than other approaches. However, MSCV still relies on trusted data sources, indicating the need for future research on reducing trust dependence in cross-chain data acquisition.

Acknowledgment. This work is supported by the VeChain Foundation (No. SCNU2018-01), Industry-University-Research Innovation Fund for Chinese Universities (2020ITA09006).

References

1. Wang, G., Wang, Q., Chen, S.: Exploring blockchains interoperability: a systematic survey. ACM Comput. Surv. **55**(13s), 1–38 (2023)
2. Hei, Y., Li, D., Zhang, C., Liu, J., Liu, Y., Wu, Q.: Practical agentchain: a compatible cross-chain exchange system. Futur. Gener. Comput. Syst. **130**, 207–218 (2022)
3. Westerkamp, M.: Verifiable smart contract portability. In: 2019 IEEE International Conference on Blockchain and Cryptocurrency (ICBC), pp. 1–9. IEEE (2019)
4. Westerkamp, M., Küpper, A.: Smartsync: cross-blockchain smart contract interaction and synchronization. In: 2022 IEEE International Conference on Blockchain and Cryptocurrency (ICBC), pp. 1–9 (2022)
5. Westerkamp, M., Küpper, A.: Instant function calls using synchronized cross-blockchain smart contracts. IEEE Trans. Netw. Serv. Manag. **20**(3), 2136–2150 (2023)
6. Dai, B., Jiang, S., Zhu, M., Lu, M., Li, D., Li, C.: Research and implementation of cross-chain transaction model based on improved hash-locking. In: Blockchain and Trustworthy Systems, pp. 218–230 (2020)

7. Cai, J., Zhou, Y., Hu, T., Li, B.: PTLC: protect the identity privacy during cross-chain asset transaction more effectively. In: 2022 IEEE 22nd International Conference on Software Quality, Reliability, and Security Companion (QRS-C), pp. 70–78. IEEE (2022)
8. Nissl, M., Sallinger, E., Schulte, S., Borkowski, M.: Towards cross-blockchain smart contracts. In: 2021 IEEE International Conference on Decentralized Applications and Infrastructures (DAPPS), pp. 85–94. IEEE (2021)
9. Fynn, E., Bessani, A., Pedone, F.: Smart contracts on the move. In: 2020 50th Annual IEEE/IFIP International Conference on Dependable Systems and Networks (DSN), pp. 233–244 (2020)
10. Hou, Z., Yang, J., Lai, R., He, Y., Mo, Z., Zhao, G.: Subscription-based state access for cross-chain smart contracts. In: 2023 IEEE 29th International Conference on Parallel and Distributed Systems (ICPADS), pp. 2763–2766. IEEE (2023)

How Does Hashgraph-Based Blockchain Work in MANETs: A Theoretical Analysis Model

Junjie Zhou[1,2], Ruilin Lai[1,2], Yale He[1,2], Zhihao Hou[1,2], Qizhi Zhang[1,2(✉)], and Gansen Zhao[1,2(✉)]

[1] School of Computer Science, South China Normal University, Guangzhou 510631, Guangdong, China
zhangqizhi@m.scnu.edu.cn
[2] Key Lab on Cloud Security and Assessment Technology of Guangzhou, Guangzhou 510631, Guangdong, China

Abstract. Nowadays, the integration of blockchain and MANET improves both MANET security and blockchain scalability. Hashgraph can better support the MANET-based blockchain by its inherent features, i.e., gossip about gossip, Byzantine fault tolerance, etc. In order to understand the limitations and performance of hashgraph in MANETs, this work investigate the theoretical model with two metrics. The metrics include the degree of node isolation and witness confirmation delay. By using the differential equations and markov chain, this work quantitatively analyze the general hashgraph with an optimal contact probability and the improved hashgraph resisting eclipse attacks, as well as identifying the expressions of these performance metrics. Extensive experiments support the analysis and reveal the impact of moving nodes and Byzantine nodes on the hashgraph performance in MANETs. To the best of our knowledge, our work is the first to apply DAG (Directed Acyclic Graph) blockchain for the MANETs from a methodological perspective.

Keywords: Blockchain · MANET · Hashgraph · Stochastic process

1 Introduction

Blockchain is a promising technology to establish trust for IoT(Internet of Things) environments [1]. MANET(Mobile Ad-hoc Network) is established autonomously by mobile devices without relying on any infrastructure [2], which is one of the most popular scenarios in IoT environments. The integration of MANET and blockchain improves both MANET security and blockchain scalability. Nowadays, the blockchain is explored to build on MANETs [3], and its applications involve incentive data collection [4], secure resources sharing [5], and expansion of cryptocurrency [6].

However, most popular consensus mechanisms are not designed specifically for the MANET-based blockchain. Proof-of-X, PBFT(Practical Byzantine Fault

G. Zhao et al. (Eds.): BWTAC 2024, CCIS 2277, pp. 324–336, 2025.
https://doi.org/10.1007/978-981-97-9412-6_30

Tolerance) and RAFT require one miner/leader for transaction collection and block generation. The miner/leader is inherently the bottleneck of blockchain performance, and this is exacerbated under the opportunistic communication of MANETs. Besides, Tangle [7] does not have a guarantee of Byzantine fault tolerance, which is importance for the trustless IoT environment. Fortunately, hashgraph, which employs an asynchronous Byzantine algorithm with asynchronous communication and virtual voting mechanisms, has the capacity to support the dynamic nature of MANETs.

To insightfully understand the above observation, the mathematical model is exploited. The model involving two metrics is in aid of studying the performance and limitations of hashgraph in MANETs [8]. First, the most important performance metrics of blockchain is the block confirmation delay [9]. In hashgraph, the witness confirmation delay is related to the consensus process using *see* and *strongly see* concepts. Second, if the network is partitioned for a long time, a node's event cannot be voted continuously, as well as not be confirmed by the community. We provide a new important concept: $k - node\ isolation$, that the node is isolated such that the number of nodes voting YES on its event remains unchanged for consecutive k time slots. The larger k's value is an inducement to the longer consensus process.

In order to analyze the upper bound of k and the hashgraph performance, we investigate the general hashgraph with an optimal contact probability, and the improved hashgraph resisting eclipse attacks. Our contributions are as follows:

- To analyze the hashgraph performance and limitations in MANETs, we propose a theoretical analysis model with two metrics. For the general hashgraph, the contact probability among nodes is resolved to realize required $k - node\ isolation$. Moreover, based on differential equations of gossiping about an event, the closed-form expressions of witness confirmation delay is derived.
- Considering Byzantine nodes launching eclipse attacks, the ranger-assisted method is proposed for the improved hashgraph. We analyze how much k caused by the eclipse attack can be resisted by the proposed method. Moreover, by using a Markov Chain for the gossip process of an event, the relationship between the mobility of different types of nodes and their influence to blockchain performance are demonstrated.
- Through extensive experiments, we validate the analysis and reveal the impact of moving nodes and Byzantine nodes on the hashgraph performance in MANETs. Particularly, the fraction of Byzantine faults, contact probabilities and blockchain sizes are varied to compare the degree of node isolation and witness confirmation delay in the general hashgraph and the improved hashgraph.

2   Related Work

According to the structure of the ledger, the MANET-based blockchains are classified into the chain and the DAG. Some works utilize the chain structure for MANET-based blockchains. Jiao et al. [10] proposed a stability-aware

PoW consensus to handle the high network dynamics in mobile ad-hoc environment. Liu et al. [4] introduced a blockchain system for security data collection in MANETs. Some works utilize the DAG structure for fast MANET-based blockchains. Morales et al. [11] integrated blockgraph with RAFT consensus to cope with network partition problems. Lai et al. [12] used hashgraph to support the dynamic changing of consensus subjects. However, the above works lack, from a mathematical perspective, exploring the performance and limitations of DAG blockchains in MANETs.

3   Hashgraph Analytical Framework in MANETs

3.1   Witness Confirmation Delay Analysis

A key performance metric of hashgraph are the witness confirmation delay. According to [13], there is at least one witness in round r which is decided to be famous in round $r + 3$. The expected delay of witness confirmation of hashgraph is 3 round time, so it is as (1), where t_r is the round time.

$$Delay_c = 3 \cdot t_r \tag{1}$$

Recall the definition of *round* in [13]. The round of a witness x is defined to be $r + 1$, if r is the maximum round number of the parents of x, and x can strongly see more than $2n/3$ witnesses of round r, where n is the number of consensus nodes in the blockchain.

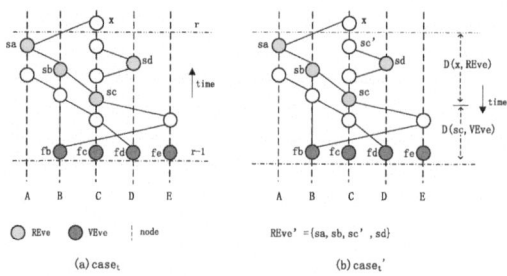

Fig. 1. $case_t$ and $case_t'$

$case_t$ indicates all round $r - 1$ events are seen by a witness x of round r. Particularly, each witness of round $r - 1$ is strongly seen by x through round $r-1$ events, $REve$. The number of round $r - 1$ witnesses($VEve$) is equal to that of $REve$, which is $2n/3 + 1$. For example, $case_t$ is depicted in Fig. 1(a), where $VEve = \{fb, fc, fd, fe\}$ and $REve = \{sa, sb, sc, sd\}$. In unicast communication, $case_t'$ indicates the case that all gossip information of $case_t$ are sent in the opposite direction. For example, $case_t'$ is depicted in Fig. 1(b). Obviously, the delay in $case_t$ is equal to that in $case_t'$. $case_t'$ makes the mathematically analysis of hashgraph performance tractable, because it is based on the propagation of an event rather than that of multiple events.

Let function $D(\theta, \Theta)$ indicate the delay when event θ propagates to nodes and the nodes vote YES on it through events Θ. In $case_t'$, $D(x, REve)$ indicates the delay between event x and events $REve$, and $D(re, VEve)$ is the delay between the last event in $REve$, re, and events $VEve$. For example, re is event sc in Fig. 1(b). Hence, the round time is given by (2).

$$t_r = D(x, REve) + D(re, VEve) \tag{2}$$

Lemma 1: *In $case_t'$, let $REve'$ be the first events of the first $2n/3 + 1$ nodes seeing witness x. The delay between x and $REve'$ is $D(x, REve')$. $D(x, REve') \leq D(x, REve)$.*

Proof: Denote the nodes generating $REve'$ and $REve$ as $nodR'$ and $nodR$, respectively. If $nodR' \cap nodR \neq \emptyset$, $D(x, REve') < D(x, REve)$, because there is at least one event in $REve$ which is generated by $nodR - nodR'$ after $REve'$. Otherwise, there may be events in $REve$ that are not the first generated events when $nodR$ seeing x. In other words, events in $REve$ may be generated after $REve'$. So $D(x, REve') \leq D(x, REve)$. The lemma is proved.

Lemma 2: *In $case_t'$, consider the delay of witness x seen by the first $2n/3 + 1 - i$ nodes, and the delay of witness x seen by the first $2n/3 + 1 + i$ nodes, where $i = 1, 2....$ $D(x, REve')$ related to the $2n/3 + 1$ nodes is closer to $D(x, REve)$, when Byzantine nodes participating.*

Proof: Denote the delay of witness x seen by the first $2n/3 + 1 - i$ nodes as $D(x, REve'')$. Because of $2n/3 + 1 > 2n/3 + 1 - i$ and $D(x, REve) \geq D(x, REve')$, $D(x, REve) \geq D(x, REve') \geq D(x, REve'')$. Besides, due to Byzantine fault tolerance of less than $1/3$ in hashgraph, the delay of x seen by the $2n/3 + 1 + i$ nodes is not considered, because the Byzantine nodes can make the delay infinitely long. The lemma is proved.

Analogously, in $case_t'$, let the delay of event re seen by the first $2n/3 + 1$ nodes be $D(re, VEve')$. $D(re, VEve')$ is also closer to $D(re, VEve)$. Thus, the expected round time t_r is $2t_f$, where t_f is the delay of an event seen by the first $2n/3 + 1$ nodes. The delay of witness confirmation is calculated in (3).

$$Delay_c = 6 \cdot t_f \tag{3}$$

3.2 Challenge of Node Isolation

Node isolation is defined based on an observed event from an honest node. If the number of nodes seeing the event does not increase during the consensus process, the network is considered fragmented. The maximum number of time slots where this remains unchanged is denoted as k, which represents the degree of node isolation ($k - node\ isolation$). A larger k indicates longer latency for the event to be seen by other nodes, affecting witness confirmation time. Therefore, node isolation must be carefully considered in analysis.

The high degree of node isolation is generally caused by low contact probabilities, or eclipse attacks. During the movement of nodes, a node has a certain probability, pr_c, to contact with another node in each time slot, $pr_c \in (0, 1]$. Events are assumed to be transmitted successfully between honest nodes in each contact, and it is rational because of the unicast transmission. When the network is lightly loaded due to low contact probabilities, it takes longer for the event to be propagated to other nodes. k will be increased. In the other hand, Byzantine nodes attempt to isolate the node by monopolizing its connections, namely eclipse attacks. In each contact, they don't gossip with the victim, or not relay the victim's events. During the successful period of this attack, the victim's event cannot be propagated to other honest nodes. Its k will be increased infinitely.

Therefore, in order to comprehensively analyze the hashgraph performance in MANETs, we investigate the general hashgraph with an optimal contact probability, and the improved hashgraph resisting eclipse attacks.

4   General Hashgraph with an Optimal Contact Probability

4.1   Node Isolation

Degree of node isolation k depends on contact probability pr_c, so pr_c needs to be resolved to realize $k - node\ isolation$. Moreover, the upper bound of pr_c is 1, meaning a node contacts with another one in each time slot. Nevertheless, it is possible that gossip information of the event is still sent to the nodes which have seen it or the Byzantine nodes, and $k > 0$. Hence, the minimum degree of node isolation also needs to be resolved.

For an observed event generated by a honest node, let $\{SEE\}$ be its state representing the number of nodes have seen it. see is the value of SEE. $see \in [1, n(1 - \lambda) - 1]$. The transition probability of state $\{SEE\}$ not changing is as (4).

$$P(see|see) = (1 - pr_c + pr_c \cdot \frac{n \cdot \lambda + see - 1}{n - 1})^{see} \tag{4}$$

In (4), if the node which has seen the event does not contact in $1 - pr_c$, contacts with Byzantine nodes in $pr_c \frac{n \cdot \lambda}{n-1}$, or contacts with the nodes which have seen the event in $pr_c \frac{see-1}{n-1}$, see is not increased by the node.

$\max P(see|see)$ indicates the highest probability that the number of nodes seeing the event remains unchanged, leading to the maximum degree of node isolation. $\max P(see|see)$ is analyzed by using MATLAB. It can be found that $P(see|see)$ has the maximum value when $see = n(1 - \lambda) - 1$ in (5).

$$\max P(see|see) = P(n(1 - \lambda) - 1|n(1 - \lambda) - 1) = (1 - \frac{pr_c}{n - 1})^{n(1-\lambda)-1} \quad (5)$$

$P(n(1-\lambda)-1|n(1-\lambda)-1)^k$ is the maximum probability of state $\{SEE\}$ not changing in consecutive k times. To keep the probability of $k - node\ isolation$ below a small threshold ε, the contact probability should be larger than $(n - 1)(1 - \varepsilon^{1/(k \cdot n(1-\lambda)-k)})$. Since $\lambda < 1/3$, the contact probability is derived by (6). For example, if $n = 100$, at least 0.87 of contact probabilities can ensure the probability of $20 - node\ isolation$ to be below $\varepsilon = 10^{-5}$. Thus, the lower bound of the contact probability in (6) does not only realize the required degree of node isolation, but also save the resource consumption of nodes.

$$pr_c > (n - 1)(1 - \varepsilon^n) \quad (6)$$
$$s.t.\ \eta = \frac{3}{(2n - 3) \cdot k}$$

Since $pr_c \leq 1$, the minimum degree of node isolation is derived by (7). For example, given $\varepsilon = 10^{-5}$ and $n = 100$, $k > 17.3$ is calculated. It means the general hashgraph only supports the node isolation which degree is larger than 17.

$$k > \frac{3 \log \varepsilon}{(2n - 3) \cdot (\log(n - 2) - \log(n - 1))} \quad (7)$$

4.2 Witness Confirmation Delay

Inspired by epidemic routing [14], ordinary differential equations are used to resolve t_f for the delay of witness confirmation. Let $i_x(t)$ be the fraction of nodes seeing an event x generated by a honest node at time t. Byzantine nodes is assumed to vote NO on x, so only the honest nodes see x. Since $1 - \lambda$ is the fraction of honest nodes in the blockchain, $1 - \lambda - i_x(t)$ is the fraction of honest nodes which donot see x at time t. As the transmission method is unicast, the dynamic equation of gossiping about event x and x being seen is given by (8).

$$n \cdot \frac{di_x(t)}{dt} = n \cdot i_x(t) \cdot pr_c \cdot (1 - \lambda - i_x(t)) \quad (8)$$

With the initial condition $i_x(0) = 1/n$, the general solution to (8) is given by (9).

$$i_x(t) = \frac{1 - \lambda}{(n - \lambda n - 1) \cdot e^{-(1-\lambda) \cdot pr_c \cdot t} + 1} \quad (9)$$

Let $n \cdot i_x(t) = 2n/3 + 1$. t is calculated and $t_f = t$ in (10).

$$t_f = (\log \frac{n - 3n - 3}{(n - \lambda \cdot n - 1)(2n - 3)})/(pr_c \cdot (\lambda - 1)) \tag{10}$$

Therefore, by integrating (3) and (10), the delay of witness confirmation is calculated in (11).

$$Delay_c = (6 \cdot \log \frac{n - 3n - 3}{(n - \lambda \cdot n - 1)(2n - 3)})/(pr_c \cdot (\lambda - 1)) \tag{11}$$

5   Improved Hashgraph Resisting Eclipse Attacks

5.1   Node Isolation

Byzantine nodes can initiate the eclipse attack to isolate victims by monopolizing their connections. It leads to higher degree of node isolation for the victims.

Based on the mobility of nodes, the ranger-assisted method is proposed to mitigate the attack. The victim as a ranger is responsible to contact with a node in each time slot. During the contact, it receives an event from and send another event to the contact node. If two rangers meet, one of them becomes a normal node again, while the other continues to contact with another node in each time slot. The state transition of nodes is depicted in Fig. 2. Besides, denote the ranger that has seen an event x as ran_x. There may be multiple ran_xs not contacting with each other. The number of ran_xs, r_x, varies from 1 to the number of victims(v). In this way, events of victims can be propagated to other nodes.

Nevertheless, it is possible that gossip information of event x is still sent to Byzantine nodes or the nodes that have seen x, and $k > 0$. Hence, the degree of node isolation for the victims needs to be resolved. In other words, it needs to find that how much victim's k caused by the eclipse attack can be resisted by the proposed method.

For an observed event x generated by a ranger, let $\{SEE\}$ be its state representing the number of nodes have seen it. see is the value of SEE, $see \in [1, n(1 - \lambda) - 1]$. The transition probability of state $\{SEE\}$ not changing is as (12).

$$P(see|see) = \eta 1^{r_x} \cdot \eta 2^{see - r_x} \tag{12}$$

$$s.t. \; \eta 1 = \frac{n \cdot \lambda + see - 1}{n - 1}$$

$$\eta 2 = 1 - pr_c + pr_c \cdot (\frac{n \cdot \lambda + see - 1 - r_x}{n - 1 - r_x})$$

$$see \in [1, n(1 - \lambda) - 1], r_x \in [1, v]$$

In (12), if a ran_x contacts with a Byzantine node in $n\lambda/(n-1)$ or the nodes that have seen x in $(see-1)/(n-1)$, see is not increased by the ran_x, and the probability is $\eta 1$. Denote the node which is not a ranger and has seen event x as nod_x. If a nod_x does not contact with other node in $1-pr_c$, contacts with a Byzantine node in $pr_c \cdot n\lambda/(n-1-r_x)$, or contacts with other nod_xs in $pr_c \cdot (see-1-r_x)/(n-1-r_x)$, see is not increased by the nod_x, and the probability is $\eta 2$. Neither the r_x ran_xs nor the $see-r_x$ nod_xs can increase values of SEE, such that the transition probability of state $\{SEE\}$ not changing is $\eta 1^{r_x} \cdot \eta 2^{see-r_x}$.

Due to $\eta 1 \in (0,1)$ and $r_x \in [1,v]$, $\max \eta 1^{r_x} = \eta 1$ when $r_x = 1$. Due to $\eta 2 \in (0,1)$, $\max \eta^{see-r_x} = 1$ when $see = r_x$. Thus, when $see = r_x = 1$, $P(see|see)$ has a maximum value in (13).

$$\max P(see|see) = P(1|1) = n \cdot \lambda/(n-1) \tag{13}$$

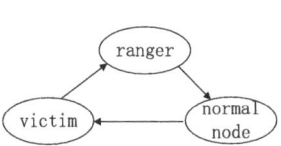

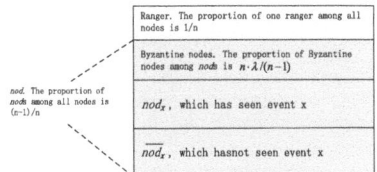

Fig. 2. State transition of nodes in the ranger-assisted method

Fig. 3. Naming of nodes in the blockchain, and their proportion in number

Since $\lambda < \frac{1}{3}$, the maximum probability of state $\{SEE\}$ not changing k consecutive times is less than $(\frac{1}{3}n/(n-1))^k$. To keep $(\frac{1}{3}n/(n-1))^k$ below a small threshold ε, k should be (14). For example, given $\varepsilon = 10^{-5}$ and $n = 100$, $k < 10.6$ is calculated. It means more than $10°$ of node isolation caused by the eclipse attack can be resisted by the ranger-assisted method.

$$k < \frac{\log \varepsilon}{\log n - \log 3(n-1)} \tag{14}$$

It is worthy to note that, the contact probability among non-ranger nodes no longer affect $k - node\ isolation$ of the victim, because only the initial state $\{SEE\}$ transition initiated by the ranger contributes to k.

5.2 Witness Confirmation Delay

The naming of nodes in the blockchain, and their proportion in number are shown in Fig. 3. The non-ranger node is named by nod. Suppose that there is one ranger in the blockchain. Since the ranger contacts with a *nod* in each time slot, the probability of a *nod* contacting with the ranger, pr_r, is $1/(n-1)$. *nods* also contact with each other in pr_c. Besides, as the ranger is a victim assumed to be honest, the proportion of the number of Byzantine nodes among *nods* is $\lambda \cdot n/(n-1)$. Among the honest *nods*, denote the *nod* which has seen an event x and the one which has not seen x, as nod_x and $\overline{nod_x}$, respectively.

Inspired by the theoretic analysis of Tangle [15], a Markov Chain is used to resolve t_f for the delay of witness confirmation. For an observed event x generated by a honest *nod*, let $\{rs(t), ns(t)\}$ be its state at time t, $t = 0, 1, 2, ...\infty$. $rs(t)$ and $ns(t)$ are stochastic processes to represent the number of rangers and *nods* which see x at time t, respectively. $rs(t) \in [0,1]$. $ns(t) \in [1, (1-\lambda)n - 1]$. $\{rs(t), ns(t)\}$ is formulated as a discrete-time markov chain in Fig. 4. The probabilities of one-step transitions from distinct state are given on Github[1].

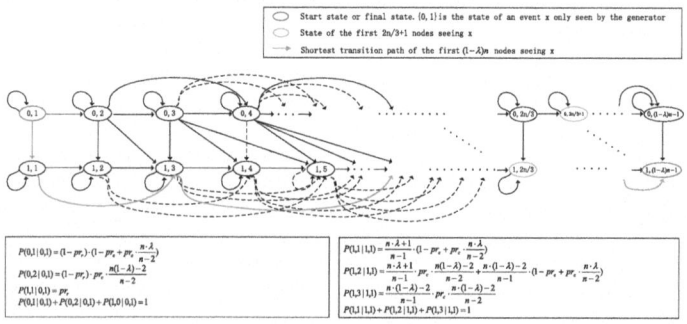

Fig. 4. Markov Chain for the process of event x being seen by the first $n(1-\lambda)$ nodes

If the number of honest nodes in the blockchain is $2n/3 + 1$, the state of the first $2n/3 + 1$ nodes seeing event x at time t is $\{rs(t), ns(t)\} = \{1, 2n/3\}$. $\{1, 2n/3\}$ is the final state. The shortest path from initial state $\{rs(0), ns(0)\} = \{0, 1\}$ to the final state has the expected minimum delay, l, $l = \lceil \log_2^{2n/3+1} \rceil$. Since the final state is an absorbing state, there is the longest path with the expected maximum delay, $L1$, when $P(rs(t) = 1, ns(t) = \frac{2n}{3} | rs(0) = 0, ns(0) = 1)$ becomes 1. Hence, t_f is calculated in (15). In the other hand, if the number of honest nodes in the blockchain is more than $2n/3+1$, the states of the first $2n/3 + 1$ nodes seeing x at time t are $\{rs(t), ns(t)\} = \{1, 2n/3\}$ and $\{rs(t), ns(t)\} = \{0, 2n/3 + 1\}$. Let $\{1, 2n/3\}$ and $\{0, 2n/3 + 1\}$ be the final states. Similarly, l is also the expected minimum delay of the shortest path from the initial state to the final states. $L2$ is its expected maximum delay, when $P(rs(t) = 1, ns(t) = \frac{2n}{3} | rs(0) = 0, ns(0) = 1) + P(rs(t) = 0, ns(t) = \frac{2n}{3} + 1 | rs(0) = 0, ns(0) = 1)$ becomes 1. Hence, t_f is calculated in (16).

$$CASE\ I:\ t_f = l \cdot P(rs(l) = 1, ns(l) = \frac{2n}{3} | rs(0) = 0, ns(0) = 1) \tag{15}$$

$$+ \sum_{t=l+1}^{L1} t \cdot (P(rs(t) = 1, ns(t) = \frac{2n}{3} | rs(0) = 0, ns(0) = 1)$$

$$-P(rs(t-1) = 1, ns(t-1) = \frac{2n}{3} | rs(0) = 0, ns(0) = 1))$$

$$CASE\ II:\ t_f = l \cdot P(rs(l) = 1, ns(l) = \frac{2n}{3} | rs(0) = 0, ns(0) = 1) \tag{16}$$

$$+l \cdot P(rs(l) = 0, ns(l) = \frac{2n}{3} + 1 | rs(0) = 0, ns(0) = 1)$$

$$+ \sum_{t=l+1}^{L2} t \cdot (P(rs(t) = 1, ns(t) = \frac{2n}{3} | rs(0) = 0, ns(0) = 1)$$

$$-P(rs(t-1) = 1, ns(t-1) = \frac{2n}{3} | rs(0) = 0, ns(0) = 1)$$

$$+P(rs(t) = 0, ns(t) = \frac{2n}{3} + 1 | rs(0) = 0, ns(0) = 1)$$

$$-P(rs(t-1) = 0, ns(t-1) = \frac{2n}{3} + 1 | rs(0) = 0, ns(0) = 1))$$

$$s.t. \quad l = \lceil \log_2^{2n/3+1} \rceil$$

Therefore, according to (3), the delay of witness confirmation is calculated in (17).

$$Delay_c = 6 \cdot t_f \tag{17}$$

$$s.t.\ t_f\ \text{is based on (15) or (16)}$$

6 Numerical Results and Discussion

The numerical results are obtained by Matlab. Some parameters are set: the contact probability are based on 1s, the average number of witnesses in a round is $n/2$. Let the number of consensus nodes, n, be the blockchain size.

6.1 Degree of Node Isolation

In the first experiment, we use (5) and (13), and let $\max P(see|see)^k$ be 10^{-5} to evaluate the degree of node isolation, k, in the general hashgrah and k for the victim in the improved hashgraph. Under different blockchain sizes and Byzantine faults, Fig. 5 presents the change of k's values. It can be observed that the degree of node isolation in the general hashgraph is larger than that of the improved hashgraph.

In Fig. 5(a), the gap of k's values between the general hashgraph and the improved hashgraph is roundly 10. Besides, the blockchain size has little effect on the degree of node isolation, because both the denominator and exponent in (5) involves n, and both the numerator and denominator of (13) contains n as well. In Fig. 5(b), as the fraction of Byzantine faults rises, the degree of node isolation increases. It is because gossip information of the event is more difficult to be sent to the honest nodes, leading to larger degrees of node isolation. Similarly, a smaller contact probability increases the degree of node isolation in the general hashgraph. Especially, with the decline of contact probabilities, the growth of k becomes faster. Besides, the contact probability among non-ranger nodes have no effect on the degree of node isolation for victims in the improved hashgraph. The reason is that only behaviors of the ranger contributes to k. Note that, when the fraction of Byzantine faults is 0, k becomes 0 and the network is not partitioned in the improved hashgraph.

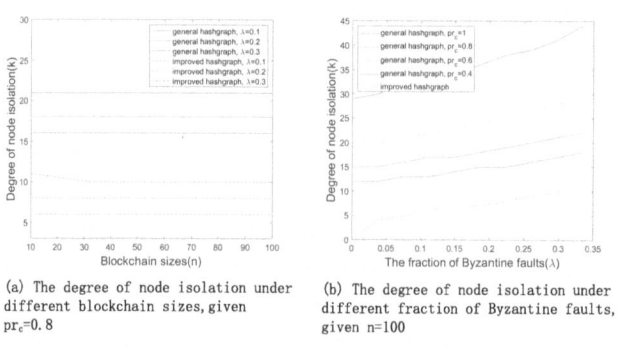

(a) The degree of node isolation under different blockchain sizes, given pr_c=0.8

(b) The degree of node isolation under different fraction of Byzantine faults, given n=100

Fig. 5. The degree of node isolation k

6.2   Witness Confirmation Delay

In the second experiment, using (11) and (17), we vary the fraction of Byzantine faults and contact probabilities to compare the delay of witness confirmation in the general hashgraph and improved hashgraph.

Figure 6 presents the delay of witness confirmation under different fraction of Byzantine faults in the general hashgraph. The delay is proportional to the fraction of Byzantine faults, because the Byzantine nodes don't gossip with the honest node or vote NO on the event, leading to latency in the event gossip. With the increase of blockchain sizes, the delay rises but its growth rate is less. Hence, the blockchain involving more nodes has better performance in MANETs, because it can achieve both high degree of decentralization and less growth rates of the delay. Figure 7 presents the delay of witness confirmation under different contact probabilities in the general hashgraph and improved hashgraph. It can be observed that the delay descends with the increase of contact probabilities, and thus the larger contact probability can be ultilized to alleviate the latency incurred by Byzantine nodes. Besides, the delay of improved hashgraph is less than that of the general hashgraph, because the ranger of improved hashgraph accelerates gossiping about the event. Especially, when the contact probability is small, e.g., 0.05, the delay of improved hashgraph is much less than that of general hashgraph. Hence, if the improved hashgraph is adopted in the case of low contact probabilities, the performance improvement of the blockchain is more significant.

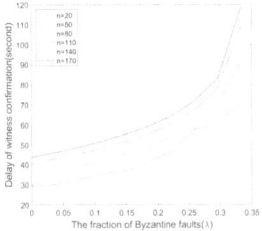

Fig. 6. The change of witness confirmation delay under different fraction of Byzantine faults

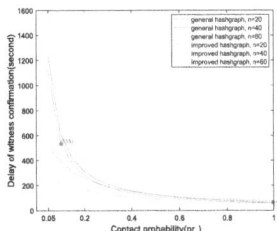

Fig. 7. The change of witness confirmation delay under different contact probabilities

7   Conclusion

We investigate the hashgraph-based blockchain in MANETs from theoretical understanding. For the general hashgraph, an optimal contact probability is resolved to realize the required degree of node isolation, such that the resource consumption of nodes can be saved. Moreover, the closed-form expressions of witness confirmation delay is derived. For the improved hashgraph resisting eclipse attacks, the ranger-assisted method is proposed, and the degree of node isolation for victims enhanced by the method is resolved. Moreover, the blockchain performance expressions associated with the mobility of the ranger and non-ranger nodes are derived. Finally, the analytical models of differential equations and markov chain are validated through numerical experiments. The results reveal the impact of moving nodes and Byzantine nodes on the hashgraph performance in MANETs. Therefore, this work can provide an analytical guideline for building an optimal and secure DAG blockchain for MANETs in the future.

Acknowledgment. This work is supported by the VeChain Foundation (No. SCNU2018-01), Industry-University-Research Innovation Fund for Chinese Universities (2020ITA09006).

References

1. Liao, Z., Pang, X., Zhang, J., Xiong, B., Wang, J.: Blockchain on security and forensics management in edge computing for IoT: a comprehensive survey. IEEE Trans. Netw. Serv. Manag. **19**(2), 1159–1175 (2021)

2. Bruzgiene, R., Narbutaite, L., Adomkus, T.: Manet network in Internet of Things system. Ad Hoc Netw. **66**, 89–114 (2017)
3. Zhou, S., Zhang, G., Meng, X.: LocTrust: a local and global consensus-combined trust model in MANETs. Peer-to-Peer Netw. Appl. 1–14 (2022)
4. Liu, G., Dong, H., Yan, Z., Zhou, X., Shimizu, S.: B4SDC: a blockchain system for security data collection in MANETs. IEEE Trans. Big Data **8**(3), 739–752 (2020)
5. Rasool, S., Iqbal, M., Dagiuklas, T., Ul-Qayyum, Z., Li, S.: Reliable data analysis through blockchain based crowdsourcing in mobile ad-hoc cloud. Mob. Netw. Appl. **25**, 153–163 (2020)
6. Chatzopoulos, D., Gujar, S., Faltings, B., Hui, P.: LocalCoin: an ad-hoc payment scheme for areas with high connectivity: poster. In: Proceedings of the 17th ACM International Symposium on Mobile Ad Hoc Networking and Computing, pp. 365–366 (2016)
7. Popov, S.: The tangle. White Paper **1**(3), 30 (2018)
8. Cao, B., et al.: Blockchain systems, technologies and applications: a methodology perspective. IEEE Commun. Surv. Tutor. **25**, 353–385 (2022)
9. Zhou, Q., Huang, H., Zheng, Z., Bian, J.: Solutions to scalability of blockchain: a survey. IEEE Access **8**, 16440–16455 (2020)
10. Jiao, Z., Zhang, B., Zhang, L., Liu, M., Gong, W., Li, C.: A blockchain-based computing architecture for mobile ad hoc cloud. IEEE Netw. **34**(4), 140–149 (2020)
11. Morales, D.C., Velloso, P.B., Laubé, A., Nguyen, T.-M.-T., Pujolle, G.: A performance evaluation of C4M consensus algorithm. Ann. Telecommun. **78**(3–4), 169–182 (2023)
12. Lai, R., Zhao, G., He, Y., Hou, Z.: A robust sharding-enabled blockchain with efficient hashgraph mechanism for MANETs. Appl. Sci. **13**(15), 8726 (2023)
13. Baird, L., Harmon, M., Madsen, P.: Hedera: a public hashgraph network & governing council. White Paper **1**, 1–97 (2019)
14. Zhang, X., et al.: The block propagation in blockchain-based vehicular networks. IEEE Internet Things J. **9**(11), 8001–8011 (2021)
15. Li, Y., et al.: Direct acyclic graph-based ledger for Internet of Things: performance and security analysis. IEEE/ACM Trans. Netw. **28**(4), 1643–1656 (2020)

Heterogeneous Graph Structure Learning Based on Feature and Topology Information Extraction

Chao Li[1], Xin Li[1($\boxtimes$)], Xiangkai Zhu[1], Qingtian Zeng[2], and Hua Duan[3]

[1] College of Electronic and Information Engineering, Shandong University of Science and Technology, Qingdao, China
lixin00120411@163.com

[2] College of Computer Science and Engineering, Shandong University of Science and Technology, Qingdao, China
qtzeng@163.com

[3] College of Mathematics and Systems Science, Shandong University of Science and Technology, Qingdao, China

Abstract. Heterogeneous Graph Structure Learning (HGSL) aims at jointly learning optimized graph structure and representation. Its purpose is to enhance the performance and robustness of Heterogeneous Graph Neural Networks (HGNNs) by solving the problems of redundancy, bias, noise, incompleteness, and unreliability in graph structures. However, the existing research is still insufficient in selecting the multi-order neighborhood information aggregation method, which leads to increased computational complexity and over-convergence of multi-layer semantics. Meanwhile, when dealing with rich node features and complex topology, previous research exhibits the problem of insufficient information utilization. To solve these problems, we propose a novel model named Heterogeneous Graph Structure Learning Based on Feature and Topology Information Extraction (**HGSL-FTIE**). First, we propose an n-hop meta-path extraction strategy. Based on this strategy, we fuse the node features to construct the feature structural subgraph and fuse the original graph structure to construct the topology structural subgraph. Then, we creatively adopt a structural subgraph fusion method based on the More Confident Fusion (MCF) strategy to guide the fusion of the feature structural subgraph and the topology structural subgraph to obtain the final graph structure and the corresponding node representation. We have conducted comprehensive experiments on three real datasets, and the results demonstrate that HGSL-FTIE outperforms the existing state-of-the-art models.

Keywords: Heterogeneous graph · Heterogeneous graph neural networks · Heterogeneous graph structure learning · Smart contract

G. Zhao et al. (Eds.): BWTAC 2024, CCIS 2277, pp. 337–349, 2025.
https://doi.org/10.1007/978-981-97-9412-6_31

1   Introduction

In recent years, Graph Neural Networks (GNNs) have gained growing attention for their strong representation abilities [1], and have been effectively utilized in real-world applications such as e-commerce [2], blockchain transactions [3] and fraud detection [4]. Nevertheless, the effectiveness of GNNs typically relies on the assumption that the original graph structure is trustworthy enough. In practice, graph structures often suffer from redundancy, bias, noise, incompleteness, and unreliability, which pose a great challenge to GNNs. Graph Structure Learning (GSL) has been proposed as a solution for the above problems [5]. GSL aims to jointly learn optimized graph structure and corresponding representations to ensure that the learned graph structure and node representations are better suited for downstream tasks. Thus, it effectively alleviates the problem of over-reliance on the original graph structures in previous models. Most current research related to GSL is designed for homogeneous graphs, such as GRCN [6], IDGL [7], and GEN [8]. These approaches achieve joint learning of graph structure and node representations by parameterizing the adjacency matrix and optimizing it for downstream tasks together with the GNN parameters. Heterogeneous Graph Neural Networks (HGNNs) are a significant branch in the field of GNNs, which are designed to deal with complex graph structure data. HGNNs show excellent performance in capturing semantic and structural information in heterogeneous graphs [9]. While facing heterogeneous graphs with rich node features and complex topology, previous HGNNs have suffered from some limitations. When exploring an effective approach to solve these limitations through heterogeneous graph structure learning, we will face the following two challenges.

Challenge 1: How to effectively aggregate the multi-order neighborhood information?

The message-passing mechanism is a fundamental concept in GNNs [10], aiming at efficiently aggregating multi-order neighborhood information and passing this information to the central node. For heterogeneous graphs with various types of nodes and edges, during the process of multi-order neighborhood information aggregation, previous HGNNs suffer from certain shortcomings in the selection of aggregation mechanism, the number of network layers, and the length of meta-paths. For example, some research followed the neighbor attention mechanism for homogeneous graphs while ignoring the effectiveness of this mechanism on heterogeneous graphs, which may lead to attention redundancy and increased computational complexity. Indeed, it has been demonstrated in [11] that the simple mean aggregation method can be as effective as aggregation with the neighbor attention module. In addition, during the aggregation process, some research chose to employ multi-layer networks and short meta-paths to aggregate neighborhood information layer by layer. However, stacking too many network layers may result in the phenomenon of over-smoothing, which makes the multi-layer semantics overly fused, thus making it difficult to distinguish between different levels of semantic information. Meanwhile, short meta-paths limit the range of semantics that can be learned.

Challenge 2: How to effectively handle node features and topology information in the heterogeneous graph?

Since the original graph often suffers from noise, bias, and redundancy, it is usually not the best choice for downstream tasks. Therefore, heterogeneous graph structure learning seeks to refine the original graph structure by exploiting the rich information in node features and topology. In [12], a heterogeneous graph structure learning framework named HGSL was proposed, which generated a feature similarity graph by computing the node feature similarity. However, this research ignored the effect of noise in high-dimensional feature vectors, which may lead to sub-optimality of the learned graph structure and affect the final performance. Additionally, some previous research performed information extraction only from the node feature perspective or only from the topology perspective while ignoring the potential connection between node features and topology. As shown in Fig. 1, in the blockchain transaction graph [3], there are two types of nodes (accounts): EOA (Externally Owned Accounts) and CA (Contract Accounts). Each type can be classified into various categories according to the users' roles. The EOA category includes investor, exchange deposit, ICO Wallet, etc. The CA category includes token contracts, miners/mining pools, Phish/Hack, etc. When a new account (node) is added, the topology of this blockchain transaction graph may change due to other external factors (e.g. attribute information of other accounts or transaction types), but it is always governed by the node's own attributes (the user's own account category and attribute information). In addition, when node attributes are incomplete or missing (e.g. when the category of an account in the transaction graph is not clear), the relationship between nodes can be inferred by analyzing the topology, and then we can complement the category that the account belongs to.

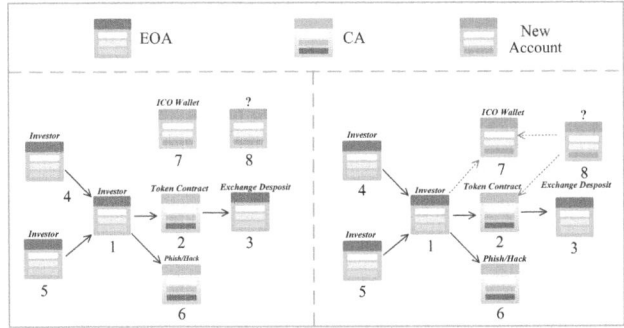

Fig. 1. Blockchain transaction graph.

To address these challenges, we introduce a novel framework called Heterogeneous Graph Structure Learning Based on Feature and Topology Information Extraction **(HGSL-FTIE)**. The main contributions are summarized as follows:

1) We propose an n-hop meta-path extraction strategy and learn the feature structural subgraph and topology structural subgraph based on this strategy. Finally, the original graph structure is enhanced.

2) We propose a novel MCF strategy, which can fully consider the contribution of each structural subgraph during the fusion process. By using this strategy, the final optimized graph structure is more suitable for downstream tasks.

2 Preliminaries

In this section, we present some relevant concepts for this paper and give detailed definitions.

Definition 1. Heterogeneous Graph [9] Heterogeneous graph is represented as $G = (V, E)$. There exist mapping function $\Phi : V \rightarrow \eta$ and $\Psi : E \rightarrow \xi$, η denotes the set of node types and ξ represents the set of edge types. The heterogeneous graph is required to satisfy $|\eta| + |\xi| > 2$.

Definition 2. Meta-path [13] Meta-path M defines a composite relationship of multiple edge types, denoted as $M = v_1 \xrightarrow{R_1} v_2 \xrightarrow{R_2} v_3 \xrightarrow{R_3} ... \xrightarrow{R_{i-1}} v_{i-1} \xrightarrow{R_i} v_i$, where $v_i \in \eta, R_i \in \xi$.

Definition 3. n-hop Meta-path For the set of node types $v_p \in \eta$, the n-hop meta-path P of node v_p is defined as $\mathcal{P}(v_p, v_{n+p}) = \{v_p, c_1, v_{1+p}, ..., c_n, v_{n+p}\}$, where v_{n+p} denotes the n-hop neighbor nodes of v_p, and $c_n \in \xi$ denotes the type of relationship between two adjacent nodes in the meta-path.

Problem. Heterogeneous Graph Structure Learning. Given a heterogeneous graph $G = (X, A)$ as input, the original graph structure can be represented as the adjacency matrix $A \in \{0, 1\}^{N \times N}$, and $A_{ij} > 0$ denotes $(v_i, v_j) \in E$. The goal is to determine the optimal graph structure A^* and the corresponding node embedding Z for particular downstream tasks by using the graph structure learner $S_\phi(X, A)$ and GNN encoder $f_\theta(X, A)$.

3 The Proposed Model

To achieve effective heterogeneous graph structure learning, we propose a framework named Heterogeneous Graph Structure Learning Based on Feature and Topology Information Extraction **(HGSL-FTIE)**. The overall framework of HGSL-FTIE is shown in Fig. 2, which comprises four modules: (a) n-hop meta-path extraction strategy; (b) Feature structural subgraph learning; (c) Topology structural subgraph learning; and (d) Structural subgraph fusion based on MCF strategy. We will detail the key modules of the framework in Subsects. 3.1–3.4.

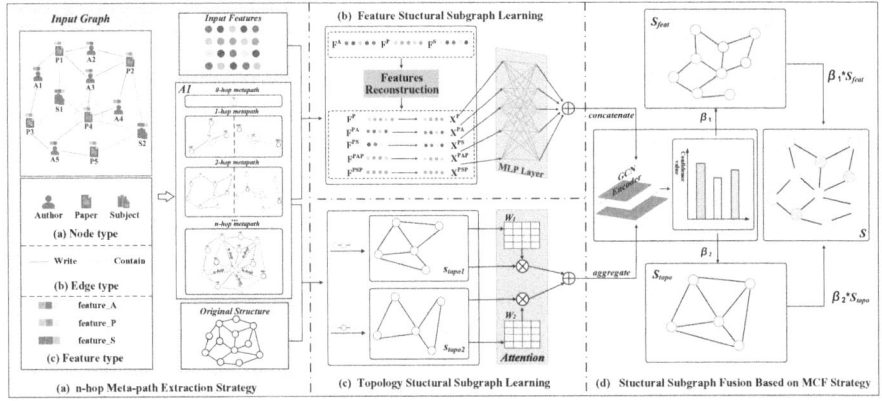

Fig. 2. The overall architecture of HGSL-FTIE.

3.1 N-Hop Meta-path Extraction Strategy

In this subsection, we propose an n-hop meta-path extraction strategy. To effectively aggregate the multi-order neighborhood information, we take into account the node features, the lower-order neighborhood (local) and the higher-order neighborhood (global) structure information of the heterogeneous graph.

First, an n-hop meta-path extraction strategy is applied to the original input graph $G = (V, E)$. The n-hop meta-path P of node $v_p \in \eta$ is defined as follows:

$$P = \mathcal{P}(v_p, v_{n+p}) = \{v_p, c_1, v_{P+1}, \ldots, c_n, v_{n+p}\} \tag{1}$$

where v_{n+p} denotes the n-hop neighbor nodes of v_p, and $c_n \in \xi$ denotes the type of relationship between two adjacent nodes in the meta-path.

The n-hop meta-paths P are obtained as shown in Fig. 2(a).A1. By using this strategy, we can obtain 0-hop meta-path (P), 1-hop meta-path (P-A/ P-S), 2-hop meta-path (P-A-P/ P-S-P), ..., n-hop meta-path (P-A(S)-...-A(S)-P).

Define the adjacency matrix based on the n-hop meta-path P as $A^P = \left[a_{ij}\right]_{n \times n}$, a_{ij} is defined as follows:

$$a_{ij} = \begin{cases} 0, & \text{if } (v_i, v_j) \in E \\ 1, & \text{if } (v_i, v_j) \notin E \end{cases} \tag{2}$$

Based on P and using a single-layer network structure, we apply a mean aggregation method to aggregate the features of neighbor nodes in multi-order neighborhood and obtain a list of feature vectors f_i,

$$f_i = \left\{ F_i^P = 1/_{\|C^P\|} \sum_{(v_i, v_j) \in C^P} f_j \right\} \tag{3}$$

where C^P denotes the set of all meta-path instances corresponding to $m(v_i, v_j)$, v_i denotes the target node, and v_j denotes the source node.

3.2   Feature Structural Subgraph Learning

In this subsection, we propose an efficient method for processing node features that aims to reconstruct node features through the edges. This approach enables us to obtain reconstructed features that convey multi-order semantic information and facilitate construction of the feature structural subgraph.

Based on the n-hop extraction strategy mentioned in (a), the reconstructed feature matrix is defined as:

$$X = \{X^P : P \in M_X\} \tag{4}$$

where M_X denotes the set of all n-hop meta-paths P.

By inputting the A^P and $\mathcal{F}^i = \{f_1^{i^T}; f_2^{i^T}; \cdots ; f_{n+1}^{i^T}\} \in \mathbb{R}^{N \times d^{\eta(i)}}$ into the feature reconstructor, we obtain the reconstructed feature matrix X^P containing semantic information.

$$X^P = \hat{A}^P \mathcal{F}^i \tag{5}$$

where $\mathcal{F}^i$ is the original feature matrix, $d^{\eta(i)}$ denotes the feature dimension, and $X^{\mathcal{P}(v_1,v_i)} = \hat{A}^{\mathcal{P}(v_1,v_i)} \mathcal{F}^i$.

For example, for the 2-hop meta-path $\mathcal{P}(v_{P_4}, v_{P_2}) = \{v_{P_4}, c_1, v_{S_2}, c_2, v_{P_2}\}$ extracted in Fig. 2(a).A1, briefly referred to as PSP in the following. After obtaining the normalized adjacency matrix $\hat{A}^{\text{PSP}}$ and the original feature matrix X^{PSP} for node type P, we can obtain the reconstructed feature $X^{\text{PSP}} = \hat{A}^{\text{PSP}} \mathcal{F}^P$ by feeding them into the feature reconstructor. Similarly, for the higher-order semantic PAPAP, which represents a paper written by similar authors, the reconstructed feature can be obtained as $X^{\text{PAPAP}} = \hat{A}^{\text{PAP}} \hat{A}^{\text{PAP}} \mathcal{F}^P = \hat{A}^{\text{PAPAP}} \mathcal{F}^P$.

To project the final reconstructed feature vector into the same potential vector space, we design a specific type of transformation matrix W_P for each meta-path P,

$$X^{P'} = W_P X^P \tag{6}$$

where $W_P \in \mathbb{R}^{d^{\eta(i)} \times d^c}$, and the reconstructed feature vector x^i has the same feature vector dimension d^c.

In order to construct the feature structural subgraph and obtain better representation ability, we first pass the reconstructed feature $X^{P'}$ through the MLP layer to obtain X_i^P,

$$X_i^P = MLP(X^{P'}) \tag{7}$$

Finally, we construct the feature structural subgraph S_f,

$$S_f = X_1^P \| X_2^P ... \| X_i^P \tag{8}$$

where $\|$ denotes the concatenate operation.

3.3   Topology Structural Subgraph Learning

In this subsection, to mine the rich information in topology, we extract primitive structures from the original graph structure that represent different semantic relations. We then assign weights to each primitive structure using the attention mechanism and construct the topology structural subgraph.

Based on the n-hop meta-path extraction strategy proposed in (a), we select the smallest transformation unit that can realize homogeneous graph transformation: the 2-hop meta-path. We define the set of 2-hop meta-paths as M_P,

$$M_P = \{P(v_p, v_{p+n}), n = 2, v_p \in \eta\} \tag{9}$$

Then, the primitive structure s_t^i is obtained as follows:

$$s_t^i = \{A^P : \quad P \in M_P\} \tag{10}$$

The attention mechanism is adopted to assign attention weights to s_t^i,

$$(\beta_t^1, ..., \beta_t^i) = att(s_t^1, ..., s_t^i) \tag{11}$$

where $att(\cdot)$ denotes the attention mechanism, the process is detailed below:

First, calculate the importance coefficient α_i for each primitive structure s_t^i,

$$\alpha_i = 1/_{|M_P|} \sum_{t \in M_P} q^T \cdot \tanh(w_T \cdot s_t^i + b_T) \tag{12}$$

where w_T and b_T are learnable parameters, q^T is semantic level attention vector.

Then, by normalizing the importance coefficient, we obtain the attention weights β_t^i,

$$\beta_t^i = \frac{\exp(\alpha_i)}{\sum_{i=1}^i \exp(\alpha_i)} \tag{13}$$

Finally, we can construct the topology structural subgraph S_t,

$$S_t = \sum_{i=1}^i \beta_t^i \cdot s_t^i \tag{14}$$

3.4   Structural Subgraph Fusion Based on MCF Strategy

In this subsection, we design the MCF strategy, which utilizes the prediction confidence as the a priori knowledge for the fusion of structural subgraphs. Then we assign a larger weight to the more confident structural subgraph so that the final graph structure can be trained more effectively.

Define the input structural subgraph as $S_i = \{S_f, S_t\}$. We first use the predictive encoder f_E to encode the prediction for each structural subgraph and compute the confidence value C_i of each subgraph,

$$C_i = f_E(S_i) \tag{15}$$

The predictive coding function $f_E(\theta)$ is implemented by using a two-layer encoder Γ_E,

$$f_E(\theta) = Softmax\left(\Gamma_E\left(\theta, \sigma(\Gamma_E(\theta, F))\right)\right) \tag{16}$$

Descending the elements of C_i yields $C_i = [c_i, c_{i-1}, ..., c_0]$. We then compute the confident weights γ_i for each structural subgraph,

$$\gamma_i = e^{\alpha(\beta \log c_i + (1-\beta) \log(c_i - c_{i-1}))} \tag{17}$$

where α and β are parameters, c_i and c_{i-1} denote the maximum and submaximum of the confidence value, respectively.

Next, the final confidence coefficient ω_i is obtained through normalization:

$$\omega_1 = \frac{\gamma_1}{\sum_{i=1}^i \gamma_i}, \omega_2 = \frac{\gamma_2}{\sum_{i=1}^i \gamma_i} \tag{18}$$

Finally, we fuse the feature structural subgraph S_f and the topology structural subgraph S_t to yield the final graph structure S,

$$S = \omega_1 \cdot S_f + \omega_2 \cdot S_t \tag{19}$$

The final representation H can be learned by using the encoder f_G,

$$H = f_G(F, S) \tag{20}$$

where the encoder f_G is encoded by using a two layers GCN.

To achieve the optimization of this model, we aim to minimize the cross-entropy loss $\mathcal{L}$, which is formulated as:

$$\mathcal{L} = \sum l(h, Y^i) = - \sum_{v_i \in V^i} \sum Y^i \log(h) \tag{21}$$

where h denotes the predicted probability vector, $v_i \in V^i$ denotes the labeled node, V^i is the set of labeled nodes, and $l(h, Y^i)$ is the cross-entropy function used.

4   Experiments

To assess the effectiveness of the proposed model, we select three heterogeneous graph datasets for extensive experiments and evaluate the results objectively and fairly.

4.1   Datasets and Baseline

We use three real-world datasets: ACM, DBLP, and YELP, to evaluate the proposed framework HGSL-FTIE. For comparison, we select eight typical HGNN models, including both traditional HGNNs and advanced HGSL: **HAN** [14] (2019), **GTN** [15] (2019), **MAGNN** [13] (2020), **HGT** [16] (2020), **HGSL** [12] (2021), **ROHE** [17] (2022), **HPN** [18] (2023), **ie-HGCN** [19] (2023). In the subsequent subsections, we compare the results of these models with our own to evaluate the performance of HGSL-FTIE.

4.2   Node Classification

To complete node classification, we classify the nodes by using a linear Support Vector Machine (SVM) classifier. We divide the test set and select different proportions of the node numbers for training. The evaluation metrics employed are Micro-F1 and Macro-F1. The experimental results are shown in Table 1, with the best results highlighted in bold and the second-best results underlined.

Table 1. Experimental results(%) on node classification

Dataset	Metrics	Ratio	HAN	MAGNN	HGT	ROHE	HPN	ie-HGCN	GTN	HGSL	OURS
ACM	Macro-F1	40%	91.33	91.39	91.68	92.01	92.27	92.14	91.36	92.58	**93.77**
		60%	91.73	92.18	91.81	92.34	92.52	92.59	91.74	92.73	**93.8**
		80%	91.91	92.67	91.82	92.5	92.52	92.79	91.81	92.83	**93.87**
	Micro-F1	60%	91.22	91.38	91.79	91.94	92.16	92.11	91.24	92.54	**93.61**
		40%	91.6	92.13	91.91	92.25	92.39	92.53	91.61	92.69	**93.65**
		80%	91.76	92.61	91.9	92.38	92.38	92.73	91.7	92.77	**93.71**
DBLP	Macro-F1	40%	92.87	93.83	88.98	91.81	92.88	93.57	94.06	93.65	**94.69**
		60%	93.05	93.81	89.22	91.96	92.99	93.66	94.15	93.81	**94.74**
		80%	93.16	94.1	89.37	92.28	93.16	94.09	94.26	94.09	**95.1**
	Micro-F1	40%	93.43	94.26	89.99	92.33	93.43	94	94.53	94.09	**95.06**
		60%	93.61	94.25	90.25	92.48	93.55	94.1	94.64	94.23	**95.13**
		80%	93.69	94.51	90.4	92.74	93.69	94.47	94.7	94.52	**95.43**
YELP	Macro-F1	40%	91.14	91.98	89.17	89.83	92.74	91.07	93.38	93.33	**93.91**
		60%	91.59	92.62	89.66	90.67	93.14	91.32	93.62	93.5	**94.08**
		80%	91.75	92.64	89.32	91.01	93.19	91.26	93.45	93.58	**94.2**
	Micro-F1	40%	90.04	90.74	89.64	89.36	92.15	90.1	92.89	92.48	**93.15**
		60%	90.48	91.45	90.04	90.26	92.51	90.33	93.14	92.64	**93.34**
		80%	90.57	91.54	90.01	90.56	92.53	90.27	93.01	92.76	**93.45**

It can be observed from the results that HGSL-FTIE surpasses the subopti- mal algorithm HGSL, with a 10.4% increase in Macro-F1 and a 9.4% increase in Micro-F1 on the ACM dataset. This result fully demonstrates the effectiveness of HGSL-FTIE and highlights its superiority in feature and topology process- ing. On the DBLP dataset, HGSL-FTIE shows 8.4% improvement on Macro-F1 and 7.3% improvement on Micro-F1 over the suboptimal algorithm GTN. This result further validates that the optimized graph structure obtained through our method is of higher quality compared to previous algorithms, proving the effec- tiveness of the n-hop meta-path extraction strategy. On the YELP dataset, our model shows 6.2% improvement over the suboptimal algorithm GTN on Macro- F1 and 4.4% improvement over the suboptimal algorithm HGSL on Micro-F1. This result further proves that our proposed HGSL-FTIE is superior compared to other methods. In summary, HGSL-FTIE outperforms the other eight algorithms, proving its effectiveness.

4.3   Clustering

We perform the clustering experiment to compare the performance of HGSL-FTIE on the clustering task. The experiment employs the K-Means algorithm and assess the results using NMI and ARI metrics. The node clustering results are presented in Table 2.

Table 2. Experimental results(%) on clustering

Datasets	Metrics	HAN	MAGNN	HGT	ROHE	HPN	ie-HGCN	GTN	HGSL	OURS
ACM	NMI	71.25	70.16	64.09	67.56	_71.85_	49.47	63.59	70.25	**76.88**
	ARI	75.15	72.14	66.46	69.79	_75.98_	34.89	68.72	74.25	**80.88**
DBLP	NMI	72.78	78.67	66.28	61.19	_79.06_	32.33	74.13	78.53	**79.67**
	ARI	78.33	84.00	65.43	67.67	**84.79**	27.21	76.07	83.62	_84.66_
YELP	NMI	39.98	47.34	53.02	53.35	32.11	17.85	49.70	_56.89_	**64.96**
	ARI	44.63	38.23	_59.81_	47.54	21.28	6.39	46.19	56.67	**67.07**

It can be seen from Table 2, that on the ACM dataset, HGSL-FTIE achieves optimal results, with a 5.03% and 4.9% improvement over HPN on NMI and ARI, respectively. The improvement of our model's performance on the DBLP dataset is not significant enough as compared to the other two datasets, with an improvement of 0.61% on NMI and slight decrease of 0.13% on ARI compared to the suboptimal algorithm. On the YELP dataset, HGSL-FTIE achieves a remarkable performance increase with NMI rising by 8.07% and ARI improving by 7.26% compared to the HGSL. Overall, these results further validate the effectiveness of HGSL-FTIE. The clustering experiment underscores that our proposed model achieves efficient heterogeneous graph structure learning, outperforming other models in key metrics.

4.4   Ablation Study

To evaluate the contribution of each module to comprehensive performance of HGSL-FTIE, we conduct an ablation study. We designed three variants, and the results of this study are shown in Fig. 3. The specific definitions of three variants are detailed below:

- **w/o-Feat:** Eliminates the feature structural subgraph learning.
- **w/o-Topo:** Eliminates the topology structural subgraph learning.
- **w/o-Fusion:** Eliminates the MCF strategy and adopts average fusion.

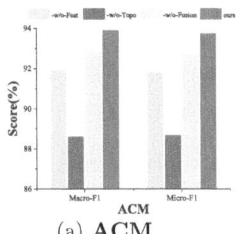
(a) **ACM**

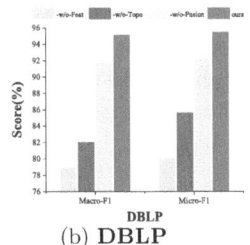
(b) **DBLP**

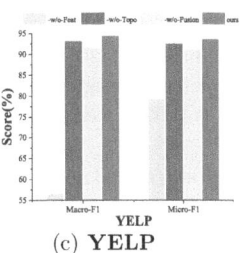
(c) **YELP**

Fig. 3. Ablation study.

As shown in the results, the overall performance of the three variants decreases across all datasets when the corresponding modules are removed. In contrast, the overall model (ours) consistently achieves the highest performance. On the ACM and DBLP datasets, the variant without topology structural subgraph learning experiences a significant decrease in performance compared to the overall model (ours), indicating that topology information significantly influences the final heterogeneous graph structure. On the DBLP and YELP datasets, the variant without feature structural subgraph learning also shows a marked decrease in performance compared to the overall model (ours), suggesting that the method of constructing feature structural subgraph through feature reconstruction is effective. These results prove that the information contained in both the feature and topology is essential for the final learned heterogeneous graph structure. Additionally, we observe that the performance of the three variants declines after removing the MCF strategy, indicating that the simple average aggregation method does not effectively leverage the contributions of the two structural subgraphs to the final graph structure and may negatively impact the model's overall performance.

5   Conclusion

In this paper, we propose a novel framework named HGSL-FTIE for heterogeneous graph structure learning. **To address the first challenge**, we propose an n-hop meta-path extraction strategy, which aims to extract meta-paths of different lengths. We then integrate node features, as well as local and global structural information of the heterogeneous graph, and use the mean aggregation method to aggregate the multi-order neighborhood information based on n-hop meta-paths. **To address the second challenge**, we fully consider the potential relationship between node features and topology, mining the rich information contained within to enhance the graph structure. We construct feature structural subgraph and topology structural subgraph, respectively. To further improve the effectiveness of structural subgraph fusion, we design the MCF strategy, which predictively encodes the input structural subgraphs and calculates the confidence value of each. Finally, we use the confidence value to guide the fusion of structural subgraphs and obtain the final graph structure.

Acknowledgments. The Natural Science Foundation of Shandong Province (Grant No. ZR2022MF268, ZR2021QG038), and the Open Research Fund Program of Key Laboratory of Agricultural Blockchain Application, Ministry of Agriculture and Rural Affairs (2022KLABA03).

Disclosure of Interests. The authors declare that there is no competing interests.

References

1. Li, Z., et al.: GSLB: the graph structure learning benchmark. In: Advances in Neural Information Processing Systems, vol. 36 (2024)
2. Yang, L.: Location-aware graph neural network supported session recommendation algorithm for e-commerce. In: The 2023 5th International Conference on Applied Machine Learning (ICAML), pp. 254–259 (2023)
3. Liu, X., Tang, Z., Li, P., Fan, X., Zhang, J.: A graph learning based approach for identity inference in DApp platform blockchain. IEEE Trans. Emerg. Top. Comput. **10**(1), 438–449 (2020)
4. Li, Z., Chen, D., Liu, Q., Wu, S.: The devil is in the conflict: disentangled information graph neural networks for fraud detection. In: 2022 IEEE International Conference on Data Mining, pp. 1059–1064 (2022)
5. Zhou, Z., et al.: OpenGSL: a comprehensive benchmark for graph structure learning. In: Advances in Neural Information Processing Systems, vol. 36 (2024)
6. Yu, D., Zhang, R., Jiang, Z., Wu, Y., Yang, Y.: Graph-revised convolutional network. In: Hutter, F., Kersting, K., Lijffijt, J., Valera, I. (eds.) ECML PKDD 2020. LNCS (LNAI), vol. 12459, pp. 378–393. Springer, Cham (2021). https://doi.org/10.1007/978-3-030-67664-3_23
7. Chen, Y., Wu, L., Zaki, M.: Iterative deep graph learning for graph neural networks: better and robust node embeddings. In: Advances in Neural Information Processing Systems, vol. 33, pp. 19314–19326 (2020)
8. Wang, R., et al.: Graph structure estimation neural networks. In: Proceedings of the Web Conference 2021, pp. 342–353 (2021)
9. Zhang, C., Song, D., Huang, C., Swami, A., Chawla, N.V.: Heterogeneous graph neural network. In: Proceedings of the 25th ACM SIGKDD International Conference on Knowledge Discovery & Data Mining, pp. 793–803 (2019)
10. Gilmer, J., Schoenholz, S.S., Riley, P.F., Vinyals, O., Dahl, G.E.: Neural message passing for quantum chemistry. In: International Conference Machine Learning, pp. 1263–1272 (2017)
11. Yang, X., Yan, M., Pan, S., Ye, X., Fan, D.: Simple and efficient heterogeneous graph neural network. In: Proceedings of the AAAI Conference on Artificial Intelligence, pp. 10816–10824 (2023)
12. Zhao, J., Wang, X., Shi, C., Hu, B., Song, G., Ye, Y.: Heterogeneous graph structure learning for graph neural networks. In: Proceedings of the AAAI Conference on Artificial Intelligence, pp. 4697–4705 (2020)
13. Fu, X., Zhang, J., Meng, Z., King, I.: MAGNN: metapath aggregated graph neural network for heterogeneous graph embedding. In: Proceedings of the Web Conference 2020, pp. 2331–2341 (2020)
14. Wang, X., et al.: Heterogeneous graph attention network. In: The World Wide Web Conference, pp. 2022–2032 (2019)

15. Yun, S., Jeong, M., Kim, R., Kang, J., Kim, H.J.: Graph transformer networks. In: Advances in Neural Information Processing Systems, vol. 32 (2019)
16. Hu, Z., Dong, Y., Wang, K., Sun, Y.: Heterogeneous graph transformer. In: Proceedings of the Web Conference 2020, pp. 2704–2710 (2020)
17. Zhang, M., Wang, X., Zhu, M., Shi, C., Zhang, Z., Zhou, J.: Robust heterogeneous graph neural networks against adversarial attacks. In: Proceedings of the AAAI Conference on Artificial Intelligence, pp. 4363–4370 (2022)
18. Ji, H., Wang, X., Shi, C., Wang, B., Philip, S.Y.: Heterogeneous graph propagation network. IEEE Trans. Knowl. Data Eng. **35**(01), 521–532 (2023)
19. Yang, Y., Guan, Z., Li, J., Zhao, W., Cui, J., Wang, Q.: Interpretable and efficient heterogeneous graph convolutional network. IEEE Trans. Knowl. Data Eng. **35**(02), 1637–1650 (2023)

A Blockchain-Based Traceable and Verifiable Digital Circuit Trade Method with Dual-Signature Strategy

Wei Wang[1,2], Zhenping Xie[1,2(✉)], and Yuan Liu[1,2]

[1] School of Artificial Intelligence and Computer Science, Jiangnan University,
Wuxi 214122, China
`xiezp@jiangnan.edu.cn`
[2] Jiangsu Key University Laboratory of Software and Media Technology under
Human-Computer Cooperation, Jiangnan University, Wuxi 214122, China

Abstract. In the integrated circuit (IC) industry, due to the inadequate protection mechanisms for IP cores, the design achievements of engineers are difficult to effectively safeguard, leading to a large number of excellent IP cores unable to legally circulate among designers. To alleviate these troubles, we propose a blockchain-based trade method. First, we design unique chain structures for storing and verifying IP core ownership and transaction contracts to reduce the misuse of intellectual property circuits. Then, we also design smart contract algorithms to automates the generation and verification process of digital identities and contract subscriptions. Additionally, we propose a dual-signature strategy to ensure the non-repudiation of contract signatures. Finally, we implement a prototype system and conduct security analysis. Experimental results demonstrate that the model can effectively resist several attacks and has good performance.

Keywords: Blockchain and smart contract · IP core trade · privacy protection

1 Introduction

The establishment of intellectual property protection mechanisms is increasingly important, especially in the face of many challenges, such as the instantaneous nature of digital goods and the ease of cross-border reproduction. The globalization of semiconductors has exacerbated the difficulty of ensuring the authenticity of IC and a reliable supply chain, allowing malicious actors to counterfeit, tamper with, or repackage IC to introduce them into the supply chain. Many semiconductor sales involve counterfeit products [3]. Most counterfeit electronic components enter the market through recycling [4].

In current supply chain management and product lifecycle management, the only feasible method to ensure data and transaction transparency is to adopt a centralized system managed by third parties. The primary task of third-party

© The Author(s), under exclusive license to Springer Nature Singapore Pte Ltd. 2025
G. Zhao et al. (Eds.): BWTAC 2024, CCIS 2277, pp. 350–361, 2025.
https://doi.org/10.1007/978-981-97-9412-6_32

management is to create a centralized data storage to facilitate the flow of trustworthy information. However, relying on third parties or a small group of collaborators to manage data storage also poses certain risks. These risks include inherent biases, fraud, and single points of failure in the system. Biases and fraud can lead to inaccurate and distorted data, thereby affecting decision-making. Meanwhile, a single point of failure can result in the entire system crashing, significantly impacting supply chain management and product lifecycle management. Therefore, we need to seek a more robust method to achieve integrated circuit traceability.

Blockchain is a distributed ledger technology first proposed in [10] and applied in Bitcoin. The ledger records are maintained by nodes across the network and propagate through the blockchain network in a peer-to-peer manner. Consensus nodes will sort and package a certain number of records to create a block. Subsequently, these blocks are added to the end of the blockchain based on the consensus algorithm. Blockchain also combines cryptography algorithms, distributed storage, and other technologies to make data stored on the blockchain easy to trace and difficult to tamper with [15, 17]. The concept of smart contracts was first proposed by N. Szabo [13] and later implemented and incorporated into the blockchain technology ecosystem by Ethereum [1]. Smart contracts can automatically and autonomously implement more business functions through predefined scripts, without human intervention. Since then, blockchain has been applied more widely. Blockchain provides security, anonymity, and data integrity without any third-party organization controlling transactions. The key to achieving this goal is the ability to achieve distributed consensus among multiple nodes in a trust-less environment by consensus algorithms [2, 6, 7].

In this paper, we propose a new method that utilizes blockchain to achieve IP core privacy protection and credible trade system. Leveraging the tamper-resistant nature of blockchain, we register digital IP information and trade details on the chain, facilitating transaction verification and copyright tracing. Combining the high-performance storage advantages of off-chain file systems, we persist file data off-chain. Meanwhile, we design smart contracts to automate the copyright registration and trade processes. Combining encryption algorithms and the elliptic curve digital signature algorithm (ECDSA), we ensure data security during transmission.

In conclusion, our contributions can be summarized as follows.

- A copyright chain and an IP trade tracking chain are designed to store and trace IP core ownership and trade records. Our method also provides two smart contracts that automate the processes of digital identity registration and contract signing.
- We design a dual-signature strategy based on the digital signature for the signing process of smart subscription contracts and provide hash digest verification to ensure contract non-repudiation and protect transaction privacy.
- Our method can resist several attacks, and the security and performance is evaluated.

2   Related Work

In the field of copyright management, Natgunanathan et al. [11] proposed a privacy protection mechanism to ensure the proper functioning of each entity in the distribution network by combining blockchain and watermarking technology for the copyright protection problem in multimedia protection distribution. An IP identity management scheme based on blockchain is proposed for privacy protection and traceability [16], achieving secure and traceable identity management and authentication of intellectual property. However, these papers did not discuss in detail the process of copyright trading, making it impossible to uncover the true value of digital objects.

In terms of digital copyright trade, an image transaction system using decentralized blockchain technology is implemented [12], which uses the InterPlanetary File System (IPFS) to realize the distributed storage of the images. Liang et al. [9] proposed a homomorphic encryption-based blockchain for circuit copyright protection, which effectively solves the problems of low security of private data, low efficiency of transaction data storage, collaboration and supervision in circuit copyright transaction protection.

In summary, contributions made by these papers demonstrate the value and practicality of blockchain technology in digital copyright protection and transactions. Blockchain has the characteristics of decentralization, not easy to be tampered with, good scalability, and flexibility, which is suitable for the requirements of copyright protection of digital integrated circuits [5]. But currently there is no complete solution for protecting and trading IP core digital objects. This thesis provides a feasible and novel approach.

3   Our Proposed Method

3.1   Attacker Model

In our proposed approach, the attacker is capable of carrying out man-in-the-middle (MiTM) attacks, single point of failure attacks, replay attacks. Additionally, the attacker may be a misbehaving participant, can obtain illicit gains.

- MiTM attacks. The attacker attempts to insert himself as an intermediary between the two communicating parties in order to steal, tamper with, or interfere with the communication data stream.
- Single point of failure attacks. Any single component of the system can be subject to mistakes or malicious attacks.
- Replay attacks. The attacker sends a packet that has already been received by the destination host to spoof the system.

3.2   Overview

As shown in Fig. 1, the proposed system mainly consists of designers, IPFS, the blockchain system, customers, the subscription module, and virtual machine. A brief description of entities is given below.

- *Designer:* The designer is the owner of the copyright of IP cores. The designer is able to obtain a copyright identifier (CID) as proof of ownership through the blockchain system.
- *IPFS:* This is a file system for off-chain storage to address the poor performance of blockchain storage of big data. IPFS is based on content addressing, which chunks files and links them by a calculated hash address. The root hash value will be published to the blockchain network along with the IP core copyright information.
- *Blockchain system:* Since data stored in a blockchain is difficult to tamper and forge, it is possible to permanently record the ownership of IP cores and transaction records. In addition, the blockchain provides traceability attributes through which it is possible to track copyright owner information and also verify the authenticity of the transaction.
- *Customer:* The customer can initiate a subscription request for IP cores. After the transaction is completed, the customer needs to check CID and verify the transaction information by blockchain, and finally obtain the IP core virtual usage environment.
- *Subscription module:* This is a module that uses encryption algorithms to ensure the trustworthy generation of transaction orders. It can ensure the privacy of subscription contracts and provide verification of transactions by the blockchain system.
- *Virtual machine:* This is a workspace used to provide isolation for IP core verification and design. IP core data will be pulled into a virtual machine environment and an open usage interface will be provided to customers.

The overall architecture of the proposed IP core trade system divides into four phases. The first phase is the registration of digital identity of designers and customers where each user has a unique digital identity. The second phase is the upload and copyright generation of digital IP circuit where each IP core has a CID and guarantee traceability of copyrights. Subscription contract signing is the third phase of the proposed system where the blockchain nodes uses ECDSA to execute a dual-signature strategy to guarantee the privacy and credibility of the subscription contract. Signed and approved subscription contracts can not

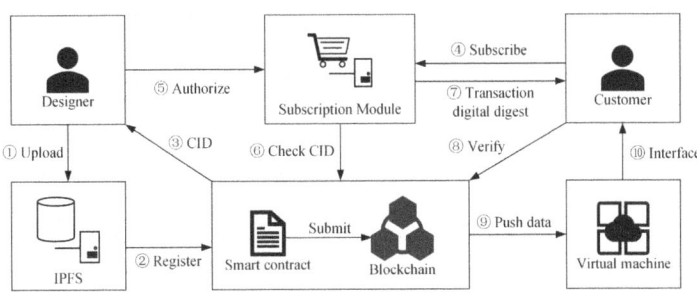

Fig. 1. Systematic architecture of proposed method

Table 1. Summary of notations

Symbol	Description
ID_i^{De}	The id of i-th designer
ID_j^{Cu}	The id of j-th customer
$Token_k$	The unique identity token for k-th designer or customer
FI_i	The file of i-th IP core
H_i^{addr}	The hash value of the storage address of i-th IP core
S_i	The size of file of i-th IP core
V_i	The version of i-th IP core
DL_i	A list of descriptions of i-th IP core
CID_i	A copyright identifier of i-th IP core
TS	Timestamp of current time
$F_{hash}()$	A secure hash algorithm
PU_k	ECDSA public key for k-th designer or customer
PR_k	ECDSA private key for k-th designer or customer
$F_{en}()$	ECDSA encryption function
$F_{de}()$	ECDSA decryption function
DD_m	The digital digest of m-th transaction
STA_m	The status of m-th transaction
K_m^{aes}	A key of AES algorithm for m-th transaction

be denied. In the fourth phase, the system can verify contracts and CID, and then push data after encryption to virtual machines for customers. The detail description of all these phase are given in following sections. All the used symbols and their meaning are shown in Table 1.

3.3   Digital Identity Registration Phase

In this phase, we design a workflow for digital identity registration to ensure a secure mutual authentication mechanism in the decentralized system architecture. The designer i can register as legitimate participants in digital circuit trade system by function *Register* in Algorithm 1, which needs to send personal basic information (PBI) to the blockchain network. After receiving identity information, blockchain miner nodes generate random ID_i^{De} by using UUID that can guarantee the uniqueness of generated random identifier in distributed systems. Then, select a hash encryption algorithm type Typ_i, and compute a unique identity token $Token_i = F_{hash}(PBI \parallel Typ_i)$. Next, publish $(ID_i^{De}, Token_i, TS)$ to the peer to peer network, and other miner nodes verify $(ID_i^{De}, Token_i, TS)$ by the consensus mechanism. Finally, $(ID_i^{De}, Token_i, TS)$ is written into a new block and linked to the tail of blockchain. The blockchain system returns $Token_i$ to the designer. When trying to enter the system next time, the designer can carry $Token_i$ to pass the blockchain's identity verification. The process of digital identity registration of customers is the same as the designer's.

Algorithm 1. Smart digital identity generation contract

1: **function** REGISTER(PBI)
2:      $ID_i^{De} \leftarrow$ generate random number using UUID
3:      $Typ_i \leftarrow$ select a hash encryption algorithm type
4:      $Token_i \leftarrow F_{hash}(PBI \parallel Typ_i)$
5:      $data \leftarrow$ package $(ID_i^{De}, Token_i, TS)$
6:      Publish $data$ to the blockchain network
7:      Miner nodes in blockchain vote for the validity of $data$
8:      **if** the number of votes $>$ half of total number of nodes **then**
9:          Create a new block that contains a Merkle tree which loads $data$
10:         Link the new block to the tail of blockchain
11:         **return** $Token_i$
12:     **else**
13:         **return** Null
14:     **end if**
15: **end function**

3.4 Copyright Generation Phase

In this phase, we primarily design the IP core information entry process to ensure the secure and reliable upload of IP core files and the registration of metadata, while providing automated digital IP generation for enduring copyright protection. First of all, the designer whose id is ID_k^{De} uploads the IP core file FI_x and its metadata (V_x, DL_x), and carries $Token_k$ to verify identity. First the system check $Token_k$ and count the size of FI_x to obtain S_x. Then, FI_x is deposited into the off-chain IPFS (a file system based on content hash indexing) and FI_x is split into multiple data blocks and each block is not exceeding 256 KB. The data blocks are managed by the Merkle DAG data structure in IPFS. IPFS sends H_x^{addr} of FI_x to the blockchain system for copyright registration. The blockchain miner node generates timestamp TS and generate CID_x. When multiple designers claim ownership of copyright CID_x, the decision can be made by TS, which means that the designer who registered the copyright first is determined to be the owner of the IP core. This is based on the immutable nature of blockchain data.

$$CID_x = F_{hash}(ID_k^{De} \parallel V_x \parallel S_x \parallel DL_x \parallel H_x^{addr} \parallel TS) \qquad (1)$$

Next, the miner nodes in blockchain write the copyright data into blockchain. We design a copyright chain used for storing and tracking copyright and the structure of the chain is shown in Table 2.

3.5 Subscription Contract Signing Phase

In this phase, we introduce a dual-signature strategy and primarily design the IP core transaction process between the customer n and the designer m to ensure privacy and security, automate contract generation, and guarantee contract trustworthiness. This subscription contract processing flow is mainly

Table 2. Structure of the copyright chain

Attribute	Definition
CID_x	Copyright unique identifier of x-th IP core
V_x	The version of x-th IP core
ID_k^{De}	Id of the k-th designer and owns CID_x
H_x^{addr}	The hash of storage address of x-th IP core
S_x	The file size of x-th IP core
TS	Timestamp of creating the copyright CID_x
DL_x	The list of descriptions of x-th IP core

implemented by the smart subscription contract (see Algorithm 2). As shown in Table 3, we also design a IP trade tracking chain.

Algorithm 2. Smart subscription contract

1: **function** SUBSCRIBE($ID_m^{De}, ID_n^{Cu}, CID_x, V_x, STA_j$)
2:     **if** $STA_j = Approved$ **then**
3:         Authenticate digital identity ($ID_m^{De}, Token_m$) and ($ID_n^{Cu}, Token_n$)
4:         Query H_x^{addr} according to CID_x, V_x and Get FI_x from IPFS
5:         Compute the size of FI_x to output S_x'
6:         **if** $S_x = S_x'$ **then**
7:             Randomly generate K_j^{aes} and TS for current transaction
8:             $DF_j \leftarrow F_{hash}(K_j^{aes} \parallel CID_x \parallel V_x \parallel ID_m^{De} \parallel ID_n^{Cu} \parallel H_x^{addr})$
9:             Generate (PU_n, PR_n) for customer n and (PU_m, PR_m) for designer m
10:             $DD_j \leftarrow F_{en}(PR_m, F_{en}(PR_n, DF_j))$
11:             $STA_j \leftarrow Signed$
12:             Submit ($DD_j \parallel data \parallel STA_j \parallel TS$) and DF_j to IP trade tracking chain
13:             return DD_j to the customer
14:         **else**
15:             return failure
16:         **end if**
17:     **else**
18:         return failure
19:     **end if**
20: **end function**

First, the transaction j should be approved by the designer and customer, that is, STA_j is *Approved*. Then, ($ID_m^{De}, Token_m$) and ($ID_n^{Cu}, Token_n$) need to be provided for identity authentication through the blockchain system. Next, the blockchain system checks the integrity of the IP core file with copyright CID_x, which is finished by calculating the file size. The system then generates a random AES key K_j^{aes} (AES is a symmetric encryption algorithm) that is set to 256 bits, and a timestamp TS of creating the transaction j.

To ensure credibility, we propose a dual-signature strategy using ECDSA for the generation of smart subscription contract. First, use $F_{hash}()$ to compute a

Table 3. Structure of the IP trade tracking chain

Attribute	Definition
DD_j	The digital digest of j-th transaction
K_j^{aes}	A key of AES algorithm for j-th transaction
CID_x	The copyright unique identifier of x-th IP core
V_x	The version of x-th IP core
ID_m^{De}	Id of the m-th designer and owns CID_x
ID_n^{Cu}	Id of the n-th customer and subscribes CID_x
H_x^{addr}	The hash of storage address of x-th IP core
TS	The timestamp of creating j-th transaction
STA_j	The status of j-th transaction

digital fingerprint DF_j and then separately use the customer's ECDSA private key PR_n and the designer's ECDSA private key PR_m to sign DF_j and obtain a digital digest DD_j. Finally, return DD_j to the customer.

$$DF_j = F_{hash}(K_j^{aes} \parallel CID_x \parallel V_x \parallel ID_m^{De} \parallel ID_n^{Cu} \parallel H_x^{addr}) \qquad (2)$$

$$DD_j = F_{en}(PR_m, F_{en}(PR_n, DF_j)) \qquad (3)$$

3.6 Delivery Phase

As shown in Fig. 2, we design a reliable workflow for IP core delivery after the subscription contract j is signed. First, the designer m sends $(PU_m, ID_m^{De}, Token_m)$ and the customer n sends $(DD_j, PU_n, ID_n^{Cu}, Token_n)$ and to the blockchain system to verify their digital identity. Then, the blockchain system check the validity of DD_j of the transaction j. The miner nodes separately use the customer's ECDSA public key PU_n and the designer's ECDSA public key PU_m to decrypt DD_j, and obtain DF_j^1.

$$DF_j^1 = F_{de}(PU_n, F_{de}(PU_m, DD_j)) \qquad (4)$$

Next, the miner nodes determine the validity of DD_j based on whether DF_j and DF_j^1 are the same, and they vote on the validation results. If the number of affirmative votes exceeds half of the total nodes, the subscription contract is validated. Next, the blockchain system get file data FI_j from IPFS according to H_x^{addr}. Before pushing FI_j to target virtual machine, the system should use the AES key of the current subscription transaction (K_m^{aes}) to encrypt FI_j. This process can guarantee the privacy security of the design's IP core data. Finally, the customer n use K_j^{aes} to decrypt FI_j. In addition, the ip address of the target virtual machine and the digital identity of the customer ($ID_n^{De}, Token_n$) must be verified again before decryption. The target virtual machine provide interfaces for the customer to work.

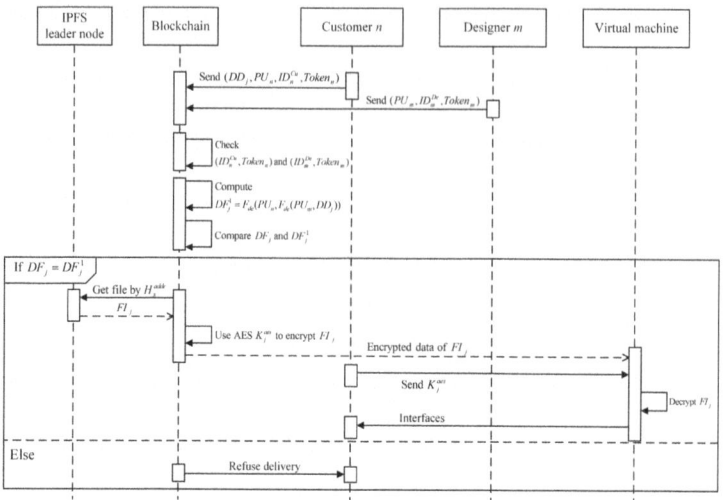

Fig. 2. Sequence diagram of delivery.

4   Analysis

4.1   Security Analysis

Our method can resist many common attacks which are analyzed as follows.

- MiTM attacks. The transaction DD_j is generated by $F_{hash}()$ and signed by using PR_n, PR_m and the ECDSA encryption function. Therefore, if the adversary intercepts DD_j from public channel, he cannot obtain or forge a valid message. Moreover, if an adversary c tries to publish fake ECDSA keys or DD_j, his digital identity $(ID_c^{De}, Token_c)$ should be successfully verified by at least half of miner nodes and his transactions are traced in blockchain. This is costly for the attacker c and impossible to realize.
- Single point of failure attacks. Our method uses blockchain that does not rely on a trusted third party (TTP). Any user can automatically complete transactions through smart contract algorithms without interference from a central authority.
- Replay attacks. Every contract or chain has a unique timestamp TS in our method. For example, $(DD_j \parallel data \parallel STA_j \parallel TS)$ is submitted to the IP trade tracking chain and $CID_x = F_{hash}(ID_k^{De} \parallel V_x \parallel S_x \parallel DL_x \parallel H_x^{addr} \parallel TS)$. If an attacker attempts to replay previously generated contracts, the recipient can easily detect the attack because the current time and a random number will not match the information.

4.2   Performance Analysis

We deploy our prototype system on virtual machines equipped with a 2-Core CPU, 2 GB memory, and 60 GB SCSI, running Ubuntu server. We use Hyperledger Fabric as the blockchain, and choose Golang as the programming language.

In our blockchain system, raft consensus algorithm applied. In raft, nodes reach consensus among themselves by voting for a leader which brings the advantages of low latency and high throughput. Our designed chain structures are applied in our blockchain system that improve the performance. As shown in Fig. 3, comparing to the works [5] and [9], our method significantly improves the throughput of the system. From the results in Fig. 3, one can see that as the number of transactions increases, the response latency time becomes sharply longer. But our approach exhibits shorter latency.

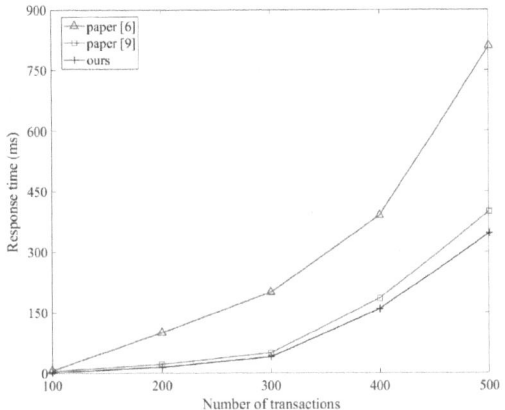

Fig. 3. Comparison of time overload.

As shown in Table 4, we compare our scheme with a number of relevant references on integrity verification of copyright, privacy protection, identity authentication, traceability, transaction non-repudiation and the time complexity of algorithms. The results demonstrate the advantages of our method.

Table 4. Comparison of related blockchain-based methods

Works	Integrity verification	Identity authentication	privacy protection	Traceability Traceability	Transaction non-repudiation	Time complexity
[5]	×	×	×	✓	×	$O(log2n)$
[9]	×	✓	✓	✓	×	$O(n)$
Ours	✓	✓	✓	✓	✓	$O(n)$

Compared to RSA-based scheme [14], our proposed dual-signature strategy inherits the advantages of short key and high performance of digital signature

Table 5. Comparable key sizes (bits)

Symmetric	Our ECDSA-based scheme	RSA-based scheme [14]
80	163	1024
112	233	2240
128	283	3072
192	409	7680
256	571	15360

algorithm. As shown in Table 5, we design different sizes of key used for comparison testing based on similar key strength, suggested from [8].

As shown in Fig. 4, we compare the time consumed for key generation and signature generation under different key strengths. The experimental data show that our ECDSA-based dual signature policy requires a much smaller key length to provide the same security as RSA-based scheme. This help reduce storage space, power consumption and processing power.

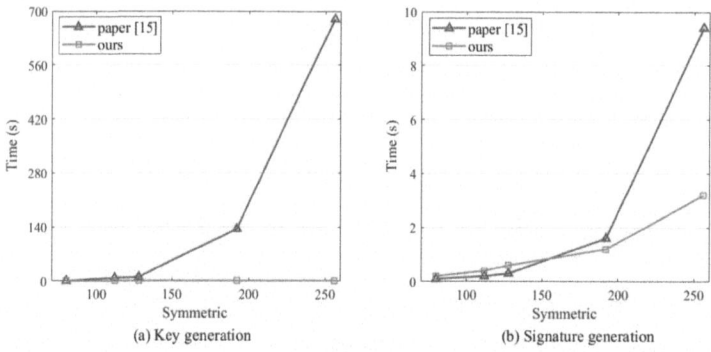

(a) Key generation   (b) Signature generation

Fig. 4. Comparison of key generation and signature generation.

5   Conclusion

In this paper, we propose a blockchain-based method for the protection and transaction of IP core digital objects, aiming to alleviate issues of trust, copyright infringement, and misuse in multi-party IP core transactions. In this method, the copyright of the IP core is automatically generated and is traceable and verifiable. Then, unique chain structures are designed to efficiently store trading records, and smart subscription contracts of IP cores are credibly generated. Additionally, a dual-signature strategy based on ECDSA ensures that the signed subscription contracts are not repudiated by participants. Finally, our method employs a decentralized architecture but does not rely on any TTP. In future research, we focus on the application of artificial intelligence in blockchain IP transactions.

References

1. Buterin, V., et al.: Ethereum white paper. GitHub repository **1**, 22–23 (2013)
2. Fahim, S., Rahman, S.K., Mahmood, S.: Blockchain: a comparative study of consensus algorithms PoW, PoS, PoA, PoV. Int. J. Math. Sci. Comput. **3**, 46–57 (2023)
3. Guin, U., Huang, K., DiMase, D., Carulli, J.M., Tehranipoor, M., Makris, Y.: Counterfeit integrated circuits: a rising threat in the global semiconductor supply chain. Proc. IEEE **102**(8), 1207–1228 (2014)
4. Islam, M.N., Kundu, S.: Modeling residual lifetime of an IC considering spatial and inter-temporal temperature variations. In: 2016 IEEE 25th Asian Test Symposium (ATS), pp. 240–245. IEEE (2016)
5. Islam, M.N., Patii, V.C., Kundu, S.: On IC traceability via blockchain. In: 2018 International Symposium on VLSI Design, Automation and Test (VLSI-DAT), pp. 1–4. IEEE (2018)
6. King, S., Nadal, S.: PPCoin: peer-to-peer crypto-currency with proof-of-stake (2012). Self-published paper
7. Larimer, D.: Delegated proof-of-stake (DPoS). Bitshare whitepaper **81**, 85 (2014)
8. Lenstra, A.K., Verheul, E.R.: Selecting cryptographic key sizes. J. Cryptol. **14**, 255–293 (2001)
9. Liang, W., Zhang, D., Lei, X., Tang, M., Li, K.C., Zomaya, A.Y.: Circuit copyright blockchain: blockchain-based homomorphic encryption for IP circuit protection. IEEE Trans. Emerg. Top. Comput. **9**(3), 1410–1420 (2020)
10. Nakamoto, S.: Bitcoin: a peer-to-peer electronic cash system (2008)
11. Natgunanathan, I., Praitheeshan, P., Gao, L., Xiang, Y., Pan, L.: Blockchain-based audio watermarking technique for multimedia copyright protection in distribution networks. ACM Trans. Multimed. Comput. Commun. Appl. (TOMM) **18**(3), 1–23 (2022)
12. Ning, J., Feng, L., Yuan, G., Yang, X.: Research on image trading system based on blockchain and IPFS. In: International Conference on Network Communication and Information Security (ICNCIS 2021), vol. 12175, pp. 51–58. SPIE (2022)
13. Szabo, N.: Smart contracts: building blocks for digital markets. EXTROPY J. Transhumanist Thought **18**(2), 28 (1996)
14. Ugochukwu, N.A., Goyal, S., Rajawat, A.S., Islam, S.M., He, J., Aslam, M.: An innovative blockchain-based secured logistics management architecture: utilizing an RSA asymmetric encryption method. Mathematics **10**(24), 4670 (2022)
15. Zheng, Z., Xie, S., Dai, H., Chen, X., Wang, H.: An overview of blockchain technology: architecture, consensus, and future trends. In: 2017 IEEE International Congress on Big Data (BigData Congress), pp. 557–564. IEEE (2017)
16. Zhuang, C., Dai, Q., Zhang, Y.: BCPPT: a blockchain-based privacy-preserving and traceability identity management scheme for intellectual property. Peer-to-Peer Netw. Appl. **15**(1), 724–738 (2022)
17. Zyskind, G., Nathan, O., et al.: Decentralizing privacy: using blockchain to protect personal data. In: 2015 IEEE Security and Privacy Workshops, pp. 180–184. IEEE (2015)

Personalized Medical Federated Learning Based on Mutual Knowledge Distillation in Object Heterogeneous Environment

Lina Ni[1,2], Chenglin Song[1], Hanmo Zhao[1], Yuncan Tang[1], Yunshen Ma[1], and Jinquan Zhang[1(✉)]

[1] College of Computer Science and Engineering, Shandong University of Science and Technology, Qingdao 266590, China
tjzhangjinquan@126.com
[2] Key Laboratory of the Ministry of Education for Embedded System and Service Computing, Tongji University, Shanghai 201804, China

Abstract. Federated Learning (FL), hailed as a potent approach in merging medical expertise, promises to elevate collaborative efforts among healthcare institutions while safeguarding the privacy and security of sensitive medical data, thereby energizing the trajectory of intelligent healthcare advancements. However, the diversity in training objectives across medical institutions can diminish their active participation in a unified federated training process. To address this issue of waning enthusiasm due to diverse training goals, in this paper, we propose Personalized Medical Federated Learning method based on Mutual Distillation Knowledge (pFedMKD). Specifically, we propose a similarity-based mutual distillation model selection algorithm that reduces interference among medical institutions with notably diverse data distributions. Moreover, we develop a server-side local model update method leveraging mutual knowledge distillation, enabling each local model to gain beneficial insights for personalization from analogous models. Additionally, we formulate a personalized model update method utilizing knowledge distillation from specifically labeled samples, thereby improving the performance of personalized models. Experimental results demonstrate that compared to the baseline algorithm, pFedMKD can more effectively address the target heterogeneity problem among different medical institutions, enabling each institution to achieve higher personalized performance in federated learning tasks.

Keywords: Federated learning · Heterogeneous Objectives · Mutual Knowledge Distillation · Personalized Federated Learning

1 Introduction

With the rapid advancement of intelligent healthcare, the volume of medical data has grown exponentially. This surge imposes considerable computational

G. Zhao et al. (Eds.): BWTAC 2024, CCIS 2277, pp. 362–374, 2025.
https://doi.org/10.1007/978-981-97-9412-6_33

burdens on traditional cloud data centers, resulting in unsustainable data transmission costs. Furthermore, in recent years, centralized processing of medical data has often compromised user privacy [1], intensifying concerns regarding the protection of medical data privacy. The escalating volume of medical data and the imperative for privacy protection present formidable challenges to the conventional centralized medical data processing model in data centers [2].

To effectively tackle these challenges, the concept of federated learning was introduced by McMahan *et al.* [3] from the Google team in 2016. Unlike traditional data centers that collect and process data centrally, each participant performs the model training tasks locally in federated learning [4]. The central server merely aggregates the parameters of the local models trained by participants without requiring access to the participants' raw data. As an innovative distributed machine learning approach, federated learning not only alleviates the burden on the central server to process massive amounts of data but also enhances user data privacy by keeping data localized, thereby preventing privacy breaches during data transmission [5]. Consequently, federated learning rapidly garnered significant attention from the research community upon its introduction.

Currently, most research on federated learning primarily focuses on the server's perspective, aiming to achieve a global model with robust generalization performance across all participating client datasets [6]. However, variations in medical fields, patient populations, medical equipment, and procedures across different healthcare institutions lead to significant differences in the medical data they collect. These variations consequently create divergent objectives for these institutions when engaging in federated learning [7].

To ensure that all clients derive benefits from federated learning and to enhance their participation enthusiasm, researchers are investigating personalized federated learning.

1) Personalized global model. Several researchers have explored personalized federated learning by adapting the global model. Wu *et al.* [11] developed a cloud-edge-based federated learning framework for home health monitoring called FedHome, which employs generative convolutional autoencoder models to facilitate personalized operations on locally enhanced, class-balanced datasets at each client.

2) Clustering. Several researchers have investigated personalized federated learning through clustering approaches. He *et al.* [12] introduced the FedGKT scheme, which employs alternating minimization and knowledge distillation to train edge models alongside a server model, thus achieving personalized local models.

3) Personalized Local Models. Some researchers have proposed federated learning schemes that train personalized models for each client to meet the different needs of various clients. Arivazhagan *et al.* [13] introduced a federated transfer learning scheme, FedPer, which segregates the local model into base layers and personalized layers. The base layers are collaboratively trained by all clients involved in federated training, while the personalized layers are updated locally in each client.

In summary, in exploring personalized federated learning within heterogeneous objectives environments, researchers have predominantly employed three strategies to cater to the personalized model requirements of clients: personalized global model, clustering, and training personalized models for clients. However, these approaches often overlook the interactions among various local models. Consequently, In this paper, we introduce a personalized medical federated learning scheme based on mutual knowledge distillation, which trains personalized models for each client. This scheme is initiated by training a distinct personalized model for each client and comprises two phases: mutual knowledge distillation among similar local models on the server side and knowledge distillation of specific labeled samples on the client side. This technique facilitates the transfer of essential knowledge from other clients' local models to the personalized models, which not only prevents the catastrophic forgetting of local knowledge during training but also minimizes the mutual interference among local models with substantial differences, thus fulfilling the personalized requirements of medical institutions.

The contributions of this paper are outlined as follows:

1. We designed a similarity-based mutual distillation model selection algorithm whereby the server computes the logits output of each local model to identify a set of -most similar models for each local model, forming a distillation model set and mitigating mutual interference among local models.
2. We introduced a server-side model updating algorithm based on mutual knowledge distillation, enabling each local model to acquire beneficial knowledge for personalization from other local models exhibiting high similarity. This fosters mutual cooperation among similar models and ensures the return of the locally updated models, post mutual knowledge distillation, to the respective medical institutions, thus preventing catastrophic forgetting during model training.
3. We investigated a personalized model update algorithm based on knowledge distillation of specific labeled samples. The personalized model employs generated specific labeled samples to learn knowledge from the local model distributed by the server through knowledge distillation. This approach not only diminishes the risk of overfitting but also substantially enhances the performance of the personalized model on specific tasks.

2   Personalized Medical Federated Learning Based on Mutual Knowledge Distillation

2.1   Algorithm Architecture

Before delving into the architecture of the personalized medical federated learning based on mutual knowledge distillation, it is essential to clarify the concepts of the local model and the personalized model.

Local Model (w_k)**:** The local model refers to the model that each medical institution trains locally and interacts with the server.

Personalized Model (v_k)**:** The personalized model is unique to each medical institution participating in federated training and performs better on local data. Unlike the local model, the personalized model is retained solely within the medical institution and does not interact with the server or other participants.

Personalized medical federated learning based on mutual knowledge distillation (pFedMKD) can be described from the perspectives of the server and the clients. In pFedMKD, the server primarily selects similar models from those uploaded by each medical institution and conducts mutual knowledge distillation. The server then sends the distilled models back to the respective clients. As clients, the medical institutions are responsible not only for training and uploading their local models but also for maintaining their personalized models.

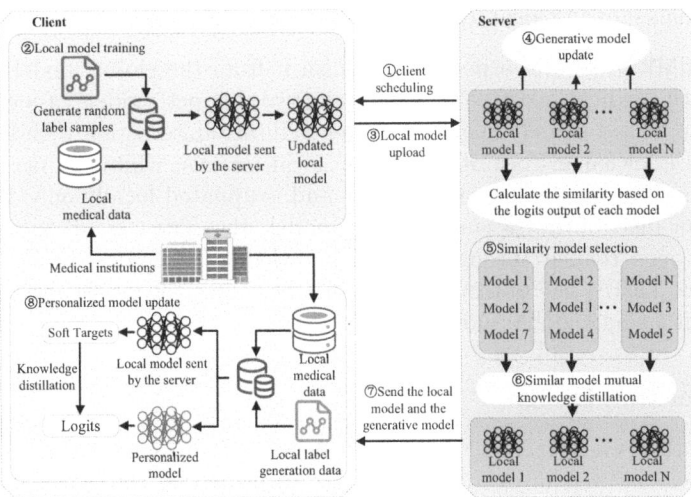

Fig. 1. Personalized medical federated learning based on mutual knowledge distillation (pFedMKD).

As shown in Fig. 1, pFedMKD mainly consists of eight steps.

1. Client Scheduling: The central server randomly selects some medical institutions to participate in the current training round.
2. Local Model Training: The medical institutions assigned to the scheduling task generate training samples using locally retained generative models and use these samples along with their local data for training and updating the local models.
3. Local Model Upload: After local training, the participating medical institutions upload their local models to the server.

4. Generative Model Update: The server aggregates the received local models using an aggregation algorithm and updates the generative models adversarially.

5. Similar Model Selection: The server calculates the similarity between local models based on the generated samples and selects a set of -most similar models for each local model.

6. Mutual Knowledge Distillation of Similar Models: The server conducts mutual knowledge distillation among the set of similar models using the generated samples, enabling each local model to acquire beneficial knowledge from similar models while retaining their local data privately.

7. Model Distribution: The server sends the updated local models and generative models back to the respective medical institutions.

8. Personalized Model Training: Upon receiving the models, the medical institutions use the generative models to produce specific labeled training samples for knowledge distillation. They then update their personalized models under the guidance of the local models to enhance performance.

In pFedMKD, several aspects distinguish it from the global model training. Firstly, each medical institution must train two distinct models: a local model and a personalized model. The local model facilitates interaction with the server and learns knowledge from other clients' local models, while the personalized model is used for local personalized tasks and is updated locally only. Secondly, rather than distributing a single global model, the server sends local models that have been refined through mutual knowledge distillation to the medical institutions. Lastly, the outcome of pFedMKD is a set of personalized models, rather than a single global model.

2.2   Algorithm Design

To ensure that every medical institution benefits from federated learning and achieves personalized objectives, pFedMKD utilizes two rounds of knowledge distillation to transfer essential knowledge from other local models to the personalized models.

On the server side: Through similar model selection and mutual knowledge distillation, each local model can learn beneficial knowledge for personalization from local models trained by medical institutions with similar data distributions.

On the client side: Through knowledge distillation using specific labeled samples, knowledge is transferred from the local models distributed by the server to the personalized models, enhancing the performance of the personalized models.

Server-Side Local Models Update Based on Mutual Knowledge Distillation. Deep learning models tend to favor labels with larger sample sizes because more samples provide more comprehensive information, allowing the model to capture the features of the data more accurately. Consequently, local models trained by different medical institutions exhibit unique characteristics; they may perform significantly better on specific labeled samples than other local models. This variability between models can significantly benefit the training of personalized models. Therefore, In this section, we employ mutual distillation to capitalize on this variability, enhancing the personalized performance of local models through mutual knowledge distillation among similar models.

1. **Similar models selection.**

   To enhance cooperation among medical institutions with similar data distributions and minimize interference from institutions with significantly different data distributions, In this section, we propose a similarity-based mutual distillation model selection algorithm (Fed-SDM). This algorithm selects the k-most similar models for each local model to undergo mutual knowledge distillation.

   First, we introduce the concept of cosine similarity to measure the similarity between local models.

Definition 1 (Cosine Similarity) [14]: Cosine similarity measures the similarity between two vectors by calculating the cosine of the angle between them. Let vector $A = [a_1, a_2, \cdots\cdots a_n]$ and vector $B = [b_1, b_2, \cdots\cdots b_n]$; then, the cosine similarity between A and B is defined as:

$$s(A, B) = \frac{\sum\limits_{i=1}^{n} a_i \times a_i}{\sqrt{\sum\limits_{i=1}^{n} (b_i)^2} \times \sqrt{\sum\limits_{i=1}^{n} (b_i)^2}}. \tag{1}$$

where a_i and b_i represent the respective components of vector A and B.

Since the generative model provides the server with IID (independent and identically distributed) training samples, we calculate the similarity by comparing the cosine similarity of the logits outputs between different models, that is, representing the similarity between local models with the similarity of knowledge. On one hand, using the logits outputs of local models to calculate similarity significantly reduces computational costs; on the other hand, compared to directly comparing model parameters, the logits outputs of a model are more indicative of the local model's data distribution. Let the input sample be x, and let the output of the local model w_i be $logits_i(x)$; then, the similarity between model w_i and model w_j as follows.

$$s(w_i, w_j) = \frac{logits_i(x) \times logits_j(x)}{\sqrt{(logits_i(x))^2} \times \sqrt{(logits_j(x))^2}}. \tag{2}$$

By calculating the similarity between the local models uploaded by various medical institutions, we can identify the k-most similar models to the local model w_i, thus forming the mutual distillation model set KD_i for w_i.

2. **Mutual knowledge distillation.**

   To effectively utilize the knowledge contained in local models trained by medical institutions with similar data distributions, In this section, we introduce pFed-MMKD, a server-side local models updating algorithm based on mutual knowledge distillation. The server conducts mutual knowledge distillation within each set of similar models, enabling the local models to learn beneficial personalized knowledge from each other, thereby enhancing personalized performance.

After obtaining the mutual distillation model set KD_i for each w_i, the server generates training samples again using the generative model and conducts mutual knowledge distillation within each mutual distillation model set. This process enables each local model to learn from similar models, acquiring knowledge that is beneficial for personalization. The update target for the models in the mutual distillation model set KD_i can be formulated as follows:

$$\underset{\{w_1, w_2 \cdots w_{|KD_i|}\}}{\arg \min} \sum_{k=1}^{|KD_i|} \lambda_k \mathcal{L}_{KL}(\sigma(\tilde{x}, w_i), \sigma(\tilde{x}, w_k)) + \mathcal{L}_{CE}(\sigma(\tilde{x}, w_i), y). \quad (3)$$

$$\lambda_k = \frac{1}{|KD_i| - 1}(1 - \frac{\exp(\mathcal{L}_{CE}(\sigma(\tilde{x}, w_k), y))}{\sum_{j \in KD_i,} \exp(\sum \mathcal{L}_{CE}(\sigma(\tilde{x}, w_j), y))}). \quad (4)$$

where $\tilde{x}$ represents the training samples generated by inputting random labels y into the generative model, $\sigma(\tilde{x}, w_k)$ is the logits output of the local model w_k, and λ_k is the weight of the knowledge provided by the local model w_k uploaded by each medical institution when it acts as a teacher model.

The schematic diagram of mutual knowledge distillation of similar models is shown in Fig. 2.

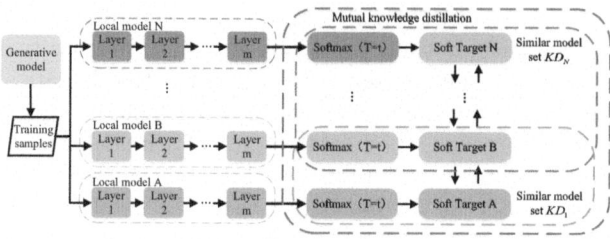

Fig. 2. Schematic diagram of the server model update based on knowledge mutual distillation.

Personalized Model Update Based on Knowledge Distillation of Specific Tag Samples. During the process of mutual knowledge distillation, each local model may inadvertently learn some knowledge that could potentially diminish its personalized performance. To mitigate the impact of such knowledge on personalized models, medical institutions update their personalized models through knowledge distillation, utilizing samples with specific labels. This approach enables personalized models to learn beneficial knowledge from the local models distributed by the server, thereby further enhancing the performance of personalized models on local medical data.

Overview of pFedMKD. The pFedMKD method completes the training of personalized models through two steps of knowledge distillation. The first step of knowledge distillation occurs server-side, where models are selected based on similarity for mutual distillation, and local models on the server are updated through mutual knowledge distillation. This process enables local models trained by medical institutions with similar data distributions to learn from each other and enrich their knowledge. The second step of knowledge distillation takes place locally, where specific labeled samples are utilized to deliberately learn the knowledge necessary for personalized models from the local models distributed by the server, thereby enhancing personalized performance. The overall pseudo-code for the pFedMKD method is presented as Algorithm 1.

Algorithm 1 : Personalized medical federated learning architecture based on mutual knowledge distillation (pFedMKD).

Input: Number of communication rounds T, number of local training iterations E, global model w, generative model w_G.

Output: Collection of personalized models $\left\{v_k^{T+1}\right\}$.

1: Initialize model parameters w, w_G
2: **for** epoch communication round $t = 12 \cdots T$ **do**
3:     $S_t \leftarrow$ The server randomly selects clients to participate in the current round of training with a sampling rate of q.
4:     **for** epoch client $k \in S$ in parallel **do**
5:         **for** epoch round $e = 1$ to E **do**
6:             Update the local model using local data and generated samples : $w_k^t \leftarrow w_k^{t-1}$
7:         **end for**
8:         Send w_k^t to server
9:     **end for**
10:    Generative model is updated adversarially against the aggregated model : $w_G^t \leftarrow w_G^{t-1}$
11:    Simiar models selection: $\{KD_i\}_{i=1}^{|S|} \leftarrow (\{w_i\}_{i\in|S|}, w_G^t, k)$
12:    Mutual Knowledge Distillation: $\{w_i\}_{i\in|S|} \leftarrow (\{w_i\}_{i\in|S|}, \{KD_i\}_{i=1}^{|S|})$
13:    Send $\{w_i\}_{i\in|S|}$, w_G to client U_i.
14:    **for** epoch client $k \in S$ in parallel **do**
15:        $\{v_k^t\} \leftarrow pFed - SLKD(w_G, \eta, E_p, D_k, v_k)$
16:    **end for**
17: **end for**
18: **return** $\left\{v_k^{T+1}\right\}$

---

3   Experiment and Analysis

3.1   Experimental Environment Configuration

Experimental Environment: Our experiment is based on the PyTorch deep learning framework in Python 3.8 for federated learning simulation. Select the colon pathology dataset and abdominal CT classification as the training tasks, and use convolutional neural networks (CNN) as the training model. We evaluated our model using two commonly used datasets for federated learning experiments, the PathMNIST dataset and the OrganMNIST (Axial) dataset.

Dataset Processing: Since personalized federated learning is predominantly applied in non-IID scenarios, this paper limits simulation experiments to conditions of data heterogeneity. To better simulate the heterogeneous objectives of clients, experiments are conducted under two types of data heterogeneity environments: (1) The dataset is partitioned using a Dirichlet distribution with parameter $\beta = 1$, where each client possesses training samples from various classes with significant differences in quantity. (2) The PathMNIST dataset, containing 9 classes, and the OrganMNIST dataset, containing 11 classes, are divided such that the training data for each class is evenly split into four parts and distributed among 18 and 22 clients, respectively. Each client randomly selects data from two of these classes as their local data. In both partitioning methods, 70% of each client's local data is designated as the training set, and 30% as the test set.

Baseline: To verify the effectiveness of the personalized model proposed in this paper, we compare it with three federated learning methods-FedAvg [3], FedRep [15], and APFL [16]—on two datasets using a single machine for simulation experiments.

3.2   Experimental Results and Analysis

Table 1 illustrates the average accuracy of personalized models for clients across two datasets using four distinct methods. Observations indicate that after 100 rounds of global iterations, the method proposed in this paper achieves the best performance under both data distribution scenarios. The average accuracy of the pFedMKD method improved by 3%–8% compared to the FedAvg method, and by approximately 1%–3% compared to the FedRep and APFL methods.

Table 1. Comparison of method performance under different data sets and data distribution.

Dataset	Data distribution	FedAvg	FedRep	APFL	pFedMKD
PathMNIST	Non-IID 1	73.14%	74.08%	74.64%	75.79%
	Non-IID 2	69.84%	76.59%	76.34%	77.61%
OrganMNIST	Non-IID 1	70.62%	72.97%	72.11%	73.39%
	Non-IID 2	71.54%	76.84%	75.93%	78.51%

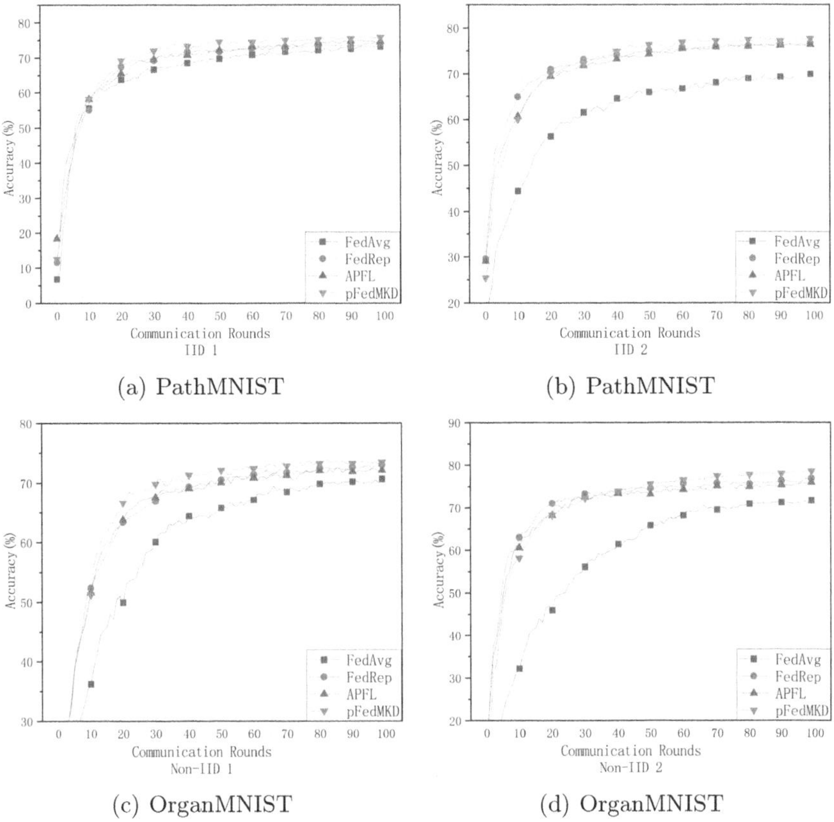

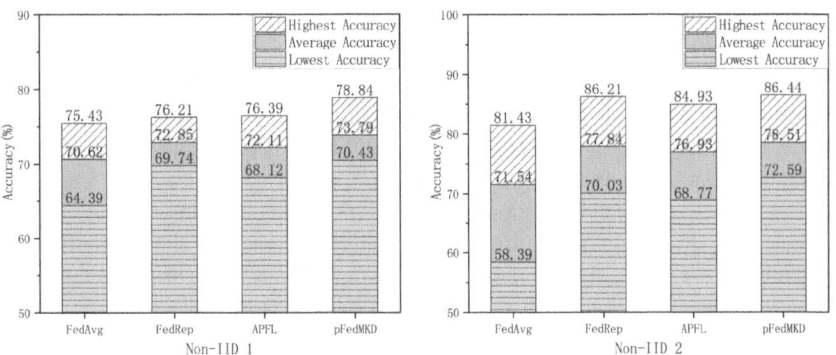

Fig. 3. Comparison of method performance under different data distributions.

Fig. 4. Schematic diagram of client highest lowest and average accuracy under different data distributions.

Figure 3 shows the changes in average accuracy of personalized models for the four methods over 100 rounds of training. Figure 3 indicates that the method proposed in this paper achieves the best model performance under both data distribution scenarios. By conducting knowledge distillation both at the server and at the clients, the personalized models trained with pFedMKD can assimilate global knowledge from other models while preserving the integrity of local models and minimizing the influence of irrelevant knowledge, thus enhancing the performance of personalized models.

Figure 4 shows the highest, average, and lowest accuracy of personalized models for all clients participating in federated training after 100 rounds of training on the OrganMNIST dataset using the four methods. It is evident that the FedAvg method results in significant variance in model performance across different clients under both data distribution scenarios. In the first data distribution scenario, the personalized models trained with the FedRep method exhibit the smallest performance difference. In the second data distribution scenario, the personalized models trained with the pFedMKD method proposed in this paper show the smallest performance difference.

In summary, with an appropriately chosen value of k, the pFedMKD method proposed in this paper achieves excellent personalized performance across various data distribution scenarios. The greater the differences in data distribution, the more substantial the improvement in personalized performance.

4   Conclusions

In this paper, we first briefly summarize the problem of heterogeneous objectives among medical institutions participating in federated learning, and propose a personalized medical federated learning method based on mutual knowledge distillation (pFedMKD). This method also employs a generative model trained at the server to generate training data for various medical institutions and the server itself. Initially, the server selects the k-most similar local models for each local model by computing the logits output from the local models uploaded by each medical institution. Subsequently, each local model undergoes mutual knowledge distillation with its set of similar models, facilitating mutual learning among similar models. After the mutual knowledge distillation is completed, the server sends the updated local models back to the corresponding medical institutions. Then, using the generative model to generate specific labeled samples, using knowledge distillation, knowledge from the local model is transferred to the personalized model, enhancing the performance of these models on local medical tasks. Finally, simulation experiments demonstrate that the pFedMKD algorithm effectively addresses the objective heterogeneity problem among medical institutions, allowing each institution to benefit from the federated learning task.

Acknowledgments. This work was supported in part by the National Science Foundation of Shandong Province under Grant ZR2022MF338, ZR2023LZH018, the Humanity and Social Science Fund of the Ministry of Education under Grant 20YJAZH078 and Grant 20YJAZH127, Open Project of Tongji University Embedded System and Service Computing of Ministry of Education of China under Grant ESSCKF2022-02.

Disclosure of Interests. The authors have no competing interests to declare that are relevant to the content of this article.

References

1. Sattler, F., Wiedemann, S., Müller, K.-R., Samek, W.: Robust and communication-efficient federated learning from non-IID data. IEEE Trans. Neural Netw. Learn. Syst. **31**(9), 3400–3413 (2019)
2. Ramani, R., Mary, A.R., Raja, S.E., Shunmugam, D.A.: Optimized data management and secured federated learning in the Internet of Medical Things (IoMT) with blockchain technology. Biomed. Sig. Process. Control **93**, 106213 (2024)
3. McMahan, B., Moore, E., Ramage, D., Hampson, S., y Arcas, B.A.: Communication-efficient learning of deep networks from decentralized data. In: Artificial Intelligence and Statistics. PMLR, pp. 1273–1282 (2017)
4. Tang, Y., Liang, Y., Liu, Y., Zhang, J., Ni, L., Qi, L.: Reliable federated learning based on dual-reputation reverse auction mechanism in Internet of Things. Future Gener. Comput. Syst. **156**, 269–284 (2024)
5. Ni, L., Gong, X., Li, J., Tang, Y., Luan, Z., Zhang, J.: rFedFW: secure and trustable aggregation scheme for byzantine-robust federated learning in Internet of Things. Inf. Sci. **653**, 119784 (2024)
6. Imteaj, A., Thakker, U., Wang, S., Li, J., Amini, M.H.: A survey on federated learning for resource-constrained IoT devices. IEEE Internet Things J. **9**(1), 1–24 (2021)
7. Qi, P., Chiaro, D., Guzzo, A., Ianni, M., Fortino, G., Piccialli, F.: Model aggregation techniques in federated learning: a comprehensive survey. Future Gener. Comput. Syst. **150**, 272–293 (2023)
8. Guduri, M., Chakraborty, C., Margala, M., et al.: Blockchain-based federated learning technique for privacy preservation and security of smart electronic health records. IEEE Trans. Consum. Electron. **70**(1), 2608–2617 (2023)
9. Antunes, R.S., André da Costa, C., Küderle, A., Yari, I.A., Eskofier, B.: Federated learning for healthcare: systematic review and architecture proposal. ACM Trans. Intell. Syst. Technol. (TIST) **13**(4), 1–23 (2022)
10. Namakshenas, D., Yazdinejad, A., Dehghantanha, A., Srivastava, G.: Federated quantum-based privacy-preserving threat detection model for consumer Internet of Things. IEEE Trans. Consum. Electron. (2024)
11. Wu, Q., Chen, X., Zhou, Z., Zhang, J.: FedHome: cloud-edge based personalized federated learning for in-home health monitoring. IEEE Trans. Mob. Comput. **21**(8), 2818–2832 (2020)
12. He, C., Annavaram, M., Avestimehr, S.: Group knowledge transfer: federated learning of large CNNs at the edge. In: Advances in Neural Information Processing Systems, vol. 33, pp. 14068–14080 (2020)
13. Arivazhagan, M.G., Aggarwal, V., Singh, A.K., Choudhary, S.: Federated learning with personalization layers. arXiv preprint arXiv:1912.00818 (2019)
14. Sattler, F., Müller, K.-R., Samek, W.: Clustered federated learning: model-agnostic distributed multitask optimization under privacy constraints. IEEE Trans. Neural Netw. Learn. Syst. **32**(8), 3710–3722 (2020)

15. Husnoo, M.A., Anwar, A., Hosseinzadeh, N., Islam, S.N., Mahmood, A.N., Doss, R.: FedREP: towards horizontal federated load forecasting for retail energy providers. In: 2022 IEEE PES 14th Asia-Pacific Power and Energy Engineering Conference (APPEEC), pp. 1–6. IEEE (2022)
16. Liu, X., Li, H., Xu, G., Lu, R., He, M.: Adaptive privacy-preserving federated learning. Peer-to-Peer Netw. Appl. **13**(6), 2356–2366 (2020). https://doi.org/10.1007/s12083-019-00869-2

Cryptocurrency Transaction Anomaly Detection Based on Chebyshev Graph Neural Network

Chao Li[1], Xiangkai Zhu[1(✉)], Jike Li[1], Nengfu Xie[2], and Qingtian Zeng[1,3]

[1] School of Electronic and Information Engineering, Shandong University of Science and Technology, Qingdao 266590, China
1551502509@qq.com

[2] Key Laboratory of Agricultural Blockchain Application, Ministry of Agriculture and Rural Affairs, Agricultural Information Institute Chinese Academy of Agricultural Sciences, Beijing, China
xienengfu@caas.cn

[3] School of Computer Science and Engineering, Shandong University of Science and Technology, Qingdao 266590, China

Abstract. Recent research has focused on effectively combining blockchain with graph neural networks, utilizing the efficient computing methods of graph neural networks to promote the application and development of blockchain technology in more fields. However, traditional GNN methods only focus on the neighborhood information around the account, ignoring global topology and high-order neighborhood information. Additionally, the importance of different fraudulent accounts with the same neighborhood cannot be distinguished during the aggregation process. To address these above challenges, we propose a research model for anomaly detection in cryptocurrency transactions based on Chebyshev graph neural networks. Specifically, we use the Chebyshev kernel function to obtain high-order neighborhood information and differentiate the importance of accounts with the same neighborhood through the Laplace operator. We demonstrate through lemma that unreasonable coefficients lead to Chebyshev networks being inferior to other methods and penalize the learned outlier coefficients to mitigate the impact on higher-order neighborhood approximations. Subsequently, we aggregate multi-layer neighbor information through attention mechanisms to achieve comprehensive information integration. The effectiveness of the model has been verified through multiple experiments on the Elliptical dataset.

Keywords: Blockchain · Cryptocurrency · Anomaly detection · Graph neural network

1 Introduction

Recent research has focused on effectively combining blockchain with graph neural networks. Specifically, blockchain provides a decentralized data storage

G. Zhao et al. (Eds.): BWTAC 2024, CCIS 2277, pp. 375–386, 2025.
https://doi.org/10.1007/978-981-97-9412-6_34

method, while graph neural networks can handle these distributed stored data. By applying graph neural networks to blockchain data, complex data analysis, mining, and prediction can be carried out, thereby revealing hidden associations and patterns between data. This analysis can help identify abnormal behavior [1], manage risks [2], or provide smarter decision support for smart contracts [3]. As shown in Fig. 1, blockchain data can be naturally depicted as a graph network, with nodes corresponding to addresses and edges denoting transactions and other activities. Once the transaction graph is formed, the model can derive high-dimensional structural features from the graph, leading to effective performance in downstream learning tasks. By utilizing graph neural networks to analyze and mine blockchain data, more business opportunities can be discovered, and the efficiency and security of smart contracts can be improved, thereby promoting the application and development of blockchain technology in more fields.

Graph neural network is a machine learning model used for processing graph data. Unlike traditional deep learning models, graph neural networks can effectively handle unstructured and relational data, such as social networks, knowledge graphs, etc. They can capture complex relationships between nodes and perform inference and learning on graph structures. Graph neural networks have been applied in recommendation systems, social network analysis [4,5], and bioinformatics [6,7].

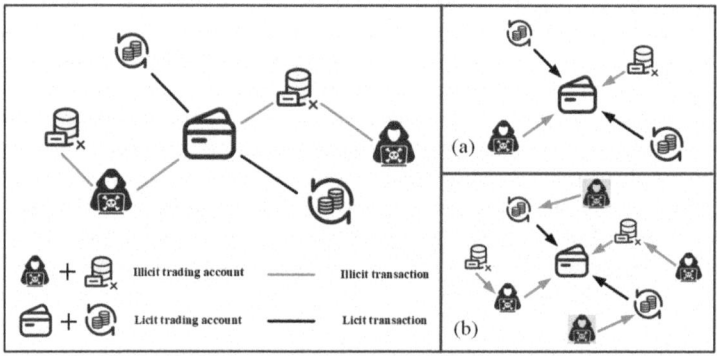

Fig. 1. A toy example of cryptocurrency transaction graph (a) Schematic diagram of first layer network aggregation. (b) Schematic diagram of multi-layer network aggregation

As shown in Fig. 1(a), in previous studies introduces the Elliptic dataset, a large-scale dataset and employs GCN method to aggregate neighborhood information and predict user information. However, they only focus on first-order neighborhood information and overlook the effective information of higher-order neighborhoods. As shown in Fig. 1(b), orange nodes have the same graph topology, making it difficult to distinguish their importance during message transmission. Moreover, coupling multiple layers of neighborhood information can result in all financial account information becoming smooth, making it difficult to correctly distinguish different account entities.

In order to accurately infer the identity of account entities, we combine blockchain and graph neural networks with Chebyshev convolution kernels. Firstly, we analyze the traditional Chebyshev function in deriving K-order neighborhoods. Due to learning illegal coefficients, the effect is not as good as the truncated GCN [8]. We punish the illegal coefficients, and then, using the Chebyshev convolution kernel to broaden the receptive field as a depth first encoder, effectively aggregating high-order neighborhood information, and distinguishing the importance between account entities with the same neighborhood with the Laplace operator to achieve correct account entity classification and prediction.

The contribution of this article is as follows:

- We derive and analyze the effectiveness of applying polynomial functions to cryptocurrency detection from the spectral GNN and distinguished the importance of accounts with the same neighborhood information through Laplace operator.
- We use Chebyshev kernel function to export high-order neighborhood information, and then fuse all neighborhood information with learnable linear parameters, alleviating the problem of indistinguishable account entity information after multi-layer coupling.
- We prove that the suboptimal performance of ChebNet is due to overfitting caused by learned illegal coefficients with experiments, and penalized the learned illegal coefficients to obtain effective node representations.

2   Related Work

In this section, we will cover the fundamental concepts of blockchain and graph neural networks.

2.1   Blockchain

Blockchain is a distributed ledger technology that uses encryption and decentralized methods to record and verify digital transactions. Recently, some studies have begun to combine blockchain and graph neural networks, utilizing their ability to effectively capture the relationships and topological structures between nodes in graph data, and to transmit and learn information on these relationships for fraud detection and prediction of account entity types. [9] extracted partial entity composition graphs from the Elliptic dataset and for the first time utilized classic methods of graph neural networks such as GCN and MLP to achieve node representation learning for large-scale datasets. R-GCN [10] proposes a new convolutional model called residual gated recurrent unit convolutional network for analyzing transactions in blockchain based platforms using Random Gradient Boosting (SGB) technology. ABGRL [11] extracts different feature information from nodes through multiple graph representations, uses adaptive attention mechanisms to capture potential relationships between different features, and selects the feature information that has the greatest impact on downstream tasks for fusion. Meanwhile, this method utilizes self supervised regression models to enhance the feature representation of tail nodes.

However, the above methods only focus on neighboring information and ignore global information. Additionally, in the multi-layer aggregation process, due to the exponential growth of node neighborhoods and the inability to distinguish the neighborhoods of adjacent nodes ultimately leads to the inability to distinguish different account entities.

2.2   Graph Neural Network

Graph Neural Networks (GNNs) [12] learn the low dimensional vector representation of each node by recursively aggregating and passing information from neighboring nodes, thereby capturing complex relationships and features in the graph structure. Spectral GNNs and spatial GNNs are the two main classifications of graph neural networks. Spectral GNNs learn node representations by performing convolution operations in the Fourier domain of the graph and using the Laplacian matrix of the graph for feature decomposition. GCN [8] empolys polynomial approximation of Laplacian matrix to avoid calculating complete eigendecomposition, thereby improving computational efficiency while retaining important frequency information to effectively learn node representations. NFGNN [13] designs a learnable filter for each node and reduced computational complexity through low rank matrix and parameter decoupling. Spatial GNNs [14,15] directly convolve on the graph and learn node representations by aggregating neighbor information of nodes. SUGRL [15] utilizes a triplet loss function to generate positive samples using GCN, and constructs a simple and effective self supervised learning method by sampling the neighbors of the positive samples and shuffling the anchor samples. TopoGCL [16] propose a new contrast mode that extracts the potential shape attributes of the graph at multiple resolutions to generate the topology of two enhanced views in the same graph.

Due to the lack of theoretical guidance, spatial GNN can result in aggregation of multiple layers that cannot be distinguished. The illegal coefficients of high-order neighborhood information in the learning process of spectral GNN lead to poor performance. How to balance the power between the two methods is currently a challenge for GNN.

3   Preparatory Work

In this section, a overview of the definitions and problem explanations related to the symbols used in graph neural networks are provided.

3.1   Notations

Definition [13]. The graph can be defined as $\mathcal{G} = (\mathcal{V}, \mathcal{E})$, $\mathcal{V}$ and $\mathcal{E}$ denote the nodes set and edges set. The graph structure in $\mathcal{G}$ can be represented as $A \in$

$\mathbb{R}^{n \times n}$. If there is an edge connection between nodes, the corresponding value is 1; otherwise, the value is 0. In this paper, we utilize a normalized Laplacian matrix for derivation operations, defined as $L = I - D^{-\frac{1}{2}} A D^{-\frac{1}{2}}$, L is the Laplacian matrix, I and D is the identity matrix and degree matrix.

The neighboring nodes can be represented by $N(v)$ and Neighbors in the k-th hop can use $N_k(v)$. The graph signal can be represented as $x = [x_1, \cdots, x_n]^T \in \mathbb{R}^n$. If each signal is associated with f signal channels, we can form a nodes attributes matrix $X = [X_1, \dots, X_n]^T \in \mathbb{R}^{n \times f}$.

For node classification tasks, node $v \in \mathcal{V}$ is associated with a class label $y_v \in \mathcal{Y} = \{1, \dots, \mathcal{C}\}$, where $\mathcal{C}$ represents the number of different classes.

Problem. The graph $\mathcal{G} = (\mathcal{V}, \mathcal{E})$ and the associated function $f : \mathcal{V} \to \mathbb{R}^d$, graph representation learning seeks to learn this mapping function f to project node V into low-dimensional space and $d \ll |\mathcal{V}|$. The aim of this paper is to optimize the mapping function f using a cross-entropy loss function.

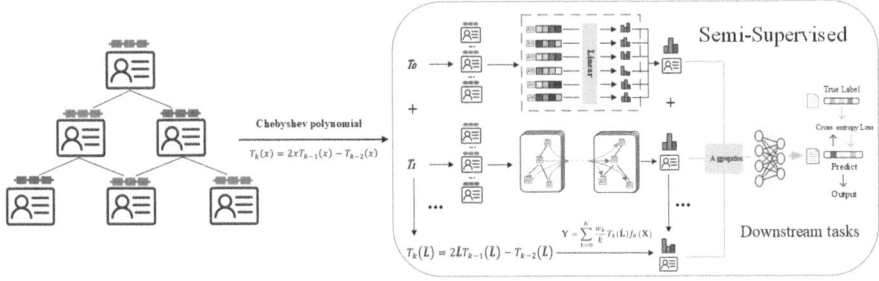

Fig. 2. The overall framework of ChebyGNN

4   Method

In this section, we will elaborate on our proposed cryptocurrency transaction anomaly detection based on **Cheby**shev **G**raph **N**eural **N**etwork (ChebyGNN). We use the Chebyshev kernel function as the network subject. Specifically, we first use the characteristics of Chebyshev and functions to derive K-order neighborhood representations. We have demonstrated through experiments that the presence of illegal coefficients leads to a decrease in our network performance. Therefore, we applied hierarchical constraints to it and adaptively learned the importance of different neighborhoods through linear attention. The model is shown in Fig. 2:

4.1   Graph Fourier Transform

The Laplacian matrix $\mathbf{L}$ can be represented as $\mathbf{U \Lambda U}^T$, U is composed of n orthogonal feature vectors $\{u_l\}_{l=1}^n \in \mathbb{R}^{n \times n}$, Λ is the diagonal matrix of the eigenvalues $\{\lambda_l\}_{l=1}^{n} \subseteq \mathbb{R}$, $\lambda_l \in [0, 2]$. The graph Fourier transform of a signal x is defined as $\hat{x} = U^T x$, while the inverse transformation is given by $x = U\hat{x}$. The signal x resulting from the filter $\hat{g}$ can be expressed using the following formula:

$$z = \sum_{l=1}^{n} \hat{g}(\lambda_l) u_l u_l^T x = U\hat{g}U^T x, \tag{1}$$

where $\hat{g} = \text{diag}\,[\hat{g}(\lambda_1), \cdots, \hat{g}(\lambda_l), \cdots, \hat{g}(\lambda_n)]$, $g = U\hat{g}$.

4.2   Spectral Filtering

In contrast to spatial GNNs, spectral GNNs focus on learning tailored spectral filters that maintain the necessary frequency components for downstream tasks based on the graph structure and node labels. This method utilizes the Laplacian eigenvalue decomposition of the graph to transform its representation into the frequency domain, enabling the propagation and updating of node features through filtering of frequency domain signals. To bypass feature decomposition, a K-order polynomial approximation $\widehat{P_K}(\cdot)$ is utilized to parameterize the general filter:

$$\hat{g}(\lambda_l) \approx \widehat{P_K}(\lambda_l) = \sum_{k=0}^{K} \gamma_k \widehat{p_k}(\lambda_l), \tag{2}$$

where $\widehat{P_K}(\cdot)$ is an approximation of K-order neighborhood. γ_k is the attention coefficient of K-order neighborhood. By substituting Eq. 2 into Eq. 1, the spectral filtering can be reformulated as:

$$U\hat{g}U^T x = U \left(\sum_{k=0}^{K} \gamma_k \widehat{p_k}(\Lambda) \right) U^T x = \left(\sum_{k=0}^{K} \gamma_k \widehat{p_k}(L) \right) x. \tag{3}$$

For efficiency, different polynomial bases are employed for parameterizing spectral filtering, including the Bernstein basis [17] and the Jacobi basis [18].

4.3   Chebyshev Convolution Kernel

Given the computational complexity involved in calculating the eigenvalues of the Laplacian matrix, we suggest using Chebyshev polynomials for approximate calculations. This does not affect the computational properties of the eigenvalues, but simplifies the eigenvalue matrix calculation to L using the Chebyshev polynomial as the kernel function, thus skipping the step of eigenvalue calculation. In theory, if the order K is sufficiently high, the Chebyshev polynomial can approximate any filter.

$$z = \sum_{k=0}^{K} \theta_k T_k(\widetilde{\mathbf{L}})x, \tag{4}$$

where $\widetilde{\mathbf{L}} = 2 \times \frac{\lambda_i}{\lambda_{\max}} - 1$, The Chebyshev K-order polynomial can be derived from the formula:

$$T_k(x) = 2xT_{k-1}(x) - T_{k-2}(x),$$
$$T_0 = 0, T_1 = 1 \tag{5}$$

In this paper $T_0 = H$, $T_1 = \widetilde{\mathbf{L}}H$, H is the node attributes. We can obtain an approximate representation of the K-order neighborhood:

$$T_k(\widetilde{\mathbf{L}}) = 2\widetilde{\mathbf{L}}T_{k-1}(\widetilde{\mathbf{L}}) - T_{k-2}(\widetilde{\mathbf{L}}) \tag{6}$$

Specifically, when K=1 and $\theta_0 = -\theta_1 = \theta$:

$$\begin{aligned} z &= (\theta I - \theta(L - I))x \\ &= \theta(2I - L)x \\ &= \theta\left(I - D^{-\frac{1}{2}}AD^{-\frac{1}{2}}\right)x \end{aligned} \tag{7}$$

This is the spectral domain filtering expression of GCN.

ChebNetII [19] points out that the suboptimal performance of ChebNet is due to overfitting caused by learned illegal coefficients. For any continuous function $f(x)$ within the interval $[-1,1]$, the Chebyshev function is defined as $f(x) = \sum_{k=0}^{\infty} \theta_k T_k(x)$. We will demonstrate through the following theorem that in order to obtain better approximations, we must apply constraints near the coefficients.

Theorem 1. When the function $f(x)$ exhibits weak singularity at the boundary and is analytic within the interval $(-1,1)$, for some positive constant q, the coefficients w_k in Chebyshev may decrease in proportion to $1/k^q$ as $k \to \infty$.

Here, "weak singularity" refers to the possibility of the derivative of f disappearing at the boundary, while "analytic" indicates that f is represented by a convergent power series. Larger values of k in the Chebyshev polynomial $T_k(x)$ correspond to higher frequency oscillations.

The ability to approximate analytical functions is essential when approximating spectral filters. For instance, Chebyshev-based methods, like Chebase, learn coefficients through gradient descent without constraints, potentially resulting in poor performance if these coefficients do not satisfy Theorem 1. To validate this hypothesis, we conducted an empirical analysis on Chebase, we devise a novel propagation process.

$$Y = \sum_{k=0}^{K} \frac{\theta_k}{k} T_k(\widetilde{\mathbf{L}})x, \tag{8}$$

where θ_k represents the Chebyshev coefficients achieved by reparameterizing the learnable parameter θ_k.

As shown in Table 1, Cora, PubMed, WiKiCSD, and Elliptic datasets are employed to verify experimental hypotheses. It is evident that by applying simple penalties on the weak signals, chebase/k outperforms both chebase and GCN.

Table 1. Comparative experimental results after punishing Chebyshev's illegal coefficients

Method	Metric	Cora	PubMed	Wiki-CS	Elliptic
GCN	Macro-F1	0.8101	0.837	0.7871	0.7881
	Micro-F1	0.8412	0.8444	0.8167	0.9308
	AUC	0.8287	0.8456	0.8334	0.8931
chebase	Macro-F1	0.8257	0.8724	0.7777	0.8723
	Micro-F1	0.8129	0.876	0.8113	0.9514
	AUC	0.8389	0.8854	0.8484	0.9076
chebase/k	Macro-F1	0.827	0.8829	0.7912	0.9016
	Micro-F1	0.8486	0.8875	0.8191	0.9631
	AUC	0.8727	0.893	0.8509	0.9142

5 Experiment

In this section, we will provide a detailed introduction to the dataset used in our experiment and validate the effectiveness of our proposed model through various experiments.

5.1 Elliptic Dataset

The Elliptic dataset comprises 203,769 nodes and 234,355 edges. These nodes represent various trading entities, including exchanges, wallet providers, miners, and potential money laundering groups. The edges signify the flow of Bitcoin transactions between two trading entities. Each node is associated with 166 transaction-related features. Among these features, the first 94 are local features, which encompass derived attributes such as time steps, in and out degrees, payment expenses, and average transaction amounts of Bitcoin. The remaining 72 features are aggregated attributes, obtained by aggregating information from neighboring transactions, including maximum, minimum, standard deviation, and correlation coefficient data. Approximately 2% of the nodes in the dataset are classified as fraudulent, 21% as non-fraudulent, while the labels for the remaining nodes are unavailable.

5.2 Experimental Settings

We use classic graph neural network models such as GAT [20], GCN [8], APPNP [21], SGC [22], GIN [23], GCN2conv [24](GCNII), NFGNN [13] for comparison. Except for the Elliptic dataset, all other datasets in this paper are from the official DGL library. In the experiment, we used labeled node classification, with approximately 2% of nodes in the data being fraudulent nodes, 21% being non fraudulent nodes, and the remaining nodes having no labels. Due to the imbalanced distribution of different types in the dataset (label = 1: label = 2 is 1:10), in order to prevent model misclassification, we have divided the training set validation set and testing set again, with a ratio of 1:3 for different types of labels.

5.3   Node Classification and Accuracy

We evaluate the effectiveness of ChebyGNN through node classification tasks. Specifically, we divided the number of node test sets into 20%, 40%, 60%, and 80% and inputted them into SVM for node classification. Micro-F1, Macro-F1, and AUC were used as evaluation metrics, with the best results highlighted in bold and the second results indicated by underline.

As shown in Table 2, our model demonstrated excellent performance on the Elliptic dataset. Compared to the methods of Spatial GNNs, our model has achieved good performance in node classification and accuracy. One important reason is that our Chebyshev kernel can derive and approximate high-order neighborhood information, and can distinguish the importance between accounts with the same neighborhood information. Compared to spectral GNNs, our node classification has achieved good performance with a slight advantage in accuracy. This is because both our method and NFGNN can approximate high-order neighborhoods, but we penalize the weight coefficients between the learned representations of different neighborhoods.

Table 2. Node classification on Elliptic dataset

Dataset	Metric	Split	GAT	GCN	APPNP	GIN	SGC	GCNII	NFGNN	OURS
ELLIPTIC	Macro-F1	80%	90.47	86.42	89.04	91.56	89.97	90.45	<u>92.04</u>	**92.72**
		60%	90.28	86.56	88.82	91.42	89.86	90.23	<u>92.11</u>	**92.65**
		40%	89.71	86.49	88.49	91.03	89.74	89.64	<u>92.21</u>	**92.43**
		20%	89.03	86.31	88.04	90.37	89.42	88.49	**92.33**	<u>92.02</u>
	Micro-F1	80%	92.98	90.16	91.89	93.81	92.71	92.98	<u>94.31</u>	**94.67**
		60%	92.82	90.24	91.71	93.71	92.62	92.78	<u>94.35</u>	**94.59**
		40%	92.37	90.21	91.45	93.41	92.53	92.31	**94.42**	**94.42**
		20%	91.85	90.09	91.09	92.87	92.28	91.38	**94.52**	<u>94.11</u>
	AUC		94.28	92.97	93.19	<u>95.22</u>	94.77	94.28	94.11	**95.37**

5.4   Layer Analysis

Our proposed chebyGNN can effectively derive node representations of K-order neighborhoods, alleviating the problem of node information being too smooth after multi-layer coupling. As shown in the Fig. 3, we visualized Micro-F1 and AUC for different baselines at different layers in the Cora dataset. As the number of layers increased, the method based on GCN reached a peak and gradually decreased, while our chebyGNN still maintained good robustness.

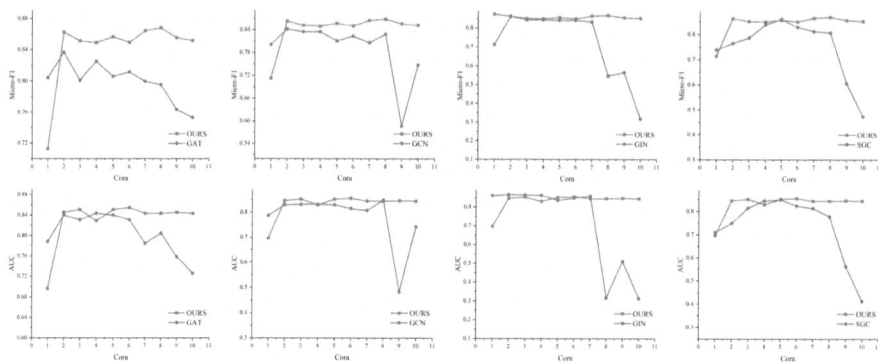

Fig. 3. Layer analysis

6 Conclusion and Future Work

In this article, we propose a cryptocurrency transaction anomaly detection based on chebyshev graph neural network. We derived the representation of K-order neighborhoods based on the Chebyshev kernel function and explained through Lemma 1 that the suboptimal performance of ChebNet is due to overfitting caused by learned illegal coefficients. Therefore, we constrained the coefficients learned from higher-order neighborhoods, alleviated the impact of illegal coefficients on K-order approximation, and alleviated the oversmooth problem caused by multiple layers of node information coupling, achieving efficient computation while maintaining effectiveness. The effectiveness of our model has been validated through multiple experiments on a large blockchain dataset like Elliptic.

In future work, we will attempt to fit our K-order neighborhood information by combining more polynomial bases, and set a learnable filter for each node in the form of a spectrogram filter to achieve targeted filtering and validate the effectiveness of our model by multiple blockchain datasets.

Declarations

Acknowledgments. This work is supported by National Key R&D Program of China (Grant No. 2022ZD0119501); National Natural Science Foundation of China (Grant No. 52374221); the Natural Science Foundation of Shandong Province (Grant No. ZR2022MF268, ZR2021QG038); the Taishan Scholar Program of Shandong Province (Grant No. ts20190936), and the Open Research Fund Program of Key Laboratory of Agricultural Blockchain Application, Ministry of Agriculture and Rural Affairs (2022KLABA03).

Disclosure of Interests. The authors declare that there is no competing interests.

References

1. Wei, S., Lee, S.: Financial anti-fraud based on dual-channel graph attention network. J. Theor. Appl. Electron. Commer. Res. **19**(1), 297–314 (2024)

2. Yudhistira, A., Fajar, A.N.: Integrating togaf and big data for digital transformation: case study on the lending industry. Sinkron: jurnal dan penelitian teknik informatika, 8(2), 1215–1225 (2024)

3. Zhen, Z., Zhao, X., Zhang, J., Wang, Y., Chen, H.: DA-GNN: a smart contract vulnerability detection method based on dual attention graph neural network. Comput. Netw. **242**, 110238 (2024)

4. Chen, X., Jian, Y., Ke, L., Qiu, Y., Chen, X., Song, Y., Wang, H.: A deep semantic-aware approach for cantonese rumor detection in social networks with graph convolutional network. Expert Syst. Appl. **245**, 123007 (2024)

5. He-xuan, H., Cao, C., Qiang, H., Zhang, Y.: Federated learning enabled graph convolutional autoencoder and factorization machine for potential friendship prediction in social networks. Inf. Fus. **102**, 102042 (2024)

6. Sun, X., Jia, X., Lu, Z., Tang, J., Li, M.: Drug repositioning with adaptive graph convolutional networks. Bioinformatics **40**(1), btad748 (2024)

7. Xuan, P., et al.: Multi-scale topology and position feature learning and relationship-aware graph reasoning for prediction of drug-related microbes. Bioinformatics **40**(2), btae025 (2024)

8. Kipf, T.N., Welling, M.: Semi-supervised classification with graph convolutional networks. In: International Conference on Learning Representations (2016)

9. Weber, M., et al.: Anti-money laundering in bitcoin: experimenting with graph convolutional networks for financial forensics. Technical report (2019)

10. Rajmohan, R., Ananth Kumar, T., Sandhya, S.G., Hu, Y-C.: R-GCN: a residual-gated recurrent unit convolution network model for anomaly detection in blockchain transactions. Multimed. Tools Appl. 1–25 (2024)

11. Sun, H., Liu, Z., Wang, S., Wang, H.: Adaptive attention-based graph representation learning to detect phishing accounts on the Ethereum blockchain. IEEE Trans. Netw. Sci. Eng. (2024)

12. Lei, R., Wang, Z., Li, Y., Ding, B., Wei, Z.: Evennet: ignoring odd-hop neighbors improves robustness of graph neural networks. Adv. Neural. Inf. Process. Syst. **35**, 4694–4706 (2022)

13. Zheng, S., Zhu, Z., Liu, Z., Li, Y., Zhao, Y.: Node-oriented spectral filtering for graph neural networks. IEEE Trans. Pattern Anal. Mach. Intell. **01**, 1–15 (2023)

14. Yang, L., et al.: Self-supervised graph neural networks via diverse and interactive message passing. In: Proceedings of the AAAI Conference on Artificial Intelligence, vol. 36, pp. 4327–4336 (2022)

15. Mo, Y., Peng, L., Jie, X., Shi, X., Zhu, X.: Simple unsupervised graph representation learning. In: Proceedings of the AAAI Conference on Artificial Intelligence, vol. 36, pp. 7797–7805 (2022)

16. Chen, Y., Frias, J., Gel, Y.R.: Topological graph contrastive learning. In: Proceedings of the AAAI Conference on Artificial Intelligence, vol. 38, pp. 11453–11461 (2024)

17. He, M., Wei, Z., Hongteng, X., et al.: Bernnet: learning arbitrary graph spectral filters via bernstein approximation. Adv. Neural. Inf. Process. Syst. **34**, 14239–14251 (2021)

18. Wang, X., Zhang, M.: How powerful are spectral graph neural networks. In: International Conference on Machine Learning, pp. 23341–23362. PMLR (2022)

19. He, M., Wei, Z., Wen, J.-R.: Convolutional neural networks on graphs with chebyshev approximation, revisited. Adv. Neural. Inf. Process. Syst. **35**, 7264–7276 (2022)

20. Veličković, P., Cucurull, G., Casanova, A., Romero, A., Lio, P., Bengio, Y.: Graph attention networks. In: International Conference on Learning Representations (2018)
21. Gasteiger, J., Bojchevski, A., Günnemann, S.: Predict then propagate: graph neural networks meet personalized pagerank. In: International Conference on Learning Representations (2018)
22. Wu, F., Souza, A., Zhang, T., Fifty, C., Yu, T., Weinberger, K.: Simplifying graph convolutional networks. In: International Conference on Machine Learning, pp. 6861–6871. PMLR (2019)
23. Yifan, H., et al.: Measuring and improving the use of graph information in graph neural networks. In: International Conference on Learning Representations (2019)
24. Chen, M., Wei, Z., Huang, Z., Ding, B., Li, Y.: Simple and deep graph convolutional networks. In: Proceedings of the 37th International Conference on Machine Learning, pp. 1725–1735 (2020)

Validating the Integrity for Deep Learning Models Based on Zero-Knowledge Proof and Blockchain

Qianyi Zhan[1], Yuanyuan Liu[2(✉)], Zhenping Xie[1], and Yuan Liu[1]

[1] Jiangsu Key Laboratory of Media Design and Software Technology, Jiangnan University, Wuxi, China
[2] School of Artificial Intelligence and Computer Science, Jiangnan University, Wuxi, China
LYuan_JN@163.com

Abstract. With the development of MLaaS in recent years, the integrity and data security have also faced challenges. Ensuring the consumers receive correct services and safeguarding the data security is important. In this paper, we designed algorithms for each module, using depthwise separable convolution to optimize the convolution module and using the minimum polynomial method to optimize the circuit design of the activation function. Additionally, this paper proposes the SSHC algorithm for deeper network connections and combines blockchain to verify the correctness of the proofs. The experimental results demonstrate that our approach reduces proof time by 54.6% and storage by 58.1% compared to the original solution, while maintaining high efficiency and practicality.

Keywords: MLaaS · Machine Learning · Zero-knowledge Proof · Blockchain

1 Introduction

Since the proposal of deep learning models, significant progress has been made in pattern recognition, speech recognition, and text processing [1–3]. However, while the performance of the models has improved, the complexity of their structure and training algorithms has also increased. As a result, many consumers of ML models outsource the training and inference of ML models to service providers, typically referred to as MLaaS [4]. Some cloud computing companies, such as Google, Amazon, and Microsoft, offer training and inference services for deep learning models.

Machine learning models are deployed in the cloud and users can use the services provided by these models, but at the same time, there are some problems: (1) Model Tampering: Algorithmic models are essential intellectual property models with specific business value, as a black-box model, once the model integrity is compromised, the model's predictions may deviate from the expected results. (2) Deceptive Services: How can the model consumer (MC) verify the model providers (MP) correctly provide predictions? In untrustworthy environments, the MP may provide random, incorrect, or even malicious predictions to minimize the actual cost or to achieve other purposes

[5]. (3) Privacy Leakage: whether the MC and MP will leak the private information of individuals in the process.

Ensuring the integrity of the model and the privacy of information is crucial [6, 7], but addressing this challenge poses several difficulties: (1) The model holds certain intellectual property rights, with key parameters that cannot be exposed to the MC. (2) Proving the model's integrity and trustworthiness within the cloud service environment, establishing a trusting relationship between the MC and the MP, presents challenges. (3) The continuous production and transmission of large amounts of data to the cloud for model training and data processing [8] are time-consuming and inefficient. (4) It's essential to guarantee personal privacy and secure data storage [9].

In this paper, we propose a scheme based on non-interactive zero-knowledge proofs (ZKP) and blockchain to accomplish the work of model integrity verification and data protection. Based on the ZKP, the model is verified and computed, and the private information of the model is kept confidential during the whole process, which guarantees the "zero-knowledge" of the information. The non-interactive approach eliminates the need for real-time communication between MC and MP, and the MC can complete the verification of the proof at any moment, thus establishing a trust relationship in the cloud service environment. Through the ZKP algorithm, the complex calculation of data is transferred to off-chain processing, while the calculation results are verified and processed through the blockchain's smart contract to achieve efficiency improvement and the security of data storage.

The main contributions of this paper are as follows:

(1) We propose a neural network model integrity verification scheme based on zk-SNARK and blockchain.
(2) We propose several algorithms for transforming neural network modules into R1CS circuits, converting convolutional layer, normalization layer, activation layer, and pooling layers into simple first-order arithmetic expressions, and optimizing them with circuit characteristics.
(3) We propose a scheme of SHCC (Serial hash circuit connection) algorithm to deal with the circuit design of large-scale machine learning models, which can complete the verification and connection between complex circuits concisely and efficiently.
(4) Experiments show that our scheme can significantly reduce the time and storage overheads, while achieving on-chain model integrity verification in an Ethereum environment.

2 Related Work

For the verifiable computation in the MLaaS, the MC submits the verification request P and data X to the MP, then the MP performs the verified computation and the generation of the proof file, and ultimately the MC verifies the completeness of the MP's computational task execution by returning the proof file.

In recent years, Lee [10] designed an efficient verifiable convolutional neural network (vCNN) framework. However, the framework only implements ReLU activation and average pooling. Takabi [11] accelerates the performance of machine learning algorithms through a combination of fully homomorphic encryption and graphical processing units, but the solution is costly and requires additional hardware. Huang [12] proposed a two-round polling response for the random sampling protocol. This work reduces the time cost of proof generation and ensures the integrity of the training process. However, the method employs a random sampling scheme and can only detect some specific attacks.

Blockchain is difficult to meet the market demand due to performance constraints [13, 14], and there are numerous studies and applications for Layer2 scaling schemes represented by ZKP. For example, Lavaur [15] proposed z k-rollup modular verification scheme, which allows multiple proofs to be executed on a single contract. Thereby increasing the throughput of the system. Liu [16] proposed information sharing and fast verification in IoT environment through ZKP, while proving its practicality based on Ethereum. Besides, ZKP has applications in democratic voting, bidding auctions, and blockchain finance [17].

With the challenges and previous research in mind, this paper proposes a non-interactive integrity verification scheme based on zk-SNARK (Zero-Knowledge Succinct Non-Interactive Argument of Knowledge) and blockchain. The scheme is designed for the integrity proofing process of CNN models, and the process can be accomplished simply and quickly.

3 Preliminaries

3.1 Zero Proof of Knowledge

Let R be an efficiently computable binary relation. For a pair of binary groups $(x, w) \in R$, x is a statement, w is a secret witness. For a binary arithmetic relation R, the proof system includes system parameter $SysGen$, proof (P) and verification (V).

A specific knowledge proof protocol $ZK\{w|(x, w) \in R\}$ consists of five polynomial time algorithms, system parameter generation $SysGen$, $commitment$, $challenge$, $response$ and $verification$. For a fixed security parameter λ run as follows.

$$\left\{ \begin{array}{c} CRS \leftarrow SysGen(1^\lambda) \\ C \leftarrow Com(x,w;r) \\ P \leftarrow Random(e) \\ Z \leftarrow Response(x,w;e,r) \\ Valid/Invalid \leftarrow Verify(x,C;e,z) \end{array} \right. \tag{1}$$

3.2 R1CS Circuit

In the proof circuit design, we have used R1CS (Rank-1 Constraint System) to represent the computational process and constraints of the circuit. R1CS is a commonly used formal description method to represent the constraint relationships in the computational process [18]. The computational process as a first-order equation can be expressed as:

$$A_z \times B_z = C_z \tag{2}$$

where A, B, C is the sparse matrix and $\times$ denotes the accumulation step by step.

The conversion is achieved by unifying the computational expressions, and using arithmetic circuit gates in combination with the circom library [19]. In the actual design process, the connections between the circuit gates are designed according to the logical structure of the expression, and usually the R1CS expression consists of $+$, $-$, and $*$ to represent the circuit operation. For example, when the expression is $x^3 + x^2 + x = 10$, the whole circuit consists of several multiplication gates and two addition gates. Then the expression can be expressed as two expressions to the R1CS constraints in formula (3), and the expression on the right is simpler than the one on the left.

$$R(x) = \begin{cases} s_1 = x * x \\ s_2 = s_1 * x \\ s_3 = s_1 + x \\ 10 = s_2 + s_3 \end{cases} \text{ or } R(x) = \begin{cases} s_1 = x * x \\ 10 - (s_1 + x) = s_1 * x \end{cases} \tag{3}$$

4 Algorithm Design

In this section, we have designed algorithms for multiple modules, each optimized for convolution operations, normalization, activation functions, and pooling operations. We use Depthwise Separable Convolution (DSC) and Adaptive Average Pooling (AAP) to optimize the convolution modules, employ the minimum polynomial method to optimize the circuit design of activation functions, and incorporate hash functions to handle the connections between modules. Additionally, we introduced a serial hash circuit connection to ensure the integrity and correctness of the network. The following subsections will detail the design of each module.

4.1 CSSP (Conv2dStaticSamePadding) Circuit Design

As an operation used in two-dimensional CNNs, the main purpose of padded convolution is to keep the dimensions of the inputs and outputs consistent. The convolution operation without padding results in a reduction of the output size, which may lead to loss of information or require additional processing to keep the size consistent. The CSSP solves this problem by padding the input with an appropriate number of zeros around the input. This padding is determined prior to training, where the formula for the number of paddings is calculated as follows:

$$p_h = \lfloor ((H_{out} - 1) * S + K - H_{in})/2 \rfloor \tag{4}$$

$$p_w = \lfloor ((W_{out} - 1) * S + K - W_{in})/2 \rfloor \tag{5}$$

where H_{out} is the height of the output, S is the step size, K is the size of the convolution kernel, and H_{in} is the height of the input.

Convolution operations are typically used to extract features from the input data by sliding a convolution kernel over the input data, and performing dot product and summation operations at each position to compute the output. When the input is (N, C_{in}, H, W), the computation process after regular convolution is

$$out(N_i, C_{outj}) = bias(C_{outj}) + \sum_{k=0}^{C_{in}-1} weight(C_{outj}, k) \circ input(N_i, k) \tag{6}$$

where o is a cross-correlation operation, N is the size of the input, and C is the number of channels.

Algorithm 1 CSSP Convert to R1CS Circuit Algorithm

Input: feature vector X, kernel W_d, convolution weight W_p

Output: convolution output $cLayer$

1./* Calculate CSSP */

2. for $i \in (0, (nRows - kSize)/strides + 1)$ do

3.   for $j \in (0, (nCols - kSize)/strides + 1)$ do

4.   for $k \in (0, nChannels - 1)$ do

5. $Y_d = X * W_d$ // Calculate DC

6. $Y = Y_d * W_p$ // Calculate PC

7. /* Calculate the output */

8. $pRows = nRows + ((nRows - 1) * strides + kSize - nRows)/2$

9. $pCols = nCols + ((nCols - 1) * strides + kSize - nCols)/2$

10. $cLayer = DSC((X_{pRows,pCols}, W_d, W_p)$

11. $cLayer.dWeights = dWeights$

12. $cLayer.pWeights = pWeights$

Due to the difficulty of representing the regular convolution using polynomial equations, we chose Depthwise Separable Convolution (DSC) [20] to complete the process, which mainly consists of two operations, Deepwise Convolution (DC) and Pointwise Convolution (PC), and the whole process is formulated as:

$$Y = (weight(C_d, k) * input(N_i, k)) \cdot weight(C_p, k) \tag{7}$$

where the DC operation $*$ is performed first followed by the PC operation $\cdot$, C_d is the channel for DC, and C_p is the channel for the PC.

The process of transforming the DC to the R1CS is shown in Fig. 1, PC using 1 × 1 for convolution is similar to this process.

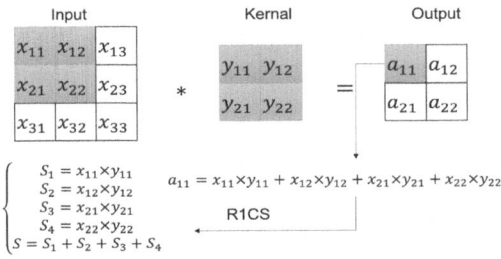

Fig. 1. The process of the Depthwise Convolution

Finally, the circuit expression for the conversion of DC and PC is converted to the R1CS circuit, and the whole process is shown in Algorithm 1.

4.2   BN2D (BatchNorm2d) Circuit Design

The function of the BN2d layer is to normalize the input to ensure a stable distribution during the training process, which helps in deeper network training. For an input feature map, BN2d first calculates its mean and standard deviation over the mini-batch, then normalizes the input feature map by the operation of subtracting the mean and dividing by the standard deviation, and finally scales and translates it with learnable parameters, described by the mathematical formula:

$$\hat{x}_i = \frac{x_i - \mu}{\sqrt{\sigma^2 + \epsilon}} \tag{8}$$

$$y_i = \gamma \hat{x}_i + \beta \tag{9}$$

where $\hat{x}_i$ is the normalised value of the i th element in the input feature map, μ is the mean of the mini-batch, σ is the standard deviation of the mini-batch, ϵ is a very small constant (to avoid divide-by-zero errors), γ and β are learnable parameters, and y_i is the final output.

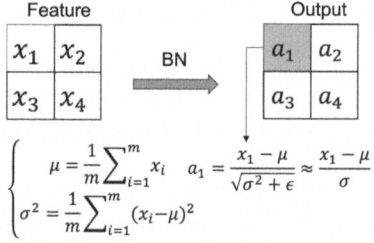

Fig. 2. The process of the BatchNorm2d

Considering the requirements of actual circuit design, we have omitted the scaling factor and bias factor. This allows for better adaptation to the range and distribution of various input data. Through linear transformation, we can simplify the circuit design process and improve the efficiency, and this process is illustrated in Fig. 2. Although it may not be possible to fully consider all details in actual circuit design, we are still able to successfully implement the BatchNorm2d function in the circuit.

4.3   MES (Memory Efficient Swish) Circuit Design

Compared to the traditional activation function, the MES function provides better nonlinear characteristics by smoothing the activation curve, making the neural network easier to train and optimize. This improvement is important as it enhances the model's ability to capture complex patterns, it is defined by the formula as follows:

$$MES(x) = x \cdot sigmoid(\beta x) \tag{10}$$

where β is a learnable parameter that is adjusted through the training process.

Due to the inability of design languages to handle floating-point arithmetic, the division operation in the Sigmoid function may pose challenges during the circuit design process. In this paper, we refer to Hesamifard's scheme of using the approximate activation function [21], and use the method of the smallest polynomial to approximate the expression of the Swish function. At the same time, for the floating-point operations involved, we round them to integers while ensuring a certain level of accuracy, thus avoiding potential issues. The final function approximation is equivalent to:

$$Swish_{approx}(x) = x \cdot (0.5 + 0.25x - \frac{1}{48}x^3 + \frac{1}{480}x^5 - \frac{17}{80640}x^7) \tag{11}$$

4.4 AAP (AdaptiveAvgPool2d) Circuit Design

The function of AAP is to adaptively average pool the input feature maps according to the specified output size. Unlike traditional average pooling, instead of pooling the input according to a fixed pooling size, AAP automatically calculates the size and step size of the pooling region according to the output size, ensuring that the size of the output feature map is consistent with the specified size.

When the size of the input feature map is $H \times W$, and the size of the output is $h \times w$, then AAP will divide the input feature map into $h \times w$ regions, each of which has a size of $\frac{H}{h} \times \frac{W}{w}$, and then average the values in each region to get the corresponding output value. In this way, AAP ensures that the size of the output feature map is same as the specified output size, while maintaining the average information of the input feature map. The formula is described as:

$$output[i,j] = \frac{1}{C_{input(i,j)}} \sum_{area} input[i,j] \tag{12}$$

where $C_{input(i,j)}$ is the number of pixels in the i th row and j th column area of the input feature map.

In this way, we are able to implement the AAP operation and ensure that we get the correct results. The following is the circuit design in Algorithm 2.

Algorithm 2 AAP Convert to R1CS Circuit Algorithm

Input: feature vector X, expected output parameters $outH, outW$
Output: feature vector X_{out}

1./* Calculate the size and step of the pooling*/
2. $pool(H, W) = nRows / outH, nCols / out$ //calculate the size of the area
3. $s(H, W) = poolSizeH, poolSizeW$ //calculate the length of the step
4./*AAP operations*/
5. $Pooling2D = SumPooling2D(X, pool(H, W), s(H, W))$
6. for $i \in (0, nRows)$ do
7.   for $j \in (0, nCols)$ do
8.   for $k \in (0, nChannels)$ do
9. $out[i][j][k] <== Pooling2D.out[i][j][k] / (poolH * poolW)$

4.5 SHCC (Serial Hash Circuit Connection) Design

The large-scale neural network model consists of multiple modules, which cannot be uniformly designed into a single circuit due to circuit limitations, and thus the overall network structure is divided into three parts for combinatorial design: the head, the backbone, and the tail. The head and tail sections are mainly for the beginning input and the final fully connected output, while the backbone section is for each layer of the module, which includes convolution, normalization and so on. And for the connection between them, we introduce the hash function for processing. For example, in the backbone network, the circuit output of the i th module is

$$H(M_i) = H(M_{n-1}) || H(out_i) \tag{13}$$

The hash of the current module is calculated from the hash of the previous module and the hash of the current module. Similarly, the head and the tail hash is interconnected with the backbone part.

If the integrity of the network is compromised by tampering with $H(out)$ or $H(Mn-1)$, it cannot pass the next layer of verification, thus ensuring the integrity and correctness of the entire circuit design. The design flow of the whole process is shown in Fig. 3.

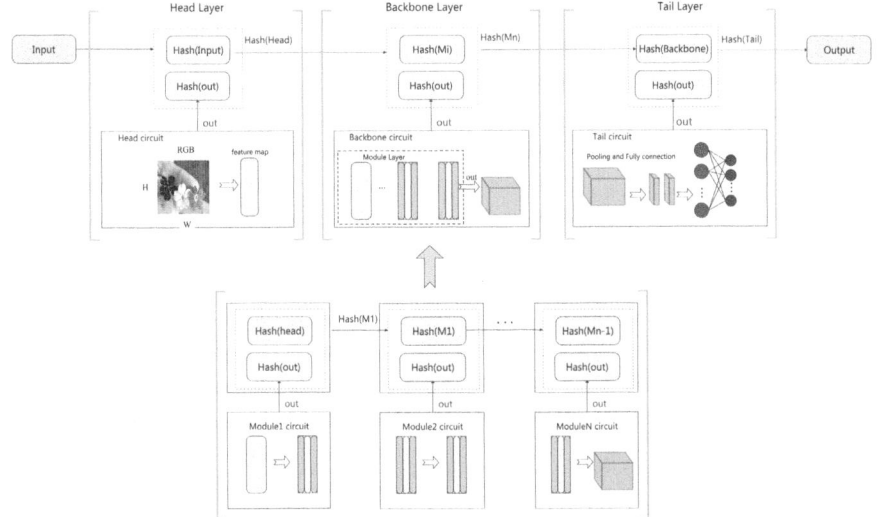

Fig. 3. The process of the SHCC algorithm

5 Experiments

5.1 Experimental Environment and Test Model

We mainly circom and snark libraries to complete the experimental part, where circom is the implementation language of the circuit and snark is used for terminal execution of the circuit file. Eventually, during the compilation process, the circuit file R1CS, the ZKEY and WASM files for proofs, and the verification file for validation are generated. Python is used to write the network and to obtain the model parameters. The main environment for the experiment is shown in Table 1.

Table 1. The Experimental Environment

Name	Version	Description
Macos	Macos12.5	computer environment
Python	V3.7	compose the network, get the parameters
circom	V2.1.8	programming circuits
snarkjs	V0.7.3	compile the circuist

We use the MBConv layer in EfficientNet [22] for the construction of the network, and the structure is shown in Fig. 4(a). The MBConv includes basic convolution, normalization, activation and other components. EfficientNet consists of 16 MBConv modules and input and output sections. We have removed some same structures and retained 6 MBConvs for the backbone network in Fig. 4(b), but there are still nearly 3M parameters overall.

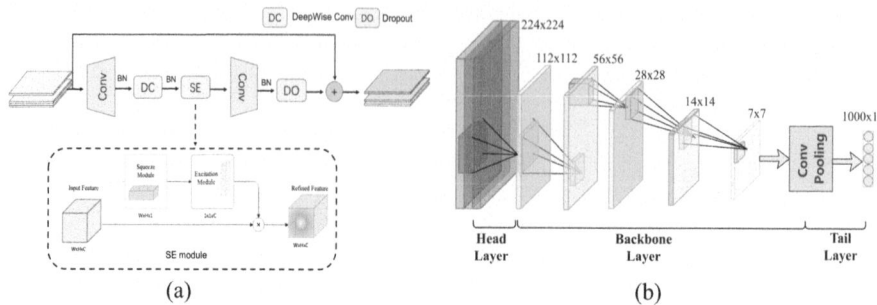

Fig. 4. The Structure of the MBConv and the EfficientNet

5.2 Basic Circuit Testing

We adjust the inputs to (3, 64, 64) and test the verification time and storage consumption of the basic circuits in the MBConv module for both the conventional and optimised scenario cases. The time results for each stage are shown in Table 2.

Table 2. The MBConv Module Time Test

Model	plan	Setup(/s)	Proving(/s)	Verify(/s)
MBConv	Original [10]	316.7	46.8	0.4
	ours	143.7	19.2	0.4

According to the results in Table 2, our approaches significantly reduce the setup time to 143.7/s as compared to 316.7/s for the original scheme. In terms of proof generation time, our scheme also outperforms with only 19.2/s as compared to 46.8/s for the original scheme. The validation time is the same for both. By calculation, our scheme improves about 54.6% in setup time and 58.1% in proof generation time relative to the original scheme.

Table 3. The MBConv Module Storage Test

Layer	R1CS	ZKEY	WASM	Verify	Total
Conv-ori [10]	268.4 MB	882.1 MB	6.8 MB	4 KB	1159.3 MB
Conv-ours	134.9 MB	368.1 MB	3.2 MB	4 KB	510.2 MB

We recorded the storage overheads under the two model structure inputs, which are shown in Table 3. For the MBConv module, the total generated file size is reduced by 55.9% compared to the original scheme and our proposed scheme, which reduces the pressure on the server-side response storage and caching by nearly half. Due to the simplicity of the protocol Groth16 used in generating ZKP, the proof file size of its entire circuit is relatively constant at 4 KB.

5.3 Network Testing

In order to verify the feasibility and properly of our scheme on large networks, we use Efficient-b0 as our overall network. The network consists of an input module (consisting of the input and the first MBConv module), a backbone module (consisting of 6 MBConvs), and an output module (pooling layer and full connectivity layer). The timing of the three parts is in Table 4 and the storage testing is in Table 5.

Table 4. The EfficientNet Time Test

Model	Layer	Setup(/s)	Proving(/s)	Verify(/s)
EfficientNet-b0	Head	7.0	0.9	0.4
	Backbone	157.8	70.4	0.4
	Tail	164.9	40.6	0.4

Among these three parts, the Tail section has the longest setup time because it holds the largest proportion of parameters in the network. Similarly, the backbone network layer is deeper than the head and tail sections, requiring longer time and incurring the highest storage consumption during the proof process. All three parts ultimately completed the proofs using the Groth16 algorithm, taking approximately 0.4 s. Additionally, we successfully executed the circuits for each part and conducted necessary tests, thereby verifying the feasibility of the SHCC algorithm.

Table 5. The EfficientNet Storage Test

Layer	R1CS	ZKEY	WASM	Verify	Total
Head	979 KB	4.4 MB	115 KB	4 KB	5.5 MB
Backbone	235.5 MB	1064 MB	10.1 MB	4 KB	1309.6 MB
Tail	134.4 MB	535.1 MB	4.8 MB	4 KB	674.3 MB

5.4 Cost Testing

We used snarkjs to complete the generation of the Solidity smart contract and allowed the proof to be verified on Ethereum. The contract was successfully deployed and the example executed correctly. The successful deployment and execution demonstrate the effectiveness of our approach, and the results of the contract gas consumption test are shown in Table 6.

Table 6. The contract gas consumption test

Contract	Transaction Cost(gas)	Execution cost (gas)	Price (10–3 Ether)
Head	422072	341578	5.06
Backbone	482312	397434	5.79
Tail	422060	341578	5.06
Head_verify	/	202483	2.43
Backbone_verify	/	222424	2.67
Tail_verify	/	202483	2.43

By verifying proofs on Ethereum, we not only enhance the trustworthiness and transparency of proofs, but also provide a safe and reliable way for users to verify the information they need. The whole process does not require users to reveal their identities, and MP does not need to expose the private data of the model, providing a new solution for model integrity verification.

6 Conclusion

This paper proposes a model integrity verification scheme based on non-interactive ZKP to effectively deal with model tampering and deceptive service problems in cloud service environments. Through experiments of each module and the entire network, our scheme significantly reduces the proof generation time and storage overhead while protecting user privacy. This enhances the credibility and data security of models in cloud services, providing a secure foundation for the use of deep learning models in cloud environments. In future work, we will focus on extending the solution to edge computing and other deep learning models, and on further optimizing the algorithmic processes.

References

1. Bai, X., Wang, X., Liu, X., et al.: Explainable deep learning for efficient and robust pattern recognition: a survey of recent developments. Pattern Recogn. **120**, 108102 (2021)
2. Weng, Z., Qin, Z., Tao, X., et al.: Deep learning enabled semantic communications with speech recognition and synthesis. IEEE Trans. Wirel. Commun. (2023)
3. Minaee, S., Kalchbrenner, N., Cambria, E., et al.: Deep learning–based text classification: a comprehensive review. ACM Comput. Surv. (CSUR) **54**(3), 1–40 (2021)
4. Kang, D., Hashimoto, T., Stoica, I., et al.: Scaling up trustless DNN inference with zero-knowledge proofs. arXiv preprint arXiv:2210.08674 (2022)
5. Fan, Y., Xu, B., Zhang, L., et al.: Validating the integrity of convolutional neural network predictions based on zero-knowledge proof. Inf. Sci. **625**, 125–140 (2023)
6. Li, F., Li, Q., Zhang, J., et al.: Detection and diagnosis of data integrity attacks in solar farms based on multilayer long short-term memory network. IEEE Trans. Power Electron. **36**(3), 2495–2498 (2020)

7. Peng, L., Feng, W., Yan, Z., et al.: Privacy preservation in permissionless blockchain: a survey. Digit. Commun. Netw. **7**(3), 295–307 (2021)

8. Zhang, F., Chen, Z., Zhang, C., et al.: An efficient parallel secure machine learning framework on GPUs. IEEE Trans. Parallel Distrib. Syst. **32**(9), 2262–2276 (2021)

9. Kaissis, G.A., Makowski, M.R., Rückert, D., et al.: Secure, privacy-preserving and federated machine learning in medical imaging. Nat. Mach. Intell. **2**(6), 305–311 (2020)

10. Lee, S., Ko, H., Kim, J., et al.: VCNN: verifiable convolutional neural network based on zk-snarks. IEEE Trans. Dependable Secure Comput. **21**(4), 4254–4270 (2024)

11. Takabi, D., et al.: Privacy preserving neural network inference on encrypted data with GPUs. arXiv preprint arXiv:1911.11377 (2019)

12. Huang, C., Wang, J., Chen, H., Si, S., Huang, Z., Xiao, J.: zkMLaaS: a verifiable scheme for machine learning as a service. In: 2022 IEEE Global Communications Conference, GLOBE-COM 2022, Rio de Janeiro, Brazil, pp. 5475–5480 (2022). https://doi.org/10.1109/GLOBEC OM48099.2022.10000784

13. Khan, K.M., Arshad, J., Khan, M.M.: Investigating performance constraints for blockchain based secure e-voting system. Futur. Gener. Comput. Syst. **105**, 13–26 (2020)

14. Bamakan, S.M.H., Motavali, A., Bondarti, A.B.: A survey of blockchain consensus algorithms performance evaluation criteria. Expert Syst. Appl. **154**, 113385 (2020)

15. Lavaur, T., Detchart, J., Lacan, J., et al.: Modular zk-rollup on-demand. J. Netw. Comput. Appl. **217**, 103678 (2023)

16. Liu, Y., Hao, X., Ren, W., et al.: A blockchain-based decentralized, fair and authenticated information sharing scheme in zero trust Internet-of-Things. IEEE Trans. Comput. **72**(2), 501–512 (2022)

17. Sun, X., Yu, F.R., Zhang, P., et al.: A survey on zero-knowledge proof in blockchain. IEEE Netw. **35**(4), 198–205 (2021)

18. Beullens, W., Seiler, G.: Labrador: compact proofs for R1CS from module-SIS. In: Hand-schuh, H., Lysyanskaya, A. (eds.) CRYPTO 2023. LNCS, vol. 14085, pp. 518–548. Springer, Cham (2023). https://doi.org/10.1007/978-3-031-38554-4_17

19. Bellés-Muñoz, M., Isabel, M., Muñoz-Tapia, J.L., Rubio, A., Baylina, J.: Circom: a cir-cuit description language for building zero-knowledge applications. IEEE Trans. Dependable Secure Comput. **20**(6), 4733–4751 (2023). https://doi.org/10.1109/TDSC.2022.3232813

20. Chollet, F.: Xception: deep learning with depthwise separable convolutions. In: Proceedings of the IEEE Conference on Computer Vision and Pattern Recognition (2017)

21. Hesamifard, E., Takabi, H., Ghasemi, M.: Deep neural networks classification over encrypted data. In: Proceedings of the Ninth ACM Conference on Data and Application Security and Privacy (CODASPY 2019) (2019)

22. Tan, M., Le, Q.: EfficientNet: rethinking model scaling for convolutional neural networks. In: International Conference on Machine Learning. PMLR (2019)

CLB-BAFL: Critical Learning Behaviour Verification Mechanism for Blockchain-Based Asynchronous Federated Learning

Yifei Tang[1], Zhaohui Zhang[1]([🖂]), Jiawei Hu[1], and Man Qi[2]

[1] Donghua University, Shanghai 201620, China
zhzhang@dhu.edu.cn
[2] Christ Church University, Canterbury CT1 1QU, UK

Abstract. Federated learning (FL) addresses the issue of data privacy in collaborative learning environments. Blockchain and asynchronous aggregation have been combined to address the issues of centralisation and efficiency. However, the lack of regulation of data makes FL models vulnerable to poisoning attacks. Therefore, we propose a new secure blockchain-based FL framework. The framework employs an asynchronous critical learning behaviour verification mechanism to defend against poisoning attacks. Clients construct the asynchronous learning behaviour models to illustrate its gradient variation pattern and the characteristics during local learning. Miners choose the honest client by the performance on the test dataset and remove malicious clients by comparing their critical learning behaviours with the honest client. The asynchronous weighted aggregation is employed to mitigate the impact of low-quality models during the aggregation phase. Experiments indicate that the proposed mechanism is effective against more than half of malicious attackers and outperforms existing defence algorithms, such as Foolsgold, RLR and multi-krum. Meanwhile, our proposed framework also exhibits good learning performance compared to other asynchronous federated learning frameworks, such as BAFL and FedAsync.

Keywords: Blockchain federated learning · Poisoning attack · Critical Learning Behaviour · Behaviour verification · Secure aggregation

1 Introduction

With the rise of deep learning and edge computing, the training of models usually requires a large amount of data support, which is usually distributed on different parties, and these distributed data form "data silos" due to data privacy and other issues [1]. Federated learning (FL) as an emerging distributed learning framework [2] allows participants to collaboratively train the model with a central server while safeguarding their data privacy. However, the central server is prone to various trust issues [3,4], such as a single point of failure and privacy leakage.

G. Zhao et al. (Eds.): BWTAC 2024, CCIS 2277, pp. 400–411, 2025.
https://doi.org/10.1007/978-981-97-9412-6_36

Blockchain, a distributed and transparent shared ledger, has been utilised to address the centralization problem [5,6]. Existing research has used blockchain to build decentralised FL, exploiting the properties of blockchain to effectively solve the limitations of traditional FL applied in networks [7–9]. In addition, existing studies have introduced asynchronous aggregation to speed up model aggregation between clients, such as BAFL and FedAsync [10–13]. However, malicious individuals may appear among the participants to carry out poisoning attacks by poisoning the local data and modifying the classification boundaries of the local models [14].

Existing research is broadly divided into two categories to defend the attack; one is to construct specific secure aggregation algorithms such as Krum, Multi-Krum [15], RLR [16] and Foolsgold [17] aggregation algorithms. The idea of these secure aggregation is to weaken the effect of malicious parameters during aggregation. Another category is to prevent malicious parameters from participating in aggregation. This is done by comparing differences in certain dimensions, such as data distribution and model parameters, through anomaly detection algorithms to identify malicious parameters [18,19]. However, it is challenging to perform secure model aggregation only for some backdoor attacks whose effects are not particularly obvious [20]. In an asynchronous environment, it also makes detection of malicious models more difficult.

To address the above issues, we propose a new mechanism for secure blockchain-based asynchronous FL based on the previous work [21]. In an asynchronous environment, we compare clients to different students, each of whom may learn at a different pace, but we do not assume that the student with low learning effectiveness is not a good learner. If the intelligent and responsive student has already finished the second chapter and the student with slow responses has only finished the first chapter, then when verifying whether a student is good or bad, we only compare the two students' performance in the first chapter. Then when all the other students have an understanding of the critical knowledge of each chapter that is consistent with that of the good students, the whole class can get a good grade. The main contributions of this paper are as follows:

- We propose a blockchain-based asynchronous FL framework with secure verification mechanism, which solves the security problem of poisoning attacks on clients in asynchronous scenarios and effectively guarantees the reliability of the global model.
- We propose an asynchronous learning behaviour model that can portray the behaviour consistency pattern of honest clients or abnormal clients in the asynchronous scenario during local training.
- We propose an asynchronous critical learning behaviour verification algorithm based on the asynchronous learning behavior model, which can effectively identify local models with malicious components.
- We propose an asynchronous quality weighted aggregation algorithm that assigns weights to global updates based on the training quality of local models, effectively reducing the impact of low-quality local models on global models.

2   New Secure Framework for Blockchain-Based Asynchronous Federated Learning

In this section, we present our proposal, a blockchain-based asynchronous FL framework with the critical learning behaviour verification mechanism(CLB-BAFL), and describe the workflow of the framework. As shown in Fig. 1, the blockchain-based asynchronous FL with a critical learning behaviour verification mechanism (CLB-BAFL) consists of clients, miners and the blockchain. The blockchain with miners, as an alternative structure to the traditional central server of FL, is responsible for the functions of collecting and verifying local models and aggregating, updating and distributing global models in the whole federation learning process. The operation under one global iteration consists of the following steps:

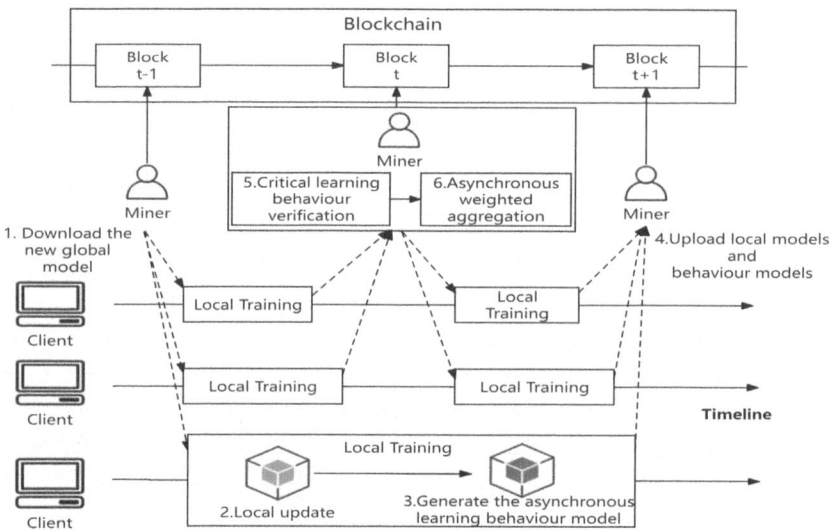

Fig. 1. The workflow of CLB-BAFL.

Step 1 : Download the new global model. The client downloads the latest global model from the latest block of the blockchain and initialises its own local model to this model.

Step 2 : Local update. The clients perform the local training on the local model based on their local training sets. The training iteration is a continuous search for the optimal solution of the model parameters that minimize the local loss value, and finally, the local model is updated.

Step 3 : Generate the asynchronous learning behaviour model. The clients generate the learning behaviour pace after local training and then construct asynchronous learning behaviour models based on the learning behaviour pace, iterations of the initial local model and the final local model (see Sect. 3 for details).

Step 4 : Upload local models and behaviour models. After generating local model updates and asynchronous learning behaviour models locally, the clients upload them to the blockchain network.

Step 5 : Critical learning behaviour verification. When the waiting phase is over, miners activate the verification mechanism. Miners verify the local models, mark the clients corresponding to the asynchronous learning behaviour models that pass the validation as honest clients. (See Sect. 4 for details).

Step 6 : Asynchronous weighted aggregation. The update weights of the local models of each honest client are calculated by a specific weight function. (See Sect. 5 for details). After calculating the weights of each honest model, these honest models will be aggregated into a new global model based on the weights.

In the following, the three core parts of the framework are described in detail: modelling of asynchronous learning behaviour, verification of asynchronous critical learning behaviour, and asynchronous weighted aggregation.

3   Asynchronous Learning Behaviour Modelling

This section describes how to model the asynchronous learning behaviour of clients. The specific modelling process is shown in Algorithm 1. The model presented in this paper is based on previous work [21], and the definitions 1–2 that will be presented below have been given in the previous literature. For the sake of completeness, we repeat here the definitions already available in previous work.

In the tth global iteration of asynchronous FL, since asynchronous aggregation does not wait for all participants to finish training the local models. Therefore, in this iteration, the local models participating in the aggregation are trained based on the global model $\Phi_G^{(k)}$ of the kth iteration, where the range of k is [0, t−1]. In other words, the global model $\Phi_G^{(k)}$ is the initial local model $\Phi_i^{(t,0)}$ trained locally by client D_i. For efficiency, it is usually iterated locally E_i times. Here, the stochastic gradient descent (SGD) optimization algorithm is used for the local model update [22].

Definition 1 (Local Model Update). The local model update refers to the process of updating the local model by performing SGD on the mini-batch data samples B_i in the global iteration t and the local iteration e. It can be calculated as follows:

$$\Phi_i^{(t,e)} = \Phi_i^{(t,e-1)} - \eta_i \cdot \delta(\Phi_i^{(t,e-1)}, B_i), i = 0, 1, 2, ...N \qquad (1)$$

where $\delta(\Phi_i^{(t,e-1)}, B_i)$ represents the gradient of the local model in global iteration t and local iteration e. B_i represents the mini-batch data samples used for

SGD and $\delta(\Phi_i^{(t,e-1)}, B_i) = \frac{1}{|B_i|} \sum_{j=1}^{|B_i|} \frac{\partial Loss(y,\hat{y})}{\partial \Phi_i^{(t,e-1)}}$. η_i represents the learning rate of model training for client D_i.

The essence of local training is to continuously update the local model parameters to minimise model loss. This means the behaviour of the clients in local training will be reflected in the local gradients. To build a portrait of the client's learning behaviour, the change rules of the gradient values can reflect the learning behaviour rules of the client. In order to prevent the weakening of the similarity between honest clients due to the different number of local iterations E_i, the average calculation of the gradient change value is used here. Since it is a reflection of the common behaviour of clients in local training, it is here referred to as the pacing of learning behaviour.

Definition 2 (Learning Behaviour Pace). The learning behaviour pace refers to the average gradient value of the client D_i after local iteration E_i in the tth global iteration. It can be calculated as follows:

$$BP_i^{(t)} = \frac{\sum_{e=1}^{E_i} \delta(\Phi_i^{(t,e-1)}, B_i)}{E_i}, i = 0, 1, 2, ...N \qquad (2)$$

where $\delta(\Phi_i^{(t,e-1)}, B_i)$ is the gradient of the local model $\Phi_i^{(t,e-1)}$ in the global iteration t and the local iteration e. From Eq. (1), the training behaviour pace $BP_i^{(t)}$ can be obtained by calculating the difference between the local model of the client D_i before and after the local iteration divided by the learning rate η_i and the number of local iterations E_i, that is, $BP_i^{(t)} = \frac{\Phi_i^{(t,E_i)} - \Phi_i^{(t,0)}}{\eta_i E_i}$.

However, in the asynchronous scenario, the initial local models of clients and the final time of participation in aggregation may not be consistent. Here, we construct an asynchronous training behaviour model to characterize the learning behaviour of clients in asynchronous scenarios.

Definition 3 (Asynchronous learning Behaviour Model). The training behaviour model refers to the triad consisting of the training behaviour pace, the training behaviour direction, the global iteration k in which the client's initial local model is located, and the global iteration t in which the client's final local model is located, in the tth global iteration. It can be represented as follows:

$$AH_i^{(t)} = (BP_i^{(t)}, k, t), i = 0, 1, 2, ...N \qquad (3)$$

where $AH_i^{(t)}$ represents the kth asynchronous learning behaviour model of the client D_i in the tth global iteration, including its learning behaviour pace.

Algorithm 1. Generate asynchronous learning behaviour model

Input: $D_i, \Phi_G^{(t-1)}, \eta_i, B_i, t$
Output: $\Phi_i^{(t)}, AH_i^{(t)}$
1: //1. Update Local model
2: Download the global model $\Phi_G^{(k)}$
3: Initialize the local model $\Phi_i^{(t,0)} \leftarrow \Phi_G^{(k)}$
4: **for** each $e \in E_i$ **do**
5:     Update local model:$\Phi_i^{(t,e)} = \Phi_i^{(t,e-1)} - \eta_i \cdot \delta(\Phi_i^{(t,e-1)}, B_i)$
6: **end for**
7: Generate local model updates $\Phi_i^{(t)} = \Phi_i^{(t,E_i)}$
8: //2. Generate learning behaviour pace
9: Compute the local model difference :$\Delta\Phi_i^{(t)} = \Phi_i^{(t,E_i)} - \Phi_i^{(t,0)}$
10: Compute training behaviour pace :$BP_i^{(t)} = \Delta\Phi_i^{(t)}/\eta_i E_i$
11: //3. Generate asynchronous learning behaviour model
12: Get the global iteration of the initial and final local model: k, t
13: Generate training behaviour model:$AH_i^{(t)} = (BP_i^{(t)}, k, t)$
14: **return** $\Phi_i^{(t)}, AH_i^{(t)}$

---

4   Asynchronous Critical Learning Behaviour Verification

After local training, the client D_i uploads the local model $\Phi_i^{(t)}$, asynchronous learning behaviour model $AH_i^{(t)}$. The miner will first validate the local model submitted by the client, selecting an honest client to benchmark against its performance on the test set. Here we have an intuition that when a malicious client performs a targeted attack, the model will be more inclined to predict the target class when it makes an error in its prediction, which will lead to a rise in the amount of errors that are predicted to be in the target class. We verified our intuition on the MNIST dataset [23]. We set the client to turn on the attack on round 5 and the target class is set to "7". As shown in Fig. 2, compared to normal learning, the amount of errors in the target class rises significantly once an attack occurs on the client side, and this effect is even more pronounced in label-flipping attacks.

Based on the above, the miner selects the highest ranked client as the honest client based on accuracy and the amount of errors in each category, and uses this as a benchmark to select the honest model for this round. There are two cases: the initial local model of the client is the global model of the previous round of global iterations (k = t−1) or the global model before the previous round of global iterations (k<t−1). When k = t−1, honest and malicious clients are discriminated by comparing the similarity of critical learning behaviour between client D_i and the selected honest client D_h. When k<t−1, the block with iteration k is found by backtracking from the current latest block. Then compare the similarity between client D_i and select the honest client $D_h^{(k)}$ of iteration k.

Definition 4 (Critical Learning Behaviour Pace). When there are more features of a certain type in the dataset, this leads to a larger change in the gradient of the

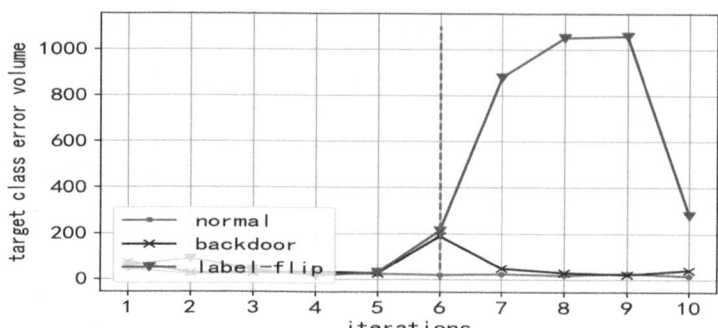

Fig. 2. The amount of target class error in the MNIST dataset in different scenarios.

corresponding parameter to better recognise such features. The critical learning behavioural paces illustrate the focus of the model during updating. It can be calculated as follows:

$$CBP_h^{(t)} = Top(BP_h^{(t)}, \theta), 0 \leq i \leq N \tag{4}$$

where $BP_h^{(t)}$ is the learning behaviour pace of the honest client D_h in the t global iteration, $Top(BP_h^{(t)}, \theta)$ denotes the parameter in $BP_h^{(t)}$ with update size in the top percent θ.

Definition 5 (Critical Learning Behaviour Direction). Critical learning behaviour direction indicates the direction of change in the pace of the critical learning behaviours, i.e., the direction of this client's local optimum with respect to the global model. It can be calculated as follows:

$$CBD_h^{(t)} = Sgn(CBP_h^{(t)}), 0 \leq i \leq N \tag{5}$$

where $Sgn(\cdot)$ is the symbolic function.

After calculating the critical learning behaviour of honest client, the similarity of the critical behaviours of the other clients between the honest client will be calculated.

Definition 6 (Asynchronous Learning Behaviour Honesty). Asynchronous learning behaviour honesty is the similarity between client D_i and the honest client $D_h^{(t)}$ or $D_h^{(k)}$ asynchronous training behaviour model in the tth global iteration, which is used to measure the degree of honesty of the client. It can be calculated as follows:

$$ABH_i^{(t)} = \frac{1}{2}(\rho(CBP_h, BP_i^{(t)}) + \rho(CBD_h, Sgn(BP_i^{(t)}))), 0 \leq i \leq N \tag{6}$$

where $\rho(CBP_h, BP_i^{(t)})$ represents the similarity between the critical learning behaviour pace of the honest client $D_h^{(t)}$ or $D_h^{(k)}$ and the learning behaviour pace of D_i at the corresponding location, and $\rho(CBD_h, Sgn(BP_i^{(t)}))$ represents the similarity between the critical learning behaviour direction of the honest client and the learning behaviour direction of D_i at the corresponding location. In this paper, we use the Pearson correlation coefficient to measure similarity.

After calculating the honesty of each client, the honesty list is clustered and the category with the highest honesty is selected to be added to the aggregated list. The specific algorithm process is shown in Algorithm 2.

Algorithm 2. Verification algorithm of critical learning behaviour

---

Input: $D = \cup_{i=1}^N D_i, \Phi^{(t)} = \cup_{i=1}^N \Phi_i^{(t)}, AH^{(t)} = \cup_{i=1}^N AH_i^{(t)}, t, \theta$
Output: $D_H = \cup_{i=1}^M D_i$
1: //1. Choose the honest client
2: **for** $\Phi_i^{(t)} \in \Phi^{(t)}$ **do**
3:     Get asynchronous learning behavior model :$AH_i^{(t)}$
4:     Compute the accuracy and volume of errors in each class of $\Phi_i^{(t)}$ on the global test dataset
5: **end for**
6: Get the honest client $D_h^{(t)}$ based on the accuracy and volume of errors in each class
7: Add $D_h^{(t)}$ into D_H
8: //2.Compute critical learning behaviour of the honest client
9: Compute the critical learning behaviour pace: $CBP_h^{(t)} = Top(BP_h^{(t)}, \theta)$
10: Compute the critical learning behaviour direction: $CBD_h^{(t)} = Sgn(CBP_h^{(t)})$
11: **for** $AH_i^{(t)} \in AH^{(t)}$ **do**
12:     //3.Compute client learning behaviour honesty
13:     Compute the asynchronous learning behavior honesty:
14: $ABH_i^{(t)} = \frac{1}{2}(\rho(CBP_h, BP_i^{(t)}) + \rho(CBD_h, Sgn(BP_i^{(t)})))$
15:     Add $ABH_i^{(t)}$ into Set_{ABH}
16: **end for**
17: //4.Get aggregated list
18: Clustering Set_{ABH} and get the category with the highest honesty Set_H
19: **for** $D_i \in Set_H$ **do**
20:     Add D_i into D_H
21: **end for**
22: **return** D_H

---

5 Asynchronous Weighted Aggregation

After verifying the legitimacy of the clients, the next step is the aggregation. Among these legitimate clients involved in aggregation, some clients have their local models outdated due to computational resources or time allocation problems, and these local models play a negative role in the aggregation of the global model.

The changes due to local model training can be reflected by the distance between the final and initial local models. In the asynchronous case, in each round of aggregation, even though the initial situation of the aggregated local models may be inconsistent, the changes in these models after aggregation are relative to the global model of the previous round. To better participate in the calculation, the distance is normalized and called the training quality of the local model, i.e., the local learning quality.

Definition 7 (Local Learning Quality). The local learning quality refers to the Euclidean distance between the local and global models normalized to the previous round in the tth global iteration. It can be calculated as follows:

$$Q_i^{(t)} = \frac{d(\Phi_i^{(t)}, \Phi_G^{(t-1)}) - d(\Phi_{min}^{(t)}, \Phi_G^{(t-1)})}{d(\Phi_{max}^{(t)}, \Phi_G^{(t-1)}) - d(\Phi_{min}^{(t)}, \Phi_G^{(t-1)})} \tag{7}$$

where $Q_i^{(t)}$ represents the learning quality of the client D_i in the tth global iteration. $\Phi_{min}^{(t)}, \Phi_{max}^{(t)}$ respectively denote the local models with the minimum and maximum distance from the global model of the previous round.

To better evaluate model performance, the accuracy of the local model on the global test set, $A_i^{(t)}$, is used here as another quality indicator called local evaluation quality.

Definition 8 (Global Update Weight). The global update weight refers to the weight of the local model $\Phi_i^{(t)}$ of client D_i when it participates in the global model aggregation in the tth global iteration, it can be calculated as follows:

$$W_i^{(t)} = (1 - \beta)A_i^{(t)} + \beta Q_i^{(t)} \tag{8}$$

where $\beta(0 < \beta < 1)$ is a moderating factor to balance the relationship between local training quality and local evaluation quality.

After the miner gets the global update weights of the local models, it aggregates and obtains a new global model.

6   Experiments

To verify the effectiveness of CLB-BAFL, we conducts experiments on the public dataset MNIST dataset [23]. Training data is distributed to 20 clients as i.i.d, and the number of local iterations $E_i = 3$. To simulate the distributed and asynchronous scenario, we used four servers equipped with 8 GB RAM and 2.40 GHz Intel(R) Core (TM) i5-1135G7 processors for the experiment, and each server started five processes to simulate the participating nodes. We assume that at least one normal client participates in each round of aggregation. We use a CNN model with two convolutional layers. We compared efficiency of CLB-BAFL with BAFL [13] and FedAsync [12], as shown in Fig. 3, the global model reached convergence at iteration 15, and the efficiency of CLB-BAFL is similar to FedAsync and better than BAFL.

Next we compared the CLB-BAFL with other defence methods in the face of backdoor and label-flipping attacks. Both attacks have a target class of "7"

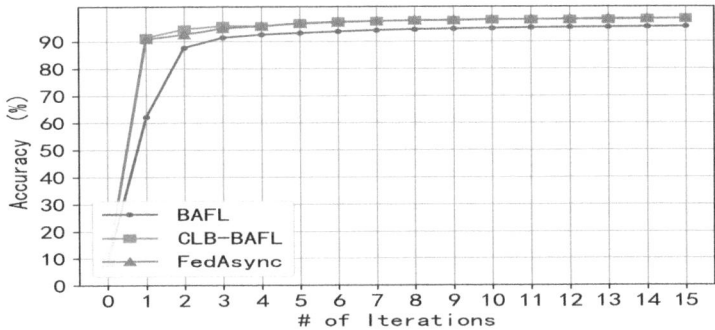

Fig. 3. The Comparison of CLB-BAFL with Other Asynchronous Federated Learning Frameworks.

and the proportion of data poisoning in the backdoor attack is 0.5. The global iteration number is still set to 15. p_c denotes the percentage of clients attacked. And there are two evaluation indicators: main task accuracy(MTA) and attack success rate(ASR). We use FedAsync as a baseline since it has good performance in asynchronous scenarios.

Table 1. Results of Backdoor Attacks on the MNIST Dataset.

Algorithm	$p_c = 0.2$		$p_c = 0.4$		$p_c = 0.6$		$p_c = 0.8$	
	MTA	ASR	MTA	ASR	MTA	ASR	MTA	ASR
FedAsync [12]	98.4%	97.3%	98.4%	99.9%	98.2%	100%	98.3%	100%
krum [15]	97.2%	0.0%	97.2%	0.0%	97.0%	0.1%	97.0%	98.6%
MultiKrum [15]	98.5%	0.0%	**98.5%**	0.0%	98.1%	99.7%	98.3%	99.7%
RLR [16]	**98.6%**	94.6%	98.2%	91.0%	98.4%	99.9%	97.9%	97.1%
Foolsgold [17]	98.4%	0.0%	98.4%	99.2%	**98.5%**	99.7%	98.4%	99.7%
CLB-BAFL(ours)	98.5%	0.0%	98.4%	0.0%	98.3%	**0.0%**	98.3%	**14.4%**

As shown in Table 1, for FedAsync, we can see that model's attention is easily shifted towards backdoor pattern. While the other defences are effective when the attack ratio is low, their effectiveness plummets when the attack ratio exceeds half. CLB-BAFL, on the other hand, achieves the best defence results in all scenarios and had little effect on the main task. For label-flipping attack, as shown in Table 2, similarly, when the percentage of attacks is more than half, the attacks will achieve significant results on the other methods. While the other defences are effective when the attack ratio is low, their effectiveness plummets when the attack ratio exceeds half. And CLB-BAFL defended perfectly in all scenarios with little or no impact on the main task.

Table 2. Results of Label-flipping Attacks on the MNIST Dataset.

Algorithm	$p_c = 0.2$		$p_c = 0.4$		$p_c = 0.6$		$p_c = 0.8$	
	MTA	ASR	MTA	ASR	MTA	ASR	MTA	ASR
FedAsync [12]	98.3%	0.0%	98.2%	0.0%	90.9%	64.4%	87.3%	97.9%
krum [15]	97.0%	0.0%	97.8%	0.0%	87.8%	97.6%	85.8%	97.9%
MultiKrum [15]	98.3%	0.0%	98.4%	0.0%	87.2%	99.4%	87.2%	99.4%
RLR [16]	98.4%	0.0%	98.4%	0.0%	87.4%	92.0%	87.0%	98.1%
Foolsgold [17]	**98.5%**	0.0%	98.4%	0.0%	96.3%	19.4%	87.3%	98.3%
CLB-BAFL(ours)	98.2%	0.0%	98.3%	0.0%	**98.3%**	**0.0%**	**98.2%**	**0.0%**

7   Conclusion

In this paper, we propose a blockchain-based asynchronous FL framework with critical learning behaviour verification mechanism, CLB-BAFL, which can identify malicious nodes through learning behavior and eliminate the effect of malicious nodes to fundamentally prevent malicious parameters from participating in aggregation. We have also experimentally demonstrated the effectiveness of the method. In the future, we will consider more cases, such as non-i.i.d data and multiple attacks.

Acknowledgments. This work was supported by Shanghai Science and Technology Innovation Action Plan Project (no.22511100700).

References

1. Li, Q., Diao, Y., Chen, Q., He, B.: Federated learning on non-iid data silos: an experimental study. In: 2022 IEEE 38th International Conference on Data Engineering (ICDE), pp. 965–978 (2022). https://doi.org/10.1109/ICDE53745.2022.00077
2. Yang, Q., Liu, Y., Cheng, Y., Kang, Y., Chen, T., Yu, H.: Federated Learning, Synthesis Lectures on Artificial Intelligence and Machine Learning. Morgan & Claypool Publishers, San Rafael (2019)
3. Ma, C., et al.: On safeguarding privacy and security in the framework of federated learning. IEEE Netw. **34**(4), 242–248 (2020). https://doi.org/10.1109/MNET.001.1900506
4. Lyu, L., Yu, H., Zhao, J., Yang, Q.: Threats to federated learning. In: Yang, Q., Fan, L., Yu, H. (eds.) Federated Learning. LNCS (LNAI), vol. 12500, pp. 3–16. Springer, Cham (2020). https://doi.org/10.1007/978-3-030-63076-8_1
5. Hunt, A.D.: Bitcoin: a peer-to-peer electronic cash system (2008). https://api.semanticscholar.org/CorpusID:236214795
6. Rawat, D.B., Chaudhary, V., Doku, R.: Blockchain technology: emerging applications and use cases for secure and trustworthy smart systems. J. Cybersecur. Priv. **1**(1), 4–18 (2021). https://doi.org/10.3390/jcp1010002, https://www.mdpi.com/2624-800X/1/1/2

7. Kim, H., Park, J., Bennis, M., Kim, S.L.: Blockchained on-device federated learning. IEEE Commun. Lett. **24**(6), 1279–1283 (2020). https://doi.org/10.1109/LCOMM.2019.2921755

8. Li, Y., Lai, Y., Chen, C., Zheng, Z.: VeryFL: a verify federated learning framework embedded with blockchain (2023)

9. Bao, X., Su, C., Xiong, Y., Huang, W., Hu, Y.: Flchain: a blockchain for auditable federated learning with trust and incentive. In: 2019 5th International Conference on Big Data Computing and Communications (BIGCOM), pp. 151–159 (2019). https://doi.org/10.1109/BIGCOM.2019.00030

10. Hu, C.H., Chen, Z., Larsson, E.G.: Scheduling and aggregation design for asynchronous federated learning over wireless networks. IEEE J. Sel. Areas Commun. **41**(4), 874–886 (2023). https://doi.org/10.1109/JSAC.2023.3242719

11. Li, Z., et al.: Asyfed: accelerated federated learning with asynchronous communication mechanism. IEEE Internet Things J. **10**(10), 8670–8683 (2023). https://doi.org/10.1109/JIOT.2022.3231913

12. Xie, C., Koyejo, S., Gupta, I.: Asynchronous federated optimization (2020)

13. Feng, L., Zhao, Y., Guo, S., Qiu, X., Li, W., Yu, P.: BAFL: a blockchain-based asynchronous federated learning framework. IEEE Trans. Comput. **71**(5), 1092–1103 (2022). https://doi.org/10.1109/TC.2021.3072033

14. Fang, M., Cao, X., Jia, J., Gong, N.Z.: Local model poisoning attacks to byzantine-robust federated learning (2021)

15. Blanchard, P., El Mhamdi, E.M., Guerraoui, R., Stainer, J.: Machine learning with adversaries: byzantine tolerant gradient descent. In: Proceedings of the 31st International Conference on Neural Information Processing Systems, pp. 118-128. NIPS 2017, Curran Associates Inc., Red Hook, NY, USA (2017)

16. Ozdayi, M.S., Kantarcioglu, M., Gel, Y.R.: Defending against backdoors in federated learning with robust learning rate. ArXiv **abs/2007.03767** (2020)

17. Fung, C., Yoon, C.J.M., Beschastnikh, I.: Mitigating sybils in federated learning poisoning (2020)

18. Li, S., Cheng, Y., Liu, Y., Wang, W., Chen, T.: Abnormal client behavior detection in federated learning (2019)

19. Kabir, E., Song, Z., Rashid, M.R.U., Mehnaz, S.: Flshield: a validation based federated learning framework to defend against poisoning attacks. ArXiv **abs/2308.05832** (2023)

20. Bagdasaryan, E., Veit, A., Hua, Y., Estrin, D., Shmatikov, V.: How to backdoor federated learning. In: Chiappa, S., Calandra, R. (eds.) Proceedings of the Twenty Third International Conference on Artificial Intelligence and Statistics. Proceedings of Machine Learning Research, vol. 108, pp. 2938–2948. PMLR (2020)

21. Zhang, Z., Hu, J., Ma, L., Pei, R., Wang, P.: BVFB: training behavior verification mechanism for secure blockchain-based federated learning. Comput. Informatics **41**, 1401–1424 (2022). https://api.semanticscholar.org/CorpusID:257677115

22. Zhang, T.: Solving large scale linear prediction problems using stochastic gradient descent algorithms. In: Proceedings of the Twenty-First International Conference on Machine Learning, p. 116. ICML 2004, Association for Computing Machinery, New York, NY, USA (2004). https://doi.org/10.1145/1015330.1015332

23. Lecun, Y., Bottou, L., Bengio, Y., Haffner, P.: Gradient-based learning applied to document recognition. Proc. IEEE **86**(11), 2278–2324 (1998). https://doi.org/10.1109/5.726791

GeePT: Governance of Efficient and Extensible Privacy-Preserving Transaction for Blockchain

Liying Wang[1(✉)], Hongyu Gui[2], Xiao Zhang[2], Song Shang[2], and Lei Sai[2]

[1] College of Electronic and Information Engineering, Tongji University, Shanghai, China
wangliying@tongji.edu.cn
[2] Wuxi Geely Blockchain Technology Co., Ltd., Wuxi, China

Abstract. Privacy-preserving transactions are currently an important direction for the development of Blockchain. Traditional blockchain transactions record the information of all participants, which leads to privacy leakage of user information and behavior. Privacy preserving methods such as Ring Confidential Transactions lose efficiency, while Zero-Knowledge Proof is limited to the range proof. To fix the aforementioned issues, we propose and implement a high efficiency, strong privacy, and flexible scalability privacy-preserving transactions framework, which adopts a master-slave chain design and supports contract parallelism. By reducing pseudo commitments and the dimensionality of the signature matrix, the transaction efficiency and privacy protection level are improved while ensuring transaction anonymity. Furthermore, the improved scope proof function enables it to provide proof within any range, providing strong transaction supervision for regulatory authorities. Finally, through comparative experiments with well-known privacy-preserving trading projects, the results prove that our method is superior to existing methods.

Keywords: Privacy-preserving Transactions · Ring Confidential · Pedersen Commitment · Zero-Knowledge Proof · Blockchain

1 Introduction

Blockchain, with its unique decentralized characteristics, provides participants with a transparent and secure platform. However, this transparency also poses a risk of privacy leakage, as all transaction records are publicly visible. This may expose the user's financial information and transaction behavior. This type of information may be used to identify users, track fund flows, and even manipulate prices. Privacy trading, as an important branch of blockchain technology, aims to solve this contradiction. The core goal of privacy trading is to provide higher levels of privacy protection without sacrificing the decentralization, security, and transparency of blockchain. To this end, researchers have proposed various privacy protection techniques, including Zero Knowledge proofs, Ring Signatures and Homomorphic Encryption [1–3]. However, privacy transactions

G. Zhao et al. (Eds.): BWTAC 2024, CCIS 2277, pp. 412–418, 2025.
https://doi.org/10.1007/978-981-97-9412-6_37

typically involve using encryption techniques to encrypt transaction data and decrypting it when needed. These encryption and decryption operations may increase the computational cost and time consumption of transactions, resulting in lower transaction performance. Secondly, privacy transactions make it difficult for regulatory agencies to track and monitor illegal activities such as money laundering and terrorist financing. Regulatory agencies typically rely on monitoring transaction traffic and analyzing transaction patterns to identify suspicious activities, but privacy transactions make these activities more difficult to detect and prevent.

Our Contribution are as follows. Firstly, we have designed and implemented a high efficiency, strong privacy, and flexible scalability privacy-preserving transactions framework called GeePT. It is a privacy transaction governance framework that combines main and sub chains while also supporting heterogeneous cross chain models and parallel contracts. To prevent transaction tracking and analysis, and reduce the risk of exposing financial information to users. Secondly, performance improvement. We have increased TPS through contract parallelism. By reducing the minimum amount of data provided by the original ring signature, the signature verification process is accelerated. By removing the blind factor difference, the data size of ring signature issuance and verification are greatly reduced, while improving the efficiency of blockchain carrying ring signature technology on the chain. Finally, scalable and enhanced regulatory capabilities. By improving the scope of proof, the transfer amount can be controlled within a certain range, and regulatory requirements for users to narrow down the range of transfer amounts can enhance regulatory compliance.

2   Related Work

Blockchain and Pseudoanonymity. As the first widely used cryptocurrency, Bitcoin's design provides a certain degree of anonymity, but it is not truly privacy protection. Scholars have demonstrated how to identify user identities through address clustering and traffic analysis by analyzing Bitcoin transaction graphs, revealing the issue of pseudo anonymity in Bitcoin and proposing anonymous protocols to protect nodes that play an important role in the network, such as anonymous emails and text data [4–6].

Cryptography and Privacy-Preserving Transactions. Zero knowledge proof is a cryptographic technique that allows the verifier to prove the correctness of a statement without leaking any useful information. Researchers apply zero knowledge proofs to blockchain and propose multiple privacy transaction solutions [7–9]. Monero uses ring signature technology to hide the sender of the transaction, while Zcash provides a method for private transactions through mixed currency services [10,11]. In terms of meeting regulatory requirements. Scholars have proposed various solutions such as privacy enhancement protocols, threshold signatures, and lightweight consensus mechanisms to improve its scalability [12–14].

3   The Proposed Scheme

GeePT and the underlying architecture of blockchain are shown (see Fig. 1). We adopt a multi-level, pluggable, highly scalable, high-performance, and highly private blockchain design architecture. The architecture is currently divided into five layers: Interface layer, GeePT layer, Protocol layer, Adaptation layer, and Resource layer. The interface layer includes APIs and SDKs provided to users. The protocol layer includes a consensus mechanism, P2P networks and distributed ledgers. The adaptation layer includes light nodes and adapters. The resource layer includes physical machines, encryption cards and cloud platforms.

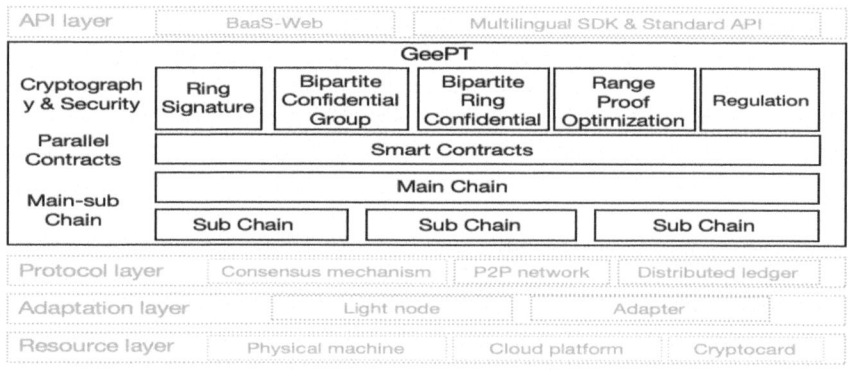

Fig. 1. GeePT and the underlying architecture of blockchain.

Main-Sub Chain Structure and Contract Parallelism. Our designed chain supports not only a homogeneous main-sub chain model but also a heterogeneous chain model. We have designed a verifiable main-sub chain association mechanism that allows correct verification of sub-chain data without requiring the main chain nodes to store all the sub-chain data. The main chain records the key information of sub-chain blocks, including the list of sub-chain verification nodes, block header information, simplified payment verification and cross-chain receipts. After the main chain accepts a proposed sub-chain block, it must accept challenges from challengers within a specified period. If there are no challenges or the challenges fail, the sub-chain block is considered valid and the block confirmation is finalized. If a challenge is successful, it reverts to the last correct block position. In a dual-layer polymorphic main-sub chain system, using a unified ledger and challenger mechanisms, and employing a verifiable main-sub chain association method, the overall performance of the blockchain is enhanced without compromising the security of the sub-chain.

Privacy-Preserving Transactions. Consider a scenario where user A transfers funds to user B. First, user A creates the necessary public and private key pairs for RingCT (Ring Confidential Transactions) in their wallet (or offline service). Next, A creates Pedersen commitments and selects an appropriate mix of public keys from the blockchain. Then, A obtains a one-time address for B and creates a two-party ring confidential transaction. Under the GeePT mechanism (see Fig. 2), the transaction amount is not displayed in plaintext but rather shown as a commitment $C(r, a)$, which is the obfuscated amount.

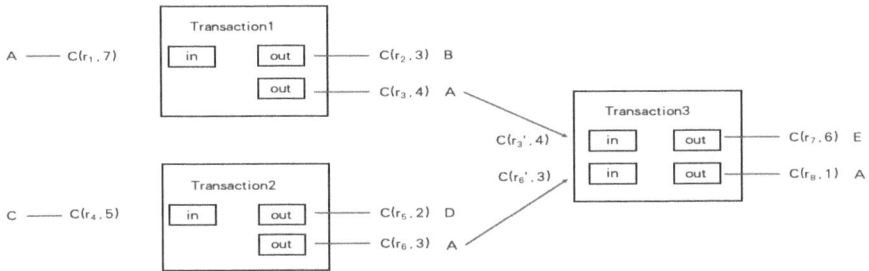

Fig. 2. Details of constructing ring confidential transactions.

During the construction of the ring confidential matrix by the sender, the quantity of randomly generated values is decreased. In GeePT, only one pseudo-commitment needs to be randomly generated, thereby reducing the computation process and enhancing efficiency. Merely a bipartite matrix needs to be supplied, and the verification does not require the blinding factor difference between outputs and inputs, reducing the computation process and decreasing storage requirements. Since the blinding factor difference between outputs and inputs is not necessary, the bipartite matrix can be directly verified, shortening the verification process and improving efficiency.

In the process of constructing transactions, improvements have been made to the functionality of range proofs in zero-knowledge proofs, enabling them to provide proofs of any greater-than or less-than intervals, such as [15, 20]. This is achieved through relational operators applied to a certain attribute (e.g., age-AGE). In the process of constructing ring signatures, the Pedersen Commitment corresponds to $C = r * G + v * H$. When proving that a certain amount (e.g., 15) is greater than or equal to 10, a Pedersen Commitment for 15 is first constructed as $C_1 = r_1 * G + 15 * H$. Then, $C_2 = C_1 - 10 * H$ is computed. Since G and H are generator points and publicly known, anyone can verify this step. Next, a zero-knowledge range proof is applied to prove that C_2 satisfies greater than or equal to zero, thus proving that C_1 is greater than or equal to 10. When proving that a certain amount (e.g., 15) is less than or equal to 20, a Pedersen Commitment for 15 is first constructed as $C_1 = r_1 * G + 15 * H$. We can easily construct C_1 within [0,16], [0,32], [0,64], [0,128]. To prove that $C_1 \leq 20$, it is sufficient to prove that $C_2 = C_1 + (64 - 20) * H$ lies within [0,64]. Therefore, the improved proof can demonstrate that a certain amount is within any real interval, facilitating the realm of privacy protection in blockchain systems. For instance, when regulations mandate that the transfer amount must be less than 500, the sender needs to construct the corresponding proof for authentication through the blockchain. Subsequently, user B can filter transactions relevant to themselves through their wallet, decrypt the specific amount and commitment value transferred by A, and can spend this amount in the next transaction.

4   Experiment and Analysis

Experiment on TPS of Parallel Contracts. Local area network, database and nodes deployed on the same machine. There are four hosts have the same configuration (Intel Xeon Gold 6271C CPU 2.60 GHz, 8 Cores, 16 GB Memory, 500 GB HD, Ubuntu 20.04 operating system). Execute the testing script to send transactions to the nodes with transaction type being contract invocation. Record the number of transactions processed by the nodes, the number of blocks generated, and the time taken, then calculate the averages. Examine the underlying transaction processing capacity by sending a large number of requests to the underlying layer and observing the number of transactions processed in each block and the average transactions processed per second (Table 1).

Table 1. Experiment on TPS of Parallel Contracts

Mode	Block Count	Transactions	Time Taken(s)	Average Block Time(s)	TPS
Parallel	20	121,130	200	10	605.65
Non-Parallel	20	73,167	200	10	365.83

Privacy Transaction Signing and Verification Experiment. The scheme was implemented using Rust language to further evaluate the project's performance in terms of communication and computation costs. The scheme runs on an Intel Core i7-13700H 2.40 GHz machine. Well-known privacy-preserving transaction projects Monero and Zcash serve as comparative baselines. The mixing inputs were based on 6 addresses, while outputs were based on 2 addresses. The optimized RingCT matrix was utilized in this scheme. The data represents the average results obtained from 5*100,000 iterations (Table 2).

Table 2. Privacy Transaction Signing and Verification Experiment

Project	Signature Size (Bytes)	Signing Rate (ms)	Verification Rate (ms)
Monero	10840	380	121
Zcash	3840	19580	11.5
Our Scheme	7776	212	82

5 Conclusion

In conclusion, our proposed scheme, governance of efficient and extensible privacy-preserving transaction, has achieved significant advantages in efficiency and scalability compared to well-known privacy protection transaction schemes. With the deep practice of GeePT in the industry, we will continue to improve its performance in the future.

References

1. Fiege, U., Fiat, A., Shamir, A.: Zero knowledge proofs of identity. In: Proceedings of the Nineteenth Annual ACM Symposium on Theory of Computing, pp. 210–217 (1987)
2. Bender, A., Katz, J., Morselli, R.: Ring signatures: stronger definitions, and constructions without random oracles. In: Halevi, S., Rabin, T. (eds.) TCC 2006. LNCS, vol. 3876, pp. 60–79. Springer, Heidelberg (2006). https://doi.org/10.1007/11681878_4
3. Yi, X., Paulet, R., Bertino, E.: Homomorphic encryption. In: Homomorphic Encryption and Applications. SCS, pp. 27–46. Springer, Cham (2014). https://doi.org/10.1007/978-3-319-12229-8_2
4. Narayanan, A., Bonneau, J., Felten, E., et al.: Bitcoin and cryptocurrency technologies (2016)
5. Rachedi, A., Benslimane, A.: Security and pseudo-anonymity with a cluster-based approach for MANET. In: IEEE GLOBECOM 2008-2008 IEEE Global Telecommunications Conference, pp. 1–6. IEEE (2008)
6. Eckert, C., Pircher, A.: Internet anonymity: problems and solutions. In: Dupuy, M., Paradinas, P. (eds.) SEC 2001. IIFIP, vol. 65, pp. 35–50. Springer, Boston, MA (2002). https://doi.org/10.1007/0-306-46998-7_3
7. Bitansky, N., Canetti, R., Chiesa, A., et al.: Recursive composition and bootstrapping for SNARKS and proof-carrying data. In: Proceedings of the Forty-Fifth Annual ACM Symposium on Theory of Computing, pp. 111–120 (2013)
8. Zhou, L., Diro, A., Saini, A., et al.: Leveraging zero knowledge proofs for blockchain-based identity sharing: a survey of advancements, challenges and opportunities[J]. J. Inf. Secur. Appl. **80**, 103678 (2024)
9. Mouris, D., Tsoutsos, N.G.: Zilch: a framework for deploying transparent zero-knowledge proofs. IEEE Trans. Inf. Forensics Secur. **16**, 3269–3284 (2021). https://doi.org/10.1109/TIFS.2021.3074869
10. Noether, S.: Ring signature confidential transactions for monero (2015)

11. Sasson, E.B., Chiesa, A., Garman, C., et al.: Zerocash: decentralized anonymous payments from bitcoin. In: 2014 IEEE Symposium on Security and Privacy, pp. 459–474. IEEE (2014)
12. Buterin, V., Illum, J., Nadler, M., et al.: Blockchain privacy and regulatory compliance: towards a practical equilibrium. Blockchain Res. Appl. **5**(1), 100176 (2024)
13. Zhou, Q., Huang, H., Zheng, Z., et al.: Solutions to scalability of blockchain: a survey. IEEE Access **8**, 16440–16455 (2020)
14. Rao, I.S., Kiah, M.L., Hameed, M.M., et al.: Scalability of blockchain: a comprehensive review and future research direction. Cluster Comput. 1–24 (2024)

HetGNN-TF: Self-supervised Learning on Heterogeneous Graph Neural Network via Topology and Feature Reconstruction

Chao Li[1(✉)], Xinming Liu[1], Jinhu Fu[1], Zhongying Zhao[2], and Qingtian Zeng[1,2]

[1] College of Electronic and Information Engineering, Shandong University of Science and Technology, Qianwangang Road, Qingdao 266590, Shandong, China
`lichao@sdust.edu.cn`
[2] College of Computer Science and Engineering, Shandong University of Science and Technology, Qianwangang Road, Qingdao 266590, Shandong, China

Abstract. Heterogeneous graph neural networks (HGNNs) are emerging techniques with remarkable capabilities in handling heterogeneous graphs. Self-supervised HGNN models have garnered significant attention. Contrastive learning, due to its excellent performance, is widely employed in heterogeneous graph representation learning. However, existing methods may lead to the loss of original topology and feature information, and there are limitations in positive and negative sample selection. To address these issues, we present a self-supervised learning approach, HetGNN-TF, on heterogeneous graph neural networks via topology and feature reconstruction. We specifically reconstruct semantic structure using an encoder-decoder to guide the model to learn original structural information. We also construct a feature similarity graph to reconstruct node features through specific encoders, guiding them to fully grasp feature information. Additionally, we design an adaptive sample selection mechanism for iterative optimization of samples. Experimental results demonstrate the superior performance of our approach over existing state-of-the-art methods. The source code and data are available on GitHub (https://github.com/LiuXMaa/HetGNN-TF.git).

Keywords: Heterogeneous Graph Neural Network · Contrastive Learning · Self-supervised Learning

1 Introduction

In real-world scenarios, heterogeneous graphs can effectively model the multiple types of nodes and complex interactions. Heterogeneous graph neural networks have demonstrated a great advantage in handling heterogeneous graph data. However, existing models require a large amount of labeled data [17–19], and it is difficult to take advantage of the nodes themselves when labels are sparse or missing. Self-supervised heterogeneous graph neural networks can improve the

G. Zhao et al. (Eds.): BWTAC 2024, CCIS 2277, pp. 419–430, 2025.
https://doi.org/10.1007/978-981-97-9412-6_38

expressive capability of models by mining their own information, thereby reducing their dependency on manually labeled data. Contrastive learning, a typical self-supervised learning method, optimizes node representations by distancing target nodes from negative samples and approaching positive samples in different views. It has shown outstanding performance in self-supervised heterogeneous graph representation learning. Nevertheless, there are two main problems with the current HGNN methods based on contrastive learning, which are as follows.

(1) Contrastive learning can lead to the loss of the original structure and feature information in heterogeneous graphs. In terms of topology, previous HGNNs directly input the original structure into the GNN encoder to capture semantic information inherent [5,16]. However, as shown in the literature [13], the node representations obtained after passing the original structure through the GNN encoder cannot fully encode the rich topological information in the heterogeneous graph, and they deviate from the original structure in terms of data distribution, resulting in the loss of some structural information. In terms of features, previous contrastive learning approaches either ignored the feature information in the heterogeneous graph [16] or used it solely as auxiliary information to train node embeddings [20]. However, the feature information in the heterogeneous graph plays a significant role in node embedding [1,6]. Hence, there is a limitation in existing contrastive learning methods in fully utilizing feature information to establish a contrastive perspective. Therefore, how to fully utilize the original structure and feature information is an urgent issue to be addressed.

(2) Choosing high-quality positive and negative samples to enhance model expression is a challenge. Existing self-supervised representation learning methods mainly adopt two approaches for selecting positive and negative samples. One is to select positive and negative samples based solely on topology [16]. The other is to select positive and negative samples by combining topology and features [5]. Heco [16] sets a threshold based on the number of meta-paths to complete the selection of positive samples for contrastive learning; HGCL [5] incorporates feature information to further restrict the selection of positive samples based on HeCo, and the results show that this method is effective in improving the quality of the selected positive samples. Although these methods can improve the quality of positive samples to some extent, they all rely on pre-trained information to complete the selection of positive samples, and their selected positive samples cannot be optimized based on specific downstream tasks. Therefore, it is necessary to optimize and enhance the method of positive sample selection.

To address the above problems, in this paper, we propose a self-supervised learning on heterogeneous graph neural network via topology and feature reconstruction (HetGNN-TF). Firstly, we propose an encoder-decoder architecture based on topological reconstruction, enabling encoders to fully learn the original structure of heterogeneous graphs by designing the reconstruction loss. Secondly, we design the encoders based on various semantics. By constructing the reconstruction loss between the feature similarity graph and the original feature similarity graph under different semantics, The encoders can adequately learn the original feature information. Finally, based on the contrastive learning strategy between topological reconstructed view and feature reconstructed view, we propose a sample selection mechanism that enables positive and negative samples to be optimized with specific downstream task, to achieve high-quality embedding of the target nodes.

The contributions of this study are summarized as follows.

- We propose a self-supervised heterogeneous graph neural network model based on topology and feature reconstruction. We reconstruct the topology and features by designing specific encoders, and guide the encoders to learn the original structure and features through the reconstruction loss.
- We present an positive sample selection strategy, which enables the positive sample selection to optimize with specific downstream tasks, allowing us to increase the quality of positive and negative samples.

2   Related Work

2.1   Self-supervised Graph Neural Network

Self-supervised graph neural networks enhance model expressiveness by mining features through reasonable agent tasks (e.g., mutual information maximization [11,14]). DGI [14] maximizes mutual information of target nodes with graph-level representation and minimizes negative samples after disrupting features. AMIL [2] reconstructs topology to aggregate node information. SUBLIME [9] constructs an anchor graph to guide structural optimization and maximizes mutual information between anchor graph and learned structure. SUGRL [10] uses mutual information on structural and neighborhood information to increase inter-class variance and constrains intra-class variance with multiple state loss constraints. STABLE [8] preprocesses graphs by similarity metrics, generates enhanced graphs by random recovery to improve data robustness by maximizing mutual information between positive samples. MT-MVGCN [4] uses multiple views and tasks with attention mechanisms and an auxiliary task enhancement model. GraphMAE [3] encodes and decodes input node features with mask tokens and optimizes the model by scaling cosine error as the objective function.

The self-supervised graph neural network is only applicable to homogeneous graphs, but when there are multiple types and complex node and edge relationships in the graph, the homogeneous graph approach is difficult, so the emergence of self-supervised heterogeneous graph neural networks (SL-HGNNs) extends the scope of self-supervised graph neural networks.

2.2   Self-supervised Heterogeneous Graph Neural Network

Self-supervised heterogeneous graph neural networks excel in effectively modeling multiple node types and complex interactions in real networks. HDGI

[12] generates positive and negative sample node representations via semantic attention fusion, and optimizes the model using the mutual information between positive and negative samples and the graph level. DMGI [11] constrains node embedding similarity and maximizes/minimizes mutual information between samples and graph-level representations. NSHE [20] samples instances and constructs multitask learning models. HDMI [7] learns the relationship between node embeddings, graph-level representations, and node attributes through higher-order mutual information and fuses node information via an attention-based module. HeCo [16] aggregates local and higher-order information through different views and jointly optimizes node information by contrastive learning. CKD [15] samples semantic context subgraphs and generates collaborative distillation within and across meta-paths.

3   Preliminaries

In this section, we define some important concepts and problem definitions related to self-supervised heterogeneous graph neural networks.

Definition 1 HGs. The HG can be represented by a network $G = (V, E, X)$, where V denotes the set of nodes, E denotes the set of edges, and X denotes the set of features. G contains three different mapping functions: the node-type, edge-type, and feature-type mapping functions $\Phi : V \to T, \Upsilon : E \to R$, and $\Omega : X \to F$, respectively; where T, R, and F represent the node-type sets, edge-type sets and feature-type sets, respectively $|T| + |R| > 2$.

Definition 2 Meta-path. A meta-path is a special path $P: v_1 \xrightarrow{r_1} v_2 \xrightarrow{r_2} \cdots \xrightarrow{r_l} v_{l+1}$ in the HG with predefined type patterns, where $v \in V$ and $r \in R$. This composite pattern represents the complex semantic information in the HG.

Definition 3 Reconstruction learning. We construct a node representation that matches the original information distribution based on the original information o, and the encoded vector representation $d(o)$, by $L = \min \Sigma_{i \in V}(o, d(o))$ to make the learned representation more closely resemble the original information.

Problem 1 Self-supervised heterogeneous graph embeddings. Given the HG $G = (V, E, X)$ and a mapping function $f : v_i \to \mathbb{R}^d$, each node v_i is projected onto a d-dimensional ($d \ll |V|$) euclidean space. The purpose of HG embeddings are to learn f and to transform the nodes into low-dimensional vectors while maximizing the preservation of the heterogeneous topological and semantic information.

4   HetGNN-TF Model

In this section, we propose a self-supervised heterogeneous graph neural network model based on topology and feature reconstruction. It includes three key parts. The overall framework is shown in Fig. 1.

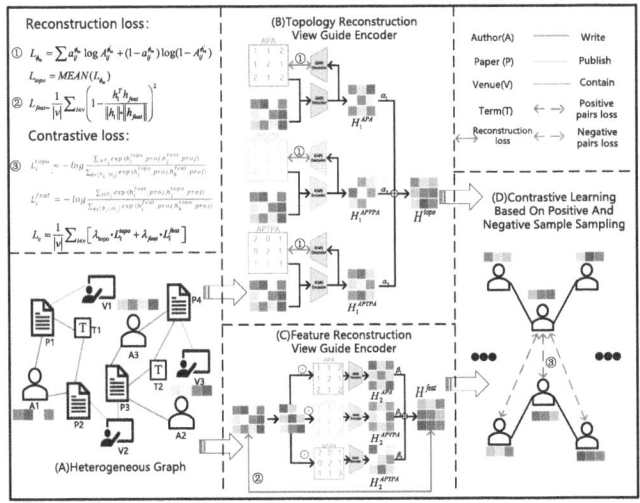

Fig. 1. Overall architecture of the proposed HetGNN-SF.

4.1 Topology Reconstruction View Guided Encoder

The main purpose of topology reconstruction view guided encoder is to learn the embedding of target nodes by constraining the reconstructed topology with the real topology. The first step is the encoding and decoding of the node representations. Since each meta-path ϕ_m represents different semantic information, we use GCN as an encoder to learn the embeddings of the nodes separately. Given the adjacency matrix A_{ϕ_m} and the features X of the nodes under different meta-paths of the network, the model is constructed as

$$H_1^{\phi_m} = f_E\left(A_{\phi_m}, X\right), \tag{1}$$

the convolutional layer is represented as:

$$f_E\left(A_{\phi_m}, X\right) = \sigma\left(\widetilde{D}_{\phi_m}^{\frac{1}{2}} \widetilde{A}_{\phi_m} \widetilde{D}_{\phi_m}^{-\frac{1}{2}} XW\right), \tag{2}$$

In this paper, we use the embedding from the encoder output and obtain the reconstructed topology representation by inner product, i.e., we obtain the reconstructed topology based on each meta-path after decoding.

$$A^{\phi_m{}'} = \sigma(H_1^{\phi_m} \cdot \left(H_1^{\phi_m}\right)^T). \tag{3}$$

After decoding the reconstructed topology based on each meta-path is obtained, we constrain the reconstructed topology by cross-entropy loss and take the mean value of all meta-paths as the reconstructed topology loss.

$$L_{\phi_m} = \sum \left[\alpha_{ij}^{\phi_m} \log A_{ij}^{\phi_m{}'} + \left(1 - \alpha_{ij}^{\phi_m}\right) \log\left(1 - A_{ij}^{\phi_m{}'}\right)\right], \tag{4}$$

$$L_{topo} = MEAN(L_{\phi_m}), \tag{5}$$

Finally, we obtain the node representation of each target node under the topological reconstruction view by semantic attention fusion of node representations under different meta-paths.

$$H^{topo} = \sum_{m=0}^{P} \beta_{\phi_m}^{topo} \cdot H_1^{\phi_m}, \tag{6}$$

$$\omega_{\phi_m} = \frac{1}{|\mathcal{V}|} \sum_{i \in \mathcal{V}} p^T \cdot \sigma\left(W_p \cdot H_1^{\Phi_m} + b_p\right), \tag{7}$$

$$\beta_{\phi_m}^{topo} = \frac{exp\left(\omega_{\phi_m}^{topo}\right)}{\sum_{m=0}^{P} exp\left(\omega_{\phi_m}^{topo}\right)}, \tag{8}$$

4.2   Feature Reconstruction View Guided Encoder

The main purpose of feature reconstruction view guided encoder is to learn the embedding of target nodes by constraining the similarity of reconstructed features to the original features. As shown in Fig. 1(C), firstly, the feature similarity graph is generated. Subsequently, the degree of similarity between each target node by calculating the K-head weighted cosine similarity between them, which is calculated as follows

$$\Gamma_{ij} = \frac{1}{K} \sum_{k=0}^{K} \cos\left(w_h \odot x_i, w_h \odot x_j\right), \tag{9}$$

The degree of similarity $A_{sim}^{\phi_m}$ between the target node and its neighbors under each meta-path is obtained by doing the Hadamard product of the K-head weighted cosine similarity with each meta-path, which reduces the burden of manually selecting high-quality neighbor nodes and enables the feature information learned by topological contrastives.

$$A_{sim}^{\phi_m} = \Gamma \odot A_{\phi_m}. \tag{10}$$

Next is the encoded node representation. We input the similarity degree $A_{sim}^{\phi_m}$ under each meta-path and the feature X of the target node to the encoder to obtain the node embedding of each meta-path for the feature reconstruction view.

$$H_2^{\phi_m} = f_E\left(A_{sim}^{\phi_m}, X\right). \tag{11}$$

Then, the semantic fusion feature representation is obtained by aggregating the node representations under different meta-paths.

$$H^{feat} = \sum_{m=0}^{P} \beta_{\phi_m}^{feat} \cdot H_2^{\phi_m}, \tag{12}$$

$$\omega_{\phi_m}^{feat} = \frac{1}{|\mathcal{V}|} \sum_{i \in \mathcal{V}} q^T \cdot \sigma \left(W_q \cdot H_2^{\phi_m} + b_q \right), \tag{13}$$

$$\beta_{\phi_m}^{feat} = \frac{exp \left(\omega_{\phi_m}^{feat} \right)}{\sum_{m=0}^{P} exp \left(\omega_{\Phi_m}^{feat} \right)}, \tag{14}$$

Finally, the node representation is constrained by reconstructing the feature representation. We use scaled cosine error to further improve the quality of the reconstructed features is calculated as follows:

$$L_{feat} = \frac{1}{|\mathcal{V}|} \sum_{i \in \mathcal{V}} \left(1 - \frac{x_i^T h_{feat}}{\|x_i\| \cdot \|h_{feat}\|} \right)^2 \tag{15}$$

4.3   Contrastive Learning Based On Sample Sampling

After obtaining the topological reconstruction view and feature reconstruction view bootstrap codes, we introduce a contrastive learning strategy with the goal of bringing the similarity of positive samples between different views closer and the similarity of negative samples between different views farther.

Firstly, the node representations under different perspectives contain different semantics, so they need to be projected under the same semantic space by MLP, as shown in Eqs. 16 to 17:

$$h_i^{topo}\_proj = W^{(2)} \sigma \left(W^{(1)} h_i^{topo} + b^{(1)} \right) + b^{(2)}, \tag{16}$$

$$h_i^{feat}\_proj = W^{(2)} \sigma \left(W^{(1)} h_i^{feat} + b^{(1)} \right) + b^{(2)}, \tag{17}$$

where $W^{(1)}, W^{(2)}$ and $b^{(1)}, b^{(2)}$ are trainable weights and biases, which are shared in the representation of the two views. σ is the activation function.

Secondly, we design a positive and negative sample selection strategy with model training to start learning the node representation for the target node itself and gradually increase the number of positive samples as the model is trained.

The specific sample sampling is shown in Fig. 2(a), that is, when we start training the model, the positive sample is only the target node itself, when after m rounds of training, we continue training by finding the similarity $S_{ij} = (x_i, x_j)$ respectively for the topological representation and feature representation after semantic fusion and then filter the first n nodes that are similar to the target node as positive samples S_{sample} (Fig. 2(b)), the set of positive samples is $\mathbb{P}_i = \{i \cup j \mid i, j \in \mathcal{V} \cup j \in S_{sample}, i \neq j\}$, and the set of negative samples is $\mathbb{N}_i = \{j \mid j \in \mathcal{V} \cup j \notin S_{sample}, i \neq j\}$. In this way, n positive samples close to the target node are added every m rounds, which not only expands the range of positive samples, but also the trained positive and negative samples can facilitate the downstream tasks more effectively. After that, a cross-view contrastive is achieved by constraining the representation $h_i^{topo}\_proj$ of the target node under

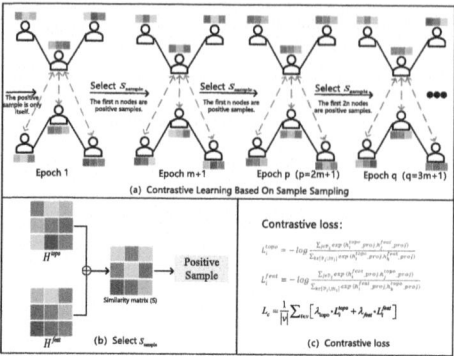

Fig. 2. Contrastive Learning Based On Sample Sampling

the topological reconstruction view with the representation $h_i^{feat}\_proj$ of the positive sample under the feature reconstruction view, as shown in Fig. 2(c):

$$L_i^{topo} = -log\frac{\Sigma_{j\epsilon\mathbb{P}_i}exp\langle h_i^{topo}\_proj, h_j^{feat}\_proj\rangle}{\Sigma_{k\epsilon\{\mathbb{P}_i\cup\mathbb{N}_i\}}exp\langle h_i^{topo}\_proj, h_k^{feat}\_proj\rangle},\qquad(18)$$

where $\langle h_i^{topo}\_proj, h_j^{feat}\_proj\rangle = cos(h_i^{topo}\_proj, h_i^{feat}\_proj)/\tau$ is the temperature parameter. Similarly, the cross-view ctrastiverast is achieved by constraining the representation $h_i^{feat}\_proj$ of the target node under the feature reconstruction view with the representation $h_i^{topo}\_proj$ of the positive sample under the feature reconstruction view as follows:

$$L_i^{feat} = -log\frac{\Sigma_{j\epsilon\mathbb{P}_i}exp\langle h_i^{feat}\_proj, h_j^{topo}\_proj\rangle}{\Sigma_{k\epsilon\{\mathbb{P}_i\cup\mathbb{N}_i\}}exp\langle h_i^{feat}\_proj, h_k^{topo}\_proj\rangle}.\qquad(19)$$

Finally, the objective function L_c for sample sampling-based contrastive learning is as follows:

$$L_c = \frac{1}{|\mathcal{V}|}\sum_{i\in\mathcal{V}}[\lambda \cdot L_i^{topo} + (1-\lambda) \cdot L_i^{feat}],\qquad(20)$$

where λ is the coefficient to balance the topological reconstruction perspective and the feature reconstruction perspective. $|\mathcal{V}|$ is the number of nodes. The overall objective function L_{final} of HetGNN-TF includes the contrastive learning loss L_c, reconstruction topological loss L_{topo} and reconstruction feature loss L_{feat}.

$$L_{final} = L_c + \beta \cdot L_{topo} + \gamma \cdot L_{feat},\qquad(21)$$

We use the semantic fusion topology representation H^{topo} and the semantic fusion feature representation H^{feat} to stitch together for downstream tasks.

5   Experiments

5.1   Datasets

In this paper, three real-world heterogeneous graph datasets are used to evaluate the effectiveness of our model. Table 1 shows the details of the datasets.

Table 1. Dataset statistics.

Dataset	Nodes	Edges	Meta-paths
ACM	P: 4019 A: 7167 S: 60	P-A: 13407 P-S: 4019	PAP PSP
DBLP	A: 4057 P: 14328 V: 20 T: 7723	P-A: 19645 P-V: 14328 P-T: 85810	APA APVPA APTPA
YELP	B: 2614 U: 1286 S: 4 L:9	B-U: 30838 B-S: 2614 B-L: 2614	BUB BSB BLB

5.2   Baselines

We compared the proposed HetGNN-TF with three types of baselines: the self-supervised homogeneous graph neural network methods {AMIL, DGI}, the self-supervised heterogeneous graph neural network methods {HDGI, HeCo, HDMI, NSHE} and the semi-supervised heterogeneous graph neural network methods {RoHe}.

5.3   Node Classification

In this section, we pass the node representation through a linear support vector machine (SVM) and divide 20%, 40%, 60% and 80% of the number of nodes as the training set for node classification, use Macro-F1 and Micro-F1 to evaluate the quality of node classification, and take the average score of 10 results as the final result. The results are shown in Table 2, the best results are bolded and the second best results are underlined.

5.4   Node Clustering

In this section, we evaluate the quality of node clustering by normalized mutual information (NMI) and adjusted rand index index (ARI) are shown in Table 3.

Table 2. Node classification results (%) compared to baselines.

Datasets	metric	split	AMIL	DGI	HDGI	HeCo	HDMI	NSHE	DMGI	RoHe	our
ACM	Macro-F1	80%	89.80	91.20	92.48	89.37	_92.60_	83.18	92.20	92.50	**93.16**
		60%	89.45	91.19	92.37	88.63	_92.47_	83.21	92.28	92.34	**93.05**
		40%	89.12	90.61	91.73	87.84	_92.01_	82.78	91.68	92.00	**92.44**
		20%	88.4	89.96	89.4	86.37	91.5	82.07	90.84	_91.57_	**92.01**
	Micro-F1	80%	89.87	91.09	92.46	89.49	_92.48_	83.47	92.10	92.38	**93.06**
		60%	89.48	91.08	_92.37_	88.75	92.36	83.47	92.10	92.25	**92.92**
		40%	89.16	90.53	91.80	88.07	91.92	82.99	91.54	_91.94_	**92.33**
		20%	88.49	89.88	89.73	86.96	91.44	82.35	90.71	_91.47_	**91.88**
DBLP	Macro-F1	80%	92.08	91.66	90.63	93.13	92.87	_93.95_	92.87	92.28	**95.11**
		60%	91.70	91.51	90.26	92.91	92.76	_93.65_	92.47	91.96	**94.88**
		40%	91.30	91.15	90.06	92.72	92.50	_93.55_	92.05	91.81	**94.84**
		20%	90.22	90.86	89.36	92.34	92.14	_93.46_	91.22	91.57	**94.55**
	Micro-F1	80%	92.68	92.25	91.18	93.66	93.34	_94.42_	93.36	92.74	**95.41**
		60%	92.35	92.14	90.84	93.46	93.25	_94.14_	93.02	92.48	**95.22**
		40%	91.97	91.78	90.65	93.26	93.01	_94.04_	92.62	92.33	**95.18**
		20%	91.11	91.49	90.07	92.91	92.69	_93.95_	91.87	92.11	**94.94**
YELP	Macro-F1	80%	61.49	62.02	55.75	53.72	56.36	56.00	75.00	_91.01_	**93.28**
		60%	61.53	62.29	55.60	53.96	55.99	55.67	74.69	_90.67_	**92.85**
		40%	61.03	62.62	55.54	53.99	55.78	55.46	73.25	_89.83_	**92.07**
		20%	59.18	61.39	55.73	53.95	55.81	56.16	71.42	_88.23_	**91.4**
	Micro-F1	80%	72.37	71.85	78.10	72.80	79.08	78.33	83.42	_90.56_	**92.88**
		60%	71.89	71.43	77.59	72.97	78.09	77.52	82.73	_90.26_	**92.37**
		40%	71.64	71.35	77.52	72.98	77.87	77.09	82.12	_89.36_	**91.62**
		20%	70.75	70.07	77.84	72.89	77.9	76.71	81.27	_87.66_	**90.96**

We input the test set node representation into K-means and take the average score of 10 results as the final result. The node clustering results are shown in Table 5, where the best results are bolded and the second best results are underlined. As we can see, HetGNN-TF shows better results on all datasets, which illustrates the effectiveness of HetGNN-TF from the perspective of node clustering. In particular, on the DBLP dataset, the NMI and ARI are 5.22% and 6.32% higher than the suboptimal AMIL model, respectively.

Table 3. Node clustering results (%) compared to baselines.

Datasets	Metrics	AMIL	DGI	HDGI	HeCo	HDMI	NSHE	DMGI	RoHe	our
ACM	NMI	60.81	51.83	59.38	63.16	51.60	41.32	66.24	**67.56**	66.36
	ARI	65.45	43.74	49.08	66.49	42.22	33.39	68.50	69.79	**70.56**
DBLP	NMI	76.37	66.37	64.46	69.42	47.90	70.31	65.65	60.43	**81.59**
	ARI	80.47	68.38	68.76	74.83	41.95	65.26	65.06	67.32	**86.8**
YELP	NMI	6.32	39.42	33.68	39.42	45.10	5.70	42.95	**53.35**	45.63
	ARI	6.32	42.60	38.84	42.62	49.40	6.59	48.56	47.54	**49.39**

6   Conclusion

In this paper, we present a novel self-supervised heterogeneous graph method, HetGNN-TF. It reconstructs semantic structure and node features via specific encoders, and designs an adaptive sample selection mechanism. Experiments demonstrate that our method outperforms baseline and semi-supervised models. Future work will focus on leveraging model learning importance for scalability improvement.

Acknowledgments. A bold run-in heading in small font size at the end of the paper is used for general acknowledgments, for example: This study was funded by X (grant number Y).

References

1. Fu, X., Zhang, J., Meng, Z., King, I.: MAGNN: metapath aggregated graph neural network for heterogeneous graph embedding. In: Proceedings of The Web Conference 2020, pp. 2331–2341 (2020)
2. He, D., et al.: Adversarial mutual information learning for network embedding. In: IJCAI, pp. 3321–3327 (2020)
3. Hou, Z., et al.: Graphmae: self-supervised masked graph autoencoders. In: Proceedings of the 28th ACM SIGKDD Conference on Knowledge Discovery and Data Mining, pp. 594–604 (2022)
4. Huang, H., Song, Y., Wu, Y., Shi, J., Xie, X., Jin, H.: Multitask representation learning with multiview graph convolutional networks. IEEE Trans. Neural Netw. Learn. Syst. **33**(3), 983–995 (2020)
5. Jin, D., et al.: Heterogeneous graph neural networks using self-supervised reciprocally contrastive learning. arXiv preprint arXiv:2205.00256 (2022)
6. Jin, D., Huo, C., Liang, C., Yang, L.: Heterogeneous graph neural network via attribute completion. In: Proceedings of the Web Conference 2021, pp. 391–400 (2021)
7. Jing, B., Park, C., Tong, H.: HDMI: high-order deep multiplex infomax. In: Proceedings of the Web Conference 2021 (2021)
8. Li, K., et al.: Reliable representations make a stronger defender: unsupervised structure refinement for robust GNN. In: Proceedings of the 28th ACM SIGKDD Conference on Knowledge Discovery and Data Mining, pp. 925–935 (2022)

9. Liu, Y., Zheng, Y., Zhang, D., Chen, H., Peng, H., Pan, S.: Towards unsupervised deep graph structure learning. In: Proceedings of the ACM Web Conference 2022, pp. 1392–1403 (2022)
10. Mo, Y., Peng, L., Xu, J., Shi, X., Zhu, X.: Simple unsupervised graph representation learning. In: Proceedings of the AAAI Conference on Artificial Intelligence, vol. 36, pp. 7797–7805 (2022)
11. Park, C., Kim, D., Han, J., Yu, H.: Unsupervised attributed multiplex network embedding. In: Proceedings of the AAAI Conference on Artificial Intelligence, vol. 34, pp. 5371–5378 (2020)
12. Ren, Y., Liu, B., Huang, C., Dai, P., Bo, L., Zhang, J.: Heterogeneous deep graph infomax. arXiv preprint arXiv:1911.08538 (2019)
13. Tian, Y., Dong, K., Zhang, C., Zhang, C., Chawla, N.V.: Heterogeneous graph masked autoencoders. arXiv preprint arXiv:2208.09957 (2022)
14. Velickovic, P., Fedus, W., Hamilton, W.L., Liò, P., Bengio, Y., Hjelm, R.D.: Deep graph infomax. ICLR (Poster) 2(3), 4 (2019)
15. Wang, C., et al.: Collaborative knowledge distillation for heterogeneous information network embedding. In: Proceedings of the ACM Web Conference 2022, pp. 1631–1639 (2022)
16. Wang, X., Liu, N., Han, H., Shi, C.: Self-supervised heterogeneous graph neural network with co-contrastive learning. In: Proceedings of the 27th ACM SIGKDD Conference on Knowledge Discovery & Data Mining, pp. 1726–1736 (2021)
17. Yang, Y., Guan, Z., Li, J., Zhao, W., Cui, J., Wang, Q.: Interpretable and efficient heterogeneous graph convolutional network. IEEE Trans. Knowl. Data Eng. (2021)
18. Zhang, M., Wang, X., Zhu, M., Shi, C., Zhang, Z., Zhou, J.: Robust heterogeneous graph neural networks against adversarial attacks. In: Proceedings of the AAAI Conference on Artificial Intelligence, vol. 36, pp. 4363–4370 (2022)
19. Zhao, J., Wang, X., Shi, C., Hu, B., Song, G., Ye, Y.: Heterogeneous graph structure learning for graph neural networks. In: Proceedings of the AAAI Conference on Artificial Intelligence, vol. 35, pp. 4697–4705 (2021)
20. Zhao, J., Wang, X., Shi, C., Liu, Z., Ye, Y.: Network schema preserving heterogeneous information network embedding. In: International Joint Conference on Artificial Intelligence (IJCAI) (2020)

Cooperative Perception and Decision-Making in Internet of Vehicles: A Comprehensive Review of Federated Learning and Blockchain Technology

Wenjie Long$^{(\boxtimes)}$ and Lejun Zhang

Guangzhou University, Guangzhou 510006, China
longwenjie007@e.gzhu.edu.cn, zhanglejun@gzhu.edu.cn

Abstract. In this review, we delve into the intricate interplay between Federated Learning (FL) and blockchain technology within the cooperative perception and decision-making frameworks of the Internet of Vehicles (IoV). As Intelligent Transportation Systems (ITS) continue to advance, IoV emerges as a pivotal component in driving significant improvements in traffic management, safety protocols, and environmental stewardship. However, integrating these technologies presents challenges, particularly in data privacy, communication optimization, and decision-making accuracy. This study sheds light on the promising potential of Blockchain-enhanced Federated Learning (BFL) within IoV contexts, offering insights into practical applications and exploring various implementation strategies. Furthermore, the review critically examines the obstacles and opportunities for refining system efficiency and concludes by charting future research directions in this rapidly evolving technological landscape.

Keywords: Internet of Vehicles · Federated Learning · Blockchain · Cooperative Perception · Decision-Making · Intelligent Transportation System

1 Introduction

In the past few years, the swift progression of Intelligent Transportation Systems (ITS) has driven the transition from conventional Vehicular Ad-Hoc Networks (VANETs) to the broader concept of the Internet of Vehicles (IoV) [1]. IoV facilitates real-time data exchange, significantly enhancing traffic management, safety, and autonomous driving. Cooperative perception in IoV depends on direct communication between vehicles and infrastructure elements, with Roadside Units (RSUs) processing data to support decision-making. Despite these advancements, challenges such as maintaining real-time performance, ensuring

G. Zhao et al. (Eds.): BWTAC 2024, CCIS 2277, pp. 431–437, 2025.
https://doi.org/10.1007/978-981-97-9412-6_39

data security, and managing system heterogeneity still persist [2]. Federated Learning (FL), functioning as a decentralized and collaborative learning approach, addresses these issues by reducing communication burdens and improving system performance [5]. The integration of blockchain technology further enhances FL, resulting in the Blockchain-based Federated Learning (BFL) framework, which boosts system responsiveness [6]. This paper aims to review the present application landscape, obstacles, and potential research avenues of the BFL framework in cooperative perception and decision-making in IoV.

2   BFL Application Advantages and Fields of Applications

Given the growing interest in integrating advanced technologies within IoV, BFL stands out as a particularly promising approach. Through the automatic execution of smart contracts, this framework ensures strict control over data ownership and seamless integration of cross-organizational collaboration, enhancing the accuracy and generalization ability of models [5,17]. It prevents data tampering and malicious attacks, while distributed model training optimizes data resource usage, reduces central server load, and accelerates model updates [18]. BFL demonstrates its broad application prospects in various IoV scenarios, including unmanned aerial vehicles, intrusion detection systems, traffic flow prediction, and autonomous driving, as illustrated in Table 1.

Table 1. BFL Application Scenarios and Roles in IoV

Application Scenarios	Functions
Unmanned Aerial Vehicles (UAV)	Data collection, computational offloading, parking management, traffic monitoring, data aggregation, facilitating coverage and flexible deployment [7–9]
Intrusion Detection System (IDS)	Detecting malicious traffic flows, handling poisoning attacks, while also protecting privacy [10,11]
Traffic Flow Prediction (TFP)	Providing decentralized traffic models, improving prediction reliability [12,13]
Autonomous Driving	Enhancing data sharing efficiency, optimizing model training speed and reducing latency to increase decision accuracy [14–16]

3   BFL Implementation Strategies

This section outlines the implementation strategies of BFL in the context of cooperative perception and decision-making in the IoV, as illustrated in Fig. 1. Task publishers like ITS operators or research institutions deploy FL tasks, initial global models, and test datasets to the blockchain. Vehicles retrieve the global model and conduct local training with datasets sourced from real-time sensory data, essential for maintaining shared awareness. After training, vehicles upload their updates to the blockchain, with RSUs participating as nodes in data collection and recording. Miners consolidate these updates and aggregate them into a new global model. Vehicles then download the updated model, with iterations continuing until the desired accuracy or convergence is reached, enhancing decision-making within the IoV. Table 2 summarizes the latest research on BFL strategies in IoV.

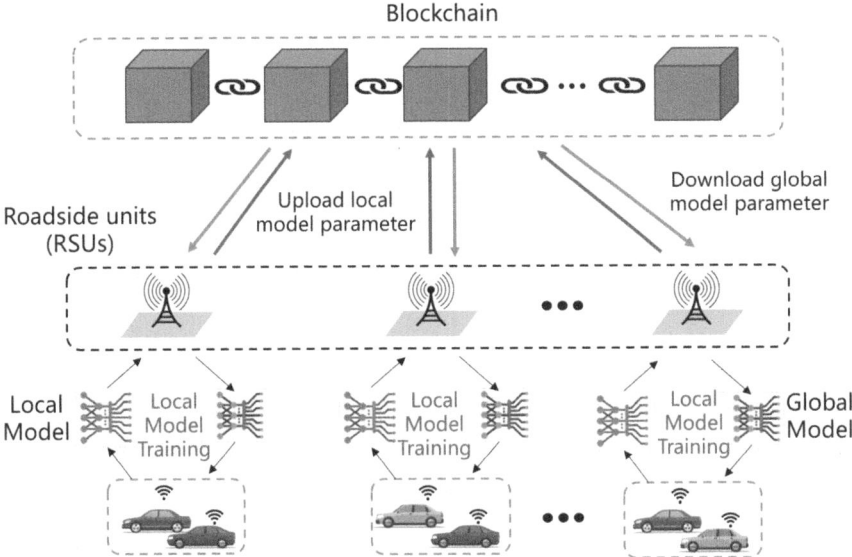

Fig. 1. Typical BFL-Based IoV Perception and Decision-Making Framework

Table 2. BFL Strategies for Cooperative Perception and Decision-Making in IoV

Strategies	Descriptions
Efficient Cooperative Communication Strategies	Adaptive sharding mechanism based on Deep Reinforcement Learning (DRL), reducing high communication costs between chains [19]
	A partial consensus lightweight blockchain architecture, controlled by smart contracts to manage model staleness [20]
	An asynchronous BFL framework, addressing differences in learning speeds among vehicles [21]
Resource Allocation and Data Management	DRL algorithms for managing resources and pricing in blockchain-as-a-service with mobile edge computing [9]
	Resource management in 5G IoV using SDN and fog computing [22]
	Resource scheduling on containerized edge computing platforms [23]
Security, Reliability, Robustness, Auditability	Enhanced resistance to asynchronous poisoning attacks through signature logs and consensus algorithms [7]
	BFL validates updates to on-Vehicle Machine Learning (oVML) models, with a focus on boosting privacy for self-driving vehicles [15]
	Various Byzantine robust aggregation rules combined with interplanetary file system (IPFS) for distributed storage [16]
Trust Management and Reputation Mechanisms	Enhancing participation incentives through synthetic data without revealing private data [21]
	Proof of Reputation (PoR) consensus ensures reliable node performance and directly impacts network-wide decision accuracy [24]
	Dynamic assessment of node reliability, based on their contribution to the learning process and adherence to the consensus protocols [25]

4   Challenges and Future Prospects

Although BFL has made progress in IoV, it still faces many obstacles. The real-time performance and scalability of the system require further improvement to adapt to the dynamic IoV environment; mechanisms for model synthesis and data sharing need optimization to enhance efficiency and accuracy. Additionally, ensuring the security of edge devices and transaction integrity is crucial. Future research should focus on developing more precise incentive mechanisms to attract more vehicle participation in BFL, enhancing experiments with real data to increase the practical value of the solutions, and developing more secure consensus algorithms to improve system security and protect user privacy. Addressing vehicle and system heterogeneity will improve the efficiency and stability of the BFL framework, thereby enhancing the overall system reliability and performance.

5   Conclusion

This review has explored the integration of BFL in cooperative perception and decision-making within the IoV. BFL stands out as a crucial technology, enhancing security, efficiency, and accuracy in data processing while addressing significant challenges such as data privacy and real-time communication in IoV. BFL combines blockchain and federated learning to enable decentralized data management and seamless inter-institutional collaboration. Its applications, from intrusion detection to traffic flow prediction and autonomous driving, demonstrate its transformative potential in intelligent transportation systems. While obstacles remain, BFL's continued development and optimization are key to fully leveraging its capabilities in advancing IoV.

Acknowledgments. This work is sponsored by the National Natural Science Foundation of China No. 62172353, No. 62302114 and No. U20B2046. Innovation Fund Program of the Engineering Research Center for Integration and Application of Digital Learning Technology of Ministry of Education No. 1331007 and No. 1311022. Natural Science Foundation of Guangdong Province No. 2024A1515010177.

References

1. Zhou, H., Xu, W., Chen, J., Wang, W.: Evolutionary V2X technologies toward the internet of vehicles: challenges and opportunities. Proc. IEEE **108**(2), 308–323 (2020). https://doi.org/10.1109/JPROC.2019.2961937
2. Schwarting, W., Alonso-Mora, J., Rus, D.: Planning and decision-making for autonomous vehicles. Ann. Rev. Control Robot. Autonom. Syst. **1**(1), 187–210 (2018). https://doi.org/10.1146/annurev-control-060117-105157
3. Lim, K., Tuladhar, K.M.: LIDAR: lidar information based dynamic V2V authentication for roadside infrastructure-less vehicular networks. In: 2019 16th IEEE Annual Consumer Communications & Networking Conference (CCNC), pp. 1–6 (2019). https://doi.org/10.1109/CCNC.2019.8651684

4. Lu, J., et al.: Analytical offloading design for mobile edge computing-based smart internet of vehicle. EURASIP J. Adv. Sig. Process. **2022**(1), 44 (2022). https://doi.org/10.1186/s13634-022-00867-2

5. Wahab, O.A., Mourad, A., Otrok, H., Taleb, T.: Federated machine learning: survey, multi-level classification, desirable criteria and future directions in communication and networking systems. IEEE Commun. Surv. Tutorials **23**(2), 1342–1397 (2021). https://doi.org/10.1109/COMST.2021.3058573

6. Liu, Z., Xu, Y., Zhang, C., Elahi, H., Zhou, X.: A blockchain-based trustworthy collaborative power trading scheme for 5G-enabled social internet of vehicles. Digital Commun. Netw. **8**(6), 976–983 (2022). https://doi.org/10.1016/j.dcan.2022.10.014

7. Wang, Y., Su, Z., Zhang, N., Benslimane, A.: Learning in the air: secure federated learning for UAV-assisted crowdsensing. IEEE Trans. Netw. Sci. Eng. **8**(2), 1055–1069 (2021). https://doi.org/10.1109/TNSE.2020.3014385

8. He, X., Chen, Q., Tang, L., Wang, W., Liu, T.: CGAN-based collaborative intrusion detection for UAV networks: a blockchain-empowered distributed federated learning approach. IEEE Internet Things J. **10**(1), 120–132 (2023). https://doi.org/10.1109/JIOT.2022.3200121

9. Asheralieva, A., Niyato, D.: Distributed dynamic resource management and pricing in the IoT systems with blockchain-as-a-service and UAV-enabled mobile edge computing. IEEE Internet Things J. **7**(3), 1974–1993 (2020). https://doi.org/10.1109/JIOT.2019.2961958

10. Ghimire, B., Rawat, D.B.: Secure, privacy preserving, and verifiable federating learning using blockchain for internet of vehicles. IEEE Consum. Electron. Mag. **11**(6), 67–74 (2022). https://doi.org/10.1109/MCE.2021.3097705

11. Liu, H., et al.: Blockchain and federated learning for collaborative intrusion detection in vehicular edge computing. IEEE Trans. Veh. Technol. **70**(6), 6073–6084 (2021). https://doi.org/10.1109/TVT.2021.3076780

12. Qi, Y., Hossain, M.S., Nie, J., Li, X.: Privacy-preserving blockchain-based federated learning for traffic flow prediction. Futur. Gener. Comput. Syst. **117**, 328–337 (2021). https://doi.org/10.1016/j.future.2020.12.003

13. Meese, C., Chen, H., Asif, S.A., Li, W., Shen, C.C., Nejad, M.: BFRT: Blockchained federated learning for real-time traffic flow prediction. In: 2022 22nd IEEE International Symposium on Cluster, Cloud and Internet Computing (CCGrid), pp. 317–326 (2022). https://doi.org/10.1109/CCGrid54584.2022.00041

14. Kansra, B., Diddee, H., Sheikh, T.H., Khanna, A., Gupta, D., Rodrigues, J.J.P.C.: BlockFITS: a federated data augmentation modelling for blockchain-based IoVT systems. In: Khanna, A., Gupta, D., Bhattacharyya, S., Hassanien, A.E., Anand, S., Jaiswal, A. (eds.) International Conference on Innovative Computing and Communications. AISC, vol. 1388, pp. 253–262. Springer, Singapore (2022). https://doi.org/10.1007/978-981-16-2597-8_21

15. Pokhrel, S.R., Choi, J.: Federated learning with blockchain for autonomous vehicles: analysis and design challenges. IEEE Trans. Commun. **68**(8), 4734–4746 (2020). https://doi.org/10.1109/TCOMM.2020.2990686

16. He, Y., Huang, K., Zhang, G., Yu, F.R., Chen, J., Li, J.: Bift: a blockchain-based federated learning system for connected and autonomous vehicles. IEEE Internet Things J. **9**(14), 12311–12322 (2022). https://doi.org/10.1109/JIOT.2021.3135342

17. Hou, D., Zhang, J., Man, K.L., Ma, J., Peng, Z.: A systematic literature review of blockchain-based federated learning: architectures, applications and issues. In: 2021 2nd Information Communication Technologies Conference (ICTC), pp. 302–307 (2021). https://doi.org/10.1109/ICTC51749.2021.9441499

18. Hildebrand, B., et al.: A comprehensive review on blockchains for internet of vehicles: challenges and directions. Comput. Sci. Rev. **48**, 100547 (2023). https://doi.org/10.1016/j.cosrev.2023.100547

19. Lin, Y., Gao, Z., Du, H., Kang, J., Niyato, D., Wang, Q., Ruan, J., Wan, S.: DRL-based adaptive sharding for blockchain-based federated learning. IEEE Trans. Commun. **71**(10), 5992–6004 (2023). https://doi.org/10.1109/TCOMM.2023.3288591

20. Zhang, J., Li, S.: Blockchain-empowered vehicular intelligence: a perspective of asynchronous federated learning. IEEE Internet Things Mag. **7**(1), 74–80 (2024). https://doi.org/10.1109/IOTM.001.2300092

21. Lu, Y., Huang, X., Zhang, K., Maharjan, S., Zhang, Y.: Blockchain empowered asynchronous federated learning for secure data sharing in internet of vehicles. IEEE Trans. Veh. Technol. **69**(4), 4298–4311 (2020). https://doi.org/10.1109/TVT.2020.2973651

22. Cao, B., Sun, Z., Zhang, J., Gu, Y.: Resource allocation in 5G IoV architecture based on SDN and fog-cloud computing. IEEE Trans. Intell. Transp. Syst. **22**(6), 3832–3840 (2021). https://doi.org/10.1109/TITS.2020.3048844

23. Cui, L., et al.: A blockchain-based containerized edge computing platform for the internet of vehicles. IEEE Internet Things J. **8**(4), 2395–2408 (2021). https://doi.org/10.1109/JIOT.2020.3027700

24. Haddaji, A., Ayed, S., Chaari, L.: Federated learning with blockchain approach for trust management in IoV. In: Barolli, L., Hussain, F., Enokido, T. (eds.) AINA 2022. LNNS, vol. 449, pp. 411–423. Springer, Cham (2022). https://doi.org/10.1007/978-3-030-99584-3_36

25. Chen, H., Chen, N., Liu, H., Zhang, H., Xu, J., Chen, H., Li, Y.: RepBFL: reputation based blockchain-enabled federated learning framework for data sharing in internet of vehicles. In: Shen, H., Sang, Y., Zhang, Y., Xiao, N., Arabnia, H.R., Fox, G., Gupta, A., Malek, M. (eds.) PDCAT 2021. LNCS, vol. 13148, pp. 536–547. Springer, Cham (2022). https://doi.org/10.1007/978-3-030-96772-7_50

ETGuard: Malicious Encrypted Traffic Detection in Blockchain-Based Power Grid Systems

Peng Zhou[1], Yongdong Liu[2]([✉]), Lixun Ma[2], Weiye Zhang[2], Haohan Tan[2], Zhenguang Liu[2], and Butian Huang[2]

[1] State Grid Zhejiang Electric Power Company, Ltd., Information and Communication Branch, Hangzhou, China
[2] Zhejiang University, Hangzhou, Zhejiang, China
yongdongliu2024@163.com, malx@zju.edu.cn

Abstract. The escalating prevalence of encryption protocols has led to a concomitant surge in the number of malicious attacks that hide in encrypted traffic. Power grid systems, as fundamental infrastructure, are becoming prime targets for such attacks. Conventional methods for detecting malicious encrypted packets typically use a *static* pre-trained model. We observe that these methods are not well-suited for blockchain-based power grid systems. More critically, they fall short in *dynamic* environments where new types of encrypted attacks continuously emerge.

Motivated by this, in this paper we try to tackle these challenges from two aspects: (1) We present a novel framework that is able to automatically detect malicious encrypted traffic in blockchain-based power grid systems and incrementally learn from new malicious traffic. (2) We mathematically derive incremental learning losses to resist the forgetting of old attack patterns while ensuring the model is capable of handling new encrypted attack patterns. Empirically, our method achieves state-of-the-art performance on three different benchmark datasets. We also constructed the first malicious encrypted traffic dataset for blockchain-based power grid scenario. Our code and dataset are available at https://github.com/PPPmzt/ETGuard, hoping to inspire future research.

Keywords: Blockchain · Network security · Malicious encrypted traffic detection · Incremental learning

1 Introduction

The *immutable* and *decentralized* nature of blockchain has led to applications such as Bitcoin, decentralized crowdfunding, and cross-industry finance [31]. While research often focuses on system and software issues like *consensus mechanisms* [29], *smart contracts* [18], and *virtual machines*, cybersecurity challenges, particularly malicious traffic attacks, are often neglected.

© The Author(s), under exclusive license to Springer Nature Singapore Pte Ltd. 2025
G. Zhao et al. (Eds.): BWTAC 2024, CCIS 2277, pp. 438–450, 2025.
https://doi.org/10.1007/978-981-97-9412-6_40

In blockchain-based power systems, critical national infrastructure, malicious traffic poses severe risks such as *widespread power outages* and *energy data breaches*. Although encryption protocols are widely adopted to secure data, they can be exploited by attackers to hide malicious activities. Detecting malicious encrypted traffic in power systems involves distinguishing attack patterns from benign packets [15]. Research in this area generally follows two approaches: one [7,9,12] uses decryption analysis to reveal clues in encrypted sequences, while another [22,23] examines statistical differences using deep learning. Current methods face two main issues: poor performance on blockchain-based power grids, leading to a significant drop in F1 scores, and difficulties with novel attack sequences due to reliance on static models.

To address these challenges, we propose a novel approach incorporating incremental learning to adapt to new attacks. Our method involves training a model with self-supervised learning to extract detailed packet features and deriving incremental learning losses to preserve old data while learning new attack patterns. We update the model using replayed samples combined with these losses. Additionally, we introduce the GridET-2024 dataset, which includes real-world traffic data from the State Grid of China, to evaluate detection in blockchain-based power grid scenarios. To evaluate our method, we conducted extensive experiments on three benchmark datasets, as well as ablation studies to assess key components. Our method demonstrates state-of-the-art performance on these datasets. In summary, our contributions are as follows:

- We propose ETGuard, a novel framework for detecting malicious encrypted traffic in blockchain-based power grids. It is the first method to automatically identify these attacks and adapt to new traffic patterns incrementally.
- We derive a loss function for effective incremental learning, supported by rigorous theoretical analysis, to manage new attack patterns while mitigating catastrophic forgetting. Additionally, we introduce a sample buffer for efficient storage and replay of representative traffic samples.
- We have collected real-world data from blockchain-based power grid systems and created the GridET-2024 dataset, the first of its kind for detecting malicious encrypted traffic in this context. Our method achieves state-of-the-art performance on several benchmark datasets.

2   Problem Statement

Problem Formulation. Given a sequence of encrypted packets $s = \{p_1, p_2, \ldots, p_n\}$, we are interested in developing a fully automated model to determine whether the packet sequence is malicious. Put differently, we aim to estimate the label $\hat{y}$ for each encrypted packet sequence s, where $\hat{y} = 1$ represents s is a malicious sequence, and $\hat{y} = 0$ indicates that s is benign.

3   Method

Method Overview. The detailed architecture of our proposed framework is outlined in Fig. 1. Overall, the framework consists of three key components:

- *Data Preprocessing*: Raw packets are cleaned and processed, ensuring that the packets from an individual client are sorted into a packet sequence and are separated from the packets of other clients. To extract features from these sequences, we use an unsupervised auto-encoder with stacked bi-GRUs.
- *Incremental Learning Module*: To adapt to novel attacks while preventing catastrophic forgetting, we introduce an incremental learning module and mathematically derive the incremental learning losses.
- *Detection Module*: The detection module learns the feature distinctions between benign and malicious sequences to continuously identify potential attacks. The learning process is supervised by the classification loss and incremental learning losses.

In what follows, we will elaborate on the details of these components one by one.

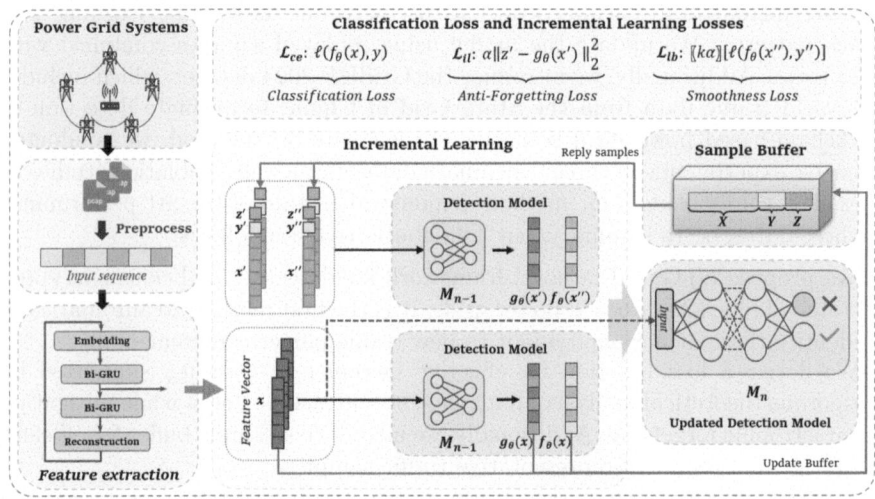

Fig. 1. The framework of ETGuard.

3.1   Data Preprocessing

The preprocessing module aims to clean and process raw packet data into distinct sequences for different clients. Since packet sequences cannot be directly input into a network, we employ an unsupervised auto-encoder with stacked bi-GRUs to extract features from each client's packet sequence.

Specifically, raw traffic data consists of packets organized by a five-tuple (*i.e.*, source and destination IP addresses, source and destination ports, and transport layer protocol). We group packets with the same five-tuple into sequences s and sort them chronologically. Irrelevant packet information, such as IP addresses and port numbers, is removed from each sequence.

The resulting sequences, s_{input}, are formatted with components l, d, and t_m, where: $l = \{b_1, b_2, \ldots, b_n\}$ denotes the packet length sequence, $d = t_n - t_1$ represents the duration of s_{input}, t_m is the mean time interval between packets.

The feature extractor uses an auto-encoder with multiple bi-directional Gated Recurrent Units (bi-GRUs) [8], serving as both encoder and decoder. The encoder transforms the input sequence into a feature vector, which the decoder uses to reconstruct the sequence. A multi-layer perceptron in the reconstruction layer restores the original embedded sequence. The encoder learns an accurate representation of encrypted network traffic by minimizing reconstruction loss during training.

Compared to traditional methods [2,3,16] that focus on specific versions of TLS handshake metadata or message types [23], our approach captures the fine-grained behavior of network traffic more effectively.

3.2 Mathematical Derivation of Incremental Learning Objectives

In this subsection, we introduce the incremental learning module, and provide the key mathematical derivations of incremental learning objectives within this module.

We use the incremental learning method based on empirical replay [6,24,27] with targeted modifications for encrypted traffic scenarios to realize the incremental update of the model when facing new types of traffic attack. Specifically, we maintain a sample buffer to store representative traffic samples. When new malicious encrypted traffic arises, we incrementally update the model through a anti-forgetting loss function to detect new attack patterns. The new traffic samples are updated into the buffer using a reservoir sampling algorithm [28], serving as a representative sample set for subsequent incremental model updates.

Sample Buffer. The sample buffer is used to store representative traffic samples to achieve experience replay during incremental learning. When the model learns new traffic patterns, it replays previous samples from the sample buffer to effectively prevent catastrophic forgetting. We implement the update of the sample buffer using the reservoir sampling algorithm. When new traffic samples arrive, the sample buffer is dynamically updated to ensure diversity and representativeness.

Incremental Learning Loss Function. The goal of the incremental learning module is to detect the ongoing emergence of new malicious traffic attacks. To enable the model to learn from new datasets, the loss function and optimization objectives are defined as follows:

$$\min_{\theta} \mathcal{L}_{ce} = \mathbb{E}_{(x,y) \sim D}[\ell(f_\theta(x), y)], \tag{1}$$

where θ denotes the model parameters, $\mathcal{L}_{ce}$ represents the loss function using cross-entropy, D denotes the dataset, $f_\theta(x)$ denotes the detection model, and y denotes the true target of the sample.

To mitigate catastrophic forgetting, we introduce a new loss function aimed at balancing the learning between new and old data. We use the past data on the updated model to obtain an output $f_\theta(x)$ that closely approximates the output of the pre-update model trained on past traffic data, denoted as $f_{\theta*t}$.

$$\mathcal{L}_{il} = \alpha \mathbb{E}_{(x,z) \sim \mathcal{M}} \left[D_{KL}(\text{softmax}(z) \| f_\theta(x)) \right]. \tag{2}$$

In the above equation, z represents the output logits of the model on the past traffic data. In order to reduce the resource consumption, we use z to replace the model output $f_{\theta*t}$. The logits z are softmaxed to obtain the probability vector, which is used to calculate the KL scatter with the model output $f_\theta(x)$.

Theorem 1. *If two logits output by the model are similar, the KL divergence between them can be approximated as the Euclidean distance.*

Proof. Assume logits z_1 and logits z_2 are two close vectors, we set the sample space of logits z, $R = \{1, ..., n\}$, n is the dimension of logits z, so we can express z_2 as:

$$z_2 = z_1 + \epsilon \Delta z, \tag{3}$$

for some small $\epsilon > 0$ and perturbation vector $\Delta z = [\Delta z(1) \cdots \Delta z(n)]^T$. Next, we approximate the KL divergence locally.

$$D_{KL}(z_1 \| z_2) = \sum_{i \in R} z_1(i) \log \left(\frac{z_1(i)}{z_2(i)} \right). \tag{4}$$

Substituting $z_2(i) = z_1(i) + \epsilon \Delta z(i)$ into the KL divergence formula gives:

$$D_{KL}(z_1 \| z_2) = \sum_{i \in R} z_1(i) \log \left(\frac{z_1(i)}{z_1(i) + \epsilon \Delta z(i)} \right). \tag{5}$$

Applying the second-order Taylor approximation to $\log \left(\frac{z_1(i)}{z_1(i) + \epsilon \Delta z(i)} \right)$:

$$D_{KL}(z_1 \| z_2) = \frac{\epsilon^2}{2} \sum_{i \in R} \frac{\Delta z(i)^2}{z_1(i)} + o(\epsilon^2). \tag{6}$$

This implicitly assumes $z_1(i) > 0$ for all $i \in R$. Introducing the weighted Euclidean norm, the KL divergence becomes:

$$D_{KL}(z_1 \| z_2) = \frac{\epsilon^2}{2} \|\Delta z\|_{z_1}^2 + o(\epsilon^2) = \|z_1 - z_2\|. \tag{7}$$

Thus, under the local approximation, the KL divergence approximates a weighted Euclidean distance.

By Theorem 1, $\mathcal{L}_{il}$ can be simplified to:

$$\mathcal{L}_{il} = \alpha \mathbb{E}_{(x,z) \sim \mathcal{M}} \left[\|z' - g(x')\|_2^2 \right]. \tag{8}$$

To handle significant changes in new attack patterns and avoid bias towards previous patterns, we introduce a smoothness loss function:

$$\mathcal{L}_{lb} = \beta \mathbb{E}_{(x'',y'',z'') \sim \mathcal{M}} \left[\ell(y'', h(x'')) \right]. \tag{9}$$

To balance the contributions of $\mathcal{L}_{il}$ and $\mathcal{L}_{lb}$, we use a coefficient k:

$$k = 0.5 + \mathrm{softmax}(\mathcal{L}_{il} \cdot \gamma). \tag{10}$$

The final loss function is:

$$\mathcal{L}_{ce} + \alpha \mathbb{E}_{(x',y',z') \sim \mathcal{M}} \left[\|z' - g(x')\|_2^2 \right] + k\alpha \mathbb{E}_{(x'',y'',z'') \sim \mathcal{M}} \left[\ell(y'', h(x'')) \right]. \tag{11}$$

3.3 Detection Module

Due to the substantial volume of traffic data and the high traffic rate in the blockchain-based power grid scenario, the real-time performance and resource consumption of the model are critically demanding. The MLP model architecture, being relatively simple, requires lower computing resources and offers faster training speeds. It is capable of monitoring traffic data in real time, and experiments have demonstrated that the MLP model is sufficient to meet the task requirements. Therefore, the MLP model is chosen to detect malicious traffic.

4 Evaluations

In this section, we conduct extensive experiments on multiple malicious encrypted traffic detection datasets to evaluate our framework. Next, we introduce the experimental setup, followed by presenting the comprehensive empirical results.

4.1 Experimental Setup

Datasets

- **CIRA-CIC-DoHBrw-2020 (DoHBrw)** [21]: The DoHBrw dataset provides a mix of benign and malicious DNS-over-HTTPS (DoH) traffic, all data is encrypted traffic. The normal traffic is generated by querying benign DNS servers using the DoH protocol. Tunneling tools such as dns2tcp, DNSCat2, and Iodine are used to generate malicious DoH traffic.
- **CIC-AndMal2017 (CIC)** [14]: CIC collected a rich variety of malicious attacks from several sources. The malicious traffic samples come from 42 unique malware families, which can be classified into four categories: Adware, Ransomware, Scareware, and SMS Malware.
- **GridET-2024 (GridET)**: To better detect the encrypted attacks of real-world blockchain-based power grid scenario, we create the dataset GridET-2024. Benign traffic samples are collected by capturing power grid system interaction traffic data. Malicious traffic data samples are sourced from malware-traffic-analysis.net and USTC-TFC2016 dataset to ensure the diversity of malicious traffic attack patterns.

Implementation Details. We implement our detection framework and all baselines by using Python 3.8.5. We run these models on a Linux server with NVIDIA GeForce RTX 3090 GPU. We list all the parameters used by our framework in Table 2. In particular, we set $n = 50$ and $d = 32$ to make a better capability of capturing fine-grained behaviors of network traffic. Then, we apply Grid Search to find the appropriate values for α and γ. The values of α and γ are 0.5 and 10, respectively. In particular, buffer size is a hyperparameter manually tuned to best fit the specific scenario. We conduct comprehensive experiments to evaluate the performance of ETGuard with various buffer sizes (Table 1).

Table 1. Statistics of Datasets

Dataset	Normal	Malicious
DoHBrw	688,489	6,112
CIC	894,367	62,972
GridET	43,611	27,141

Table 2. Parameter Settings of ETGuard

Module	Para.	Value	Description
Feature Extraction	n	50	Number of used head packets
	V	32	Embedding size of GRU-AE
	H	8	Hidden size of each GRU layer
	B	2	Number of GRU layers
Incremental Learning	α	0.5	Coefficient of loss L_2
	γ	10	Coefficient to balance loss L_2 and loss L_3

Evaluation Metrics. We use *ACC* and *F1 Score* as metrics to evaluate the malicious traffic detection and incremental learning performance of ETGuard.

4.2   Performance on Malicious Encrypted Traffic Detection

In this section, we benchmark our method against state-of-the-art malicious encrypted traffic detection methods for two public dataset and one power grad scenario dataset GridET.

In public dataset evaluations, we train and test methods on DoHBrw, and CIC, respectively. Figure 2 presents public dataset comparison results. From Fig. 2, we observe that our method is capable of consistently outperforming existing methods on all five benchmarks. For example, the F1 score of our method is 0.92 on DoHBrw while the state-of-the-art detection method RAPIER [23] is 0.88. The F1 score of our method is also outperformed FS [17] in all datasets. In addition, we also use the CoinFlip algorithm and PacketLen algorithm, which simulate randomly guess and only utilize packet length, respectively, to detect encrypted traffic.

Table 3. F1 scores of Malicious Encrypted Traffic Detection Methods

Dataset	RAPIER	FS	CoinFlip	PacketLen	ETGuard (Ours)
DoHBrw	0.88	0.76	0.28	0.56	**0.92**
CIC	0.84	0.71	0.27	0.46	**0.86**
GridET	0.83	0.73	0.31	0.49	**0.94**

The blockchain-based power grid scenario malicious traffic detection is more challenging for existed detection methods. To evaluate the detection abilities of the methods on this scenario, we train and test the models on the GridET dataset. Table 3 demonstrate the state-of-the-art malicious encrypted traffic detection methods still suffer from relatively low F1 score on the GridET dataset, which reveals that such methods are fall short to extract the critical features of traffic sample in the blockchain-based power grid scenario.

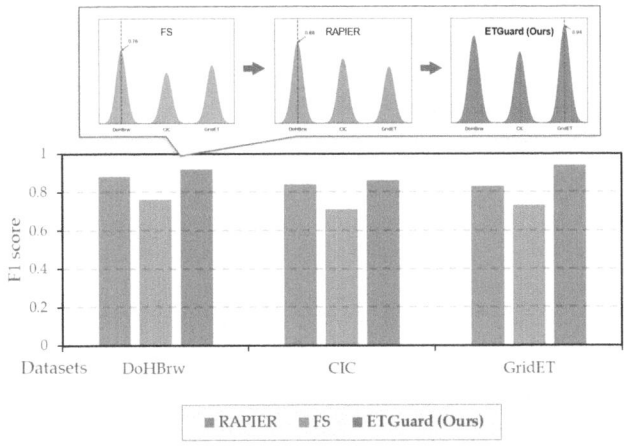

Fig. 2. Performance on Malicious Encrypted Traffic Detection.

Overall, our method achieves state-of-the-art general scenarios and blockchain-based power grid scenario malicious encrypted traffic detection performance. For general scenarios comparisons, our method improves the F1 score on DoHBrw from 0.88 to 0.92, and on CIC from 0.84 to 0.86. In contrast with general scenarios methods, our method also attains 0.94 F1 score on GridET, outperforming the current state-of-the-art method RAPIER.

4.3   Performance on Incremental Learning

To evaluate the performance of our method on incremental learning, we create a new dataset *DoHBrw/CIC*. Specifically, we combine all benign samples from the DoHBrw dataset with a selection of malicious samples from the CIC dataset. We further divide the datasets into six sub-datasets $\{A_0, A_1, A_2, A_3, A_4, A_5\}$. In each of these sub-datasets, the benign traffic is all of the same type DoHBrw, while the malicious traffic all consists of different types of malicious attacks. We use A_0 for pre-training the model, while the other sub-datasets are used for incremental updates to the model. We established a separate test set for each round, where the test set for round i includes all attack types observed from rounds 0 to i.

We compare ETGuard against five incremental learning methods (ER [25], DER [6], DER++ [6], GSS [1], SI [30]) on DoHBrw/CIC. To assess the efficacy of the incremental learning module within our approach, we extracted this component from ETGuard, resulting in a variant dubbed ETGuard-V. We then evaluated the performance of ETGuard-V to conduct an ablation study. We further provide an upper bound given by training all attack samples (FULL).

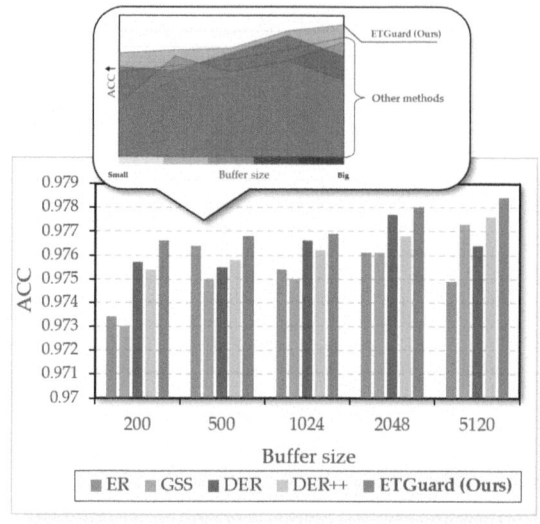

Fig. 3. The Performance of Incremental Learning Methods.

Figure 3 reports performance in terms of average accuracy across all rounds. Experimental evidence ETGuard achieve state-of-the-art performance in almost all settings (Fig. 4).

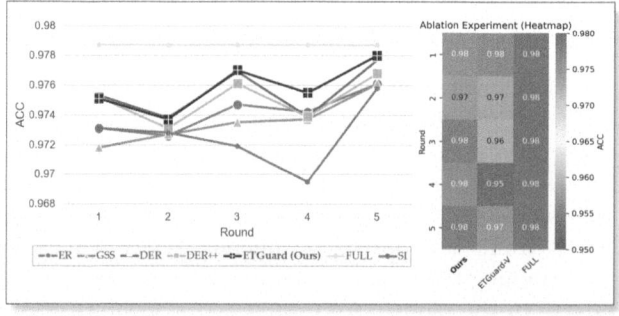

Fig. 4. The Performance of Incremental Learning Methods in Different Round.

At the same time, we observe that the performance of ETGuard is almost always better than that of ETGuard-V. And as the number of rounds increases, the gap in detection performance between ETGuard-V and ETGuard gradually widens, which further proves the effectiveness of our incremental learning module.

5   Related Work

5.1   Malicious Encrypted Traffic Detection

Traditional malicious encrypted traffic detection mainly uses signature-based methods [7,9,12] to detect malicious encrypted traffic. However, the method relies heavily on the quality of decryption operations and rules for traffic [4,13]. With the growth of artificial intelligence technology [19,26], machine learning is increasingly being adopted for detecting malicious encrypted traffic. Machine learning enhances detection by extracting statistical features from traffic, offering faster and more accurate results compared to traditional methods. For example, Fu et al., utilized frequency domain features for real-time detection [11]. Barradas et al., detect attacks by applying random forests [5]. In addition to traditional traffic detection or packet inspection [3,20], Fang et al. [10], on the other hand, detects TLS traffic by collecting features of the traffic communication channel (packets consisting of the same destination IP and destination port) and uses Random Forest (RF) to enhance malware traffic detection performance. All these methods are not effective in detecting attacks on new encrypted traffic.

5.2   Incremental Learning

The core challenge of incremental learning is to balance the conflict between remembering information about old tasks and absorbing information about new tasks, the so-called catastrophic forgetting problem. To overcome this problem, existing methods fall into two main categories: replay-based methods and parameter optimization-based methods. Replay-based methods mitigate Catastrophic Forgetting by replaying some samples of old tasks while learning new ones. The replayed samples can be real historical data, *i.e.*, empirical replay. It can also be pseudo-samples generated by generative models (*e.g.*, Generative Adversarial Networks, GAN), *i.e.*, generative replay. iCaRL [24] is a representative of the empirical replay-based approach, which combines knowledge distillation methods to update the model parameters on a representative sample pool. However, iCaRL updates the parameters of old tasks and therefore suffers from overfitting to old data.

6   Conclusion

In this paper, we try to tackle the malicious encrypted traffic detection problem from two aspects: (1) We propose a novel framework termed ETGuard, which to our knowledge is the first approach tailored for automatically identifying malicious traffic attacks in blockchain-based power grid systems. (2) We lay the mathematical foundation for establishing an incremental learning model that can effectively adapt to new types of attacks. We utilized real data collected from the State Grid and constructed the malicious encrypted traffic dataset GridET. We extensively evaluated the proposed method on three benchmark datasets. Empirical results show that our method consistently delivers state-of-the-art performance on malicious encrypted traffic detection across general scenarios and the blockchain-based power grid scenario.

Acknowledgments. This work was supported by State Grid Zhejiang Electric Power Company, LTD. Information and Communication Branch, China (Grant number 5211XT 24000D).

References

1. Aljundi, R., Lin, M., Goujaud, B., Bengio, Y.: Gradient based sample selection for online continual learning. In: Advances in Neural Information Processing Systems, vol. 32 (2019)
2. Anderson, B., McGrew, D.: Identifying encrypted malware traffic with contextual flow data. In: Proceedings of the 2016 ACM Workshop on Artificial Intelligence and Security, pp. 35–46 (2016)
3. Anderson, B., McGrew, D.: Machine learning for encrypted malware traffic classification: accounting for noisy labels and non-stationarity. In: Proceedings of the 23rd ACM SIGKDD International Conference on Knowledge Discovery and Data Mining, pp. 1723–1732 (2017)
4. Azeez, N.A., Bada, T.M., Misra, S., Adewumi, A., Van der Vyver, C., Ahuja, R.: Intrusion detection and prevention systems: an updated review. In: Data Management, Analytics and Innovation: Proceedings of ICDMAI 2019, vol. 1, pp. 685–696 (2020)
5. Barradas, D., Santos, N., Rodrigues, L., Signorello, S., Ramos, F.M., Madeira, A.: Flowlens: enabling efficient flow classification for ml-based network security applications. In: NDSS (2021)
6. Buzzega, P., Boschini, M., Porrello, A., Abati, D., Calderara, S.: Dark experience for general continual learning: a strong, simple baseline. Adv. Neural. Inf. Process. Syst. **33**, 15920–15930 (2020)
7. Chiba, Z., Abghour, N., Moussaid, K., Omri, A.E., Rida, M.: Newest collaborative and hybrid network intrusion detection framework based on suricata and isolation forest algorithm. In: Proceedings of the 4th International Conference on Smart City Applications, pp. 1–11 (2019)
8. Chung, J., Gulcehre, C., Cho, K., Bengio, Y.: Empirical evaluation of gated recurrent neural networks on sequence modeling. arXiv preprint arXiv:1412.3555 (2014)
9. Dong, C., Lu, Z., Cui, Z., Liu, B., Chen, K.: Mbtree: detecting encryption rats communication using malicious behavior tree. IEEE Trans. Inf. Forensics Secur. **16**, 3589–3603 (2021)
10. Fang, Y., Li, K., Zheng, R., Liao, S., Wang, Y.: A communication-channel-based method for detecting deeply camouflaged malicious traffic. Comput. Netw. **197**, 108297 (2021)

11. Fu, C., Li, Q., Shen, M., Xu, K.: Realtime robust malicious traffic detection via frequency domain analysis. In: Proceedings of the 2021 ACM SIGSAC Conference on Computer and Communications Security, pp. 3431–3446 (2021)
12. Gupta, A., Sharma, L.S.: A categorical survey of state-of-the-art intrusion detection system-snort. Int. J. Inf. Comput. Secur. **13**(3–4), 337–356 (2020)
13. Khraisat, A., Gondal, I., Vamplew, P., Kamruzzaman, J.: Survey of intrusion detection systems: techniques, datasets and challenges. Cybersecurity **2**(1), 1–22 (2019). https://doi.org/10.1186/s42400-019-0038-7
14. Lashkari, A.H., Kadir, A.F.A., Taheri, L., Ghorbani, A.A.: Toward developing a systematic approach to generate benchmark android malware datasets and classification. In: 2018 International Carnahan conference on security technology (ICCST), pp. 1–7. IEEE (2018)
15. Li, Y., Guo, H., Hou, J., Zhang, Z., Jiang, T., Liu, Z.: A survey of encrypted malicious traffic detection. In: 2021 International Conference on Communications, Computing, Cybersecurity, and Informatics (CCCI), pp. 1–7. IEEE (2021)
16. Liu, C., Cao, Z., Xiong, G., Gou, G., Yiu, S.M., He, L.: MaMPF: encrypted traffic classification based on multi-attribute Markov probability fingerprints. In: 2018 IEEE/ACM 26th International Symposium on Quality of Service (IWQoS), pp. 1–10. IEEE (2018)
17. Liu, C., He, L., Xiong, G., Cao, Z., Li, Z.: Fs-net: a flow sequence network for encrypted traffic classification. In: IEEE INFOCOM 2019-IEEE Conference On Computer Communications, pp. 1171–1179. IEEE (2019)
18. Liu, Z., et al.: Rethinking smart contract fuzzing: fuzzing with invocation ordering and important branch revisiting. IEEE Trans. Inf. Forensics Secur. (TIFS) **18**, 1237–1251 (2023). https://doi.org/10.1109/TIFS.2023.3237370
19. Liu, Z., Wu, S., Xu, C., Wang, X., Zhu, L., Wu, S., Feng, F.: Copy motion from one to another: fake motion video generation. In: IJCAI, pp. 1223–1231 (2022). https://doi.org/10.24963/IJCAI.2022/171
20. Mirsky, Y., Doitshman, T., Elovici, Y., Shabtai, A.: Kitsune: an ensemble of autoencoders for online network intrusion detection. arXiv preprint arXiv:1802.09089 (2018)
21. MontazeriShatoori, M., Davidson, L., Kaur, G., Lashkari, A.H.: Detection of doh tunnels using time-series classification of encrypted traffic. In: 2020 IEEE International Conference on Dependable, Autonomic and Secure Computing, International Conference on Pervasive Intelligence and Computing, International Conference on Cloud and Big Data Computing, International Conference on Cyber Science and Technology Congress (DASC/PiCom/CBDCom/CyberSciTech), pp. 63–70. IEEE (2020)
22. Ni, J., Chen, W., Tong, J., Wang, H., Wu, L.: High-speed anomaly traffic detection based on staged frequency domain features. J. Inf. Secur. Appl. **77**, 103575 (2023)
23. Qing, Y., et al.: Low-quality training data only? a robust framework for detecting encrypted malicious network traffic. arXiv preprint arXiv:2309.04798 (2023)
24. Rebuffi, S.A., Kolesnikov, A., Sperl, G., Lampert, C.H.: ICARL: incremental classifier and representation learning. In: Proceedings of the IEEE conference on Computer Vision and Pattern Recognition, pp. 2001–2010 (2017)
25. Riemer, M., Cases, I., Ajemian, R., Liu, M., Rish, I., Tu, Y., Tesauro, G.: Learning to learn without forgetting by maximizing transfer and minimizing interference. arXiv preprint arXiv:1810.11910 (2018)
26. Shuai, C., et al.: Locate and verify: a two-stream network for improved deepfake detection. In: ACM MM, pp. 7131–7142 (2023). https://doi.org/10.1145/3581783.3612386

27. Van de Ven, G.M., Siegelmann, H.T., Tolias, A.S.: Brain-inspired replay for continual learning with artificial neural networks. Nat. Commun. **11**(1), 4069 (2020)
28. Vitter, J.S.: Random sampling with a reservoir. ACM Trans. Math. Softw. (TOMS) **11**(1), 37–57 (1985)
29. Yadav, A.K., Singh, K., Amin, A.H., Almutairi, L., Alsenani, T.R., Ahmadian, A.: A comparative study on consensus mechanism with security threats and future scopes: Blockchain. Comput. Commun. **201**, 102–115 (2023)
30. Zenke, F., Poole, B., Ganguli, S.: Continual learning through synaptic intelligence. In: International Conference on Machine Learning, pp. 3987–3995. PMLR (2017)
31. Zheng, Z., Xie, S., Dai, H.N., Chen, X., Wang, H.: Blockchain challenges and opportunities: a survey. Int. J. Web Grid Serv. **14**(4), 352–375 (2018)

Self-supervised Heterogeneous Graph Neural Network Based on Deep and Broad Neighborhood Encoding

Chao Li[1,3], Qianyu Song[1(⊠)], Jinhu Fu[1], Nengfu Xie[3], and Qingtian Zeng[1,2]

[1] College of Electronic and Information Engineering, Shandong University of Science and Technology, Qingdao, China
15054534283@163.com

[2] College of Computer Science and Engineering, Shandong University of Science and Technology, Qingdao, China

[3] Key Laboratory of Agricultural Blockchain Application, Ministry of Agriculture and Rural Affairs, Agricultural Information Institute Chinese Academy of Agricultural Sciences, Beijing, China
xienengfu@caas.cn

Abstract. Self-supervised heterogeneous graph neural networks have demonstrated remarkable effectiveness in addressing the challenge of limited labeled data. However, current contrastive learning methods face limitations in exploiting neighborhood information for each node. Some methods only utilize the local information of the target node, ignoring useful signals from deeper neighborhoods. On the other hand, certain methods fail to consider the differences among neighbors at various distances. In this paper, we propose HGNN-DB, a self-supervised heterogeneous graph neural network based on depth and breadth neighborhood encoding. Specifically, HGNN-DB aims to effectively capture features from deep and broad neighborhoods. We introduce a deep neighborhood encoder using a distance-weighted strategy to capture deep features of target nodes. Additionally, we utilize a single-layer graph convolutional network for the broad neighborhood encoder to aggregate broad features of target nodes. We furthermore employ a collaborative contrastive algorithm to learn the complementarity and potential invariance between the two views of neighborhood information. The results demonstrate that HGNN-DB performs better than other state-of-the-art methods on various tasks.

Keywords: Heterogeneous Graphs · Self-supervised Learning · Graph Neural Network · Graph Contrastive Learning

1 Introduction

In recent years, Heterogeneous Graph Neural Networks (HGNNs) have received significant attention among researchers due to their powerful ability to handle heterogeneous graph data. Heterogeneous graphs can represent complex relationships, thereby enabling them to model diverse real-world systems, such as

G. Zhao et al. (Eds.): BWTAC 2024, CCIS 2277, pp. 451–462, 2025.
https://doi.org/10.1007/978-981-97-9412-6_41

transportation networks [1], cryptocurrency trading network [2] and e-commerce [3]. HGNNs can effectively aggregate graph topology and node attributes to learn representations of nodes, leading to outstanding successes in various graph analysis tasks [4], including node classification, node clustering, link prediction, and recommendation algorithms. These advantages have led HGNN to gain extensive attention from researchers, making it one of the popular research directions in the field of graph analysis and data mining.

Most existing Graph Neural Network (GNN) methods rely on supervised learning, leveraging labeled node information and yield excellent performance during training. Representative studies include Graph Convolutional Networks [6], message passing algorithms [5], graph attention networks [7], and various techniques such as neighbor aggregation with recurrent neural networks [8]. However, these methods only aggregate local neighborhood information of nodes, and modeling deeper-range graphs has not been thoroughly explored.

In fact, expanding the receptive field of target nodes can provide richer topological and attribute information, which is particularly crucial for boundary nodes and nodes in sparse graphs. Nevertheless, simply stacking graph convolutional layers leads to two main issues: (1) The embedding between nodes tend to converge [11], which refers to the issue of over-smoothing. (2) Training difficulties due to gradient vanishing.

Furthermore, in most real-world scenarios, labeling nodes often requires specialized personnel, making the collection of node labels both costly and difficult. Therefore, some existing methods are capable of extracting supervised signals from the data itself with contrastive learning. For example, DGI [10] builds local patches from encoding the original graph and global summary as positive pairs. The objective is to maximize mutual information between these representations to optimize the objective. HeCo [12] treats network schame and metapaths as different perspectives to capture local and high order structures, conducting contrastive learning between the two structures. HetGNN-SF [13] generates weights for different metapaths with Feature and Topology Comparison (FTC), then, it divides the original diverse graph into various semantically distinct subgraphs by following metapaths. However, these methods require the construction of effective contrastive learning mechanisms to comprehensively capture rich semantics in heterogeneous graphs. Based on the above analysis, there's still two fundamental problems that require us to address.

Challenge 1: How to differentiate the importance of neighbors at different distances during message passing? Current Graph Neural Networks (GNNs) are inherently flat and do not possess the capacity to aggregate node information in a hierarchical fashion. [19]. Moreover, the information provided by neighbors at different distances varies, with directly connected first-hop neighbors typically providing the most crucial information. In contrast, distant nodes have a smaller impact on the target node. Existing methods, such as APPNP [9] and GraphSage [14], often overlook the differences in the influence of neighbors at different distances during propagation. Therefore, it is essential to design an effective approach to clearly distinguish the importance of neighbors at different distances. Such an approach should leverage the information from neighboring nodes to accurately characterize the features of the target node.

Challenge 2: How to extend the propagation range of GNNs? Traditional GNN models aggregate limited neighbor information via message passing, but their expressive power is inherently limited by the depth of the network. When the depth is excessive, message passing by GNNs tends to make node representations more similar, leading to oversmoothing [15]. Furthermore, the number of trainable parameters can also result in the issue of parameter expansion as the depth of layers increases. This requires striking a balance between expanding the propagation range and preventing oversmoothing. Specifically, there is a need to design an efficient message propagation mechanism to enhance the expressive power of nodes by facilitating effective long-range information fusion.

To solve the above challenges, we propose a Self-Supervised Heterogeneous Graph Neural Network based on deep and broad neighborhood encoding. The main contributions of our work are summarized as follows:

- We propose a cross-view contrastive learning framework. It consists of depth and breadth neighborhood views, enabling us to acquire node representations from different perspectives and supervise each other. The depth neighborhood encoder leverages a designed distance-weighted mechanism to capture high-order information, while the breadth neighborhood encoder focuses on first-hop neighbors to capture low-order information.
- We present an approximate PageRank propagation scheme named Distance-weighted Approximate PageRank Propagation (DAPP). This scheme inherits the advantages of a few learnable parameters from APPNP, effectively expands the propagation range of message passing. Additionally, it incorporates a distance-weighted mechanism to distinguish the importance of neighbors at different distances.
- We conduct diverse experiments on four public datasets, and the proposed HGNN-DB outperforms the states-of-the-arts methods, which demonstrates the effectiveness of our proposed HGNN-DB from various aspects.

The rest of this paper is organized as follows. In Sect. 2, we introduce the relevant concepts and formal definitions of heterogeneous graphs. In Sect. 3, we provide the framework of HGNN-DB and detailed definitions of each encoding module. In Sect. 4, we evaluate the effectiveness of HGNN-DB with experimental results and analysis. In Sect. 5, we summarize the research work of this paper and offers future prospects.

2 Preliminaries

Definition 1 (Heterogeneous Graph [11]). *A heterogeneous graph is represented as a network $G = (V, E, X)$, where V denotes the set of nodes, E denotes the set of edges, and X denotes the set of features. G contains three different mapping functions: the node type mapping function $\Phi = V \rightarrow T$, the edge type* *mapping function $\psi : E \to R$, and the feature type mapping function $\Omega : X \to F$, where T, R, and F represent the sets of node types, edge types, and feature types, respectively. Note that $|T| + |R| > 2$.*

Definition 2 (Meta path [7]). *A meta-path in graph-structured data is a specific path connecting two entities, represented as $A_1 \xrightarrow{R_1} A_2 \xrightarrow{R_2} \cdots \xrightarrow{R_l} A_{l+1}$. It captures the composite relationship between nodes A_1 and A_{l+1}, where $A_1, A_2, \cdots A_{l+1} \in A$ and $R_1, R_2, \cdots R_l \in R$. This composite pattern represents the complex semantic information in a heterogeneous graph.*

Definition 3 (Message passing [17]). *Generalizing the convolution operator to graph-structured data is typically expressed as a message passing scheme with neighborhood aggregation. For a node i with features $x_i^{(k-1)}$ at layer $k-1$, message passing graph neural networks can be described as:*

$$x_i^k = \rho_i^k(x_i^{k-1}, \sum_{j \in N(i)} \phi^{k-1}(x_i^{k-1}, x_j^{k-1}, e_{j,i})), \tag{1}$$

where $N(i)$ denotes the neighbors of node i. $e_{j,i} \in \mathbb{R}^d$ represents the edge features between node i and node j. ρ and ϕ denote different types of aggregation functions. The summation symbol in the equation can also be replaced by other operations, e.g., sum, max or mean.

Problem (Heterogeneous Graph Representation Learning): Given a heterogeneous graph (HG) with a corresponding set of mapping functions $\left\{ \Phi_k : V_k \to \mathbb{R}^d \right\}_{k=1}^K$, where K denotes the number of node types, each mapping function Φ_k defines latent representations for all nodes of type k. Heterogeneous graph representation learning aims to learn a set of mapping functions Φ_k that project nodes V into d-dimensional vectors, where $d \ll V$. The objective of this study on heterogeneous graph representation learning is to jointly optimize the mapping functions Φ_k using self-supervised losses.

3   The Proposed Method

We present a self-supervised heterogeneous graph neural network based on deep and broad neighborhood encoding named HGNN-DB. The framework of HGNN-DB as shown in Fig. 1, which consists of three main modules: (a) Deep Neighborhood Encoder. (b) Broad Neighborhood Encoder. (c) Collaborative Contrastive Optimization Module. In the following sections, we will elaborate in detail on the above three components of HGNN-DB.

3.1   Broad Neighborhood Encoder

Heterogeneous graphs consist of a variety of node and edge types, which means their attributes typically reside in distinct dimensions. Consequently, it is essential to initially map the features of all node types into a unified latent vector space:

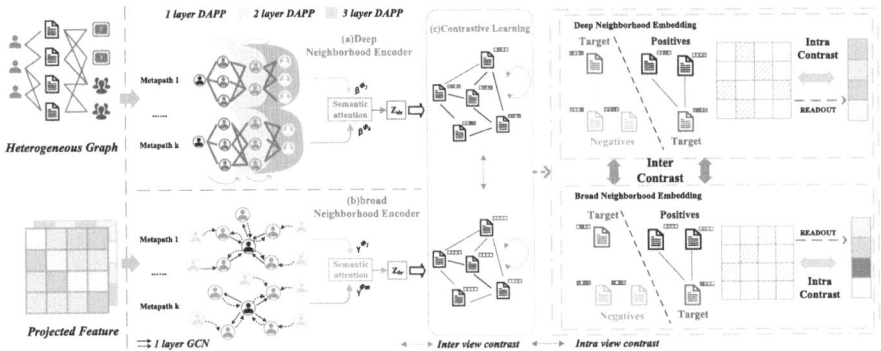

Fig. 1. The overall architecture of the proposed HGNN-DB.

$$h_i = \sigma(W^{(1)} \cdot x_i + b^{(1)}), \tag{2}$$

where $h_i \in \mathbb{R}^d$ represents the projected embedding vector of the features of node i, $\sigma(\cdot)$ is an activation function, $W^{(1)}$ represents the node mapping matrix and $b^{(1)}$ represents the bias vector.

Existing studies [18] have shown that for an l-layer graph convolutional network, the influence of input node x on node y is proportional to the probability of a random walk starting from node y and terminating at node x. The first-hop neighbors of the target node will provide the most crucial information.

In a single layer of GCN propagation, for meta-path Φ_m, the formula is as follows:

$$H_{br}^{\Phi_m} = softmax((\widehat{D}^{\Phi_m -\frac{1}{2}} \widehat{A}^{\Phi_m} \widehat{D}^{\Phi_m -\frac{1}{2}})h_i W_{br}^{\Phi_m}), \tag{3}$$

where $\widehat{A} = A + I_N$ represents the adjacency matrix with self-loops added, and $\widehat{D}^{\Phi_m}$ denotes the degree matrix of the graph under meta-path Φ_m, i.e., $\widehat{D}_{ii} = \sum_j \widehat{A}_{ij}$. W^{Φ_m} represents the learnable parameter matrix corresponding to the meta-path.

To obtain more general representations, we need to learn the weights of different meta-paths with a semantic-level attention layer for the embeddings of each learned meta-path, and aggregate them together. Specifically, we first calculate the importance of each meta-path β^{Φ_m}:

$$e^{\Phi_m} = \frac{1}{|N|} \sum_{i=1}^{N} tanh(q_{br}^{\top} \cdot [W_{br} H_{br_i}^{\Phi_m} + b_{br}]), \tag{4}$$

$$\beta^{\Phi_m} = softmax(e^{\Phi_m}) = \frac{exp(e^{\Phi_m})}{\sum_{i=1}^{P} exp(e^{\Phi_i})}, \tag{5}$$

where W_{br} is the parameter matrix for linear transformation, $q_{br}^{\top}$ is the learnable shared attention vector, and b_{br} represents the bias.

β^{Φ_m} represents the importance of metapath Φ_m. Utilizing the acquired weights as multipliers, we amalgamate these diverse embeddings to derive the ultimate embedding Z_{br} in the following manner:

$$Z_{br} = \sum_{i=1}^{P} \beta^{\Phi_i} \cdot H_{br}^{\Phi_i}. \tag{6}$$

The aggregated Z_{br} encapsulates information from all first-hop neighbors of the target node, encoding both local structure and feature information. It provides semantic support from the breadth of the neighborhood for downstream tasks.

3.2 Deep Neighborhood Encoder

To expand the receptive field of GNNs, we have developed a deep neighborhood encoder submodule with an optimized PageRank.

Approximate Personalized Propagation of Predictions (APPNP). Most existing message-passing schemes employ learnable parameter matrices at each layer, inevitably increasing the depth of neural networks during multi-layer propagation. APPNP [9] establishes an inherent link between the steady-state distribution and the PageRank algorithm. Specifically, APPNP iteratively approaches the goal of the global personalized PageRank:

$$Z^{(0)} = H = f_\theta(h_i),$$
$$Z^{(k+1)} = (1 - \alpha)\widetilde{\widehat{A}}Z^{(k)} + \alpha H, \tag{7}$$
$$Z^{(K)} = softmax((1 - \alpha)\widetilde{\widehat{A}}Z^{(K-1)} + \alpha H),$$

where α represents the probability of restarting to the root node, and $k \in [0, K - 2]$ denotes the number of iterations.

However, this method conducts propagation based on the previous layer without distinguishing the contribution of each layer's neighbors to the target node. To address this issue, we attempt to differentiate the impact of embeddings from different layers during propagation by employing an aggregation function.

Distance-weighted Approximate PageRank Propagation (DAPP). In the HGNN-DB framework, the broad neighborhood encoder has already captured the information of first-hop neighbors. However, the embeddings produced by APPNP's propagation retain excessive information from these first-hop neighbors due to the restart probability α. This retention is not conducive to obtaining the complementary views necessary for contrastive learning within HGNN-DB. Therefore, there is no longer a need to retain information from the root node during propagation. Reconsidering Eq. 7, we remove the influence of the parameter α:

$$Z^{(0)} = H = f_\theta(h_i),$$

$$Z^{(k+1)} = \widetilde{A} Z^{(k)},$$ (8)

$$Z^{(K)} = softmax(\widetilde{A} Z^{(K-1)}).$$

Moreover, because it is impossible to predetermine the contribution of k-hop neighbors to the target node, we conduct experiments using the propagation method in Eq. 8 within the HGNN-DB model. Then we aggregate the embeddings of each layer of the broad neighborhood encoder using layer attention. We observe that the weights of every layer approximately follow logarithmic distributions.

Based on the above analysis, we propose a **distance-weighted approximate PageRank propagation (DAPP)** to estimate the weight distribution of different layers. Specifically, in the propagation process of DAPP, we distinguish the importance of each layer with a logarithmic function.

$$H_{de} = \frac{log(\eta + 1)}{\sum_{i=1}^{K} log(\eta + i)} Z^{(0)} + \frac{log(\eta + 2)}{\sum_{i=1}^{K} log(\eta + i)} Z^{(1)} + \cdots \frac{log(\eta + 1)}{\sum_{i=1}^{K} log(\eta + k)} Z^{(K)},$$ (9)

where η ($\eta > 0$) is used to control the rate of weight increase.

In this manner, we can simulate the parameter distribution between different layers, thereby reducing the computational cost of HGNN-DB without compromising the model's performance.

Finally, the deep neighborhood information from different meta-paths is fused with semantic-level attention:

$$y^{\Phi_m} = \frac{1}{|N|} \sum_{i=1}^{N} tanh(q_{de}^\top \cdot [W_{de} H_{de_i}^{\Phi_m} + b_{br}]),$$ (10)

$$\gamma^{\Phi_m} = softmax(y^{\Phi_m}) = \frac{exp(y^{\Phi_m})}{\sum_{i=1}^{P} exp(y^{\Phi_i})},$$ (11)

where W_{de} and b_{de} represent learnable parameters, and q_{de} is a learnable shared attention vector.

Weighted aggregation of the representations propagated with each meta-path yields the final embedding under the deep neighborhood perspective:

$$Z_{de} = \sum_{i=1}^{P} \gamma^{\Phi_i} \cdot H_{de}^{\Phi_i}.$$ (12)

3.3   Collaboratively Contrastive Optimization

To extract rich semantics from heterogeneous graphs, inspired by HGCML [16], we adopt a collaborative optimization strategy involving intra-view and inter-view contrasts.

Inter-view Contrastive Learning. This contrastive approach is designed to acquire distinctive node representations that enhance subsequent node-specific tasks. In particular, within this study, a contrastive loss is applied between two perspectives to either maximize or minimize the certainty between analogous (or dissimilar) nodes:

$$L_{inter}^{(m,n)} = \frac{\sum_{v \in \mathbb{P}} sim(Z_u^m, Z_v^n)}{\sum_{v \in \mathbb{P}} sim(Z_u^m, Z_v^n) + \sum_{v \in (V/\mathbb{P})} sim(Z_u^m, Z_v^m) + \sum_{v \in (v/\mathbb{P})} sim(Z_u^m, Z_v^n)},$$
$$(13)$$

note that m and n represent different views. To capture the intra-view relationships, we allow m and n to take the same value (comparing against themselves). $\mathbb{P}$ denotes the selected positive samples.

We employ a similarity function to compute the distances between different views: $sim(Z_u^m, Z_v^m) = e^{\varphi(\rho(Z_u^m), \rho(Z_v^n))/\tau}$. Here, $\phi(\cdot, \cdot)$ measures the cosine distance between two vectors, $\rho(\cdot)$ denotes a non-linear projection enhancing representational capacity, and τ controls the data distribution.

Intra-view Contrastive Learning. Different from inter-view contrastive learning, we also incorporate intra-view contrast as an auxiliary task, which is defined as follows:

$$L_{intra}^{(m,n)} = \sum_{m=1}^{2} \sum_{n=1}^{2} \left(-\log(D(Z_m, S_m)) - \log(1 - D(Z_n, S_m)) \right), \qquad (14)$$

in this contrastive view, we still allow m and n to be the same value. Additionally, Z_m represents the local information of each view, while S_m is the global information of the view obtained with the $READOUT(\cdot)$ function average pooling. Here, $D(h, s) = \omega(\rho(h), \rho(s))$, where $\omega(\cdot, \cdot)$ is a discriminator composed of a bilinear layer $Bilinear(\cdot)$ and a sigmoid function $\sigma(\cdot)$. By maximizing the local and global information of the same view, discriminative node representations within each view can be learned.

The overall objective $\mathfrak{L}$ is defined as the aggregation of all views, formulated as:

$$\mathfrak{L} = \sum_{m \in M} \sum_{n \in M} (\delta \cdot L_{intra}^{(m,n)} + (1 - \delta) \cdot L_{inter}^{(m,n)}), \qquad (15)$$

here, M represents the set of different views, and δ serves as a balancing factor for the losses across the two perspectives. We can refine the proposed model and acquire node embeddings by the process of backpropagation. To perform downstream tasks, we utilize the sum of embeddings from different views and adjust them using parameter λ:

$$Z = (1 - \lambda) \cdot Z_{de} + \lambda \cdot Z_{br}. \qquad (16)$$

Table 1. Quantitative results (%) on node classification.

Dataset	Metrics	Split	Mp2vec	GAT	HAN	HDGI	HeCo	MEOW	HGCML	Ours
ACM	Macro-F1	40	76.47	87.69	91.33	87.18	88.62	91.43	92.52	**93.04**
		60	77.65	88.89	91.73	86.59	87.06	91.75	92.77	**93.13**
		80	78.01	89.53	91.79	88.95	89.95	92.83	92.98	**93.32**
	Micro-F1	40	77.36	87.48	91.22	87.5	86.19	91.50	92.46	**92.96**
		60	78.23	88.67	91.6	87.81	88.73	91.79	92.70	**93.04**
		80	78.77	89.57	91.69	88.78	89.29	92.04	92.90	**93.05**
Aminer	Macro-F1	40	65.25	64.77	62.65	62.65	64.15	**68.51**	66.08	66.59
		60	60.53	60.65	64.48	66.48	65.41	**70.03**	66.23	66.91
		80	64.24	61.35	65.53	65.23	65.46	**70.54**	66.3	67.01
	Micro-F1	40	69.34	71.34	82.39	82.53	81.07	75.67	84.14	**84.24**
		60	63.51	67.7	82.73	82.84	81.75	76.92	84.26	**84.28**
		80	65.74	68.73	83.11	82.89	82.45	75.98	83.50	**84.38**
Yelp	Macro-F1	40	63.89	54.66	79.49	42.26	80.62	52.01	63.79	**92.50**
		60	63.69	54.45	78.57	42.38	79.83	52.53	62.91	**93.04**
		80	63.46	54.32	79.84	42.39	79.67	53.64	62.08	**93.45**
	Micro-F1	40	76.69	73.16	79.48	66.89	85.09	72.90	77.97	**92.12**
		60	78.59	72.47	79.97	66.94	84.52	73.55	78.07	**92.59**
		80	78.22	72.42	81.33	67.03	84.65	73.89	78.42	**92.96**
DBLP	Macro-F1	40	83.27	90.61	92.41	90.53	89.99	91.53	91.63	**92.73**
		60	85.17	90.47	92.39	90.63	91.14	93.42	91.96	**93.45**
		80	84.49	91.12	91.55	90.62	91.64	93.19	91.62	**93.24**
	Micro-F1	40	82.49	91.26	92.81	90.05	90.31	91.36	91.40	**93.34**
		60	85.73	91.49	93.02	90.43	91.99	93.59	91.72	**93.60**
		80	84.97	92.01	92.53	91.79	92.47	**94.05**	92.31	93.79

4   Experiments

In this section, we assess the performance of the HGNN-DB framework across four diverse heterogeneous graphs (ACM[1], DBLP[2], Aminer[3], Yelp[4]) and compare HGNN-DB with seven representative models, including three semi-supervised models (Metapath2vec (2017) [20], GAT (2017) [21], HAN (2019) [7]) and four self-supervised models(HDGI (2019) [11], HECO (2021) [8], MEOW (2023) [17], HGCML (2023) [16]).

4.1   Node Classification

In this section, we evaluate the outcomes of node classification for the HGNN-DB framework when applied to datasets on ACM, Aminer, DBLP, and Yelp.

---

[1] http://dl.acm.org/.

[2] https://dblp.unitrier.de.

[3] https://www.aminer.cn/aminernetwork.

[4] https://www.yelp.com/dataset.

Specifically, we feed the node representations into a Support Vector Machine (SVM) for classification, partitioning 40%, 60%, and 80% of the nodes as training sets, and employing Micro-F1 and Macro-F1 as evaluation metrics. The best performance results are highlighted in bold, whereas the results that rank next in terms of performance are underlined, as shown in Table 1.

HGNN-DB shows an average increase of 0.6% in Macro-F1 and 0.47% in Micro-F1 on ACM, and a significant improvement of 12.44% in Macro-F1 and 14.91% in Micro-F1 on Yelp. On DBLP, it also outperforms the best baseline with an average gain of 0.43% in Macro-F1 and 0.64% in Micro-F1. This is attributed to: (1) Within the same view, we focus on learning the local-global mutual information to obtain discriminative node representations. (2) We capture the complementarity between deep and broad neighborhood views to fully learn the neighborhood information of nodes at different distances.

4.2   Ablation Study

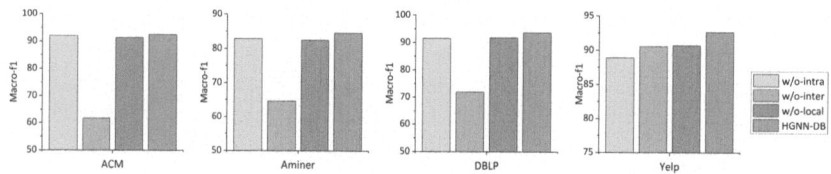

Fig. 2. The comparison of HGNN-DB and its variants.

In this section, we perform an ablation analysis on our HGNN-DB framework to assess the efficacy of the suggested encoding components. Specifically, in HGNN-DB$_{-w/o-intra}$, we ignore intra-view collaboration contrast. In HGNN-DB$_{-w/o-inter}$, we ignore inter-view cross-contrast. In HGNN-DB$_{-w/o-local}$, we no longer allow m and n in Eq. 13 and 14 to be the same value, i.e., each view is not allowed to be contrasted with itself. As shown in Fig. 2, we observe that HGNN-DB consistently outperforms these variants, providing ample evidence of the effectiveness of each encoding module.

4.3   DAPP Performance Improvement

To verify the effectiveness of the proposed DAPP, we compare it against the original APPNP, as illustrated in Fig. 3. The HGNN-DB method utilizing DAPP propagation consistently outperformed the original APPNP.

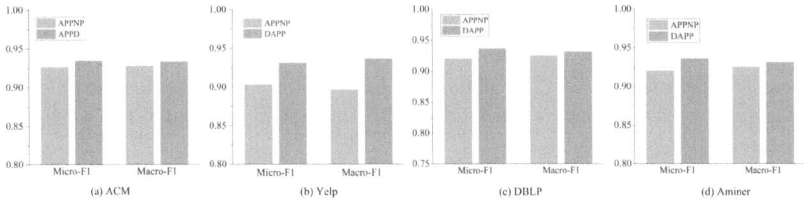

Fig. 3. The comparison of performance between DAPP and APPNP on node classification tasks.

5   Conclusion

We propose a self-supervised heterogeneous graph neural network HGNN-DB based on depth and breadth neighborhood encoding. To address the first challenge, we simulate the distribution trend of neighbors at different distances with layer attention and design a distance-weighted approximate PageRank propagation scheme DAPP based on this trend. It fully considers the difference in the influence of neighbors at different distances, ensures the model couples the depth neighborhood while avoiding the issue of node over-smoothing. To solve the second challenge, we separately design the breadth neighborhood view and the depth neighborhood view, allowing the model to capture the complementarity and potential invariances of these two views simultaneously, effectively extending the GNN's propagation range. Experiments on multiple datasets show that the HGNN-DB model outperforms several advanced baselines. In the future, we will further explore how to distinguish the influence relationships among nodes in the same-hop neighborhoods.

Declarations

Acknowledgement. This work is supported by National Natural Science Foundation of China (Grant No.52374221); the Natural Science Foundation of Shandong Province (Grant No. ZR2021QG038); the Taishan Scholar Program of Shandong Province (Grant No. ts20190936), and the Open Research Fund Program of Key Laboratory of Agricultural Blockchain Application, Ministry of Agriculture and Rural Affairs(2022KLABA03).

Disclosure of Interests. The authors declare that there is no competing interests. The authors declare that there is no competing interests.

References

1. Zhang, Q., et al.: Graph neural network-driven traffic forecasting for the connected internet of vehicles. IEEE Trans. Netw. Sci. Eng. **9**, 3015–3027 (2022)
2. Jing, L., Kang, Y.: Automated cryptocurrency trading approach using ensemble deep reinforcement learning: learn to understand candlesticks. Expert Syst. Appl. (Mar. Pt.A) **237**, 121373 (2024)

3. Zhang, G., et al.: eFraudCom: an e-commerce fraud detection system via competitive graph neural networks. ACM Trans. Inf. Syst.(TOIS) **40**, 1–29 (2022)
4. Rong, Y., Huang, W., Xu, T., Huang, J.: DropEdge: towards deep graph convolutional networks on node classification. In: International Conference on Learning Representations (2019)
5. Giovanni, F.D., Giusti, L., Barbero, F., Luise, G., Lio', P., Bronstein, M.M.: On over-squashing in message passing neural networks: the impact of width, depth, and topology. ArXiv, abs/2302.02941 (2023)
6. Chen, M., Wei, Z., Huang, Z., Ding, B., Li, Y.: Simple and deep graph convolutional networks. In: International Conference on Machine Learning (2020)
7. Jiang, N., Wen, J., Li, J., Liu, X., Jin, D.: GATrust: a multi-aspect graph attention network model for trust assessment in OSNs. IEEE Trans. Knowl. Data Eng. **35**, 5865–5878 (2023)
8. Dai, H., Kozareva, Z., Dai, B., Smola, A., Song, L.: Learning steady-states of iterative algorithms over graphs. In: International Conference on Machine Learning (2018)
9. Klicpera, J., Bojchevski, A., Günnemann, S.: Predict then propagate: graph neural networks meet personalized PageRank. In: International Conference on Learning Representations (2018)
10. Velickovic, P., Fedus, W., Hamilton, W.L., Lio', P., Bengio, Y., Hjelm, R.D.: Deep graph infomax. ArXiv, abs/1809.10341 (2018)
11. Ren, Y., Liu, B., Huang, C., Dai, P., Bo, L., Zhang, J.: Heterogeneous deep graph infomax. ArXiv, abs/1911.08538 (2019)
12. Wang, X., Liu, N., Han, H., Shi, C.: Self-supervised heterogeneous graph neural network with co-contrastive learning. In: Proceedings of the 27th ACM SIGKDD Conference on Knowledge Discovery & Data Mining (2021)
13. Li, C., Liu, X., Yan, Y., Zhao, Z., Zeng, Q.: HetGNN-SF: self-supervised learning on heterogeneous graph neural network via semantic strength and feature similarity. Appl. Intell. **53**, 21902–21919 (2023)
14. Hamilton, W.L., Ying, Z., Leskovec, J.: Inductive representation learning on large graphs. In: Neural Information Processing Systems (2017)
15. Maskey, S., Paolino, R., Bacho, A., Kutyniok, G.: A fractional graph laplacian approach to versmoothing. ArXiv, abs/2305.13084 (2023)
16. Wang, Z., Li, Q., Yu, D., Han, X., Gao, X., Shen, S.: Heterogeneous graph contrastive multi-view learning. ArXiv, abs/2210.00248 (2022)
17. Feng, J., Chen, Y., Li, F., Sarkar, A., Zhang, M.: How powerful are k-hop message passing graph neural networks. ArXiv, abs/2205.13328 (2022)
18. Li, Y., Shen, Y., Chen, L., Yuan, M.: Zebra: when temporal graph neural networks meet temporal personalized PageRank. Proc. VLDB Endow. **16**, 1332–1345 (2023)
19. Ranjan, E., Sanyal, S., Talukdar, P.P.: ASAP: adaptive structure aware pooling for learning hierarchical graph representations. ArXiv, abs/1911.07979 (2019)
20. Dong, Y., Chawla, N., Swami, A.: metapath2vec: scalable representation learning for heterogeneous networks. In: Proceedings of the 23rd ACM SIGKDD International Conference on Knowledge Discovery and Data Mining (2017)
21. Wang, X., et al.: Heterogeneous graph attention network. In: The World Wide Web Conference (2019)

Batch Validation Scheme of Data Feature Requirement in Blockchain-Based Data Trading Platform

Junlang Zhang⬤, Zeyu Yu⬤, Tianrong Chen⬤, Jiawen Fang⬤,
Chufeng Liang⬤, and Hua Tang$^{(\boxtimes)}$⬤

School of Computer Science, South China Normal University, Guangzhou 510631,
China
tanghua@m.scnu.edu.cn

Abstract. In traditional data trading process, data is sent directly to the demand side, leading to resale risks. To solve this problem, some researchers have proposed trading platforms that trade the right to use data, while data reamins local. However, due to the data invisibility, how to verify whether the data features meet the requirements of the Data requester without compromising the data privacy becomes a key issue. To address the issues above, this work propose a scheme for batch verification of data feature requirement fulfillment, where data holders organize and deposit data features using sparse feature Merkle trees (SFMT), and multiple data feature zero-knowledge proofs are aggregated using SnarkPack aggregation technology for data, thus enabling efficient verification of data feature zero-knowledge proofs on the chain. In addition, to avoid redundant verification of the same data features, this work propose a multi-way sparse Merkle tree (MSMT) to achieve efficient storage and verification of zero-knowledge proofs. Experimental results based on this scheme demonstrate that our proposed scheme significantly reduces the size of zero-knowledge proofs on the chain and decreases the gas consumption for verifying data requirement proofs on the chain, and MSMT also shows better performance in terms of insertion efficiency and generation and verification of Merkle paths, which improves the efficiency of verifying proofs of data feature requirement satisfaction on blockchain.

Keywords: Data trading · Data feature validation · Sparse feature Merkle tree · multi-ary sparse Merkle tree

1 Introduction

With the continuous development of the Internet, mobile devices, industrial sensors, and other technologies, the scale of global data has been increasing significantly. Vast amounts of data, which hold immense value for organizations and enterprises, have been accumulated by providers. In traditional data transactions, data is directly sent to the data requester after a deal, leading to the risk

G. Zhao et al. (Eds.): BWTAC 2024, CCIS 2277, pp. 463–474, 2025.
https://doi.org/10.1007/978-981-97-9412-6_42

of data resale. To mitigate this, a data transaction platform has been proposed [4] that enables transactions without the data leaving its local environment. Building on this, we consider a data trading platform based on a reverse auction mechanism, as illustrated in Fig. 1. Data owners sell usage rights without transferring the data itself. Data requesters post their requirements to a blockchain smart contract, and data owners bid based on their data. The winning data owner performs local computations and sends the results to the data requester, completing the transaction.

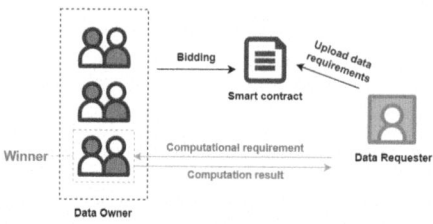

Fig. 1. Data trading platform framework.

In the trading process described above, the difficulty lies in verifying the data's features without direct access, yet it is crucial to ensure that the data held by data owners meets the requirements of data requesters. To address this, we developed an efficient framework for verifying data feature requirement satisfaction. Data owners generate a Merkle tree of their data feature(SFMT) and upload the Merkle root to the blockchain for save. Generate a Merkle path ZKP to verify the data feature saved in SFMT without accessing the data. Using SnarkPack-based proof aggregation scheme, we achieve efficient aggregation and verification, reducing on-chain verification time and blockchain storage space. Additionally, to avoid repeated verification for the same data requirements, we use an MSMT structure to organize and store original ZKP proofs, enhancing the efficiency of insertion, path proof generation and verification.

The contributions of this paper are threefold: 1) We implemented an efficient framework for verifying data requirement satisfaction based on data feature Merkle trees and SnarkPack aggregation scheme; 2) We propose a specialized data features depository structure based on Spare Merkle trees SFMT; 3) To prevent repeated verification of the same data requirements, we develop an enhanced sparse Merkle tree structure MSMT for storing verified original proofs and enhancing the efficiency of sparse Merkle tree generation and verification.

2   Related Work

Data trading is a popular research area, with many researchers proposing blockchain-based platforms to address the centralization issue [4,9,11,12,14]. Su et al. [11] proposed the STDP platform, leveraging SGX and blockchain to create a decentralized data trading platform, using TEE for fair data transmission. To prevent data resale risks, Dai et al. [4] introduced the SDTE system, which also uses blockchain and SGX to ensure data brokers and buyers cannot access the seller's raw data, with buyers receiving only the necessary analysis results.

Zero-knowledge proofs (ZKPs) have become widely used in Web3 and cryptography, with the Groth16 protocol [7] being notable for its small proof size, extensively used in applications like Zcash, ZkSync, and File Coin. ZKPs are crucial for privacy protection in data trading platforms. For example, Lorünser et al. [10] proposed a decentralized data market framework combining secure multi-party computation and ZKPs for flexible sealed-bid auctions. In medical data trading, Xue et al. [13] suggested a model where buyers publish their data requirements in advance, and sellers provide ZKPs to prove they possess the necessary electronic medical records.

The storage and verification of ZKPs incur significant space and time costs, leading to scalability issues in blockchain systems. Researchers have proposed various compression and aggregation schemes for ZKPs, such as SnarkPack [5], aPLONK [1], and BulletProofs [2]. SnarkPack based on Groth16 proofs, uses random linear combinations to verify n Groth16 proofs with a single pairing operation, significantly reducing time and space overhead.

Sparse Merkle Trees (SMTs) use a hash function to determine leaf node positions, facilitating existence and non-existence proofs for data elements. Existence proofs require a hash path from leaf to root, while non-existence proofs verify a leaf node's default value. To improve efficiency, default node values are cached at each level. Dahlberg et al. [3] introduced caching strategies like B-caching, B–caching, and B++-caching to optimize space and time. Haider et al. [8] developed the Compact Sparse Merkle Tree (C-SMT), employing a minimum distance path algorithm, defining distance as the binary interval between two keys. Gao et al. [6] developed the Jellyfish Merkle Tree (JMT) based on the Addressable Radix Merkle Tree, using version-based keys for adaptability to version-based sharding. JMT classifies nodes into internal and leaf nodes, reducing complexity, and increasing storage and computational efficiency.

3   System Model

Our proposed system model, as shown in Fig. 2, includes five roles: Data Owner (DO), Data Requester (DR), Data Trading Platform (DP), Proof Aggregator (PA), and Challenger (CH).

1. **Data Owners** hold and intend to sell data in the data trading platform. They aim to trade the value of the data without revealing or reselling the dataset itself.
2. **Data Requesters** are the entities seeking target data in the data trading market.
3. **Data Trading Platform** is a decentralized on-chain data trading platform composed of multiple smart contracts.

4. **Proof Aggregators** are selected randomly by the smart contract, proof aggregators aggregate the ZKPs of data request satisfaction submitted by data owners. Aggregators need to deposit collateral with the smart contract to preverent evil behavior. Honest aggregators get paid From deal amounts.
5. **Challengers** verify and challenge the work of proof aggregators. They can be either data owners or data requesters.

We describe the flow of the system in detail in Sect. 4.2.

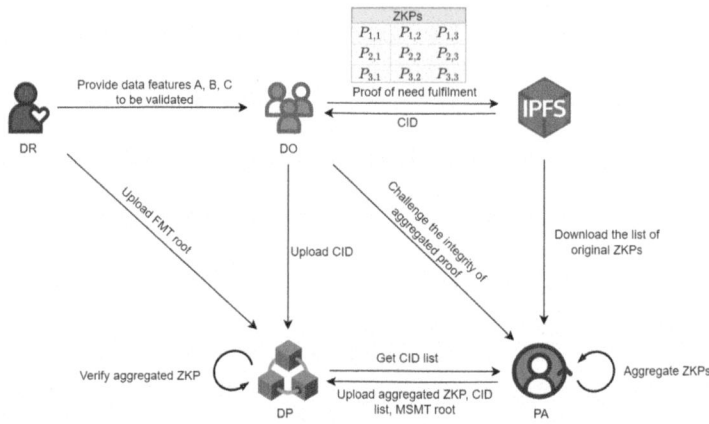

Fig. 2. Blockchain-based Batch Verification Scheme for Data Feature Requirement Proofs.

4   Proposed Blockchain-Based Batch Verification Scheme for Data Feature Requirement Proofs

In this section, we introduce the detailed process and relevant data structures of our proposed blockchain-based batch verification scheme for data feature requirement proofs. Within this scheme, our fundamental assumption is that, influenced by a reputation mechanism, DOs with poor historical transaction records will find it difficult to conclude transactions. Therefore, all DOs will honestly upload the data features they possess.

4.1   Data Feature Depository Structure: SFMT

The dataset D held by the DO has a feature set $F = \{f_1, f_2, \ldots, f_n\}$. To store data features and provide a reliable and efficient on-chain certification mechanism, we propose the SFMT structure. SFMT stores specified data features in the leaves of a sparse Merkle tree and depository the data features by recording the root of the generated Merkle tree on the blockchain.

The structure of SFMT is illustrated in Fig. 3, where each leaf node value is calculating by the hash function $H(f, r, m)$, where r is a random number. Incorporating a random number in the hash computation helps prevent brute force attacks on data features, thereby avoiding the leakage of related data characteristics. The m represents the category identifier of the feature, preventing DOs from impersonating the data feature requirements with mismatched category features. To prevent DOs from uploading multiple values of the same type of data feature to the leaf nodes, the types of data features stored, the number of features, the number of layers in the Merkle tree, and the default values for empty leaf nodes are specified by the data trading platform. DOs are required to provide a zero-knowledge proof of non-existence for empty nodes.

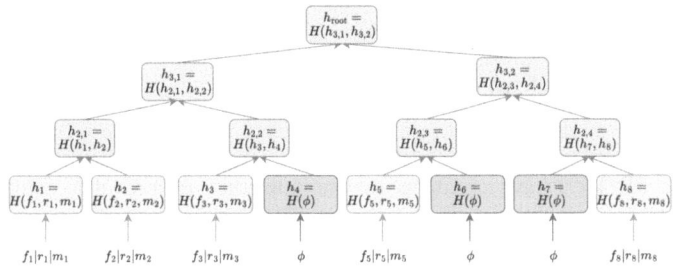

Fig. 3. Structure of Sparse Feature Merkle Tree

When verification is required for the data features stored in the SFMT by a DO, it is performed through a ZKP circuit. The public inputs for this circuit include: the leaf node hash value $leaf_{FMT} = H(f, r, m)$, the feature attribute category identifier m, the root of SFMT $root_{FMT}$, the data feature to be verified f^*, and the comparison method w (greater than, less than, or equal to). The secret inputs include: the feature value f, the random number r, the Merkle path $path$, the Merkle path index $pathIndex$. The corresponding verification circuit, as shown in Algorithm 1, first compares f and f^* according to the comparison method w. It then checks whether $Hash(f, r, m)$ matches $leaf_{FMT}$, verifying the correctness of f, r, and m. Subsequently, it generates and verifies the root node value using the Merkle path, thus validating the correctness of the Merkle proof.

4.2 ZKP Generation and Batch Verification Process for Data Feature Requirement

In this section, we describe the details of the proposed scheme, which includes five roles: DO, DR, DP, PA, and CH. The system's smart contracts consist of a Depository Contract (DC), Verification Contract (VC), and Payment Contract (PC). The batch verification process for data requirement satisfaction is illustrated in Fig. 2, with the detailed process as follows:

Algorithm 1. FMT Features Verification Circuits

Input: Public Input: $leaf_{FMT} = H(f, r, m)$, feature attribute m, root of FMT $root_{FMT}$, data feature to be verified f^*, comparison method w

Input: Witness: f, r, Merkle path $path$, path index $pathIndex$

1: $comparisons \leftarrow [f < f^*, f = f^*, f > f^*]$
2: $assert(comparisons[w])$
3: $assert(H(f, r, m) = leaf_{FMT})$
4: $INode \leftarrow leaf_{FMT}$
5: **for** $i \in [0, \ldots, l_p - 1]$ **do**
6:    $left \leftarrow path[i]$
7:    $right \leftarrow INode$
8:    **if** $pathIndex[i] = 1$ **then**
9:       $left, right \leftarrow right, left$
10:   **end if**
11:   $INode \leftarrow H(left, right)$
12: **end for**
13: $assert(INode = root_{FMT})$

Initially, all DOs participating in the auction organize the features $F = \{f_1, f_2, \ldots, f_n\}$ of the dataset D into an SFMT, according to the platform's required layering and feature types, and upload the root R_{SFMT} of the SFMT to DC to certify the data features of dataset D.

After DR publish their data requirements $F^* = \{f_1^*, f_2^*, f_3^*\}$, multiple DOs generate a batch of ZKPs $P = \{P_{1,1}, P_{1,2}, P_{1,3}, \ldots, P_{m,1}, P_{m,2}, P_{m,3}\}$ that proof their data features saved in SFMT meet the data requirements. These ZKPs are uploaded to IPFS, obtaining a list of CIDs $List_{CID1}, List_{CID2}, \ldots, List_{CIDm}$, which are then certified in the SC.

To reduce the cost of verifying all data feature requirement ZKPs on-chain, a qualified PA is randomly selected. After paying a deposit to PC, the PA uses $List_{CID1}, List_{CID2}, \ldots, List_{CIDm}$ to download the original ZKPs from IPFS. By employing SnarkPack scheme, PA aggregates ZKPs of the same circuit uploaded by each user and simultaneously verifies the correctness of the ZKPs. The hash values of each valid original ZKP are organized into a sparse Merkle tree to obtain the root R_{MSMT}, which, along with the aggregated ZKP P_{agg} and the qualified list $List_{CIDagg}$, is uploaded to DC for depository.

After CH verifies the work of PA, and if it is found that the PA has not aggregated correctly, CH provides evidence and the smart contract forfeits the PA's deposit. Once the challenge phase concludes, VC verifies P_{agg}, thereby confirming that all DOs' datasets meet the DR's data requirements.

4.3   Aggregation and Challenge Scheme for SFMT Path ZKPs

As shown in Algorithm 2, to prevent PA from acting maliciously or not performing the aggregation diligently, after PA has completed aggregation, CH can challenge the work of the PA. The detailed challenge steps are as follows:

1. CH download P_{agg}, $publicInputs$, pvk, $verSRS$, and $List_{CIDagg}$ that PA uploaded to the blockchain from DC, and download the original ZKPs through $List_{CID1}, List_{CID2}, \ldots, List_{CIDm}$.

2. CH first verifies the validity of P_{agg}. If the verification fails, evidence is submitted and the smart contract forfeits the aggregator node's deposit.

3. By examining the public inputs (SFMT Merkle roots and leaf nodes) of the downloaded original ZKPs and comparing them, if any public inputs of the original ZKPs are not included in P_{agg}, verify the validity of such original ZKPs. If the original ZKP is valid, it indicates an error in the aggregator's process, leading to the forfeiture of the aggregator's deposit.

4. Identify the CIDs of the valid ZKPs from the P_{agg}'s publicInputs and compare it with the $List_{CIDagg}$ uploaded by PA to determine whether the aggregator has included ZKPs not uploaded by the DOs.

5. CH requests that the PA provide Merkle path ZKPs for nodes storing valid ZKPs and non-existence path ZKPs for nodes of invalid ZKPs in MSMT, ensuring that the content stored in MSMT accurately reflects the verification status of the original ZKPs.

Algorithm 2. Challenge Aggregate ZKP Integrity Verification Algorithms

---

Output: If the aggregation node pass the check
Input: P_{agg}, $publicInputs$, pvk, $verSRS$, $List_{CID}$, $CIDProofMap$
 1: **if** not AGG.Verify(P_{agg}, $publicInputs$, pvk, $verSRS$) **then**
 2:    **return** false
 3: **end if**
 4: $List_{verifiedCIDs} \leftarrow \{\}$
 5: **for** $(cid, proof)$ in $CIDProofMap$ **do**
 6:    $root_{FMT}, leaf_{FMT} \leftarrow proof.getPublicInput()$
 7:    **if** $(root_{FMT}, leaf_{FMT}) \notin publicInputs \wedge \neg Groth16.Verify(proof)$ **then**
 8:       **return** false
 9:    **end if**
10:    $List_{verifiedCIDs}.add(cid)$
11: **end for**
12: **return** $List_{verifiedCIDs} = Set(List_{CID})$
Output: If the aggregation node passes the check

4.4 Original ZKP Storage Structure: MSMT

Different DRs may need data features with inclusion relationships, allowing the same batch of data from DO to be sold to multiple DRs. For instance, in the first transaction, DR_A need 1,000 data points. DO_C, DO_D, and DO_E, after proving their datasets meet the requirements and passing on-chain aggregation verification, can sell their data. In another auction, DR_B may need 800 data points. Since DO_C, DO_D, and DO_E have already verified their datasets contain over 1,000 points, it is naturally verified that they meet DR_B's requirements. Thus, DO_C, DO_D, and DO_E, can provide ZKPs stored in MSMT leaf nodes and corresponding Merkle paths, proving their data features have already been verified on-chain, avoiding repeated verification and conserving resources.

In order to improve the efficiency of generating SMTs and reduce the verification cost of Merkle paths, our proposed MSMT reduces the number of layers of a sparse Merkle tree by improving the original SMTs to 2-bit branching and uses a path compression mechanism that encodes paths as binary strings and then converts them to byte representations, which improves the efficiency of generating and verifying the Merkle tree and reduces the storage space required to store nodes. Theoretically, the height of the sparse Merkle tree can be optimized from $\log_2 n$ to $\log_4 n$ by improving it to 2-bit branching, which improves the efficiency of node insertion and the efficiency of generating and verifying the path proofs.

The structure of MSMT is shown in Fig. 4. Blue nodes represent stored nodes, while yellow nodes indicate empty nodes. Each intermediate node has 4 branches. Due to varying node density within different tree regions, we classify nodes as flexible or rigid, similiar as the JMT [6] implementation. Rigid nodes encode branch nodes and store multiple child nodes, reducing access times. Flexible nodes, representing a single valid child node on the path, compress paths and save storage space. For instance, the last two digits in nodes $h(P_1)$, $h(P_4)$, and $h(P_5)$ are represented in a compressed manner.

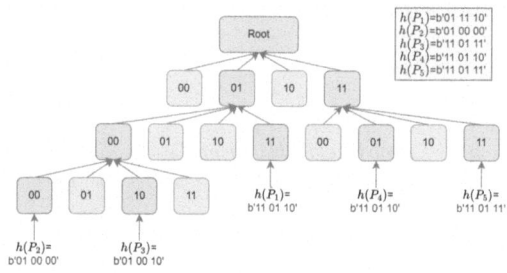

Fig. 4. Structure of MSMT.

5   Experiments

5.1   Experimental Preparations

We conducted our experiments using a computer equipped with an Intel Xeon CPU 2.40 GHz processor and 64 GB of memory, operating on a 64-bit system. The on-chain experiments were performed on the Arbitrum Stylus Layer 2 network. We utilized Groth16 as the ZKP protocol, and the SnarkPack protocol, which is based on Groth16 ZKPs, for the aggregation of ZKP. We tested the performance of our proposed method both locally and on-chain.

5.2   Batch Verification of Data Requirement Satisfaction ZKPs

In an SFMT with 128 leaf nodes and a constraint circuit of size 2562 for SFMT
Merkle path proofs, time, space, and gas consumption comparisons for different
batch sizes of original Groth16 ZKPs are illustrated in Fig. 5. Figure (a) shows
that as the batch size increases, the generation time for original ZKPs also
rises, but the time required for aggregation remains relatively low. For instance,
generating 1024 Groth16 ZKPs takes 1208 ms, while aggregating them takes
only 92 ms.

In terms of ZKP verification time, as shown in Fig. (b), the time to verify
individual ZKPs increases with the number of ZKPs, whereas verifying aggregated ZKPs takes significantly less time. For instance, verifying 1024 ZKPs after
aggregation takes only 8.6% of the original time, thanks to SnarkPack's method
of verifying all Groth16 ZKPs simultaneously using random linear combinations,
requiring only one pairing operation instead of n.

Figure (c) compares the spatial efficiency of aggregated ZKPs. While the size
of aggregated ZKPs is initially larger for small numbers of original ZKPs, the
advantage becomes clear after exceeding 128 ZKPs. When the number reaches
1024, the aggregated ZKP uses only about 20% of the space compared to the
original ZKPs, demonstrating spatial efficiency.

We implement the smart contract logic of Groth16 algorithm verification and
Snarkpack aggregated ZKP verification based on Arbitrum layer 2. The experimental results of the relevant Groth16 ZKP batch verification and aggregated
ZKP verification are shown in Fig. (d), after the number of original ZKPs is more
than 16, the gas fee of using aggregated ZKP for verification is significantly lower
than the gas fee of verifying original ZKP one-by-one, and the gas for verifying
the aggregated proof is only 5% of that of verifying one by one when the number
of original ZKPs is 256, which reflects the advantage of this scheme in saving
on-chain computing resources.

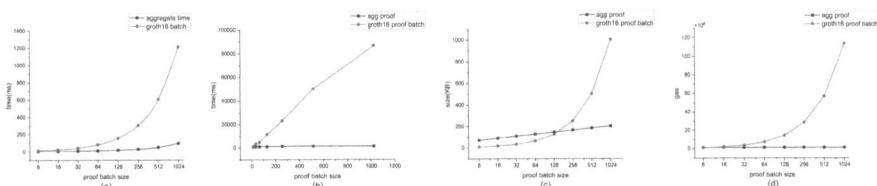

Fig. 5. Experiments related to time, space, and gas consumption were conducted for
different batch sizes of original ZKPs.

5.3   MSMT Performance Comparison

To evaluate the performance of MSMT structures, we compare them with the
following state-of-the-art SMT structures:

1. **Vanilla SMT** is the simplest sparse Merkle tree, a complete binary tree storing values of all leaf nodes, existing or not.
2. **Cached SMT** improves Vanilla SMT by caching default node values at each level.
3. **C-SMT** [8] utilizes a minimum distance path algorithm where the distance is defined as the binary interval between two keys which reduce tree height.
4. **JMT** [6] uses version-based keys to adapt to version-based sharding and classifies nodes into internal and leaf nodes, reducing the complexity of the tree structure.

Comparative experimental results of MSMT against Vanilla SMT, Cashed SMT, C-SMT and JMT in terms of insertion efficiency, Merkle path generation efficiency, and Merkle path verification efficiency are shown in Fig. 6. The key length is 32 bytes, all keys and values inserted were randomly generated, with each value representing the average of 20 experimental runs in python.

Figure (a) compares insertion times for MSMT and other structures across different batch sizes. MSMT significantly outperforms Vanilla SMT and Cached SMT, reducing average insertion time by 92.1% compared to C-SMT, which requires repeated shortest path calculations. Compared to JMT, MSMT achieves a 35.7% reduction in insertion time due to its simpler branch node structure, which streamlines path selection.

Figure (b) shows the comparison of the time required to generate Merkle Paths at different batch sizes. Due to the shorter paths generated, MSMT reduces the average generation time by 22.4% compared to C-SMT and by 48.6% compared to JMT.

Figure (c) shows the comparison of the time required to verify Merkle Paths at different verification batch sizes. MSMT reduces the average verification time by 93.2% compared to C-SMT and by 25.5% compared to JMT. The more complex node structure of C-SMT increases the computational complexity at each level. Additionally, the longer path lengths in JMT result in greater computational overhead compared to MSMT.

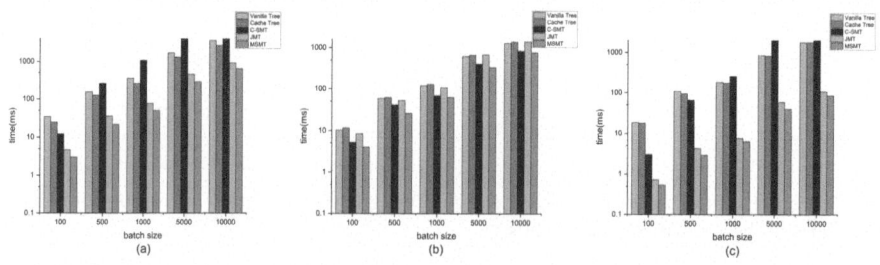

Fig. 6. The performance on insertion, Merkle path proof generation and Merkle path proof verification of different data structures at different batch sizes.

To analyze the operational efficiency of MSMT with different branching factors, we compared the average insertion time, average path generation time, and average path verification time for MSMTs with 2-bit to 5-bit branching factors under different batch sizes. The experimental results are shown in Fig. 7.

Figure(a) illustrates insertion efficiency variations under different branching factors. Figure (b) shows changes in Merkle path generation efficiency, while Fig. (c) depicts variations in Merkle path verification efficiency. It can be observed that as the branching factor increases, the insertion efficiency, Merkle path generation efficiency, and Merkle path verification efficiency of MSMT gradually deteriorate. This is due to the increased number of branches stored in each internal node with higher branching factors, which increases the complexity of processing rigid nodes. Additionally, the increased number of branches also leads to longer hash computation times, resulting in decreased efficiency.

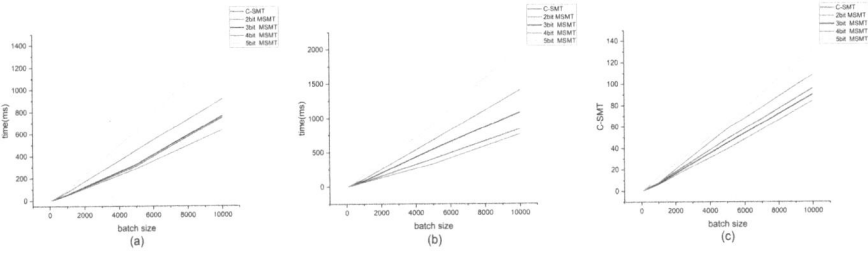

Fig. 7. Performance of MSMT under different number of forks.

6   Conclusion

We propose an efficient scheme for batch verification of data feature requirements in blockchain-based data trading platforms. This scheme enables data owners to verify that their data meets buyers' requirements without revealing the data itself and significantly improves proof verification efficiency on the blockchain platform. Specifically, we introduce SFMT for trusted storage of data requirements, construct an aggregation-verification process for ZKPs of data features to achieve batch verification on-chain based on SnarkPack, and use the MSMT structure to avoid redundant verification. Together, these solutions address the data feature fulfillment problem, ensuring privacy and efficiency.

Experimental results show that our scheme significantly reduces the time, space, and gas consumption associated with data feature ZKP verification on blockchain platforms. Compared to traditional and other advanced SMT structures, the proposed MSMT structure demonstrates superior performance in terms of insertion efficiency, Merkle path generation, and verification efficiency. We experimentally explored the effect of different branching factors of MSMT on insertion efficiency, Merkle path generation, and verification, and verified that MSMT with 2-bit branching yields the best results.

In summary, our scheme provides a scalable and secure solution for data feature verification in decentralized data trading markets, paving the way for

more efficient and privacy-preserving data transactions. In future work, we aim
to explore reputation mechanisms within this framework and apply the proof
aggregation and challenge process to a broader range of data-driven applications
and industries.

Acknowledgments. This work was financially supported by the National Natural
Science Foundation of China (No. 82271267).

References

1. Ambrona, M., Beunardeau, M., Schmitt, A.L., Toledo, R.R.: a p lon k: aggregated
p lon k from multi-polynomial commitment schemes. In: Shikata, J., Kuzuno, H.
(eds.) Advances in Information and Computer Security, IWSEC 2023, LNCS, vol.
14128, pp. 195–213. Springer, Cham (2023). https://doi.org/10.1007/978-3-031-
41326-1_11
2. Bünz, B., Bootle, J., Boneh, D., Poelstra, A., Wuille, P., Maxwell, G.: Bulletproofs:
short proofs for confidential transactions and more. In: 2018 IEEE Symposium on
Security and Privacy (SP), pp. 315–334. IEEE (2018)
3. Dahlberg, R., Pulls, T., Peeters, R.: Efficient Sparse Merkle Trees. In: Brumley,
B.B., Röning, J. (eds.) NordSec 2016. LNCS, vol. 10014, pp. 199–215. Springer,
Cham (2016). https://doi.org/10.1007/978-3-319-47560-8_13
4. Dai, W., Dai, C., Choo, K.K.R., Cui, C., Zou, D., Jin, H.: SDTE: a secure
blockchain-based data trading ecosystem. IEEE Trans. Inf. Forensics Secur. **15**,
725–737 (2019)
5. Gailly, N., Maller, M., Nitulescu, A.: SnarkPack: practical sNARK aggregation.
In: Eyal, I., Garay, J. (eds.) Financial Cryptography and Data Security, FC 2022,
LNCS, vol. 13411, pp. 203–229. Springer, Cham (2022). https://doi.org/10.1007/
978-3-031-18283-9_10
6. Gao, Z., Hu, Y., Wu, Q.: Jellyfish merkle tree (2021)
7. Groth, J.: On the size of pairing-based non-interactive arguments. In: Fischlin, M.,
Coron, J.-S. (eds.) EUROCRYPT 2016. LNCS, vol. 9666, pp. 305–326. Springer,
Heidelberg (2016). https://doi.org/10.1007/978-3-662-49896-5_11
8. Haider, F.: Compact sparse merkle trees. Cryptology ePrint Archive (2018)
9. Li, Y., et al.: Toward decentralized fair data trading based on blockchain. IEEE
Network **35**(1), 304–310 (2020)
10. Lorünser, T., Wohner, F., Krenn, S.: A privacy-preserving auction platform with
public verifiability for smart manufacturing. ICISSP **2022**, 637–647 (2022)
11. Su, G., Yang, W., Luo, Z., Zhang, Y., Bai, Z., Zhu, Y.: Bdtf: a blockchain-based
data trading framework with trusted execution environment. In: 2020 16th International Conference on Mobility, Sensing and Networking (MSN), pp. 92–97. IEEE
(2020)
12. Xiong, W., Xiong, L.: Smart contract based data trading mode using blockchain
and machine learning. IEEE Access **7**, 102331–102344 (2019)
13. Xue, L., Ni, J., Liu, D., Lin, X., Shen, X.: Blockchain-based fair and fine-grained
data trading with privacy preservation. IEEE Trans. Comput. **72**(9), 2440–2453
(2023)
14. Zheng, S., Pan, L., Hu, D., Li, M., Fan, Y.: A blockchain-based trading platform
for big data. In: IEEE INFOCOM 2020-IEEE Conference on Computer Communications Workshops (INFOCOM WKSHPS), pp. 991–996. IEEE (2020)

Business Process Representation Based on Graph Convolutional Network

Qingtian Zeng[1,3], Lin Zhang[1(✉)], Rui Cao[2], Wenyan Guo[3], and Chao Li[1]

[1] College of Electronic and Information Engineering, Shandong University of Science and Technology, Shandong, Qingdao, China
qtzeng@163.com, 3245128274@qq.com, lichao@sdust.edu.cn
[2] School of Information and Control Engineering, Qingdao University of Technology, Qingdao, China
ruicaoqing@163.com
[3] College of Computer Science and Engineering, Shandong University of Science and Technology, Qingdao, China
gwy995926315@163.com

Abstract. The effective representation of business processes is a key problem of predictive monitoring based on deep learning networks. Most of the existing business process representation methods are unable to accurately reflect the characteristics and node information aggregation of events in the graph structure. Therefore, a business process representation method based on graph convolutional network is proposed. Firstly, the diagram structure is constructed based on the same prefix window event of the business process. Secondly, on the basis of the constructed graph structure data, the node vectorization representation based on graph convolutional network model is given, and the information is aggregated through the graph convolutional network. Then, the depth representation of nodes is applied to the downstream prediction task of the business process. Finally, five real datasets are used for experimental evaluation. The experimental results show that the proposed event log graph construction strategy and process representation method are effective in business process prediction. The source code of this work is available at https://github.com/LinZhang0/GCNp.

Keywords: Business process · Prediction of next event · Deep learning · Graph neural network

1 Introduction

Predictive business process monitoring technology analyzes the historical event logs of business processes to build a prediction model for future process behavior, which is used to optimize process execution, reduce the risk of process violations, and improve the ability of enterprises to schedule resources. Business process vector representation maps high-dimensional business process data to

© The Author(s), under exclusive license to Springer Nature Singapore Pte Ltd. 2025
G. Zhao et al. (Eds.): BWTAC 2024, CCIS 2277, pp. 475–486, 2025.
https://doi.org/10.1007/978-981-97-9412-6_43

low-dimensional vector space through embedding technology to effectively capture the correlation between process elements, which is a key part of predictive business process monitoring and lays a foundation for accurate process data analysis and process optimization. In recent years, deep learning models have been widely used in the field of predictive business process monitoring, models such as Convolutional Neural Networks (CNN) and Long Short Term Memory (LSTM) networks are widely used in predictive business process mining tasks [1–3]. The business process vector representation is the basic step to complete the predictive business process mining task.

Traditional convolutional neural networks only deal with Euclidean spatial datasets, while graph data can be used to represent non-Euclidean spatial data. Graphs can naturally express complex relationships and data structures in real life, demonstrating powerful expressiveness in many fields, such as transportation networks, social networks, and protein interaction networks. In recent years, GNN have been used in business process prediction tasks and achieved good results [4–6]. Graph Convolutional Networks (GCN) [7] is a kind of neural network, its core idea is to extend convolution operation from the traditional grid data to graph data, through the aggregation node characteristics information to update the neighbor node. The method can be used to describe the structure of the business process model. At present, the business process representation method based on GCN has two problems: (1) The graph structure constructed by an event log dataset regards each activity type as a node, which cannot accurately reflect the characteristics of each event in the log; (2) The main purpose of GCN algorithm is information aggregation, and the existing GCN calculation method in business process monitoring tasks is more similar to event coding rather than information aggregation.

In order to solve the above problems, a business process representation method based on GCN is proposed. First of all, an innovative graph structure construction strategy based on prefix window connection is proposed. In this strategy, each event in the dataset is regarded as a node in the graph, and two nodes are connected by the prefix window, so as to construct the effective graph structure of the business process data. On this basis, the performance of the other two variants is studied. The experiment results on five business process datasets show that the proposed method is superior to existing methods in business process prediction based on graph convolutional networks.

The remainder of this paper is organized as follows. Section 2 briefly reviews the related work. In Sect. 3, we present business process representation based on graph convolutional network. Section 4 evaluates the effectiveness of the method with the experimental results and analysis. Finally, Sect. 5 summarizes the research work of this work.

2   Related Work

The research status of graph neural network and business process representation learning in recent years is introduced.

2.1 Graph Neural Network

Graph neural network is a cross product of graph theory and deep learning, which can learn complex nonlinear relationships in graphs and effectively fuse the structure and feature information of nodes. It is a research hotspot in machine learning. There are two main categories of graph neural networks: Graph neural network models in the spectral domain [8,9] and spatial graph neural network model [10,11]. In spectral domain, Performing graph convolution in the Fourier domain of graph is the core idea of graph neural network model. Bruna et al. [12] discussed how to extend convolutional neural networks to non-Euclidean domains (as shown in the graph), and proposes two methods: one based on graph hierarchical clustering and the other based on graph Laplace spectrum. Through these methods, the convolution layer can be learned efficiently, making the number of parameters independent of the input size, especially for low-dimensional graphs. Gilmer et al. [10] discusses the graph data structure for a universal framework for learning, Message Passing Neural Networks (MPNNs) messaging. In this paper, the existing model is unified under MPNNs framework, and on this basis, a new variant is proposed. With this approach, the researchers had demonstrated state-of-the-art results in molecular property prediction benchmarks, with significant potential for predicting molecular properties in particular.

Compared with the spectral domain method, in the spatial domain, the graph neural network model directly performs graph aggregation operations on the original network structure, without explicitly calculating the graph spectrum. The method aggregates the information of neighbor nodes at the node level. Hamilton et al. [13] proposed a framework named GraphSAGE for inductive representation learning on large-scale graphs. GraphSAGE generates embedded representations of nodes by sampling and aggregating features of local neighbors of nodes, which can effectively deal with new nodes and graph structures that have not been seen before. Veličković et al. [14] introduces the attention mechanism into graph neural networks and assigns different weights to different nodes. Liang et al. [15] proposes a semi-supervised inductive graph convolution algorithm to complement information and predict node labels by assigning different weights.

2.2 Business Process Representation Learning

Existing business process representation learning uses deep neural networks to obtain process vector representation. The method is used in tasks such as predicting process execution results, next activity, and remaining time. Gated graph sequential neural networks (GGNN) are used to experiment three different concepts of process example graphs [5]. Rama-Maneiro et al. [16] proposes a method that combines GCN and Recurrent Neural Network (RNN) to predict the next activity using information from event logs and process models. Venugopal et al. [4] uses the inductive mining method of Directly Follows Graphs (DGF) to build the graph structure, which is generated by the PM4PY tool developed in Berti et al. [17]. By combining the adjacency matrix and node attributes, they obtained the vector representation of the nodes through the one-layer GCN and the multi-layer perception (MLP).

Tax et al. [18] uses the LSTM architecture to predict the next activity and timestamp, the remaining cycle time, and the order of remaining events in the process instance. This work converts input activities into feature vectors via one-hot encoding and enriches the representation with specific features generated by timestamps. Camargo et al. [19] proposes a method of learning accurate business process models based on LSTM model. By using event sequence data in business processes, LSTM model is trained to automatically capture patterns and rules in the processes. Pasquadibisceglie et al. [20] uses CNN to combines gray image coding with CNN processing activities and time stamps, and trains a 2DCNN to predict the next activity of the event trace.

In terms of business process monitoring based on GNN, Weinzierl et al. [5] explores the method of using GGNN to predict the next process activity. By representing the process as a graph structure, neural network model is used to learn the graph structure and achieve accurate prediction of the next activity. Rama-Maneiro et al. [16] proposes a method combining GCN and RNN to predict the next activity using information from datasets and process models. Venugopal et al. [4] combines traditional process mining with deep learning techniques and designs four variants of GCN for predictive business process monitoring tasks.

The existing flowchart construction methods are difficult to fully consider the close relationship between events and process instances, resulting in the failure of one-to-one correspondence between some events and nodes in the diagram. The limitation of flowchart is that it can not fully capture the organic connection between events and instances, resulting in the deviation and missing between nodes and events. To solve this problem, we design a business process representation method based on graph convolutional network, presents a new graph structure construction method of datasets, and inputs the graph structure information into graph convolutional network to improve the performance of business process prediction.

3   Business Process Representation Based on Graph Convolutional Network

The overall framework of business process representation method based on graph convolutional network is shown in Fig. 1, which includes building module (A) based on prefix window graph structure, information aggregation module (B) based on graph convolutional network and downstream task-driven model training module (C).

3.1   The Graph Structure Building Module Based on Prefix Window

The process of building a graph structure based on a prefix window generates a directed graph where an earlier event points to a later event through a directed edge, and there is no reverse. The reason for choosing to build a directed graph

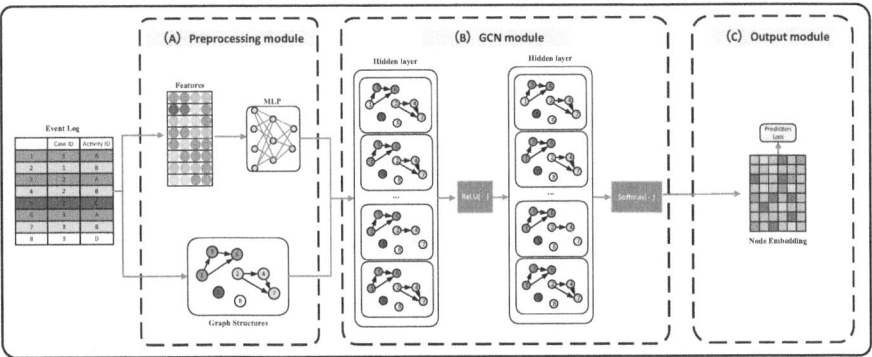

Fig. 1. Business process representation method framework based on GCN

rather than an undirected graph is that graph convolutional networks aim to achieve efficient aggregation of information. In an undirected graph structure, earlier events attempt to aggregate information about subsequent events; however, information about subsequent events is unknown to earlier events, so known events cannot aggregate information about unknown events. Next, this section details how nodes and edges are generated.

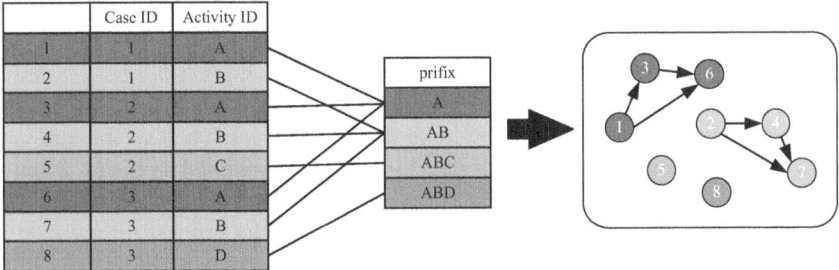

Fig. 2. Example of generation process of representation method based on GCN

Node Generation: This method treats each event in the event log as a node in the graph with the same node number as the event log number. $\forall i \in |1, \cdots , |\sigma_{log}||$, for $1 \leq i \leq |\sigma_{log}|$, node v_i is generated. Figure 2 shows the generation of the node set $V = \{v_1, v_2, v_3, v_4, v_5, v_6, v_7, v_8\}$. The attributes of the node are obtained by passing through an MLP layer on the basis of generating prefix window encoding.

Edge Generation: Node connections are determined based on the similarity of prefix windows. Events with the same prefix window are connected, while events with different prefix windows are unconnected. The edge formed in this process is a directed edge, and the connection direction is from the node with a low number to the node with a high number. $\forall i, j \in \{1, \cdots, |\sigma_{log}|\}$, for $1 \leq i < j \leq |\sigma_{log}|$, if v_i and v_j have the same prefix window, then v_i and v_j have a directed edge e_{ij}. Figure 2 shows the generation of the edge set $E = \{e_{13}, e_{16}, e_{36}, e_{24}, e_{27}, e_{47}\}$. This connection is referred to as Graph_p.

Two variants of the prefixed window graph structure representation are designed to compare the performance of these variants with the Graph_p representation proposed by experiments. The following sections describe both variants in detail:

1) Graph_a (graph structure containing only the above connection relation): The connection of events in the graph structure is not based on the same prefix window, but on two events in the same process instance that are adjacent to each other. The event that happened first points to the event that happened later, but the event that happened later does not point to the event that happened first. This connection allows events in the same event trace to be connected in a directed graph subgraph.

2) Graph_pa (graph structure containing the above connection and prefix relationship): Graph_pa This graph structure is the edge of Graph_p type and the edge of Graph_a type at the same time to connect the event log event together. This variant of the graph structure combines the way Graph_p and Graph_a are connected. Graph_pa contains all the edges of Graph_p and Graph_a. This connection basically connects all the events in the event log in a single graph.

3.2   Information Aggregation Module Based on Graph Convolutional Network

In the core mechanism of GCN, graph structure is cleverly used to converge and integrate node information, thus giving birth to a new node representation. In essence, both the graph convolution of the graph method and the graph convolution of the spatial method show common points in the process of aggregating the features of the surrounding nodes, so as to transmit and diffuse the information of the neighboring nodes, and finally generate new node information. Aggregation is performed using 2-layer GCN. The expression of the first layer GCN is:

$$H^{(1)} = ReLU\left(\tilde{D}^{-1}\tilde{A}XW^{(0)}\right),\qquad(1)$$

where W is the weight parameter, X is the initial feature of the node, $ReLU\left(\cdot\right)$ is the activation function, $A = A + I$, I is the identity matrix, and A is the adjacency matrix. D is a degree matrix whose diagonal element $\tilde{D}_{ii} = \sum_j \tilde{A}_{ii}$.

The expression for GCN on the second layer is:

$$H^{(2)} = softmax\left(\tilde{D}^{-1}\tilde{A}H^{(1)}W^{(1)}\right),\qquad(2)$$

where W is the weight parameter, X is the node feature, and $softmax\left(\cdot\right)$ is the activation function.

3.3   Downstream Task-Driven Model Training Module

How to optimize the parameters of the model to the greatest extent in the training process is the key to realize the node classification or graph level task. In this process, we not only pay attention to the expression form of loss function, but also focus on the information principle behind it. First, node features are extracted from the graph data and transported to the GCN model. Then, by using adjacency matrix, weight matrix and activation function operation, the original node features are transformed and updated continuously, so as to obtain more abundant node representation.

When the model is trained, the cross entropy loss function is used as the optimization objective. This loss function can not only quantify the difference between the model prediction result and the real label, but also guide the model towards the accurate classification result in the training process. Specifically, the accuracy of the model output is measured by calculating the cross entropy between the probability distribution of the predicted label and the distribution of the real label.

4   Experiment and Result Analysis

The adopted datasets, data preprocessing, and detailed metrics are introduced. It then compares the performance of the proposed representation, other variations of the design, and representations in other literature on five business process datasets. Finally, the contrast experiment and ablation study of different prefix window lengths will be introduced.

4.1   Datasets

Five datasets are used in this study, including two classical business process datasets (Helpdesk and BPIC12 (W)) and three medical business process datasets (Sepsis Cases, Hospital Billing, Drug).

(1) **Helpdesk dataset:** This dataset is derived from the event logs of Helpdesk, an Italian software company, and contains 3840 process instances and 13,710 events. There are 9 activity types, and the longest process instance contains 14 events.

(2) **BPIC2012 (W) Dataset:** Real data from Dutch financial institutions used in the Business Process Intelligence Challenge 2012 (BPIC2012). The W subprocess event log, BPIC2012 (W), contains 96,598 process instances and 72,413 events involving six activity types. The longest process instance contains 74 events.

(3) **Sepsis Cases dataset:** the Enterprise Resource Planning (ERP) dataset from the hospital system of the actual event logs, on behalf of the patient's path. The dataset includes 560 process instances and 8135 events, covering 14 activity types. The longest process instance contains 23 events.

(4) **Hospital Billing dataset:** This dataset is derived from the financial module of the regional hospital ERP system and records the medical service fee collection activities. Contains 10,000 process instances and 49,951 events across 16 activity types. The study used 1,768 of these process instances and 10,000 events with eight activity types. The longest process instance contains 6 events.

(5) **Drug dataset:** This dataset comes from the data of the hospital's special management drug loss process, and each group of process instances represents the loss process of a drug. The dataset contains 48,320 process instances and 1111,360 events, totaling 23 activity types. This study used 431 of these process instances and 10,005 events, with the longest process instance containing 23 events.

4.2   Data Preprocessing

The dataset contains three attributes: "Case ID", "Activity ID", and "Complete Timestamp". Only "Case ID" and "Activity ID" are used for data encoding in the study. The encoding process involves encoding the activity type for each event in the dataset and extracting the prefix window for each event as input. These prefix Windows, stored in a vector matrix of the same size, contain all events from a particular part of the event trace up to the previous activity. The label is determined according to the activity type of the event next to the current event. If there are no subsequent events after this event in the trace, the label is specified as 0.

4.3   Training Setup

In the experiment, all the datasets are evenly divided into three parts: $1/3$ as the training set, $1/3$ as the verification set, and $1/3$ as the test set. After entering all the data into the graph convolutional network model, the cross entropy loss is calculated using the results of the training set data and the original training set data. The learning rate is set to 0.001, the number of iterations is 1000, the optimizer adopts Adam, and the evaluation index is the accuracy. The experiment is run 5 times to take the average value. Layer 1 GCN uses $ReLU\left(\cdot\right)$ as the activation function, and Layer 2 GCN uses $softmax\left(\cdot\right)$.

4.4   Business Processes Represent Experimental Results and Analysis

This section compares the performance of the representation of the design, its different variants with the four variants designed in [4], and the MLP method for predicting the next activity on five business process datasets. In a particular dataset, the prefix window length of HospitalBilling and BPIC2012(W) is set to 6, Helpdesk to 5, Sepsis Cases to 4, and Drug to 3. In GCN_W, GCN_B, GCN_LB and GCN_LW experiments, the graphs generated by the three business process datasets cannot show the connection points in the adjacency matrix, which has an impact on normal normalization. To address this problem, the normalization process of the adjacency matrix is reconstructed: If all elements of a column in the adjacency matrix are 0, then each element of that column is assigned the value 0.000001.

The experimental results of this section are shown in Table 1, where the best performance results are shown in bold font and the second-best results are underlined. Table 1 shows that the Graph_p representation method achieves optimal or suboptimal results on all five datasets, indicating that its graph structure representation has advantages over other variants. In particular, the MLP method is 8.33% more accurate than Graph_p on the Drug dataset. Similarly, Graph_pa has a 0.28% higher accuracy on the Hospital Billing dataset than Graph_p. Graph_p has the best performance on the remaining three datasets. Experimental results show that the Graph_p representation method can achieve excellent performance on most process mining datasets. The experimental results show that good graph structure representation can achieve excellent results in business process prediction based on graph convolutional networks. However, if the graph structure representation is not properly constructed, the performance of business process prediction will be compromised. This performance degradation may be due to the fact that the graph convolutional network cannot extract useful information from the poor graph structure, and may even aggregate wrong information, while the effective graph structure representation can aggregate a large amount of beneficial information. Therefore, the business flowchart structure representation based on graph convolutional networks is a key factor in achieving excellent performance.

Table 1. Different variations of the representation are compared

model	Accuracy for Event Predict				
	Helpdesk	BPIC20212(W)	Sepsis Cases	Hospital Billing	Drug
GCN_W	0.7487	0.5398	0.4804	0.6285	0.2936
GCN_B	0.6836	0.5344	0.4535	0.6334	0.2313
GCN_LB	0.7391	0.5693	0.4712	0.6907	0.4253
GCN_LW	0.719	0.5001	0.4398	0.6414	0.3856
MLP	0.8163	0.6552	0.5433	0.8846	**0.5617**
$Graph\_a$	0.5158	0.6036	0.2282	0.6209	0.1209
$Graph\_pa$	0.8072	0.6792	0.5667	**0.9426**	0.4691
$Graph\_p$	**0.8236**	**0.6802**	**0.5922**	0.9398	0.4784

4.5   Ablation Experiment

In order to explore the influence of different components of the graph convolutional network designed in this paper on the experimental results, ablation studies are conducted in this section, and the following variants were compared:

1) *Graph_p*-w/o MLP: The method removes the MLP layer that deals with prefix window vector features in the graph convolutional network architecture.

2) *Graph_p*-w/o Graph: The method removes the graph structure part of the architecture, which is the main comparison object in this section, because it is related to the graph structure representation method designed in this paper.

3) *Graph_p*-w/o MLP&Graph: The method removes the MLP layer and the graph structure at the same time.

Ablation experiments are conducted on 5 business process datasets, and the results of ablation experiments are shown in Fig. 3.

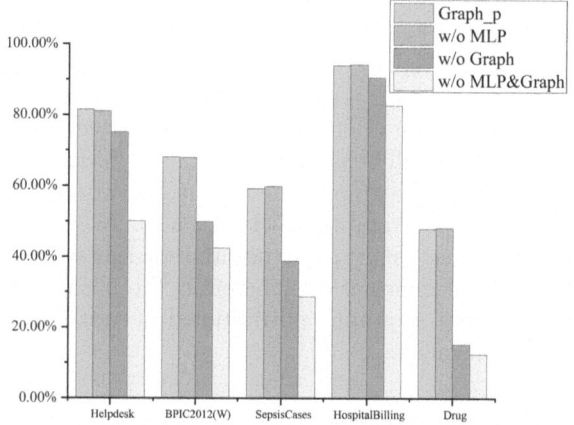

Fig. 3. Results of ablation experiments on five datasets

The experimental results in Fig. 3 show that the MLP layer has a small impact on the experimental results of all datasets, while the graph structure has a significant impact on the results. In Helpdesk and BPIC2012(W) datasets, the MLP layer improves experimental results, but in Sepsis Cases, Hospital Billing, and Drug datasets, it slightly degrades performance. By comparing the results of *Graph_p*-w/o Graph and *Graph_p*-w/o MLP&Graph, the MLP layer significantly improves the experimental performance, so it is decided to add the MLP layer in the experiment. Comparing the results of *Graph_p* and *Graph_p*-w/o MLP&Graph on five datasets, the graph structure representation method designed in this paper significantly improved the experimental performance, especially in the Drug dataset, where the graph structure increased the accuracy of predicting the next activity by more than two times.

5   Conclusion

In this paper, a business process representation method based on graph convolutional network is proposed. Theoretical exploration is carried out from the connection relationship of graph structure. The method is applied to the prediction task of the next activity, and five business process datasets are analyzed experimentally. A graph representation method is proposed to construct the graph structure of business process dataset by taking events as nodes and using the event connection edge of the same prefix window. The study also deals with the downstream task of predicting the next activity as an example. Experimental results show that the proposed method can effectively improve the accuracy of business process prediction based on graph convolution.

Future research will focus on exploring more efficient ways to represent business process data, with the aim of revealing underlying patterns and structures in datasets. On this basis, we will continue to optimize and innovate deep learning models to significantly improve the performance of business process prediction and push the field to new heights.

Declarations

Acknowledgments. This work is supported by National Natural Science Foundation of China (Grant No.52374221); the Natural Science Foundation of Shandong Province (Grant No. ZR2021QG038); the Taishan Scholar Program of Shandong Province (Grant No. ts20190936), and the Open Research Fund Program of Key Laboratory of Agricultural Blockchain Application, Ministry of Agriculture and Rural Affairs (2022KLABA03).

Disclosure of Interests. The authors declare that there is no competing interests.

References

1. Da, T.N., Cho, M.-Y., Thanh, P.N.: Hourly load prediction based feature selection scheme and hybrid CNN-LSTM method for building's smart solar microgrid. Expert Syst. e13539 (2024)
2. Altarawneh, L., Wang, H., Jin, Y.: Covid-19 vaccine prediction based on an interpretable CNN-LSTM model with three-stage feature engineering. Health Technol. 1–21 (2024)
3. Mushtaq, S., Singh, O.: Convolution neural networks for disease prediction: applications and challenges. Scalable Comput. Pract. Exp. **25**(1), 615–636 (2024)
4. Venugopal, I., Töllich, J., Fairbank, M., Scherp, A.: A comparison of deep-learning methods for analysing and predicting business processes. In: 2021 International Joint Conference on Neural Networks (IJCNN), pp. 1–8. IEEE (2021)
5. Weinzierl, S.: Exploring gated graph sequence neural networks for predicting next process activities. In: Marrella, A., Weber, B. (eds.) BPM 2021. LNBIP, vol. 436, pp. 30–42. Springer, Cham (2022). https://doi.org/10.1007/978-3-030-94343-1_3
6. Duong, L.T., Travé-Massuyès, L., Subias, A., Merle, C.: Remaining cycle time prediction with graph neural networks for predictive process monitoring. In: Proceedings of the 2023 8th International Conference on Machine Learning Technologies, pp. 95–101 (2023)
7. Kipf, T.N., Welling, M.: Semi-supervised classification with graph convolutional networks. arXiv preprint arXiv:1609.02907 (2016)

8. Levie, R., Monti, F., Bresson, X., Bronstein, M.M.: Cayleynets: graph convolutional neural networks with complex rational spectral filters. IEEE Trans. Signal Process. **67**(1), 97–109 (2018)
9. Defferrard, M., Bresson, X., Vandergheynst, P.: Convolutional neural networks on graphs with fast localized spectral filtering. In: Advances in Neural Information Processing Systems, vol. 29 (2016)
10. Gilmer, J., Schoenholz, S.S., Riley, P.F., Vinyals, O., Dahl, G.E.: Neural message passing for quantum chemistry. In: International Conference on Machine Learning, pp. 1263–1272. PMLR (2017)
11. Monti, F., Boscaini, D., Masci, J., Rodola, E., Svoboda, J., Bronstein, M.M.: Geometric deep learning on graphs and manifolds using mixture model CNNs. In: Proceedings of the IEEE Conference on Computer Vision and Pattern Recognition, pp. 5115–5124 (2017)
12. Bruna, J., Zaremba, W., Szlam, A., LeCun, Y.: Spectral networks and locally connected networks on graphs. arXiv preprint arXiv:1312.6203 (2013)
13. Hamilton, W., Ying, Z., Leskovec, J.: Inductive representation learning on large graphs. In: Advances in Neural Information Processing Systems, vol. 30 (2017)
14. Veličković, P., Cucurull, G., Casanova, A., Romero, A., Lio, P., Bengio, Y.: Graph attention networks. arXiv preprint arXiv:1710.10903 (2017)
15. Liang, J., Jacobs, P., Sun, J., Parthasarathy, S.: Semi-supervised embedding in attributed networks with outliers. In: Proceedings of the 2018 SIAM International Conference on Data Mining, pp. 153–161. SIAM (2018)
16. Rama-Maneiro, E., Vidal, J.C., Lama, M.: Embedding graph convolutional networks in recurrent neural networks for predictive monitoring. IEEE Trans. Knowl. Data Eng. **36**(1), 137–151 (2023)
17. Berti, A., Van Zelst, S.J., van der Aalst, W.: Process mining for python (pm4py): bridging the gap between process-and data science. arXiv preprint arXiv:1905.06169 (2019)
18. Tax, N., Verenich, I., La Rosa, M., Dumas, M.: Predictive business process monitoring with LSTM neural networks. In: Dubois, E., Pohl, K. (eds.) CAiSE 2017. LNCS, vol. 10253, pp. 477–492. Springer, Cham (2017). https://doi.org/10.1007/978-3-319-59536-8_30
19. Camargo, M., Dumas, M., González-Rojas, O.: Learning accurate LSTM models of business processes. In: Hildebrandt, T., van Dongen, B.F., Röglinger, M., Mendling, J. (eds.) BPM 2019. LNCS, vol. 11675, pp. 286–302. Springer, Cham (2019). https://doi.org/10.1007/978-3-030-26619-6_19
20. Pasquadibisceglie, V., Appice, A., Castellano, G., Malerba, D.: Using convolutional neural networks for predictive process analytics. In: International Conference on Process Mining (ICPM), pp. 129–136. IEEE (2019)

Membership Data Privacy Protection and Poisoning Detection Scheme for Federated Learning

Yafeng Li[1] , Zhijun Sun[2,3] , and Lichuan Ma[2,3(✉)]

[1] China CETC Key Laboratory of Technology on Data Link, Xi'an 710068, China
[2] State Key Laboratory of Integrated Services Networks, Xidian University,
Xi'an 710071, China
lcma@xidian.edu.cn
[3] Shaanxi Key Laboratory of Blockchain and Secure Computing, Xi'an 710071,
China

Abstract. In the era of big data, data privacy and security are highly valued, leading to the phenomenon of "data islands", which hinders the effective utilization of data. Federated learning, as a privacy-preserving distributed machine learning method, allows model training without sharing raw data, addressing the privacy concerns in cross-organizational data cooperation. Although federated learning protects data privacy, participants' gradient parameters can still potentially leak sensitive information. As a result, extensive research has focused on conducting federated learning while protecting the privacy of gradient parameters and reducing the communication and computational overhead for participants. These efforts assume that each participant adheres honestly to the protocol; however, malicious submissions of incorrect gradient parameters can significantly bias the federated learning model. This paper proposes a federated learning scheme for privacy-protected gradient aggregation and poison detection that defends against malicious poisoning attacks while safeguarding data privacy, and optimizes computational and communication overheads. By employing inner product triples, the computation process is further optimized, enhancing system performance. The security of the scheme is demonstrated, and its efficiency is validated through practical tests, showing that the optimized solution significantly outperforms the basic scheme in terms of performance.

Keywords: Federated learning · privacy preservation · secure aggregation · poisoning attacks · secure multi-party computation

1 Introduction

With the rapid advancement of information technology, big data has emerged as a key hallmark of modern times, garnering unprecedented attention across various industries due to its value. Machine learning, a crucial data processing

G. Zhao et al. (Eds.): BWTAC 2024, CCIS 2277, pp. 487–498, 2025.
https://doi.org/10.1007/978-981-97-9412-6_44

tool, is extensively utilized in diverse fields. However, the presence of sensitive information within data has made data privacy protection a critical societal issue, particularly in sectors like healthcare and financial services where data security is paramount.

As concerns over data security and privacy grow, data owners have become more cautious, leading to the phenomenon of "data islands" where vast amounts of data are underutilized, causing resource wastage. Machine learning, limited by these data accessibility issues, often cannot operate optimally. Federated learning, a distributed machine learning approach, has gained attention as a solution to these challenges. It allows local training of models on clients' end, with only model gradients—rather than raw data—being uploaded, reducing the risks of privacy breaches associated with centralized data processing. This technique not only protects individual data privacy but also facilitates data collaboration and sharing across different organizations, helping to bridge data islands.

However, the widespread application of federated learning has highlighted significant security issues. Despite its design preventing direct data sharing among clients, indirect leakage about original data can occur through shared model gradients, known as inversion attacks. For example, Yang et al. [1] explored model inversion attacks that extract training or testing data information from model outputs. Another critical security concern is poisoning attacks, where attackers manipulate model gradients to bias the global model. Zhou et al. [2] discussed stealthy, persistent methods of poisoning attacks that subtly alter local model weights to remain undetected without compromising the main task's accuracy. These attacks threaten both the accuracy of the model and the integrity of the system. Other potential security threats include privacy inference attacks and traditional network threats like man-in-the-middle attacks, which can compromise both data security and model integrity.

To combat these threats, researchers have developed various defensive measures. For data and privacy protection, common strategies include differential privacy, secure multi-party computation, homomorphic encryption, and secret sharing. For instance, Rassouli et al. [3] discussed encryption techniques in vertical federated learning to defend against inference attacks and protect data during training and prediction. To specifically address poisoning attacks, strategies like anomaly detection algorithms are employed to identify and filter out malicious gradients before model aggregation, as highlighted by Zhang et al. [4] who developed a system to prevent poisoning by detecting malicious clients. A comprehensive review by Sagar et al. [5] categorized federated learning defense strategies into anomaly detection, robust aggregation, and perturbation mechanisms.

This paper focuses on privacy protection and poisoning detection in federated learning, aiming to safeguard members' data privacy while countering internal threats from malicious actors. The contributions of this paper are:

- A privacy-protected federated learning scheme that effectively safeguards data privacy and defends against poisoning. This involves deploying two servers in different trust domains to which clients upload divided gradients. The servers then use multiplication triples with secure two-party computation for poisoning detection. Detection methods include L_2 Norm Bound, Norm Ball, Zeno++, and Cosine Similarity, supporting both static and dynamic threshold settings.

- The optimization of the basic scheme through the introduction of inner product triples, which reduce the computational overhead by minimizing the generation and usage of multiplication triples. This optimization compresses the number of communications and the volume of data processed, enhancing system performance.
- A rigorous security analysis confirming that the non-colluding servers maintain data privacy during gradient aggregation and poisoning detection. The optimized scheme, proven to outperform the basic scheme significantly, supports dynamic threshold settings based on actual training data, enhancing both security and performance.

2   Related Works

Currently, there has been extensive research focused on secure aggregation in federated learning, which involves using privacy-preserving technologies to aggregate model gradients from different participants in an encrypted state, without exposing the specific data or gradient details of each participant.

In the area of Trusted Execution Environments, Kalapaaking et al. [6] proposed a blockchain-based federated learning framework that integrates Intel Software Guard Extension (SGX)-based TEEs to securely aggregate local models in Industrial Internet of Things (IIoTs).

Regarding encryption algorithms, Flamingo [7] is a system for securely aggregating data, designed for multi-round federated learning settings. It reduces the number of interactions between clients and the server through a new lightweight robust early-exit protocol and client neighborhood selection techniques, significantly decreasing the end-to-end runtime of a full training session. It utilizes various encryption techniques, including ElGamal encryption and digital signature algorithms. Bell [8] introduced a new secure single-server aggregation protocol that significantly reduces the communication and computational overhead between clients and the server while ensuring data privacy, with each client's communication and computation complexity being logarithmic, addressing the linear overhead issues previously raised by Bonawitz [9]. Hahn et al. [10] proposed a new protocol named VERSA, aimed at achieving privacy protection and secure aggregation in cross-device federated learning. VERSA does not require a trusted setup among users and uses lightweight pseudorandom generators to prove and verify the correctness of model aggregation, significantly reducing verification costs.

In the field of secret sharing technology, Jahani-Nezhad et al. [11] proposed a novel secure aggregation protocol, SwiftAgg+, which significantly reduces communication overhead in federated learning systems while ensuring information-theoretic security, achieving optimal communication load. Bonawitz et al. [12]

developed a practical and efficient secure aggregation protocol for federated learning on user-held data, designing an efficient and fault-tolerant aggregation algorithm suitable for mobile devices and low-bandwidth networks. Kadhe et al. [13] introduced a highly efficient secure aggregation protocol called FastSecAgg, utilizing a novel multi-secret sharing scheme based on Fast Fourier Transform (FFT) called FastShare, which effectively reduces computational and communication costs and is robust against client dropouts. So et al. [14] introduced the first secure aggregation framework Turbo-Aggregate, which achieves efficient model aggregation while protecting user privacy, reducing secure aggregation overhead to and tolerating up to 50% user dropout rates.

There is also a substantial body of work focused on defense strategies against poisoning attacks in federated learning environments. These involve a range of measures and technologies designed to prevent malicious participants from corrupting the overall model's learning process or accuracy by altering their local training data or model gradients.

Tolpegin et al. [16] addressed targeted data poisoning attacks in federated learning systems and introduced an effective defense strategy that helps identify malicious participants in FL to avoid poisoning attacks. Lu et al. [17] proposed an effective defense paradigm against local model poisoning attacks in federated learning, which does not require an auxiliary dataset and enhances the robustness of Byzantine fault-tolerant aggregation rules, with experiments demonstrating better detection performance and shorter detection times. Li et al. [18] introduced a personalized federated learning framework named Ditto, aimed at balancing robustness against data and model poisoning attacks with fairness in device performance across statistically heterogeneous networks. Through theoretical analysis and empirical validation, they demonstrated its competitiveness and superiority in achieving fairness and robustness. Shejwalkar et al. [19] proposed a generic framework for federated learning model poisoning attacks and designed a "divide-and-conquer" defense mechanism, showing stronger resistance capabilities than existing Byzantine-robust federated learning algorithms. Mo et al. [20] proposed a privacy-preserving federated learning framework (PPFL), utilizing trusted execution environments to implement secure training and aggregation on both client and server sides, effectively protecting model updates from adversary attacks while keeping system overhead low.

In existing research, there are solutions that consider both secure aggregation and defense against poisoning attacks, addressing two major security issues with a comprehensive approach: firstly, ensuring the privacy of each participant's data during collaborative model training (secure aggregation), and secondly, preventing malicious participants from injecting harmful information into training data or model gradients, thus compromising model accuracy or integrity.

Roy et al. [21] proposed the EIFFeL system for federated learning, which is a method to ensure the integrity of the process. This system uses non-interactive zero-knowledge proofs (SNIP) and verifiable secret sharing (VSS) techniques to validate client-submitted updates and has extended SNIP to accommodate malicious threat models. This method not only protects the privacy of each participant's data but also ensures that the received data has not been tampered with, thereby enhancing the security and reliability of the federated learning model.

Rathee et al. [22] introduced the ELSA protocol for secure aggregation in federated learning, which ensures data privacy and system security even in the presence of malicious participants. The key contribution of this protocol is that it uses multiplication triples generated by the users and validated by the servers to enhance efficiency. Specifically, ELSA uses two servers for distributed computing to protect the privacy of client updates. Even in the face of joint attacks by malicious servers and clients, as long as at least one server remains honest, data privacy is assured.

Bell et al. [23] presented the ACORN protocol for secure aggregation with input validation capabilities, utilizing zero-knowledge proofs to verify the integrity of inputs. This work also introduced a new zero-knowledge proof construction to prove L_∞ norm bounds. The protocol, while protecting privacy, allows servers to verify that client vector data meets specific constraints. By introducing input validation, the ACORN protocol effectively enhances the security and credibility of data aggregation.

3   System Model

This paper identifies two types of system roles: servers and clients. Clients are multiple cross-device users or different organizational entities that do not wish to share their local datasets, while servers aim to train a model using distributed datasets. In the training process, clients train using their datasets, and after each training round, they send updates back to the servers. The servers perform poisoning data detection and secure aggregation of updates from all clients to update the global model, which is then sent back to all clients. For security reasons, the system employs two servers, each deployed in a separate trust domain. The two servers use secure multi-party computation to detect and aggregate updates from clients. The structure of the system model is shown in Fig. 1. The objectives of the system design are as follows:

- To ensure smooth training progress: Each client C_i conducts its local training normally, and clients C_i can upload their updates to servers S_0 and S_1 without issues. Servers S_0 and S_1 smoothly conduct joint checks through secure two-party computation and detection algorithms to determine if the updates uploaded by client C_i are normal data and not poisoned, and can distribute updates to the global model correctly.
- To ensure the privacy of clients: Local data from each client C_i is not shared. The updates uploaded to the two servers are secret shares, and a single server cannot reconstruct the original data.
- To ensure the security of training results: Poisoning detection algorithms are used. The two servers use detection functions to assess whether the data uploaded by clients is poisoned. If a client's update for a round is normal, it is included in the aggregation; if it is poisoned, it is removed and does not participate in the aggregation for that round.

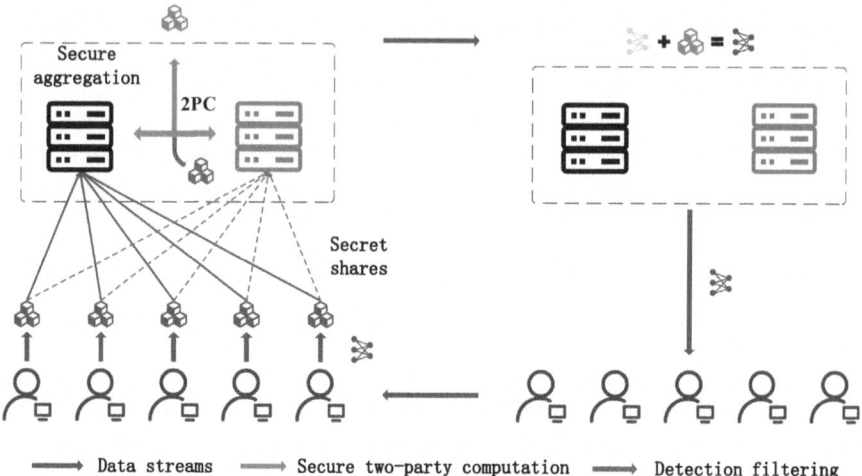

Fig. 1. System Model

4   The Proposed Scheme

The horizontal federated learning process in this paper involves five stages: data preprocessing, client model update uploads, server-side poisoning detection, model update aggregation, and global model distribution. This paper focuses on three key stages: data preprocessing, client model update uploads, and server-side poisoning detection. During the data preprocessing phase, designs are based on two techniques: Paillier homomorphic encryption and Oblivious Transfer (OT). Specifically, the server first performs data preprocessing to prepare for secure two-party computation, each client then uploads their model updates to the server, which carries out poisoning detection and aggregation, and finally, the server distributes the global model to the clients. This process ensures the privacy and security of the model update aggregation process, with the aggregated new global model being used for the next round of federated learning.

4.1   Data Preprocessing Based on Paillier Homomorphic Encryption

During the data preprocessing phase, the two servers first generate several necessary multiplication triples for use in executing multiplication operations during secure two-party computations.

Suppose servers S_0 and S_1 hold secret shares $\langle a \rangle_0$, $\langle b \rangle_0$ and $\langle a \rangle_1$, $\langle b \rangle_1$ respectively, then the process of generating multiplication triples involves the following steps:

a. Server S_0 encrypts its secret shares $\langle a \rangle_0$ and $\langle b \rangle_0$, and sends the encrypted information to server S_1.

b. Server S_1 then chooses a random number r, calculates $d = Enc(\langle a \rangle_0)^{\langle b \rangle_1} \times Enc(\langle b \rangle_0)^{\langle a \rangle_1} \times Enc(r)$, and sends the result d back to server S_0.

c. Server S_0 decrypts d and adds it to the locally computed $\langle a \rangle_0 \langle b \rangle_0$ to compute its secret share $\langle c \rangle_0$.

d. Simultaneously, server S_1 locally calculates $\langle a \rangle_1 \langle b \rangle_1$ minus the random number r, obtaining $\langle c \rangle_1$.

By repeating steps a. through d., a sufficient number of multiplication triples $c_i = a_i b_i$ are obtained for subsequent poisoning detection and collaborative computing between the servers.

4.2   Data Preprocessing Based on Oblivious Transfer

Suppose servers S_0 and S_1 hold secret shares $\langle a \rangle_0$, $\langle b \rangle_0$ and $\langle a \rangle_1$, $\langle b \rangle_1$ respectively.

Taking the calculation of $\langle a \rangle_0 \langle b \rangle_1$ as an example, a Correlated Oblivious Transfer (COT) protocol communication is established between S_0 and S_1. In the i-th round of the COT communication, the specific steps are as follows:

a. S_0, as the sender, inputs a correlation function $f_{\Delta_i}(x) = (\langle a \rangle_0 \cdot 2^i - x) \mod 2^l$.

b. Then, S_1, as the receiver, inputs its choice bit for the current round i, $\langle b \rangle_1[i]$.

c. Based on the above inputs, S_0 calculates and obtains a pair of values $(s_{i,0}, s_{i,1})$, where $s_{i,0} \in_R \mathbb{Z}_{2^L}$, and $s_{i,1}$ is calculated through the correlation function f_{Δ_i}, $s_{i,1} = f_{\Delta_i}(s_{i,0}) = (\langle a \rangle_0 \cdot 2^i - s_{i,0}) \mod 2^l$.

d. S_1 retrieves the computation result corresponding to its input choice bit $\langle b \rangle_1[i]$, $s_{i,\langle b \rangle_1[i]} = (\langle b \rangle_1[i] \cdot \langle a \rangle_0 \cdot 2^i - s_{i,0}) \mod 2^l$.

After a total of l rounds of communication, S_0 and S_1 respectively obtain the secret shares $\langle u \rangle_0 = (\sum_{i=0}^{l-1} s_{i,0}) \mod 2^l$ and $\langle u \rangle_1 = (\sum_{i=0}^{l-1} s_{i,\langle b \rangle_1[i]}) \mod 2^l$, and thus $\langle a \rangle_0 \langle b \rangle_1$ can be computed as $\langle u \rangle_0 + \langle u \rangle_1$. Similarly, $\langle a \rangle_1 \langle b \rangle_0$ can be computed as $\langle v \rangle_0 + \langle v \rangle_1$, allowing the two servers to locally compute $\langle c \rangle_i = \langle a \rangle_i \langle b \rangle_i + \langle u \rangle_i + \langle v \rangle_i$. Finally, both servers hold the secret shares of the multiplication triple, providing a basis for subsequent secure computations.

By repeating the above steps, a sufficient number of multiplication triples are obtained for subsequent poisoning detection and collaborative computing between the servers.

4.3   Client's Update Upload

Each client, using the Shamir Secret Sharing algorithm, divides their updates into secret shares. This section describes the process of a client uploading their updates, taking one client as an example.

Suppose the updates from this client consist of a series of parameters $x_1, x_2, \ldots, x_n$, forming the vector $\mathbf{x} = (x_1, x_2, \ldots, x_n)$. According to the Shamir Secret Sharing algorithm introduced in Chapter 2, the client splits each update parameter into two parts, namely $\langle x_1 \rangle_0, \langle x_2 \rangle_0, \ldots, \langle x_n \rangle_0$ and $\langle x_1 \rangle_1, \langle x_2 \rangle_1, \ldots, \langle x_n \rangle_1$, and uploads them to servers S_0 and S_1 respectively.

4.4　Server-Side Poisoning Detection

In this phase, the two servers use detection functions and multiplication triples generated during the preprocessing stage to perform data checks on the gradients uploaded by clients. This paper utilizes four detection methods introduced in Chapter 2: L_2 Norm Bound, Norm Ball, Zeno++, and Cosine Similarity. Among these detection algorithms, correctly setting the threshold ρ is a key factor ensuring effective algorithm implementation. This paper adopts two threshold setting methods: (1) Static threshold setting: This method sets a fixed threshold, typically determined based on experience or previous experimental results. For example, the threshold could be set to a predefined constant. (2) Dynamic threshold setting: Compared to the static method, the dynamic setting adjusts the threshold based on statistical information from real-time training data, adding flexibility and adaptability. This is often done by calculating the mean and standard deviation of the gradient norms, and then setting the threshold by adding or subtracting several standard deviations to the mean as needed.

4.5　Model Update Aggregation and Global Model Distribution

After excluding poisoned data, the remaining updates from various clients are aggregated. The model's aggregation method, such as simple averaging (averaging across all participating clients) or weighted averaging (based on the quality of the model or the quantity of its training data), is not considered in detail here.

The servers distribute the aggregated global model parameters to each client for the next round of local training by the clients.

4.6　Inner Product Triple Optimization

In the scheme described in the previous section, basic multiplication triples are chosen to assist in the homomorphic multiplication calculations in the secret sharing process. The four detection functions selected in this paper, L_2 Norm Bound, Norm Ball, Zeno++, and Cosine Similarity, each require consuming n triples, n triples, $\frac{n(n+1)}{2}$ triples, and $\frac{n(n+1)}{2}$ triples respectively for their calculations. If the model has a large number of parameters (i.e., model weights), n will be large, and both scenarios will require a significant amount of multiplication operations between servers, consuming a large number of multiplication triples. Since both the generation of multiplication triples and the multiplication calculations require interactive communication between the two servers, extensive use of multiplication triples will lead to significant communication overhead, affecting the overall performance of the system. Therefore, this section introduces the concept of the inner product triple, which is generated based on Paillier homomorphic encryption technology. The inner product triple is used to compress the substantial amount of communication required during the generation phase.

5   Experiments

The server and client environments used in this paper are deployed on traditional physical servers, equipped with the 64-bit Ubuntu 20.04 operating system to ensure the stability of the experimental environment. The server's CPU is an Intel Core i5-9500, with 16 GB of RAM to support complex data processing and computational tasks.

5.1   Data Preprocessing

In the implementation of the scheme, the time overhead for generating multiplication triples during the data preprocessing phase is determined by the dimension of the client updates (which corresponds to the dimension of the model weights) and the chosen detection algorithm. The tables below compares the time overhead for data preprocessing using different technologies, across various dimensions and detection algorithms. It is evident from the comparison that as the dimension increases, the time overhead for Zeno++ and Cosine Similarity algorithms is significantly higher than for the L_2 Norm Bound and Norm Ball algorithms. This is because the number of multiplication triples required by the Zeno++ and Cosine Similarity detection algorithms is of a square order relative to the other two algorithms, which makes optimization of the scheme crucial (Tables 1 and 2).

Table 1. Time Overhead During the Data Preprocessing Stage Based on Paillier Homomorphic Encryption

Detection Algorithm	Dimension			
	700	800	900	1000
L_2 Norm Bound	8168 ms	9334 ms	10509 ms	11668 ms
Norm Ball	8174 ms	9329 ms	10497 ms	11676 ms
Zeno++	2862.53 s	3737.87 s	4731.03 s	5840.34 s
Cosine Similarity	2862.41 s	3739.09 s	4729.86 s	5838.98 s

5.2   Poison Detection

According to the scheme, the server-side uses four detection algorithms-L_2 Norm Bound, Norm Ball, Zeno++, and Cosine Similarity-for poison detection, testing the scheme using these four methods and different update dimensions, including the communication time overhead inherent in the scheme. Figure 2 reflects the time overhead of server-side detection using L_2 Norm Bound, Norm Ball, Zeno++, and Cosine Similarity methods.

Table 2. Time Overhead During the Data Preprocessing Stage Based on Oblivious Transfer

Detection Algorithm	Dimension			
	700	800	900	1000
L_2 Norm Bound	28.67 ms	29.02 ms	29.33 ms	29.70 ms
Norm Ball	28.75 ms	28.94 ms	29.38 ms	29.67 ms
Zeno++	10.082 s	16.860 s	26.633 s	40.193 s
Cosine Similarity	10.084 s	16.858 s	26.634 s	40.192 s

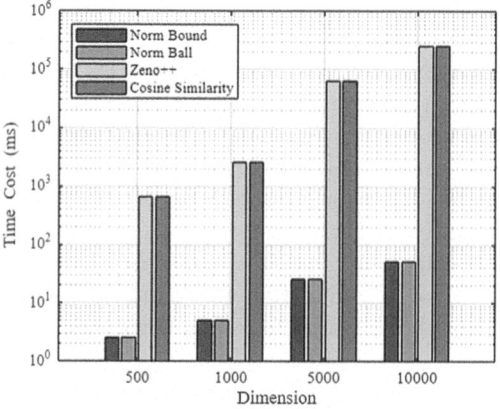

Fig. 2. Example of a figure caption.

5.3   Optimization of Inner Product Triple

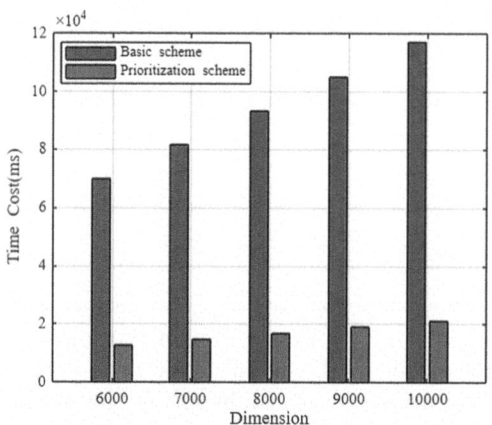

Fig. 3. Comparison of Time Overhead for the Scheme

This part compares the effects of the optimization scheme presented in this paper with the basic scheme. First, we compare the time overhead in the data preprocessing stage when the update dimensions are 6000, 7000, 8000, 9000, and 10000 respectively. As shown in Fig. 3, the optimization scheme based on Paillier homomorphic encryption significantly reduces the time overhead in the data preprocessing stage, indicating that the optimization effects are outstanding.

Based on the comparative test results, it can be concluded that the optimization scheme based on Paillier homomorphic encryption is extremely effective in optimizing the data preprocessing stage.

6   Conclusion

In the context of rapid advancements in information technology, data security and privacy protection have become especially important. Federated learning, as a distributed machine learning method, has attracted widespread attention because it processes cross-domain data while reducing privacy leak risks. However, as its applications increase, the security issues associated with federated learning have also become more evident, including model inversion attacks, privacy inference attacks, and model poisoning attacks. This paper proposes a federated learning system that effectively prevents malicious actors from conducting poisoning attacks while protecting member data privacy, employing multiple privacy protection technologies such as Shamir's secret sharing, Paillier homomorphic encryption, and Oblivious Transfer, and introducing an inner product triple-based optimization scheme to enhance system efficiency and performance.

References

1. Yang, Z., Zhang, J., Chang, E.C., et al.: Neural network inversion in adversarial setting via background knowledge alignment. In: Proceedings of the ACM SIGSAC Conference on Computer and Communications Security, pp. 225–240 (2019)
2. Zhou, X., Xu, M., Wu, Y., et al.: Deep model poisoning attack on federated learning. Future Internet **13**(3), 73 (2021)
3. Rassouli, B., Varasteh, M., Gunduz, D.: Privacy against inference attacks in vertical federated learning. arXiv preprint arXiv:2207.11788 (2022)
4. Zhang, Z., Cao, X., Jia, J., et al.: FLDetector: defending federated learning against model poisoning attacks via detecting malicious clients. In: Proceedings of the 28th ACM SIGKDD Conference on Knowledge Discovery and Data Mining, pp. 2545–2555 (2022)
5. Sagar, S., Li, C.S., Loke, S.W., et al.: Poisoning attacks and defenses in federated learning: a survey. arXiv preprint arXiv:2301.05795 (2023)
6. Kalapaaking, A.P., Khalil, I., Rahman, M.S., et al.: Blockchain-based federated learning with secure aggregation in trusted execution environment for Internet-of-Things. IEEE Trans. Ind. Inf. **19**(2), 1703–1714 (2022)
7. Ma, Y., Woods, J., Angel, S., et al.: Flamingo: multi-round single-server secure aggregation with applications to private federated learning. In: 2023 IEEE Symposium on Security and Privacy (SP), 477–496. IEEE (2023)

8. Bell, J.H., Bonawitz, K.A., Gascón, A., et al.: Secure single-server aggregation with (poly) logarithmic overhead. In: Proceedings of the 2020 ACM SIGSAC Conference on Computer and Communications Security, pp. 1253–1269 (2020)

9. Bonawitz, K., Ivanov, V., Kreuter, B., et al.: Practical secure aggregation for privacy-preserving machine learning. In: Proceedings of the ACM SIGSAC Conference on Computer and Communications Security, pp. 1175–1191 (2017)

10. Hahn, C., Kim, H., Kim, M., et al.: Versa: verifiable secure aggregation for cross-device federated learning. IEEE Trans. Dependable Secure Comput. **20**(1), 36–52 (2021)

11. Jahani-Nezhad, T., Maddah-Ali, M.A., Li, S., et al.: SwiftAgg+: achieving asymptotically optimal communication loads in secure aggregation for federated learning. IEEE J. Sel. Areas Commun. **41**(4), 977–989 (2023)

12. Bonawitz, K., Ivanov, V., Kreuter, B., et al.: Practical secure aggregation for federated learning on user-held data. arXiv preprint arXiv:1611.04482 (2016)

13. Kadhe, S., Rajaraman, N., Koyluoglu, O.O., et al.: FastSecAgg: scalable secure aggregation for privacy-preserving federated learning. arXiv preprint arXiv:2009.11248 (2020)

14. So, J., Güler, B., Avestimehr, A.S.: Turbo-aggregate: breaking the quadratic aggregation barrier in secure federated learning. IEEE J. Sel. Areas Inf. Theory **2**(1), 479–489 (2021)

15. Kairouz, P., Liu, Z., Steinke, T.: The distributed discrete gaussian mechanism for federated learning with secure aggregation. In: International Conference on Machine Learning. PMLR, pp. 5201–5212 (2021)

16. Tolpegin, V., Truex, S., Gursoy, M.E., Liu, L.: Data poisoning attacks against federated learning systems. In: Chen, L., Li, N., Liang, K., Schneider, S. (eds.) ESORICS 2020. LNCS, vol. 12308, pp. 480–501. Springer, Cham (2020). https://doi.org/10.1007/978-3-030-58951-6_24

17. Lu, S., Li, R., Chen, X., et al.: Defense against local model poisoning attacks to byzantine-robust federated learning. Front. Comput. Sci. **16**(6), 166337 (2022)

18. Li, T., Hu, S., Beirami, A., et al.: Ditto: fair and robust federated learning through personalization. In: International Conference on Machine Learning. PMLR, pp. 6357–6368 (2021)

19. Shejwalkar, V., Houmansadr, A.: Manipulating the byzantine: optimizing model poisoning attacks and defenses for federated learning. In: NDSS (2021)

20. Mo, F., Haddadi, H., Katevas, K., et al.: PPFL: privacy-preserving federated learning with trusted execution environments. In: Proceedings of the 19th Annual International Conference on Mobile Systems, Applications, and Services, pp. 94–108 (2021)

21. Roy Chowdhury, A., Guo, C., Jha, S., et al.: Eiffel: ensuring integrity for federated learning. In: Proceedings of the ACM SIGSAC Conference on Computer and Communications Security, pp. 2535–2549 (2022)

22. Rathee, M., Shen, C., Wagh, S., et al.: Elsa: secure aggregation for federated learning with malicious actors. In: 2023 IEEE Symposium on Security and Privacy (SP), pp. 1961–1979. IEEE (2023)

23. Bell, J., Gasc, A., Lepoint, T., et al.: ACORN: input validation for secure aggregation. In: 32nd USENIX Security Symposium (USENIX Security 2023), pp. 4805–4822 (2023)

Code-Based Blockchain Light Node Data Availability Guarantee Method

Zirui Wu[✉]

University of Electronic Science and Technology of China, Chengdu, China
zirui_wu@126.com

Abstract. As the focus on blockchain scaling research intensifies, the security of light nodes has become a prominent concern. Bitcoin employs Simple Payment Verification (SPV) to ensure the trustworthiness of light nodes by verifying transactions through a proof-of-existence process. Light nodes broadcast confirmation requests to neighboring full nodes, who respond with Merkle proofs for the requested transactions. This system is dependable when the network is predominantly honest, but vulnerabilities arise when an attacker controls a majority of nodes, enabling them to deceive light nodes with fabricated proofs. This paper introduces erasure code to enhance data redundancy and combines it with Merkle proofs to detect protocol rule violations. By integrating coding patterns with random sampling, we verify the integrity of data blocks and enable light nodes to detect fraud by receiving and verifying invalid block proofs from full nodes. We validate the efficacy of our coding-based random sampling model using simulations and probabilistic calculations.

Keywords: Blockchain · Erasure Code · Data Availability

1 Introduction

Since its inception, blockchain technology has revolutionized financial transactions, smart contracts, and various other sectors with its decentralized nature and distributed ledger principles. However, as user numbers grow, scalability challenges have emerged as a critical bottleneck for further development [1]. In this context, light nodes, as key participants in blockchain networks, offer low-resource requirements, making it easier for users to access and utilize blockchain services [2,9]. However, concerns over their security, particularly their vulnerability during transaction validation, have garnered significant attention.

The prevalent SPV mechanism in Bitcoin networks serves as a standard solution for light nodes, enabling them to verify transactions without downloading the entire blockchain by providing existence proofs. While SPV is effective when honest nodes predominate, its security relies on the network's honesty, which can be exploited by malicious nodes, leading to potential fraud when they control a majority of the nodes and present false transaction proofs.

G. Zhao et al. (Eds.): BWTAC 2024, CCIS 2277, pp. 499–510, 2025.
https://doi.org/10.1007/978-981-97-9412-6_45

The original Bitcoin whitepaper [3] briefly mentions the possibility of 'alerts', which are messages sent by full nodes to alert light clients that a block is invalid, prompting them to download the full block to verify the inconsistency. Little further exploration has been done on this, partly due to the data availability problem.

To address this issue, several studies have proposed enhancements to light node validation [10]. [4] has advocated the employment of erasure coding for enabling light clients to contribute voluntarily to blockchain storage by participating in partial data sharing without the need for downloading the entire ledger. However, these methods often come with additional communication costs or performance sacrifices, without fundamentally addressing the vulnerability of light nodes against large-scale attacks.

Erasure codes have been employed on blockchains primarily as a distributed storage solution, wherein the fundamental concept is to encode data into coded blocks that are distributed across numerous nodes within the system. A comparable concept is utilized by the Storjs system [7], which stores coded and encrypted data in a peer-to-peer network. Data is stored in a P2P network that can be connected to the blockchain. [5] proposes a combination of PBFT and censoring codes to partition blocks for all nodes on a blockchain system, with the objective of reducing storage complexity and read efficiency. In all these systems, PBFT strikes a balance between data availability and the amount of stored data.

This paper proposes a novel light node validation mechanism that combines erasure codes and Merkle proofs. Erasure codes, traditionally used in data storage to ensure redundancy and fault tolerance, are introduced into the blockchain context as a viable means for data availability checks. This application significantly enhances the security of transaction verification for light nodes. By adding redundancy to data and employing coding patterns and probabilistic sampling, our approach enables light nodes to detect fraudulent activities within data blocks and verify the availability of blockchain data. The integration of erasure codes not only bolsters the robustness of light nodes against adversarial threats but also ensures the integrity and availability of blockchain data.

2   Preliminaries

2.1   Network Model

In order to meet the scalability needs, blockchain systems require light nodes that do not fully download blocks, which may face the risk of data fraud. Typically, because the security of light nodes depends on full nodes, ensuring the connection of light nodes with honest nodes is crucial; this chapter makes a weaker assumption about the "honest majority" and designs a block data random sampling model based on two-dimensional RS codes under the network structure shown in Fig. 1 to provide data availability assurance for light nodes.

As shown in Fig. 1, each honest node (represented in green) is connected to at least one honest full node (represented in square shape). A light node (represented in circular shape) may be connected to more malicious full nodes (represented in shaded red squares) than honest full nodes.

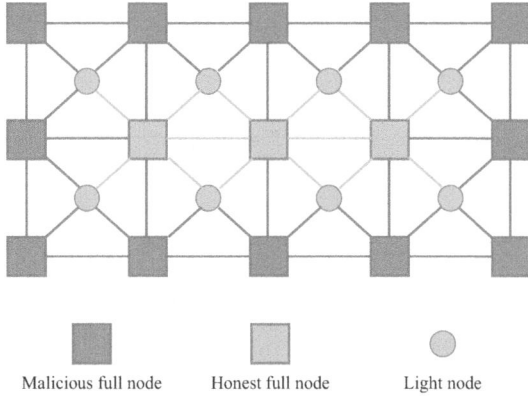

Malicious full node   Honest full node   Light node

Fig. 1. Network model-A light node may be connected to more malicious full nodes than honest full nodes.

2.2 2D-RS Code

RS codes have been generalized to multidimensional codes in various ways [6]. In p-multidimensional codes [8], messages are encoded p times along p orthogonal axes, i.e., along different dimensions in a multidimensional array.

In this paper, it is assumed that a malicious block producer may construct the extended data incorrectly, such that even if more than 50% of the data is available, incomplete block data is not covered from the extended data. In the event that standard Reed-Solomon encoding is employed, the validation and recovery of both arbitrary extended data and original data necessitates the availability of the full data set as a guarantee. Consequently, the node is compelled to locally recode all the data in order to verify the match with the given extended data, thereby requiring $O(n)$data. In this paper, we propose a multidimensional encoding scheme that restricts the proofs about the encoded data to one axis in a particular direction, thus reducing the size of the proofs to $O(\sqrt[d]{n})$, where d is the number of dimensions of the encoding. For simplicity, we consider only 2D-RS coding in this paper, but the scheme can be generalized to higher dimensions. The two-dimensional encoding organizes the original data in a two-dimensional matrix. The extended data are obtained by RS code computation by rows and columns, respectively. The $k * k$ original data matrix is extended to a $2k * 2k$ matrix, i.e., $(2k, k)$ RS codes are used in each row and each column. The data expansion method is shown in Fig. 2.

In accordance with the fundamental principles of RS codes, the complete irrecoverability of a data matrix is inevitable in the event that a malicious block maker withholds at least $k+1$ copies of data from any given column or row. This results in a total of $(k+1)^2$ copies of data being withheld, thereby rendering the data matrix irrecoverable.

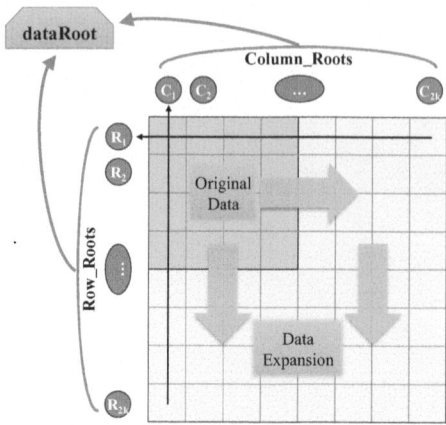

Fig. 2. Data expansion and Merkle tree construction

Theorem 1. *Given a $2k*2k$ matrix E as shown in Fig. 3, the entire data matrix is irrecoverable if there exist at least $k + 1$ columns or rows, each of which has at least $k + 1$ unavailable data blocks. In this case, the minimum number of unavailable data copies from which the matrix cannot be recovered is $(k + 1)^2$.*

Proof. Suppose a malicious block producer wants to make the data $E_{(i,j)}$ in a $2k * 2k$ matrix E irrecoverable. Since RS codes using $(2k, k)$ allow all $2k$ data to be recovered from any k data, the block producer would have to make at least $k + 1$ data from row $E_{(i,*)}$ irrecoverable, or at least $k + 1$ data from column $E_{(*,j)}$ irrecoverable.

Because of the transposable nature of the matrix, it is sufficient to prove the row irrecoverability condition: the malicious block producer withholds at least $k + 1$ copies from row $E_{(i,*)}$. However, the data $(E_{(i,c_1)}, ..., E_{(i,C_{(k+1)})}) \in E_{(i,*)}$ withheld from each of these k+1 rows can be recovered from the data available in their respective columns $E_{(*,c_1)}, E_{(*,c_2)}, ..., E_{(*,c_{(k+1)})}$. Therefore, the malicious block producer must also withhold at least $k + 1$ copies of data from each of these columns to ensure irrecoverability. This leaves a total of $(k+1)*(k+1) = (k+1)^2$ copies of data to be withheld.

In summary, if a malicious block maker wants a data matrix to be irrecoverable, at least $k + 1$ copies of the columns or rows of data need to be withheld, that is, a total of $(k + 1)^2$ copies of data need to be withheld, and such a matrix is called a minimum irrecoverable matrix.

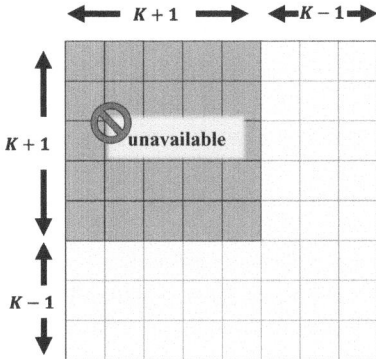

Fig. 3. Minimum irrecoverable matrix

3   Light Node Data Availability Guarantee Method

3.1   Merkle Tree Construction

In order to provide Merkle proofs for block data, in this paper, the data blocks are constructed into a 2D- RS encoded Merkle tree in the following way:

1. Divide the original data into fixed-size blocks and arrange them into a $k * k$ data matrix; if the last block is not large enough, or there is not enough data to fill the matrix, then 0-filling is performed.
2. Extend the data horizontally and vertically by applying Reed-Solomon coding to each row and column of the $k*k$ matrix, i.e., to each row and column. Then apply a third RS encoding to the vertical extension of the matrix horizontally to create a $2k * 2k$ matrix, as shown in Fig. 2
3. Compute the root of the Merkle tree for each row and column of the $2k * 2k$ matrix, where the leaves of the Merkle tree are the data blocks of the matrix. Obtain the row root $rowRoot_i = root((M_{(}i, 1), M_{(}i, 2), ..., M_{(}i, 2k)))$ and the column root $colRoot_i = root((M_{(}1, i), M_{(}2, i), ..., M_{(}2k, i)))$, where $M_{(}x, y)$ represents the data in the xth row and yth column of the matrix.
4. Based on the root of the row and column Merkle tree computed in step 3, dataRoot is computed: $dataRoot = root((rowRoot_1, rowRoot_2, ..., rowRoot_{2k}, colRoot_1, colRoot_2, ..., colRoot_{2k}))$

The Merkle tree generated by the encoding shown in Fig. 2 has $2k$ row roots and $2k$ column roots, each of which is obtained by the computation of $2k$ data blocks, and the entire Merkle tree has $dataLength = 2 * (2k)^2$ leaf nodes, each of which will appear as both a leaf below the row root and a leaf below the column root. Similar to the Merkle proof procedure, a Merkle proof can be generated from dataRoot to a single data block, but in addition to this, because a data block appears in both the part of the row root and the part of the column root, and because the generation of the row root and the generation of the column root are independent of each other, there are also different parts of the Merkle path involved in calling the $VerifyMerkleProof$ twice.

Another way to verify is to only verify the Merkle proofs for the dataRoot to the row root and column root, not the following chunks of data, then it can be assumed that this dataRoot's Merkle tree has $2 * matrixWidth = 2 * 2k$ leaves when verifying the Merkle proofs for the row root or the column root, and these leaves are these row roots and column roots.

Light nodes or full nodes are able to rebuild the dataRoot from all row roots and column roots by re-executing step 4. to obtain a guarantee of data availability, all light nodes should at least download all the row roots and column roots needed to rebuild the dataRoot and check that step 4 is calculated correctly.

3.2 Random Sampling

In order for any data in the matrix encoded by a 2D-RS code to be unrecoverable, then at least $(k + 1)^2$ out of the $(2k)^2$ data blocks must be unavailable (see Theorem 1), whereas a 1D-RS code only needs to hide $k + 1$ out of $2k$. In order to enable light nodes to obtain the required block data on demand and to achieve data availability guarantee, this section designs a random sampling pattern for light nodes, which makes full use of the 2D-RS code and the Merkle tree generation and Merkle proof process for data blocks proposed in Sect. 3.1. When a light client receives a new block header from the network, they are supposed to randomly sample $0 < s \leq (2k)^2$ distinct data blocks from the extended matrix and accept the block only if they receive all of them. The larger s is, the higher the light node's confidence that the data is available (this will be analyzed in Sect. 3.3). In addition, light nodes broadcast the data blocks they receive to the network so that the complete block can be recovered by an honest full node. The protocol between a light node and the full node it is connected to works as follows:

1. The light node receives from the full node the block header h, and the set of row roots and columns $R = rowRoot_1, rowRoot_2, ..., rowRoot_2k$, $colRoot_1, colRoot_2, ..., colRoot_2k$);
2. If $root(R) \neq dataroot$, otherwise reject block header;
3. Light node sends a coordinate request to the full node for a block of data in the corresponding matrix: the light node randomly selects a set of unique (x, y) coordinates corresponding to the points $S = (x_0, y_0), (x_1, y_1), ..., (x_s, y_s)$ on the extended matrix, where $0 < x \leq matrixWidth, 0 < y \leq matrixWidth$, and then sends them to one or more full nodes to which it is connected to request blocks in the corresponding matrix;
4. The full node receives the request to send to the light node the data blocks corresponding to the coordinates and the corresponding Merkle paths: if the full node has all the data blocks corresponding to the coordinates in the set S and their associated Merkle proofs, then for each coordinate (x_a, y_b), the full node uses the return data $M_{(x_a, y_b)}$ and the corresponding Merkle proof $M_{(x_a, y_b)} \rightarrow rowRoot_a$ or $M_{(x_a, y_b)} \rightarrow colRoot_a$. Since there are two possible

Merkle proofs for each data block, one from the row root and the other from the column root, here the full node may provide Merkle proofs in both directions must also specify for each Merkle proof whether it is associated with the row root or the column root.

5. Light node verifies received data blocks and Merkle paths: for each data block $M_{(x_a, y_b)}$ already received by the light node, if the Merkle path comes from the self-root, the light node performs the check $VerifyMerkleProof$ $(M_{(x_a, y_b)}, M_{(x_a, y_b)}) \rightarrow rowRoot_a, rowRoot_a, matrixWidth, b)$ is true; if the proof is from a column root, perform a check to see if $VerifyMerkleProof$ $(M_{(x_a, y_b)}, M_{(x_a, y_b)}) \rightarrow colRoot_b, colRoot_b, matrixWidth, a)$ is true;

6. If the received data block is valid, the light node broadcasts the received block and the valid Merkle proof to the connected full nodes; these full nodes also broadcast further if they do not already have these blocks;

7. If the requests sent in step 3 have all received the corresponding data block and have been successfully verified by step 5, and no other fraud proofs have been received for this block within 2σ time, then this block will be accepted by the light node.

Step 5 states that the data received by the light nodes can be broadcasted in the network, and through this behavior, the cooperation between the nodes is strengthened and the security of the whole system is improved.

3.3 Security Probability Analysis

Section 3.2 devises a random sampling pattern for light nodes, this pattern specifies the behavior that a single light node adopts in order to obtain data availability guarantees, also, Step 5 illustrates that multiple light nodes in the network can establish cooperation and randomly sample data from a block at the same time, the high probability of data availability guarantees obtained by light nodes in this pattern will be analyzed in this section.

Random Sampling of a Single Node. Theorem 1 has proved that the entire data matrix is irrecoverable by the nature of RS codes if there exists at least $k+1$ columns or rows of the extended $2k * 2k$ matrix, each of them having at least $k + 1$ unusable data blocks. That means a malicious full node needs to cause the data obtained by a light node to be unavailable by hiding at least $(k+1)*(k+1)$ data blocks. In the mode of random sampling by a single light node, Theorem 2 gives the probability that a single light node detects data unrecoverability by random sampling under the condition that a malicious full node hides the least number of data blocks:

Theorem 2. *As shown in Fig. 3, there is a $2k * 2k$ matrix E in which $(k + 1)^2$ data blocks are unavailable. If a light node randomly draws $s(0 < s < (k + 1)^2)$ blocks from E, the probability of drawing at least one unusable block is:*

$$P_1(X \geq 1) = 1 - \prod_{i=0}^{s-1} 1 - \left(\frac{(k+1)^2}{4k^2 - i} \right) \tag{1}$$

Proof. Given a $2k * 2k$ matrix with $(k+1)^2$ data blocks are unavailable the probability of randomly drawing $s(0 < s < (k+1)^2)$ blocks with 0 unavailable block is:

$$P_1(X = 0) = \frac{\binom{4k^2-(k+1)^2}{s}}{\binom{4k^2}{s}} \tag{2}$$

So.

$$P_1(X \geq 1) = 1 - P_1(X = 0) = 1 - \prod_{i=0}^{s-1} 1 - \left(\frac{(k+1)^2}{4k^2 - i}\right) \tag{3}$$

Prove the end.

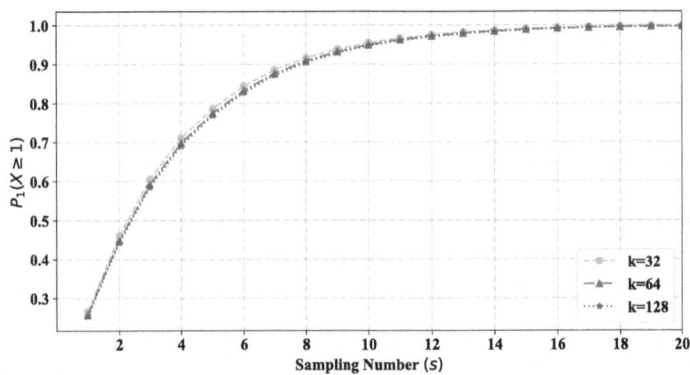

Fig. 4. Variation of probability $P_1(X \geq 1)$ with the number of samples s (computed for k = 32, k = 64, k = 128)

Figure 4 illustrate the variation of this probability with the number of samples s (taken at k = 32, k = 64 and k = 128 respectively). A single light node is able to sample at least one unavailable data block in the minimum unrecoverable matrix with approximately 60% probability after 3 samples (i.e., after sampling 0.07% of the data blocks for k = 32, 0.02% of the data blocks for k = 64 and 0.005% of the data blocks for k = 128, respectively); and after 15 samples (i.e., after sampling 0.4% of the data blocks for k = 32, 0.4% of the data blocks for k = 64 and 0.005% of the data blocks for k = 256, respectively); the probability is about 60%. 0.09% data blocks for k = 64, and 0.023% data blocks at k = 256) it is possible to sample at least one unavailable data block in the minimum unrecoverable matrix with more than 99% probability.

It is also easy to see from Figs. 4 that the size of k affects the probability $P_1(X \geq 1)$ to a very small extent, and Eq. (4) shows an even more pronounced result: for sufficiently large values of k, the probability $P_1(X \geq 1)$ is almost independent of k; therefore, using a large matrix size (i.e., $k \geq 128$) is appropriate because it reduces the amount of data that must be downloaded by the light nodes.

$$\lim_{k \to \infty} P_1(X \geq 1) = \lim_{k \to \infty} 1 - \left(\frac{(k+1)^2}{4k^2 - i} \right) = 1 - (\frac{3}{4})^s \tag{4}$$

Random Sampling of Multiple Nodes In the case of random sampling by a single light node, a malicious full node can link a sampling request to the same light node and on that basis release data selectively against it. To address this problem, this section enables a sufficient number of honest light nodes to make requests, which disseminate their acquired data to each other by broadcasting, such that more than $(k+1)^2$ chunks of data are sampled, and that each data sampling request is anonymous (i.e., the sampling request cannot be associated with the same node), and that the distribution of each sampling request received is uniformly randomized, e.g., via the using a hybrid network.

For the case where multiple light nodes cooperate in random sampling, Theorem 3 gives the probability that c light nodes have more than $\hat{c}$ nodes detecting data irrecoverability by random sampling under a malicious node-wide hidden minimum data block condition:

Theorem 3. *As shown in Fig. 3, there is a $2k * 2k$ matrix E in which $(k+1)^2$ data blocks are unavailable. If c light nodes randomly draw $s(0 < s < (k+1)^2)$ blocks from E, the probability that more than $\hat{c}$ nodes draw at least one unusable block is:*

$$P_c(Y > \hat{c}) = 1 - \sum_{j=1}^{\hat{c}} \binom{c}{j} (P_1(X \geq 1))^j (1 - P_1(X \geq 1))^{c-j} \tag{5}$$

Proof. For the above case of random sampling of c nodes, the probability that exactly j nodes draw at least one unavailable block is:

$$P_c(Y = j) = \binom{c}{j} (P_1(X \geq 1))^j (1 - P_1(X \geq 1))^{c-j} \tag{6}$$

Therefore, the probability that no more than $\hat{c}$ nodes extract at least one unavailable block is:

$$P_c(Y \leq \hat{c}) = \sum_{j=1}^{\hat{c}} \binom{c}{j} (P_1(X \geq 1))^j (1 - P_1(X \geq 1))^{c-j} \tag{7}$$

So, the probability that more than $\hat{c}$ nodes extract at least one unavailable block is:

$$P_c(Y > \hat{c}) = 1 - P_c(Y \leq \hat{c}) = 1 - \sum_{j=1}^{\hat{c}} \binom{c}{j} (P_1(X \geq 1))^j (1 - P_1(X \geq 1))^{c-j} \tag{8}$$

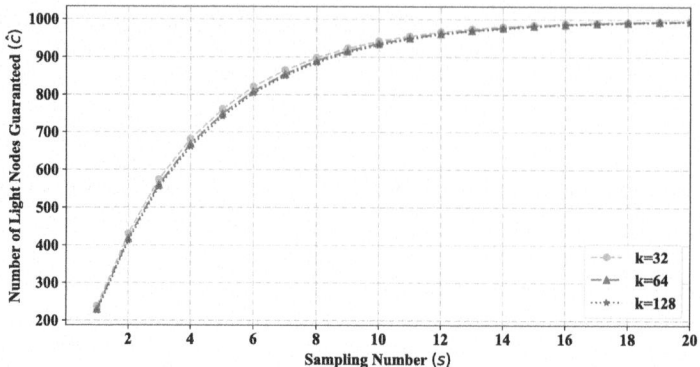

Fig. 5. Variation of the number of light nodes $\hat{c}$ with the number of samples s for obtaining high probability data availability guarantees (computed for k = 32, k = 64, k = 128)

Figures 5 show the variation of the number of light nodes $\hat{c}$ (i.e., the number of light nodes that detect the minimum irrecoverable matrix with high probability ($P_c(Y > \hat{c}) \geq 0.99$) with respect to the number of samples s. The total number of light nodes c is fixed to 1000, and the matrix sizes are k = 32, 64, 128. Equation (4) already shows that the probability $P_1(X \geq 1)$ is almost independent of k, so the probability $P_c(Y > \hat{c})$ probability is also almost independent of k. It can also be seen from the figure that the improvement in data availability guarantees for light nodes caused by increasing s beyond 15 is no longer significant.

4   Experiments

Theorem 1 has proved that if a malicious block producer selectively releases blocks of data at the request of light clients, it can release at most $(k + 1)^2$ copies of valid data. If the light node accepts this unrecoverable block, it can be said that the malicious full node jeopardizes the soundness in data availability. Another way to formulate this statement is that for a light node, it needs to obtain at least $\alpha = (2k)^2 - (k+1)^2 + 1 = k(3k+2)$ valid blocks of data in order to recover the full $2k * 2k$ data matrix.

In order to avoid malicious full nodes linking the sampling requests to the same light node, while selectively releasing data against it on this basis. In this paper, we propose that multiple light nodes initiate sampling requests for block data, and the network model designed in this section assumes that there is a collective of light nodes, each sampling a different block of data, collectively sampling out at least Z different blocks of data.

In order to study the random distribution probability $P(Z \geq \alpha)$ of multiple light nodes collectively sampling Z distinct blocks of data greater than or equal to the α data needed for the light nodes to recover the data this section uses the go language to design a program to simulate the behavior of the light nodes and the full nodes, allowing them to interact and see what happens. If this simulation is run multiple times, the random distribution probability metrics can be statistically analyzed for simulation calculations.

The full node launched in each simulation instance provides a new block matrix consisting of $(2k)^2$ data blocks. c light nodes attempt to sample different random blocks from the full node. In the worst case, the full node withholds $(k + 1)^2$ blocks, i.e., it accepts to send data to the light node until it sends $(2k)^2 - (k + 1)^2$ different data.

An iteration is considered successful when the number of simulated iterations reaches the number of times the full node decides to refuse to respond to a request to send a block of data (this means that the light node can detect data fraud or is able to recover the data). By running multiple light node iterations, the probability $P(Z \geq \alpha)$ can be estimated by calculating the proportion of light nodes that successfully iterate according to this setting (Table 1).

Table 1. The number of light nodes (c) that need to participate in random sampling cooperation to make the probability $P(Z \geq \alpha) > 0.99$

c	s = 2	s = 5	s = 10	s = 20	s = 50
k = 16	690	275	138	69	28
k = 32	2805	1122	561	280	112
k = 64	11289	4516	2258	1129	451
k = 128	>40000	>18000	>9000	>4500	1811

The table counts the number of light nodes c that need to participate in the random sampling cooperation to make the probability $P(Z \geq \alpha)$ for different data matrix size settings ($matrixWidth = 2k$) and the number of random samples s per light node.

From the table, it can be seen that, unlike Eqs. (4) and (5), the probability $P(Z \geq \alpha)$ is affected by both the matrix size (k) and the number of samples (s) as well as the number of light nodes (c). Thus, the fewer the number of random samples, the more the number of light nodes that need to participate in random sampling cooperation; the larger the data matrix size, the more the number of light nodes that need to participate in random sampling cooperation.

5   Conclusion

In this paper, we relax certain assumptions about the "honest majority", enabling lighter nodes to receive and validate fraudulent proofs of invalid blocks from the whole node and to verify the availability of block data. In order to prevent an attacker from creating a block that is either valid or invalid, but not publishing all of the data, thereby leaving no other verifier with the ability to fully compute the state or create a block associated with the part that is no longer accessible; In order to facilitate public accessibility of the data published to the blockchain, this paper increases data redundancy by encoding it with a Merkle tree, which is used in conjunction with the Merkle tree. The use of a Merkle tree in conjunction with the encoded data enables nodes to verify the validity of the data through a simple computation. In order to prevent malicious full nodes from concealing data against the will of a specific light node, this paper proposes a random sampling pattern of multiple nodes. This pattern enables honest nodes to obtain the data blocks necessary to recover the data with a high probability. The random sampling pattern is demonstrated to provide a high probability guarantee for system security through probabilistic calculations and simulations, which verify the effectiveness of the method.

References

1. Chauhan, A., Malviya, O.P., Verma, M., Mor, T.S.: Blockchain and scalability. In: 2018 IEEE International Conference on Software Quality, Reliability and Security Companion (QRS-C) (2018). https://doi.org/10.1109/qrs-c.2018.00034
2. Dorri, A., Kanhere, S.S., Jurdak, R., Gauravaram, P.: LSB: a lightweight scalable blockchain for IoT security and anonymity. J. Parallel Distrib. Comput. **134**, 180–197 (2019). https://doi.org/10.1016/j.jpdc.2019.08.005. https://www.sciencedirect.com/science/article/pii/S0743731518307688
3. Nakamoto, S.: Bitcoin: a peer-to-peer electronic cash system (2008)
4. Perard, D., Lacan, J., Bachy, Y., Detchart, J.: Erasure code-based low storage blockchain node. In: 2018 IEEE International Conference on Internet of Things (iThings) and IEEE Green Computing and Communications (GreenCom) and IEEE Cyber, Physical and Social Computing (CPSCom) and IEEE Smart Data (SmartData) (2018). https://doi.org/10.1109/cybermatics_2018.2018.00271
5. Qi, X., Zhang, Z., Jin, C., Zhou, A.: BFT-store: storage partition for permissioned blockchain via erasure coding. In: 2020 IEEE 36th International Conference on Data Engineering (ICDE), pp. 1926–1929 (2020). https://doi.org/10.1109/ICDE48307.2020.00205
6. Shen, B.Z., Tzeng, K.: Multidimensional extension of Reed-solomon codes. In: Proceedings. 1998 IEEE International Symposium on Information Theory (Cat. No. 98CH36252), p. 54. IEEE (1998)
7. Wilkinson, S.: Storj a peer-to-peer cloud storage network (2014). https://api.semanticscholar.org/CorpusID:33754813
8. Wu, J., Costello, D.: New multilevel codes over GF (q). IEEE Trans. Inf. Theory **38**(3), 933–939 (1992)
9. Xu, L., Chen, L., Gao, Z., Xu, S., Shi, W.: Efficient public blockchain client for lightweight users. ICST Trans. Secur. Saf. **4**(13), 153528 (2018). https://doi.org/10.4108/eai.4-1-2018.153528
10. Yang, C., Wang, X., Jiang, Z., Liu, Y., Lin, F., Zheng, Z.: On min-max storage for resource restricted clients in coded blockchain systems. IEEE Internet Things J. (2023)

Author Index

GPSR Compliance

The European Union's (EU) General Product Safety Regulation (GPSR) is a set of rules that requires consumer products to be safe and our obligations to ensure this.

If you have any concerns about our products, you can contact us on ProductSafety@springernature.com

In case Publisher is established outside the EU, the EU authorized representative is:

Springer Nature Customer Service Center GmbH
Europaplatz 3
69115 Heidelberg, Germany

The manufacturer's authorised representative in the EU is Springer
Nature Customer Service Centre GmbH, Europaplatz 3, 69115 Heidelberg,
Germany. If you have any concerns regarding our products, please
contact ProductSafety@springernature.com

Printed and bound by CPI Group (UK) Ltd, Croydon, CR0 4YY
29/04/2026
02099532-0018